# *SPSS® Base 11.0 User's Guide*



SPSS®

For more information about SPSS® software products, please visit our Web site at *http://www.spss.com* or contact

SPSS Inc.
233 South Wacker Drive, 11th Floor
Chicago, IL 60606-6412
Tel: (312) 651-3000
Fax: (312) 651-3668



1 2 3 4 5 6 7 8 9 0     05 04 03 02 01

ISBN 0-13-034838-4

# Preface

SPSS® 11.0 is a comprehensive system for analyzing data. SPSS can take data from almost any type of file and use them to generate tabulated reports, charts, and plots of distributions and trends, descriptive statistics, and complex statistical analyses.

SPSS makes statistical analysis accessible for the casual user and convenient for the experienced user. The Data Editor offers a simple and efficient spreadsheet-like facility for entering data and browsing the working data file. High-resolution, presentation-quality charts and plots are integral parts of the Base system. Much of the output from the Base system and Tables option takes the form of flexible pivot tables that you can modify quickly and copy directly into other applications. The Viewer makes it easy to organize and manage your tables and charts using a familiar tree structure. When you have questions about an item in a dialog box, a statistic in your output, or the steps needed to accomplish a task, help is only a click or two away. With the Draft Viewer, you can create simple text output instead of interactive pivot tables. See the overview (Chapter 1) for a list of new features and an introduction to the Base system.

This manual, the *SPSS Base 11.0 User's Guide,* documents the graphical user interface of SPSS for Windows. Complete information about using interactive graphics can be found in *SPSS Interactive Graphics 10.0*, which is compatible with release 11.0 of SPSS. Examples using the statistical procedures found in SPSS Base 11.0 are provided in the Help system, installed with the software. Algorithms used in the statistical procedures are available on the product CD-ROM.

Beneath the menus and dialog boxes, SPSS uses a command language that can be used to create and run production jobs. Dialog boxes can "paste" commands into a syntax window, where they can be modified and saved; a few features of the system can be accessed only via command syntax. Complete command syntax is documented in the *SPSS 11.0 Syntax Reference Guide,* which is included on the product CD-ROM and is available for purchase separately in print. The Help system contains brief syntax diagrams in addition to full help on the graphical user interface.

## SPSS Options

The SPSS family of products includes add-on enhancements to the SPSS Base system, which are available on several computer platforms. Contact your local SPSS office or sales representative about availability of the following options:

- **SPSS Regression Models™** provides techniques for analyzing data that do not fit traditional linear statistical models. It includes procedures for probit analysis, logistic regression, weight estimation, two-stage least-squares regression, and general nonlinear regression.
- **SPSS Advanced Models™** focuses on techniques often used in sophisticated experimental and biomedical research. It includes procedures for general linear models (GLM), linear mixed models, variance components analysis, loglinear analysis, ordinal regression, actuarial life tables, Kaplan-Meier survival analysis, and basic and extended Cox regression.
- **SPSS Tables™** creates a variety of presentation-quality tabular reports, including complex stub-and-banner tables and displays of multiple-response data.
- **SPSS Trends™** performs comprehensive forecasting and time series analyses with multiple curve-fitting models, smoothing models, and methods for estimating autoregressive functions.
- **SPSS Categories®** performs optimal scaling procedures, including correspondence analysis.
- **SPSS Conjoint™** performs conjoint analysis.
- **SPSS Exact Tests™** calculates exact *p* values for statistical tests when small or very unevenly distributed samples could make the usual tests inaccurate.
- **SPSS Missing Value Analysis™** describes patterns of missing data, estimates means and other statistics, and imputes values for missing observations.
- **SPSS Maps™** turns your geographically distributed data into high-quality maps with symbols, colors, bar charts, pie charts, and combinations of themes to present not only what is happening but where it is happening.

### *Compatibility*

The SPSS Base 11.0 system is designed to operate on computer systems running Windows 98, Windows 2000, Windows Me, or Windows NT 4.0.

### *Serial Numbers*

Your serial number is your identification number with SPSS Inc. You will need this serial number when you contact SPSS Inc. for information regarding support, payment, or an upgraded system. The serial number was provided with your Base system. Before using the system, please copy this number to the registration card.

### *Registration Card*

Don't put it off: *fill out and send us your registration card.* Until we receive your registration card, you have an unregistered system. Even if you have previously sent a card to us, please fill out and return the card enclosed in your Base system package. Registering your system entitles you to:

- Technical support services
- New product announcements and upgrade announcements

### *Customer Service*

If you have any questions concerning your shipment or account, contact your local office, listed on page vii. Please have your serial number ready for identification when calling.

### *Training Seminars*

SPSS Inc. provides both public and onsite training seminars for SPSS. All seminars feature hands-on workshops. SPSS seminars will be offered in major U.S. and European cities on a regular basis. For more information on these seminars, call your local office, listed on page vii.

## *Technical Support*

The services of SPSS Technical Support are available to registered customers of SPSS. Customers may contact Technical Support for assistance in using SPSS products or for installation help for one of the supported hardware environments. To reach Technical Support, see the SPSS Web site at *http://www.spss.com*, or call your local office, listed on page vii. Be prepared to identify yourself, your organization, and the serial number of your system.

## *Additional Publications*

Except for academic course adoptions, additional copies of SPSS product manuals may be purchased directly from SPSS Inc. Visit our Web site at *http://www.spss.com/estore*, or contact your local SPSS office, listed on page vii.

SPSS product manuals may also be purchased from Prentice Hall, the exclusive distributor of SPSS publications. To order, fill out and mail the Publications order form included with your system, or call 800-947-7700. If you represent a bookstore or have an account with Prentice Hall, call 800-382-3419. In Canada, call 800-567-3800. Outside of North America, contact your local Prentice Hall office.

Statistical introductions to procedures in the Base, Regression Models, and Advanced Models written by Marija Norušis are planned to be available from Prentice Hall. Check with the publisher or visit the SPSS Web site for announcements regarding availability.

## *Tell Us Your Thoughts*

Your comments are important. Please let us know about your experiences with SPSS products. We especially like to hear about new and interesting applications using the SPSS system. Please send e-mail to *suggest@spss.com*, or write to SPSS Inc., Attn: Director of Product Planning, 233 South Wacker Drive, 11th Floor, Chicago, IL 60606-6412.

## *Contacting SPSS*

If you would like to be on our mailing list, contact one of our offices, listed on page vii, or visit our Web site at *http://www.spss.com*. We will send you a copy of our newsletter and let you know about SPSS Inc. activities in your area.

**SSPSS Inc.**
Chicago, Illinois, U.S.A.
Tel: 1.312.651.3000
www.spss.com/corpinfo
**Customer Service:**
1.800.521.1337
**Sales:**
1.800.543.2185
sales@spss.com
**Training:**
1.800.543.6607
**Technical Support:**
1.312.651.3410
support@spss.com

**SPSS Federal Systems**
Tel: 1.703.527.6777
www.spss.com

**SPSS Argentina srl**
Tel: +5411.4814.5030
www.spss.com

**SPSS Asia Pacific Pte. Ltd.**
Tel: +65.245.9110
www.spss.com

**SPSS Australasia Pty. Ltd.**
Tel: +61.2.9954.5660
www.spss.com

**SPSS Belgium**
Tel: +32.163.170.70
www.spss.com

**SPSS Benelux BV**
Tel: +31.183.651777
www.spss.com

**SPSS Brasil Ltda**
Tel: +55.11.5505.3644
www.spss.com

**SPSS Czech Republic**
Tel: +420.2.24813839
www.spss.cz

**SPSS Denmark A/S**
Tel: +45.45.46.02.00
www.spss.com

**SPSS Finland Oy**
Tel: +358.9.524.801
www.spss.com

**SPSS France SARL**
Tel: +01.55.35.27.00 x03
www.spss.com

**SPSS Germany**
Tel: +49.89.4890740
www.spss.com

**SPSS Hellas SA**
Tel: +30.1.72.51.925/72.51.950
www.spss.com

**SPSS Hispanoportuguesa S.L.**
Tel: +34.91.447.37.00
www.spss.com

**SPSS Hong Kong Ltd.**
Tel: +852.2.811.9662
www.spss.com

**SPSS India**
Tel: +91.80.225.0260
www.spss.com

**SPSS Ireland**
Tel: +353.1.496.9007
www.spss.com

**SPSS Israel Ltd.**
Tel: +972.3.5795230
www.spss.com

**SPSS Italia srl**
Tel: +39.51.252573
www.spss.it

**SPSS Japan Inc.**
Tel: +81.3.5466.5511
www.spss.com

**SPSS Kenya Limited**
Tel: +254.2.577.262/3
www.spss.com

**SPSS Korea KIC Co., Ltd.**
Tel: +82.2.3446.7651
www.spss.co.kr

**SPSS Latin America**
Tel: +1.312.651.3539
www.spss.com

**SPSS Malaysia Sdn Bhd**
Tel: +603.7873.6477
www.spss.com

**SPSS Mexico SA de CV**
Tel: +52.5.682.87.68
www.spss.com

**SPSS Norway**
Tel: +47.22.99.25.50
www.spss.com

**SPSS Polska**
Tel: +48.12.6369680
www.spss.pl

**SPSS Russia**
Tel: +7.095.125.0069
www.spss.com

**SPSS Schweiz AG**
Tel: +41.1.266.90.30
www.spss.com

**SPSS Sweden AB**
Tel: +46.8.506.105.68
www.spss.com

**SPSS BI (Singapore) Pte. Ltd.**
Tel: +65.346.2061
www.spss.com

**SPSS South Africa**
Tel: +27.11.807.3189
www.spss.com

**SPSS Taiwan Corp.**
Taipei, Republic of China
Tel: +886.2.25771100
www.sinter.com.tw/spss/

**SPSS (Thailand) Co., Ltd.**
Tel: +66.2.260.7070, +66.2.260.7080
www.spss.com

**SPSS UK Ltd.**
Tel: +44.1483.719200
www.spss.com

# Contents

## 3 Data Files 25

# 4 Distributed Analysis 61



# 5 Data Editor 71

## 6 Data Transformations 91



## 7 File Handling and File Transformations 117

## 10 Pivot Tables 197



## 11 Working with Command Syntax 231

## 12 Frequencies 239



## 13 Descriptives 245



## 14 Explore 249



## 15 Crosstabs 257

## 16 Summarize 263



## 17 Means 267



## 18 OLAP Cubes 271



## 19 T Tests 277

## 22 Bivariate Correlations 313



## 23 Partial Correlations 319



## 24 Distances 323



## 25 Linear Regression 327

## 33 Reporting Results 419



## 34 Reliability Analysis 435

## 35 Multidimensional Scaling 441



## 36 Ratio Statistics 449



## 37 Overview of the Chart Facility 453



## 38 ROC Curves 465

## 39 Utilities 469



## 40 Options 475



## 41 Customizing Menus and Toolbars 491

## 42 Production Facility 499



## 43 Scripting Facility 513

Chapter

# 1

# Overview

SPSS for Windows provides a powerful statistical analysis and data management system in a graphical environment, using descriptive menus and simple dialog boxes to do most of the work for you. Most tasks can be accomplished simply by pointing and clicking the mouse.

In addition to the simple point-and-click interface for statistical analysis, SPSS for Windows provides:

**Data Editor.** A versatile spreadsheet-like system for defining, entering, editing, and displaying data.

**Viewer.** The Viewer makes it easy to browse your results, selectively show and hide output, change the display order results, and move presentation-quality tables and charts between SPSS and other applications.

**Multidimensional pivot tables.** Your results come alive with multidimensional pivot tables. Explore your tables by rearranging rows, columns, and layers. Uncover important findings that can get lost in standard reports. Compare groups easily by splitting your table so that only one group is displayed at a time.

**High-resolution graphics.** High-resolution, full-color pie charts, bar charts, histograms, scatterplots, 3-D graphics, and more are included as standard features in SPSS.

**Database access.** Retrieve information from databases by using the Database Wizard instead of complicated SQL queries.

**Data transformations**. Transformation features help get your data ready for analysis. You can easily subset data, combine categories, add, aggregate, merge, split, and transpose files, and more.

**Electronic distribution**. Send e-mail reports to others with the click of a button, or export tables and charts in HTML format for Internet and Intranet distribution.

**Online Help**. Detailed tutorials provide a comprehensive overview; context-sensitive Help topics in dialog boxes guide you through specific tasks; pop-up definitions in pivot table results explain statistical terms; the Statistics Coach helps you find the procedures you need; and the Results Coach helps you understand how to interpret your results.

## What's New in SPSS 11.0

New features in SPSS 11.0 include:

**Ratio Statistics**. A new procedure provides a comprehensive list of summary statistics for describing the ratio between two scale variables, including coefficient of dispersion, coefficient of variation, price-related differential, and average absolute deviation.

**Linear Mixed Models**. A new procedure enables you to construct predictive models when you have a nested data structure. You can formulate a wide variety of models, including Fixed Effects ANOVA Model, Randomized Complete Blocks Design, Split-Plot Design, Purely Random Effects Model, Random Coefficient Model, Multilevel Analysis, Unconditional Linear Growth Model, Linear Growth Model with a person-level covariate, Repeated Measures Analysis, and Repeated Measures Analysis with time-dependent covariate. In addition, you can work with repeated measure designs, such as incomplete repeated measurements in which the number of observations varies across subjects. Available in the Advanced Models option.

**Performance enhancements**. General Linear Models, Proximities, Hierarchical Cluster Analysis (Base system), and Multinomial Logistic Regression (Regression Models) now run much faster than in previous releases.

**Data management**. Restructure data to create a single case (record) from multiple cases or create multiple cases from a single case.

**Database Wizard**. Now allows you to automatically recode categorical string values to numeric variables (using the original values as value labels), auto-join tables using primary/foreign key relationships, and obtain random samples from large data sources.

**Text Wizard**. Now allows you to read CSV-format text data that contains text qualifiers (such as, "1,000", "2,000", ...).

**OLAP Cubes**. Now allows you to calculate arithmetic and percentage differences between categories of a grouping variable or between separate variables.

**One-way ANOVA**. Now includes the Brown-Forsythe and Welch tests.

**Scientific notation for small numbers**. You can choose not to see it in your output (from the Edit menu, choose Options, and then click the General tab).

**Aggregate**. Median has been added to the list of available Aggregate functions.

**Arithmetic functions**. Available functions in arithmetic expressions are expanded to include density functions for continuous and discrete distributions.

**Multinomial Logistic Regression**. New functionality added to this procedure allows you to save estimated response probabilities, predicted response categories, probability of predicted response categories, and probability of actual response categories. Available in the Regression Models option.

**Categorical Regression**. This procedure has been redesigned to make it more powerful and easier to use. Available in the Categories option.

**Categorical Principal Components Analysis**. Improvements in this procedure now make results easier to understand. Available in the Categories option.

## *Windows*

There are a number of different types of windows in SPSS:

**Data Editor.** This window displays the contents of the data file. You can create new data files or modify existing ones with the Data Editor. The Data Editor window opens automatically when you start an SPSS session. You can have only one data file open at a time.

**Viewer.** All statistical results, tables, and charts are displayed in the Viewer. You can edit the output and save it for later use. A Viewer window opens automatically the first time you run a procedure that generates output.

**Draft Viewer.** You can display output as simple text (instead of interactive pivot tables) in the Draft Viewer.

**Pivot Table Editor.** Output displayed in pivot tables can be modified in many ways with the Pivot Table Editor. You can edit text, swap data in rows and columns, add color, create multidimensional tables, and selectively hide and show results.

**Chart Editor.** You can modify high-resolution charts and plots in chart windows. You can change the colors, select different type fonts or sizes, switch the horizontal and vertical axes, rotate 3-D scatterplots, and even change the chart type.

**Text Output Editor.** Text output not displayed in pivot tables can be modified with the Text Output Editor. You can edit the output and change font characteristics (type, style, color, size).

**Syntax Editor.** You can paste your dialog box choices into a syntax window, where your selections appear in the form of command syntax. You can then edit the command syntax to utilize special features of SPSS not available through dialog boxes. You can save these commands in a file for use in subsequent SPSS sessions.

**Script Editor.** Scripting and OLE automation allow you to customize and automate many tasks in SPSS. Use the Script Editor to create and modify basic scripts.

Figure 1-1
*Data Editor and Viewer*

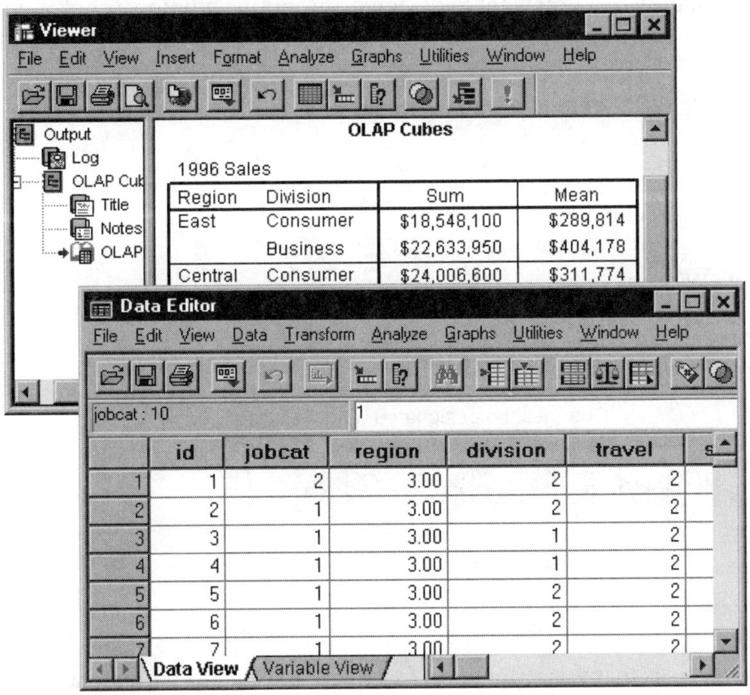

## Designated versus Active Window

If you have more than one open Viewer window, output is routed to the **designated** Viewer window. If you have more than one open Syntax Editor window, command syntax is pasted into the designated Syntax Editor window. The designated windows are indicated by an exclamation point (!) in the status bar. You can change the designated windows at any time.

The designated window should not be confused with the **active** window, which is the currently selected window. If you have overlapping windows, the active window appears in the foreground. If you open a new Syntax Editor or Viewer window, that window automatically becomes the active window and the designated window.

#### To Change the Designated Viewer or Syntax Editor Window

▶ Make the window that you want to designate the active window (click anywhere in the window).

▶ Click the Designate Window tool on the toolbar (the one with the exclamation point).

*or*

▶ From the menus choose:

Utilities
  Designate Window

Figure 1-2
*Designate Window tool*

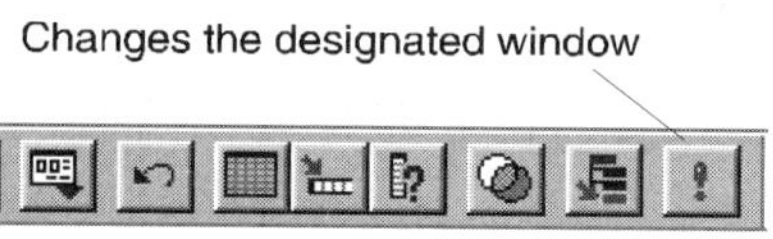


## Menus

Many of the tasks that you want to perform with SPSS start with menu selections. Each window in SPSS has its own menu bar with menu selections appropriate for that window type.

The Analyze and Graphs menus are available on all windows, making it easy to generate new output without having to switch windows.

## Toolbars

Each SPSS window has its own toolbar that provides quick, easy access to common tasks. Some windows have more than one toolbar. ToolTips provide a brief description of each tool when you put the mouse pointer on the tool.

Figure 1-3
*Toolbar with ToolTip Help*

You can control the display of toolbars in several ways:

- Show or hide toolbars.
- Display toolbars vertically or horizontally, attached to the left, right, top, or bottom of the window.
- Display toolbars as floating palettes anywhere inside or outside the window.
- Customize toolbars to contain the features that you use most often, including scripts.

### To Show or Hide a Toolbar

▶ From the menus choose:

View
 Toolbars...

▶ In the Show Toolbars dialog box, select the toolbars that you want to show (or hide).

### To Move a Toolbar

▶ Click anywhere in the toolbar outside the toolbar buttons.

▶ Drag the toolbar where you want it.

- Dragging the toolbar to the left or right side of the window attaches a toolbar vertically to that side.
- Dragging the toolbar to the top or bottom of the window attaches the toolbar horizontally.
- Dragging the toolbar anywhere other than the window borders creates a detached, floating toolbar.

Figure 1-4
*Floating toolbars*

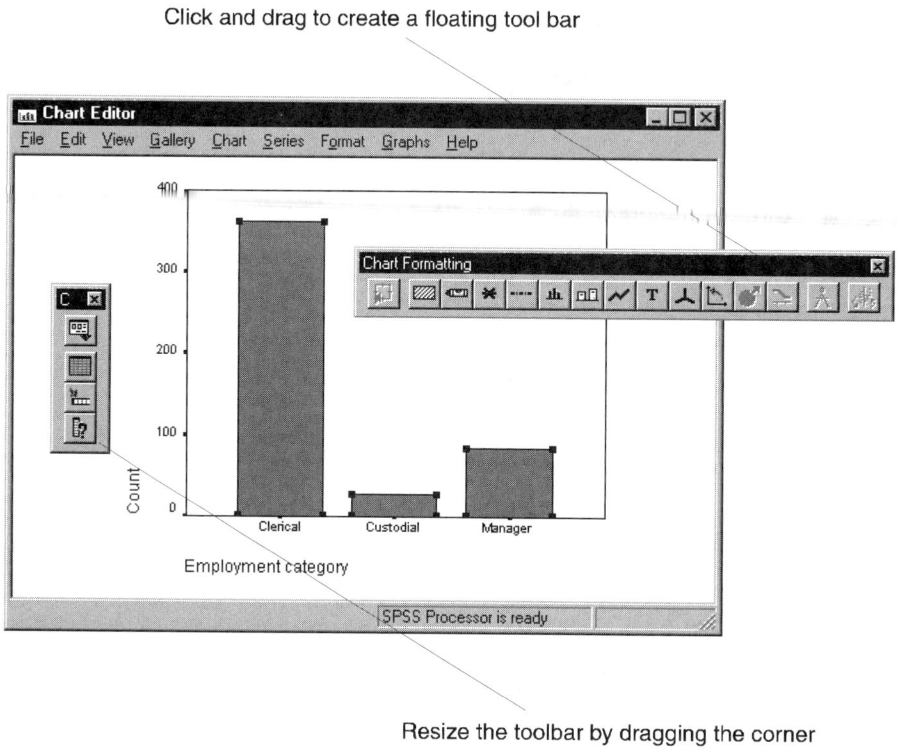


# Status Bar

The status bar at the bottom of each SPSS window provides the following information:

**Command status.** For each procedure or command that you run, a case counter indicates the number of cases processed so far. For statistical procedures that require iterative processing, the number of iterations is displayed.

**Filter status.** If you have selected a random sample or a subset of cases for analysis, the message Filter on indicates that some type of case filtering is currently in effect and not all cases in the data file are included in the analysis.

**Weight status.** The message Weight on indicates that a weight variable is being used to weight cases for analysis.

**Split File status.** The message Split File on indicates that the data file has been split into separate groups for analysis, based on the values of one or more grouping variables.

### *To Show or Hide the Status Bar*

- From the menus choose:

  View
  Status Bar

## *Dialog Boxes*

Most menu selections open dialog boxes. You use dialog boxes to select variables and options for analysis.

Each main dialog box for statistical procedures and charts has several basic components:

**Source variable list.** A list of variables in the working data file. Only variable types allowed by the selected procedure are displayed in the source list. Use of short string and long string variables is restricted in many procedures.

**Target variable list(s).** One or more lists indicating the variables that you have chosen for the analysis, such as dependent and independent variable lists.

**Command pushbuttons.** Buttons that instruct the program to perform an action, such as run the procedure, display Help, or open a subdialog box to make additional specifications.

For information on individual controls in a dialog box, click the control with the right mouse button.

Figure 1-5
*Dialog box controls*

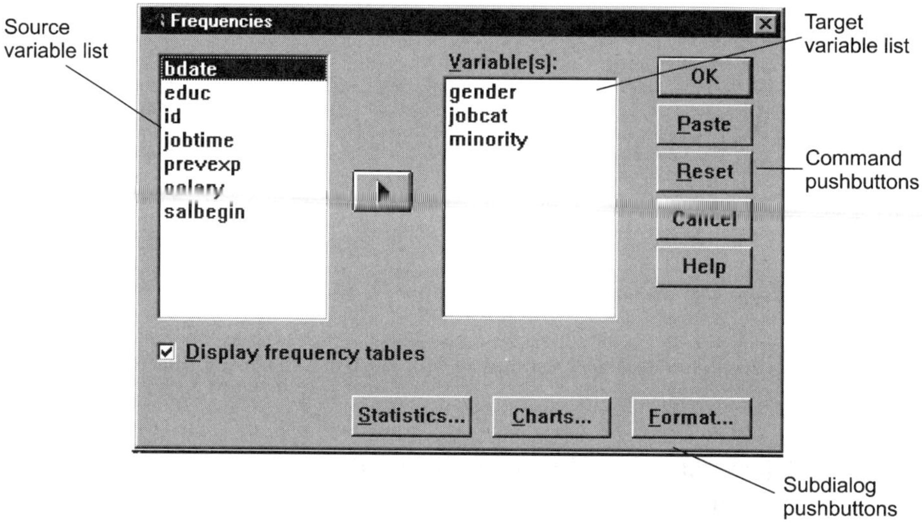


## Variable Names and Variable Labels in Dialog Box Lists

You can display either variable names or variable labels in dialog box lists. Since variable names are limited to eight characters, variable labels often provide more descriptive information.

- To control the display of variable names or labels, choose Options from the Edit menu in any window.
- To define or modify variable labels, use Variable View in the Data Editor.
- For data imported from database sources, field names are used as variable labels.
- For long labels, position the mouse pointer over the label in the list to view the entire label.
- If no variable label is defined, the variable name is displayed.

Figure 1-6
*Variable labels displayed in a dialog box*

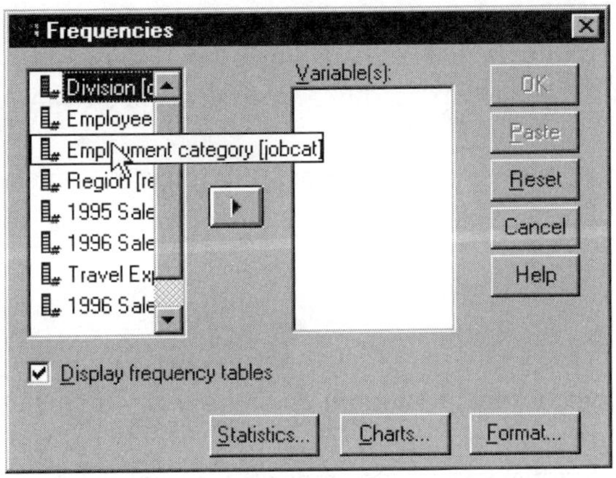


## *Dialog Box Pushbuttons*

There are five standard command pushbuttons in most dialog boxes:

**OK.** Runs the procedure. After you select your variables and choose any additional specifications, click OK to run the procedure. This also closes the dialog box.

**Paste.** Generates command syntax from the dialog box selections and pastes the syntax into a syntax window. You can then customize the commands with additional features not available from dialog boxes.

**Reset.** Deselects any variables in the selected variable list(s) and resets all specifications in the dialog box and any subdialog boxes to the default state.

**Cancel.** Cancels any changes in the dialog box settings since the last time it was opened and closes the dialog box. Within a session, dialog box settings are persistent. A dialog box retains your last set of specifications until you override them.

**Help.** Context-sensitive Help. This takes you to a standard Microsoft Help window that contains information about the current dialog box. You can also get help on individual dialog box controls by clicking the control with the right mouse button.

## Subdialog Boxes

Since most procedures provide a great deal of flexibility, not all of the possible choices can be contained in a single dialog box. The main dialog box usually contains the minimum information required to run a procedure. Additional specifications are made in subdialog boxes.

In the main dialog box, pushbuttons with an ellipsis (...) after the name indicate that a subdialog box will be displayed.

## Selecting Variables

To select a single variable, you simply highlight it on the source variable list and click the right arrow button next to the target variable list. If there is only one target variable list, you can double-click individual variables to move them from the source list to the target list.

You can also select multiple variables:

- To select multiple variables that are grouped together on the variable list, click the first one and then Shift-click the last one in the group.
- To select multiple variables that are not grouped together on the variable list, use the Ctrl-click method. Click the first variable, then Ctrl-click the next variable, and so on.
- To select all variables in the list, press Ctrl-A.

Figure 1-7
*Selecting multiple variables with Shift-click*

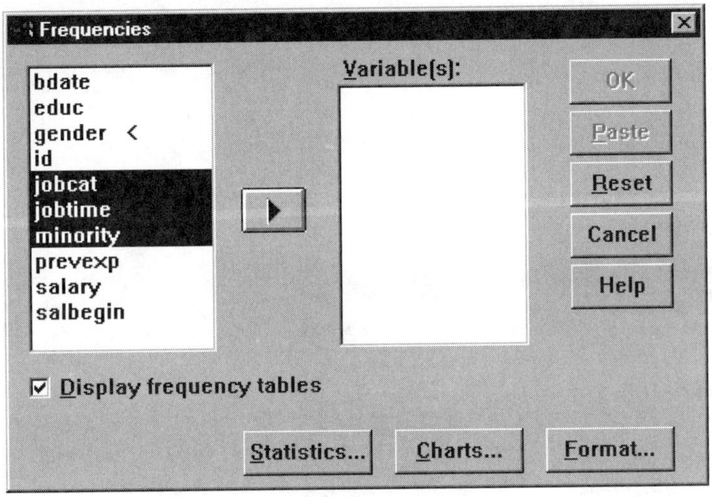


Figure 1-8
*Selecting multiple noncontiguous variables with Ctrl-click*

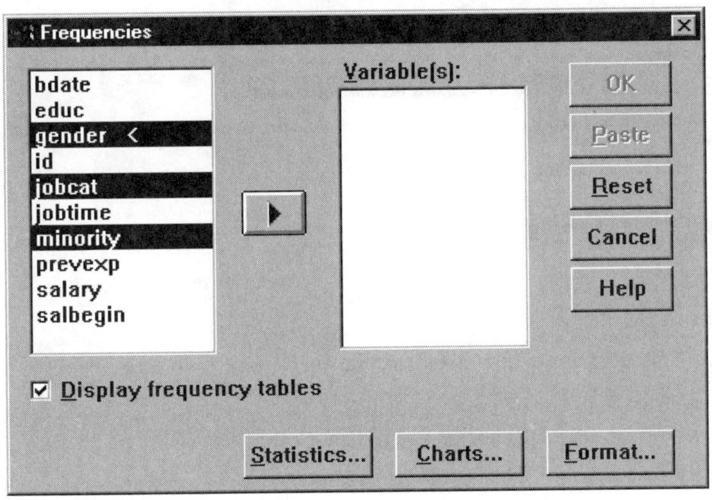

### To Get Information about Variables in a Dialog Box

- ▶ Left-click a variable in a list to select it.
- ▶ Right-click anywhere in the list.
- ▶ Select Variable Information in the pop-up context menu.

Figure 1-9
*Variable Information with right mouse button*

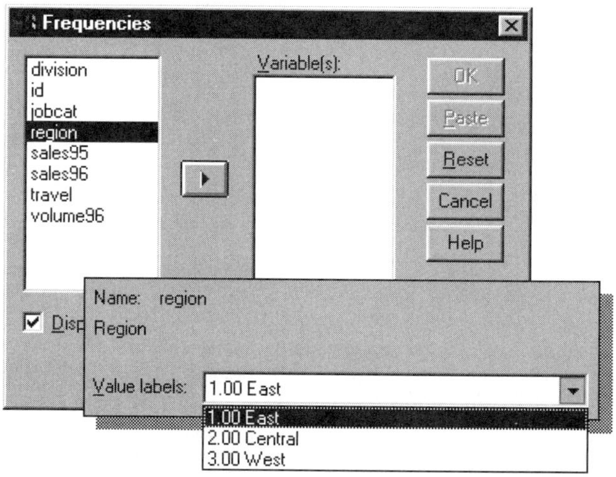


### To Get Information about Dialog Box Controls

- ▶ Right-click the control you want to know about.
- ▶ Select What's This? on the pop-up context menu.

A pop-up window displays information about the control.

Figure 1-10
*Right mouse button "What's This?" pop-up Help for dialog box controls*

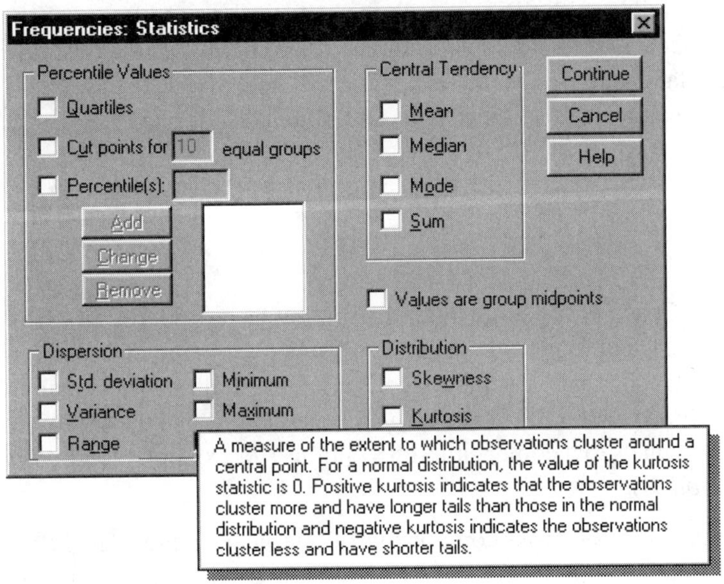


## Basic Steps in Data Analysis

Analyzing data with SPSS is easy. All you have to do is:

**Get your data into SPSS.** You can open a previously saved SPSS data file; read a spreadsheet, database, or text data file; or enter your data directly in the Data Editor.

**Select a procedure.** Select a procedure from the menus to calculate statistics or to create a chart.

**Select the variables for the analysis.** The variables in the data file are displayed in a dialog box for the procedure.

**Run the procedure and look at the results.** Results are displayed in the Viewer.

## Statistics Coach

If you are unfamiliar with SPSS or with the statistical procedures available in SPSS, the Statistics Coach can help you get started by prompting you with simple questions, nontechnical language, and visual examples that help you select the basic statistical and charting features that are best suited for you data.

To use the Statistics Coach, from the menus in any SPSS window choose:

Help
  Statistics Coach

The Statistics Coach covers only a selected subset of procedures in the SPSS Base system. It is designed to provide general assistance for many of the basic, commonly used statistical techniques. For detailed discussions of all the statistical procedures available in SPSS, see the *SPSS Base Applications Guide* and the applications sections of the SPSS manuals that come with SPSS options (for example, *Regression Models* or *Advanced Models*).

*Note*: The Statistic Coach uses components of Internet Explorer. The SPSS installation CD provides both an upgrade to Internet Explorer 4 and a full, installable version of Internet Explorer 5.

## Finding Out More about SPSS

For a comprehensive overview of SPSS basics, see the online tutorial. From any SPSS menu choose:

Help
  Tutorial

Chapter
2

# Getting Help

Online Help in provided in several ways:

**Help menu.** Every window has a Help menu on the menu bar. Topics provides access to the Contents, Index, and Find tabs, which you can use to find specific Help topics. Tutorial provides access to the introductory tutorial.

**Dialog box context menu Help.** Right-click on any control in a dialog box and select What's This? from the context menu to display a description of the control and directions for its use.

**Dialog box Help buttons.** Most dialog boxes have a Help button that takes you directly to a Help topic for that dialog box. The Help topic provides general information and links to related topics.

**Pivot table context menu Help.** Right-click on terms in an activated pivot table in the Viewer and select What's This? from the context menu to display definitions of the terms.

**Results Coach**. Double-click a pivot table or a chart to activate it, and then select Results Coach from the Help menu to get information that can help you interpret your results.

**Tutorial.** Select Tutorial on the Help menu in any window to access the online introductory tutorial.

**CD-ROM Syntax Reference Guide.** Detailed syntax reference information is available online with the CD-ROM version. The Syntax Reference Guide is available from the Help menu. If you did not install the Syntax Reference Guide when you installed this software, you will need the CD-ROM to access it. (It is not available with some versions.) To install the Syntax Reference Guide, in the Setup program select Custom for the type of installation and then select Syntax Guide.

### To Use the Help Table of Contents

- In any window, from the menus choose:

  Help
   Topics

- Click the Contents tab.

- Double-click items with a book icon to expand or collapse the contents.

- Double-click an item to go to that Help topic.

Figure 2-1
*Contents tab and Help topic*

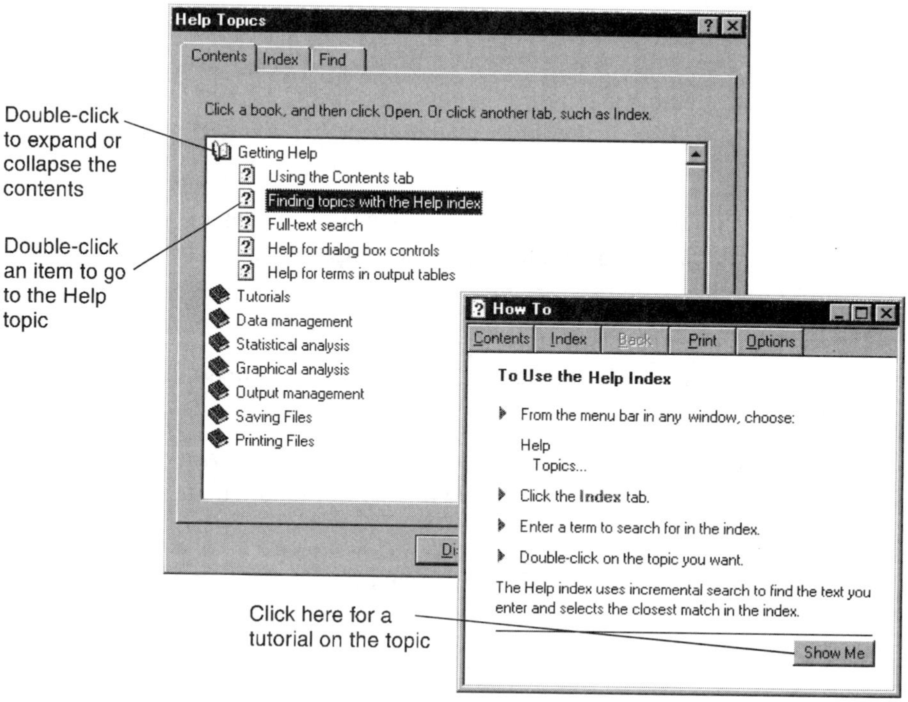

### To Use the Help Index

▶ In any window, from the menus choose:

Help
 Topics

▶ Click the Index tab.

▶ Enter a term to search for in the index.

▶ Double-click the topic you want.

The Help index uses incremental search to find the text you enter and selects the closest match in the index.

Figure 2-2
*Index tab and incremental search*

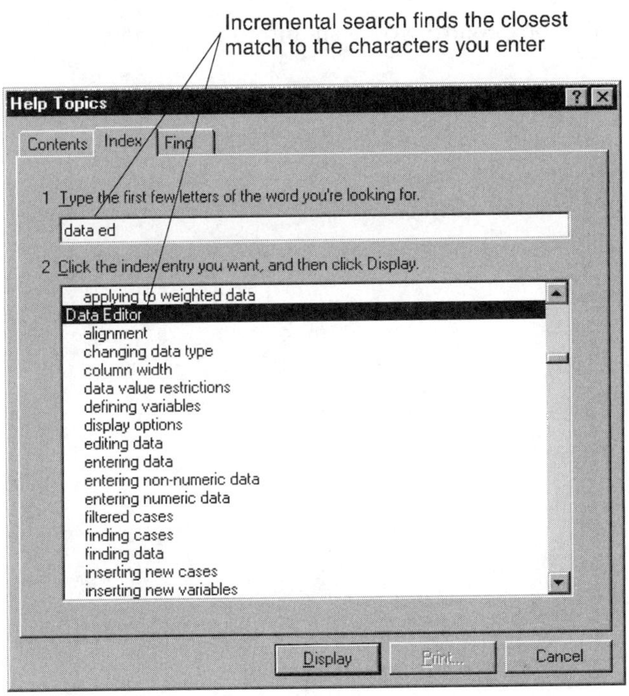

### To Use Full-Text Search in Help

▶ In any window, from the menus choose:

Help
  Topics

▶ Click the Find tab.

▶ Use the Find Setup Wizard to create a database of text in the Help system.

▶ Enter the word or words you want to find.

▶ Double-click one of the listed topics to display that topic.

### To Get Help for Dialog Box Controls

▶ Right-click on the dialog box control you want information about.

▶ Choose What's This? from the pop-up context menu.

A description of the control and how to use it is displayed in a pop-up window. General information about a dialog box is available from the Help button in the dialog box.

Figure 2-3
*Dialog box control Help with right mouse button*

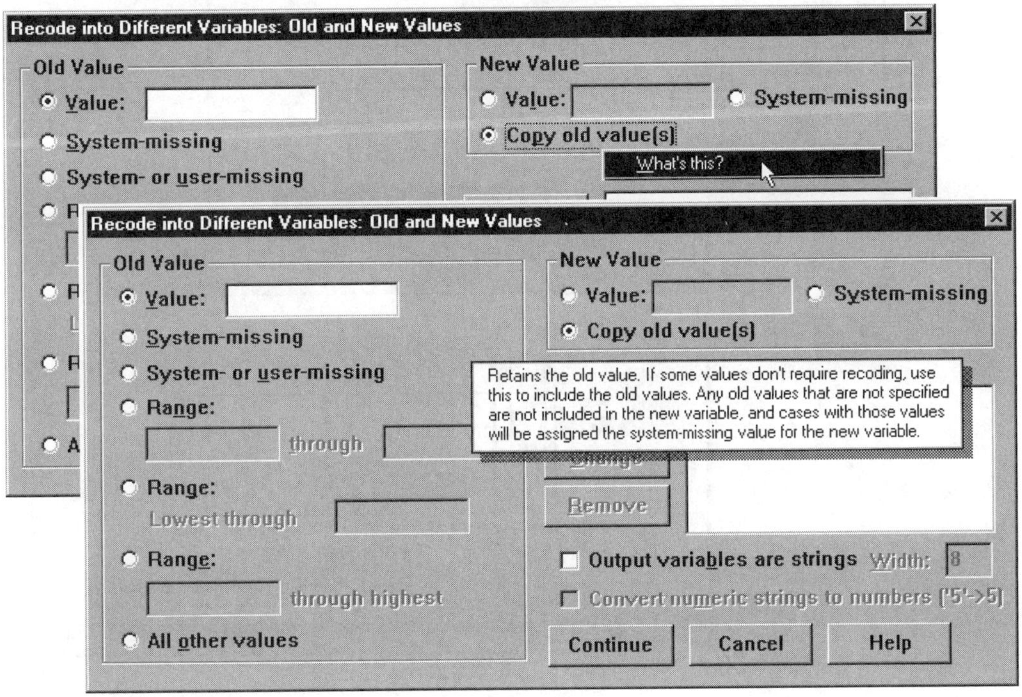


### *To Get Information about Terms in Output Pivot Tables*

- ▶ Double-click the pivot table to activate it.
- ▶ Right-click on the term that you want to be explained.
- ▶ Choose What's This? from the context menu.

  A definition of the term is displayed in a pop-up window.

Figure 2-4
*Activated pivot table glossary Help with right mouse button*

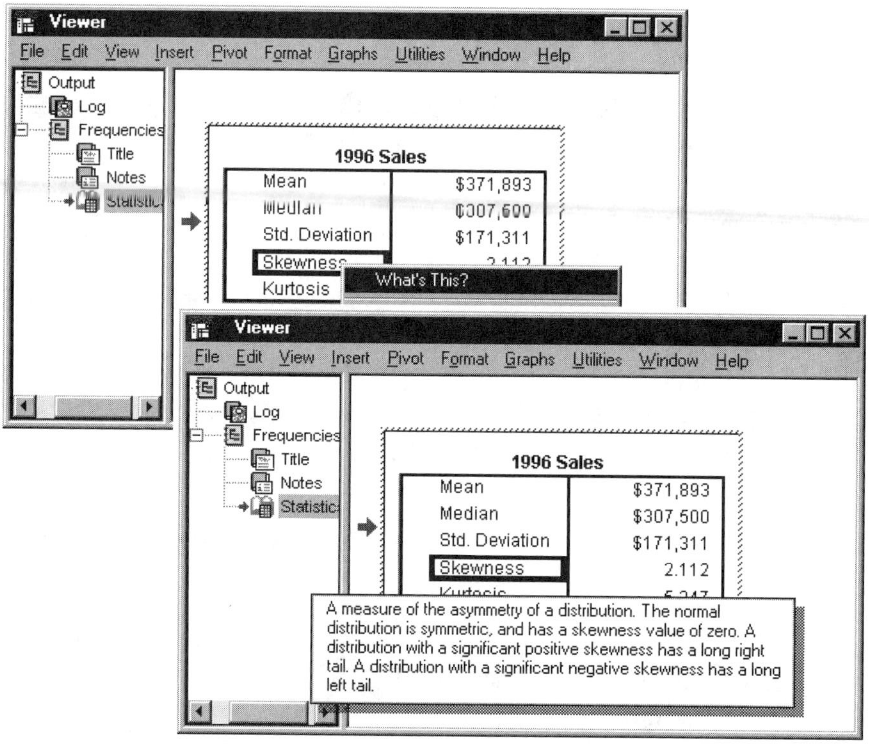


### To Use the Results Coach

▶ Double-click a pivot table or a chart to activate it.

▶ Choose Results Coach from the Help menu.

# Copying Help Text

You can copy text from the Help system and paste it into other applications.

- You can copy whole topics or selected portions of topics in Help windows.
- You can copy the text of Help pop-ups accessed from Help windows, dialog boxes, and pivot tables.

## To Copy Help Text from a Help Window

▶ Click and drag to select the text you want to copy.

▶ Click the Options button and select Copy from the menu.

*or*

▶ Press Ctrl-C.

If no text is selected, the entire Help topic is copied. In Help windows that do not have an Options button, use the Ctrl-C method.

## To Copy Help Text from a Pop-Up Window

▶ Right-click the button in the pop-up window.

▶ Choose Copy on the context menu.

The entire text of the pop-up window is copied.

Chapter

3

# Data Files

Data files come in a wide variety of formats, and this software is designed to handle many of them, including:

- Spreadsheets created with Lotus 1-2-3 and Excel
- Database files created with dBASE and various SQL formats
- Tab-delimited and other types of ASCII text files
- Data files in SPSS format created on other operating systems
- SYSTAT data files

## Opening a Data File

In addition to files saved in SPSS format, you can open Excel, Lotus 1-2-3, dBASE, and tab-delimited files without converting the files to an intermediate format or entering data definition information.

### To Open an SPSS, SYSTAT, Spreadsheet, or dBASE File

▶ From the menus choose:

File
 Open
  Data...

▶ In the Open File dialog box, select the file that you want to open.

▶ Click Open.

Optionally, you can:

- Read variable names from the first row for spreadsheet and tab-delimited files.
- Specify a range of cells to read for spreadsheet files.
- Specify a sheet within an Excel file to read (Excel 5 or later).

## Data File Types

**SPSS.** Opens data files saved in SPSS format, including SPSS for Windows, Macintosh, UNIX, and also the DOS product SPSS/PC+.

**SPSS/PC+.** Opens SPSS/PC+ data files.

**SYSTAT.** Opens SYSTAT data files.

**SPSS portable.** Opens data files saved in SPSS portable format. Saving a file in portable format takes considerably longer than saving the file in SPSS format.

**Excel.** Opens Excel files.

**Lotus 1-2-3.** Opens data files saved in 1-2-3 format for release 3.0, 2.0, or 1A of Lotus.

**SYLK.** Opens data files saved in SYLK (symbolic link) format, a format used by some spreadsheet applications.

**dBASE.** Opens dBASE format files for either dBASE IV, dBASE III or III PLUS, or dBASE II. Each case is a record. Variable and value labels and missing-value specifications are lost when you save a file in this format.

## Opening File Options

**Read variable names.** For spreadsheets, you can read variable names from the first row of the file or the first row of the defined range. If the names are longer than eight characters, they are truncated. If the first eight characters do not create a unique variable name, the name is modified to create a unique variable name.

**Worksheet.** Excel 5 or later files can contain multiple worksheets. By default, the Data Editor reads the first worksheet. To read a different worksheet, select the worksheet from the drop-down list.

**Range.** For spreadsheet data files, you can also read a range of cells. Use the same method for specifying cell ranges as you would with the spreadsheet application.

## How the Data Editor Reads Excel 5 or Later Files

The following rules apply to reading Excel 5 or later files:

**Data type and width.** Each column is a variable. The data type and width for each variable is determined by the data type and width in the Excel file. If the column contains more than one data type (for example, date and numeric), the data type is set to string, and all values are read as valid string values.

**Blank cells.** For numeric variables, blank cells are converted to the system-missing value, indicated by a period. For string variables, a blank is a valid string value, and blank cells are treated as valid string values.

**Variable names.** If you read the first row of the Excel file (or the first row of the specified range) as variable names, names longer than eight characters are truncated, non-unique names are converted to unique ones, and the original names are used as variable labels. If you do not read variable names from the Excel file, default variable names are assigned.

## How the Data Editor Reads Older Excel Files and Other Spreadsheets

The following rules apply to reading Excel files prior to version 5 and other spreadsheet data:

**Data type and width.** The data type and width for each variable are determined by the column width and data type of the first data cell in the column. Values of other types are converted to the system-missing value. If the first data cell in the column is blank, the global default data type for the spreadsheet (usually numeric) is used.

**Blank cells.** For numeric variables, blank cells are converted to the system-missing value, indicated by a period. For string variables, a blank is a valid string value, and blank cells are treated as valid string values.

**Variable names.** If you do not read variable names from the spreadsheet, the column letters (*A*, *B*, *C*, ...) are used for variable names for Excel and Lotus files. For SYLK files and Excel files saved in R1C1 display format, the software uses the column number preceded by the letter *C* for variable names (*C1*, *C2*, *C3*, ...).

## How the Data Editor Reads dBASE Files

Database files are logically very similar to SPSS-format data files. The following general rules apply to dBASE files:

- Field names are automatically translated to variable names.
- Field names should comply with variable naming conventions for SPSS format. Field names longer than eight characters are truncated. If the first eight characters of the field name do not produce a unique name, the field is dropped.
- Colons used in dBASE field names are translated to underscores.
- Records marked for deletion but not actually purged are included. The software creates a new string variable, *D_R*, which contains an asterisk for cases marked for deletion.

# Reading Database Files

You can read data from any database format for which you have a database driver. In local analysis mode, the necessary drivers must be installed on your local computer. In distributed analysis mode (available with the server version), the drivers must be installed on the remote server. For more information about distributed analysis, see Chapter 4.

### To Read Database Files

▶ From the menus choose:

File
  Open Database
    New Query...

▶ Select the data source.

▶ Depending on the data source, you may need to select the database file and/or enter a login name, password, and other information.

▶ Select the table(s) and fields.

▶ Specify any relationships between your tables.

Optionally, you can:

- Specify any selection criteria for your data.
- Add a prompt for user input to create a parameter query.
- Define any variable attributes.
- Save the query you have constructed before running it.

### *To Edit a Saved Database Query*

▶ From the menus choose:

File
  Open Database
    Edit Query...

▶ Select the query file (**.spq*) that you want to edit.

▶ Follow the instructions for creating a new query.

### *To Read Database Files with a Saved Query*

▶ From the menus choose:

File
  Open Database
    Run Query...

▶ Select the query file (**.spq*) that you want to run.

▶ Depending on the database file, you may need to enter a login name and password.

▶ If the query has an embedded prompt, you may need to enter other information (for example, the quarter for which you want to retrieve sales figures).

## Selecting a Data Source

Use the first dialog box to select the type of data source to read into the software. After you have chosen the file type, the Database Wizard may prompt you for the path to your data file.

If you do not have any data sources configured, or if you want to add a new data source, click Add Data Source. In distributed analysis mode (available with the server version), this button is not available. To add data sources in distributed analysis mode, see your system administrator.

**Data sources.** A data source consists of two essential pieces of information: the driver that will be used to access the data and the location of the database that you want to access. To specify data sources, you must have the appropriate drivers installed. For local analysis mode, you can install drivers from the CD-ROM for this product:

- **SPSS Data Access Pack.** Installs drivers for a variety of database formats. Available on the AutoPlay menu.
- **Microsoft Data Access Pack.** Installs drivers for Microsoft products, including Microsoft Access. To install the Microsoft Data Access Pack, double-click Microsoft Data Access Pack in the Microsoft Data Access Pack folder on the CD-ROM.

Figure 3-1
*Database Wizard dialog box*

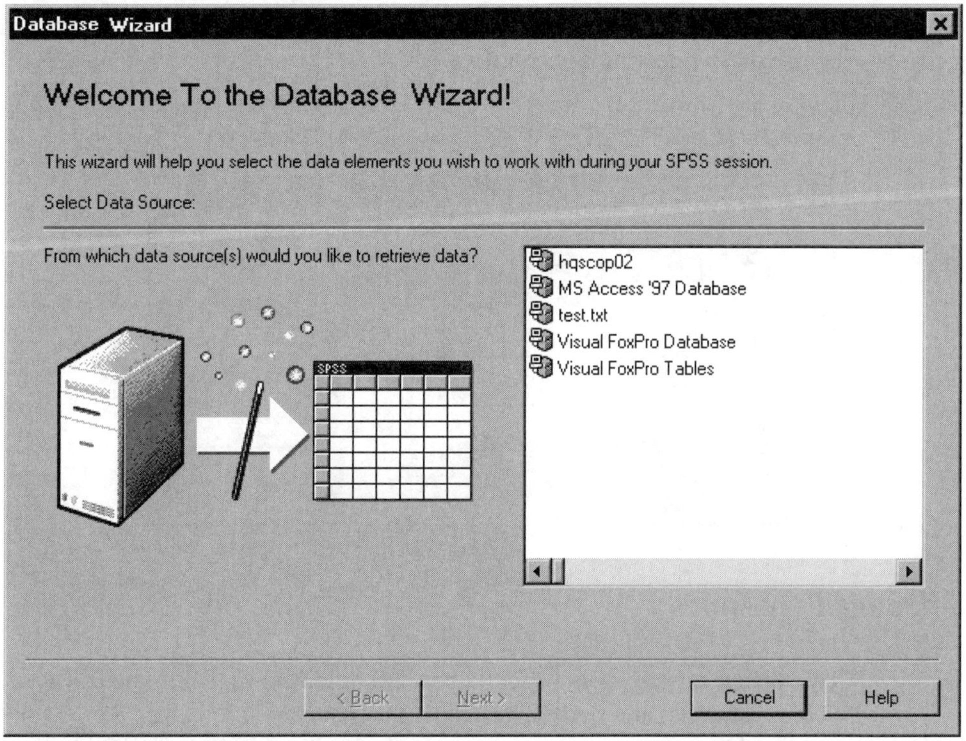


**Example.** Let's say you have a Microsoft Access 7.0 database that contains data about your employees and about the regions in which they work, and you want to import that data. Select the MS Access 7.0 Database icon, and click Next to proceed. You will see the Select Database dialog box. Specify the path to your database and click OK.

## Database Login

If your database requires a password, the Database Wizard will prompt you for one before it can open the data source.

Figure 3-2
*Login dialog box*

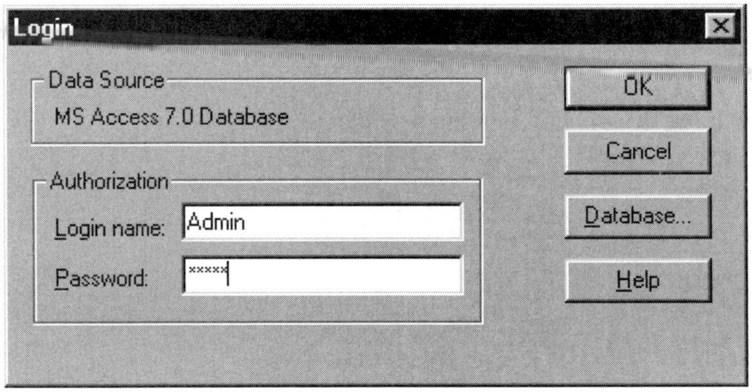


## Selecting Data Fields

This dialog box controls which tables and fields are read into the software. Database fields (columns) are read as variables.

If a table has any field(s) selected, *all* of its fields will be visible in the following Database Wizard windows, but only those fields selected in this dialog box will be imported as variables. This enables you to create table joins and to specify criteria using fields that you are not importing.

Figure 3-3
*Select Data dialog box*

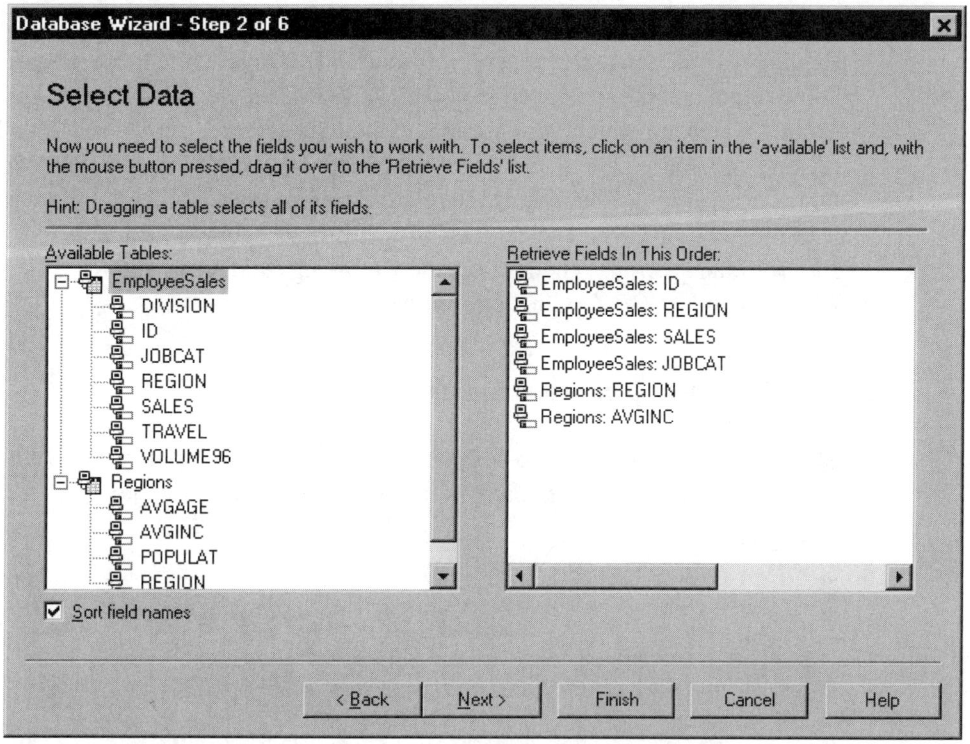


**Displaying field names.** To list the fields in a table, click the plus sign (+) to the left of a table name. To hide the fields, click the minus sign (–) to the left of a table name.

**To add a field.** Double-click any field in the Available Tables list, or drag it to the Retrieve Fields in This Order list. Fields can be reordered by dragging and dropping them within the selected fields list.

**To remove a field.** Double-click any field in the Retrieve Fields in This Order list, or drag it to the Available Tables list.

**Sort field names.** If selected, the Database Wizard will display your available fields in alphabetical order.

**Example.** Assume that you want to import from a database with two tables, Employees and Regions. The Employees table contains information about your company's employees, including the region they work in, their job category, and their annual sales. Employees are each assigned a region code (*REGION*), while those who do not have a home region get the special code of 0. The Regions table holds a large amount of data about the areas in which your company operates and prospective markets. It uses a region code (*REGION*) to identify the area and provides the average per capita income for the area, among other things. To relate each employee's sales to the average income in the region, you would select the following fields from the Employees table: *ID*, *REGION*, and *SALES*. Then, select the following fields from the Regions table: *REGION* and *AVGINC*. Click Next to proceed.

### *Creating a Relationship between Tables*

This dialog box allows you to define the relationships between the tables. If fields from more than one table are selected, you must define at least one join.

Figure 3-4
*Specify Relationships dialog box*

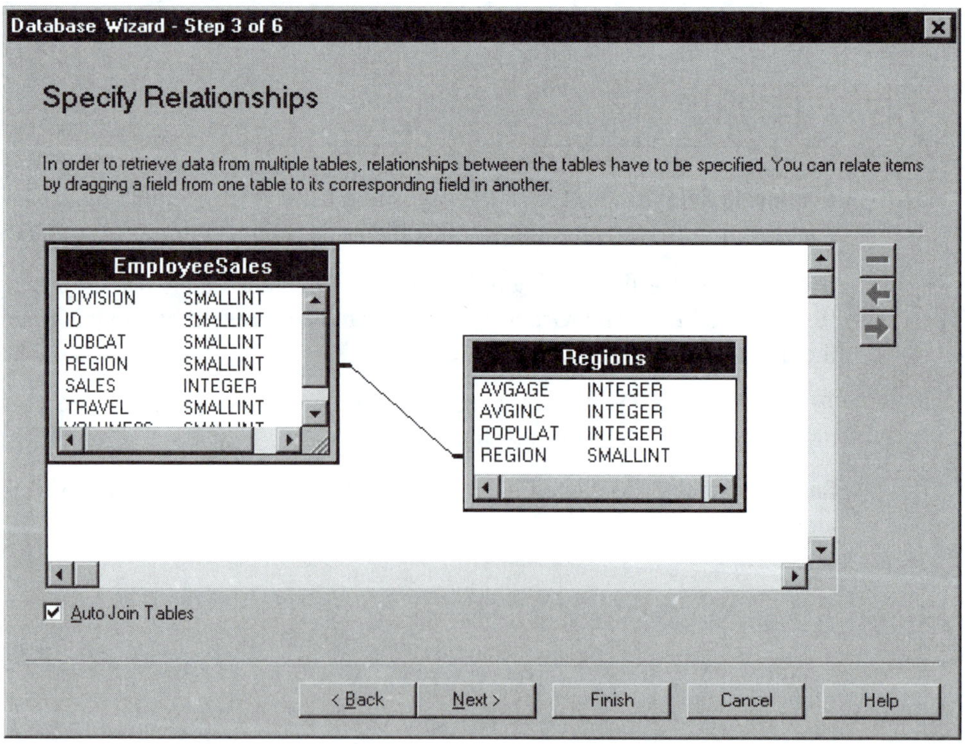

**Establishing relationships.** To create a relationship, drag a field from any table onto the field to which you want to join it. The Database Wizard will draw a **join line** between the two fields, indicating their relationship. These fields must be of the same data type.

**Auto Join Tables.** Attempts to automatically join tables based on primary/foreign keys or matching field names and data type.

**Specifying join types.** If outer joins are supported by your driver, you can specify either inner joins, left outer joins, or right outer joins. To select the type of join, click the join line between the fields, and the software will display the Relationship Properties dialog box.

You can also use the icons in the upper right corner of the dialog box to choose the type of join.

## Relationship Properties

This dialog box allows you to specify which type of relationship joins your tables.

Figure 3-5
*Relationship Properties dialog box*

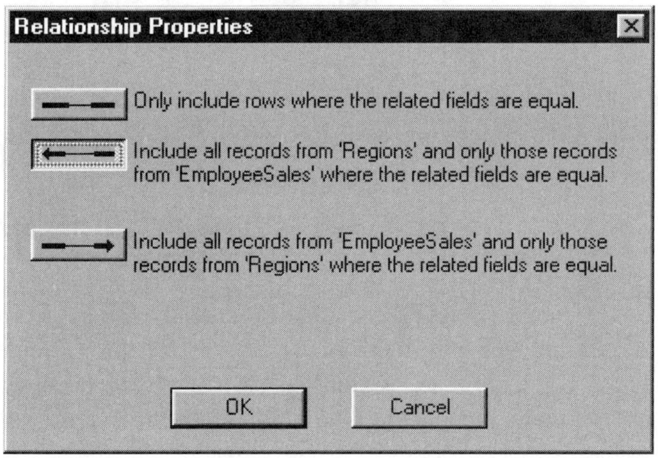


**Inner joins.** An inner join includes only rows where the related fields are equal.

**Example.** Continuing with our data, suppose that you want to import data only for those employees who work in a fixed region and only for those regions in which your company operates. In this case, you would use an inner join, which would exclude traveling employees and would filter out information about prospective regions in which you do not currently have a presence.

Completing this would give you a data set that contains the variables *ID*, *REGION*, *SALES95*, and *AVGINC* for each employee who worked in a fixed region.

Figure 3-6
*Creating an inner join*

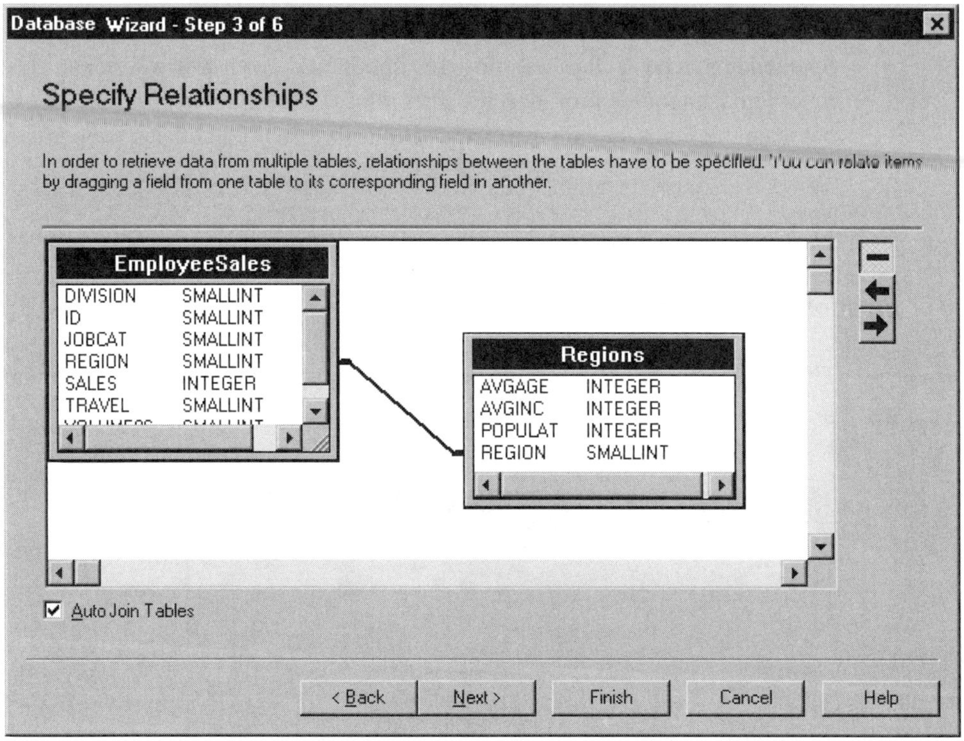


**Outer joins.** A left outer join includes all records from the table on the left and only those records from the table on the right in which the related fields are equal. In a right outer join, this relationship is switched, so that the software imports all records from the table on the right and only those records from the table on the left in which the related fields are equal.

**Example.** If you wanted to import data only for those employees who worked in fixed regions (a subset of the Employees table) but needed information about *all* of the regions, a right outer join would be appropriate. This results in a data set that contains the variables *ID*, *REGION*, *SALES95*, and *AVGINC* for each employee who worked in a fixed region, plus data on the remaining regions in which your company does not currently operate.

Figure 3-7
*Creating a right outer join*

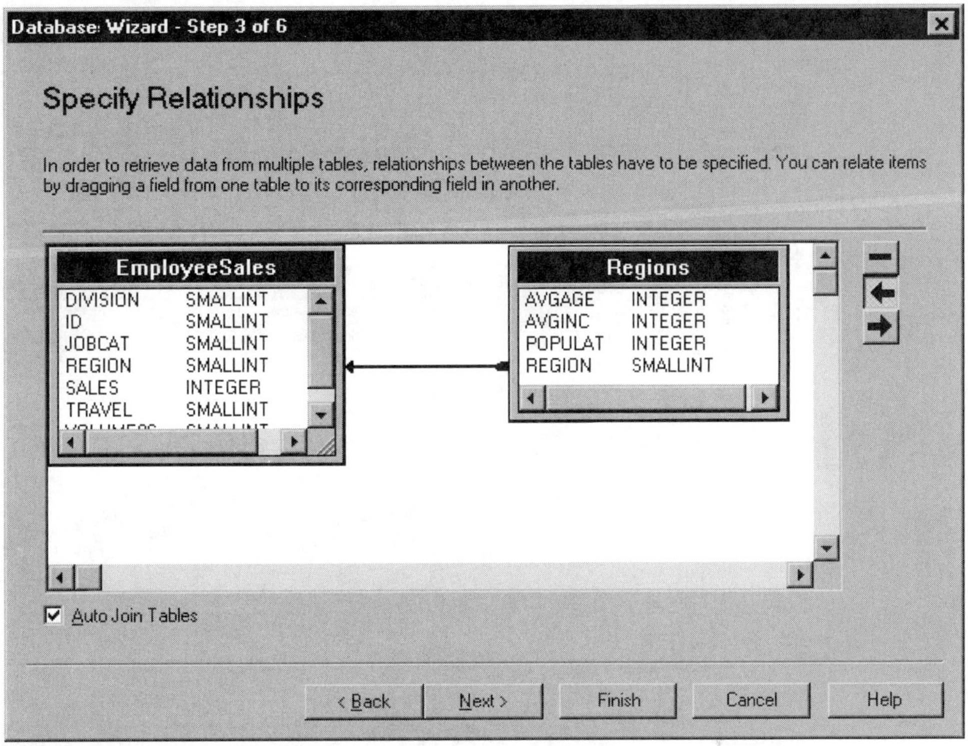


## *Limiting Retrieved Cases*

The Limit Retrieved Cases dialog box allows you to specify the criteria to select subsets of cases (rows). Limiting cases generally consists of filling the criteria grid with one or more criteria. Criteria consist of two expressions and some relation between them. They return a value of *true*, *false*, or *missing* for each case.

- If the result is *true*, the case is selected.
- If the result is *false* or *missing*, the case is not selected.
- Most criteria use one or more of the six relational operators (<, >, <=, >=, =, and <>).
- Expressions can include field names, constants, arithmetic operators, numeric and other functions, and logical variables. You can use fields that you do not plan to import as variables.

Figure 3-8
*Limit Retrieved Cases dialog box*

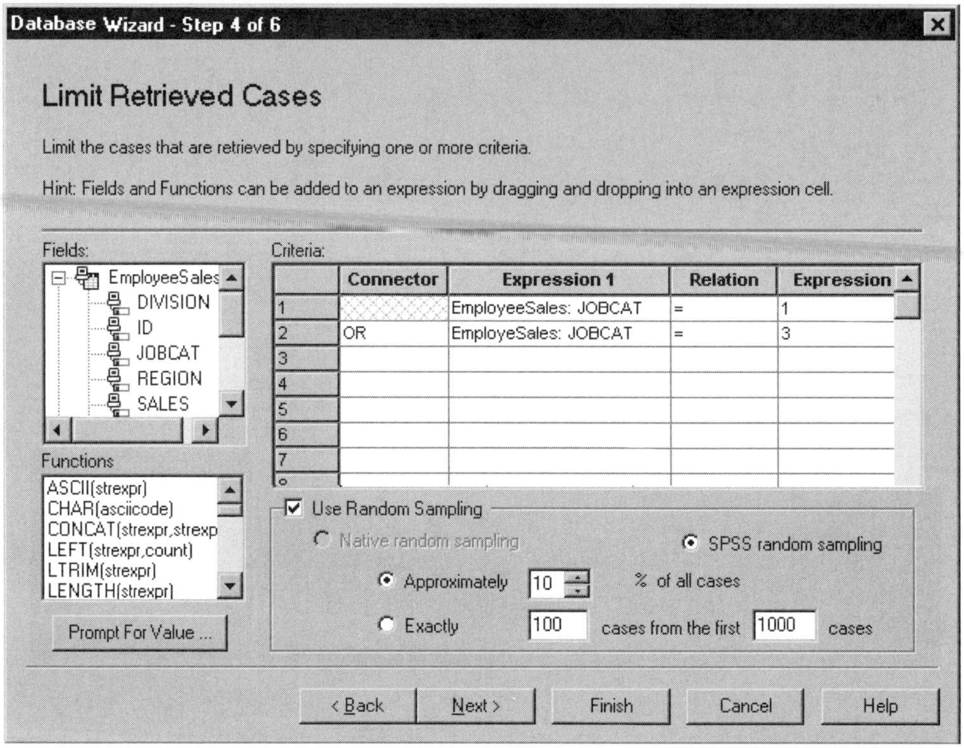


To build your criteria, you need at least two expressions and a relation to connect them.

- To build an expression, put your cursor in an Expression cell. You can type field names, constants, arithmetic operators, numeric and other functions, and logical variables. Other methods of putting a field into a criteria cell include double-clicking the field in the Fields list, dragging the field from the Fields list, or selecting a field from the drop-down menu that is available in any active Expression cell.

- The two expressions are usually connected by a relational operator, such as = or >. To choose the relation, put your cursor in the Relation cell and either type the operator or select it from the drop-down menu.

To modify our earlier example to retrieve data only about employees who fit into job categories 1 or 3, create two criteria in the criteria grid, and prefix the second criteria with the connector OR.

Criteria 1: 'EmployeeSales'.'JOBCAT' = 1
Criteria 2: 'EmployeeSales'.'JOBCAT' = 3

**Functions.** A selection of built-in arithmetic, logical, string, date, and time SQL functions are provided. You can select a function from the list and drag it into the expression, or you can enter any valid SQL function. See your database documentation for valid SQL functions.

**Use Random Sampling.** Selects a random sample of cases from the data source. For large data sources, you may want to limit the number of cases to a small, representative sample. This can significantly reduce the time to it takes to run procedures. Native random sampling, if available for the data source, is faster than SPSS random sampling, since SPSS random sampling must still read the entire data source to extract a random sample.

**Prompt for Value.** You can embed a prompt in your query to create a **parameter query**. When users run the query, they will be asked to enter information specified here. You might want to do this if you need to see different views of the same data. For example, you may want to run the same query to see sales figures for different fiscal quarters. Place your cursor in any Expression cell, and click Prompt for Value to create a prompt.

## *Creating a Parameter Query*

Use the Prompt for Value dialog box to create a dialog that solicits information from users each time someone runs your query. It is useful if you want to query the same data source using different criteria.

Figure 3-9
*Prompt for Value dialog box*

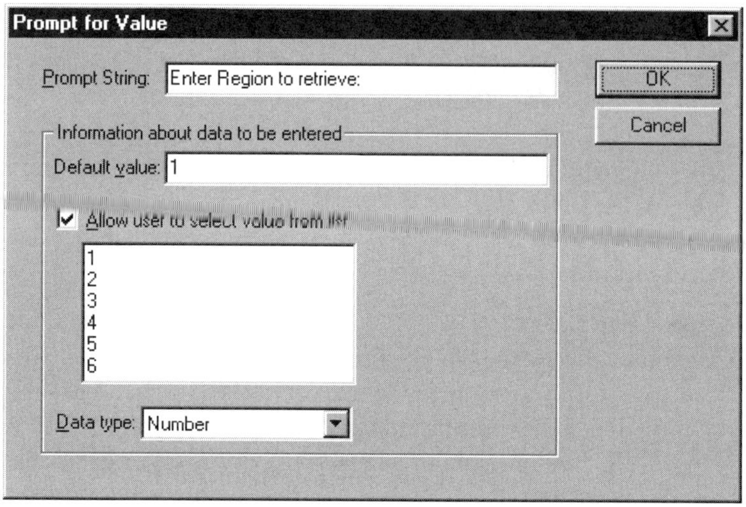


To build a prompt, you need to enter a prompt string and a default value. The prompt string is displayed each time a user runs your query. It should specify the kind of information to enter, and, if the user is not selecting from a list, it should give hints about how the input should be formatted. For example, "Enter a Quarter (Q1, Q2, Q3, ...):".

**Allow user to select value from list.** If this is selected, you can limit the user to the values you place here, which are separated by carriage returns.

**Data type.** Specify the data type here, either number, string, or date.

The final result looks like this:

Figure 3-10
*User-defined prompt dialog box*

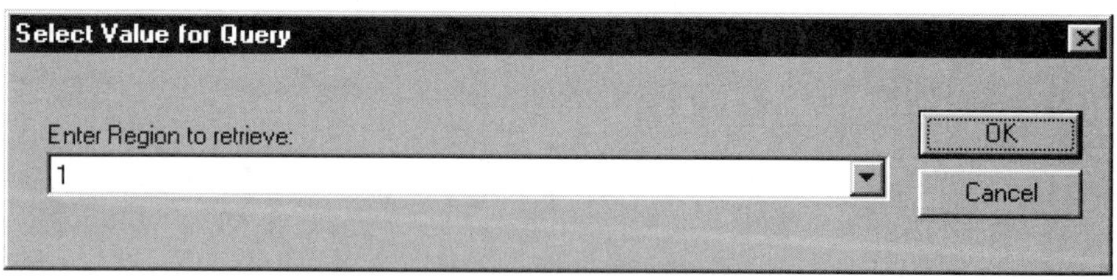

## Defining Variables

**Variable names and labels.** The complete database field (column) name is used as the variable label. Unless you modify the variable name, the Database Wizard assigns variable names to each column from the database in one of two ways:

- If the name of the database field (or the first eight characters) forms a valid, unique variable name, it is used as the variable name.
- If the name of the database field does not form a valid, unique variable name, the software creates a unique name.

Click any cell to edit the variable name.

**Converting strings to numeric values.** Check the Value Labels box for a string variable if you want to automatically convert it to a numeric variable. String values are converted to consecutive integer values based on alphabetic order of the original values. The original values are retained as value labels for the new variables.

Figure 3-11
*Define Variables dialog box*

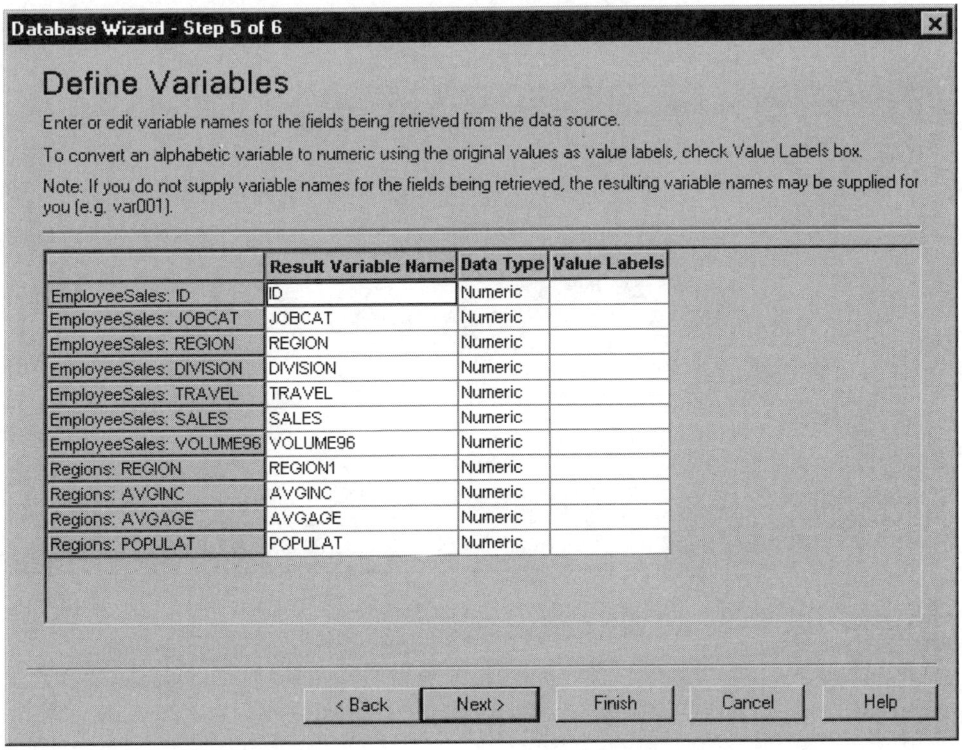

## *Results*

The Results dialog box displays the SQL Select statement for your query.

- You can edit the SQL Select statement before you run the query, but if you click the Back button to make changes in previous steps, the changes to the Select statement will be lost.
- You can save the query for future use with Save query to a file.
- Select Paste it into the syntax editor for further modification to paste complete GET DATA syntax into a syntax window. Copying and pasting the Select statement from the Results window will not paste the necessary command syntax.

Figure 3-12
*Results dialog box*

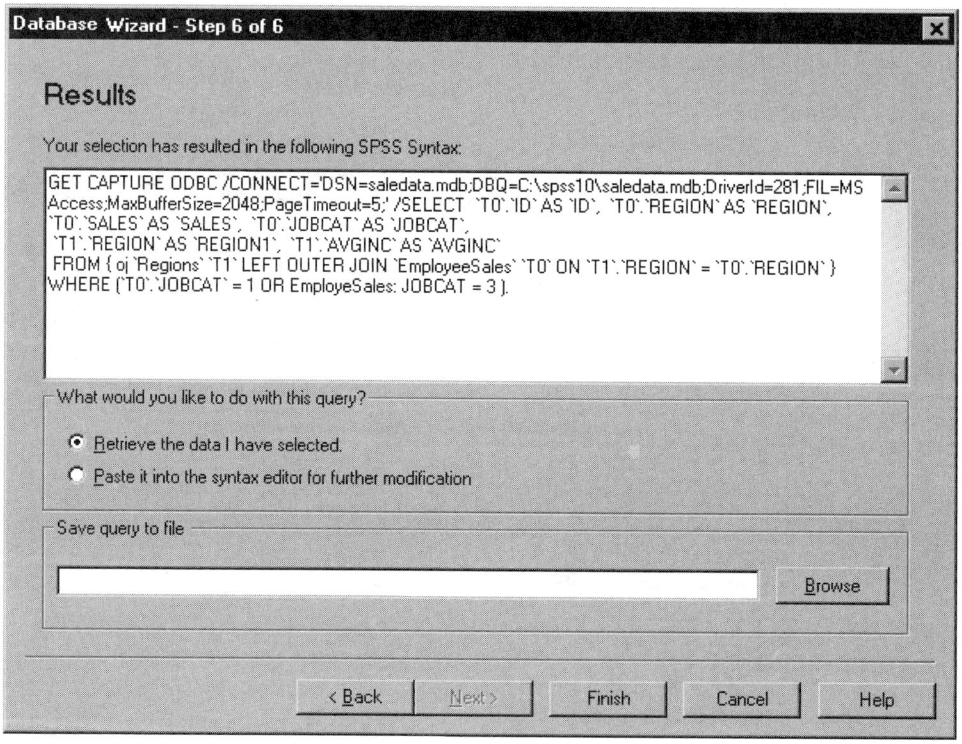

# Reading Text Data Files

The Text Wizard can read text data files formatted in a variety of ways:

- Tab-delimited files
- Space-delimited files
- Comma-delimited files
- Fixed-field format files

For delimited files, you can also specify other characters as delimiters between values, and you can specify multiple delimiters.

## To Read Text Data Files

▶ From the menus choose:

File
  Read Text Data

▶ Select the text file in the Open dialog box.

▶ Follow the steps in the Text Wizard to define how to read the data file.

## Text Wizard Step 1

Figure 3-13
*Text Wizard Step 1*

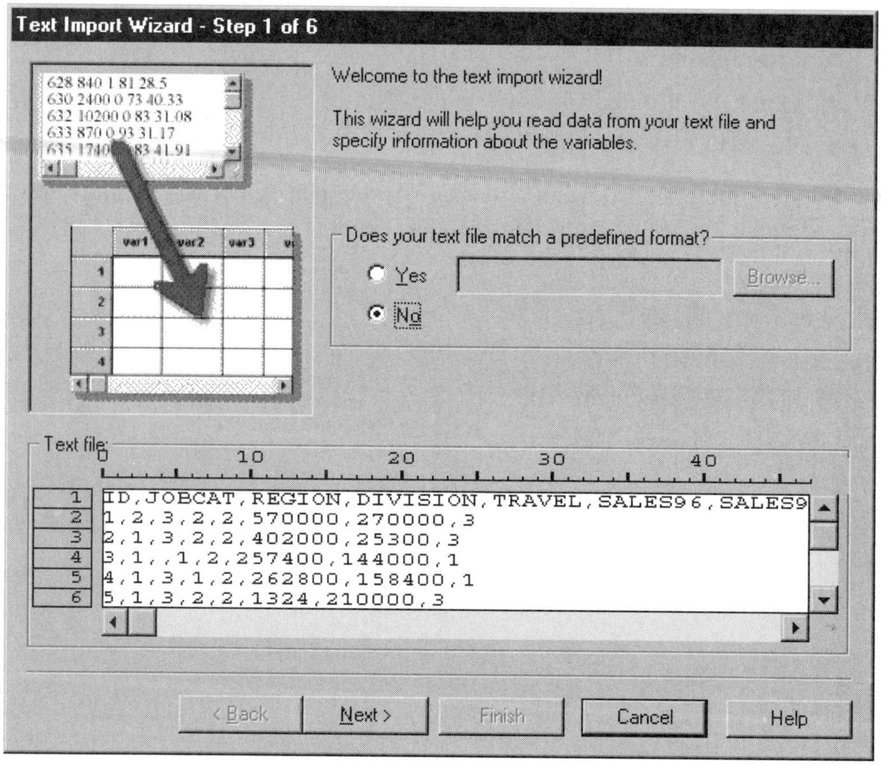


The text file is displayed in a preview window. You can apply a predefined format (previously saved from the Text Wizard) or follow the steps in the Text Wizard to specify how the data should be read.

## Text Wizard Step 2

Figure 3-14
*Text Wizard Step 2*

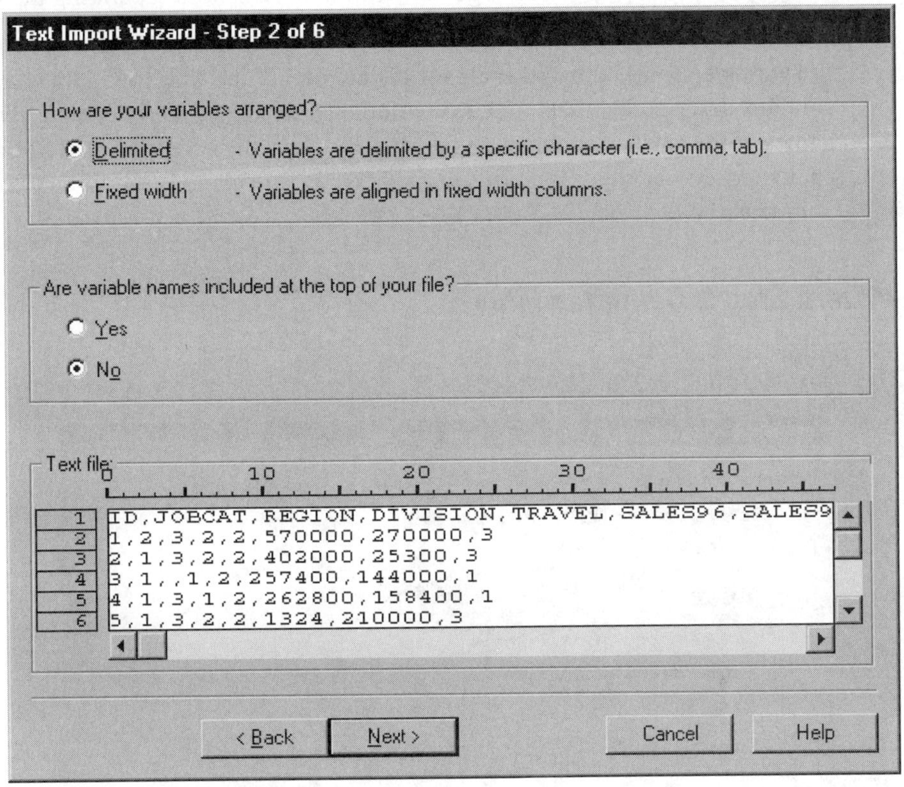


This step provides information about variables. A variable is similar to a field in a database. For example, each item in a questionnaire is a variable.

**How are your variables arranged?** To read your data properly, the Text Wizard needs to know how to determine where the data value for one variable ends and the data value for the next variable begins. The arrangement of variables defines the method used to differentiate one variable from the next.

- **Delimited.** Spaces, commas, tabs, or other characters are used to separate variables. The variables are recorded in the same order for each case but not necessarily in the same column locations.

- **Fixed width.** Each variable is recorded in the same column location on the same record (line) for each case in the data file. No delimiter is required between variables. In fact, in many text data files generated by computer programs, data values may appear to run together without even spaces separating them. The column location determines which variable is being read.

**Are variable names included at the top of your file?** If the first row of the data file contains descriptive labels for each variable, you can use these labels as variable names. If the labels are longer than eight characters, they are truncated. If the first eight characters do not create a unique variable name, the name is modified to create a unique variable name.

## Text Wizard Step 3: Delimited Files

Figure 3-15
*Text Wizard Step 3 for delimited files*

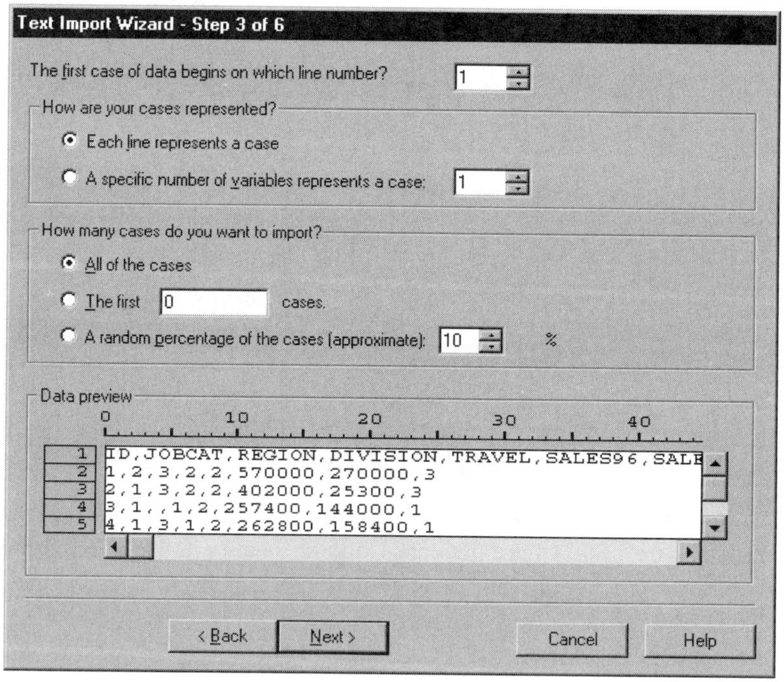


This step provides information about cases. A case is similar to a record in a database. For example, each respondent to a questionnaire is a case.

**The first case of data begins on which line number?** Indicates the first line of the data file that contains data values. If the top line(s) of the data file contain descriptive labels or other text that does not represent data values, this will *not* be line 1.

**How are your cases represented?** Controls how the Text Wizard determines where each case ends and the next one begins.

- **Each line represents a case.** Each line contains only one case. It is fairly common for each case to be contained on a single line (row), even though this can be a very long line for data files with a large number of variables. If not all lines contain the same number of data values, the number of variables for each case is determined by the line with the greatest number of data values. Cases with fewer data values are assigned missing values for the additional variables.
- **A specific number of variables represents a case.** The specified number of variables for each case tells the Text Wizard where to stop reading one case and start reading the next. Multiple cases can be contained on the same line, and cases can start in the middle of one line and be continued on the next line. The Text Wizard determines the end of each case based on the number of values read, regardless of the number of lines. Each case must contain data values (or missing values indicated by delimiters) for all variables, or the data file will be read incorrectly.

**How many cases do you want to import?** You can import all cases in the data file, the first *n* cases (*n* is a number you specify), or a random sample of a specified percentage. Since the random sampling routine makes an independent pseudo-random decision for each case, the percentage of cases selected can only approximate the specified percentage. The more cases there are in the data file, the closer the percentage of cases selected is to the specified percentage.

## Text Wizard Step 3: Fixed-Width Files

Figure 3-16
*Text Wizard Step 3 for fixed-width files*

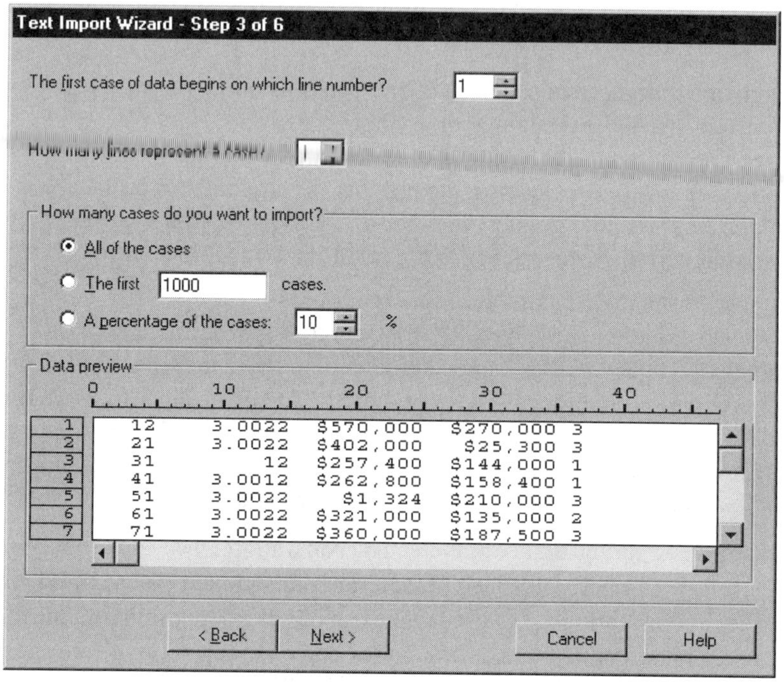


This step provides information about cases. A case is similar to a record in a database. For example, each respondent to questionnaire is a case.

**The first case of data begins on which line number?** Indicates the first line of the data file that contains data values. If the top line(s) of the data file contain descriptive labels or other text that does not represent data values, this will *not* be line 1.

**How many lines represent a case?** Controls how the Text Wizard determines where each case ends and the next one begins. Each variable is defined by its line number within the case and its column location. You need to specify the number of lines for each case to read the data correctly.

**How many cases do you want to import?** You can import all cases in the data file, the first *n* cases (*n* is a number you specify), or a random sample of a specified percentage. Since the random sampling routine makes an independent pseudo-random decision for each case, the percentage of cases selected can only approximate the specified percentage. The more cases there are in the data file, the closer the percentage of cases selected is to the specified percentage.

## Text Wizard Step 4: Delimited Files

Figure 3-17
*Text Wizard Step 4 for delimited files*

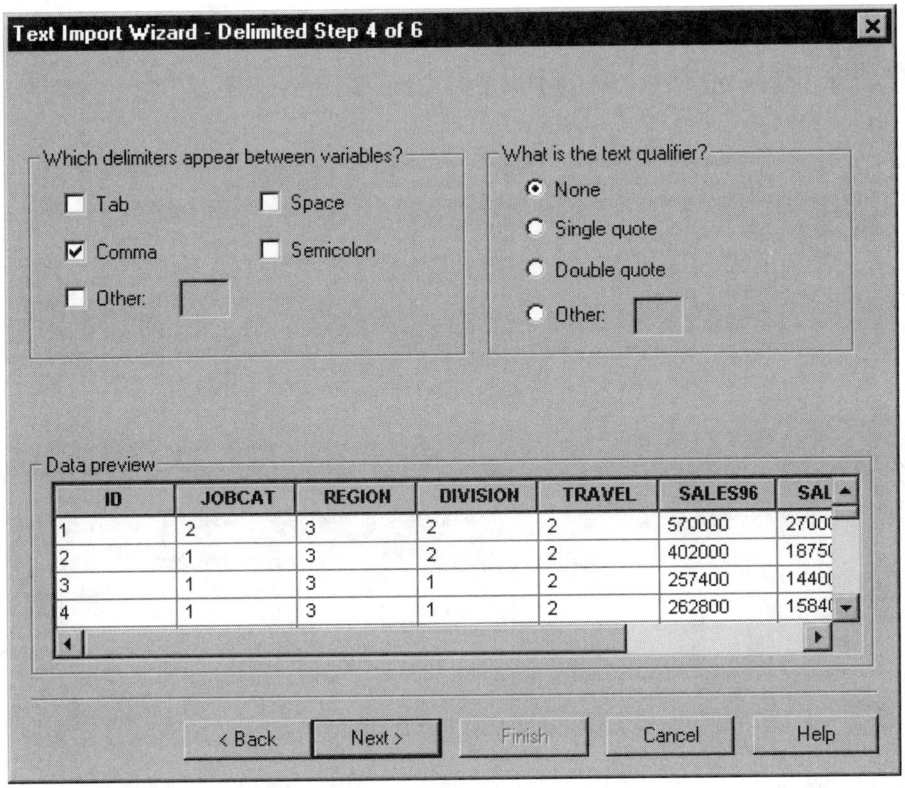


This step displays the Text Wizard's best guess on how to read the data file and allows you to modify how the Text Wizard will read variables from the data file.

**Which delimiters appear between variables?** Indicates the characters or symbols that separate data values. You can select any combination of spaces, commas, semicolons, tabs, or other characters. Multiple, consecutive delimiters without intervening data values are treated as missing values.

**What is the text qualifier?** Characters used to enclose values that contain delimiter characters. For example, if a comma is the delimiter, values that contain commas will be read incorrectly unless there is a text qualifier enclosing the value, preventing the commas in the value from being interpreted as delimiters between values. CSV-format data files exported from Excel use a double quotation mark (") as a text qualifier. The text qualifier appears at both the beginning and the end of the value, enclosing the entire value.

## *Text Wizard Step 4: Fixed-Width Files*

Figure 3-18
*Text Wizard Step 4 for fixed-width files*

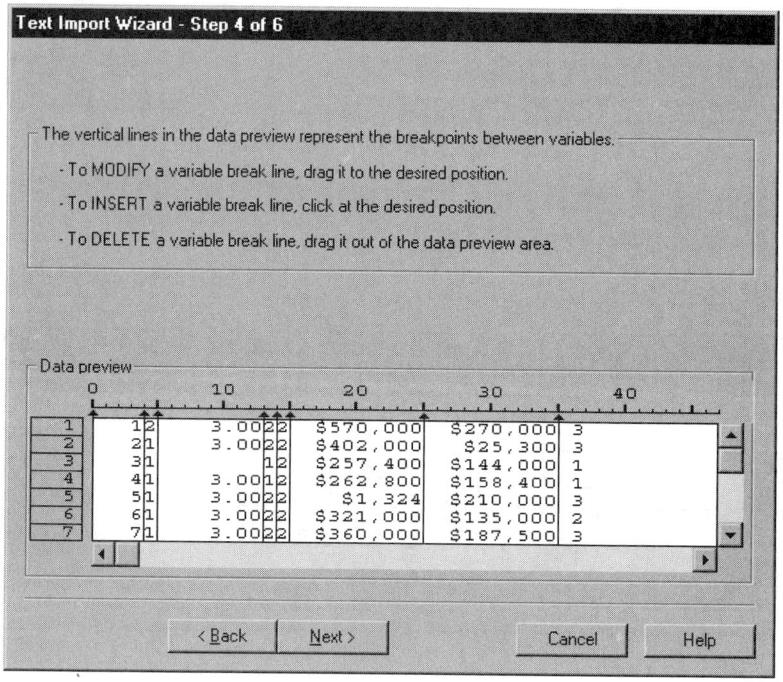


This step displays the Text Wizard's best guess on how to read the data file and allows you to modify how the Text Wizard will read variables from the data file. Vertical lines in the preview window indicate where the Text Wizard currently thinks each variable begins in the file.

Insert, move, and delete variable break lines as necessary to separate variables. If multiple lines are used for each case, select each line from the drop-down list and modify the variable break lines as necessary.

*Note*: For computer-generated data files that produce a continuous stream of data values with no intervening spaces or other distinguishing characteristics, it may be difficult to determine where each variable begins. Such data files usually rely on a data definition file or some other written description that specifies the line and column location for each variable.

## Text Wizard Step 5

Figure 3-19
*Text Wizard Step 5*

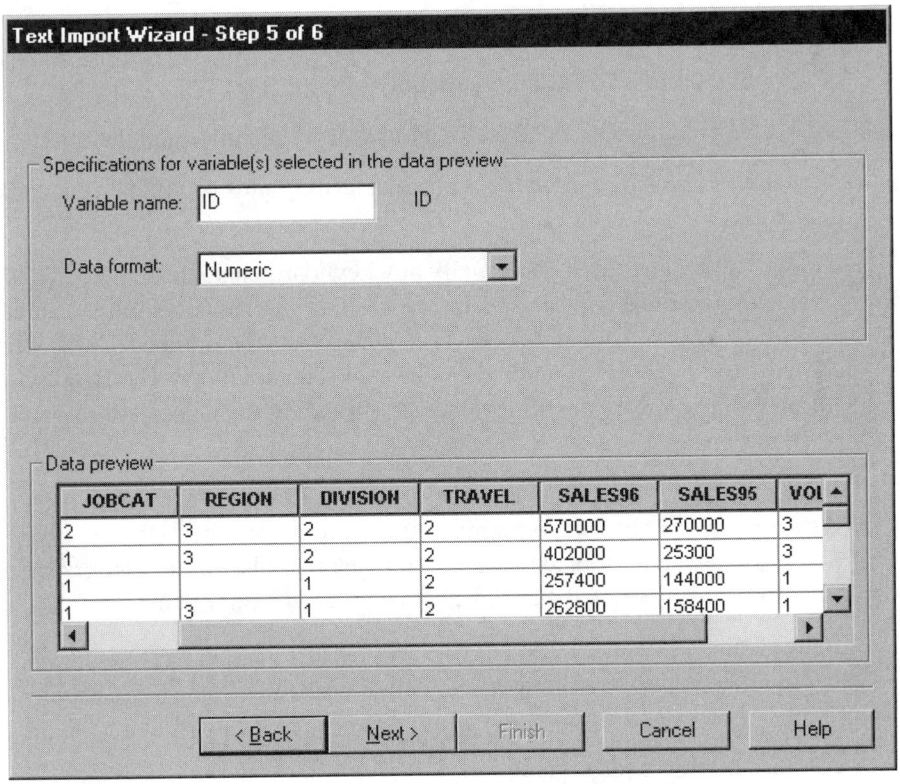

This steps controls the variable name and the data format that the Text Wizard will use to read each variable and which variables will be included in the final data file.

**Variable name.** You can overwrite the default variable names with your own variable names. If you read variable names from the data file, the Text Wizard will automatically modify variable names that are longer than eight characters or are not unique. Select a variable in the preview window and then enter a variable name. Variable names cannot exceed eight characters, cannot start with a number or the pound sign (#), and cannot contain spaces.

**Data format.** Select a variable in the preview window and then select a format from the drop-down list. Shift-click to select multiple contiguous variables or Ctrl-click to select multiple noncontiguous variables.

### Text Wizard Data Formatting Options

Formatting options for reading variables with the Text Wizard include:

**Do not import.** Omit the selected variable(s) from the imported data file.

**Numeric.** Valid values include numbers, a leading plus or minus sign, and a decimal indicator.

**String.** Valid values include virtually any keyboard characters and embedded blanks. For delimited files, you can specify the number of characters in the value, up to a maximum of 255. By default, the Text Wizard sets the number of characters to the longest string value encountered for the selected variable(s). For fixed-width files, the number of characters in string values is defined by the placement of variable break lines in step 4.

**Date/Time.** Valid values include dates of the general format *dd-mm-yyyy*, *mm/dd/yyyy*, *dd.mm.yyyy*, *yyyy/mm/dd*, *hh:mm:ss*, and a variety of other date and time formats. Months can be represented in digits, Roman numerals, or three-letter abbreviations, or they can be fully spelled out. Select a date format from the list.

**Dollar.** Valid values are numbers with an optional leading dollar sign and optional commas as thousands separators.

**Comma.** Valid values include numbers that use a period as a decimal indicator and commas as thousands separators.

**Dot.** Valid values include numbers that use a comma as a decimal indicator and periods as thousands separators.

*Note*: Values that contain invalid characters for the selected format will be treated as missing. Values that contain any of the specified delimiters will be treated as multiple values.

## Text Wizard Step 6

Figure 3-20
*Text Wizard Step 6*

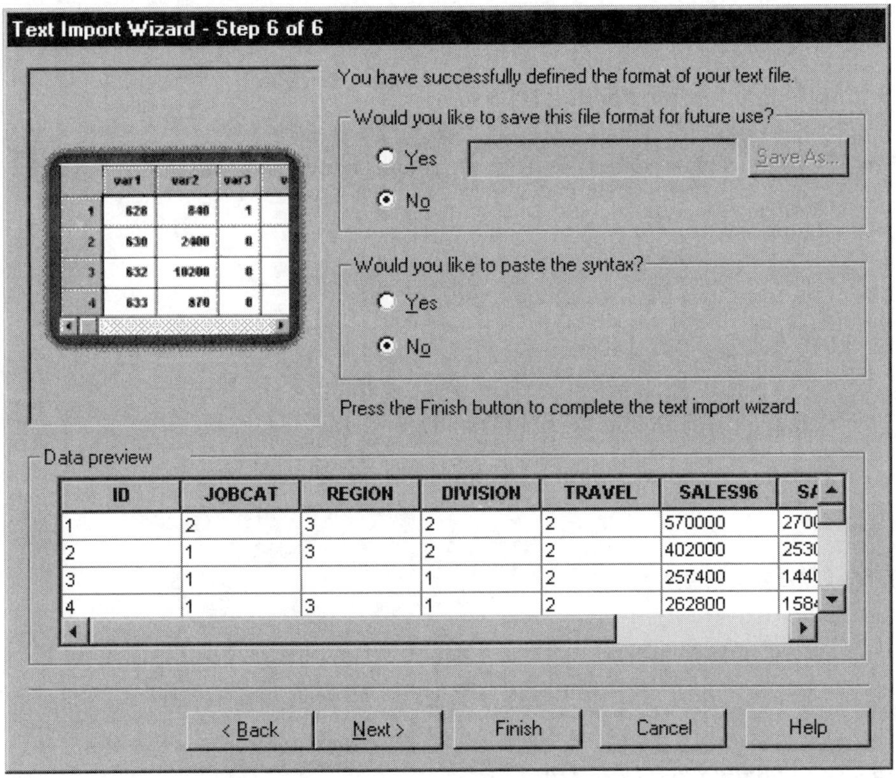


This is the final step of the Text Wizard. You can save your specifications in a file for use when importing similar text data files. You can also paste the syntax generated by the Text Wizard into a syntax window. You can then customize and/or save the syntax for use in other sessions or in production jobs.

# File Information

A data file contains much more than raw data. It also contains any variable definition information, including:

- Variable names
- Variable formats
- Descriptive variable and value labels

This information is stored in the dictionary portion of the data file. The Data Editor provides one way to view the variable definition information. You can also display complete dictionary information for the working data file or any other data file.

### To Obtain Information about a Data File

▶ For the working data file, from the menus choose:

Utilities
 File Info

▶ For other data files, from the menus choose:

File
 Display Data Info...

▶ Select a file from the Display Data Info dialog box.

The data file information is displayed in the Viewer.

# Saving Data Files

Any changes that you make in a data file last only for the duration of the current session—unless you explicitly save the changes.

### To Save Changes to a Data File

▶ Make the Data Editor the active window (click anywhere in the window to make it active).

▶ From the menus choose:

File
 Save

The modified data file is saved, overwriting the previous version of the file.

### To Save a New Data File or Save Data in a Different Format

▶ Make the Data Editor the active window (click anywhere in the window to make it active).

▶ From the menus choose:

File
 Save As...

▶ Select a file type from the drop-down list.

▶ Enter a filename for the new data file.

To write variable names to the first row of a spreadsheet or tab-delimited data files:

▶ Click Write variable names to spreadsheet in the Save Data As dialog box.

### Saving Data: Data File Types

You can save data in the following formats:

**SPSS (*.sav).** SPSS format. Data files saved in SPSS format cannot be read by versions of the software prior to version 7.5.

**SPSS 7.0 (*.sav).** SPSS 7.0 for Windows format. Data files saved in SPSS 7.0 format can be read by SPSS 7.0 and earlier versions of SPSS for Windows but do not include defined multiple response sets or Data Entry for Windows information.

**SPSS/PC+ (*.sys).** SPSS/PC+ format. If the data file contains more than 500 variables, only the first 500 will be saved. For variables with more than one defined user-missing value, additional user-missing values will be recoded into the first defined user-missing value.

**SPSS portable (*.por).** SPSS portable format that can be read by versions of SPSS on other operating systems (for example, Macintosh or UNIX).

**Tab-delimited (*.dat).** ASCII text files with values separated by tabs.

**Fixed ASCII (*.dat).** ASCII text file in fixed format, using the default write formats for all variables. There are no tabs or spaces between variable fields.

**Excel (*.xls).** Microsoft Excel 4.0 spreadsheet file. The maximum number of variables is 256.

**1-2-3 Release 3.0 (*.wk3).** Lotus 1-2-3 spreadsheet file, release 3.0. The maximum number of variables you can save is 256.

**1-2-3 Release 2.0 (*.wk1).** Lotus 1-2-3 spreadsheet file, release 2.0. The maximum number of variables you can save is 256.

**1-2-3 Release 1.0 (*.wks).** Lotus 1-2-3 spreadsheet file, release 1A. The maximum number of variables you can save is 256.

**SYLK (*.slk).** Symbolic link format for Microsoft Excel and Multiplan spreadsheet files. The maximum number of variables you can save is 256.

**dBASE IV (*.dbf).** dBASE IV format.

**dBASE III (*.dbf).** dBASE III format.

**dBASE II (*.dbf).** dBASE II format.

## Saving Subsets of Variables

Figure 3-21
*Save Data As Variables dialog box*

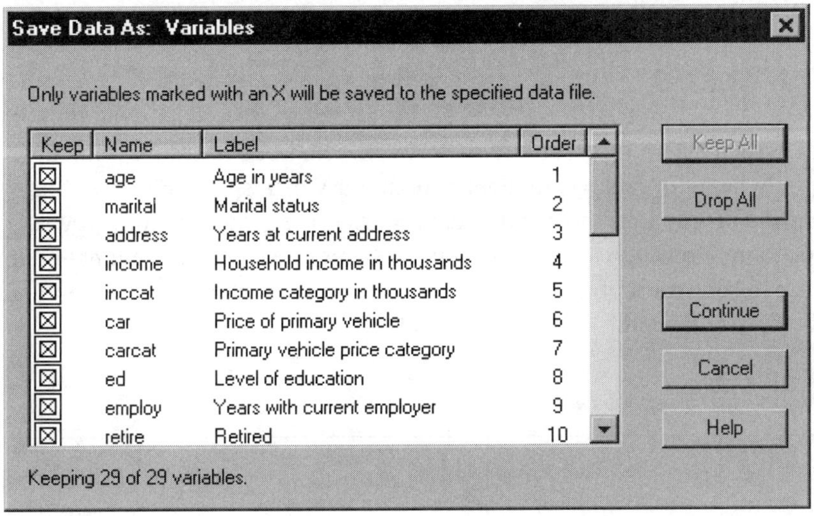


For data saved as an SPSS data file, the Save Data As Variables dialog box allows you to select the variables that you want saved in the new data file. By default, all variables will be saved. Deselect the variables that you don't want to save, or click Drop All and then select the variables that you want to save.

### To Save a Subset of Variables

- Make the Data Editor the active window (click anywhere in the window to make it active).
- From the menus choose:

  File
  Save As...

- Select SPSS (.sav) from the list of file types.
- Click Variables.
- Select the variables that you want to save.

## Saving File Options

For spreadsheet and tab-delimited files, you can write variable names to the first row of the file.

# Virtual Active File

The virtual active file enables you to work with large data files without requiring equally large (or larger) amounts of temporary disk space. For most analysis and charting procedures, the original data source is re-read each time you run a different procedure. Procedures that modify the data require a certain amount of temporary disk space to keep track of the changes, and some actions always require enough disk space for at least one entire copy of the data file.

Figure 3-22
*Temporary disk space requirements*

| **Action** | GET FILE = 'v1-5.sav'.<br>FREQUENCIES... | COMPUTE v6 = ...<br>RECODE v4...<br>REGRESSION...<br>/SAVE ZPRED. | SORT CASES BY...<br>or<br>CACHE |
|---|---|---|---|
| **Virtual Active File** | v1 v2 v3 v4 v5<br>11 12 13 14 15<br>21 22 23 24 25<br>31 32 33 34 35<br>41 42 43 44 45<br>51 52 53 54 55<br>61 62 63 64 65 | v1 v2 v3 v4 v5 v6 zpre<br>11 12 13 14 15 16 1<br>21 22 23 24 25 26 2<br>31 32 33 34 35 36 3<br>41 42 43 44 45 46 4<br>51 52 53 54 55 56 5<br>61 62 63 64 65 66 6 | v1 v2 v3 v4 v5 v6 zpre<br>11 12 13 14 15 16 1<br>21 22 23 24 25 26 2<br>31 32 33 34 35 36 3<br>41 42 43 44 45 46 4<br>51 52 53 54 55 56 5<br>61 62 63 64 65 66 6 |
| **Data Stored in Temporary Disk Space** | None | v4 v6 zpre<br>14 16 1<br>24 26 2<br>34 36 3<br>44 46 4<br>54 56 5<br>64 66 6 | v1 v2 v3 v4 v5 v6 zpre<br>11 12 13 14 15 16 1<br>21 22 23 24 25 26 2<br>31 32 33 34 35 36 3<br>41 42 43 44 45 46 4<br>51 52 53 54 55 56 5<br>61 62 63 64 65 66 6 |

**Actions that don't require any temporary disk space include:**

- Reading SPSS data files
- Merging two or more SPSS data files
- Reading database tables with the Database Wizard
- Merging an SPSS data file with a database table
- Running procedures that read data (for example, Frequencies, Crosstabs, Explore)

**Actions that create one or more columns of data in temporary disk space include:**

- Computing new variables
- Recoding existing variables
- Running procedures that create or modify variables (for example, saving predicted values in Linear Regression)

**Actions that create an entire copy of the data file in temporary disk space include:**

- Reading Excel files
- Reading text data files with the Text Wizard
- Running procedures that sort data (for example, Sort Cases, Split File, Report Summaries in Rows/Columns)
- Reading data with GET TRANSLATE or DATA LIST commands
- Using the Cache Data facility or the CACHE command
- Launching other applications from SPSS that read the data file (for example, AnswerTree, DecisionTime).

*Note*: The GET DATA command provides functionality comparable to DATA LIST, without creating an entire copy of the data file in temporary disk space. The SPLIT FILE and REPORT commands in command syntax do not sort the data file and therefore do not create a copy of the data file. Both commands, however, require sorted data for proper operation, and the dialog box interface for these procedures will automatically sort the data file, resulting in a complete copy of the data file.

## *Creating a Data Cache*

Although the virtual active file can vastly reduce the amount of temporary disk space required, the absence of a temporary copy of the "active" file means that the original data source has to be re-read for each procedure. For data tables read from a database source, this means the SQL query that reads the information from the database must be re-executed for any command or procedure that needs to read the data. Since virtually all statistical analysis procedures and charting procedures need to read the data, the SQL query is re-executed for each procedure you run, which can result in a significant increase in processing time if you run a large number of procedures.

If you have sufficient disk space on the computer performing the analysis (either your local computer or a remote server), you can eliminate multiple SQL queries and improve processing time by creating a data cache of the active file. The data cache is a temporary copy of the complete data table.

### To Create a Data Cache

▶ From the menus choose:

File
 Cache Data

▶ Click OK or Cache Now.

OK creates a data cache the next time the program reads the data (for example, the next time you run a statistical procedure), which is usually what you want since it doesn't require an extra data pass. Cache Now creates a data cache immediately, which shouldn't be necessary under most circumstances. Cache Now is useful primarily for two reasons:

- A data source is "locked" and can't be updated by anyone until you end your session, open a different data source, or cache the data.
- For large data sources, scrolling through the contents of the Data view in the Data Editor will be much faster if you cache the data.

Chapter

4

# Distributed Analysis

Distributed analysis mode allows you to use a computer other than your local (or desktop) computer to do memory-intensive work for you. Since remote servers used for distributed analysis are typically more powerful and faster than your local computer, appropriate use of distributed analysis mode can significantly reduce computer processing time. Distributed analysis with a remote server can be useful if your work involves:

- Large data files, particularly data read from database sources.
- Memory-intensive tasks. Any task that seems to take a long time in local analysis mode might be a good candidate for distributed analysis.

Distributed analysis affects only data-related tasks, such as reading data, transforming data, computing new variables, and calculating statistics. It has no effect on tasks related to editing output, such as manipulating pivot tables or modifying charts.

*Note*: Distributed analysis is available only if you have both a local version and access to a licensed server version of the software installed on a remote server.

# Distributed versus Local Analysis

Following are some guidelines that you might find useful for choosing distributed or local analysis mode:

**Database access.** Jobs that perform database queries may run faster in distributed mode if the server has superior access to the database or if the server is running on the same machine as the database engine. If the necessary database access software is available only on the server, or if your network administrator does not permit you to download large data tables, you will be able to access the database only in distributed mode.

**Ratio of computation to output.** Commands that perform a lot of computation and produce small output results (for example, few and small pivot tables, brief text results, few or simple charts) have the most to gain from running in distributed mode. The degree of improvement depends largely on the computing power of the remote server.

**Small jobs.** Jobs that run quickly in local mode will almost always run slower in distributed mode because of inherent client/server overhead.

**Charts.** Case-oriented charts, such as scatterplots, regression residual plots, and sequence charts, require raw data on your local computer. For large data files or database tables, this can result in slower performance in distributed mode because the data have to be sent from the remote server to your local computer. Other charts are based on summarized or aggregated data and should perform adequately because the aggregation is performed on the server.

**Interactive graphics.** Since it is possible to save raw data with interactive graphics (an optional setting), this can result in large amounts of data being transferred from the remote server to your local computer, significantly increasing the time it takes to save your results.

**Pivot tables.** Large pivot tables may take longer to create in distributed mode. This is particularly true for the OLAP Cubes procedure and tables that contain individual case data, such as those available in the Summarize procedure.

**Text output.** The more text that is produced, the slower it will be in distributed mode because this text is produced on the remote server and copied to your local computer for display. Text results have low overhead, however, and tend to transmit quickly.

## Server Login

The Server Login dialog box allows you to select the computer that you want to use to process commands and run procedures. This can be either your local computer or a remote server.

Figure 4-1
*Server Login dialog box*

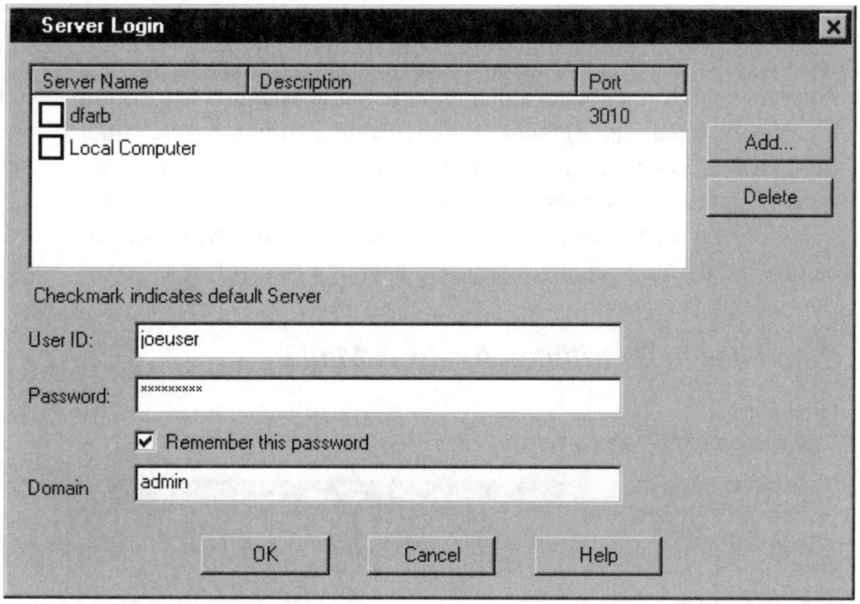


You can add or delete remote servers from the list. Remote servers usually require a user ID and a password, and a domain name may also be necessary. Contact your system administrator for information about available servers, user ID, passwords, and domain names.

You can select a default server and save the user ID, domain name, and password associated with any server. You are automatically connected to the default server when you start a new session.

### To Select, Switch, or Add Servers

▶ From the menus choose:

File
  Switch Server...

▶ Select the server from the list.

▶ Enter your user ID, domain name, and password (if necessary).

▶ If the server that you want to use isn't in the list, click Add to add the server to the list.

A server "name" can be an alphanumeric name assigned to a computer (for example, hqdev001) or a unique IP address assigned to a computer (example, 202.123.456.78). Contact your system administrator for a list of available servers and the correct way to specify server names, user ID, domain name, and password.

When you switch servers during a session, all open windows are closed. You will be prompted to save changes before the windows are closed.

## Opening Data Files in Distributed Analysis Mode

Figure 4-2
*Open Remote File dialog box*

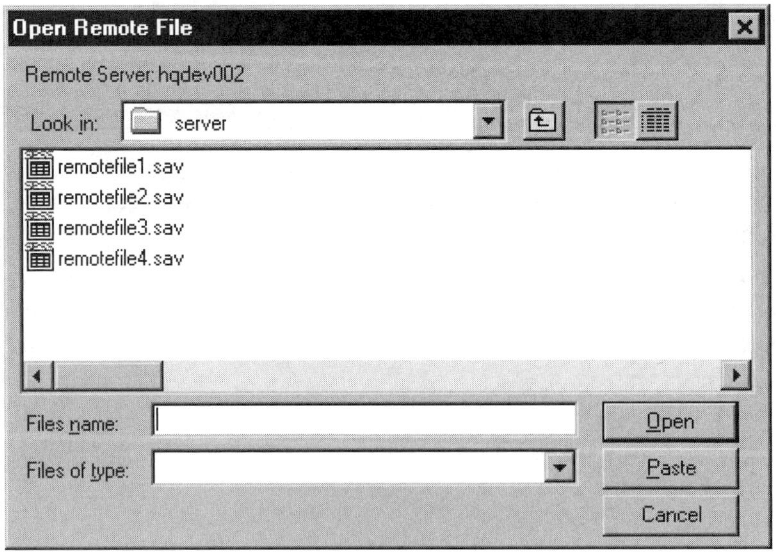

In distributed analysis mode, the Open Remote File dialog box replaces the standard Open File dialog box.

- The list of available files, folders, and drives is dependent on what is available on or from the remote server. The current server name is indicated at the top of the dialog box.
- You will not have access to files on your local computer in distributed analysis mode unless you specify the drive as a shared device or the folders containing your data files as shared folders.
- If the server is running a different operating system (for example, you are running Windows and the server is running UNIX), you probably won't have access to local data files in distributed analysis mode, even if they are in shared folders.

Only one data file can be open at a time. The current data file is automatically closed when a new data file is opened. If you want to have multiple data files open at the same time, you can start multiple sessions.

### To Open Data Files in Distributed Analysis Mode

▶ If you aren't already connected to the remote server, log in to the remote server.

▶ Depending on the type of data file that you want to open, from the menus choose:

File
  Open
    Data...

*or*

File
  Open Database

*or*

File
  Read Text Data

## Saving Data Files in Distributed Analysis Mode

Figure 4-3
*Save Remote File dialog box*

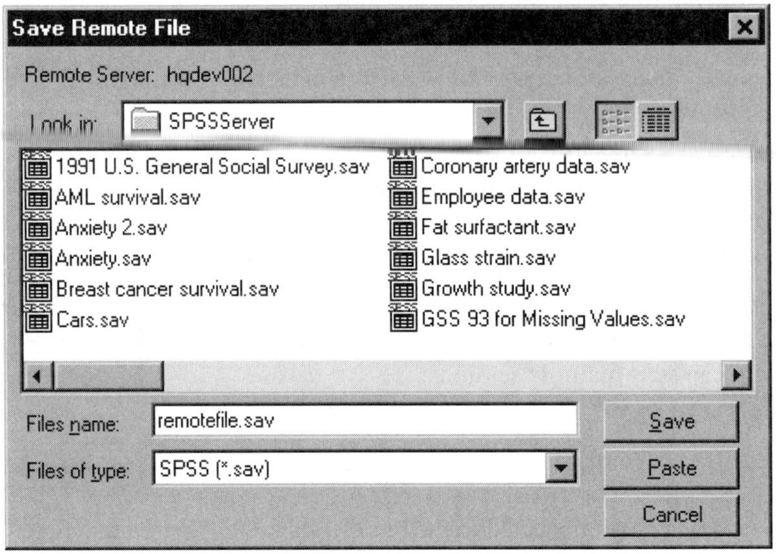


In distributed analysis mode, the Save Remote File dialog box replaces the standard Save File dialog box.

The list of available folders and drives is dependent on what is available on or from the remote server. The current server name is indicated at the top of the dialog box. You will not have access to folders on your local computer unless you specify the drive as a shared device and the folders as shared folders. If the server is running a different operating system (for example, you are running Windows and the server is running UNIX), you probably won't have access to local data files in distributed analysis mode, even if they are in shared folders. Permissions for shared folders must include the ability to write to the folder if you want to save data files in a local folder.

### To Save Data Files in Distributed Analysis Mode

▶ Make the Data Editor the active window.

▶ From the menus choose:

File
 Save (or Save As...)

## Data File Access in Local and Distributed Analysis Mode

The view of data files, folders (directories), and drives for both your local computer and the network is based on the computer you are currently using to process commands and run procedures—which is not necessarily the computer in front of you—where you select those commands and procedures and see the results.

**Local analysis mode.** When you use your local computer as your "server," the view of data files, folders, and drives that you see in the file access dialog box (for opening data files) is similar to what you see in other applications or in the Windows Explorer. You can see all of the data files and folders in your computer and any files and folders on mounted network drives that you would normally see.

**Distributed analysis mode.** When you use another computer as a "remote server" to run commands and procedures, the view of data files, folders, and drives represents the view from the perspective of the remote server computer. Although you may see familiar folder names such as *Program Files* and drives such as *C*, these are *not* the folders and drives on your computer; they are the folders and drives on the remote server.

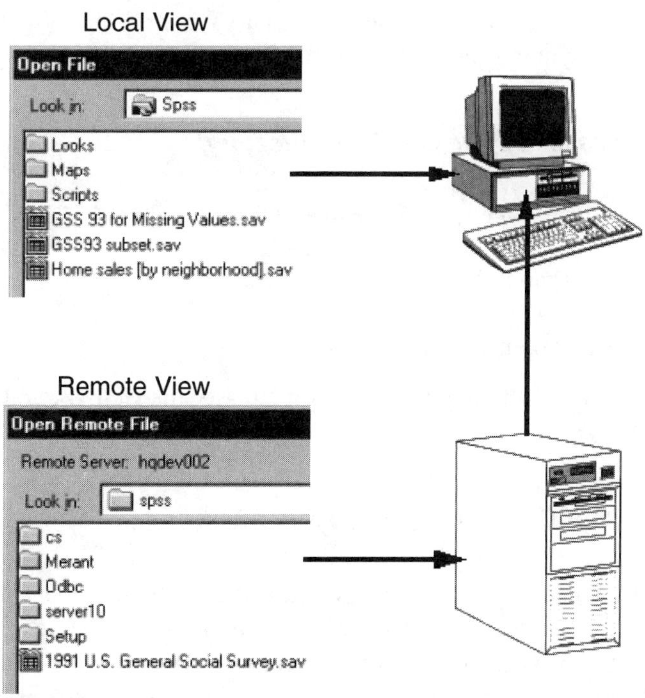

In distributed analysis mode, you will not have access to data files on your local computer unless you specify the drive as a shared device or the folders containing your data files as shared folders. If the server is running a different operating system (for example, if you are running Windows and the server is running UNIX), you probably won't have access to local data files in distributed analysis mode, even if they are in shared folders.

Distributed analysis mode is not the same as accessing data files that reside on another computer on your network. You can access data files on other network devices in local analysis mode or in distributed analysis mode. In local mode, you access other devices from your local computer. In distributed mode, you access other network devices from the remote server.

If you're not sure if you're using local analysis mode or distributed analysis mode, look at the title bar in the dialog box for accessing data files. If the title of the dialog box contains the word *Remote* (as in Open Remote File), or if the text Remote Server: [server name] appears at the top of the dialog box, you're using distributed analysis mode.

*Note*: This affects only dialog boxes for accessing data files (for example, Open Data, Save Data, Open Database, and Apply Data Dictionary). For all other file types (for example, Viewer files, syntax files, and script files), the local view is always used.

### To Set Sharing Permissions for a Drive or Folder (Directory)

- In My Computer, click the directory or drive that you want to share.
- On the File menu, click Properties.
- Click the Sharing tab, and then click Shared As.

For more information about sharing drives and folders, see the Help for your operating system.

## Availability of Procedures in Distributed Analysis Mode

In distributed analysis mode, only procedures installed on both your local version and the version on the remote server are available. You cannot use procedures installed on the server that are not also installed on your local version, and you cannot use procedures installed on your local version that are not also installed on the remote server.

While the latter situation may be unlikely, it is possible that you may have optional components installed locally that aren't available on the remote server. If this is the case, switching from your local computer to a remote server will result in the removal of the affected procedures from the menus, and the corresponding command syntax will result in errors. Switching back to local mode will restore all affected procedures.

## Using UNC Path Specifications

With the Windows NT server version of SPSS, relative path specifications for data files are relative to the current server in distributed analysis mode, not relative to your local computer. In practical terms, this means that a path specification such as *c:\mydocs\mydata.sav* does not point to a directory and file on your *C* drive; it points to a directory and file on the remote server's hard drive. If the directory and/or file don't exist on the remote server, this will result in an error in command syntax, as in:

```
GET FILE='c:\mydocs\mydata.sav'.
```

If you are using the Windows NT server version of SPSS, you can use universal naming convention (UNC) specifications when accessing data files with command syntax. The general form of a UNC specification is:

```
\\servername\sharename\path\filename
```

- *Servername* is the name of the computer that contains the data file.
- *Sharename* is the folder (directory) on that computer that is designated as a shared folder.
- *Path* is any additional folder (subdirectory) path below the shared folder.
- *Filename* is the name of the data file.

For example:

```
GET FILE='\\hqdev001\public\july\sales.sav'.
```

If the computer doesn't have a name assigned to it, you can use its IP address, as in:

```
GET FILE='\\204.125.125.53\public\july\sales.sav'.
```

Even with UNC path specifications, you can access data files only from devices and folders designated as shared. When you use distributed analysis mode, this includes data files on your local computer.

**UNIX servers.** On UNIX platforms, there is no equivalent of the UNC path, and all directory paths must be absolute paths that start at the root of the server; relative paths are not allowed. For example, if the data file is located in */bin/spss/data* and the current directory is also */bin/spss/data*, GET FILE='sales.sav' is not valid; you must specify the entire path, as in:

```
GET FILE='/bin/data/spss/sales.sav'.
```

Chapter

5

# Data Editor

The Data Editor provides a convenient, spreadsheet-like method for creating and editing data files. The Data Editor window opens automatically when you start a session.

The Data Editor provides two views of your data:

- **Data view**. Displays the actual data values or defined value labels.
- **Variable view**. Displays variable definition information, including defined variable and value labels, data type (for example, string, date, and numeric), measurement scale (nominal, ordinal, or scale), and user-defined missing values.

In both views, you can add, change, and delete information contained in the data file.

# Data View

Figure 5-1
*Data view*

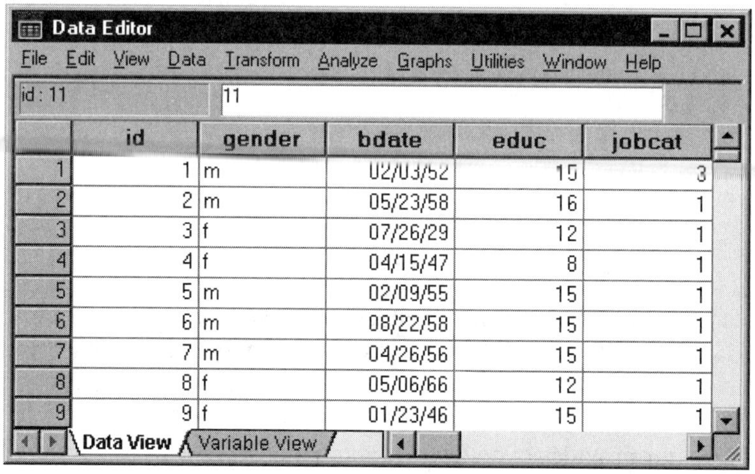


Many of the features of the Data view are similar to those found in spreadsheet applications. There are, however, several important distinctions:

- Rows are cases. Each row represents a case or an observation. For example, each individual respondent to a questionnaire is a case.
- Columns are variables. Each column represents a variable or characteristic being measured. For example, each item on a questionnaire is a variable.
- Cells contain values. Each cell contains a single value of a variable for a case. The cell is the intersection of the case and the variable. Cells contain only data values. Unlike spreadsheet programs, cells in the Data Editor cannot contain formulas.
- The data file is rectangular. The dimensions of the data file are determined by the number of cases and variables. You can enter data in any cell. If you enter data in a cell outside the boundaries of the defined data file, the data rectangle is extended to include any rows and/or columns between that cell and the file boundaries. There are no “empty” cells within the boundaries of the data file. For numeric variables, blank cells are converted to the system-missing value. For string variables, a blank is considered a valid value.

# Variable View

Figure 5-2
*Variable view*

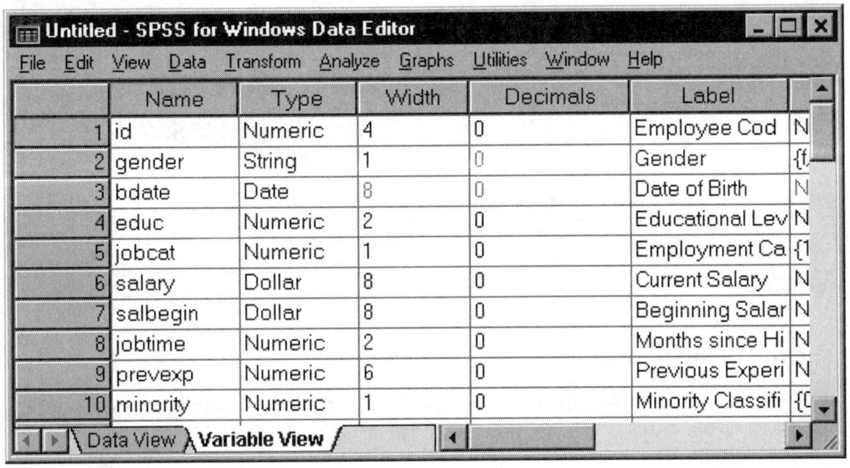


The Variable view contains descriptions of the attributes of each variable in the data file. In the Variable view:

- Rows are variables.
- Columns are variable attributes.

You can add or delete variables and modify attributes of variables, including:

- Variable name
- Data type
- Number of digits or characters
- Number of decimal places
- Descriptive variable and value labels
- User-defined missing values
- Column width
- Measurement scale

### To Display or Define Variable Attributes

▶ Make the Data Editor the active window.

▶ Double-click a variable name at the top of the column in the Data view, or click the Variable View tab.

▶ To define new variables, enter a variable name in any blank row.

▶ Select the attribute(s) you want to define or modify.

## Variable Names

The following rules apply to variable names:

- The name must begin with a letter. The remaining characters can be any letter, any digit, a period, or the symbols @, #, _, or $.
- Variable names cannot end with a period.
- Variable names that end with an underscore should be avoided (to avoid conflict with variables automatically created by some procedures).
- The length of the name cannot exceed eight characters.
- Blanks and special characters (for example, !, ?, ', and *) cannot be used.
- Each variable name must be unique; duplication is not allowed. Variable names are not case sensitive. The names *NEWVAR*, *NewVar*, and *newvar* are all considered identical.

## Measurement Level

You can specify the level of measurement as scale (numeric data on an interval or ratio scale), ordinal, or nominal. Nominal and ordinal data can be either string (alphanumeric) or numeric. Measurement specification is relevant only for:

- Chart procedures that identify variables as scale or categorical. Nominal and ordinal are both treated as categorical.
- SPSS-format data files used with AnswerTree.

Figure 5-3
*Scale and categorical variables in a chart procedure*

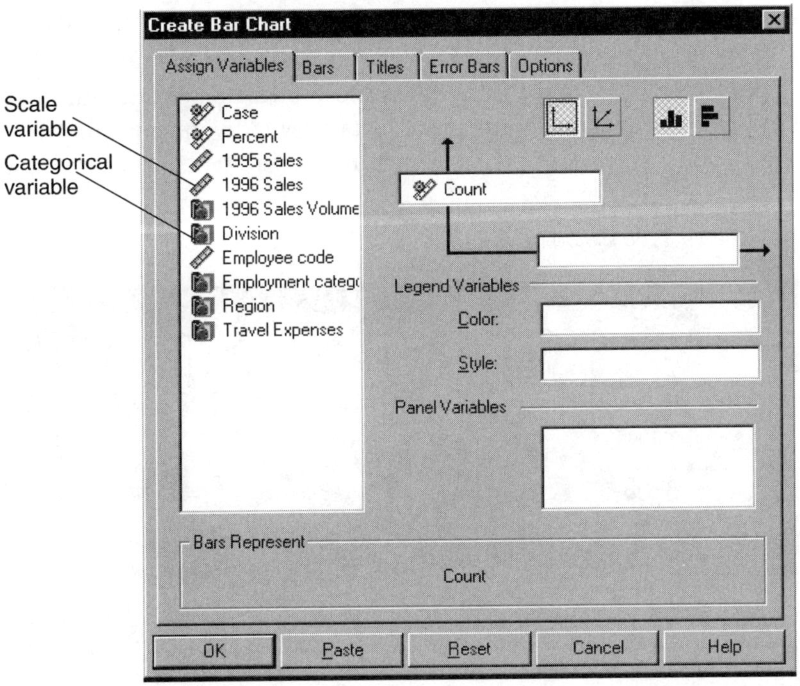


For SPSS-format data files created in earlier versions of SPSS products, the following rules apply:

- String (alphanumeric) variables are set to nominal.
- String and numeric variables with defined value labels are set to ordinal.
- Numeric variables without defined value labels but less than a specified number of unique values are set to ordinal.
- Numeric variables without defined value labels and more than a specified number of unique values are set to scale.

The default number of unique values is 24. To change the specified value, change the interactive chart options (from the Edit menu, choose Options and click the Interactive tab).

# Variable Type

Define Variable Type specifies the data type for each variable. By default, all new variables are assumed to be numeric. You can use Define Variable Type to change the data type. The contents of the Define Variable Type dialog box depend on the data type selected. For some data types, there are text boxes for width and number of decimals; for others, you can simply select a format from a scrollable list of examples.

Figure 5-4
*Define Variable Type dialog box*

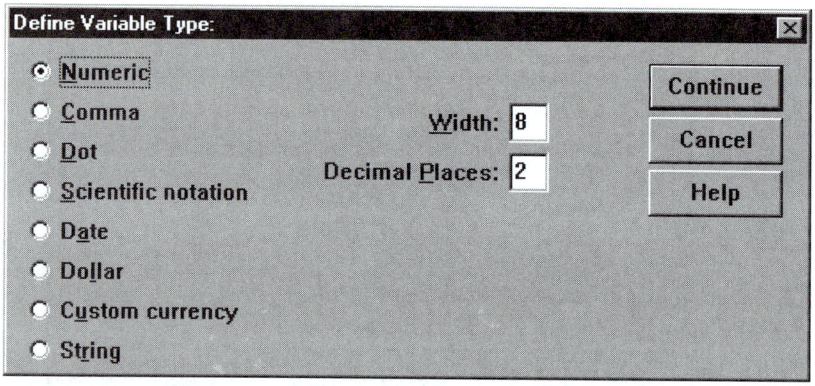


The available data types are numeric, comma, dot, scientific notation, date, dollar, custom currency, and string.

## To Define Variable Type

- ▶ Click the button in the Type cell for the variable you want to define.
- ▶ Select the data type in the Define Variable Type dialog box.

## Input versus Display Formats

Depending on the format, the display of values in the Data view may differ from the actual value as entered and stored internally. Following are some general guidelines:

- For numeric, comma, and dot formats, you can enter values with any number of decimal positions (up to 16), and the entire value is stored internally. The Data view displays only the defined number of decimal places, and it rounds values with more decimals. However, the complete value is used in all computations.

- For string variables, all values are right-padded to the maximum width. For a string variable with a width of 6, a value of 'No' is stored internally as 'No    ' and is not equivalent to '  No  '.
- For date formats, you can use slashes, dashes, spaces, commas, or periods as delimiters between day, month, and year values, and you can enter numbers, three-letter abbreviations, or complete names for month values. Dates of the general format dd-mmm-yy are displayed with dashes as delimiters and three-letter abbreviations for the month. Dates of the general format dd/mm/yy and mm/dd/yy are displayed with slashes for delimiters and numbers for the month. Internally, dates are stored as the number of seconds from October 14, 1582. The century range for dates with two-digit years is determined by your Options settings (from the Edit menu, choose Options and click the Data tab).
- For time formats, you can use colons, periods, or spaces as delimiters between hours, minutes, and seconds. Times are displayed with colons as delimiters. Internally, times are stored as the number of seconds from October 14, 1582.

## Variable Labels

Although variable names can be only 8 characters long, variable labels can be up to 256 characters long, and these descriptive labels are displayed in output.

## Value Labels

You can assign descriptive value labels for each value of a variable. This is particularly useful if your data file uses numeric codes to represent non-numeric categories (for example, codes of 1 and 2 for *male* and *female*). Value labels can be up to 60 characters long. Value labels are not available for long string variables (string variables longer than 8 characters).

Figure 5-5
*Define Value Labels dialog box*

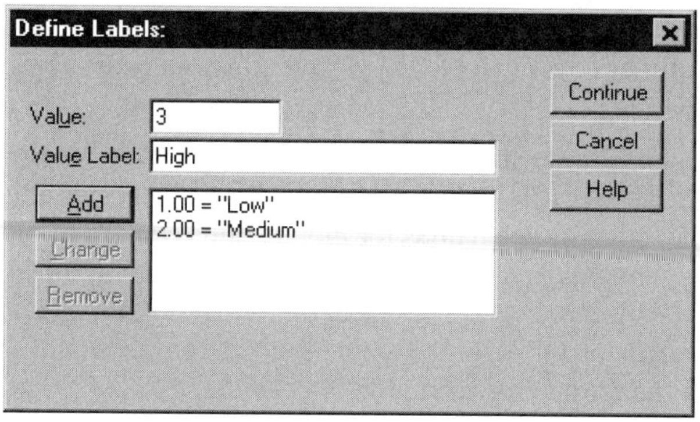


### To Specify Value Labels

- ▶ Click the button in the Values cell for the variable you want to define.
- ▶ For each value, enter the value and a label.
- ▶ Click Add to enter the value label.

## Missing Values

Define Missing Values defines specified data values as **user-missing**. It is often useful to know why information is missing. For example, you might want to distinguish between data missing because a respondent refused to answer and data missing because the question didn't apply to that respondent. Data values specified as user-missing are flagged for special treatment and are excluded from most calculations.

Figure 5-6
*Define Missing Values dialog box*

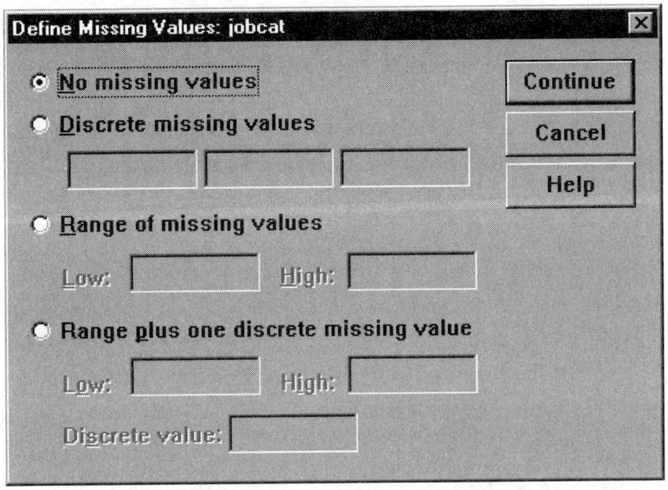


- You can enter up to three discrete (individual) missing values, a range of missing values, or a range plus one discrete value.
- Ranges can be specified only for numeric variables.
- You cannot define missing values for long string variables (string variables longer than eight characters).

**Missing values for string variables**. All string values, including null or blank values, are considered valid values unless you explicitly define them as missing. To define null or blank values as missing for a string variable, enter a single space in one of the fields for Discrete missing values.

### *To Define Missing Values for a Variable*

▶ Click the button in the Missing cell for the variable you want to define.

▶ Enter the values or range of values that represent missing data.

## Column Width

You can specify a number of characters for the column width. Column widths can also be changed in the Data view by clicking and dragging the column borders.

Column formats affect only the display of values in the Data Editor. Changing the column width does not change the defined width of a variable. If the defined and actual width of a value are wider than the column, asterisks (*) are displayed in the Data view.

## Alignment

Alignment controls the display of data values and/or value labels in the Data view. The default alignment is *right* for numeric variables and *left* for string variables. This setting affects only the display in the Data view.

## Applying Variable Definition Attributes to Other Variables

Once you have defined variable definition attributes for a variable, you can copy one or more attributes and apply them to one or more variables.

Basic copy and paste operations are used to apply variable definition attributes.

### To Apply Variable Definition Attributes to Other Variables

▶ In the Variable view, select the attribute cell(s) you want to apply to other variables.

▶ From the menus choose:

Edit
 Copy

▶ Select the attribute cell(s) to which you want to apply the attribute(s). You can select multiple target variables.

▶ From the menus choose:

Edit
 Paste

If you copy attributes to blank rows, new variables are created with default attributes for all but the selected attributes.

# Entering Data

You can enter data directly in the Data Editor in the Data view. You can enter data in any order. You can enter data by case or by variable, for selected areas or for individual cells.

- The active cell is highlighted.
- The variable name and row number of the active cell are displayed in the top left corner of the Data Editor.
- When you select a cell and enter a data value, the value is displayed in the cell editor at the top of the Data Editor.
- Data values are not recorded until you press Enter or select another cell.
- To enter anything other than simple numeric data, you must define the variable type first.

If you enter a value in an empty column, the Data Editor automatically creates a new variable and assigns a variable name.

Figure 5-7
*Working data file in the Data view*

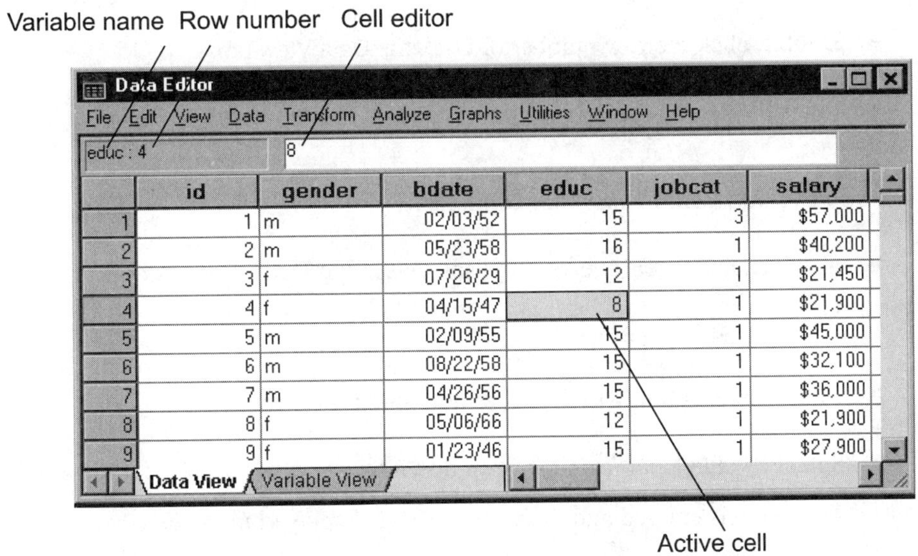

### To Enter Numeric Data

- ▶ Select a cell in the Data view.
- ▶ Enter the data value. The value is displayed in the cell editor at the top of the Data Editor.
- ▶ Press Enter or select another cell to record the value.

### To Enter Non-Numeric Data

- ▶ Double-click a variable name at the top of the column in the Data view or click the Variable View tab.
- ▶ Click the button in the Type cell for the variable.
- ▶ Select the data type in the Define Variable Type dialog box.
- ▶ Click OK.
- ▶ Double-click the row number or click the Data View tab.
- ▶ Enter the data in the column for the newly defined variable.

### To Use Defined Value Labels for Data Entry

- ▶ If value labels aren't currently displayed in the Data view, from the menus choose:

  View
  Value Labels

- ▶ Click on the cell in which you want to enter the value.
- ▶ Select a value label from the drop-down list.

  The value is entered and the value label is displayed in the cell.

  *Note*: This works only if you have defined value labels for the variable.

### Data Value Restrictions

The defined variable type and width determine the type of value that can be entered in the cell in the Data view.

- If you type a character not allowed by the defined variable type, the Data Editor beeps and does not enter the character.
- For string variables, characters beyond the defined width are not allowed.
- For numeric variables, integer values that exceed the defined width can be entered, but the Data Editor displays either scientific notation or asterisks in the cell to indicate that the value is wider than the defined width. To display the value in the cell, change the defined width of the variable. (*Note*: Changing the column width does not affect the variable width.)

## Editing Data in Data View

With the Data Editor, you can modify data values in the Data view in many ways. You can:

- Change data values.
- Cut, copy, and paste data values.
- Add and delete cases.
- Add and delete variables.
- Change the order of variables.

#### To Replace or Modify a Data Value

To delete the old value and enter a new value:

▶ In the Data view, double-click the cell. The cell value is displayed in the cell editor.

▶ Edit the value directly in the cell or in the cell editor.

▶ Press Enter (or move to another cell) to record the new value.

## Cutting, Copying, and Pasting Data Values

You can cut, copy, and paste individual cell values or groups of values in the Data Editor. You can:

- Move or copy a single cell value to another cell.
- Move or copy a single cell value to a group of cells.
- Move or copy the values for a single case (row) to multiple cases.
- Move or copy the values for a single variable (column) to multiple variables.
- Move or copy a group of cell values to another group of cells.

### Data Conversion for Pasted Values in the Data View

If the defined variable types of the source and target cells are not the same, the Data Editor attempts to convert the value. If no conversion is possible, the system-missing value is inserted in the target cell.

**Numeric or Date into String.** Numeric (for example, numeric, dollar, dot, or comma) and date formats are converted to strings if they are pasted into a string variable cell. The string value is the numeric value as displayed in the cell. For example, for a dollar format variable, the displayed dollar sign becomes part of the string value. Values that exceed the defined string variable width are truncated.

**String into Numeric or Date.** String values that contain acceptable characters for the numeric or date format of the target cell are converted to the equivalent numeric or date value. For example, a string value of 25/12/91 is converted to a valid date if the format type of the target cell is one of the day-month-year formats, but it is converted to system-missing if the format type of the target cell is one of the month-day-year formats.

**Date into Numeric.** Date and time values are converted to a number of seconds if the target cell is one of the numeric formats (for example, numeric, dollar, dot, or comma). Since dates are stored internally as the number of seconds since October 14, 1582, converting dates to numeric values can yield some extremely large numbers. For example, the date 10/29/91 is converted to a numeric value of 12,908,073,600.

**Numeric into Date or Time.** Numeric values are converted to dates or times if the value represents a number of seconds that can produce a valid date or time. For dates, numeric values less than 86,400 are converted to the system-missing value.

## Inserting New Cases

Entering data in a cell on a blank row automatically creates a new case. The Data Editor inserts the system-missing value for all the other variables for that case. If there are any blank rows between the new case and the existing cases, the blank rows also become new cases with the system-missing value for all variables.

You can also insert new cases between existing cases.

### To Insert a New Case between Existing Cases

▶ In the Data view, select any cell in the case (row) below the position where you want to insert the new case.

▶ From the menus choose:

Data
 Insert Case

A new row is inserted for the case and all variables receive the system-missing value.

## Inserting New Variables

Entering data in an empty column in the Data view or in an empty row in the Variable view automatically creates a new variable with a default variable name (the prefix *var* and a sequential number) and a default data format type (numeric). The Data Editor inserts the system-missing value for all cases for the new variable. If there are any empty columns in the Data view or empty rows in the Variable view between the new variable and the existing variables, these also become new variables with the system-missing value for all cases.

You can also insert new variables between existing variables.

### To Insert a New Variable between Existing Variables

▶ Select any cell in the variable to the right of (Data view) or below (Variable view) the position where you want to insert the new variable.

▶ From the menus choose:

Data
 Insert Variable

A new variable is inserted with the system-missing value for all cases.

### To Move Variables in the Data Editor

If you want to position the variable between two existing variables, insert a new variable in the position where you want to move the variable.

▶ For the variable you want to move, click the variable name at the top of the column in the Data view or the row number in the Variable view. The entire variable is highlighted.

▶ From the menus choose:

Edit
 Cut

▶ Click the variable name (Data view) or the row number (Variable view) where you want to move the variable. The entire variable is highlighted.

▶ From the menus choose:

Edit
 Paste

## Changing Data Type

You can change the data type for a variable at any time using the Define Variable Type dialog box in the Variable view, and the Data Editor will attempt to convert existing values to the new type. If no conversion is possible, the system-missing value is assigned. The conversion rules are the same as those for pasting data values to a variable with a different format type. If the change in data format may result in the loss of missing value specifications or value labels, the Data Editor displays an alert box and asks if you want to proceed with the change or cancel it.

# Go to Case

Go to Case goes to the specified case (row) number in the Data Editor.

Figure 5-8
*Go to Case dialog box*

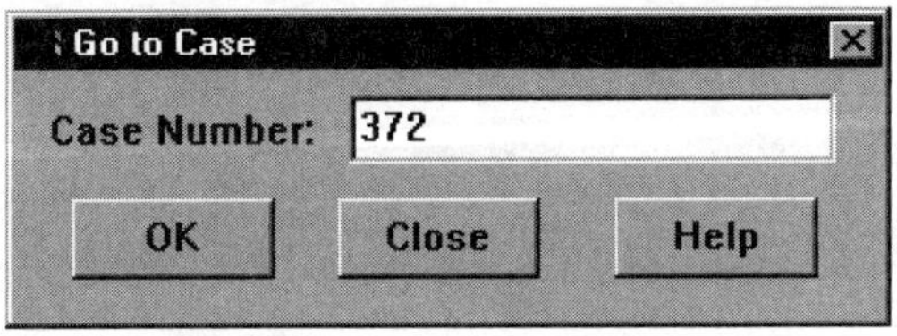


### To Go to a Case in the Data Editor

▶ Make the Data Editor the active window.

▶ From the menus choose:

Data
  Go to Case...

▶ Enter the Data Editor row number for the case.

# Case Selection Status in the Data Editor

If you have selected a subset of cases but have not discarded unselected cases, unselected cases are marked in the Data Editor with a vertical line through the row number.

Figure 5-9
*Filtered cases in the Data Editor*

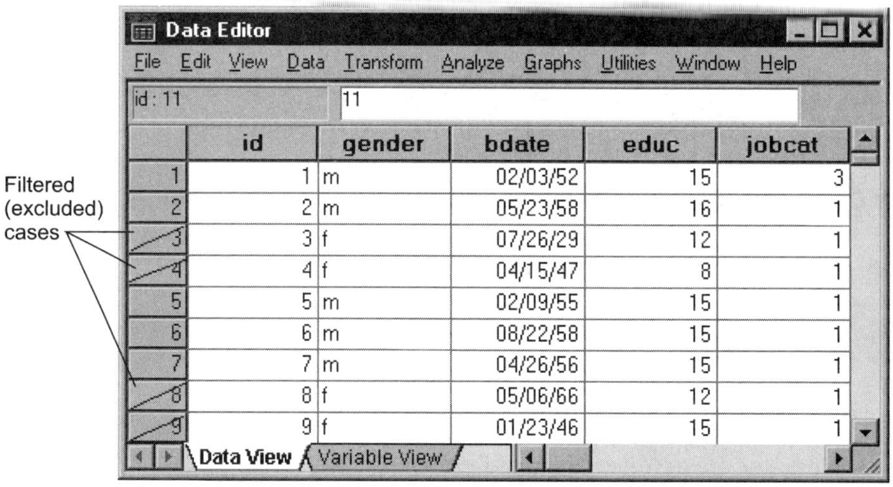


# Data Editor Display Options

The View menu provides several display options for the Data Editor:

**Fonts.** Controls the font characteristics of the data display.

**Grid Lines.** Toggles the display of grid lines.

**Value Labels.** Toggles between the display of actual data values and user-defined descriptive value labels. This is available only in the Data view.

# Data Editor Printing

A data file is printed as it appears on screen.

- The information in the currently displayed view is printed. In the Data view, the data are printed. In the Variable view, data definition information is printed.
- Grid lines are printed if they are currently displayed in the selected view.
- Value labels are printed in the Data view if they are currently displayed. Otherwise, the actual data values are printed.

Use the View menu in the Data Editor window to display or hide grid lines and toggle between the display of data values and value labels.

### To Print the Data Editor Contents

▶ Make the Data Editor the active window.

▶ Select the tab for the view you want to print.

▶ From the menus choose:

File
  Print...

Chapter

6

# Data Transformations

In an ideal situation, your raw data are perfectly suitable for the type of analysis you want to perform, and any relationships between variables are either conveniently linear or neatly orthogonal. Unfortunately, this is rarely the case. Preliminary analysis may reveal inconvenient coding schemes or coding errors, or data transformations may be required in order to coax out the true relationship between variables.

You can perform data transformations ranging from simple tasks, such as collapsing categories for analysis, to more advanced tasks, such as creating new variables based on complex equations and conditional statements.

## Compute Variable

Compute Variable computes values for a variable based on numeric transformations of other variables.

- You can compute values for numeric or string (alphanumeric) variables.
- You can create new variables or replace the values of existing variables. For new variables, you can also specify the variable type and label.
- You can compute values selectively for subsets of data based on logical conditions.
- You can use over 70 built-in functions, including arithmetic functions, statistical functions, distribution functions, and string functions.

Figure 6-1
*Compute Variable dialog box*

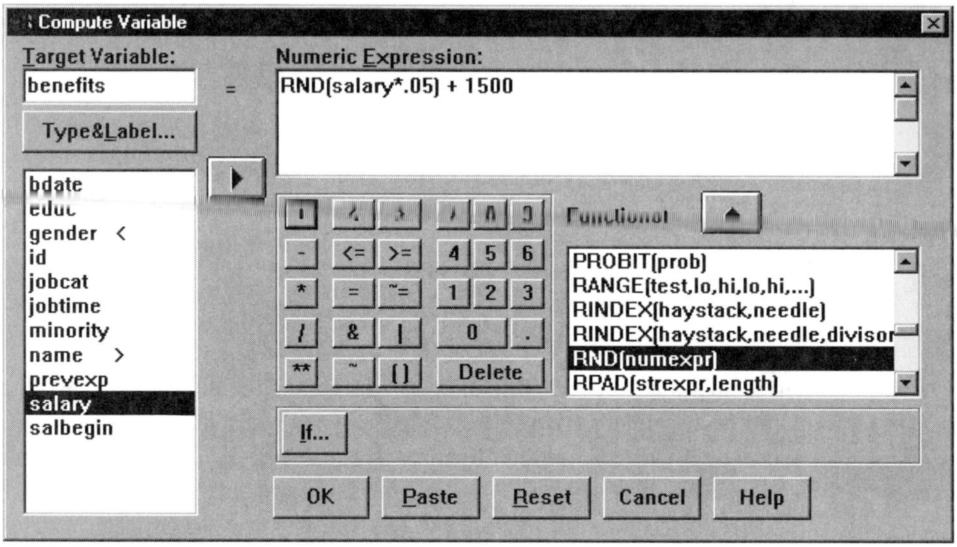


### *To Compute Variables*

▶ From the menus choose:

Transform
  Compute...

▶ Type the name of a single target variable. It can be an existing variable or a new variable to be added to the working data file.

▶ To build an expression, either paste components into the Expression field or type directly in the Expression field.

- Paste functions from the function list and fill in the parameters indicated by question marks.
- String constants must be enclosed in quotation marks or apostrophes.
- Numeric constants must be typed in American format, with the period (.) as the decimal indicator.
- For new string variables, you must also select Type & Label to specify the data type.

## Compute Variable: If Cases

The If Cases dialog box allows you to apply data transformations to selected subsets of cases, using conditional expressions. A conditional expression returns a value of *true*, *false*, or *missing* for each case.

- If the result of a conditional expression is *true*, the transformation is applied to the case.
- If the result of a conditional expression is *false* or *missing*, the transformation is not applied to the case.
- Most conditional expressions use one or more of the six relational operators (<, >, <=, >=, =, and ~=) on the calculator pad.
- Conditional expressions can include variable names, constants, arithmetic operators, numeric and other functions, logical variables, and relational operators.

Figure 6-2
*If Cases dialog box*

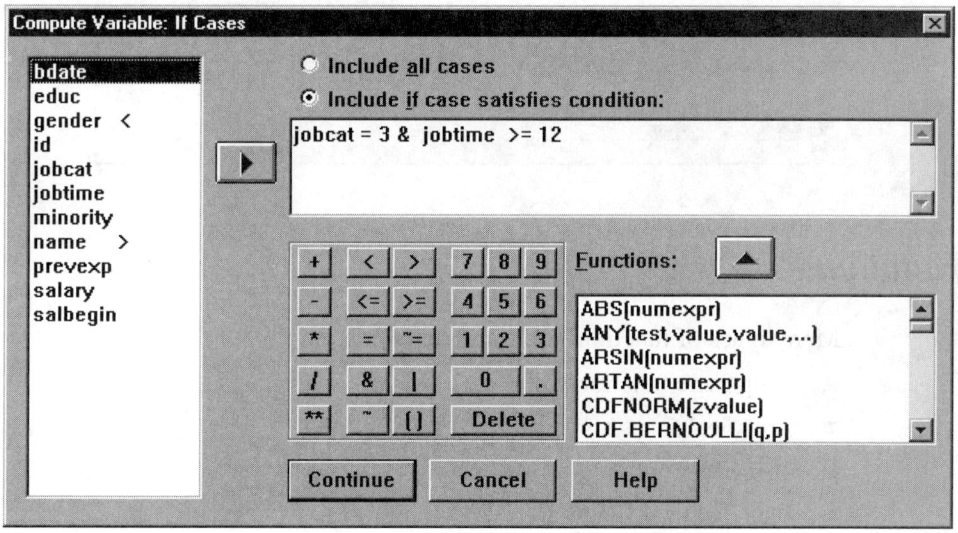

### Compute Variable: Type and Label

By default, new computed variables are numeric. To compute a new string variable, you must specify the data type and width.

**Label.** Optional, descriptive variable label up to 120 characters long. You can enter a label or use the first 110 characters of the Compute expression as the label.

**Type.** Computed variables can be numeric or string (alphanumeric). String variables cannot be used in calculations.

Figure 6-3
*Type and Label dialog box*

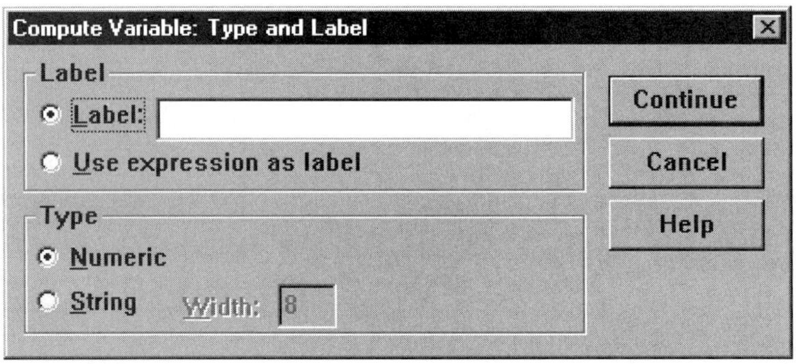


## Functions

Many types of functions are supported, including:

- Arithmetic functions
- Statistical functions
- String functions
- Date and time functions
- Distribution functions
- Random variable functions
- Missing value functions

Search for functions in the online Help system index for a complete list of functions. Right-click on a selected function in the list for a description of that function.

## Missing Values in Functions

Functions and simple arithmetic expressions treat missing values in different ways. In the expression

(var1+var2+var3)/3

the result is missing if a case has a missing value for any of the three variables.

In the expression

MEAN(var1, var2, var3)

the result is missing only if the case has missing values for all three variables.

For statistical functions, you can specify the minimum number of arguments that must have nonmissing values. To do so, type a period and the minimum number after the function name, as in

MEAN.2(var1, var2, var3)

# Random Number Seed

Random Number Seed sets the seed used by the pseudo-random number generator to a specific value so that you can reproduce a sequence of pseudo-random numbers.

The random number seed changes each time a random number is generated for use in transformations (such as the UNIFORM and NORMAL functions), random sampling, or case weighting. To replicate a sequence of random numbers, use this dialog box to reset the seed to a specific value prior to each analysis that uses the random numbers.

Figure 6-4
*Random Number Seed dialog box*

The random number seed is automatically reset to 2,000,000 every time you start a new session.

### To Set the Random Number Seed

- From the menus choose:

  Transform
  Random Number Seed...

- Select Set seed to.

- Enter a positive integer between 1 and 2,000,000,000.

## Count Occurrences of Values within Cases

This dialog box creates a variable that counts the occurrences of the same value(s) in a list of variables for each case. For example, a survey might contain a list of magazines with *yes/no* check boxes to indicate which magazines each respondent reads. You could count the number of *yes* responses for each respondent to create a new variable that contains the total number of magazines read.

Figure 6-5
*Count Occurrences of Values within Cases dialog box*

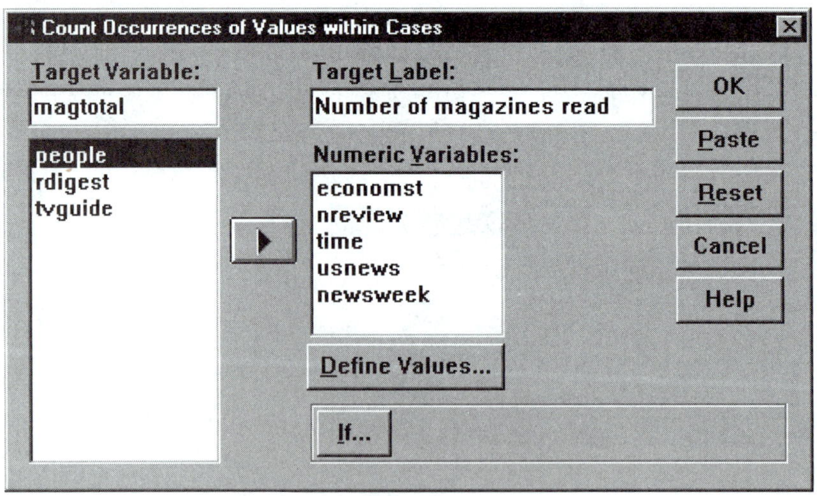

### To Count Occurrences of Values within Cases

- ▶ From the menus choose:

  Transform
   Count...

- ▶ Enter a target variable name.

- ▶ Select two or more variables of the same type (numeric or string).

- ▶ Click Define Values and specify which value or values should be counted.

  Optionally, you can define a subset of cases for which to count occurrences of values.

  The If Cases dialog box for defining subsets of cases is the same as the one described for Compute Variable.

## Count Values within Cases: Values to Count

The value of the target variable (on the main dialog box) is incremented by 1 each time one of the selected variables matches a specification in the Values to Count list here. If a case matches several specifications for any variable, the target variable is incremented several times for that variable.

Value specifications can include individual values, missing or system-missing values, and ranges. Ranges include their endpoints and any user-missing values that fall within the range.

Figure 6-6
*Values to Count dialog box*

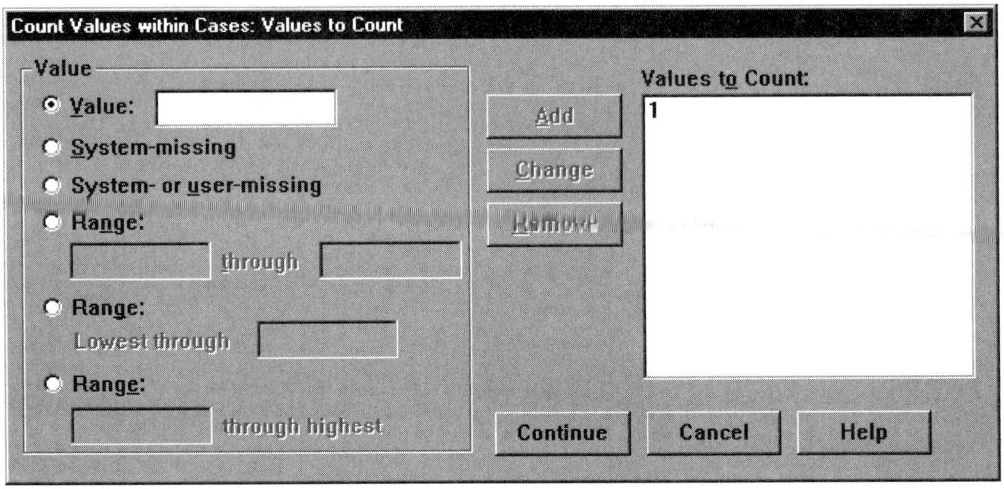


# Recoding Values

You can modify data values by recoding them. This is particularly useful for collapsing or combining categories. You can recode the values within existing variables, or you can create new variables based on the recoded values of existing variables.

## Recode into Same Variables

Recode into Same Variables reassigns the values of existing variables or collapses ranges of existing values into new values. For example, you could collapse salaries into salary range categories.

You can recode numeric and string variables. If you select multiple variables, they must all be the same type. You cannot recode numeric and string variables together.

Figure 6-7
*Recode into Same Variables dialog box*

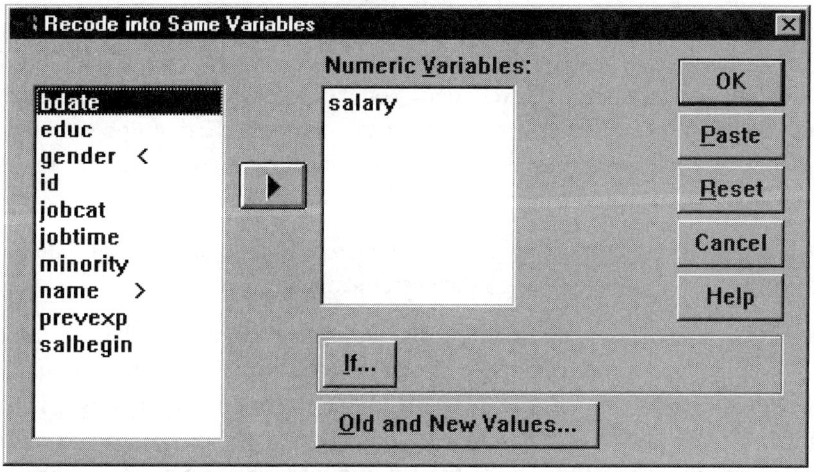


### *To Recode the Values of a Variable*

▶ From the menus choose:

Transform
  Recode
    Into Same Variables...

▶ Select the variables you want to recode. If you select multiple variables, they must be the same type (numeric or string).

▶ Click Old and New Values and specify how to recode values.

Optionally, you can define a subset of cases to recode.

The If Cases dialog box for defining subsets of cases is the same as the one described for Compute Variable.

### Recode into Same Variables: Old and New Values

You can define values to recode in this dialog box. All value specifications must be the same data type (numeric or string) as the variables selected in the main dialog box.

**Old Value**. The value(s) to be recoded. You can recode single values, ranges of values, and missing values. System-missing values and ranges cannot be selected for string variables because neither concept applies to string variables. Ranges include their endpoints and any user-missing values that fall within the range.

**New Value.** The single value into which each old value or range of values is recoded. You can enter a value or assign the system-missing value.

**Old->New.** The list of specifications that will be used to recode the variable(s). You can add, change, and remove specifications from the list. The list is automatically sorted, based on the old value specification, using the following order: single values, missing values, ranges, and all other values. If you change a recode specification on the list, the procedure automatically re-sorts the list, if necessary, to maintain this order.

Figure 6-8
*Old and New Values dialog box*

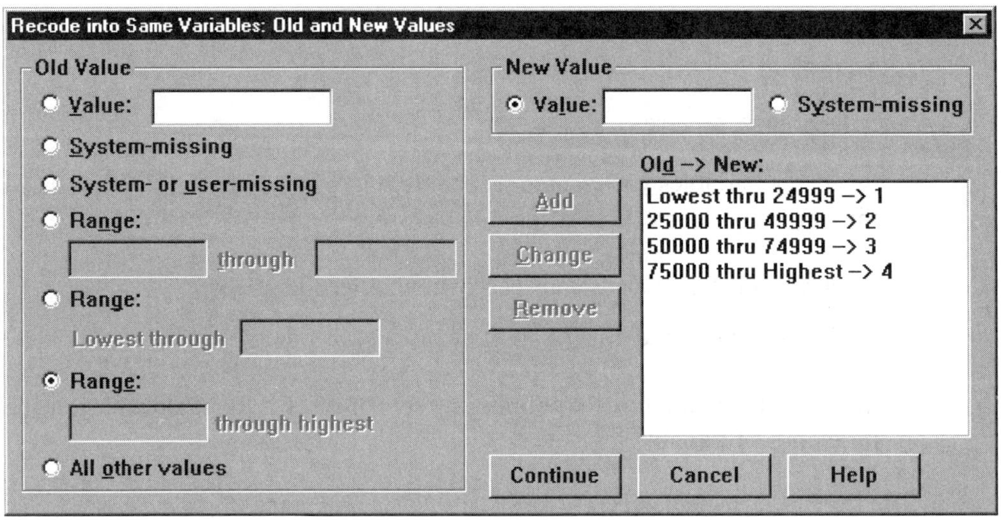

## Recode into Different Variables

Recode into Different Variables reassigns the values of existing variables or collapses ranges of existing values into new values for a new variable. For example, you could collapse salaries into a new variable containing salary-range categories.

- You can recode numeric and string variables.
- You can recode numeric variables into string variables and vice versa.
- If you select multiple variables, they must all be the same type. You cannot recode numeric and string variables together.

Figure 6-9
*Recode into Different Variables dialog box*

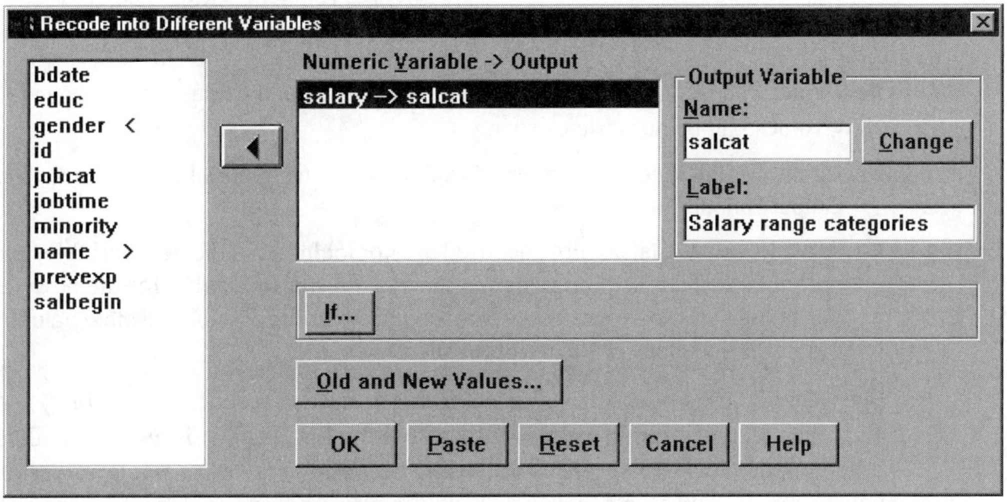


### To Recode the Values of a Variable into a New Variable

▶ From the menus choose:

Transform
 Recode
  Into Different Variables...

▶ Select the variables you want to recode. If you select multiple variables, they must be the same type (numeric or string).

▶ Enter an output (new) variable name for each new variable and click Change.

▶ Click Old and New Values and specify how to recode values.

Optionally, you can define a subset of cases to recode.

### Recode into Different Variables: Old and New Values

You can define values to recode in this dialog box.

**Old Value.** The value(s) to be recoded. You can recode single values, ranges of values, and missing values. System-missing values and ranges cannot be selected for string variables because neither concept applies to string variables. Old values must be the same data type (numeric or string) as the original variable. Ranges include their endpoints and any user-missing values that fall within the range.

**New Value.** The single value into which each old value or range of values is recoded. New values can be numeric or string.

- If you want to recode a numeric variable into a string variable, you must also select Output variables are strings.
- Any old values that are not specified are not included in the new variable, and cases with those values will be assigned the system-missing value for the new variable. To include all old values that do not require recoding, select All other values for the old value and Copy old value(s) for the new value.

**Old->New.** The list of specifications that will be used to recode the variable(s). You can add, change, and remove specifications from the list. The list is automatically sorted, based on the old value specification, using the following order: single values, missing values, ranges, and all other values. If you change a recode specification on the list, the procedure automatically re-sorts the list, if necessary, to maintain this order.

Figure 6-10
*Old and New Values dialog box*

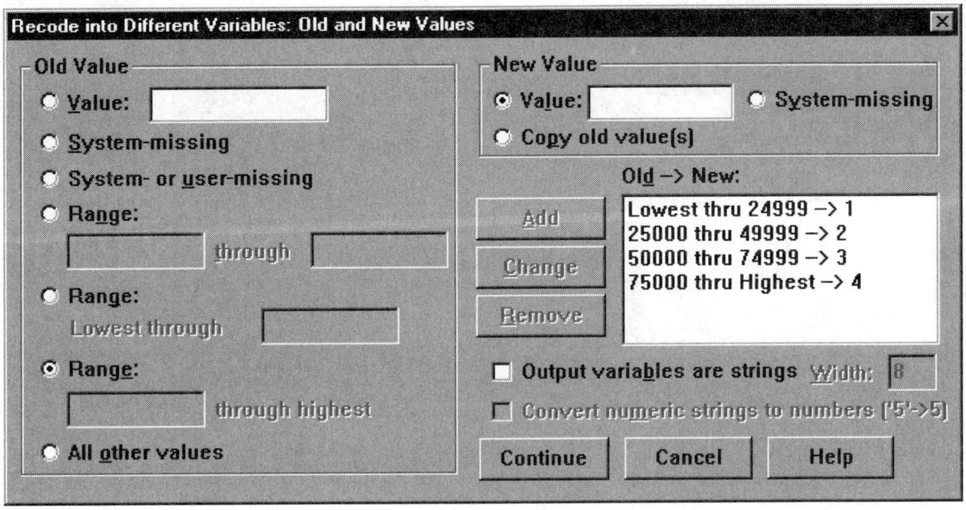


## Rank Cases

Rank Cases creates new variables containing ranks, normal and Savage scores, and percentile values for numeric variables.

New variable names and descriptive variable labels are automatically generated, based on the original variable name and the selected measure(s). A summary table lists the original variables, the new variables, and the variable labels.

Optionally, you can:

- Rank cases in ascending or descending order.
- Organize rankings into subgroups by selecting one or more grouping variables for the By list. Ranks are computed within each group. Groups are defined by the combination of values of the grouping variables. For example, if you select *gender* and *minority* as grouping variables, ranks are computed for each combination of *gender* and *minority*.

Figure 6-11
*Rank Cases dialog box*

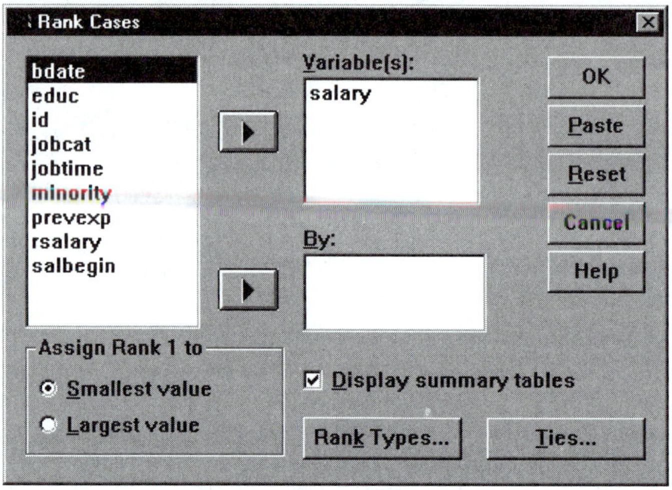


### To Rank Cases

▶ From the menus choose:

Transform
  Rank Cases...

▶ Select one or more variables to rank. You can rank only numeric variables.

Optionally, you can rank cases in ascending or descending order and organize ranks into subgroups.

## Rank Cases: Types

You can select multiple ranking methods. A separate ranking variable is created for each method. Ranking methods include simple ranks, Savage scores, fractional ranks, and percentiles. You can also create rankings based on proportion estimates and normal scores.

**Proportion Estimation Formula.** For proportion estimates and normal scores, you can select the proportion estimation formula: Blom, Tukey, Rankit, or Van der Waerden.

Figure 6-12
*Rank Cases Types dialog box*

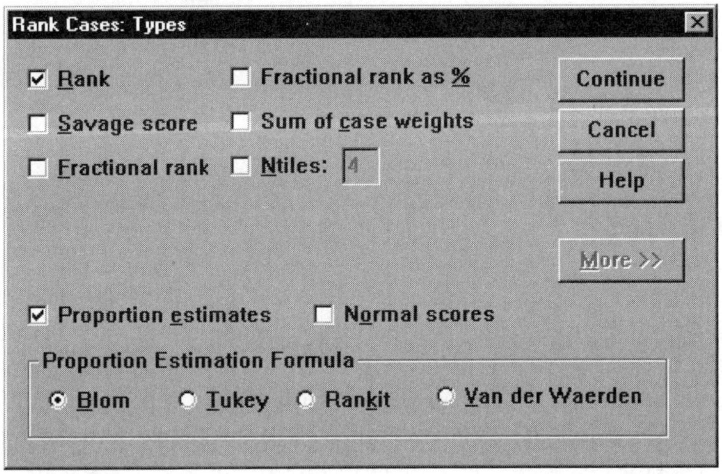


## *Rank Cases: Ties*

This dialog box controls the method for assigning rankings to cases with the same value on the original variable.

Figure 6-13
*Rank Cases Ties dialog box*

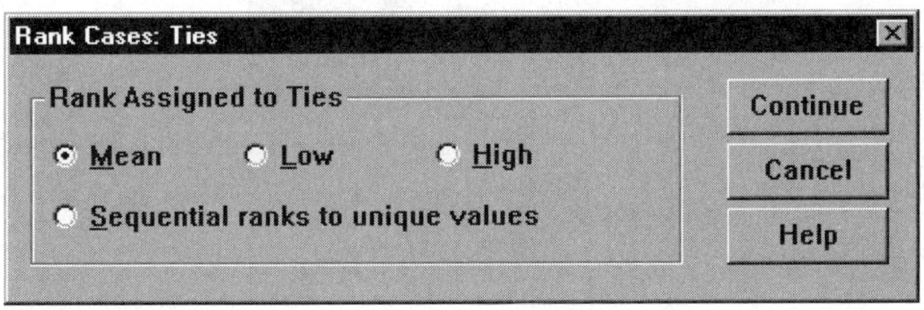

The following table shows how the different methods assign ranks to tied values:

| Value | Mean | Low | High | Sequential |
|---|---|---|---|---|
| 10 | 1 | 1 | 1 | 1 |
| 15 | 3 | 2 | 4 | 2 |
| 15 | 3 | 2 | 4 | 2 |
| 15 | 3 | 2 | 4 | 2 |
| 16 | 5 | 5 | 5 | 3 |
| 20 | 6 | 6 | 6 | 4 |

## Categorize Variables

Categorize Variables converts continuous numeric data to a discrete number of categories. The procedure creates new variables containing the categorical data. Data are categorized based on percentile groups, with each group containing approximately the same number of cases. For example, a specification of 4 groups would assign a value of 1 to cases below the 25th percentile, 2 to cases between the 25th and 50th percentile, 3 to cases between the 50th and 75th percentile, and 4 to cases above the 75th percentile.

Figure 6-14
*Categorize Variables dialog box*

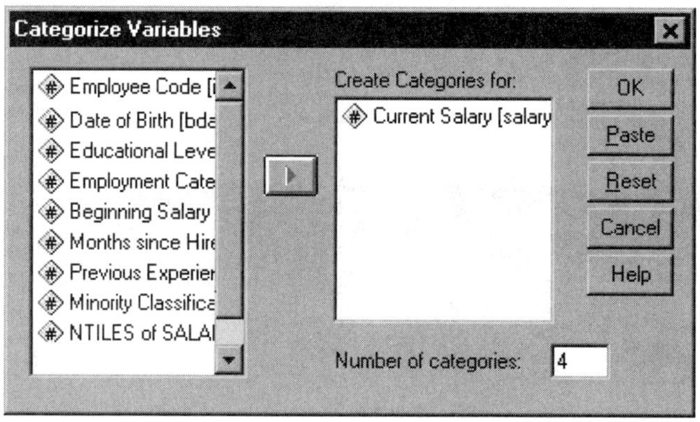

### To Categorize Variables

▶ From the menus choose:

Transform
  Categorize Variables...

▶ Select one or more numeric variables to categorize. You can categorize only numeric variables.

## Automatic Recode

Automatic Recode converts string and numeric values into consecutive integers. When category codes are not sequential, the resulting empty cells reduce performance and increase memory requirements for many procedures. Additionally, some procedures cannot use string variables, and some require consecutive integer values for factor levels.

Figure 6-15
*Automatic Recode dialog box*

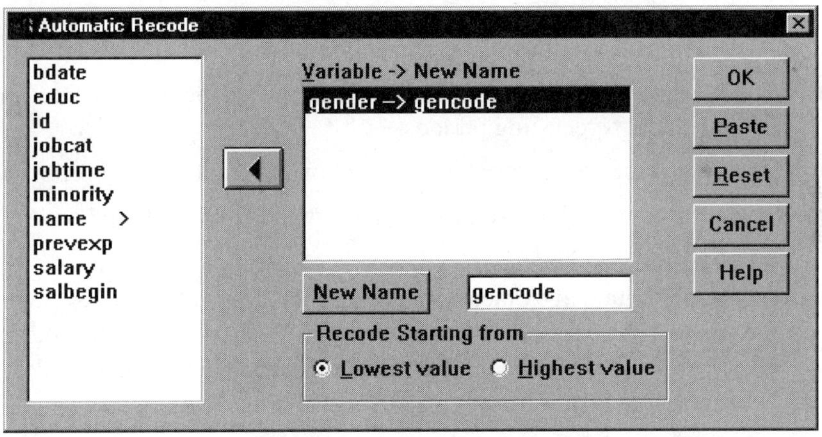


The new variable(s) created by Automatic Recode retain any defined variable and value labels from the old variable. For any values without a defined value label, the original value is used as the label for the recoded value. A table displays the old and new values and value labels.

String values are recoded in alphabetical order, with uppercase letters preceding their lowercase counterparts. Missing values are recoded into missing values higher than any nonmissing values, with their order preserved. For example, if the original variable has 10 nonmissing values, the lowest missing value would be recoded to 11, and the value 11 would be a missing value for the new variable.

### To Recode String or Numeric Values into Consecutive Integers

▶ From the menus choose:

Transform
  Automatic Recode...

▶ Select one or more variables to recode.

▶ For each selected variable, enter a name for the new variable and click New Name.

# Time Series Data Transformations

Several data transformations that are useful in time series analysis are provided:

- Generate date variables to establish periodicity and distinguish between historical, validation, and forecasting periods.
- Create new time series variables as functions of existing time series variables.
- Replace system- and user-missing values with estimates based on one of several methods.

A **time series** is obtained by measuring a variable (or set of variables) regularly over a period of time. Time series data transformations assume a data file structure in which each case (row) represents a set of observations at a different time, and the length of time between cases is uniform.

## Define Dates

Define Dates generates date variables that can be used to establish the periodicity of a time series and to label output from time series analysis.

Figure 6-16
*Define Dates dialog box*

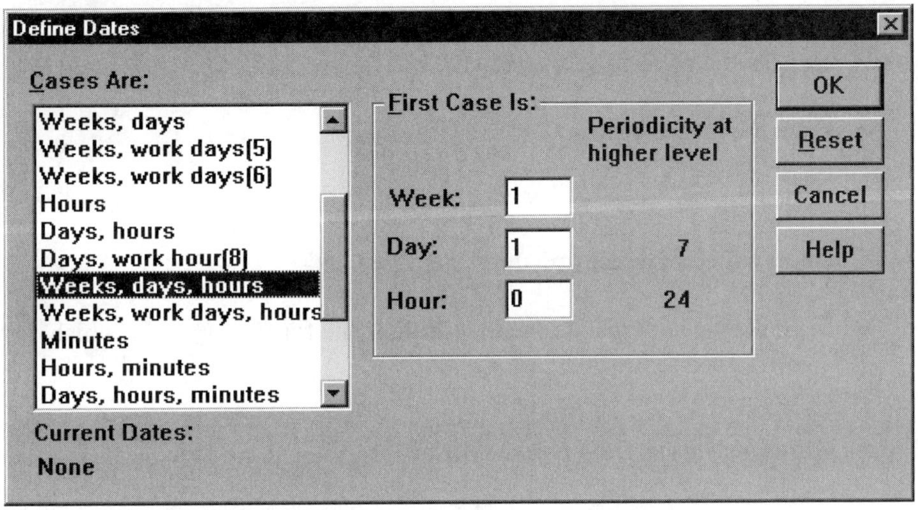


**Cases Are.** Defines the time interval used to generate dates.

- Not dated removes any previously defined date variables. Any variables with the following names are deleted: *year_*, *quarter_*, *month_*, *week_*, *day_*, *hour_*, *minute_*, *second_*, and *date_*.
- Custom indicates the presence of custom date variables created with command syntax (for example, a four-day work week). This item merely reflects the current state of the working data file. Selecting it from the list has no effect. (See the *Syntax Reference Guide* for information on using the DATE command to create custom date variables.) Custom date variables are not available with the Student version.

**First Case Is.** Defines the starting date value, which is assigned to the first case. Sequential values, based on the time interval, are assigned to subsequent cases.

**Periodicity at higher level.** Indicates the repetitive cyclical variation, such as the number of months in a year or the number of days in a week. The value displayed indicates the maximum value you can enter.

A new numeric variable is created for each component that is used to define the date. The new variable names end with an underscore. A descriptive string variable, *date_*, is also created from the components. For example, if you selected Weeks, days, hours, four new variables are created: *week_*, *day_*, *hour_*, and *date_*.

If date variables have already been defined, they are replaced when you define new date variables that will have the same names as the existing date variables.

### To Define Dates for Time Series Data

- From the menus choose:

  Data
  Define Dates

- Select a time interval from the Cases Are list.

- Enter the value(s) that define the starting date for First Case Is, which determines the date assigned to the first case.

### Date Variables versus Date Format Variables

Date variables created with Define Dates should not be confused with date format variables, defined in the Variable View of the Data Editor. Date variables are used to establish periodicity for time series data. Date format variables represent dates and/or times displayed in various date/time formats. Date variables are simple integers representing the number of days, weeks, hours, etc., from a user-specified starting point. Internally, most date format variables are stored as the number of seconds from October 14, 1582.

## Create Time Series

Create Time Series creates new variables based on functions of existing numeric time series variables. These transformed values are useful in many time series analysis procedures.

Default new variable names are the first six characters of the existing variable used to create it, followed by an underscore and a sequential number. For example, for the variable *price*, the new variable name would be *price_1*. The new variables retain any defined value labels from the original variables.

Available functions for creating time series variables include differences, moving averages, running medians, lag, and lead functions.

Figure 6-17
*Create Time Series dialog box*

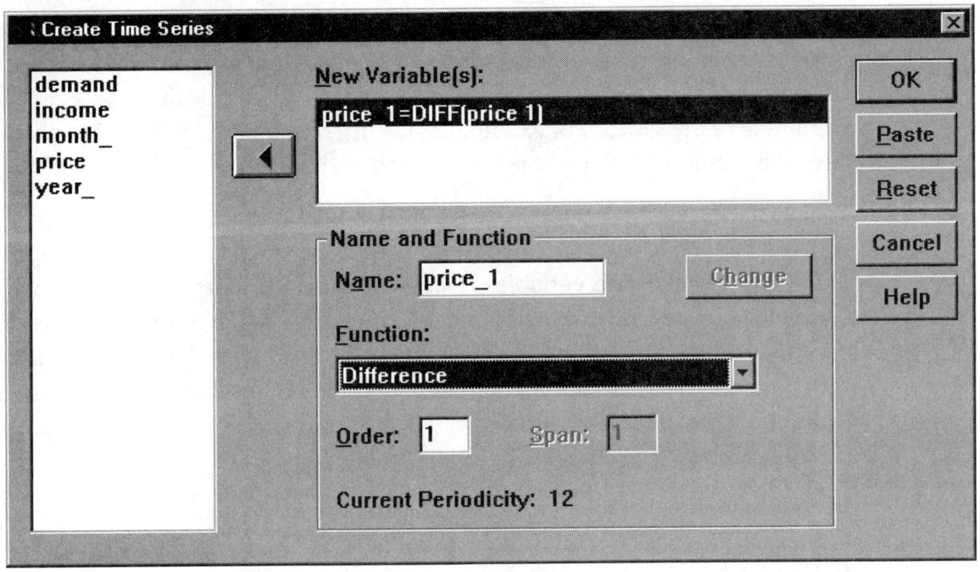


### *To Create a New Time Series Variable*

▶ From the menus choose:

Transform
  Create Time Series...

▶ Select the time series function you want to use to transform the original variable(s).

▶ Select the variable(s) from which you want to create new time series variables. Only numeric variables can be used.

Optionally, you can:

- Enter variable names to override the default new variable names.
- Change the function for a selected variable.

### *Time Series Transformation Functions*

**Difference.** Nonseasonal difference between successive values in the series. The order is the number of previous values used to calculate the difference. Because one observation is lost for each order of difference, system-missing values appear at the beginning of the series. For example, if the difference order is 2, the first two cases will have the system-missing value for the new variable.

**Seasonal difference.** Difference between series values a constant span apart. The span is based on the currently defined periodicity. To compute seasonal differences, you must have defined date variables (Data menu, Define Dates) that include a periodic component (such as months of the year). The order is the number of seasonal periods used to compute the difference. The number of cases with the system-missing value at the beginning of the series is equal to the periodicity multiplied by the order. For example, if the current periodicity is 12 and the order is 2, the first 24 cases will have the system-missing value for the new variable.

**Centered moving average.** Average of a span of series values surrounding and including the current value. The span is the number of series values used to compute the average. If the span is even, the moving average is computed by averaging each pair of uncentered means. The number of cases with the system-missing value at the beginning and at the end of the series for a span of $n$ is equal to $n/2$ for even span values and for odd span values. For example, if the span is 5, the number of cases with the system-missing value at the beginning and at the end of the series is 2.

**Prior moving average.** Average of the span of series values preceding the current value. The span is the number of preceding series values used to compute the average. The number of cases with the system-missing value at the beginning of the series is equal to the span value.

**Running median.** Median of a span of series values surrounding and including the current value. The span is the number of series values used to compute the median. If the span is even, the median is computed by averaging each pair of uncentered medians. The number of cases with the system-missing value at the beginning and at the end of the series for a span of $n$ is equal to $n/2$ for even span values and for odd span values. For example, if the span is 5, the number of cases with the system-missing value at the beginning and at the end of the series is 2.

**Cumulative sum.** Cumulative sum of series values up to and including the current value.

**Lag.** Value of a previous case, based on the specified lag order. The order is the number of cases prior to the current case from which the value is obtained. The number of cases with the system-missing value at the beginning of the series is equal to the order value.

**Lead.** Value of a subsequent case, based on the specified lead order. The order is the number of cases after the current case from which the value is obtained. The number of cases with the system-missing value at the end of the series is equal to the order value.

**Smoothing.** New series values based on a compound data smoother. The smoother starts with a running median of 4, which is centered by a running median of 2. It then resmoothes these values by applying a running median of 5, a running median of 3, and hanning (running weighted averages). Residuals are computed by subtracting the smoothed series from the original series. This whole process is then repeated on the computed residuals. Finally, the smoothed residuals are computed by subtracting the smoothed values obtained the first time through the process. This is sometimes referred to as T4253H smoothing.

## Replace Missing Values

Missing observations can be problematic in analysis, and some time series measures cannot be computed if there are missing values in the series. Replace Missing Values creates new time series variables from existing ones, replacing missing values with estimates computed with one of several methods.

Default new variable names are the first six characters of the existing variable used to create it, followed by an underscore and a sequential number. For example, for the variable *price*, the new variable name would be *price_1*. The new variables retain any defined value labels from the original variables.

Figure 6-18
*Replace Missing Values dialog box*

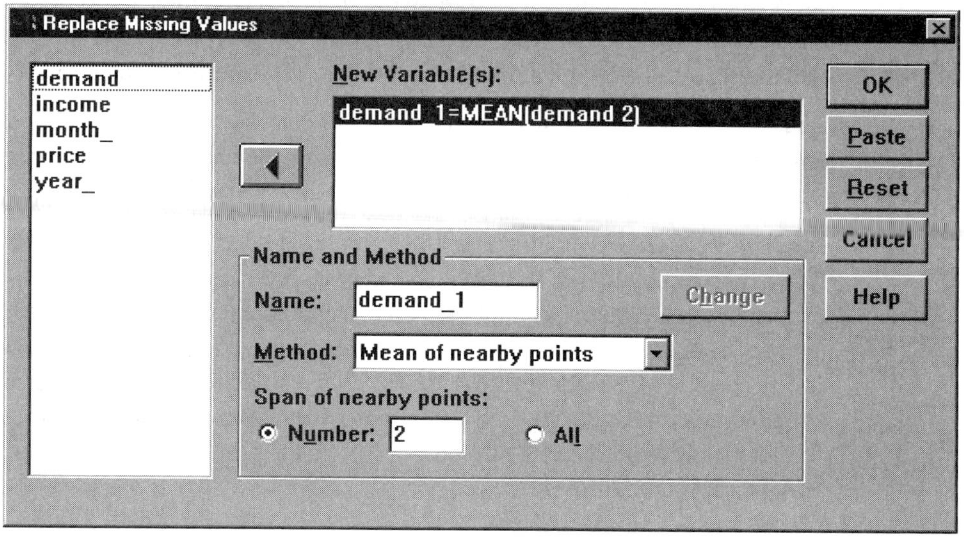


### *To Replace Missing Values for Time Series Variables*

▶ From the menus choose:

Transform
  Replace Missing Values...

▶ Select the estimation method you want to use to replace missing values.

▶ Select the variable(s) for which you want to replace missing values.

Optionally, you can:

- Enter variable names to override the default new variable names.
- Change the estimation method for a selected variable.

### *Estimation Methods for Replacing Missing Values*

**Series mean.** Replaces missing values with the mean for the entire series.

**Mean of nearby points.** Replaces missing values with the mean of valid surrounding values. The span of nearby points is the number of valid values above and below the missing value used to compute the mean.

**Median of nearby points.** Replaces missing values with the median of valid surrounding values. The span of nearby points is the number of valid values above and below the missing value used to compute the median.

**Linear interpolation.** Replaces missing values using a linear interpolation. The last valid value before the missing value and the first valid value after the missing value are used for the interpolation. If the first or last case in the series has a missing value, the missing value is not replaced.

**Linear trend at point.** Replaces missing values with the linear trend for that point. The existing series is regressed on an index variable scaled 1 to $n$. Missing values are replaced with their predicted values.

Chapter

# 7

# File Handling and File Transformations

Data files are not always organized in the ideal form for your specific needs. You may want to combine data files, sort the data in a different order, select a subset of cases, or change the unit of analysis by grouping cases together. A wide range of file transformation capabilities is available, including the ability to:

**Sort data.** You can sort cases based on the value of one or more variables.

**Transpose cases and variables.** The SPSS data file format reads rows as cases and columns as variables. For data files in which this order is reversed, you can switch the rows and columns and read the data in the correct format.

**Merge files.** You can merge two or more data files. You can combine files with the same variables but different cases or the same cases but different variables.

**Select subsets of cases.** You can restrict your analysis to a subset of cases or perform simultaneous analyses on different subsets.

**Aggregate data.** You can change the unit of analysis by aggregating cases based on the value of one or more grouping variables.

**Weight data.** Weight cases for analysis based on the value of a weight variable.

**Restructure data.** You can restructure data to create a single case (record) from multiple cases or create multiple cases from a single case.

# Sort Cases

This dialog box sorts cases (rows) of the data file based on the values of one or more sorting variables. You can sort cases in ascending or descending order.

- If you select multiple sort variables, cases are sorted by each variable within categories of the prior variable on the Sort by list. For example, if you select *gender* as the first sorting variable and *minority* as the second sorting variable, cases will be sorted by minority classification within each gender category.
- For string variables, uppercase letters precede their lowercase counterparts in sort order. For example, the string value "Yes" comes before "yes" in sort order.

Figure 7-1
*Sort Cases dialog box*

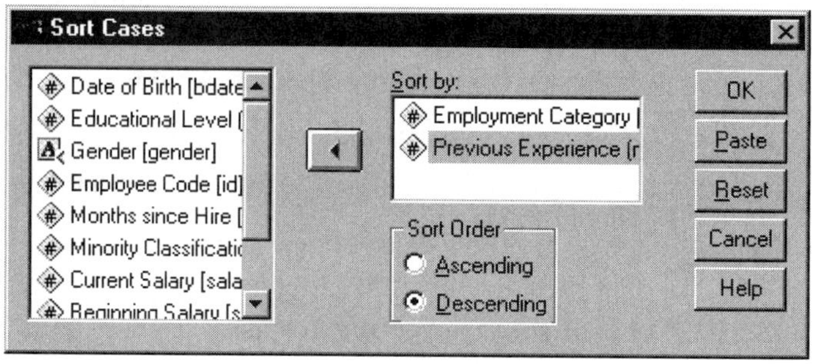


### To Sort Cases

▶ From the menus choose:

Data
  Sort Cases...

▶ Select one or more sorting variables.

# Transpose

Transpose creates a new data file in which the rows and columns in the original data file are transposed so that cases (rows) become variables and variables (columns) become cases. Transpose automatically creates new variable names and displays a list of the new variable names.

- A new string variable that contains the original variable names, *case_lbl*, is automatically created.
- If the working data file contains an ID or name variable with unique values, you can use it as the name variable, and its values will be used as variable names in the transposed data file. If it is a numeric variable, the variable names start with the letter *V*, followed by the numeric value.
- User-missing values are converted to the system-missing value in the transposed data file. To retain any of these values, change the definition of missing values (from the Data menu, choose Define Variable).

### To Transpose Variables and Cases

▶ From the menus choose:

Data
 Transpose...

▶ Select one or more variables to transpose into cases.

# Merging Data Files

You can merge data from two files in two different ways. You can:

- Merge files containing the same variables but different cases.
- Merge files containing the same cases but different variables.

## Add Cases

Add Cases merges the working data file with a second data file that contains the same variables but different cases. For example, you might record the same information for customers in two different sales regions and maintain the data for each region in separate files.

Figure 7-2
*Add Cases dialog box*

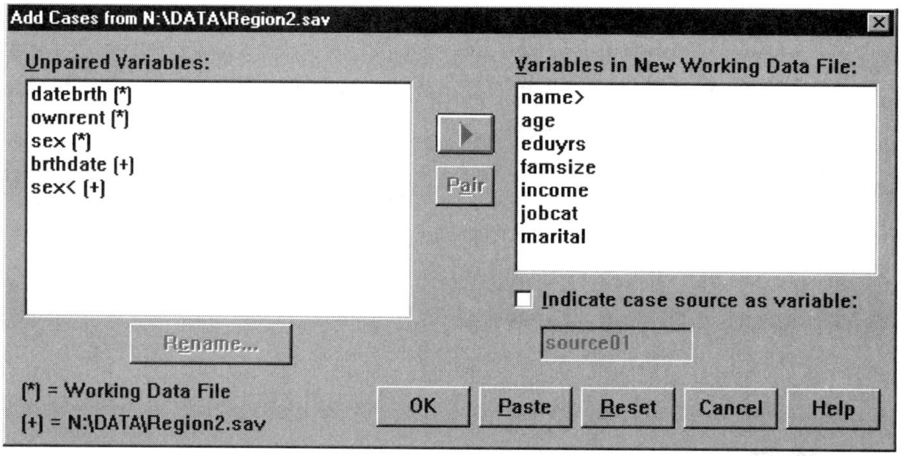


**Unpaired Variables.** Variables to be excluded from the new, merged data file. Variables from the working data file are identified with an asterisk (*). Variables from the external data file are identified with a plus sign (+). By default, this list contains:

- Variables from either data file that do not match a variable name in the other file. You can create pairs from unpaired variables and include them in the new, merged file.
- Variables defined as numeric data in one file and string data in the other file. Numeric variables cannot be merged with string variables.
- String variables of unequal width. The defined width of a string variable must be the same in both data files.

**Variables in New Working Data File.** Variables to be included in the new, merged data file. By default, all of the variables that match both the name and the data type (numeric or string) are included on the list.

- You can remove variables from the list if you don't want them to be included in the merged file.
- Any unpaired variables included in the merged file will contain missing data for cases from the file that does not contain that variable.

### To Merge Files with the Same Variables and Different Cases

- ▶ Open one of the data files. The cases from this file will appear first in the new, merged data file.

- ▶ From the menus choose:

  Data
   Merge Files
    Add Cases...

- ▶ Select the data file to merge with the open data file.

- ▶ Remove any variables you don't want from the Variables in New Working Data File list.

- ▶ Add any variable pairs from the Unpaired Variables list that represent the same information recorded under different variable names in the two files. For example, date of birth might have the variable name *brthdate* in one file and *datebrth* in the other file.

### To Select a Pair of Unpaired Variables

- ▶ Click one of the variables on the Unpaired Variables list.

- ▶ Ctrl-click the other variable on the list. (Press the Ctrl key and click the left mouse button at the same time.)

- ▶ Click Pair to move the variable pair to the Variables in New Working Data File list. (The variable name from the working data file is used as the variable name in the merged file.)

Figure 7-3
*Selecting pairs of variables with Ctrl-click*

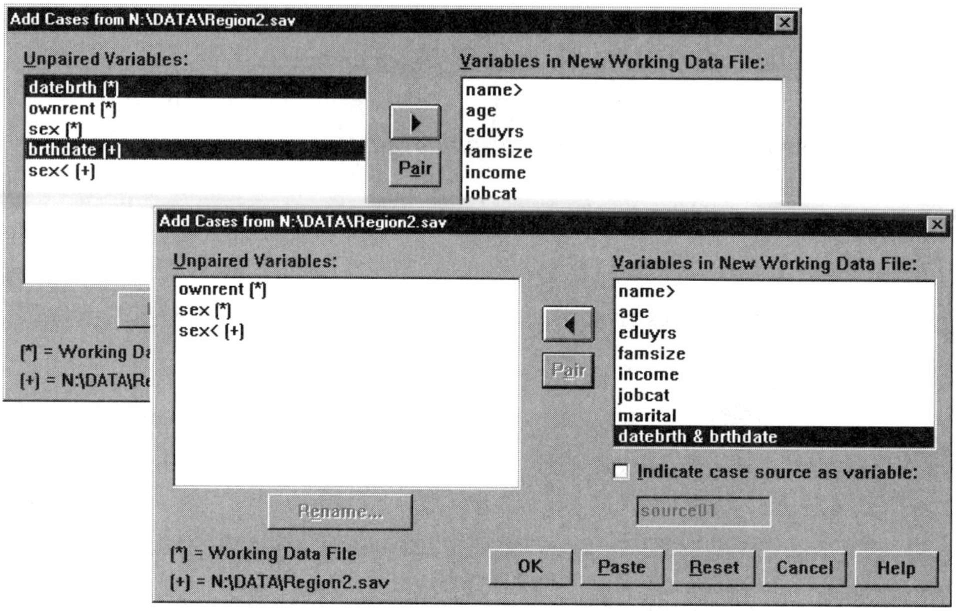


## *Add Cases: Rename*

You can rename variables from either the working data file or the external file before moving them from the unpaired list to the list of variables to be included in the merged data file. Renaming variables enables you to:

- Use the variable name from the external file rather than the name from the working data file for variable pairs.
- Include two variables with the same name but of unmatched types or different string widths. For example, to include both the numeric variable *sex* from the working data file and the string variable *sex* from the external file, one of them must be renamed first.

## *Add Cases: Dictionary Information*

Any existing dictionary information (variable and value labels, user-missing values, display formats) in the working data file is applied to the merged data file.

- If any dictionary information for a variable is undefined in the working data file, dictionary information from the external data file is used.
- If the working data file contains any defined value labels or user-missing values for a variable, any additional value labels or user-missing values for that variable in the external file are ignored.

## Add Variables

Add Variables merges the working data file with an external data file that contains the same cases but different variables. For example, you might want to merge a data file that contains pre-test results with one that contains post-test results.

- Cases must be sorted in the same order in both data files.
- If one or more key variables are used to match cases, the two data files must be sorted by ascending order of the key variable(s).
- Variable names in the second data file that duplicate variable names in the working data file are excluded by default because Add Variables assumes that these variables contain duplicate information.

Figure 7-4
*Add Variables dialog box*

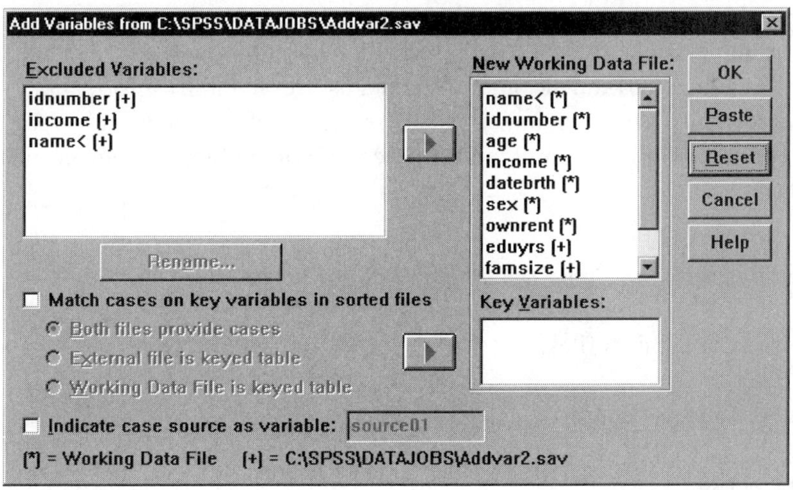

**Excluded Variables.** Variables to be excluded from the new, merged data file. By default, this list contains any variable names from the external data file that duplicate variable names in the working data file. Variables from the working data file are identified with an asterisk (*). Variables from the external data file are identified with a plus sign (+). If you want to include an excluded variable with a duplicate name in the merged file, you can rename it and add it to the list of variables to be included.

**New Working Data File.** Variables to be included in the new, merged data file. By default, all unique variable names in both data files are included on the list.

**Key Variables.** If some cases in one file do not have matching cases in the other file (that is, some cases are missing in one file), use key variables to identify and correctly match cases from the two files. You can also use key variables with table lookup files.

- The key variables must have the same names in both data files.
- Both data files must be sorted by ascending order of the key variables, and the order of variables on the Key Variables list must be the same as their sort sequence.
- Cases that do not match on the key variables are included in the merged file but are not merged with cases from the other file. Unmatched cases contain values for only the variables in the file from which they are taken; variables from the other file contain the system-missing value.

**External file or Working data file is keyed table.** A keyed table, or **table lookup file**, is a file in which data for each "case" can be applied to multiple cases in the other data file. For example, if one file contains information on individual family members (such as sex, age, education) and the other file contains overall family information (such as total income, family size, location), you can use the file of family data as a table lookup file and apply the common family data to each individual family member in the merged data file.

### *To Merge Files with the Same Cases but Different Variables*

▶ Open one of the data files.

▶ From the menus choose:

Data
  Merge Files
    Add Variables...

▶ Select the data file to merge with the open data file.

### To Select Key Variables

▶ Select the variables from the external file variables (+) on the Excluded Variables list.

▶ Select Match cases on key variables in sorted files.

▶ Add the variables to the Key Variables list.

The key variables must exist in both the working data file and the external data file. Both data files must be sorted by ascending order of the key variables, and the order of variables on the Key Variables list must be the same as their sort sequence.

### Add Variables: Rename

You can rename variables from either the working data file or the external file before moving them to the list of variables to be included in the merged data file. This is primarily useful if you want to include two variables with the same name that contain different information in the two files.

## Apply Dictionary

This dialog box applies dictionary information (labels, missing values, formats) from an external data file to the working data file. Dictionary information is applied based on matching variable names. The variables don't have to be in the same order in both files, and variables that aren't present in both files are unaffected. The following rules apply:

- If the variable type (numeric or string) is the same in both files, all of the dictionary information is applied.
- If the variable type is not the same for both files, or if it is a long string (more than eight characters), only the variable label is applied.
- Numeric, dollar, dot, comma, date, and time formats are all considered numeric, and all dictionary information is applied.
- String variable widths are not affected by the applied dictionary.
- For short string variables (eight characters or fewer), missing values and specified values for value labels are truncated if they exceed the defined width of the variable in the working data file.
- Any applied dictionary information overwrites existing dictionary information.

#### To Apply a Data Dictionary to the Working Data File

▶ From the menus choose:

File
  Apply Data Dictionary...

▶ Select the data file with the dictionary information you want to apply to the working data file.

### Applying a Dictionary to Weighted Data Files

The following rules apply when applying a data dictionary to weighted data files:

- If the working data file is weighted and the file containing the dictionary is unweighted, the working data file remains weighted.
- If the working data file is unweighted and the file containing the dictionary is weighted by a variable that exists in the working data file, the working data file is weighted by that variable.
- If both files are weighted but they are not weighted by the same variable, the weight is changed in the working data file if the weight variable in the file containing the dictionary also exists in the working data file.

## Aggregate Data

Aggregate Data combines groups of cases into single summary cases and creates a new aggregated data file. Cases are aggregated based on the value of one or more grouping variables. The new data file contains one case for each group. For example, you could aggregate county data by state and create a new data file in which state is the unit of analysis.

Figure 7-5
*Aggregate Data dialog box*

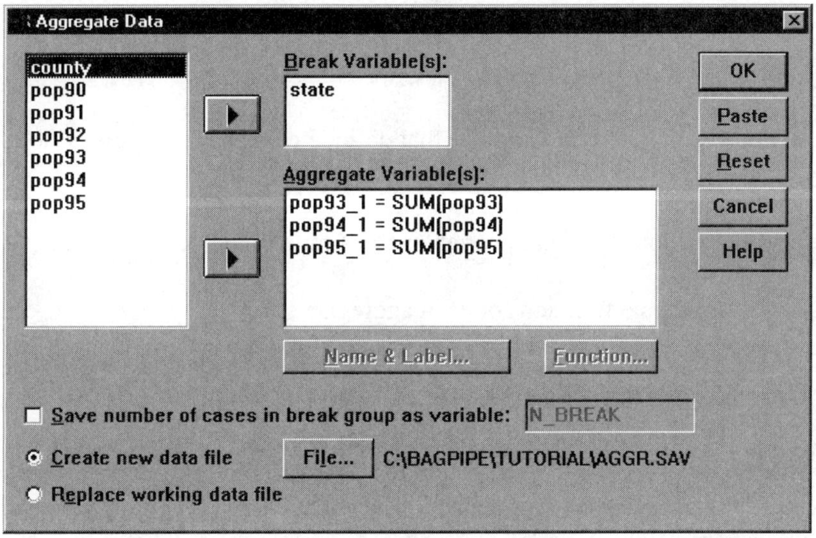


**Break Variable(s).** Cases are grouped together based on the values of the break variables. Each unique combination of break variable values defines a group and generates one case in the new aggregated file. All break variables are saved in the new file with their existing names and dictionary information. The break variable can be either numeric or string format.

**Aggregate Variable(s).** Variables are used with aggregate functions to create the new variables for the aggregated file. By default, Aggregate Data creates new aggregate variable names using the first several characters of the source variable name followed by an underscore and a sequential two-digit number. The aggregate variable name is followed by an optional variable label in quotes, the name of the aggregate function, and the source variable name in parentheses. Source variables for aggregate functions must be numeric.

You can override the default aggregate variable names with new variable names, provide descriptive variable labels, and change the functions used to compute the aggregated data values. You can also create a variable that contains the number of cases in each break group.

### To Aggregate a Data File

▶ From the menus choose:

Data
  Aggregate...

▶ Select one or more break variables that define how cases are grouped to create aggregated data.

▶ Select one or more aggregate variables to include in the new data file.

▶ Select an aggregate function for each aggregate variable.

## Aggregate Data: Aggregate Function

This dialog box specifies the function to use to calculate aggregated data values for selected variables on the Aggregate Variables list in the Aggregate Data dialog box. Aggregate functions include:

- Summary functions, including mean, standard deviation, and sum.
- Percentage or fraction of values above or below a specified value.
- Percentage or fraction of values inside or outside a specified range.

Figure 7-6
*Aggregate Function dialog box*

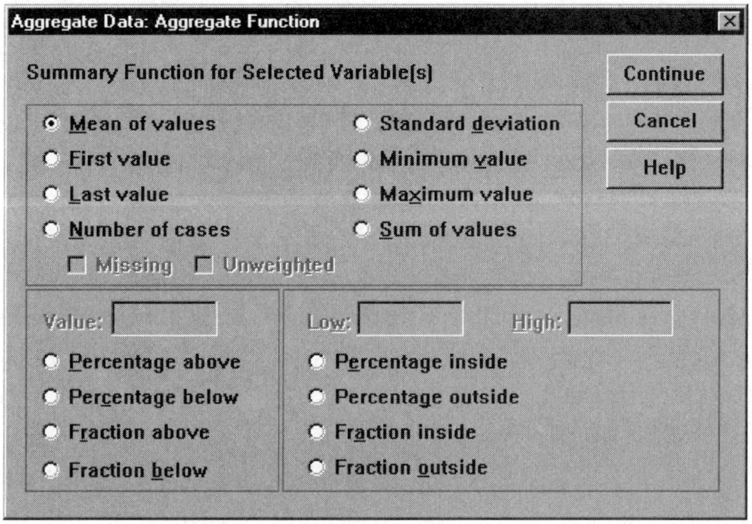


## Aggregate Data: Variable Name and Label

Aggregate Data assigns default variable names for the aggregated variables in the new data file. This dialog box enables you to change the variable name for the selected variable on the Aggregate Variables list and provide a descriptive variable label.

- Variable names cannot exceed 8 characters.
- Variable labels can be up to 120 characters.

Figure 7-7
*Variable Name and Label dialog box*

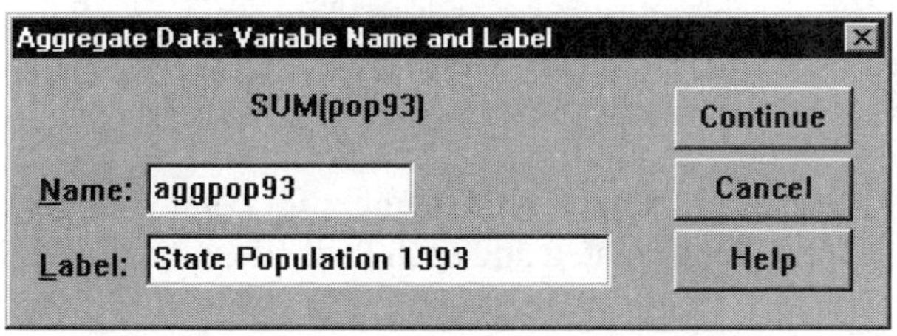

# Split File

Split File splits the data file into separate groups for analysis based on the values of one or more grouping variables. If you select multiple grouping variables, cases are grouped by each variable within categories of the prior variable on the Groups Based On list. For example, if you select *gender* as the first grouping variable and *minority* as the second grouping variable, cases will be grouped by minority classification within each gender category.

- You can specify up to eight grouping variables.
- Each eight characters of a long string variable (string variables longer than eight characters) counts as a variable toward the limit of eight grouping variables.
- Cases should be sorted by values of the grouping variables, in the same order that variables are listed in the Groups Based On list. If the data file isn't already sorted, select Sort the file by grouping variables.

Figure 7-8
*Split File dialog box*

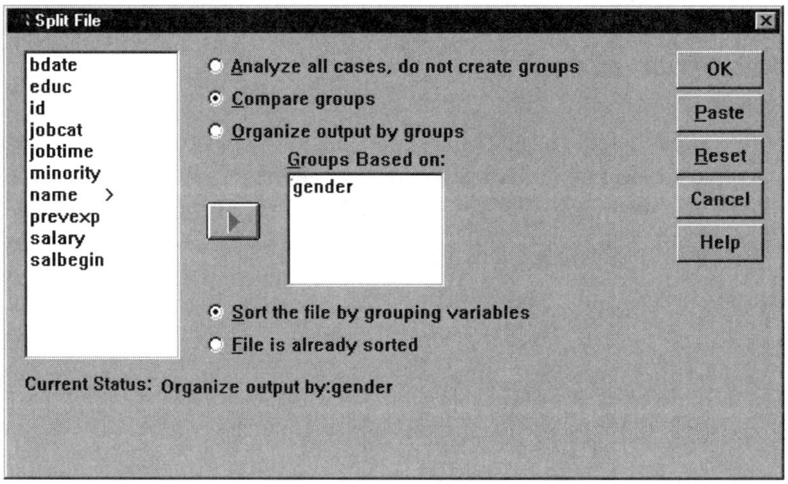


**Compare groups.** Split-file groups are presented together for comparison purposes. For pivot tables, a single pivot table is created and each split-file variable can be moved between table dimensions. For charts, a separate chart is created for each split-file group and the charts are displayed together in the Viewer.

**Organize output by groups.** All results from each procedure are displayed separately for each split-file group.

### *To Split a Data File for Analysis*

▶ From the menus choose:

Data
 Split File...

▶ Select Compare groups or Organize output by groups.

▶ Select one or more grouping variables.

## *Select Cases*

Select Cases provides several methods for selecting a subgroup of cases based on criteria that include variables and complex expressions. You can also select a random sample of cases. The criteria used to define a subgroup can include:

- Variable values and ranges
- Date and time ranges
- Case (row) numbers
- Arithmetic expressions
- Logical expressions
- Functions

**Unselected Cases.** You can filter or delete cases that don't meet the selection criteria. Filtered cases remain in the data file but are excluded from analysis. Select Cases creates a filter variable, *filter_$*, to indicate filter status. Selected cases have a value of 1; filtered cases have a value of 0. Filtered cases are also indicated with a slash through the row number in the Data Editor. To turn filtering off and include all cases in your analysis, select All cases.

Deleted cases are removed from the data file and cannot be recovered if you save the data file after deleting the cases.

Figure 7-9
*Select Cases dialog box*

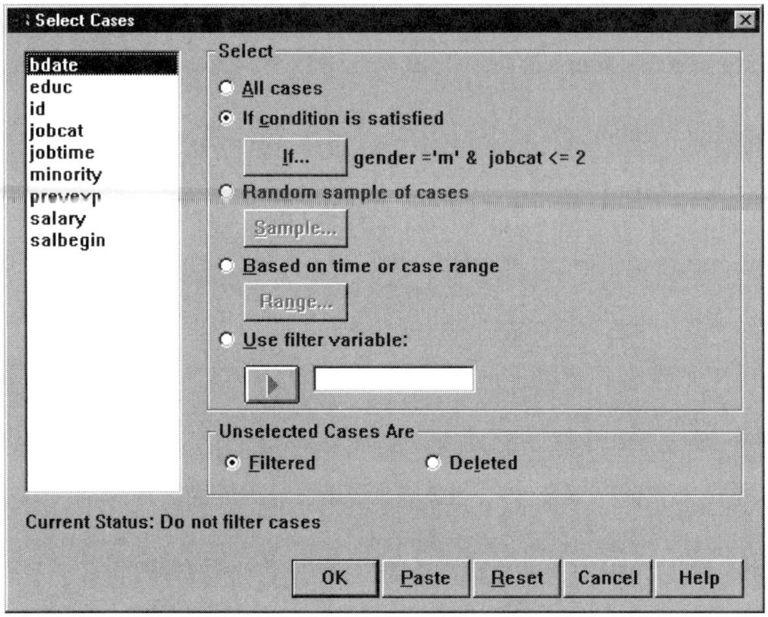


### *To Select Subsets of Cases*

- From the menus choose:

  Data
  Select Cases...

- Select one of the methods for selecting cases.
- Specify the criteria for selecting cases.

## *Select Cases: If*

This dialog box allows you to select subsets of cases using conditional expressions. A conditional expression returns a value of *true*, *false*, or *missing* for each case.

Figure 7-10
*Select Cases If dialog box*

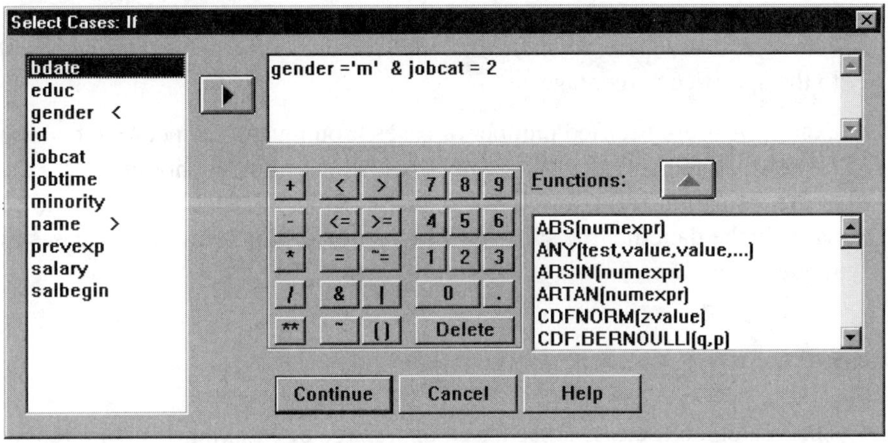


- If the result of a conditional expression is *true*, the case is selected.
- If the result of a conditional expression is *false* or *missing*, the case is not selected.
- Most conditional expressions use one or more of the six relational operators (<, >, <=, >=, =, and ~=) on the calculator pad.
- Conditional expressions can include variable names, constants, arithmetic operators, numeric and other functions, logical variables, and relational operators.

## Select Cases: Random Sample

This dialog box allows you to select a random sample based on an approximate percentage or an exact number of cases.

Figure 7-11
*Select Cases Random Sample dialog box*

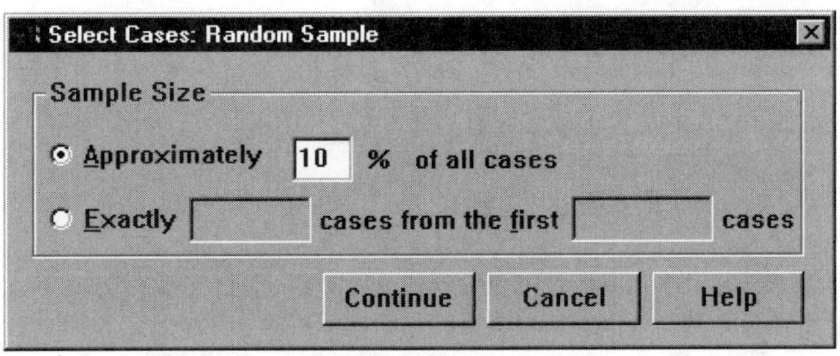

**Approximately.** Generates a random sample of approximately the specified percentage of cases. Since this routine makes an independent pseudo-random decision for each case, the percentage of cases selected can only approximate the specified percentage. The more cases there are in the data file, the closer the percentage of cases selected is to the specified percentage.

**Exactly.** A user-specified number of cases. You must also specify the number of cases from which to generate the sample. This second number should be less than or equal to the total number of cases in the data file. If the number exceeds the total number of cases in the data file, the sample will contain proportionally fewer cases than the requested number.

## Select Cases: Range

This dialog box selects cases based on a range of case numbers or a range of dates or times.

- Case ranges are based on row number as displayed in the Data Editor.
- Date and time ranges are available only for time series data with defined date variables (Data menu, Define Date).

Figure 7-12
*Select Cases Range dialog box for range of cases (no defined date variables)*

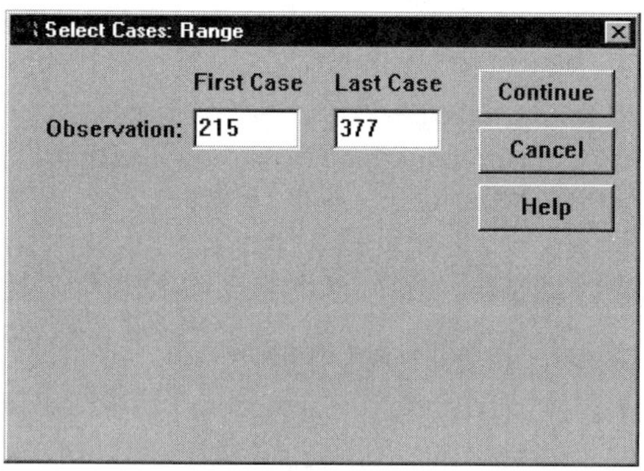

Figure 7-13
*Select Cases Range dialog box for time series data with defined date variables*

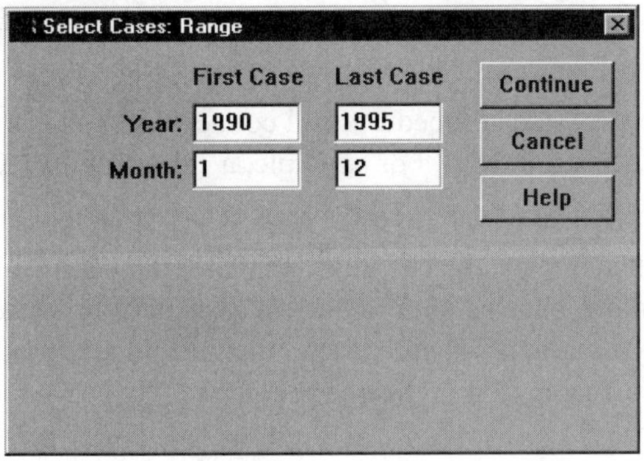


# Weight Cases

Weight Cases gives cases different weights (by simulated replication) for statistical analysis.

- The values of the weighting variable should indicate the number of observations represented by single cases in your data file.
- Cases with zero, negative, or missing values for the weighting variable are excluded from analysis.
- Fractional values are valid; they are used exactly where this is meaningful, and most likely where cases are tabulated.

Figure 7-14
*Weight Cases dialog box*

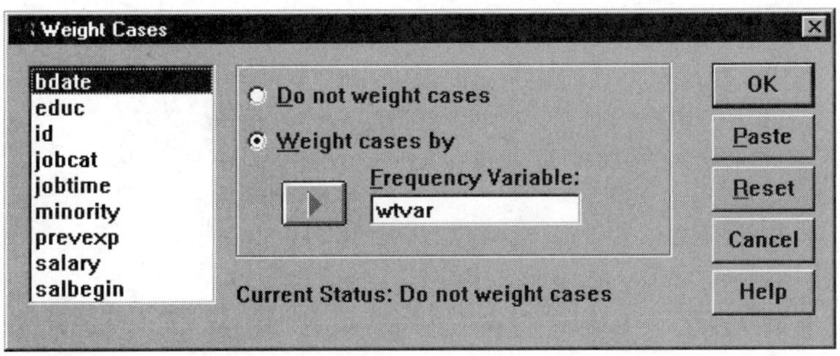

Once you apply a weight variable, it remains in effect until you select another weight variable or turn off weighting. If you save a weighted data file, weighting information is saved with the data file. You can turn off weighting at any time, even after the file has been saved in weighted form.

**Weights in Crosstabs.** In the Crosstabs procedure, cell counts based on fractional weights are rounded to the nearest integer. For example, a cell count of 4.2 based on fractional weights is rounded to 4.

**Weights in scatterplots and histograms.** Scatterplots and histograms have an option for turning case weights on and off, but this does not affect cases with zero, negative, or missing values for the weight variable. These cases remain excluded from the chart even if you turn weighting off from within the chart.

### To Weight Cases

▶ From the menus choose:

Data
 Weight Cases...

▶ Select Weight cases by.

▶ Select a frequency variable.

The values of the frequency variable are used as case weights. For example, a case with a value of 3 for the frequency variable will represent three cases in the weighted data file.

# Restructuring Data

Use the Restructure Data Wizard to restructure your data for the SPSS procedure that you want to use. The wizard replaces the current file with a new, restructured file. The wizard can:

- Restructure selected variables into cases.
- Restructure selected cases into variables.
- Transpose all data.

## To Restructure Data Files

▶ From the menus choose:

Data
  Restructure...

▶ Select the type of restructuring that you want to do.

▶ Select the data to restructure.

Optionally, you can:

- Create identification variables, which allow you to trace a value in the new file back to a value in the original file.
- Sort the data prior to restructuring.
- Define options for the new file.
- Paste the command syntax into a syntax window.

## Restructure Data Wizard: Select Type

Use the Restructure Data Wizard to restructure your data. In the first dialog box, select the type of restructuring that you want to do.

Figure 7-15
*Restructure Data Wizard*

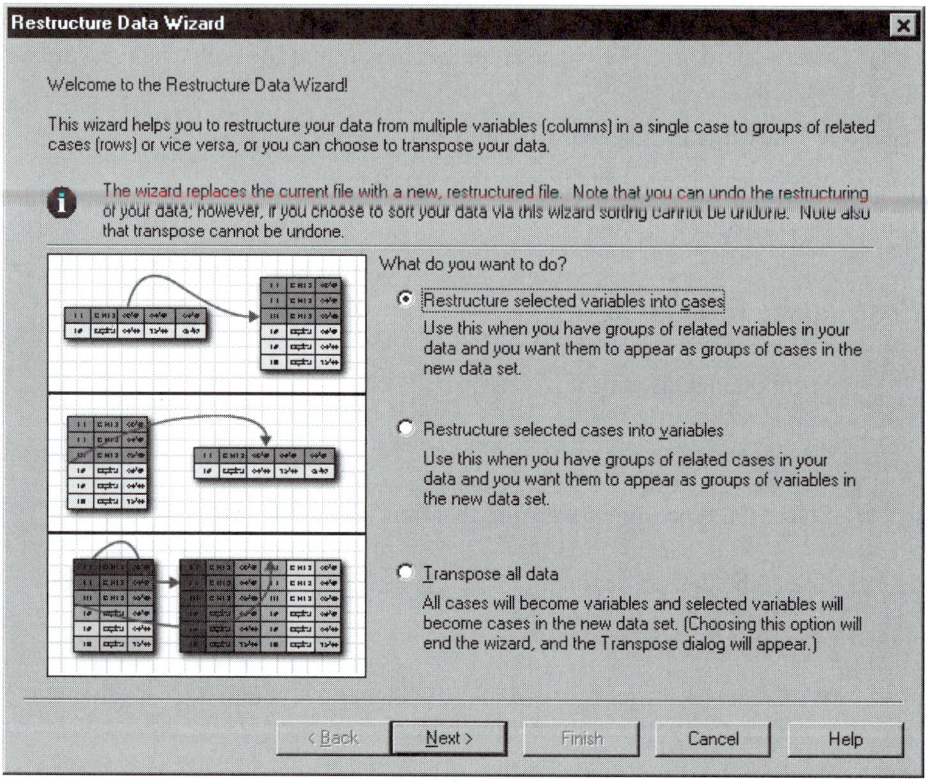


- **Restructure selected variables into cases.** Choose this when you have groups of related columns in your data and you want them to appear in groups of rows in the new data file.

  If you choose this, the wizard will display the steps for **Variables to Cases**.

- **Restructure selected cases into variables.** Choose this when you have groups of related rows in your data and you want them to appear in groups of columns in the new data file.

  If you choose this, the wizard will display the steps for **Cases to Variables**.

- **Transpose all data.** Choose this when you want to transpose your data. All rows will become columns and all columns will become rows in the new data. This choice closes the Restructure Data Wizard and opens the Transpose Data dialog box.

### Deciding How to Restructure the Data

A **variable** contains information that you want to analyze—for example, a measurement or a score. A **case** is an observation—for example, an individual. In a *simple* data structure, each variable is a single column in your data and each case is a single row. So, for example, if you were measuring test scores for all students in a class, all score values would appear in only one column, and there would be a row for each student.

When you analyze data, you are often analyzing how a variable varies according to some condition. The condition can be a specific experimental treatment, a demographic, a point in time, or something else. In data analysis, conditions of interest are often referred to as **factors**. When you analyze factors, you have a *complex* data structure. You may have information about a variable in more than one column in your data (for example, a column for each level of a factor), or you may have information about a case in more than one row (for example, a row for each level of a factor). The Restructure Data Wizard helps you to restructure files with a complex data structure.

The structure of the current file and the structure that you want in the new file determine the choices that you make in the wizard.

**How are the data arranged in the current file?** The current data may be arranged so that factors are recorded in a *separate* variable (in groups of cases) or *with* the variable (in groups of variables).

- **Groups of cases.** Does the current file have variables and conditions recorded in separate columns? For example:

  | var | factor |
  |---|---|
  | 8 | 1 |
  | 9 | 1 |
  | 3 | 2 |
  | 1 | 2 |

  In this example, the first two rows are a **case group** because they are related. They contain data for the same factor level. In SPSS data analysis, the factor is often referred to as a **grouping variable** when the data are structured this way.

- **Groups of columns.** Does the current file have variables and conditions recorded in the same column? For example:

| var_1 | var_2 |
|---|---|
| 8 | 3 |
| 9 | 1 |

In this example, the two columns are a **variable group** because they are related. They contain data for the same variable—*var_1* for factor level 1 and *var_2* for factor level 2. In SPSS data analysis, the factor is often referred to as a **repeated measure** when the data are structured this way.

**How should the data be arranged in the new file?** This is usually determined by the procedure that you want to use to analyze your data.

- **Procedures that require groups of cases.** Your data must be structured in case groups to do analyses that require a grouping variable. Examples are *univariate*, *multivariate*, and *variance components* with General Linear Model; Mixed Models; OLAP Cubes; and *independent samples* with T Test or Nonparametric Tests. If your current data structure is variable groups and you want to do these analyses, select Restructure selected variables into cases.
- **Procedures that require groups of variables.** Your data must be structured in variable groups to analyze repeated measures. Examples are *repeated measures* with General Linear Model, *time-dependent covariate* analysis with Cox Regression Analysis, *paired samples* with T Test, or *related samples* with Nonparametric Tests. If your current data structure is case groups and you want to do these analyses, select Restructure selected cases into variables.

### Example of Variables to Cases

In this example, test scores are recorded in separate columns for each factor, A and B.

Figure 7-16
*Current data for variables to cases*

| | score_a | score_b |
|---|---|---|
| 1 | 1014.00 | 864.00 |
| 2 | 684.00 | 636.00 |
| 3 | 810.00 | 638.00 |

You want to do an independent samples *t* test. You have a column group consisting of *score_a* and *score_b*, but you don't have the **grouping variable** that the procedure requires. Select Restructure selected variables into cases in the Restructure Data Wizard, restructure one variable group into a new variable named *score*, and create an index named *group*. The new data file is shown in the following figure.

Figure 7-17
*New, restructured data for variables to cases*

| | id | scor.pre | scor.pos |
|---|---|---|---|
| 1 | 1 | 1014.00 | 864.00 |
| 2 | 2 | 684.00 | 636.00 |

When you run the independent samples *t* test, you can now use *group* as the grouping variable.

### Example of Cases to Variables

In this example, test scores are recorded twice for each subject, before and after a treatment.

Figure 7-18
*Current data for cases to variables*

| | id | scor | time |
|---|---|---|---|
| 1 | 1 | 1014.00 | pre |
| 2 | 1 | 864.00 | post |
| 3 | 2 | 684.00 | pre |
| 4 | 2 | 636.00 | post |

You want to do a paired samples *t* test. Your data structure is case groups, but you don't have the **repeated measures** for the paired variables that the procedure requires. Select Restructure selected cases into variables in the Restructure Data Wizard, use *id* to identify the row groups in the current data, and use *time* to create the variable group in the new file.

Figure 7-19
*New, restructured data for cases to variables*

| | id | scor.bef | scor.aft |
|---|---|---|---|
| 1 | 1 | 1014.00 | 864.00 |
| 2 | 2 | 684.00 | 636.00 |

When you run the paired samples *t* test, you can now use *scor.bef* and *scor.aft* as the variable pair.

## Restructure Data Wizard (Variables to Cases): Number of Variable Groups

*Note*: The wizard presents this step if you choose to restructure variable groups into rows.

In this step, decide how many variable groups in the current file that you want to restructure in the new file.

**How many variable groups are in the current file?** Think about how many variable groups exist in the current data. A group of related columns, called a **variable group**, records repeated measures of the same variable in separate columns. For example, if you have three columns in the current data—*w1*, *w2*, and *w3*—that record **width**, you have one variable group. If you have an additional three columns—*h1*, *h2*, and *h3*—that record **height**, you have two variable groups.

**How many variable groups should be in the new file?** Consider how many variable groups you want to have represented in the new data file. You do not have to restructure all variable groups into the new file.

Figure 7-20
*Restructure Data Wizard: Number of Variable Groups*

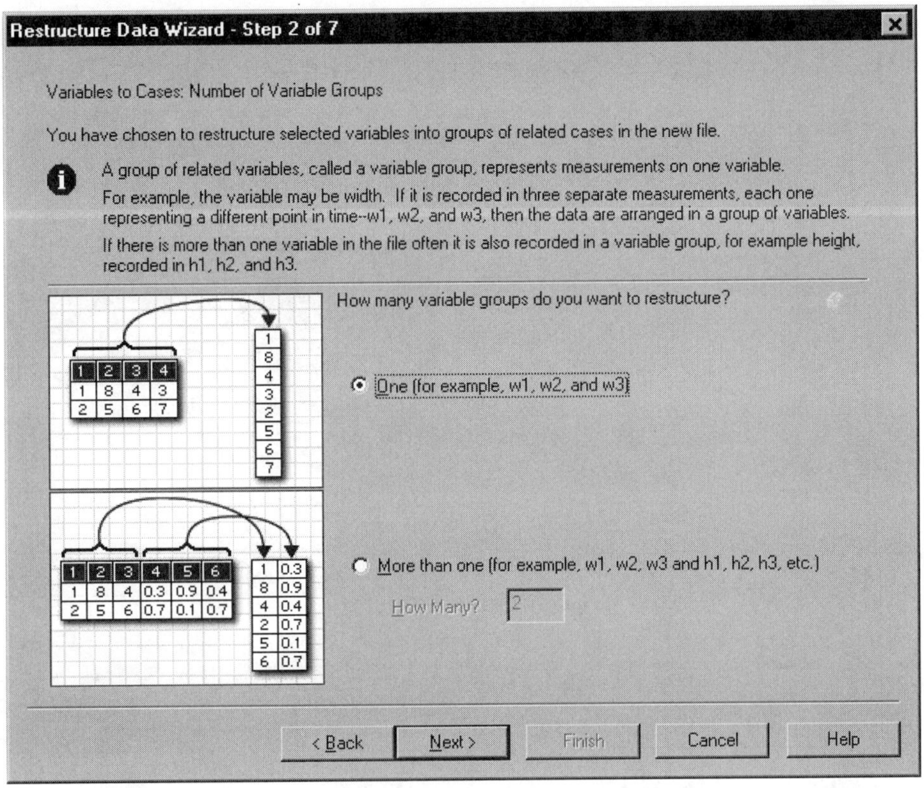


- **One.** The wizard will create a single restructured variable in the new file from one variable group in the current file.
- **More than one.** The wizard will create multiple restructured variables in the new file. The number that you specify affects the next step, in which the wizard automatically creates the specified number of new variables.

## Restructure Data Wizard (Variables to Cases): Select Variables

*Note*: The wizard presents this step if you choose to restructure variable groups into rows.

In this step, provide information about how the variables in the current file should be used in the new file. You can also create a variable that identifies the rows in the new file.

Figure 7-21
*Restructure Data Wizard: Select Variables*

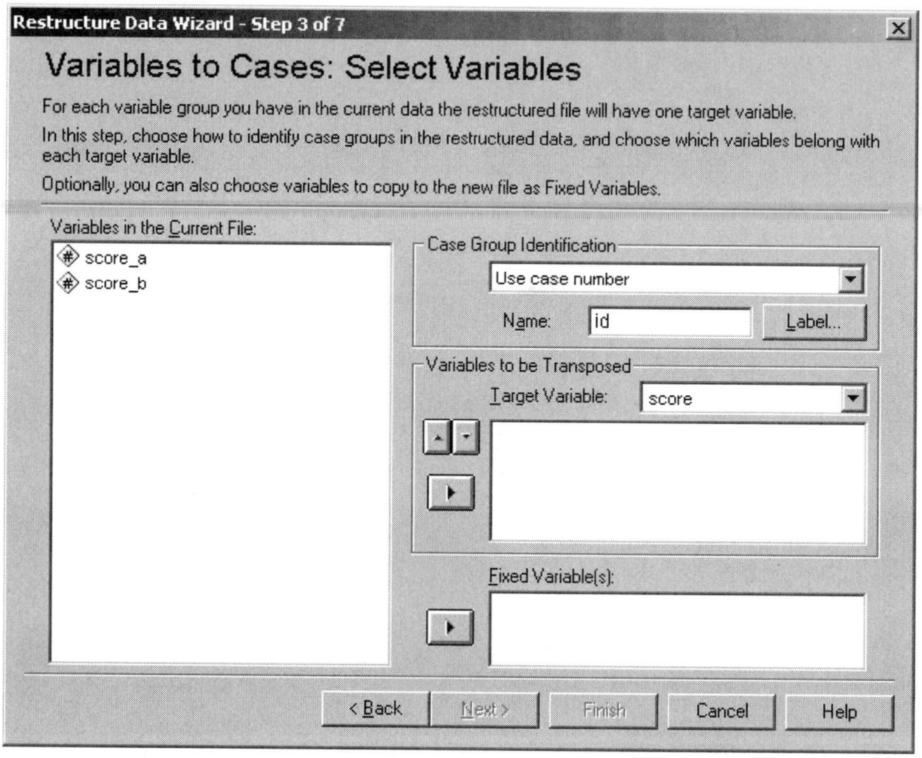


**What should be restructured in the new file?** In the previous step, you told the wizard how many variable groups that you want to restructure. The wizard created one new variable for each group. The values for the variable group will appear in that variable in the new file. Use the controls in Variables to be Transposed to define the restructured variable in the new file.

**What should be copied into the new file?** Variables that aren't restructured can be copied into the new file. Their values will be propagated in the new rows. Move variables that you want to copy into the new file into the Fixed Variable(s) list.

**How should the new rows be identified?** You can create a variable in the new data file that identifies the row in the current data file that was used to create a group of new rows. The identifier can be a sequential case number or it can be the values of the variable. Use the controls in Case Group Identification to define the identification variable in the new file. Click a cell to change the default variable name and provide a descriptive variable label for the identification variable. Variable names cannot exceed 8 characters. Variable labels can be up to 120 characters.

## Restructure Data Wizard (Variables to Cases): Create Index Variables

*Note*: The wizard presents this step if you choose to restructure variable groups into rows.

In this step, decide whether to create index variables. An index is a new variable that sequentially identifies a row group based on the original variable from which the new row was created.

Figure 7-22

*Restructure Data Wizard: Create Index Variables*

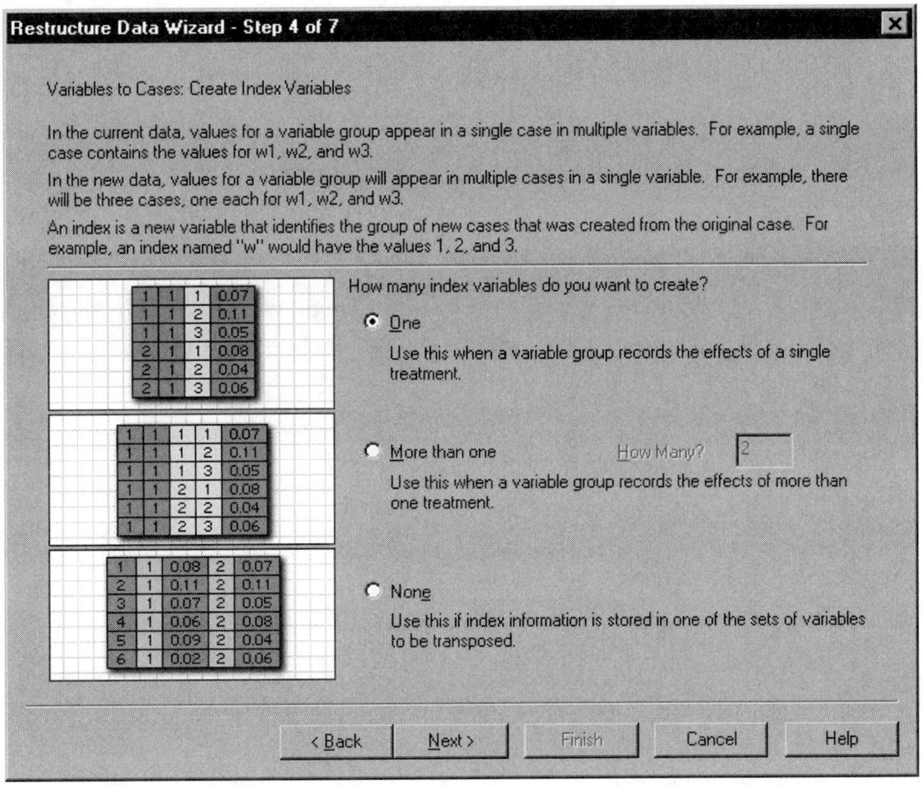

**How many index variables should be in the new file?** Index variables can be used as grouping variables in SPSS procedures. In most cases, a single index variable is sufficient; however, if the variable groups in your current file reflect multiple factor levels, multiple indices may be appropriate.

- **One.** The wizard will create a single index variable.
- **More than one.** The wizard will create multiple indices and enter the number of indices that you want to create. The number that you specify affects the next step, in which the wizard automatically creates the specified number of indices.
- **None.** Select this if you do not want to create index variables in the new file.

## *Example of One Index for Variables to Cases*

In the current data, there is one variable group, width, and one factor, time. Width was measured three times and recorded in *w1*, *w2*, and *w3*.

Figure 7-23
*Current data for one index*

| | subject | w1 | w2 | w3 |
|---|---|---|---|---|
| 1 | 1 | 6.70 | 4.30 | 5.70 |
| 2 | 2 | 7.10 | 5.90 | 5.60 |

We'll restructure the variable group into a single variable, *width*, and create a single numeric index. The new data are shown in the following table.

Figure 7-24
*New, restructured data with one index*

| | subject | width | index |
|---|---|---|---|
| 1 | 1 | 6.70 | 1 |
| 2 | 1 | 4.30 | 2 |
| 3 | 1 | 5.70 | 3 |
| 4 | 2 | 7.10 | 1 |
| 5 | 2 | 5.90 | 2 |
| 6 | 2 | 5.60 | 3 |

*Index* starts with 1 and increments for each variable in the group. It restarts for each new row. We can now analyze the restructured data in SPSS procedures that require a grouping variable.

### Example of Two Indices for Variables to Cases

When a variable group records more than one factor, you can create more than one index; however, the current data must be arranged so that the levels of the first factor are a primary index within which the levels of subsequent factors cycle. In the current data, there is one variable group, width, and two factors, A and B. The data are arranged so that levels of factor B cycle within levels of factor A.

Figure 7-25
*Original data for two indices*

| | subject | w_a1b1 | w_a1b2 | w_a2b1 | w_a2b2 |
|---|---|---|---|---|---|
| 1 | 1 | 5.50 | 6.40 | 5.80 | 5.90 |
| 2 | 2 | 7.40 | 7.10 | 5.60 | 6.70 |

We'll restructure the variable group into a single variable, *width*, and create two indices. The new data are shown in the following table.

Figure 7-26
*New data with two indices*

| | subject | width | index_a | index_b |
|---|---|---|---|---|
| 1 | 1 | 5.50 | 1 | 1 |
| 2 | 1 | 6.40 | 1 | 2 |
| 3 | 1 | 5.80 | 2 | 1 |
| 4 | 1 | 5.90 | 2 | 2 |
| 5 | 2 | 7.40 | 1 | 1 |
| 6 | 2 | 7.10 | 1 | 2 |
| 7 | 2 | 5.60 | 2 | 1 |
| 8 | 2 | 6.70 | 2 | 2 |

## Restructure Data Wizard (Variables to Cases): Create One Index Variable

*Note*: The wizard presents this step if you choose to restructure variable groups into rows and create one index variable.

In this step, decide what values you want for the index variable. The values can be sequential numbers or the names of the variables in an original variable group. You can also specify a name and a label for the new index variable.

Figure 7-27
*Restructure Data Wizard: Create One Index Variable*

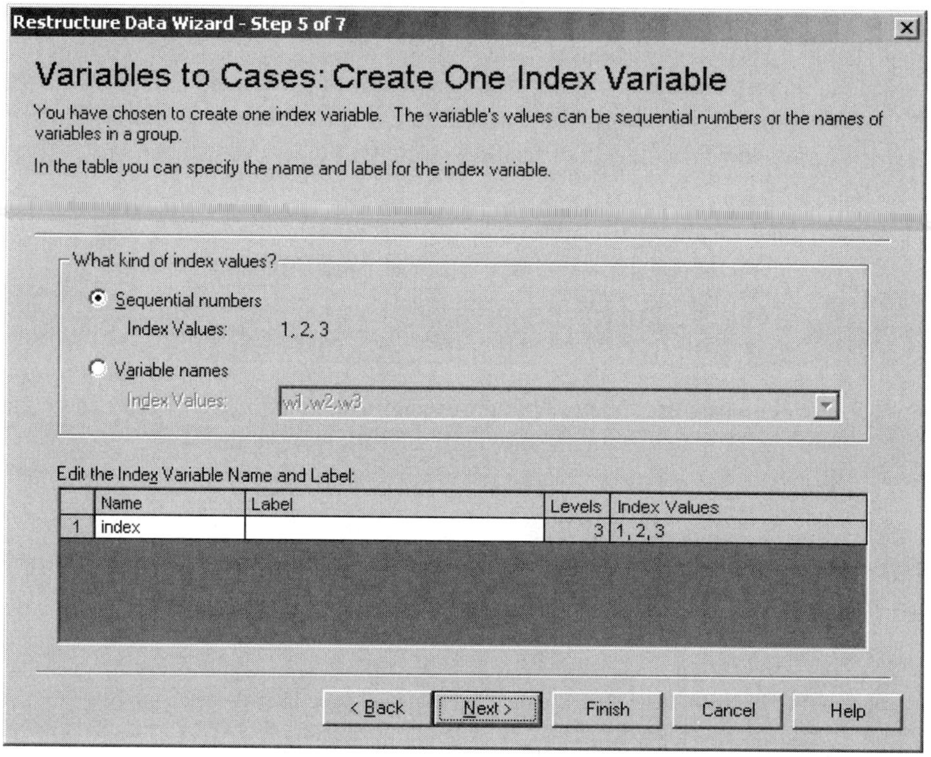


See "Example of One Index for Variables to Cases" on p. 146 for an example of a single index.

- **Sequential numbers.** The wizard will automatically assign sequential numbers as index values.
- **Variable names.** The wizard will use the names of the selected variable group as index values. Choose a variable group from the list.
- **Names and labels.** Click a cell to change the default variable name and provide a descriptive variable label for the index variable. Variable names cannot exceed 8 characters. Variable labels can be up to 120 characters.

## Restructure Data Wizard (Variables to Cases): Create Multiple Index Variables

*Note*: The wizard presents this step if you choose to restructure variable groups into rows and create multiple index variables.

In this step, specify the number of levels for each index variable. You can also specify a name and a label for the new index variable.

Figure 7-28
*Restructure Data Wizard: Create Multiple Index Variables*

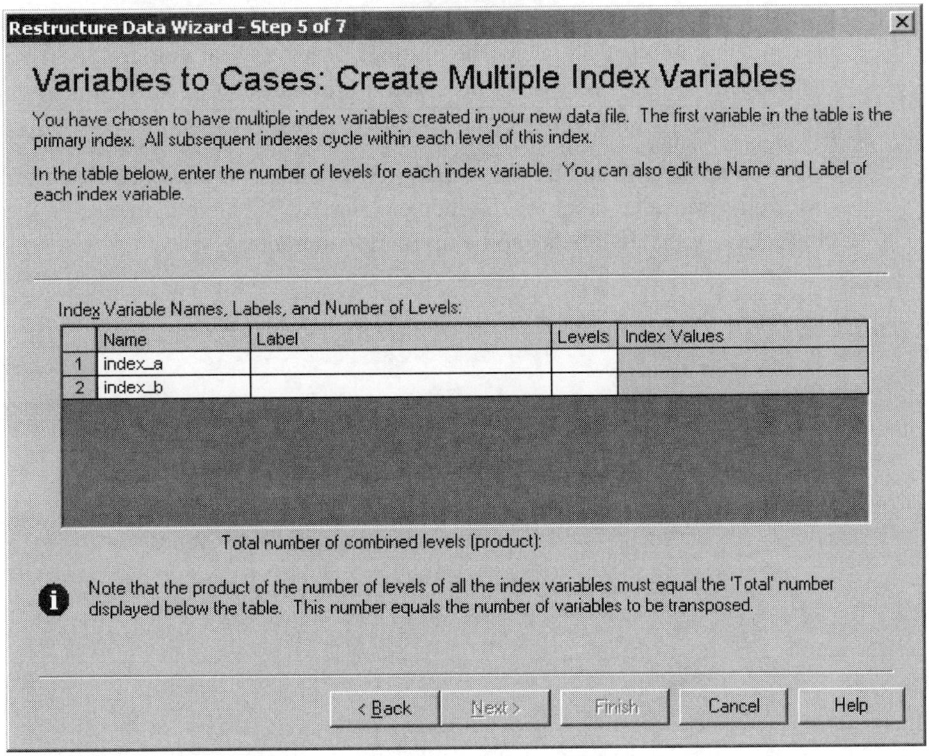


See "Example of Two Indices for Variables to Cases" on p. 147 for an example of two indices.

**How many levels are recorded in the current file?** Consider how many factor levels are recorded in the current data. A **level** defines a group of cases that experienced identical conditions. If there are multiple factors, the current data must be arranged so that the levels of the first factor are a primary index within which the levels of subsequent factors cycle.

**How many levels should be in the new file?** Enter the number of levels for each index. The values for multiple index variables are always sequential numbers. The values start at 1 and increment for each level. The first index increments the slowest, and the last index increments the fastest.

**Total combined levels.** You cannot create more levels than exist in the current data. Because the restructured data will contain one row for each combination of treatments, the wizard checks the number of levels that you create. It will compare the product of the levels that you create to the number of variables in your variable groups. They must match.

**Names and labels.** Click a cell to change the default variable name and provide a descriptive variable label for the index variables. Variable names cannot exceed 8 characters. Variable labels can be up to 120 characters.

## Restructure Data Wizard (Variables to Cases): Options

*Note*: The wizard presents this step if you choose to restructure variable groups into rows.

In this step, specify options for the new, restructured file.

Figure 7-29
*Restructure Data Wizard: Options*

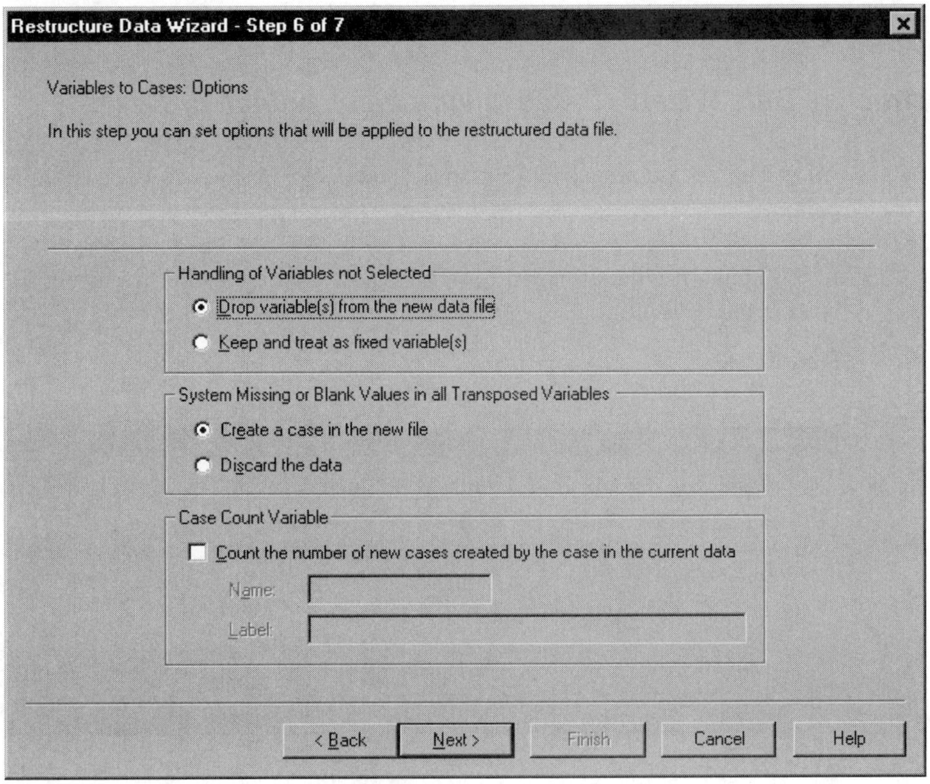


**Drop unselected variables?** In the select variables step (step 3), you selected variable groups to be restructured, variables to be copied, and an identification variable from the current data. The data from the selected variables will appear in the new file. If there are other variables in the current data, you can choose to discard or keep them.

**Keep missing data?** The wizard checks each potential row for missing values before it adds it to the new file and flags rows that contain only missing data. You can choose to keep or discard these rows.

**Create a count variable?** The wizard can create a count variable in the new file. It contains the number of new rows generated by a row in the current data. A count variable may be useful if you choose to discard missing data from the new file because that makes it possible to generate a different number of new rows for a given row in the current data. Click a cell to change the default variable name and provide a descriptive variable label for the count variable. Variable names cannot exceed 8 characters. Variable labels can be up to 120 characters.

## Restructure Data Wizard (Cases to Variables): Select Variables

*Note*: The wizard presents this step if you choose to restructure case groups into columns.

In this step, provide information about how the variables in the current file should be used in the new file.

Figure 7-30
*Restructure Data Wizard: Select Variables*

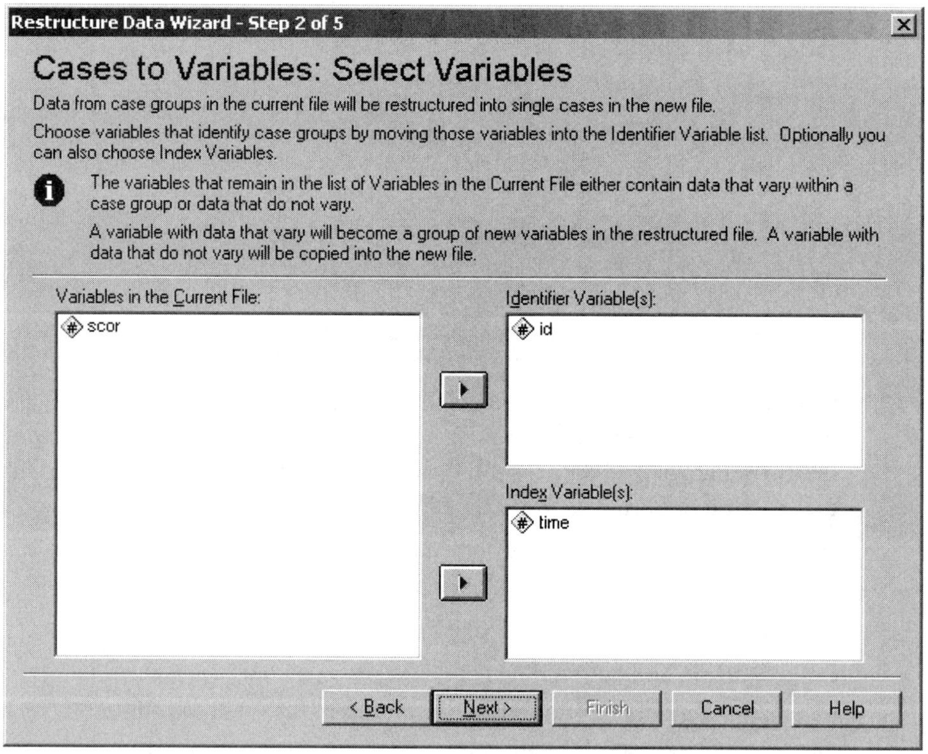

**What identifies case groups in the current data?** A case group is a group of rows that are related because they measure the same observational unit—for example, an individual or an institution. The wizard needs to know which variables in the current file identify the case groups so that it can consolidate each group into a single row in the new file. Move variables that identify case groups in the current file into the Identifier Variable(s) list. Variables that are used to split the current data file are automatically used to identify case groups. Each time a new combination of identification values is encountered, the wizard will create a new row, so cases in the current file should be sorted by values of the identification variables, in the same order that variables are listed in the Identifier Variable(s) list. If the current data file isn't already sorted, you can sort it in the next step.

**How should the new variable groups be created in the new file?** In the original data, a variable appears in a single column. In the new data file, that variable will appear in multiple new columns. **Index variables** are variables in the current data that the wizard should use to create the new columns. The restructured data will contain one new variable for each unique value in these columns. Move the variables that should be used to form the new variable groups to the Index Variable(s) list. When the wizard presents options, you can also choose to order the new columns by index.

**What happens to the other columns?** The wizard automatically decides what to do with the variables that remain in the Current File list. It checks each variable to see if the data values vary within a case group. If it does, the wizard restructures the values into a variable group in the new file. If it doesn't, the wizard copies the values into the new file.

## Restructure Data Wizard (Cases to Variables): Sort Data

*Note*: The wizard presents this step if you choose to restructure case groups into columns.

In this step, decide whether to sort the current file before restructuring it. Each time the wizard encounters a new combination of identification values, a new row is created, so it is important that the data are sorted by the variables that identify case groups.

Figure 7-31
*Restructure Data Wizard: Sort Data*

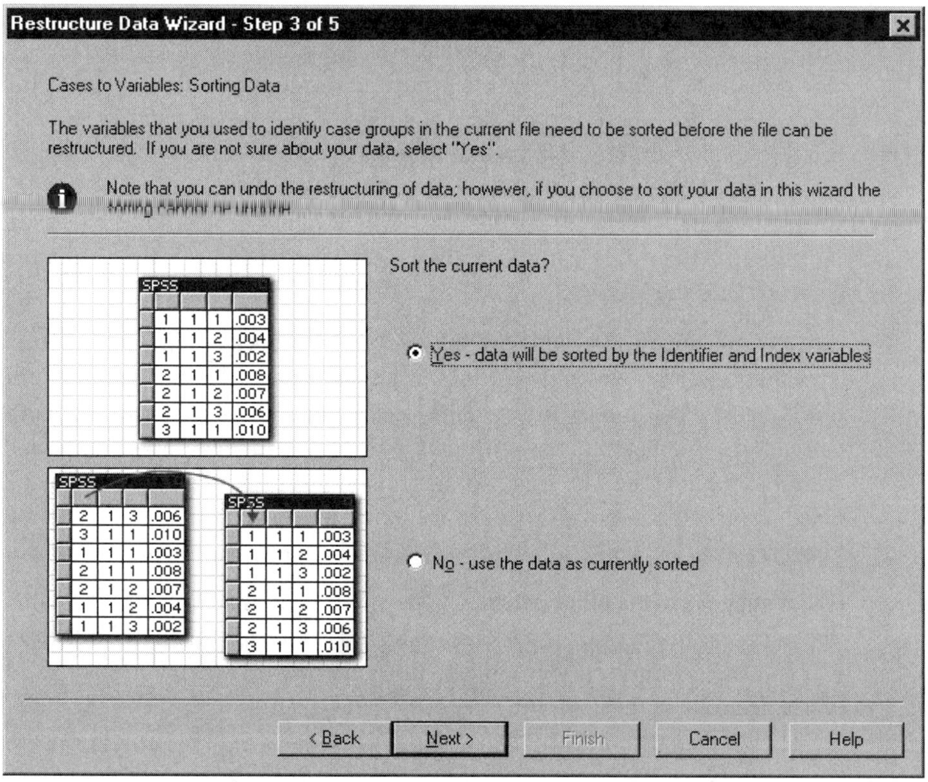


**How are the rows ordered in the current file?** Consider how the current data are sorted and which variables you are using to identify case groups (specified in the previous step).

- **Yes.** The wizard will automatically sort the current data by the identification variables, in the same order that variables are listed in the Identifier Variable(s) list in the previous step. Choose this when the data aren't sorted by the identification variables or when you aren't sure. This choice requires a separate pass of the data, but it guarantees that the rows are correctly ordered for restructuring.
- **No.** The wizard will not sort the current data. Choose this when you are sure that the current data are sorted by the variables that identify case groups.

## Restructure Data Wizard (Cases to Variables): Options

*Note*: The wizard presents this step if you choose to restructure case groups into columns.

In this step, specify options for the new, restructured file.

Figure 7-32
*Restructure Data Wizard: Options*

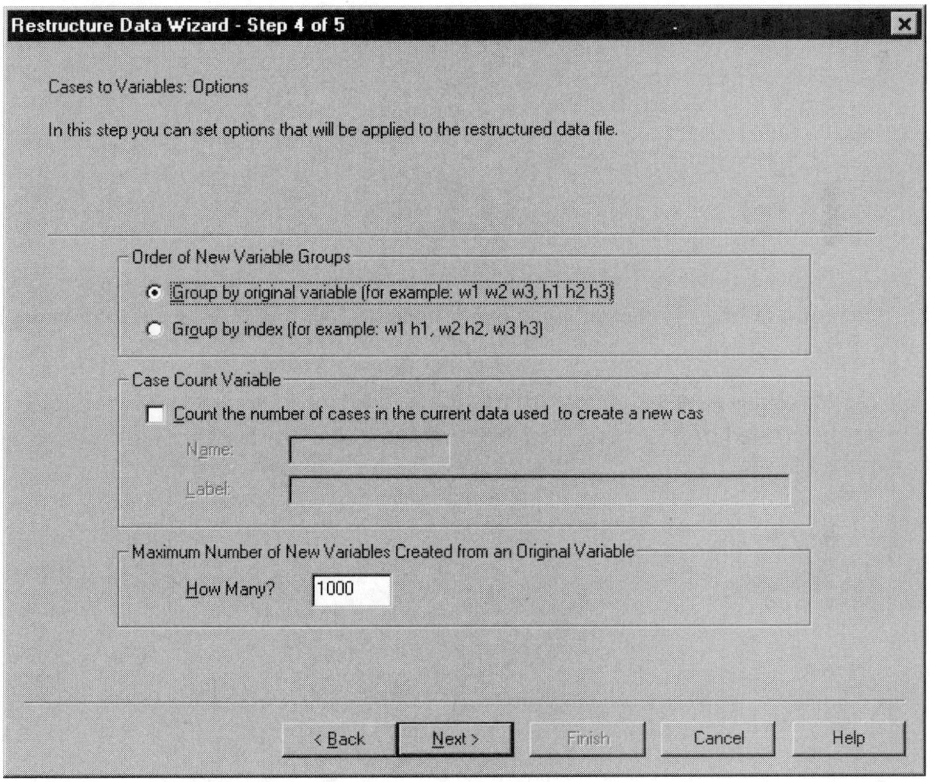

**How should the new variable groups be ordered in the new file?**

- **By variable.** The wizard groups the new variables created from an original variable together.
- **By index.** The wizard groups the variables according to the values of the index variables.

**Example.** The variables to be restructured are *w* and *h* and the index is *month*:

| *w* | *h* | *month* |
|---|---|---|

Grouping by variable results in:

| *w.jan* | *w.feb* | *h.jan* |
|---|---|---|

Grouping by index results in:

| *w.jan* | *h.jan* | *w.feb* |
|---|---|---|

**Create a count variable?** The wizard can create a count variable in the new file. It contains the number of rows in the current data that were used to create a row in the new data file.

**Maximum new variables.** Specify the maximum number of new variables that should be created from a variable in the current file. Keep the number low to avoid excessively wide files.

## Restructure Data Wizard: Finish

This is the final step of the Restructure Data Wizard. Decide what to do with your specifications.

Figure 7-33
*Restructure Data Wizard: Finish*

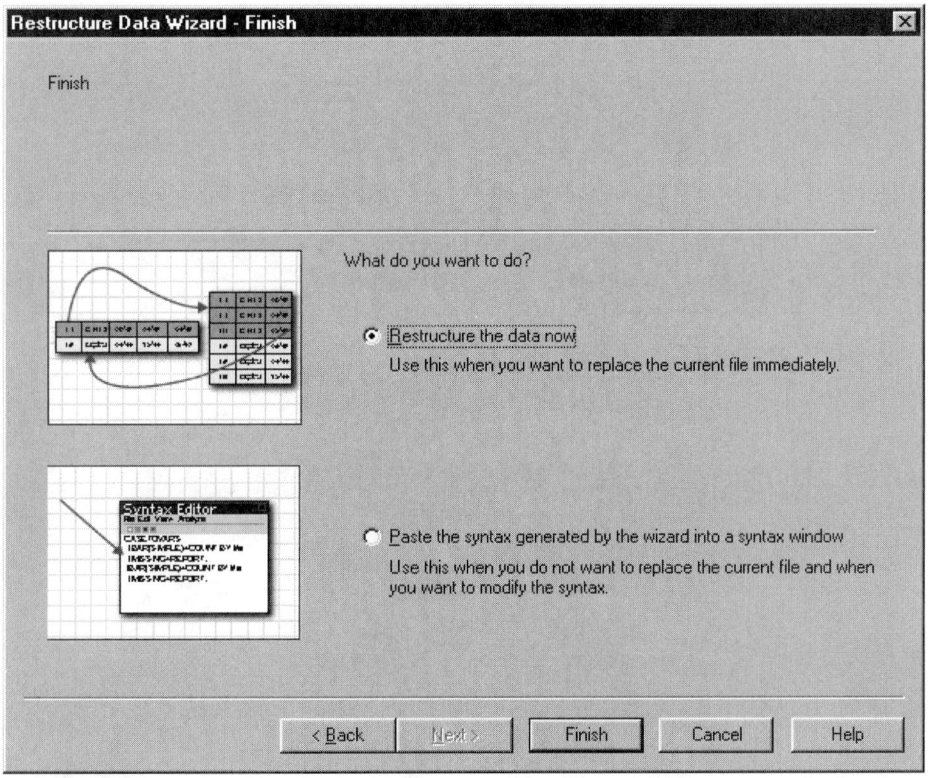


- **Restructure now.** The wizard will create the new, restructured file. Choose this if you want to replace the current file immediately. *Note*: If original data are weighted, the new data will be weighted unless the variable that is used as the weight is restructured or dropped from the new file.
- **Paste syntax**. The wizard will paste the syntax it generates into a syntax window. Choose this when you are not ready to replace the current file, when you want to modify the syntax, or when you want to save it for future use.

Chapter

**8**

# Working with Output

When you run a procedure, the results are displayed in a window called the Viewer. In this window, you can easily navigate to whichever part of the output that you want to see. You can also manipulate the output and create a document that contains precisely the output that you want, arranged and formatted appropriately.

## Viewer

Results are displayed in the Viewer. You can use the Viewer to:

- Browse results.
- Show or hide selected tables and charts.
- Change the display order of results by moving selected items.
- Move items between the Viewer and other applications.

Figure 8-1
*Viewer*

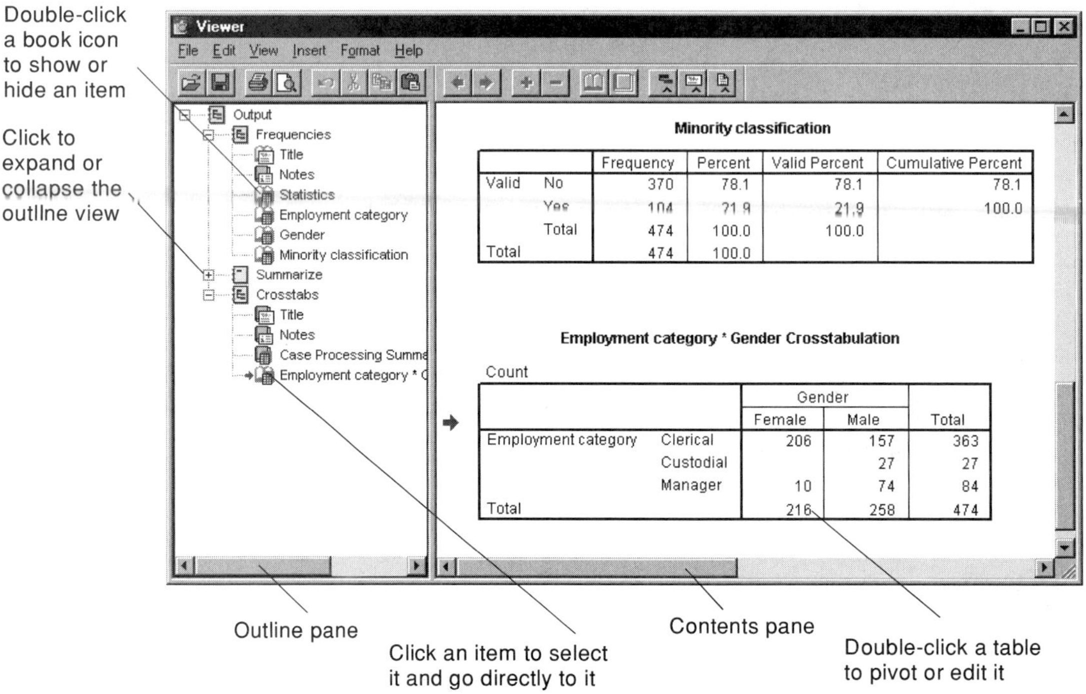


The Viewer is divided into two panes:

- The left pane of the Viewer contains an outline view of the contents.
- The right pane contains statistical tables, charts, and text output.
- You can use the scroll bars to browse the results, or you can click an item in the outline to go directly to the corresponding table or chart.
- You can click and drag the right border of the outline pane to change the width of the outline pane.

## Draft Viewer

If you prefer simple text output rather than interactive pivot tables, you can use the Draft Viewer.

To use the Draft Viewer:

▶ In any window, from the menus choose:

Edit
 Options...

▶ On the General tab, click Draft Viewer for the output type.

▶ To change the format options for Draft Viewer output, click the Draft Viewer tab.

For more information on the Draft Viewer, see Chapter 9.

▶ In any window, from the menus choose:

Help
 Topics

▶ Click the Index tab in the Help Topics window.

▶ Type draft viewer, and double-click the index entry.

## Showing and Hiding Results

In the Viewer, you can selectively show and hide individual tables or results from an entire procedure. This is useful when you want to shorten the amount of visible output in the contents pane.

### To Hide a Table or Chart without Deleting It

▶ Double-click its book icon in the outline pane of the Viewer.

*or*

▶ Click the item to select it.

▶ From the menus choose:

View
 Hide

*or*

▶ Click the closed book (Hide) icon on the Outlining toolbar.

The open book (Show) icon becomes the active icon, indicating that the item is now hidden.

### To Hide All of the Results from a Procedure

- Click the box to the left of the procedure name in the outline pane.

  This hides all of the results from the procedure and collapses the outline view.

## Moving, Copying, and Deleting Results

You can rearrange the results by copying, moving, or deleting an item or a group of items.

### To Move Results in the Viewer

- Click an item in the outline or contents pane to select it. (Shift-click to select multiple items, or Ctrl-click to select noncontiguous items.)
- Use the mouse to click and drag selected items (hold down the mouse button while dragging).
- Release the mouse button on the item just above the location where you want to drop the moved items.

  You can also move items by using Cut and Paste After on the Edit menu.

### To Delete Results in the Viewer

- Click an item in the outline or contents pane to select it. (Shift-click to select multiple items, or Ctrl-click to select noncontiguous items.)
- Press Delete.

  *or*

- From the menus choose:

  Edit
   Delete

### To Copy Results in the Viewer

▶ Click items in the outline or contents pane to select them. (Shift-click to select multiple items, or Ctrl-click to select noncontiguous items.)

▶ Hold down the Ctrl key while you use the mouse to click and drag selected items (hold down the mouse button while dragging).

▶ Release the mouse button to drop the items where you want them.

You can also copy items by using Copy and Paste After on the Edit menu or the context menu.

## Changing Alignment

By default, all results are initially left-aligned. You can change the initial alignment (choose Options on the Edit menu, then click the Viewer tab) or the alignment of selected items at any time.

### To Change the Alignment of Results

▶ Select the items that you want to align (click the items in the outline or contents pane; Shift-click or Ctrl-click to select multiple items).

▶ From the menus choose:

Format
  Align Left

Other alignment options include Center and Align Right.

*Note*: All results are displayed left-aligned in the Viewer. Only the alignment of printed results is affected by the alignment settings. Centered and right-aligned items are identified by a small symbol above and to the left of the item.

## Viewer Outline

The outline pane provides a table of contents of the Viewer document. You can use the outline pane to navigate through your results and control the display. Most actions in the outline pane have a corresponding effect on the contents pane.

- Selecting an item in the outline pane selects and displays the corresponding item in the contents pane.
- Moving an item in the outline pane moves the corresponding item in the contents pane.
- Collapsing the outline view hides the results from all items in the collapsed levels.

Figure 8-2
*Collapsed outline view and hidden results*

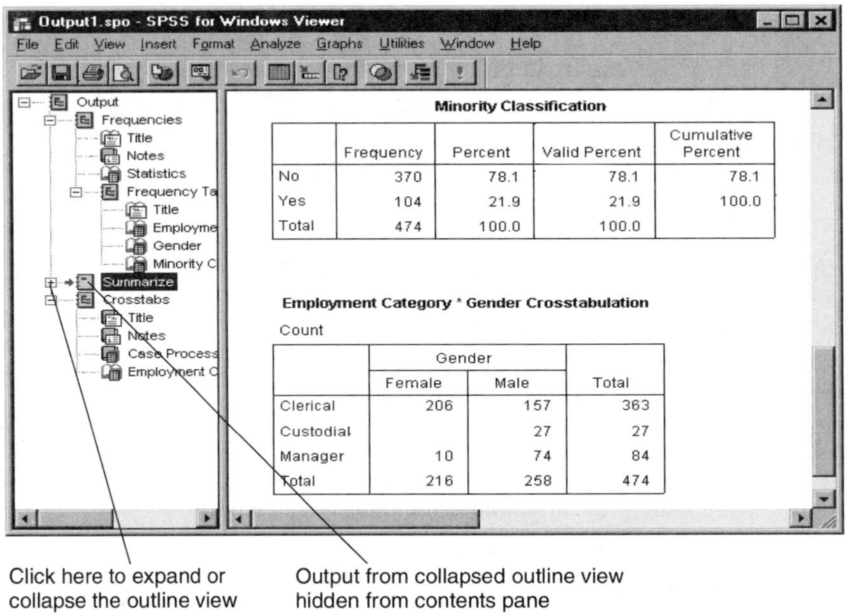


**Controlling the outline display.** To control the outline display, you can:

- Expand and collapse the outline view.
- Change the outline level for selected items.
- Change the size of items in the outline display.
- Change the font used in the outline display.

### To Collapse or Expand the Outline View

▶ Click the box to the left of the outline item that you want to collapse or expand.

*or*

▶ Click the item in the outline.

▶ From the menus choose:

View
  Collapse

*or*

View
  Expand

### To Change the Outline Level of an Item

▶ Click the item in the outline pane to select it.

▶ Click the left arrow on the Outlining toolbar to promote the item (move the item to the left).

▶ Click the right arrow on the Outlining toolbar to demote the item (move the item to the right).

*or*

From the menus choose:

Edit
  Outline
    Promote

*or*

Edit
  Outline
    Demote

Changing the outline level is particularly useful after you move items in the outline level. Moving items can change the outline level of the selected items, and you can use the left and right arrow buttons on the Outlining toolbar to restore the original outline level.

### To Change the Size of Items in the Outline

▶ From the menus choose:

View
  Outline Size
    Small

Other options include Medium and Large.

The icons and their associated text change size.

### To Change the Font in the Outline

▶ From the menus choose:

View
  Outline Font...

▶ Select a font.

### Adding Items to the Viewer

In the Viewer, you can add items such as titles, new text, charts, or material from other applications.

### To Add a New Title or Text Item to the Viewer Contents

▶ Text items that are not connected to a table or chart can be added to the Viewer.

▶ Click the table, chart, or other object that will precede the title or text.

▶ From the menus choose:

Insert
  New Title

*or*

Insert
  New Text

▶ Double-click the new object.

▶ Enter the text that you want at this location.

### To Insert a Chart into the Viewer

Charts from older versions of SPSS can be inserted into the Viewer. To insert a chart:

- Click the table, chart, or other object that will precede the chart.
- From the menus choose:

  Insert
  Old Graph...

- Select a chart file.

### To Add an Existing Text File to the Viewer

- In either the outline or the contents pane of the Viewer, click the table, chart, or other object that will precede the text.
- From the menus choose:

  Insert
  Text File...

- Select a text file.

To edit the text, double-click it.

## Using Results in Other Applications

Pivot tables and charts can be copied and pasted into another Windows application, such as a word processing program or a spreadsheet. You can paste the pivot tables or charts in various formats, including the following:

**Embedded object.** For applications that support ActiveX objects, you can embed pivot tables and interactive charts. After you paste the table, it can be activated in place by double-clicking and then edited as if in the Viewer.

**Picture (metafile).** You can paste pivot tables, text output, and charts as metafile pictures. The picture format can be resized in the other application, and sometimes a limited amount of editing can be done with the facilities of the other application. Pivot tables pasted as pictures retain all borders and font characteristics.

**RTF (rich text format)**. Pivot tables can be pasted into other applications in RTF format. In most applications, this pastes the pivot table as a table that can then be edited in the other application.

**Bitmap**. Charts can be pasted into other applications as bitmaps.

**BIFF.** The contents of a table can be pasted into a spreadsheet and retain numeric precision.

**Text.** The contents of a table can be copied and pasted as text. This can be useful for applications such as e-mail, where the application can accept or transmit only text.

### To Copy a Table or Chart

- Select the table or chart to be copied.
- From the menus choose:

Edit
 Copy

### To Copy and Paste Results into Another Application

- Copy the results in the Viewer.
- From the menus in the target application choose:

Edit
 Paste

*or*

Edit
 Paste Special...

**Paste**. Output is copied to the clipboard in a number of formats. Each application determines the "best" format to use for Paste. In many applications, Paste will paste results as a picture (metafile). For word processing applications, Paste will paste pivot tables in RTF format, which pastes the pivot table as a table. For spreadsheet applications, Paste will paste pivot tables in BIFF format. Charts are pasted as metafiles.

**Paste Special**. Results are copied to the clipboard in multiple formats. Paste Special allows you to select the format that you want from the list of formats available to the target application.

## To Embed Pivot Tables and Interactive Charts in Another Application

You can embed pivot tables and interactive charts in other applications in ActiveX format. An embedded object can be activated in place by double-clicking and can then be edited and pivoted as if in the Viewer.

If you have applications that support ActiveX objects:

▶ Run the file *objs-on.bat*, located in the directory in which the program is installed. (Double-click the file to run it.)

This turns on ActiveX embedding for pivot tables. The file *objs-off.bat* turns ActiveX embedding off.

To embed a pivot table or interactive chart in another application:

▶ In the Viewer, copy the table.

▶ From the menus in the target application choose:

Edit
  Paste Special...

▶ From the list select SPSS Pivot Table Object *or* SPSS Graphics Control Object.

The target application must support ActiveX objects. See the application's documentation for information on ActiveX support. Some applications that do not support ActiveX may initially accept ActiveX pivot tables but may then exhibit unstable behavior. Do not rely on embedded objects until you have tested the application's stability with embedded ActiveX objects.

## To Paste a Table or Chart as a Picture

- In the Viewer, copy the table or chart.
- From the menus in the target application choose:

  Edit
  Paste Special...

- From the list, select Picture.

  The item is pasted as a metafile. Only the layer and columns that were visible when the item was copied are available in the metafile. Other layers or hidden columns are not available.

## To Paste a Pivot Table as a Table

- In the Viewer, copy the pivot table.
- From the menus in the target application choose:

  Edit
  Paste Special...

- From the list select Formatted Text (RTF) or Rich Text Format.

  The pivot table is pasted as a table. Only the layer and columns that were visible when the item was copied are pasted into the table. Other layers or hidden columns are not available. You can copy and paste only one pivot table at a time in this format.

### To Paste a Pivot Table as Unformatted (ASCII) Text:

- In the Viewer, copy the table.
- From the menus in the target application choose:

  Edit
  Paste Special...

- From the list select Unformatted Text.

Unformatted pivot table text contains tabs between columns. You can align columns by adjusting the tab stops in the other application.

### To Copy and Paste Multiple Items into Another Application

- Select the tables and/or charts to be copied. (Shift-click or Ctrl-click to select multiple items.)
- From the menus choose:

  Edit
    Copy Objects

- In the target application, from the menus choose:

  Edit
    Paste

  *Note*: Use Copy Objects only to copy multiple items from the Viewer to another application. For copying and pasting within Viewer documents (for example, between two Viewer windows), use Copy on the Edit menu.

## Pasting Objects into the Viewer

Objects from other applications can be pasted into the Viewer. You can use either Paste After or Paste Special. Either type of pasting puts the new object after the currently selected object in the Viewer. Use Paste Special when you want to choose the format of the pasted object.

### Paste Special

Paste Special allows you to select the format of a copied object that is pasted into the Viewer. The possible file types for the object on the clipboard are listed.

The object will be inserted in the Viewer following the currently selected object.

Figure 8-3
*Paste Special dialog box*

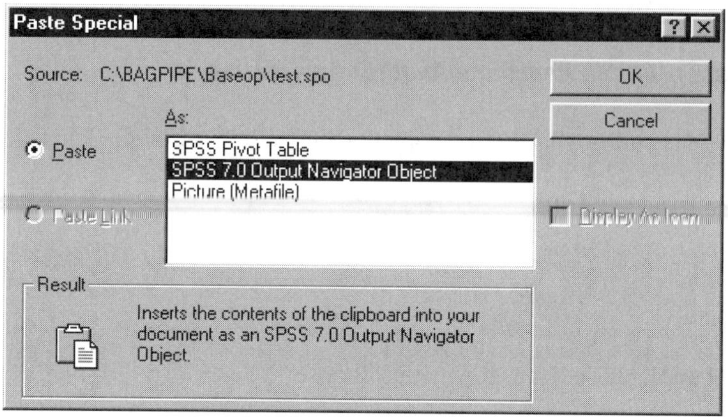


### *To Paste an Object from Another Application into the Viewer*

▶ Copy the object in the other application.

▶ In either the outline or the contents pane of the Viewer, click the table, chart, or other object that will precede the object.

▶ From the menus choose:

Edit
  Paste Special...

▶ From the list, select the format for the object.

## Export Output

Export Output saves pivot tables and text output in HTML and text format, and it saves charts in a variety of common formats used by other applications.

**Output Document**. Exports any combination of pivot tables, text output, and charts. Charts are exported in the currently selected chart export format, and a separate file is created for each chart. For HTML document format, charts are embedded by reference, and you should export charts in a suitable format for inclusion in HTML documents. For text document format, a line is inserted in the text file for each chart, indicating the filename of the exported chart.

**Output Document (No Charts)**. Exports pivot tables and text output. Pivot tables can be exported as HTML tables (HTML 3.0 or later), as tab-separated text, or as space-separated text. Text output can be exported as preformatted HTML or space-separated text. A fixed-pitch (monospaced) font is required for proper alignment of space-separated text output. (By default, most Web browsers use a fixed-pitch font for preformatted text.)

**Charts Only**. Exports charts only. Export formats include: Windows metafile (WMF), Windows bitmap (BMP), encapsulated PostScript (EPS), JPEG, TIFF, PNG, and Macintosh PICT.

**Export What**. You can export all objects in the Viewer, all visible objects, or only selected objects.

**Export Format**. For output documents, the available options are HTML and text; charts are exported in the currently selected chart format in the HTML Options or Text Options dialog box. For Charts Only, select a chart export format from the drop-down list.

## To Export Output

- ▶ Make the Viewer the active window (click anywhere in the window).
- ▶ From the menus choose:

  File
  Export...

- ▶ Enter a filename (or prefix for charts) and select an export format.

Figure 8-4
*Export Output dialog box*

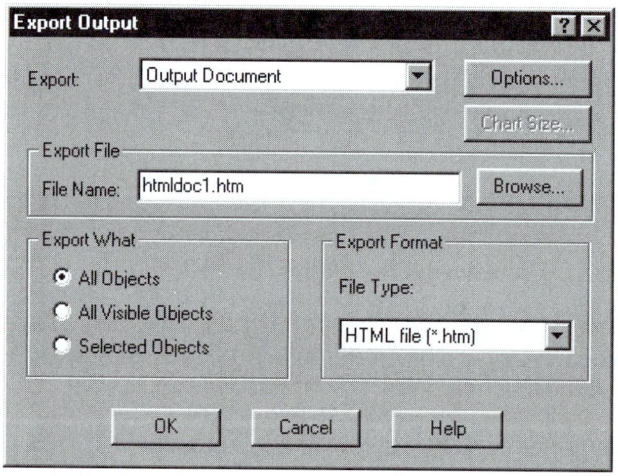

Figure 8-5
*Output exported in HTML format*

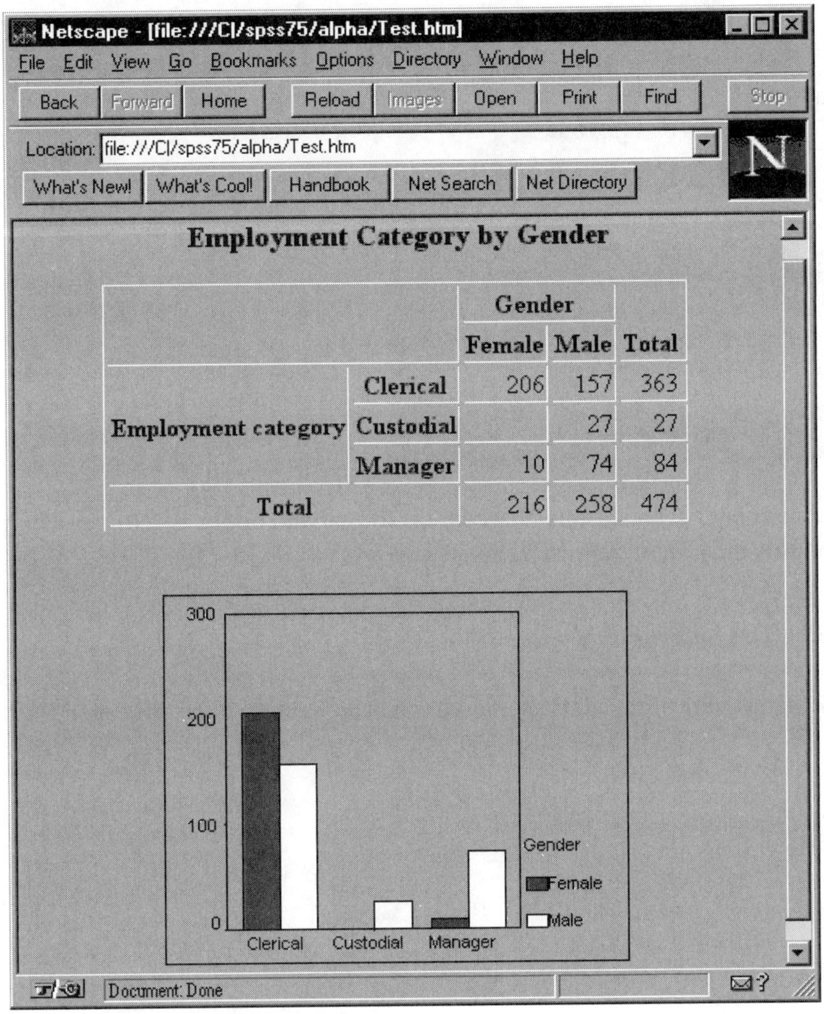

### HTML Options

HTML Options controls the chart export options and the inclusion of footnotes and captions for documents exported in HTML format.

Figure 8-6
*HTML Options dialog box*

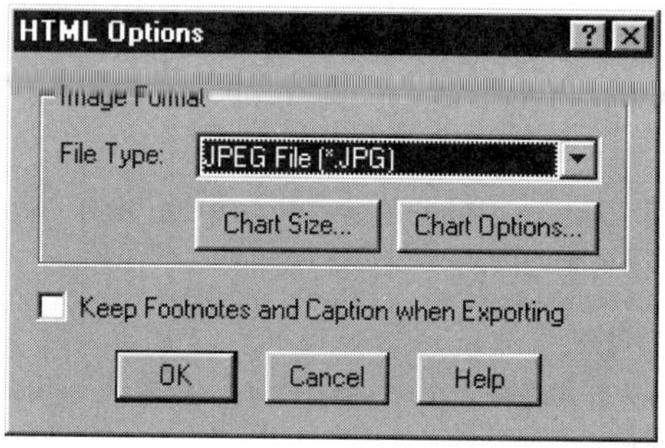


**Image Format.** Controls the chart export format and optional settings. Chart Size controls the size of exported charts.

### To Set HTML Export Options

- Make the Viewer the active window (click anywhere in the window).
- From the menus choose:

  File
  Export...
- Select HTML file as the export format.
- Click Options.

### Text Options

Text Options controls pivot table, text output, and chart format options and the inclusion of footnotes and captions for documents exported in text format.

Figure 8-7
*Text Options dialog box*

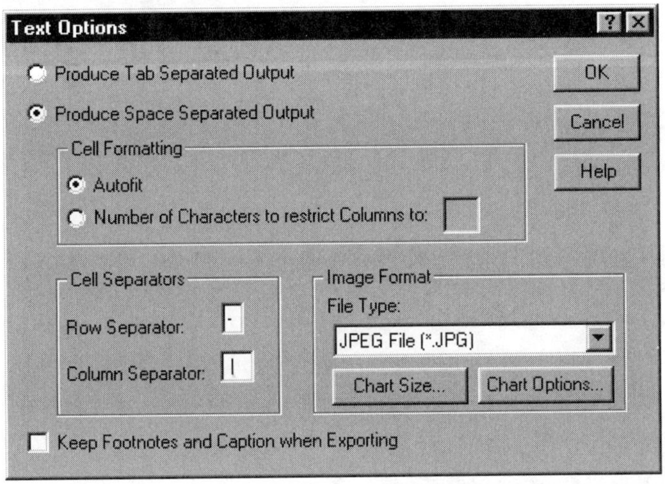


Pivot tables can be exported in tab-separated or space-separated format. For tab-separated format, if a cell is not empty, its contents and a tab character are printed. If a cell is empty, a tab character is printed.

All text output is exported in space-separated format. All space-separated output requires a fixed-pitch (monospaced) font for proper alignment.

**Cell Formatting**. For space-separated pivot tables, by default all line wrapping is removed and each column is set to the width of the longest label or value in the column. To limit the width of columns and wrap long labels, specify a number of characters for the column width. This setting affects only pivot tables.

**Cell Separators**. For space-separated pivot tables, you can specify the characters used to create cell borders.

**Image Format**. Controls the chart export format and optional settings. Chart Size controls the size of exported charts.

### To Set Text Export Options

- ▶ Make the Viewer the active window (click anywhere in the window).
- ▶ From the menus choose:

File
  Export...

- ▶ Select Text file as the export format.
- ▶ Click Options.

### Chart Size

Chart Size controls the size of exported charts. The custom percentage specification allows you to decrease or increase the size of the exported chart up to 200%.

Figure 8-8
*Chart Size dialog box*

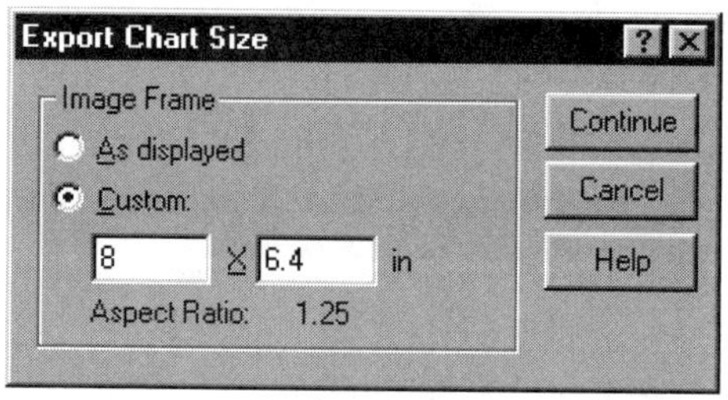


### To Set the Size of Exported Charts

- ▶ Make the Viewer the active window (click anywhere in the window).
- ▶ From the menus choose:

File
  Export...

- For output documents, click Options, select CGM metafile or Windows metafile as the export format, and click Chart Size.
- For Charts Only, select the export format, and click Chart Size.

## Printing Viewer Documents

You can control the Viewer items that print in several ways:

**All visible output.** Prints only items currently displayed in the contents pane. Hidden items (items with a closed book icon in the outline pane or hidden in collapsed outline layers) are not printed.

**All output.** Prints all output, including hidden items.

**Selection.** Prints only items currently selected in the outline and/or contents panes.

Figure 8-9
*Viewer Print dialog box*

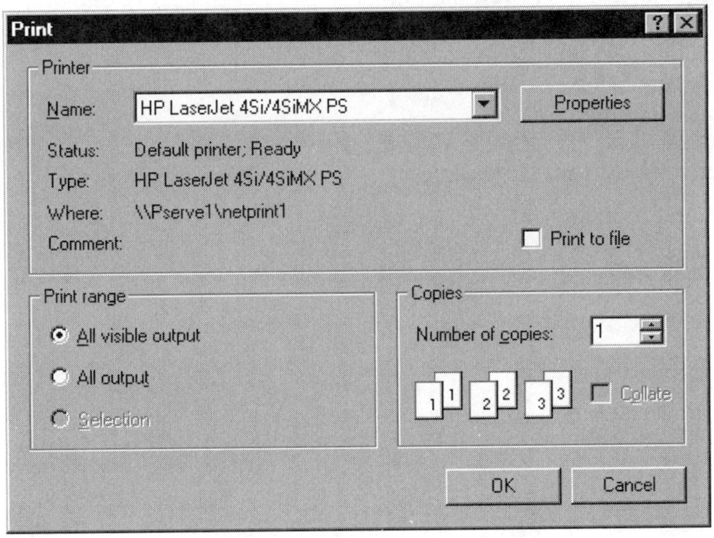

### To Print Output and Charts

▶ Make the Viewer the active window.

▶ From the menus choose:

File
 Print...

▶ Select the print settings that you want.

▶ Click OK to print.

## Print Preview

Print Preview shows you what will print on each page for Viewer documents. It is usually a good idea to check Print Preview before actually printing a Viewer document because Print Preview shows you items that may not be visible simply by looking at the contents pane of the Viewer, including:

- Page breaks
- Hidden layers of pivot tables
- Breaks in wide tables
- Complete output from large tables
- Headers and footers printed on each page

Figure 8-10
*Print Preview*

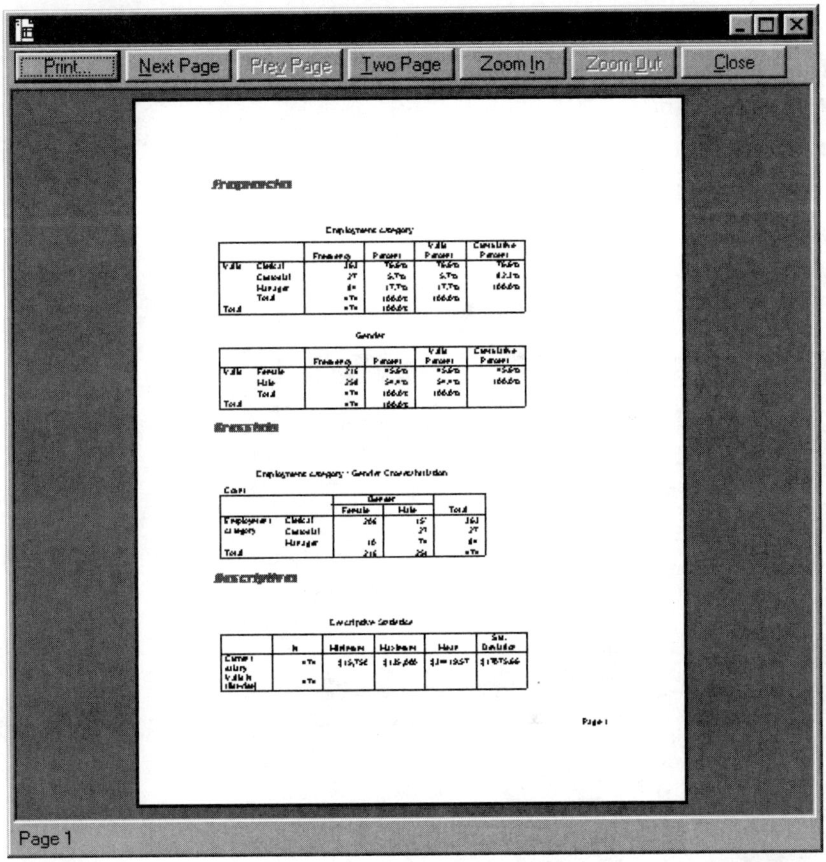


If any output is currently selected in the Viewer, the preview displays only the selected output. To view a preview for all output, make sure nothing is selected in the Viewer.

## To View a Print Preview

▶ Make the Viewer the active window.

▶ From the menus choose:

File
  Print Preview

## Page Setup

With Page Setup, you can control:

- Paper size and orientation
- Page margins
- Page headers and footers
- Page numbering
- Printed size for charts

Figure 8-11
*Page Setup dialog box*

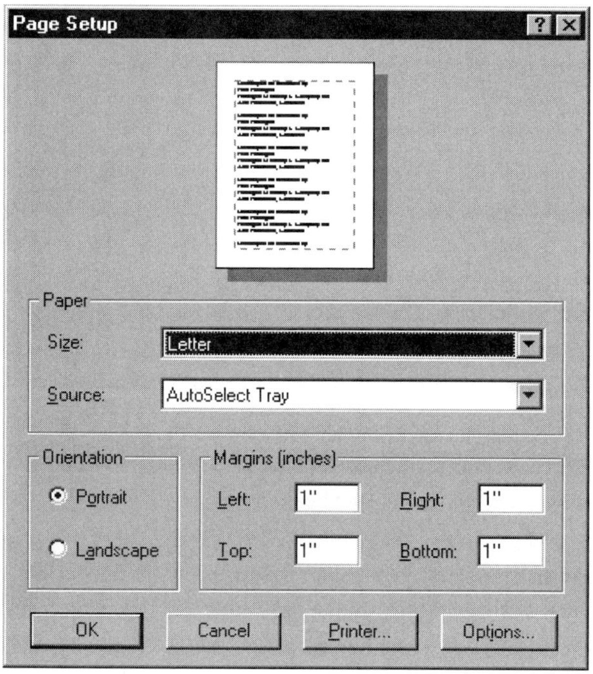


Page Setup settings are saved with the Viewer document. Page Setup affects settings for printing Viewer documents only. These settings have no effect on printing data from the Data Editor or syntax from a syntax window.

### To Change Page Setup

- ▶ Make the Viewer the active window.
- ▶ From the menus choose:

  File
    Page Setup...

- ▶ Change the settings and click OK.

### Page Setup Options: Header/Footer

Headers and footers are the information that prints at the top and bottom of each page. You can enter any text that you want to use as headers and footers. You can also use the toolbar in the middle of the dialog box to insert:

- Date and time
- Page numbers
- Viewer filename
- Outline heading labels
- Page titles and subtitles

Figure 8-12
*Page Setup Options Header/Footer tab*

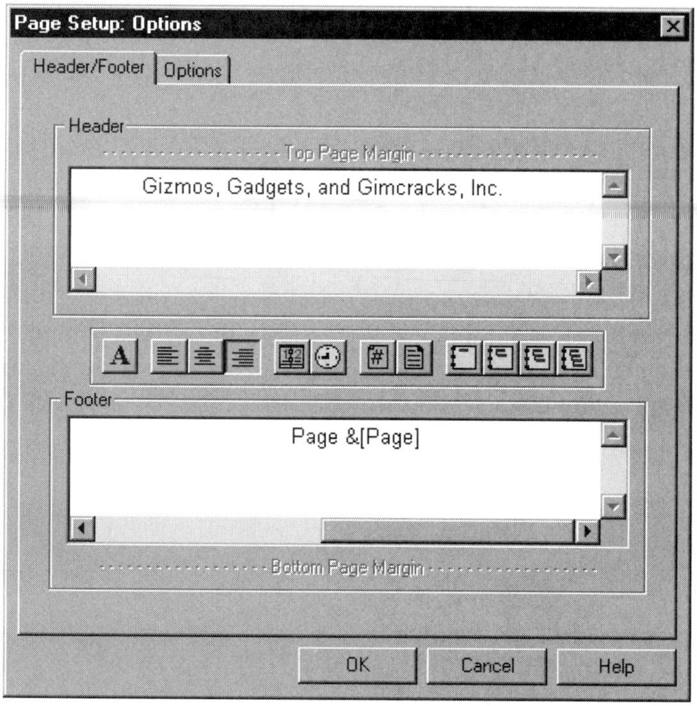


Outline heading labels indicate the first-, second-, third-, and/or fourth-level outline heading for the first item on each page.

Page titles and subtitles print the current page titles and subtitles. Page titles and subtitles are created with Insert New Page Title on the Viewer Insert menu or the TITLE and SUBTITLE commands in command syntax. If you have not specified any page titles or subtitles, this setting is ignored.

*Note*: Font characteristics for new page titles and subtitles are controlled on the Viewer tab of the Options dialog box (Edit menu). Font characteristics for existing page titles and subtitles can be changed by editing the titles in the Viewer.

Use Print Preview on the File menu to see how your headers and footers will look on the printed page.

### *Page Setup Options: Options*

This dialog box controls printed chart size, space between printed output items, and page numbering.

**Printed Chart Size**. Controls the size of the printed chart relative to the defined page size. The chart's aspect ratio (width-to-height ratio) is not affected by the printed chart size. The overall printed size of a chart is limited by both its height and width. Once the outer borders of a chart reach the left and right borders of the page, the chart size cannot increase further to fill additional page height.

**Space between items**. Controls the space between printed items. Each pivot table, chart, and text object is a separate item. This setting does not affect the display of items in the Viewer.

**Number pages starting with.** Numbers pages sequentially starting with the specified number.

Figure 8-13
*Page Setup Options tab*

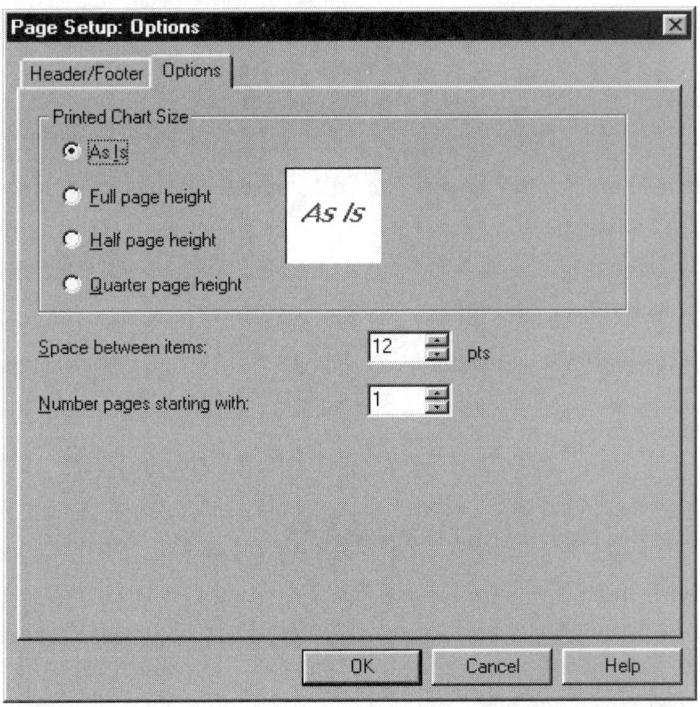

# Saving Results

The contents of the Viewer can be saved to a Viewer document. The saved document includes both panes of the Viewer window (the outline and the contents).

### To Save a Viewer Document

▶ From the Viewer window menus choose:

File
  Save

▶ Enter the name of the document and click Save.

To save results in external formats (for example, HTML or text), use Export on the File menu. (Not available in the standalone Smart Viewer.)

## Save with Password

Save with Password allows you to password-protect your Viewer files.

**Password**. The password is case sensitive and can be up to 16 characters long. If you assign a password, the file cannot be viewed without entering the password.

**OEM Code**. Leave this field blank unless you have a contractual agreement with SPSS Inc. to redistribute the Smart Viewer. The OEM license code is provided with the contract.

### To Save Viewer Files with a Password

▶ From the Viewer window menus choose:

File
  Save with Password...

▶ Enter the password.

▶ Reenter the password to confirm it and click OK.

▶ Enter a filename in the Save As dialog box.

▶ Click Save.

*Note*: Leave the OEM Code blank unless you have a contractual agreement with SPSS Inc. to redistribute the Smart Viewer.

Chapter

# 9

# Draft Viewer

The Draft Viewer provides results in draft form, including:

- Simple text output (instead of pivot tables)
- Charts as metafile pictures (instead of chart objects)

## Draft Viewer Output

Text output in the Draft Viewer can be edited, charts can be resized, and both text output and charts can be pasted into other applications. However, charts cannot be edited, and the interactive features of pivot tables and charts are not available.

Figure 9-1
*Draft Viewer window*

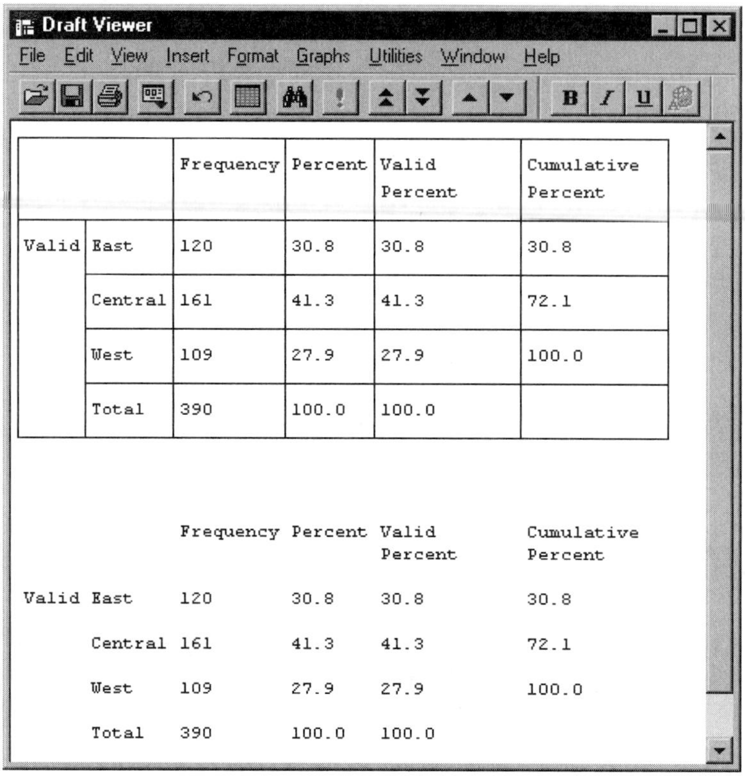


| | | Frequency | Percent | Valid Percent | Cumulative Percent |
|---|---|---|---|---|---|
| Valid | East | 120 | 30.8 | 30.8 | 30.8 |
| | Central | 161 | 41.3 | 41.3 | 72.1 |
| | West | 109 | 27.9 | 27.9 | 100.0 |
| | Total | 390 | 100.0 | 100.0 | |

| | | Frequency | Percent | Valid Percent | Cumulative Percent |
|---|---|---|---|---|---|
| Valid | East | 120 | 30.8 | 30.8 | 30.8 |
| | Central | 161 | 41.3 | 41.3 | 72.1 |
| | West | 109 | 27.9 | 27.9 | 100.0 |
| | Total | 390 | 100.0 | 100.0 | |

## To Create Draft Output

▶ From the menus choose:

File
  New
    Draft Output

▶ To make draft output the default output type, from the menus choose:

Edit
  Options...

▶ Click the General tab.

▶ Select Draft Viewer under Output Type.

*Note*: New output is always displayed in the designated Viewer window. If you have both a Viewer and Draft Viewer window open, the **designated window** is the one opened most recently or the one designated with the Designate Window tool (the exclamation point) on the toolbar.

## Controlling Draft Output Format

Output that would be displayed as pivot tables in the Viewer is converted to text output for the Draft Viewer. The default settings for converted pivot table output include:

- Each column is set to the width of the column label, and labels are not wrapped to multiple lines.
- Alignment is controlled by spaces (instead of tabs).
- Box characters from the SPSS Marker Set font are used as row and column separators.
- If box characters are turned off, vertical line characters (|) are used as column separators and dashes (–) are used as row separators.

You can control the format of new draft output using Draft Viewer Options (Edit menu, Options, Draft Viewer tab).

Figure 9-2
*Draft Viewer Options*

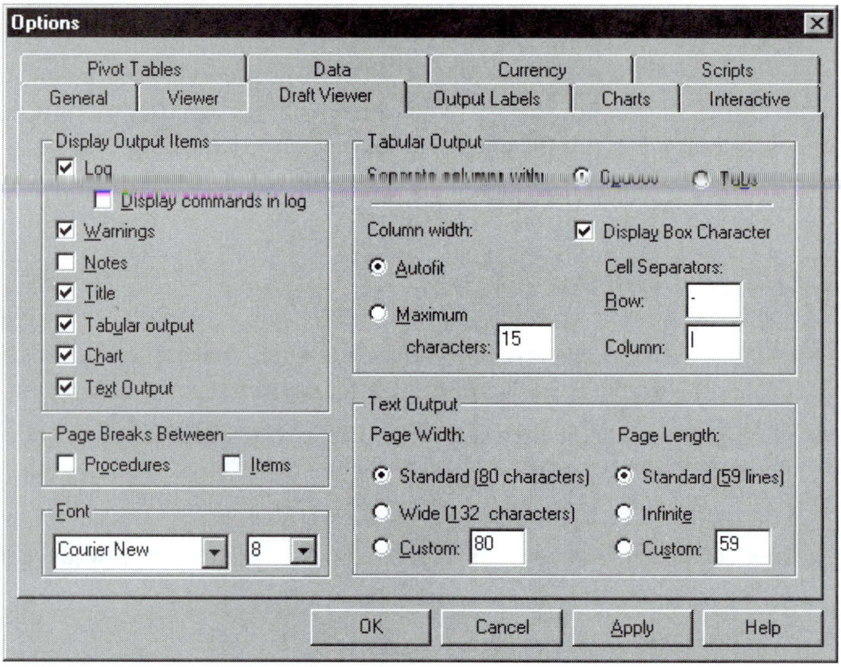


**Column width.** To reduce the width of tables that contain long labels, select Maximum characters under Column width. Labels longer than the specified width are wrapped to fit the maximum width.

Figure 9-3
*Draft output before and after setting maximum column width*

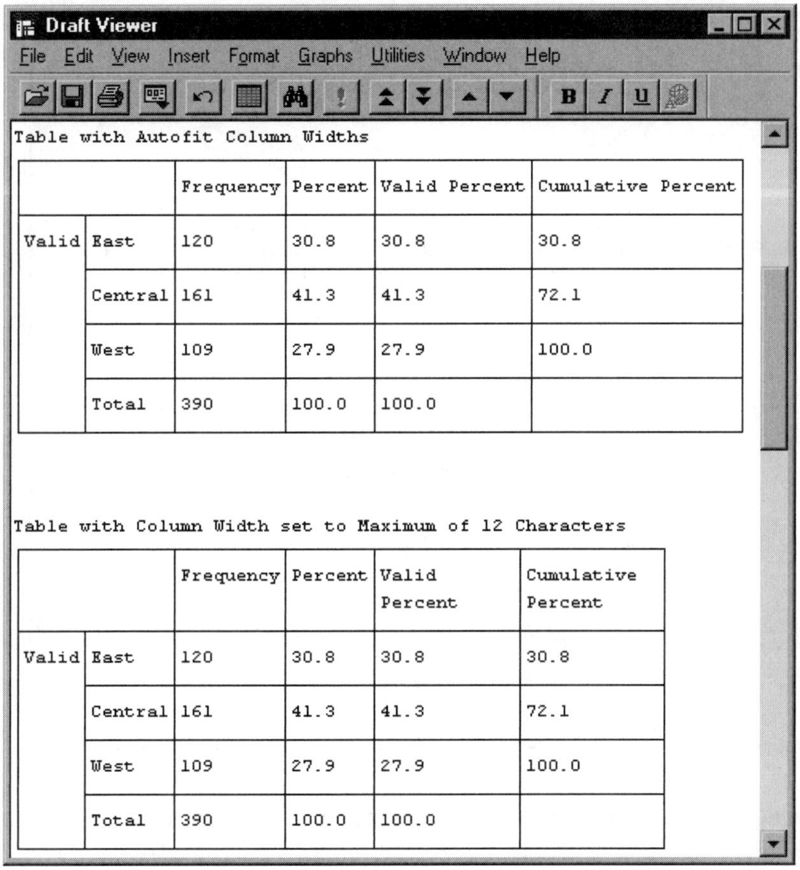


Table with Autofit Column Widths

| | | Frequency | Percent | Valid Percent | Cumulative Percent |
|---|---|---|---|---|---|
| Valid | East | 120 | 30.8 | 30.8 | 30.8 |
| | Central | 161 | 41.3 | 41.3 | 72.1 |
| | West | 109 | 27.9 | 27.9 | 100.0 |
| | Total | 390 | 100.0 | 100.0 | |

Table with Column Width set to Maximum of 12 Characters

| | | Frequency | Percent | Valid<br>Percent | Cumulative<br>Percent |
|---|---|---|---|---|---|
| Valid | East | 120 | 30.8 | 30.8 | 30.8 |
| | Central | 161 | 41.3 | 41.3 | 72.1 |
| | West | 109 | 27.9 | 27.9 | 100.0 |
| | Total | 390 | 100.0 | 100.0 | |

**Row and column separators.** As an alternative to box characters for row and column borders, you can use the Cell Separators settings to control the row and column separators displayed in new draft output. You can specify different cell separators or enter blank spaces if you don't want any characters used to mark rows and columns. You must deselect (uncheck) Display Box Character to specify cell separators.

Figure 9-4
*Draft output before and after setting cell separators*

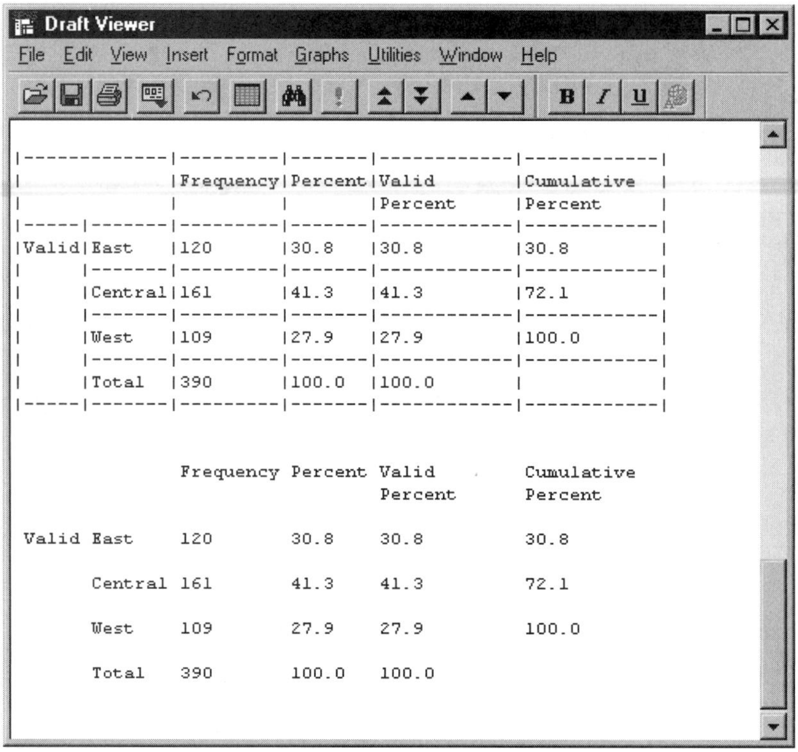


**Space-separated versus tab-separated columns.** The Draft Viewer is designed to display space-separated output in a fixed-pitch (monospaced) font. If you want to paste draft output into another application, you must use a fixed-pitch font to align space-separated columns properly. If you select Tabs for the column separator, you can use any font you want in the other application and set the tabs to align output properly. However, tab-separated output will not align properly in the Draft Viewer.

Figure 9-5
*Tab-separated output in the Draft Viewer and formatted in a word processor*

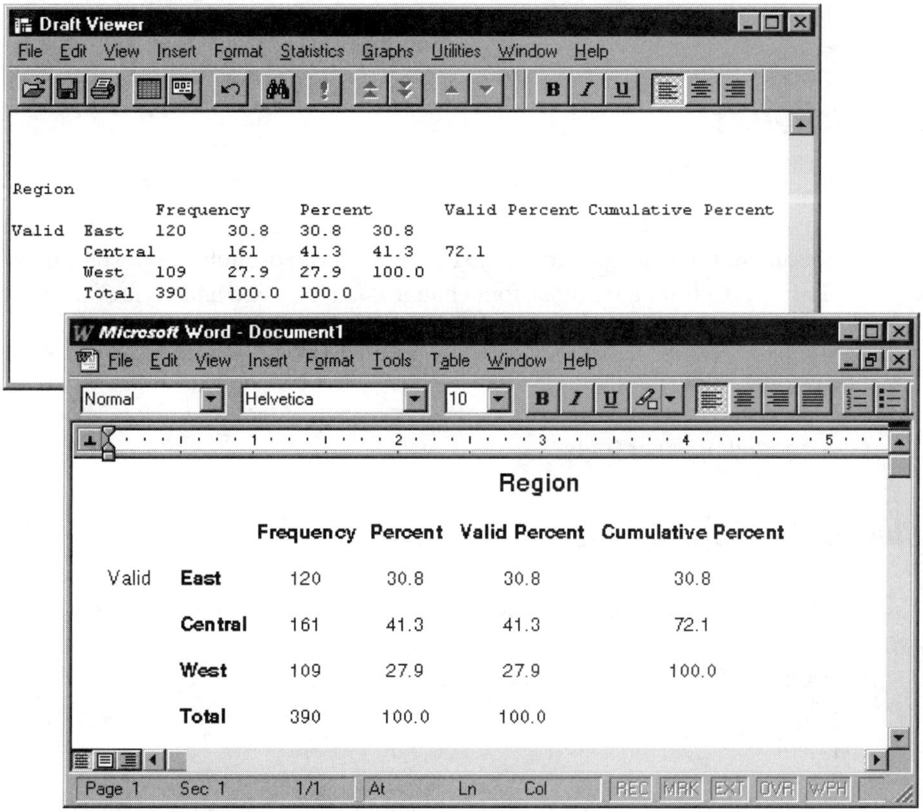

### *To Set Draft Viewer Options*

▶ From the menus choose:

Edit
 Options...

▶ Click the Draft Viewer tab.

▶ Select the settings you want.

▶ Click OK or Apply.

Draft Viewer output display options affect only new output produced after you change the settings. Output already displayed in the Draft Viewer is not affected by changes in these settings.

## Font Attributes

You can modify the font attributes (font, size, style) of text output in the Draft Viewer. However, if you use box characters for row and column borders, proper column alignment for space-separated text requires a fixed-pitch (monospaced) font, such as Courier. Additionally, other font changes, such as size and style (for example, bold, italic), applied to only part of a table can affect column alignment.

**Row and column borders.** The default solid-line row and column borders use the SPSS Marker Set font. The line-drawing characters used to draw the borders are not supported by other fonts.

### To Change Font Attributes for Draft Output

▶ Select (highlight) the text to which you want to apply the font change.

▶ From the Draft Viewer menus choose:

Format
  Font...

▶ Select the font attributes you want to apply to the selected text.

## Printing Draft Output

▶ To print Draft Viewer output, from the menus choose:

File
  Print...

▶ To print only a selected portion of the draft output, select (highlight) the output you want to print.

▶ From the menus choose:

File
 Print...

▶ Select Selection.

## Print Preview

Print Preview shows you what will print on each page for draft documents. It is usually a good idea to check Print Preview before actually printing a Viewer document because Print Preview shows you items that may not fit on the page, including:

- Long tables
- Wide tables produced by converted pivot table output without column-width control
- Text output created with the Wide page-width option (Draft Viewer Options) with the printer set to Portrait mode

Output that is too wide for the page is truncated, not printed on another page. There are several things you can do to prevent wide output from being truncated:

- Use a smaller font size (Format menu, Fonts).
- Select Landscape for the page orientation (File menu, Page Setup).
- For new output, specify a narrow maximum column width (Edit menu, Options, Draft Viewer tab).

For long tables, use page breaks (Insert menu, Page Break) to control where the table breaks between pages.

## To View a Print Preview for Draft Output

▶ From the Draft Viewer menus choose:

File
 Print Preview

## Saving Draft Viewer Output

▶ To save output from the Draft Viewer, from the menus choose:

File
  Save

Draft Viewer output is saved in rich text format (RTF).

### Saving Draft Output as Text

▶ To save draft output as text, from the Draft Viewer menus choose:

File
  Export...

You can export all text or just the selected (highlighted) text. Only text output (converted pivot table output and text output) is saved in the exported files; charts are not included.

Chapter

# 10

# Pivot Tables

Many of the results in the Viewer are presented in tables that can be pivoted interactively. That is, you can rearrange the rows, columns, and layers.

## Manipulating a Pivot Table

Options for manipulating a pivot table include:

- Transposing rows and columns
- Moving rows and columns
- Creating multidimensional layers
- Grouping and ungrouping rows and columns
- Showing and hiding cells
- Rotating row and column labels
- Finding definitions of terms

### To Edit a Pivot Table

▶ Double-click the table.

This activates the Pivot Table Editor.

### To Edit Two or More Pivot Tables at a Time

▶ Click the right mouse button on the pivot table.

▶ From the context menu choose:

SPSS Pivot Table Object
  Open

▶ Repeat for each pivot table you want to edit.

Each pivot table is ready to edit in its own separate window.

### To Pivot a Table Using Icons

▶ Activate the pivot table.

▶ From the Pivot Table menus choose:

Pivot
  Pivoting Trays

▶ Hover over each icon with the mouse pointer for a ToolTip pop-up that tells you which table dimension the icon represents.

▶ Drag an icon from one tray to another.

Figure 10-1
*Pivoting trays*

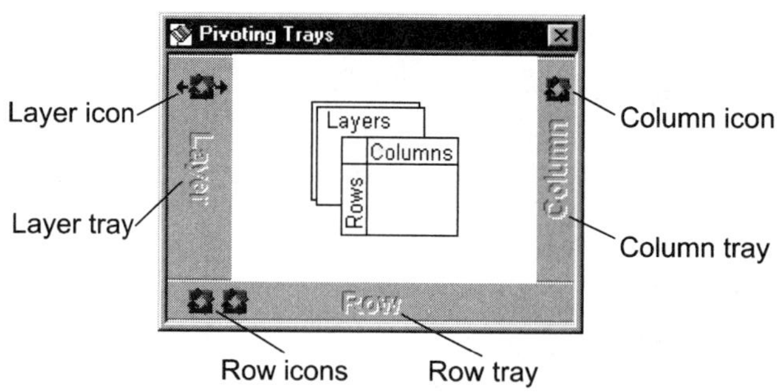


This changes the arrangement of the table. For example, suppose that the icon represents a variable with categories Yes and No and you drag the icon from the Row tray to the Column tray. Before the move, Yes and No were row labels; after the move, they are column labels.

### *To Identify Dimensions in a Pivot Table*

▶ Activate the pivot table.

▶ If pivoting trays are not on, from the Pivot Table menus choose:

Pivot
  Pivoting Trays

▶ Click and hold down the mouse button on an icon.

This highlights the dimension labels in the pivot table.

### *To Transpose Rows and Columns*

▶ From the Pivot Table menus choose:

Pivot
  Transpose Rows and Columns

This has the same effect as dragging all of the row icons into the Column tray and all of the column icons into the Row tray.

### *To Change the Display Order*

The order of pivot icons in a dimension tray reflects the display order of elements in the pivot table. To change the display order of elements in a dimension:

▶ Activate the pivot table.

▶ If pivoting trays are not already on, from the Pivot Table menus choose:

Pivot
  Pivoting Trays

▶ Drag the icons in each tray to the order you want (left to right or top to bottom).

### *To Move Rows or Columns in a Pivot Table*

▶ Activate the pivot table.

▶ Click the label for the row or column you want to move.

▶ Click and drag the label to the new position.

▶ From the context menu, choose Insert Before or Swap.

*Note*: Make sure that Drag to Copy on the Edit menu is *not* enabled (checked). If Drag to Copy is enabled, deselect it.

### To Group Rows or Columns and Insert Group Labels

▶ Activate the pivot table.

▶ Select the labels for the rows or columns you want to group together (click and drag or Shift-click to select multiple labels).

▶ From the menus choose:

Edit
 Group

A group label is automatically inserted. Double-click the group label to edit the label text.

Figure 10-2
*Row and column groups and labels*

| | | Column Group Label | | |
|---|---|---|---|---|
| | | Female | Male | Total |
| **Row Group Label** | Clerical | 206 | 157 | 363 |
| | Custodial | | 27 | 27 |
| | Manager | 10 | 74 | 84 |

*Note*: To add rows or columns to an existing group, you must first ungroup the items currently in the group; then create a new group that includes the additional items.

### To Ungroup Rows or Columns and Delete Group Labels

▶ Activate the pivot table.

▶ Select the group label (click anywhere in the group label) for the rows or columns you want to ungroup.

▶ From the menus choose:

Edit
 Ungroup

Ungrouping automatically deletes the group label.

## *To Rotate Row or Column Labels*

▶ Activate the pivot table.

▶ From the menus choose:

Format
  Rotate InnerColumn Labels

*or*

  Rotate OuterRow Labels

Figure 10-3
*Rotated column labels*

| | Frequency | Percent | Valid Percent | Cumulative Percent |
|---|---|---|---|---|
| Clerical | 363 | 76.6 | 76.6 | 76.6 |
| Custodial | 27 | 5.7 | 5.7 | 82.3 |
| Manager | | | | |
| Total | | | | |

| | Frequency | Percent | Valid Percent | Cumulative Percent |
|---|---|---|---|---|
| Clerical | 363 | 76.6 | 76.6 | 76.6 |
| Custodial | 27 | 5.7 | 5.7 | 82.3 |
| Manager | 84 | 17.7 | 17.7 | 100.0 |
| Total | 474 | 100.0 | 100.0 | |

Only the innermost column labels and the outermost row labels can be rotated.

## *To Reset Pivots to Defaults*

After performing one or more pivoting operations, you can return to the original arrangement of the pivot table.

▶ From the Pivot menu choose Reset Pivots to Defaults.

This resets only changes that are the result of pivoting row, column, and layer elements between dimensions. It does not affect changes such as grouping or ungrouping or moving rows and columns.

### To Find the Definition of a Label in a Pivot Table

You can obtain context-sensitive Help on cell labels in pivot tables. For example, if *Mean* appears as a label, you can obtain a definition of the mean.

▶ Click the right mouse button on a label cell.

▶ From the context menu, choose What's This?.

You must click your right mouse button on the label cell itself rather than on the data cells in the row or column.

Context-sensitive Help is not available for user-defined labels, such as variable names or value labels.

## Working with Layers

You can display a separate two-dimensional table for each category or combination of categories. The table can be thought of as stacked in layers, with only the top layer visible.

### To Create and Display Layers

▶ Activate the pivot table, and from the Pivot menu choose Pivoting Trays if it is not already selected.

▶ Drag an icon from the Row tray or the Column tray into the Layer tray.

Figure 10-4
*Moving categories into layers*

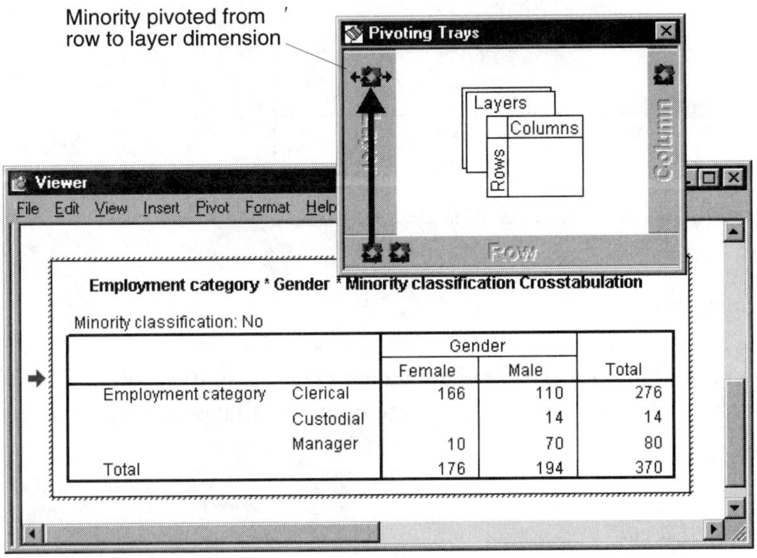


Each layer icon has left and right arrows. The visible table is the table for the top layer.

Figure 10-5
*Categories in separate layers*

Minority classification: Yes

Minority classification: No

| | | Gender | | |
|---|---|---|---|---|
| | | Female | Male | Total |
| Employment category | Clerical | 166 | 110 | 276 |
| | Custodial | 0 | 14 | 14 |
| | Manager | 10 | 70 | 80 |
| Total | | 176 | 194 | 370 |

## *To Change Layers*

▶ Click one of the layer icon arrows.

*or*

▶ Select a category from the drop-down list of layers.

Figure 10-6
*Selecting layers from drop-down lists*

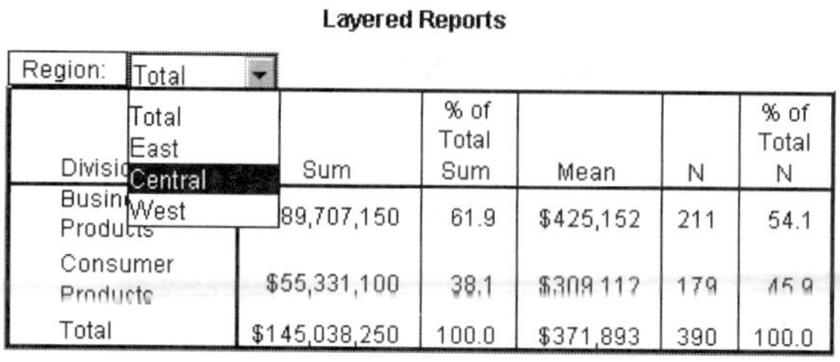


## Go to Layer Category

Go to Layer Category allows you to change layers in a pivot table. This dialog box is particularly useful when there are a large number of layers or one layer has many categories.

## To Go to a Layer of a Table

▶ From the Pivot Table menus choose:

Pivot
  Go to Layer...

Figure 10-7
*Go to Layer Category dialog box*

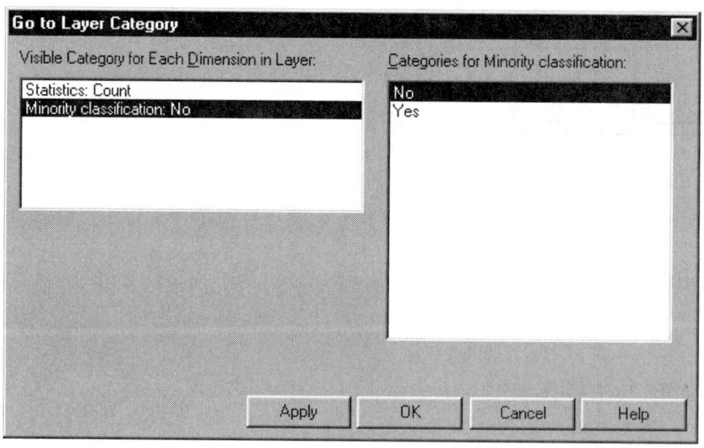

▶ Select a layer dimension in the Visible Category list. The Categories list will display all categories for the selected dimension.

▶ Select the category you want in the Categories list and click OK. This changes the layer and closes the dialog box.

To view another layer without closing the dialog box:

▶ Select the category and click Apply.

### To Move Layers to Rows or Columns

If the table you are viewing is stacked in layers with only the top layer showing, you can display all of the layers at once, either down the rows or across the columns. There must be at least one icon in the Layer tray.

▶ From the Pivot menu choose Move Layers to Rows.

*or*

▶ From the Pivot menu choose Move Layers to Columns.

You can also move layers to rows or columns by dragging their icons between the Layer, Row, and Column pivoting trays.

## Bookmarks

Bookmarks allow you to save different views of a pivot table. Bookmarks save:

- Placement of elements in row, column, and layer dimensions
- Display order of elements in each dimension
- Currently displayed layer for each layer element

### To Bookmark a Pivot Table View

▶ Activate the pivot table.

▶ Pivot the table to the view you want to bookmark.

- From the menus choose:

  Pivot
  Bookmarks...

- Enter a name for the bookmark. Bookmark names are not case sensitive.

- Click Add.

  Each pivot table has its own set of bookmarks. Within a pivot table, each bookmark name must be unique, but you can use duplicate bookmark names in different pivot tables.

### To Display a Bookmarked Pivot Table View

- Activate the pivot table.

- From the menus choose:

  Pivot
  Bookmarks...

- Click the name of the bookmark in the list.

- Click Go To.

### To Rename a Pivot Table Bookmark

- Activate the pivot table.

- From the menus choose:

  Pivot
  Bookmarks...

- Click the name of the bookmark in the list.

- Click Rename.

- Enter the new bookmark name.

- Click OK.

# Showing and Hiding Cells

Many types of cells can be hidden:

- Dimension labels
- Categories, including the label cell and data cells in a row or column
- Category labels (without hiding the data cells)
- Footnotes, titles, and captions

### To Hide Rows or Columns in a Table

▶ Ctrl-Alt-click the category label of the row or column to be hidden.

▶ From the Pivot Table menus choose:

View
 Hide

*or*

▶ Right-click the highlighted row or column to show the context menu.

▶ From the context menu choose Hide Category.

### To Show Hidden Rows or Columns in a Table

▶ Select another label in the same dimension as the hidden row or column.

For example, if the *Female* category of the Gender dimension is hidden, click the *Male* category.

▶ From the Pivot Table menus choose:

View
 Show All Categories in *dimension name*

For example, choose Show All Categories in Gender.

*or*

▶ From the Pivot Table menus choose:

View
 Show All

This displays all hidden cells in the table. (If Hide empty rows and columns is selected in Table Properties for this table, a completely empty row or column remains hidden.)

### To Hide or Show a Dimension Label in a Table

▶ Activate the pivot table.

▶ Select the dimension label or any category label within the dimension.

▶ From the menus choose:

View
 Hide (or Show) Dimension Label

### To Hide or Show a Footnote in a Table

▶ Select a footnote.

▶ From the menus choose:

View
 Hide (or Show)

### To Hide or Show a Caption or Title in a Table

▶ Select a caption or title.

▶ From the menus choose:

View
 Hide (or Show)

## Editing Results

The appearance and contents of each table or text output item can be edited. You can:

- Apply a TableLook.
- Change the properties of the current table.
- Change the properties of cells in the table.
- Modify text.
- Add footnotes and captions to tables.
- Add items to the Viewer.
- Copy and paste results into other applications.

## Changing the Appearance of Tables

You can change the appearance of a table either by editing table properties or by applying a TableLook. Each TableLook consists of a collection of table properties, including general appearance, footnote properties, cell properties, and borders. You can select one of the preset TableLooks or you can create and save a custom TableLook.

### TableLooks

A TableLook is a set of properties that define the appearance of a table. You can select a previously defined TableLook or create your own.

Before or after a TableLook is applied, you can change cell formats for individual cells or groups of cells, using cell properties. The edited cell formats will remain, even when you apply a new TableLook.

For example, you might start by applying TableLook *9POINT,* then select a data column, and from the Cell Formats dialog box, change to a bold font for that column. Later, you change the TableLook to *BOXED*. The previously selected column retains the bold font while the rest of the characteristics are applied from the *BOXED* TableLook.

Optionally, you can reset all cells to the cell formats defined by the current TableLook. This resets any cells that have been edited. If As Displayed is selected in the TableLook files list, any edited cells are reset to the current table properties.

### To Apply a TableLook

- ▶ Activate a pivot table.
- ▶ From the menus choose:

  Format
  TableLooks...

Figure 10-8
*TableLooks dialog box*

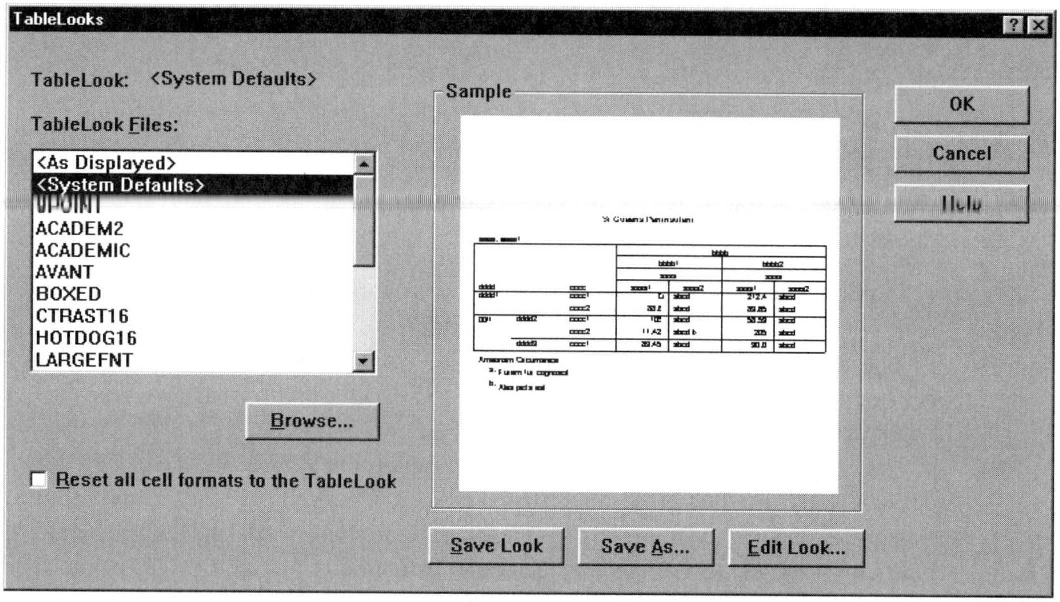


- ▶ Select a TableLook from the list of files. To select a file from another directory, click Browse.
- ▶ Click OK to apply the TableLook to the selected pivot table.

### To Edit or Create a TableLook

- ▶ Select a TableLook from the list of files.
- ▶ Click Edit Look.
- ▶ Adjust the table properties for the attributes you want and click OK.
- ▶ Click Save Look to save the edited TableLook or Save As to save it as a new TableLook.

  Editing a TableLook affects only the selected pivot table. An edited TableLook is not applied to any other tables that use that TableLook unless you select those tables and reapply the TableLook.

## Table Properties

The Table Properties dialog box allows you to set general properties of a table, set cell styles for various parts of a table, and save a set of those properties as a TableLook. Using the tabs on this dialog box, you can:

- Control general properties, such as hiding empty rows or columns and adjusting printing properties.
- Control the format and position of footnote markers.
- Determine specific formats for cells in the data area, for row and column labels, and for other areas of the table.
- Control the width and color of the lines forming the borders of each area of the table.
- Control printing properties.

### To Change Pivot Table Properties

▶ Activate the pivot table (double-click anywhere in the table).

▶ From the Pivot Table menus choose:

Format
 Table Properties...

▶ Select a tab (General, Footnotes, Cell Formats, Borders, or Printing).

▶ Select the options you want.

▶ Click OK or Apply.

The new properties are applied to the selected pivot table. To apply new table properties to a TableLook instead of just the selected table, edit the TableLook (Format menu, TableLooks).

### Table Properties: General

Several properties apply to the table as a whole. You can:

- Show or hide empty rows and columns. (An empty row or column has nothing in any of the data cells.)
- Control the placement of row labels. They can be in the upper left corner or nested.
- Control maximum and minimum column width (expressed in points).

Figure 10-9
*Table Properties General tab*

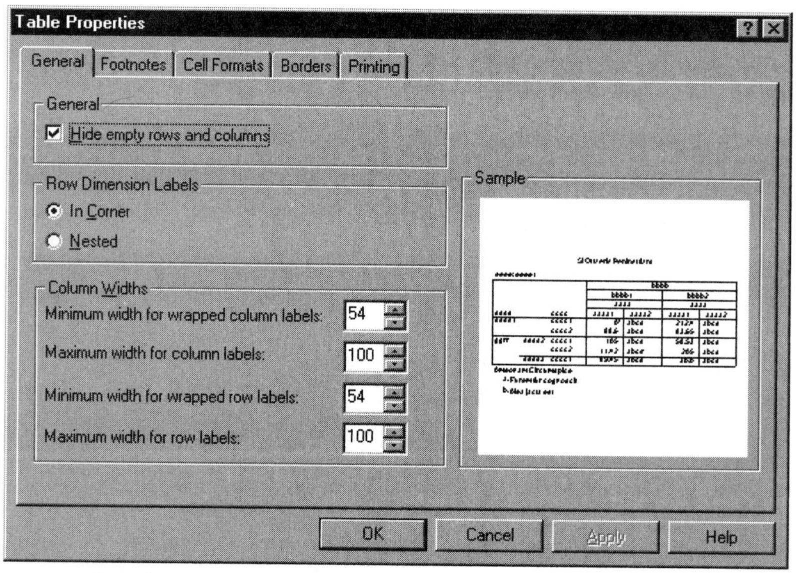


### To Change General Table Properties

- ▶ Select the General tab.
- ▶ Select the options you want.
- ▶ Click OK or Apply.

### Table Properties: Footnotes

The properties of footnote markers include style and position in relation to text.

- The style of footnote markers is either numbers (1, 2, 3...) or letters (a, b, c...).
- The footnote markers can be attached to text as superscripts or subscripts.

Figure 10-10
*Table Properties Footnotes tab*

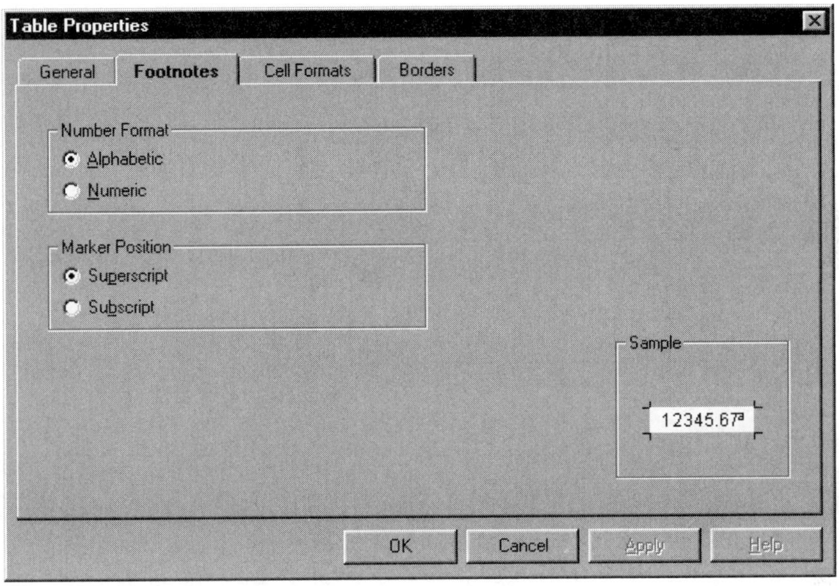


### To Change Footnote Marker Properties

- ▶ Select the Footnotes tab.
- ▶ Select a footnote marker format.
- ▶ Select a marker position.
- ▶ Click OK or Apply.

### Table Properties: Cell Formats

For formatting, a table is divided into areas: Title, Layers, Corner Labels, Row Labels, Column Labels, Data, Caption, and Footnotes. For each area of a table, you can modify the associated cell formats. Cell formats include: text characteristics (font, size, color, style), horizontal and vertical alignment, cell shading, foreground and background colors, and inner cell margins.

Figure 10-11
*Areas of a table*

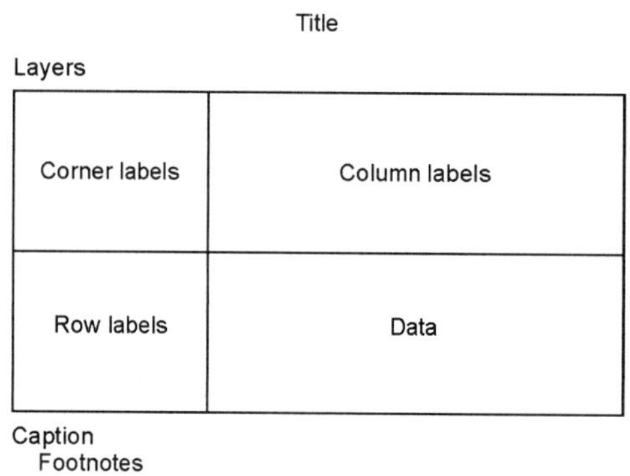


Cell formats are applied to areas (categories of information). They are not characteristics of individual cells. This distinction is an important consideration when pivoting a table.

For example:

- If you specify a bold font as a cell format of column labels, the column labels will appear bold no matter what information is currently displayed in the column dimension—and if you move an item from the column dimension to another dimension, it does not retain the bold characteristic of the column labels.
- If you make column labels bold simply by highlighting the cells in an activated pivot table and clicking the Bold button on the toolbar, the contents of those cells will remain bold no matter what dimension you move them to, and the column labels will not retain the bold characteristic for other items moved into the column dimension.

Figure 10-12
*Table Properties Cell Formats tab*

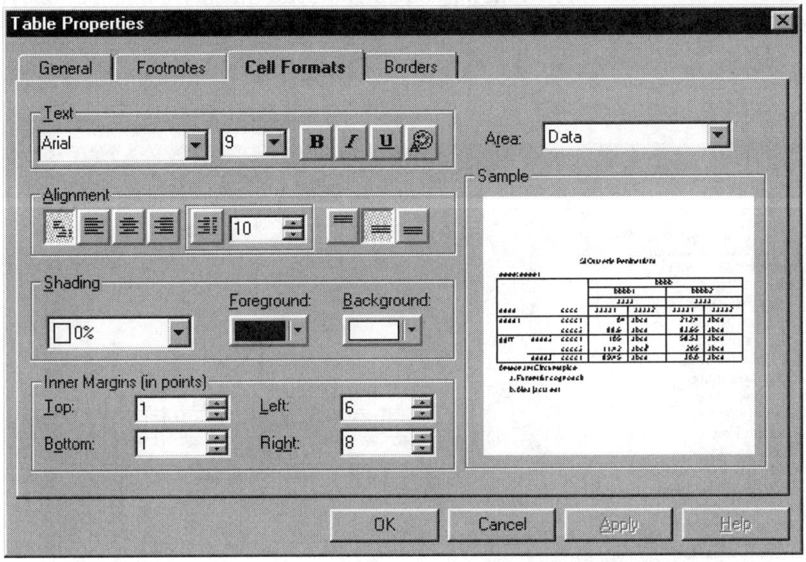


### *To Change Cell Formats*

- Select the Cell Formats tab.
- Select an area from the drop-down list or click an area of the sample.
- Select characteristics for the area. Your selections are reflected in the sample.
- Click OK or Apply.

## Table Properties: Borders

For each border location in a table, you can select a line style and a color. If you select None as the style, there will be no line at the selected location.

Figure 10-13
*Table Properties Borders tab*

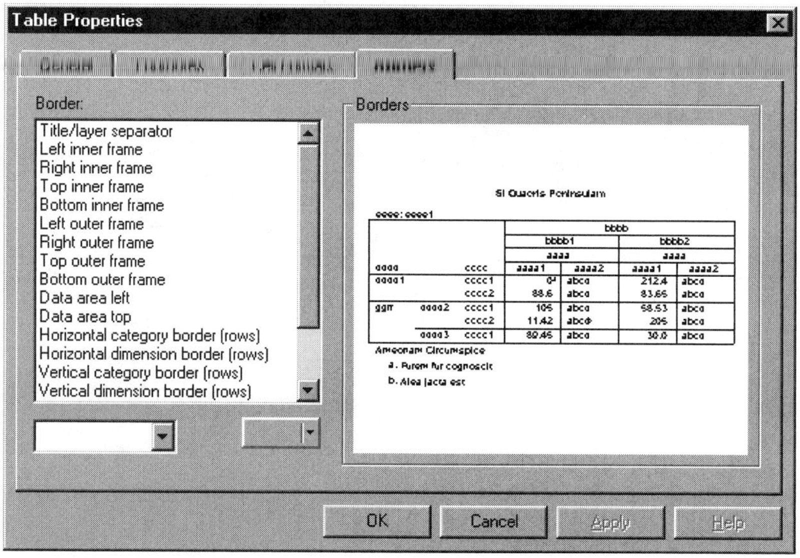


## To Change Borders in Tables

- ▶ Click the Borders tab.
- ▶ Select a border location, either by clicking its name in the list or by clicking a line in the Sample area. (Shift-click to select multiple names, or Ctrl-click to select noncontiguous names.)
- ▶ Select a line style or None.
- ▶ Select a color.
- ▶ Click OK or Apply.

### To Display Hidden Borders in a Pivot Table

For tables without many visible borders, you can display the hidden borders. This can make tasks like changing column widths easier. The hidden borders (gridlines) are displayed in the Viewer but are not printed.

▶ Activate the pivot table (double-click anywhere in the table).

▶ From the menus choose:

View
  Gridlines

### Table Properties: Printing

You can control the following properties for printed pivot tables:

- Print all layers or only the top layer of the table, and print each layer on a separate page. (This affects only printing, not the display of layers in the Viewer.)
- Shrink a table horizontally or vertically to fit the page for printing.
- Control widow/orphan lines—the minimum number of rows and columns that will be contained in any printed section of a table if the table is too wide and/or too long for the defined page size. (*Note*: If a table is too long to fit on the remainder of the current page because there is other output above it on the page but fits within the defined page length, it is automatically printed on a new page, regardless of the widow/orphan setting.)
- Include continuation text for tables that don't fit on a single page. You can display continuation text at the bottom of each page and at the top of each page. If neither option is selected, the continuation text will not be displayed.

### To Control Pivot Table Printing

▶ Click the Printing tab.

▶ Select the printing options you want.

▶ Click OK or Apply.

## Font

A TableLook allows you to specify font characteristics for different areas of the table. You can also change the font for any individual cell. Options for the font in a cell include the font type, style, and size. You can also hide the text or underline it.

If you specify font properties in a cell, they apply in all of the table layers that have the same cell.

Figure 10-14
*Font dialog box*

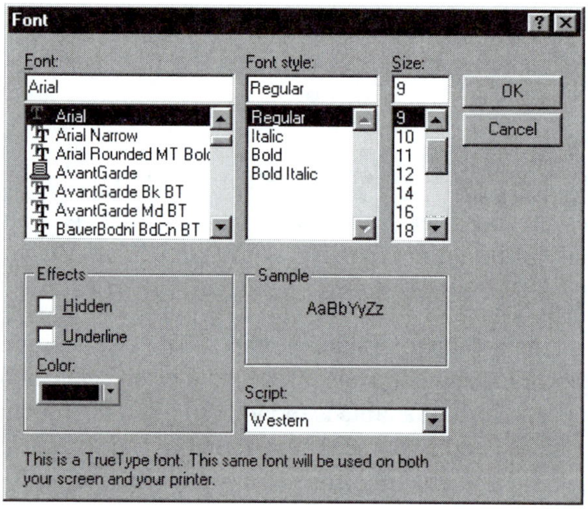


### To Change the Font in a Cell

▶ Activate the pivot table and select the text you want to change.

▶ From the Pivot Table menus choose:

Format
 Font...

Optionally, you can select a font, font style, and point size; whether you want the text hidden or underlined; a color; and a script style.

## Set Data Cell Widths

Set Data Cell Widths is used to set all data cells to the same width.

Figure 10-15
*Set Data Cell Width dialog box*

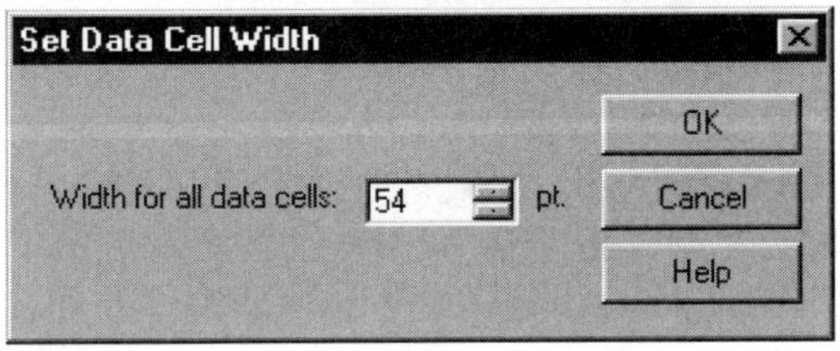


### To Change Data Cell Widths

- ▶ Activate the pivot table.
- ▶ From the menus choose:

  Format
  Set Data Cell Widths...
- ▶ Enter a value for the cell width.

### To Change the Width of a Pivot Table Column

- ▶ Activate the pivot table (double-click anywhere in the table).
- ▶ Move the mouse pointer through the category labels until it is on the right border of the column you want to change. The pointer changes to an arrow with points on both ends.
- ▶ Hold down the mouse button while you drag the border to its new position.

Figure 10-16
*Changing the width of a column*

Drag column border

| | | Gender | | |
|---|---|---|---|---|
| | | Female | Male | Total |
| Employment category | Clerical | 40 | 47 | 87 |
| | Custodial | 0 | 13 | 13 |
| | Manager | 0 | 4 | 4 |
| Total | | 40 | 64 | 104 |

You can change vertical category and dimension borders in the row labels area, whether or not they are showing.

- Move the mouse pointer through the row labels until you see the double-pointed arrow.
- Drag it to the new width.

## Cell Properties

Cell Properties are applied to a selected cell. You can change the value format, alignment, margins, and shading. Cell properties override table properties; therefore, if you change table properties, you do not change any individually applied cell properties.

### To Change Cell Properties

- Activate a table and select a cell in the table.
- From the menus choose:

Format
  Cell Properties...

### Cell Properties: Value

This dialog box tab controls the value format for a cell. You can select formats for number, date, time, or currency, and you can adjust the number of decimal digits displayed.

Figure 10-17
*Cell Properties Value tab*

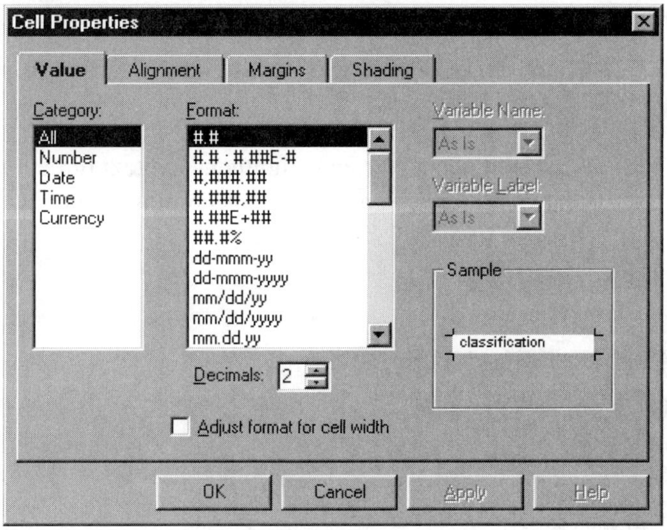


## *To Change Value Formats in a Cell*

- Click the Value tab.
- Select a category and a format.
- Select the number of decimal places.

## *To Change Value Formats for a Column*

- Ctrl-Alt-click the column label.
- Right-click the highlighted column.
- From the context menu choose Cell Properties.
- Click the Value tab.
- Select the format you want to apply to the column.

You can use this method to suppress or add percent signs and dollar signs, change the number of decimals displayed, and switch between scientific notation and regular numeric display.

### Cell Properties: Alignment

This dialog box tab sets horizontal and vertical alignment and text direction for a cell. If you choose Mixed, contents of the cell are aligned according to its type (number, date, or text).

Figure 10-18

*Cell Properties Alignment tab*

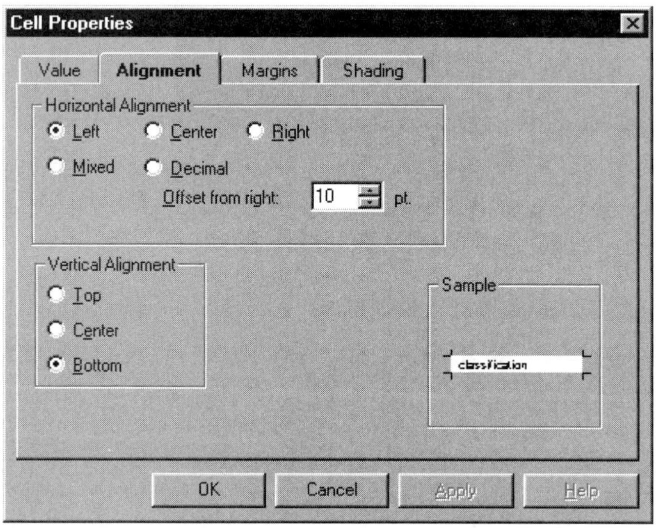


### To Change Alignment in Cells

▶ Select a cell in the table.

▶ From the Pivot Table menus choose:

Format
  Cell Properties...

▶ Click the Alignment tab.

As you select the alignment properties for the cell, they are illustrated in the Sample area.

### Cell Properties: Margins

This dialog box tab specifies the inset at each edge of a cell.

Figure 10-19
*Cell Properties Margins tab*

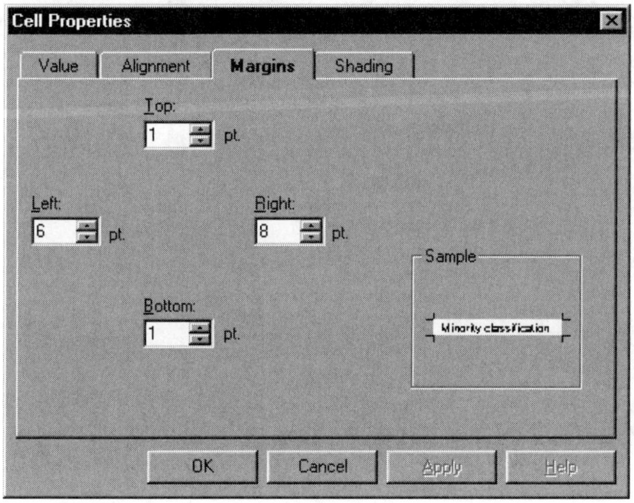


### To Change Margins in Cells

- Click the Margins tab.
- Select the inset for each of the four margins.

### Cell Properties: Shading

This dialog box tab specifies the percentage of shading or a cell outline, and foreground and background colors for a selected cell area. This does not change the color of the text. The cell outline is a selection on the Visual Highlights list.

Figure 10-20
*Cell Properties Shading tab*

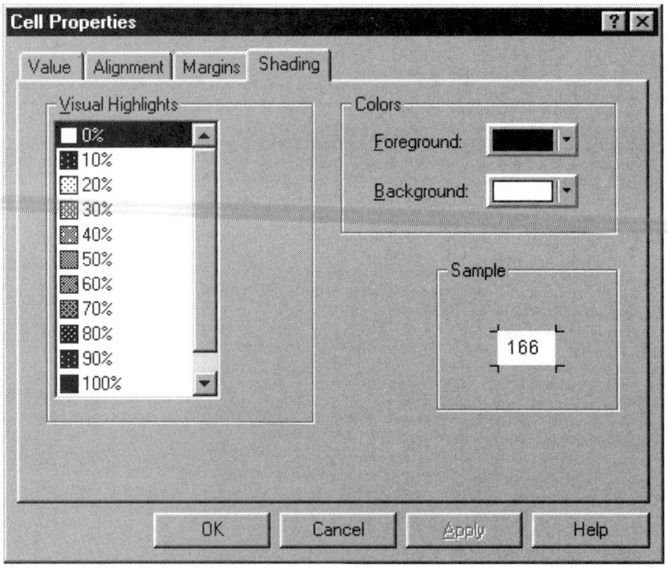


### To Change Shading in Cells

- Click the Shading tab.
- Select the highlights and colors for the cell.

## Footnote Marker

Footnote Marker changes the character(s) used to mark a footnote.

Figure 10-21
*Footnote Marker dialog box*

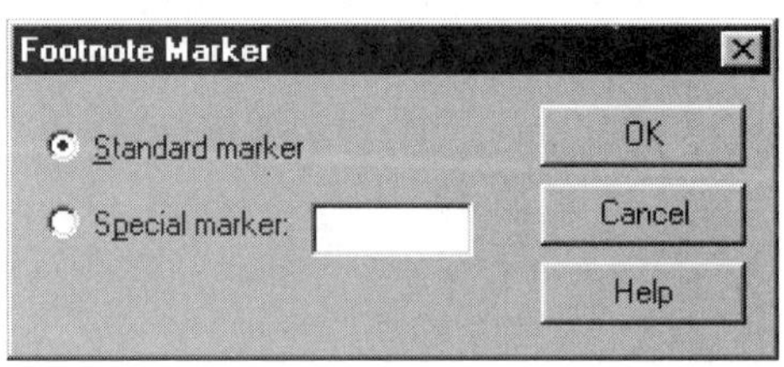

### To Change Footnote Marker Characters

- ▶ Select a footnote.
- ▶ From the Pivot Table menus choose:

  Format
  Footnote Marker...

- ▶ Enter one or two characters.

### To Renumber Footnotes

When you have pivoted a table by switching rows, columns, and layers, the footnotes may be out of order. To renumber the footnotes:

- ▶ Activate the pivot table.
- ▶ From the menus choose:

  Format
  Renumber Footnotes

## Selecting Rows and Columns in Pivot Tables

The flexibility of pivot tables places some constraints on how you select entire rows and columns, and the visual highlight that indicates the selected row or column may span noncontiguous areas of the table.

### To Select a Row or Column in a Pivot Table

- ▶ Activate the pivot table (double-click anywhere in the table).
- ▶ Click a row or column label.

▶ From the menus choose:

Edit
  Select
    Data and Label Cells

*or*

▶ Ctrl-Alt-click the row or column label.

If the table contains more than one dimension in the row or column area, the highlighted selection may span multiple noncontiguous cells.

## Modifying Pivot Table Results

Text appears in the Viewer in many items. You can edit the text or add new text.

Pivot tables can be modified by:

- Editing text within pivot table cells
- Adding captions and footnotes

### To Modify Text in a Table Cell

▶ Activate the pivot table.

▶ Double-click the cell or press F2.

▶ Edit the text.

▶ Press Enter to record your changes, or press Esc to revert to the previous contents of the cell.

### To Add Captions to a Table

▶ From the Pivot Table menus choose:

Insert
  Caption

The words Table Caption are displayed at the bottom of the table.

▶ Select the words Table Caption and enter your caption text over it.

### To Add a Footnote to a Table

A footnote can be attached to any item in a table.

▶ Click a title, cell, or caption within an activated pivot table.

▶ From the Pivot Table menus choose:

Insert
  Footnote...

▶ Select the word Footnote and enter the footnote text over it.

## Printing Pivot Tables

Several factors can affect the way printed pivot charts look, and these factors can be controlled by changing pivot table attributes.

- For multidimensional pivot tables (tables with layers), you can either print all layers or print only the top (visible) layer.
- For long or wide pivot tables, you can automatically resize the table to fit the page or control the location of table breaks and page breaks.

Use Print Preview on the File menu to see how printed pivot tables will look.

### To Print Hidden Layers of a Pivot Table

▶ Activate the pivot table (double-click anywhere in the table).

▶ From the menus choose:

Format
  Table Properties...

▶ On the Printing tab, select Print all layers.

You can also print each layer of a pivot table on a separate page.

## Controlling Table Breaks for Wide and Long Tables

Pivot tables that are either too wide or too long to print within the defined page size are automatically split and printed in multiple sections. (For wide tables, multiple sections will print on the same page if there is room.) You can:

- Control the row and column locations where large tables are split.
- Specify rows and columns that should be kept together when tables are split.
- Rescale large tables to fit the defined page size.

### To Specify Row and Column Breaks for Pivot Tables

▶ Activate the pivot table.

▶ Click the column label to the left of where you want to insert the break or click the row label above where you want to insert the break.

▶ From the menus choose:

Format
  Insert Break Here

### To Specify Rows or Columns to Keep Together

▶ Activate the pivot table.

▶ Select the labels of the rows or columns you want to keep together. (Click and drag or Shift-click to select multiple row or column labels.)

▶ From the menus choose:

Format
  Insert Keep Together

### To Rescale a Table to Fit the Page Size

▶ Activate the pivot table.

▶ From the menus choose:

Format
  Table Properties

▶ Click the Printing tab.

▶ Click Rescale wide table to fit page.

*and/or*

▶ Click Rescale long table to fit page.

Chapter

# 11

# Working with Command Syntax

Most commands are accessible from the menus and dialog boxes. However, some commands and options are available only by using the command language. The command language also allows you to save your jobs in a syntax file so that you can repeat your analysis at a later date or run it in an automated job with the Production Facility.

A syntax file is simply a text file that contains commands. While it is possible to open a syntax window and type in commands, it is easier if you let the software help you build your syntax file using one of the following methods:

- Pasting command syntax from dialog boxes
- Copying syntax from the output log
- Copying syntax from the journal file

In the online Help for a given procedure, click the Syntax pushbutton to find out what (if any) command language options are available for that procedure and to access the syntax diagram for the relevant command. For complete documentation of the command language, refer to the *SPSS Syntax Reference Guide*.

## Command Syntax Rules

Keep in mind the following simple rules when editing and writing command syntax:

- Each command must begin on a new line and end with a period (.).
- Most subcommands are separated by slashes (/). The slash before the first subcommand on a command is usually optional.

- Variable names must be spelled out fully.
- Text included within apostrophes or quotation marks must be contained on a single line.
- Each line of command syntax cannot exceed 80 characters.
- A period (.) must be used to indicate decimals, regardless of your Windows regional settings.
- Variable names ending in a period can cause errors in commands created by the dialog boxes. You cannot create such variable names in the dialog boxes, and you should generally avoid them.

Command syntax is case insensitive, and three-letter abbreviations can be used for many command specifications. You can use as many lines as you want to specify a single command. You can add space or break lines at almost any point where a single blank is allowed, such as around slashes, parentheses, arithmetic operators, or between variable names. For example,

```
FREQUENCIES
 VARIABLES=JOBCAT GENDER
 /PERCENTILES=25 50 75
 /BARCHART.
```

and

```
freq var=jobcat gender /percent=25 50 75 /bar.
```

are both acceptable alternatives that generate the same results.

**Production Facility syntax files and INCLUDE files.** For command files run via the Production Facility or the INCLUDE command, the syntax rules are slightly different:

- Each command must begin in the first column of a new line.
- Continuation lines must be indented at least one space.
- The period at the end of the command is optional.

If you generate command syntax by pasting dialog box choices into a syntax window, the format of the commands is suitable for any mode of operation.

# Creating Command Syntax from Dialog Boxes

The easiest way to build a command syntax file is to make selections in dialog boxes and paste the syntax for the selections into a syntax window. By pasting the syntax at each step of a lengthy analysis, you can build a job file allowing you to repeat the analysis at a later date or run an automated job with the Production Facility.

In the syntax window, you can run the pasted syntax, edit it, and save it in a syntax file.

## To Paste Command Syntax from a Dialog Box

▶ Open the dialog box and make the selections that you want.

▶ Click Paste.

The command syntax is pasted to the designated syntax window. If you do not have an open syntax window, a new syntax window opens automatically, and the syntax is pasted there.

Figure 11-1
*Command syntax pasted from a dialog box*

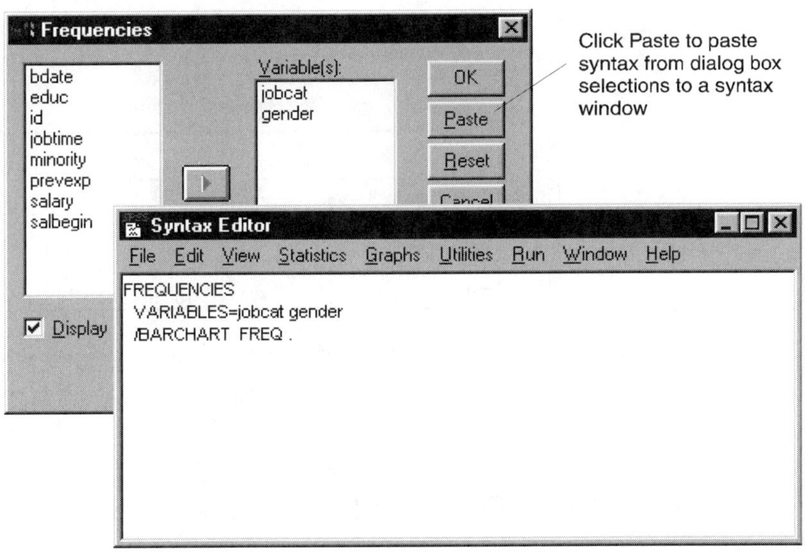


*Note*: If you open a dialog box from the menus in a script window, code for running syntax from a script is pasted into the script window.

# Using Syntax from the Output Log

You can build a syntax file by copying command syntax from the log that appears in the Viewer. To use this method, you must select Display commands in the log in the Viewer dialog box before running the analysis. Each command will then appear in the Viewer along with the output from the analysis.

In the syntax window, you can run the pasted syntax, edit it, and save it in a syntax file.

Figure 11-2
*Command syntax in the log*

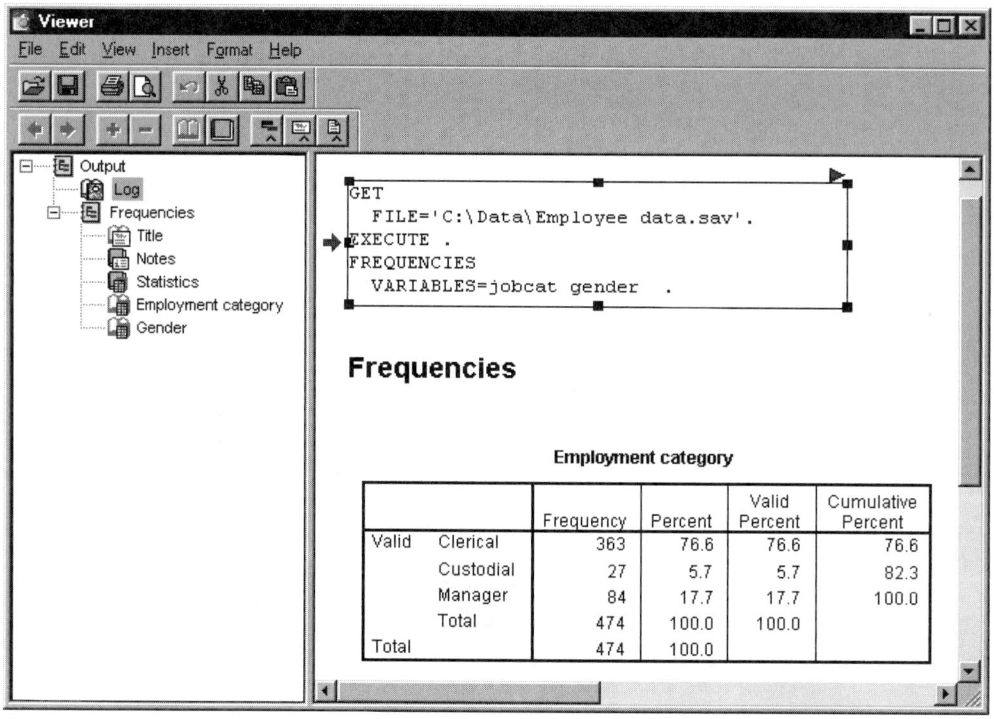


## To Copy Syntax from the Output Log

▶ Before running the analysis, from the menus choose:

Edit
  Options...

▶ On the Viewer tab, select Display commands in the log.

As you run analyses, the commands for your dialog box selections are recorded in the log.

▶ Open a previously saved syntax file or create a new one. To create a new syntax file, from the menus choose:

File
 New
  Syntax

▶ In the Viewer, double-click on a log item to activate it.

▶ Click and drag the mouse to highlight the syntax that you want to copy.

▶ From the Viewer menus choose:

Edit
 Copy

▶ In a syntax window, from the menus choose:

Edit
 Paste

## Using Syntax from the Journal File

By default, all commands executed during a session are recorded in a journal file named *spss.jnl* (set with Options on the Edit menu). You can edit the journal file and save it as a syntax file that you can use to repeat a previously run analysis, or you can run it in an automated job with the Production Facility.

The journal file is a text file that can be edited like any other text file. Because error messages and warnings are also recorded in the journal file along with command syntax, you must edit out any error and warning messages that appear before saving the syntax file. Note, however, that errors must be resolved or the job will not run successfully.

Save the edited journal file with a different filename. Because the journal file is automatically appended or overwritten for each session, attempting to use the same filename for a syntax file and the journal file may yield unexpected results.

Figure 11-3
*Editing the journal file*

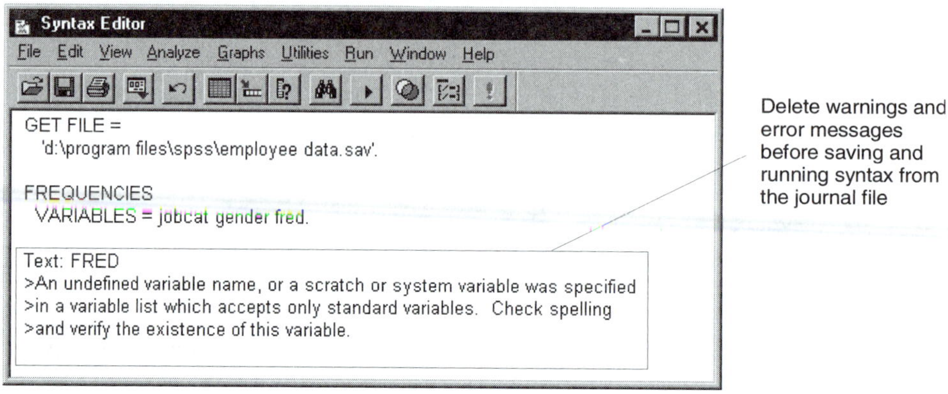


### *To Edit the Journal File*

▶ To open the journal file, from the menus choose:

File
  Open
    Other...

▶ Locate and open the journal file (by default, *spss.jnl* is located in the *temp* directory).

Select All files (*.*) for Files of Type or enter *.jnl in the File Name text box to display journal files in the file list. If you have difficulty locating the file, use Options on the Edit menu to see where the journal is saved in your system.

▶ Edit the file to remove any error messages or warnings, indicated by the > sign.

▶ Save the edited journal file using a different filename. (We recommend that you use a filename with the extension *.sps*, the default extension for syntax files.)

## To Run Command Syntax

- ▶ Highlight the commands that you want to run in the syntax window.
- ▶ Click the Run button (the right-pointing triangle) on the syntax window toolbar.

*or*

- ▶ Select one of the choices from the Run menu.
  - **All.** Runs all commands in the syntax window.
  - **Selection.** Runs the currently selected commands. This includes any commands partially highlighted.
  - **Current.** Runs the command where the cursor is currently located.
  - **To End.** Runs all commands from the current cursor location to the end of the command syntax file.

The Run button on the Syntax Editor toolbar runs the selected commands or the command where the cursor is located if there is no selection.

Figure 11-4
*Syntax Editor toolbar*

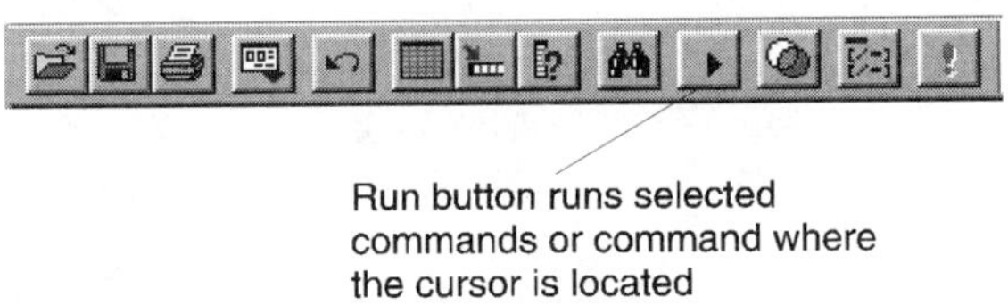


## Execute Command

Syntax pasted from dialog boxes or copied from the log or the journal may contain EXECUTE commands. When you run multiple commands from a syntax window, multiple EXECUTE commands are unnecessary and may slow performance because this command reads the entire data file.

- If the last command in the syntax file is a command that reads the data file (such as a statistical or graphing procedure), no EXECUTE commands are necessary, and they can be deleted.
- If you are unsure if the last command reads the data file, you can delete all but the last EXECUTE command in the syntax file.

Chapter

# 12

# *Frequencies*

The Frequencies procedure provides statistics and graphical displays that are useful for describing many types of variables. For a first look at your data, the Frequencies procedure is a good place to start.

For a frequency report and bar chart, you can arrange the distinct values in ascending or descending order or order the categories by their frequencies. The frequencies report can be suppressed when a variable has many distinct values. You can label charts with frequencies (the default) or percentages.

**Example.** What is the distribution of a company's customers by industry type? From the output, you might learn that 37.5% of your customers are in government agencies, 24.9% in corporations, 28.1% in academic institutions, and 9.4% in the healthcare industry. For continuous, quantitative data, such as sales revenue, you might learn that the average product sale is $3,576 with a standard deviation of $1,078.

**Statistics and plots.** Frequency counts, percentages, cumulative percentages, mean, median, mode, sum, standard deviation, variance, range, minimum and maximum values, standard error of the mean, skewness and kurtosis (both with standard errors), quartiles, user-specified percentiles, bar charts, pie charts, and histograms.

**Data.** Use numeric codes or short strings to code categorical variables (nominal or ordinal level measurements).

**Assumptions.** The tabulations and percentages provide a useful description for data from any distribution, especially for variables with ordered or unordered categories. Most of the optional summary statistics, such as the mean and standard deviation, are based on normal theory and are appropriate for quantitative variables with symmetric distributions. Robust statistics, such as the median, quartiles, and percentiles, are appropriate for quantitative variables that may or may not meet the assumption of normality.

# Sample Output

Figure 12-1
*Frequencies output*

**Industry**

| | Frequency | Percent | Valid Percent | Cumulative Percent |
|---|---|---|---|---|
| Government | 331 | 37.5 | 37.5 | 37.5 |
| Corporate | 220 | 24.9 | 24.9 | 62.5 |
| Academic | 248 | 28.1 | 28.1 | 90.6 |
| Healthcare | 83 | 9.4 | 9.4 | 100.0 |
| Total | 882 | 100.0 | 100.0 | |

**Statistics**

| | Mean | Median | Std. Deviation |
|---|---|---|---|
| Amount of Product Sale | $3,576.52 | $3,417.50 | $1,077.84 |

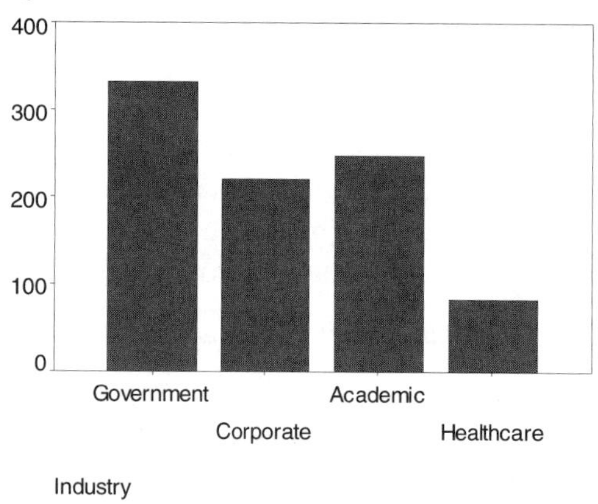


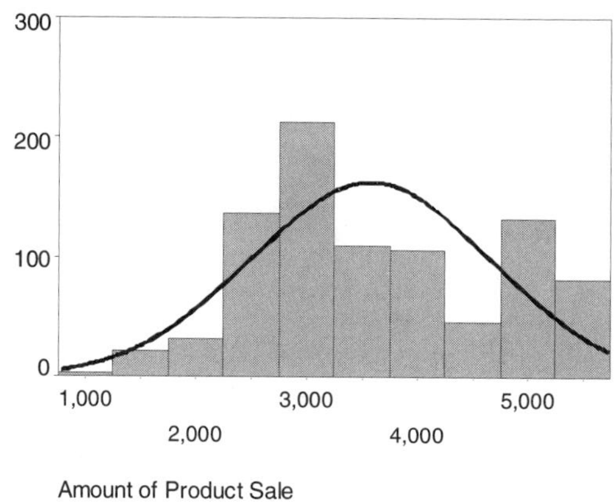

# To Obtain Frequencies and Statistics

▶ From the menus choose:

Analyze
  Descriptive Statistics
    Frequencies...

Figure 12-2
*Frequencies dialog box*

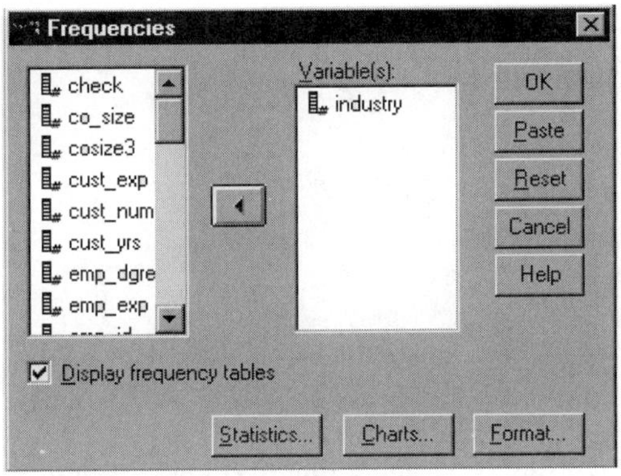


▶ Select one or more categorical or quantitative variables.

Optionally, you can:

- Click Statistics for descriptive statistics for quantitative variables.
- Click Charts for bar charts, pie charts, and histograms.
- Click Format for the order in which results are displayed.

## Frequencies Statistics

Figure 12-3
*Frequencies Statistics dialog box*

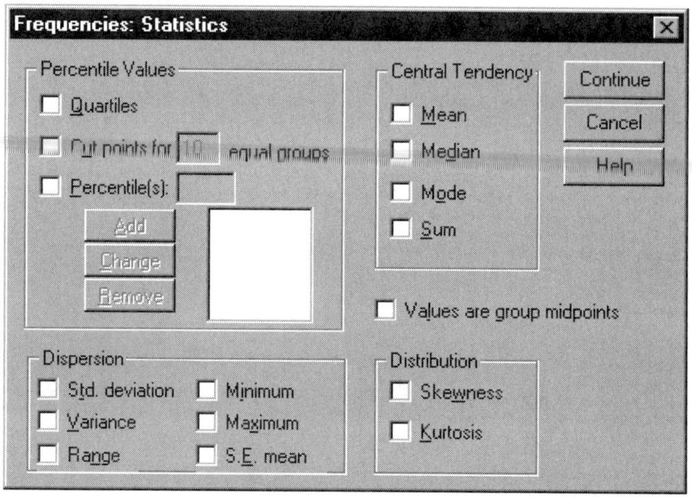


**Percentile Values.** Values of a quantitative variable that divide the ordered data into groups so that a certain percentage is above and another percentage is below. Quartiles (the 25th, 50th, and 75th percentiles) divide the observations into four groups of equal size. If you want an equal number of groups other than four, select Cut points for n equal groups. You can also specify individual percentiles (for example, the 95th percentile, the value below which 95% of the observations fall).

**Central Tendency.** Statistics that describe the location of the distribution include the mean, median, mode, and sum of all the values.

**Dispersion.** Statistics that measure the amount of variation or spread in the data include the standard deviation, variance, range, minimum, maximum, and standard error of the mean.

**Distribution.** Skewness and kurtosis are statistics that describe the shape and symmetry of the distribution. These statistics are displayed with their standard errors.

**Values are group midpoints.** If the values in your data are midpoints of groups (for example, ages of all people in their thirties are coded as 35), select this option to estimate the median and percentiles for the original, ungrouped data.

## Frequencies Charts

Figure 12-4
*Frequencies Charts dialog box*

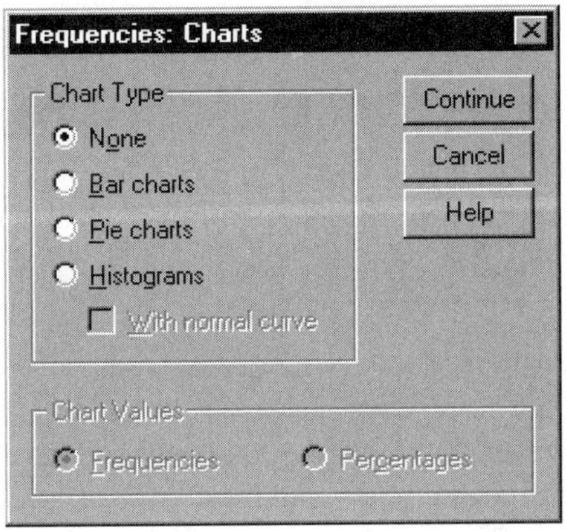


**Chart Type.** A pie chart displays the contribution of parts to a whole. Each slice of a pie chart corresponds to a group defined by a single grouping variable. A bar chart displays the count for each distinct value or category as a separate bar, allowing you to compare categories visually. A histogram also has bars, but they are plotted along an equal interval scale. The height of each bar is the count of values of a quantitative variable falling within the interval. A histogram shows the shape, center, and spread of the distribution. A normal curve superimposed on a histogram helps you judge whether the data are normally distributed.

**Chart Values.** For bar charts, the scale axis can be labeled by frequency counts or percentages.

## Frequencies Format

Figure 12-5
*Frequencies Format dialog box*

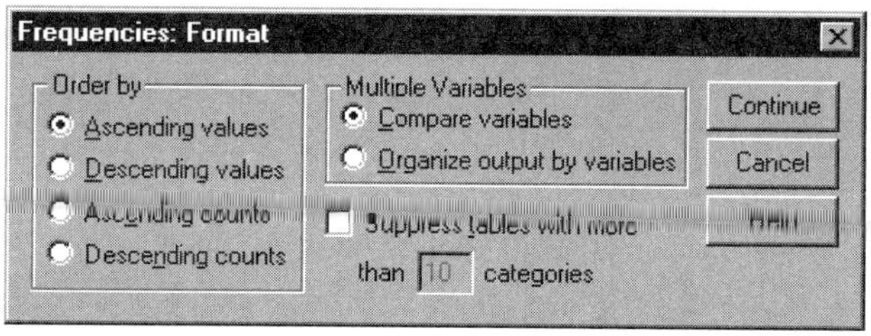


**Order by.** The frequency table can be arranged according to the actual values in the data or according to the count (frequency of occurrence) of those values, and in either ascending or descending order. However, if you request a histogram or percentiles, Frequencies assumes that the variable is quantitative and displays its values in ascending order.

**Multiple Variables.** If you produce statistics tables for multiple variables, you can either display all variables in a single table (Compare variables) or display a separate statistics table for each variable (Organize output by variables).

**Suppress tables with more than n categories.** This option prevents the display of tables with more than the specified number of values.

Chapter

# 13

# Descriptives

The Descriptives procedure displays univariate summary statistics for several variables in a single table and calculates standardized values (*z* scores). Variables can be ordered by the size of their means (in ascending or descending order), alphabetically, or by the order in which you select the variables (the default).

When *z* scores are saved, they are added to the data in the Data Editor and are available for charts, data listings, and analyses. When variables are recorded in different units (for example, gross domestic product per capita and percentage literate), a *z*-score transformation places variables on a common scale for easier visual comparison.

**Example.** If each case in your data contains the daily sales totals for each member of the sales staff (for example, one entry for Bob, one for Kim, one for Brian, etc.) collected each day for several months, the Descriptives procedure can compute the average daily sales for each staff member and order the results from highest average sales to lowest.

**Statistics.** Sample size, mean, minimum, maximum, standard deviation, variance, range, sum, standard error of the mean, and kurtosis and skewness with their standard errors.

**Data.** Use numeric variables after you have screened them graphically for recording errors, outliers, and distributional anomalies. The Descriptives procedure is very efficient for large files (thousands of cases).

**Assumptions.** Most of the available statistics (including *z* scores) are based on normal theory and are appropriate for quantitative variables (interval- or ratio-level measurements) with symmetric distributions (avoid variables with unordered categories or skewed distributions). The distribution of *z* scores has the same shape as that of the original data; therefore, calculating *z* scores is not a remedy for problem data.

# Sample Output

Figure 13-1
*Descriptives output*

Descriptive Statistics

| | N | Minimum | Maximum | Mean | Std. Deviation |
|---|---|---|---|---|---|
| Dave's Sales | 10 | 42.00 | 86.00 | 59.2000 | 14.2657 |
| Sharon's Sales | 10 | 23.00 | 85.00 | 56.2000 | 17.6623 |
| Brian's Sales | 10 | 45.00 | 71.00 | 56.0000 | 8.8819 |
| Mary's Sales | 10 | 34.00 | 83.00 | 52.9000 | 16.6029 |
| Bob's Sales | 10 | 28.00 | 89.00 | 52.9000 | 21.8858 |
| Kim's Sales | 10 | 23.00 | 73.00 | 52.1000 | 16.4617 |
| Juan's Sales | 10 | 25.00 | 85.00 | 50.5000 | 21.1305 |
| Valid N (listwise) | 10 | | | | |

# To Obtain Descriptive Statistics

▶ From the menus choose:

Analyze
  Descriptive Statistics
    Descriptives...

Figure 13-2
*Descriptives dialog box*

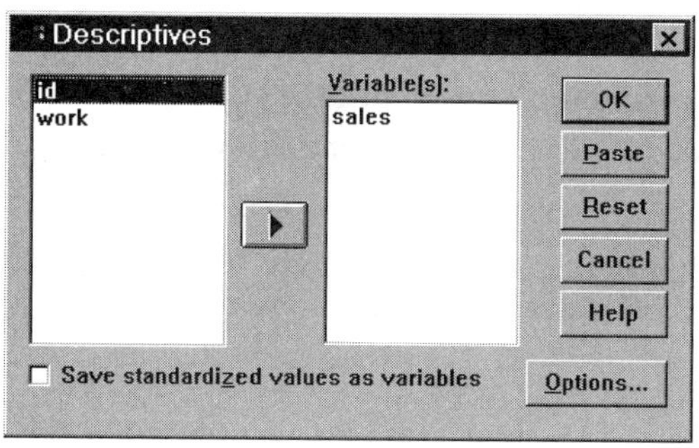


▶ Select one or more variables.

Optionally, you can:

- Click Save standardized values as variables to save *z* scores as new variables.
- Click Options for optional statistics and display order.

## Descriptives Options

Figure 13-3
*Descriptives Options dialog box*

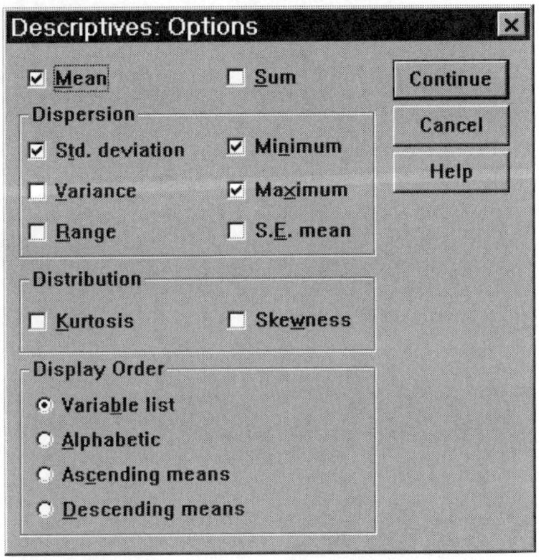


**Mean and Sum.** The mean, or arithmetic average, is displayed by default.

**Dispersion.** Statistics that measure the spread or variation in the data include the standard deviation, variance, range, minimum, maximum, and standard error of the mean.

**Distribution.** Kurtosis and skewness are statistics that characterize the shape and symmetry of the distribution. These are displayed with their standard errors.

**Display Order.** By default, the variables are displayed in the order in which you selected them. Optionally, you can display variables alphabetically, by ascending means, or by descending means.

Chapter

# 14

# Explore

The Explore procedure produces summary statistics and graphical displays, either for all of your cases or separately for groups of cases. There are many reasons for using the Explore procedure—data screening, outlier identification, description, assumption checking, and characterizing differences among subpopulations (groups of cases). Data screening may show that you have unusual values, extreme values, gaps in the data, or other peculiarities. Exploring the data can help to determine whether the statistical techniques that you are considering for data analysis are appropriate. The exploration may indicate that you need to transform the data if the technique requires a normal distribution. Or, you may decide that you need nonparametric tests.

**Example.** Look at the distribution of maze-learning times for rats under four different reinforcement schedules. For each of the four groups, you can see if the distribution of times is approximately normal and whether the four variances are equal. You can also identify the cases with the five largest and five smallest times. The boxplots and stem-and-leaf plots graphically summarize the distribution of learning times for each of the groups.

**Statistics and plots.** Mean, median, 5% trimmed mean, standard error, variance, standard deviation, minimum, maximum, range, interquartile range, skewness and kurtosis and their standard errors, confidence interval for the mean (and specified confidence level), percentiles, Huber's M-estimator, Andrews' wave estimator, Hampel's redescending M-estimator, Tukey's biweight estimator, the five largest and five smallest values, the Kolmogorov-Smirnov statistic with a Lilliefors significance level for testing normality, and the Shapiro-Wilk statistic. Boxplots, stem-and-leaf plots, histograms, normality plots, and spread-versus-level plots with Levene tests and transformations.

**Data.** The Explore procedure can be used for quantitative variables (interval- or ratio-level measurements). A factor variable (used to break the data into groups of cases) should have a reasonable number of distinct values (categories). These values may be short string or numeric. The case label variable, used to label outliers in boxplots, can be short string, long string (first 15 characters), or numeric.

**Assumptions.** The distribution of your data does not have to be symmetric or normal.

# Sample Output

Figure 14-1
*Explore output*

**Descriptives**

| | | | Time Schedule | | | |
|---|---|---|---|---|---|---|
| | | | 1 | 2 | 3 | 4 |
| Mean | | Statistic | 2.760 | 4.850 | 6.900 | 9.010 |
| | | Std. Error | .165 | .422 | .445 | .289 |
| 95.0% Confidence Interval for Mean | Lower Bound | Statistic | 2.387 | 3.895 | 5.893 | 8.357 |
| | Upper Bound | Statistic | 3.133 | 5.805 | 7.907 | 9.663 |
| 5% Trimmed Mean | | Statistic | 2.761 | 4.889 | 6.911 | 8.994 |
| Median | | Statistic | 2.850 | 4.900 | 7.050 | 9.000 |
| Variance | | Statistic | .272 | 1.783 | 1.982 | .834 |
| Std. Deviation | | Statistic | .521 | 1.335 | 1.408 | .913 |
| Minimum | | Statistic | 2.0 | 2.3 | 4.5 | 7.8 |
| Maximum | | Statistic | 3.5 | 6.7 | 9.1 | 10.5 |
| Range | | Statistic | 1.5 | 4.4 | 4.6 | 2.7 |
| Interquartile Range | | Statistic | .925 | 2.250 | 2.400 | 1.650 |
| Skewness | | Statistic | -.116 | -.559 | -.197 | .219 |
| | | Std. Error | .687 | .687 | .687 | .687 |
| Kurtosis | | Statistic | -1.210 | -.104 | -.606 | -1.350 |
| | | Std. Error | 1.334 | 1.334 | 1.334 | 1.334 |

Extreme Values

| | | | Case Number | Schedule | Value |
|---|---|---|---|---|---|
| Time | Highest | 1 | 31 | 4 | 10.5 |
| | | 2 | 33 | 4 | 9.9 |
| | | 3 | 39 | 4 | 9.8 |
| | | 4 | 32 | 4 | 9.5 |
| | | 5 | 36 | 4 | 9.3 |
| | Lowest | 1 | 2 | 1 | 2.0 |
| | | 2 | 7 | 1 | 2.1 |
| | | 3 | 1 | 1 | 2.3 |
| | | 4 | 11 | 2 | 2.3 |
| | | 5 | 3 | 1 | 2.5 |

```
Frequency    Stem &  Leaf

   7.00        2 .  0133589
   6.00        3 .  014577
   3.00        4 .  568
   5.00        5 .  05779
   4.00        6 .  1379
   3.00        7 .  268
   6.00        8 .  012237
   5.00        9 .  13589
   1.00       10 .  5

Stem width:     1.0
Each leaf:      1 case(s)
```

## To Explore Your Data

▶ From the menus choose:

Analyze
  Descriptive Statistics
    Explore...

Figure 14-2
*Explore dialog box*

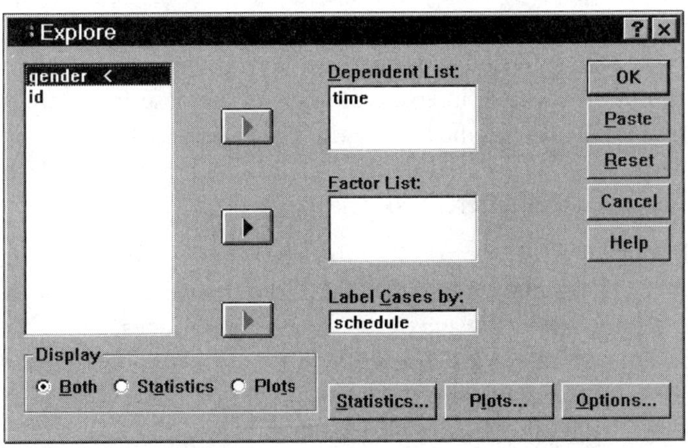


▶ Select one or more dependent variables.

Optionally, you can:

- Select one or more factor variables, whose values will define groups of cases.
- Select an identification variable to label cases.
- Click Statistics for robust estimators, outliers, percentiles, and frequency tables.
- Click Plots for histograms, normal probability plots and tests, and spread-versus-level plots with Levene's statistics.
- Click Options for the treatment of missing values.

## Explore Statistics

Figure 14-3
*Explore Statistics dialog box*

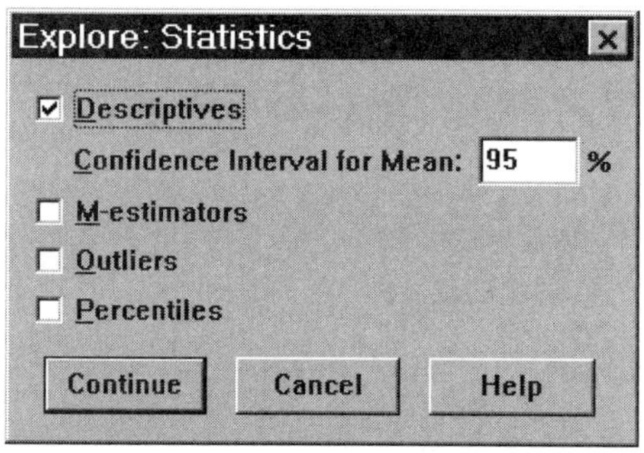


**Descriptives.** These measures of central tendency and dispersion are displayed by default. Measures of central tendency indicate the location of the distribution; they include the mean, median, and 5% trimmed mean. Measures of dispersion show the dissimilarity of the values; these include standard error, variance, standard deviation, minimum, maximum, range, and interquartile range. The descriptive statistics also include measures of the shape of the distribution; skewness and kurtosis are displayed with their standard errors. The 95% level confidence interval for the mean is also displayed; you can specify a different confidence level.

**M-estimators.** Robust alternatives to the sample mean and median for estimating the center of location. The estimators calculated differ in the weights they apply to cases. Huber's M-estimator, Andrews' wave estimator, Hampel's redescending M-estimator, and Tukey's biweight estimator are displayed.

**Outliers.** Displays the five largest and five smallest values, with case labels.

**Percentiles.** Displays the values for the 5th, 10th, 25th, 50th, 75th, 90th, and 95th percentiles.

## Explore Plots

Figure 14-4
*Explore Plots dialog box*

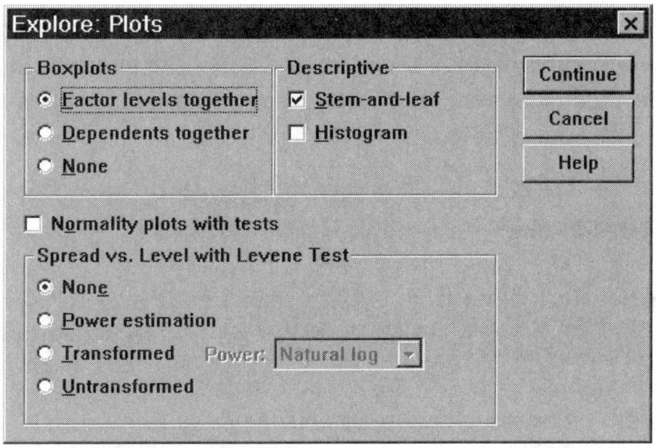


**Boxplots.** These alternatives control the display of boxplots when you have more than one dependent variable. Factor levels together generates a separate display for each dependent variable. Within a display, boxplots are shown for each of the groups defined by a factor variable. Dependents together generates a separate display for each group defined by a factor variable. Within a display, boxplots are shown side by side for each dependent variable. This display is particularly useful when the different variables represent a single characteristic measured at different times.

**Descriptive.** The Descriptive group allows you to choose stem-and-leaf plots and histograms.

**Normality plots with tests.** Displays normal probability and detrended normal probability plots. The Kolmogorov-Smirnov statistic, with a Lilliefors significance level for testing normality, is displayed. If non-integer weights are specified, the Shapiro-Wilk statistic is calculated when the weighted sample size lies between 3 and 50. For no weights or integer weights, the statistic is calculated when the weighted sample size lies between 3 and 5000.

**Spread vs. Level with Levene Test.** Controls data transformation for spread-versus-level plots. For all spread-versus-level plots, the slope of the regression line and Levene's robust tests for homogeneity of variance are displayed. If you select a transformation, Levene's tests are based on the transformed data. If no factor variable is selected, spread-versus-level plots are not produced. Power estimation produces a plot of the natural logs of the interquartile ranges against the natural logs of the medians for all cells, as well as an estimate of the power transformation for achieving equal variances in the cells. A spread-versus-level plot helps determine the power for a transformation to stabilize (make more equal) variances across groups. Transformed allows you to select one of the power alternatives, perhaps following the recommendation from power estimation, and produces plots of transformed data. The interquartile range and median of the transformed data are plotted. Untransformed produces plots of the raw data. This is equivalent to a transformation with a power of 1.

### Explore Power Transformations

These are the power transformations for spread-versus-level plots. To transform data, you must select a power for the transformation. You can choose one of the following alternatives:

- **Natural log.** Natural log transformation. This is the default.
- **1/square root.** For each data value, the reciprocal of the square root is calculated.
- **Reciprocal.** The reciprocal of each data value is calculated.
- **Square root.** The square root of each data value is calculated.
- **Square.** Each data value is squared.
- **Cube.** Each data value is cubed.

## Explore Options

Figure 14-5
*Explore Options dialog box*

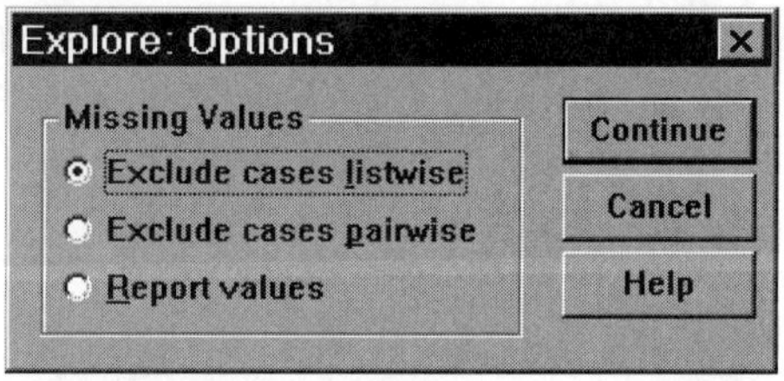


**Missing Values.** Controls the treatment of missing values.

- **Exclude cases listwise.** Cases with missing values for any dependent or factor variable are excluded from all analyses. This is the default.
- **Exclude cases pairwise.** Cases with no missing values for variables in a group (cell) are included in the analysis of that group. The case may have missing values for variables used in other groups.
- **Report values.** Missing values for factor variables are treated as a separate category. All output is produced for this additional category. Frequency tables include categories for missing values. Missing values for a factor variable are included but labeled as missing.

Chapter

15

# Crosstabs

The Crosstabs procedure forms two-way and multiway tables and provides a variety of tests and measures of association for two-way tables. The structure of the table and whether categories are ordered determine what test or measure to use.

Crosstabs' statistics and measures of association are computed for two-way tables only. If you specify a row, a column, and a layer factor (control variable), the Crosstabs procedure forms one panel of associated statistics and measures for each value of the layer factor (or a combination of values for two or more control variables). For example, if *gender* is a layer factor for a table of *married* (yes, no) against *life* (is life exciting, routine, or dull), the results for a two-way table for the females are computed separately from those for the males and printed as panels following one another.

**Example.** Are customers from small companies more likely to be profitable in sales of services (for example, training and consulting) than those from larger companies? From a crosstabulation, you might learn that the majority of small companies (fewer than 500 employees) yield high service profits, while the majority of large companies (more than 2500 employees) yield low service profits.

**Statistics and measures of association.** Pearson chi-square, likelihood-ratio chi-square, linear-by-linear association test, Fisher's exact test, Yates' corrected chi-square, Pearson's *r*, Spearman's rho, contingency coefficient, phi, Cramér's *V*, symmetric and asymmetric lambdas, Goodman and Kruskal's tau, uncertainty coefficient, gamma, Somers' *d*, Kendall's tau-*b*, Kendall's tau-*c*, eta coefficient, Cohen's kappa, relative risk estimate, odds ratio, McNemar test, and Cochran's and Mantel-Haenszel statistics.

**Data.** To define the categories of each table variable, use values of a numeric or short string (eight or fewer characters) variable. For example, for *gender*, you could code the data as 1 and 2 or as *male* and *female*.

**Assumptions.** Some statistics and measures assume ordered categories (ordinal data) or quantitative values (interval or ratio data), as discussed in the section on statistics. Others are valid when the table variables have unordered categories (nominal data). For the chi-square-based statistics (phi, Cramér's *V*, and contingency coefficient), the data should be a random sample from a multinomial distribution.

# Sample Output

Figure 15-1
*Crosstabs output*

**Service Profitability * Company Size Crosstabulation**

| Service Profitability | Company Size | | | Total |
|---|---|---|---|---|
| | 1-500 | 501-2,500 | > 2,500 | |
| Low | 200 | 85 | 135 | 420 |
| High | 251 | 106 | 105 | 462 |
| Total | 451 | 191 | 240 | 882 |

**Chi-Square Tests**

| | Value | df | Asymp. Sig. (2-sided) |
|---|---|---|---|
| Pearson Chi-Square | 9.848 | 2 | .007 |
| Likelihood Ratio | 9.852 | 2 | .007 |
| Linear-by-Linear Association | 7.869 | 1 | .005 |
| N of Valid Cases | 882 | | |

# To Obtain Crosstabulations

▶ From the menus choose:

Analyze
  Descriptive Statistics
    Crosstabs...

Figure 15-2
*Crosstabs dialog box*

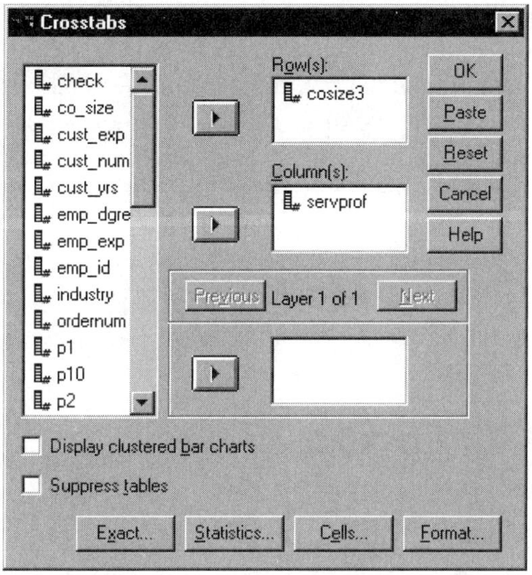


▶ Select one or more row variables and one or more column variables.

Optionally, you can:

- Select one or more control variables.
- Click Statistics for tests and measures of association for two-way tables or subtables.
- Click Cells for observed and expected values, percentages, and residuals.
- Click Format for controlling the order of categories.

## Crosstabs Layers

If you select one or more layer variables, a separate crosstabulation is produced for each category of each layer variable (control variable). For example, if you have one row variable, one column variable, and one layer variable with two categories, you get a two-way table for each category of the layer variable. To make another layer of control variables, click Next. Subtables are produced for each combination of categories for each 1st-layer variable with each 2nd-layer variable and so on. If statistics and measures of association are requested, they apply to two-way subtables only.

## Crosstabs Clustered Bar Charts

**Display clustered bar charts.** A clustered bar chart helps summarize your data for groups of cases. There is one cluster of bars for each value of the variable you specified under Rows. The variable that defines the bars within each cluster is the variable you specified under Columns. There is one set of differently colored or patterned bars for each value of this variable. If you specify more than one variable under Columns or Rows, a clustered bar chart is produced for each combination of two variables.

## Crosstabs Statistics

Figure 15-3
*Crosstabs Statistics dialog box*

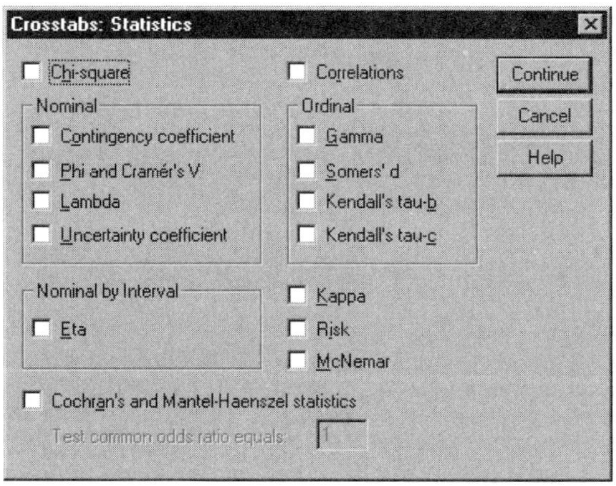


**Chi-square.** For tables with two rows and two columns, select Chi-square to calculate the Pearson chi-square, the likelihood-ratio chi-square, Fisher's exact test, and Yates' corrected chi-square (continuity correction). For $2 \times 2$ tables, Fisher's exact test is computed when a table that does not result from missing rows or columns in a larger table has a cell with an expected frequency of less than 5. Yates' corrected chi-square is computed for all other $2 \times 2$ tables. For tables with any number of rows and columns, select Chi-square to calculate the Pearson chi-square and the likelihood-ratio chi-square. When both table variables are quantitative, Chi-square yields the linear-by-linear association test.

**Correlations.** For tables in which both rows and columns contain ordered values, Correlations yields Spearman's correlation coefficient, rho (numeric data only). Spearman's rho is a measure of association between rank orders. When both table variables (factors) are quantitative, Correlations yields the Pearson correlation coefficient, *r*, a measure of linear association between the variables.

**Nominal.** For nominal data (no intrinsic order, such as Catholic, Protestant, and Jewish), you can select Phi (coefficient) and Cramér's V, Contingency coefficient, Lambda (symmetric and asymmetric lambdas and Goodman and Kruskal's tau), and Uncertainty coefficient.

**Ordinal.** For tables in which both rows and columns contain ordered values, select Gamma (zero-order for 2-way tables and conditional for 3-way to 10-way tables), Kendall's tau-b, and Kendall's tau-c. For predicting column categories from row categories, select Somers' d.

**Nominal by Interval.** When one variable is categorical and the other is quantitative, select Eta. The categorical variable must be coded numerically.

**Kappa.** For tables that have the same categories in the columns as in the rows (for example, measuring agreement between two raters), select Cohen's Kappa.

**Risk.** For tables with two rows and two columns, select Risk for relative risk estimates and the odds ratio.

**McNemar.** The McNemar test is a nonparametric test for two related dichotomous variables. It tests for changes in responses using the chi-square distribution. It is useful for detecting changes in responses due to experimental intervention in "before and after" designs.

**Cochran's and Mantel-Haenszel.** Cochran's and Mantel-Haenszel statistics can be used to test for independence between a binary factor variable and a binary response variable. The statistics are adjusted for covariate patterns defined by one or more control variables.

## Crosstabs Cell Display

Figure 15-4
*Crosstabs Cell Display dialog box*

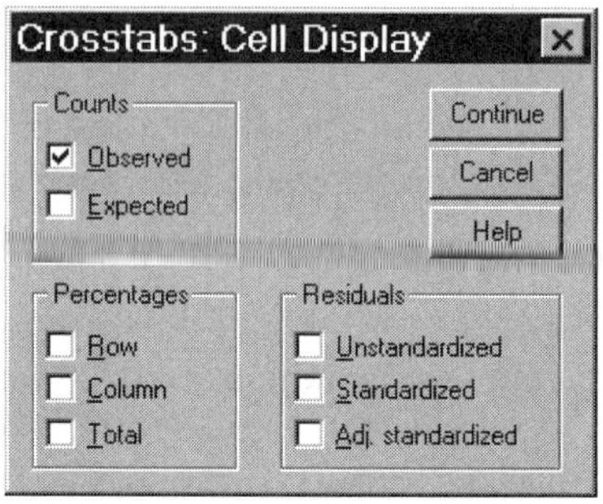


To help you uncover patterns in the data that contribute to a significant chi-square test, the Crosstabs procedure displays expected frequencies and three types of residuals (deviates) that measure the difference between observed and expected frequencies. Each cell of the table can contain any combination of counts, percentages, and residuals selected.

**Counts.** The number of cases actually observed and the number of cases expected if the row and column variables are independent of each other.

**Percentages.** The percentages can add up across the rows or down the columns. The percentages of the total number of cases represented in the table (one layer) are also available.

**Residuals.** Raw unstandardized residuals give the difference between the observed and expected values. Standardized and adjusted standardized residuals are also available. Standardized and adjusted standardized residuals are calculated as in Haberman (1978).

## Crosstabs Table Format

Figure 15-5
*Crosstabs Table Format dialog box*

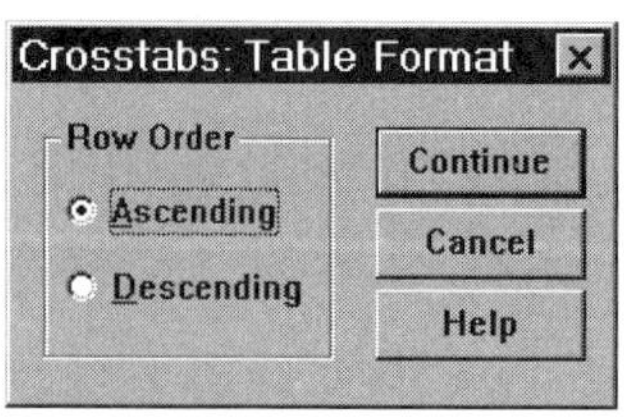


You can arrange rows in ascending or descending order of the values of the row variable.

Chapter

# 16

# Summarize

The Summarize procedure calculates subgroup statistics for variables within categories of one or more grouping variables. All levels of the grouping variable are crosstabulated. You can choose the order in which the statistics are displayed. Summary statistics for each variable across all categories are also displayed. Data values in each category can be listed or suppressed. With large data sets, you can choose to list only the first *n* cases.

**Example.** What is the average product sales amount by region and customer industry? You might discover that the average sales amount is slightly higher in the western region than in other regions, with corporate customers in the western region yielding the highest average sales amount.

**Statistics.** Sum, number of cases, mean, median, grouped median, standard error of the mean, minimum, maximum, range, variable value of the first category of the grouping variable, variable value of the last category of the grouping variable, standard deviation, variance, kurtosis, standard error of kurtosis, skewness, standard error of skewness, percentage of total sum, percentage of total N, percentage of sum in, percentage of N in, geometric mean, harmonic mean.

**Data.** Grouping variables are categorical variables whose values can be numeric or short string. The number of categories should be reasonably small. The other variables should be able to be ranked.

**Assumptions.** Some of the optional subgroup statistics, such as the mean and standard deviation, are based on normal theory and are appropriate for quantitative variables with symmetric distributions. Robust statistics, such as the median and the range, are appropriate for quantitative variables that may or may not meet the assumption of normality.

# Sample Output

Figure 16-1
*Summarize output*

**Case Summaries**
**Average Product Sale by Region and Industry**

| | Industry | | | | |
|---|---|---|---|---|---|
| Region | Government | Corporate | Academic | Healthcare | Total |
| East | $3,594.65 | $3,953.76 | $3,764.91 | $3,722.32 | $3,735.45 |
| Central | $3,370.12 | $3,268.47 | $3,317.81 | $3,165.11 | $3,305.03 |
| West | $3,552.50 | $4,649.00 | $4,276.25 | $4,027.00 | $4,079.46 |
| Total | $3,503.75 | $3,727.50 | $3,579.76 | $3,456.93 | $3,576.52 |

# To Obtain Case Summaries

▶ From the menus choose:

Analyze
  Reports
    Case Summaries...

Figure 16-2
*Summarize Cases dialog box*

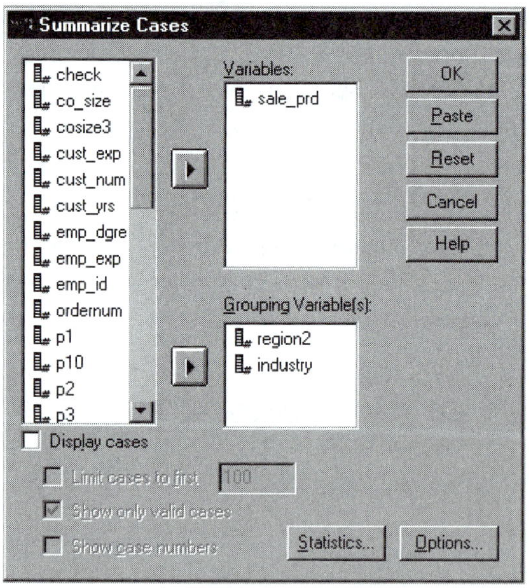

▶ Select one or more variables.

Optionally, you can:

- Select one or more grouping variables to divide your data into subgroups.
- Click Options to change the output title, add a caption below the output, or exclude cases with missing values.
- Click Statistics for optional statistics.
- Select Display cases to list the cases in each subgroup. By default, the system lists only the first 100 cases in your file. You can raise or lower the value for Limit cases to first n or deselect that item to list all cases.

## Summarize Options

Figure 16-3
*Summarize Cases Options dialog box*

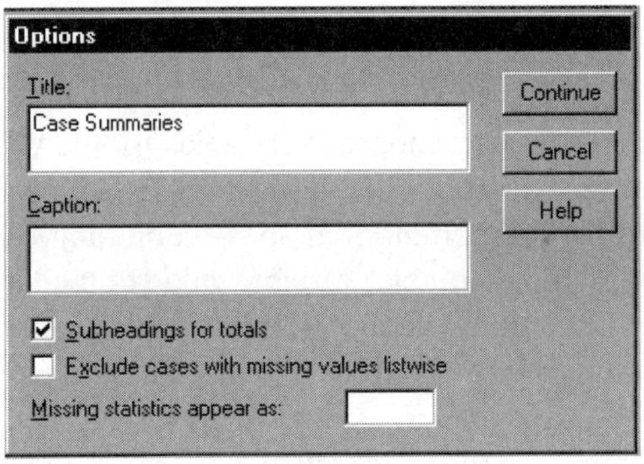


Summarize allows you to change the title of your output or add a caption that will appear below the output table. You can control line wrapping in titles and captions by typing \n wherever you want to insert a line break in the text.

You can also choose to display or suppress subheadings for totals and to include or exclude cases with missing values for any of the variables used in any of the analyses. Often it is desirable to denote missing cases in output with a period or an asterisk. Enter a character, phrase, or code that you would like to have appear when a value is missing; otherwise, no special treatment is applied to missing cases in the output.

## Summarize Statistics

Figure 16-4
*Summarize Cases Statistics dialog box*

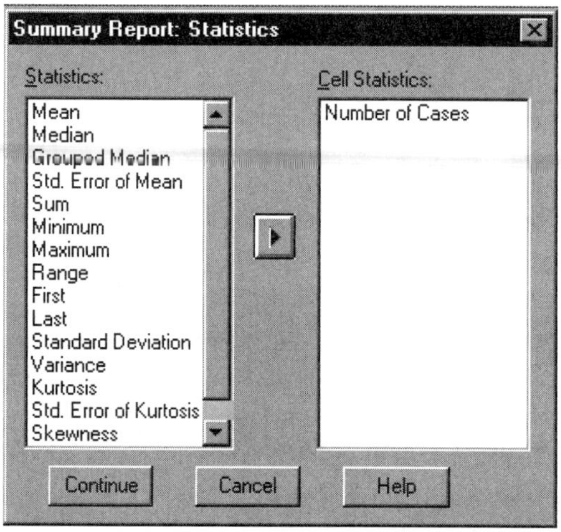


You can choose one or more of the following subgroup statistics for the variables within each category of each grouping variable: sum, number of cases, mean, median, grouped median, standard error of the mean, minimum, maximum, range, variable value of the first category of the grouping variable, variable value of the last category of the grouping variable, standard deviation, variance, kurtosis, standard error of kurtosis, skewness, standard error of skewness, percentage of total sum, percentage of total N, percentage of sum in, percentage of N in, geometric mean, harmonic mean. The order in which the statistics appear in the Cell Statistics list is the order in which they will be displayed in the output. Summary statistics are also displayed for each variable across all categories.

Chapter 17

# Means

The Means procedure calculates subgroup means and related univariate statistics for dependent variables within categories of one or more independent variables. Optionally, you can obtain a one-way analysis of variance, eta, and tests for linearity.

**Example.** Measure the average amount of fat absorbed by three different types of cooking oil and perform a one-way analysis of variance to see if the means differ.

**Statistics.** Sum, number of cases, mean, median, grouped median, standard error of the mean, minimum, maximum, range, variable value of the first category of the grouping variable, variable value of the last category of the grouping variable, standard deviation, variance, kurtosis, standard error of kurtosis, skewness, standard error of skewness, percentage of total sum, percentage of total N, percentage of sum in, percentage of N in, geometric mean, harmonic mean. Optional statistics include analysis of variance, eta, eta squared, and tests for linearity $R$ and $R^2$.

**Data.** The dependent variables are quantitative and the independent variables are categorical. The values of categorical variables can be numeric or short string.

**Assumptions.** Some of the optional subgroup statistics, such as the mean and standard deviation, are based on normal theory and are appropriate for quantitative variables with symmetric distributions. Robust statistics, such as the median and the range, are appropriate for quantitative variables that may or may not meet the assumption of normality. Analysis of variance is robust to departures from normality, but the data in each cell should be symmetric. Analysis of variance also assumes that the groups come from populations with equal variances. To test this assumption, use Levene's homogeneity-of-variance test, available in the One-Way ANOVA procedure.

# Sample Output

**Figure 17-1**
*Means output*

Report

Absorbed Grams of Fat

| | | | |
|---|---|---|---|
| Type of Oil | Peanut Oil | Mean | 72.00 |
| | | N | [illegible] |
| | | Std. Deviation | 13.34 |
| | Lard | Mean | 85.00 |
| | | N | 6 |
| | | Std. Deviation | 7.77 |
| | Corn Oil | Mean | 62.00 |
| | | N | 6 |
| | | Std. Deviation | 8.22 |
| | Total | Mean | 73.00 |
| | | N | 18 |
| | | Std. Deviation | 13.56 |

**ANOVA Table**

| | | | Sum of Squares | df | Mean Square | F | Significance |
|---|---|---|---|---|---|---|---|
| Absorbed Grams of Fat * Type of Oil | Between Groups | (Combined) | 1596.00 | 2 | 798.000 | 7.824 | .005 |
| | Within Groups | | 1530.00 | 15 | 102.000 | | |
| | Total | | 3126.00 | 17 | | | |

# To Obtain Means

▶ From the menus choose:

Analyze
  Compare Means
    Means...

Figure 17-2
*Means dialog box*

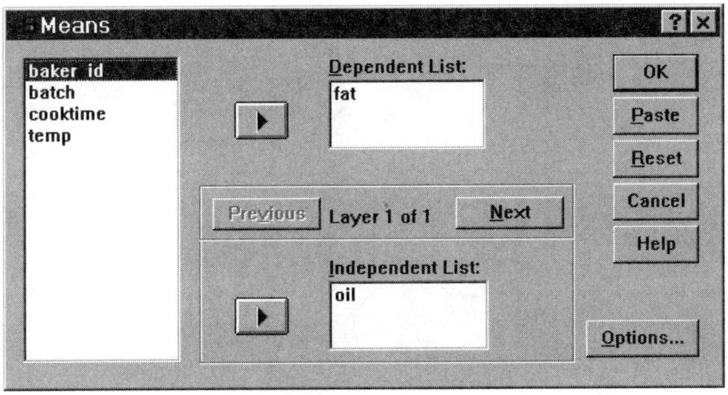


▶ Select one or more dependent variables.

▶ There are two ways to select categorical independent variables.

- Select one or more independent variables. Separate results are displayed for each independent variable.
- Select one or more layers of independent variables. Each layer further subdivides the sample. If you have one independent variable in Layer 1 and one in Layer 2, the results are displayed in one crossed table as opposed to separate tables for each independent variable.

▶ Optionally, you can:

- Click Options for optional statistics, analysis of variance table, eta, eta squared, $R$, and $R^2$.

## Means Options

Figure 17-3
*Means Options dialog box*

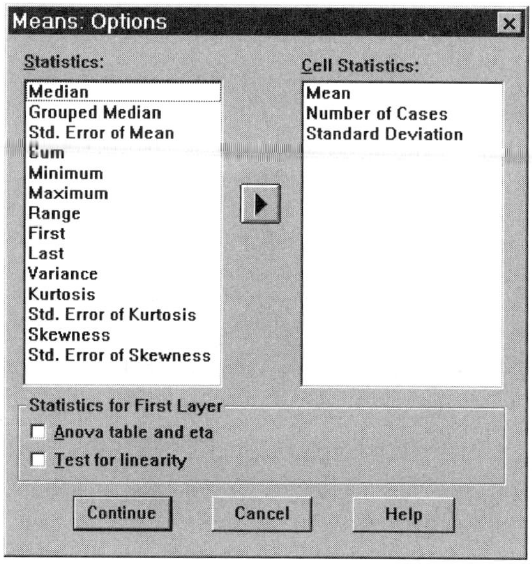


You can choose one or more of the following subgroup statistics for the variables within each category of each grouping variable: sum, number of cases, mean, median, grouped median, standard error of the mean, minimum, maximum, range, variable value of the first category of the grouping variable, variable value of the last category of the grouping variable, standard deviation, variance, kurtosis, standard error of kurtosis, skewness, standard error of skewness, percentage of total sum, percentage of total N, percentage of sum in, percentage of N in, geometric mean, harmonic mean. You can change the order in which the subgroup statistics appear. The order in which the statistics appear in the Cell Statistics list is the order in which they are displayed in the output. Summary statistics are also displayed for each variable across all categories.

Click ANOVA table and eta to obtain a one-way analysis of variance, eta, and eta squared for each independent variable in the first layer. Eta and eta squared are measures of association. Eta squared is the proportion of variance in the dependent variable that is explained by differences among groups. It is the ratio of the between-groups sum of squares and the total sum of squares. Tests for linearity yield $R$ and $R^2$, which are appropriate measures when the categories of the independent variable are ordered. $R$ and $R^2$ measure the goodness of fit of a linear model.

Chapter 18

# OLAP Cubes

The OLAP (Online Analytical Processing) Cubes procedure calculates totals, means, and other univariate statistics for continuous summary variables within categories of one or more categorical grouping variables. A separate layer in the table is created for each category of each grouping variable.

**Example.** Total and average sales for different regions and product lines within regions.

**Statistics.** Sum, number of cases, mean, median, grouped median, standard error of the mean, minimum, maximum, range, variable value of the first category of the grouping variable, variable value of the last category of the grouping variable, standard deviation, variance, kurtosis, standard error of kurtosis, skewness, standard error of skewness, percentage of total cases, percentage of total sum, percentage of total cases within grouping variables, percentage of total sum within grouping variables, geometric mean, and harmonic mean.

**Data.** The summary variables are quantitative (continuous variables measured on an interval or ratio scale), and the grouping variables are categorical. The values of categorical variables can be numeric or short string.

**Assumptions.** Some of the optional subgroup statistics, such as the mean and standard deviation, are based on normal theory and are appropriate for quantitative variables with symmetric distributions. Robust statistics, such as the median and range, are appropriate for quantitative variables that may or may not meet the assumption of normality.

# Sample Output

Figure 18-1
*OLAP Cubes output*

**1996 Sales**
**by Division and Region**

Division: Total
Region: Total

| | |
|---|---|
| Sum | $145,038,250 |
| Mean | $371,893 |
| Median | $307,500 |
| Std. Deviation | $171,311 |

**1996 Sales**
**by Division and Region**

Division: Consumer Products
Region: East

| | |
|---|---|
| Sum | $18,548,100 |
| Mean | $289,814.06 |
| Median | $273,600.00 |
| Std. Deviation | $80,674.66 |

# To Obtain OLAP Cubes

▶ From the menus choose:

Analyze
  Reports
    OLAP Cubes...

Figure 18-2
*OLAP Cubes dialog box*

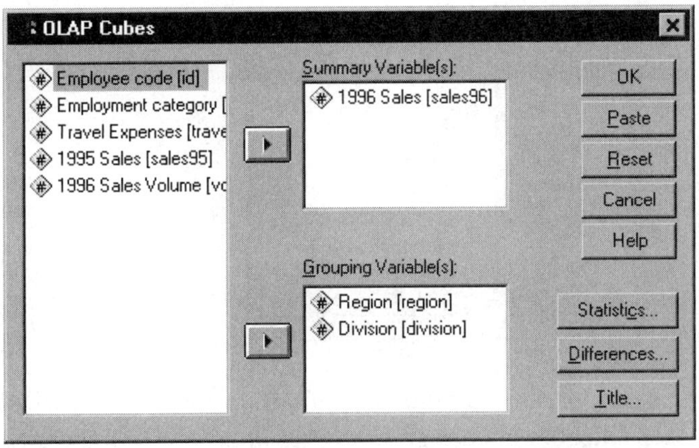


▶ Select one or more continuous summary variables.

▶ Select one or more categorical grouping variables.

Optionally, you can:

- Select different summary statistics (click Statistics).
- Calculate differences between pairs of variables and pairs of groups defined by a grouping variable (click Differences).
- Create custom table titles (click Title).

## OLAP Cubes Statistics

Figure 18-3
*OLAP Cubes Statistics dialog box*

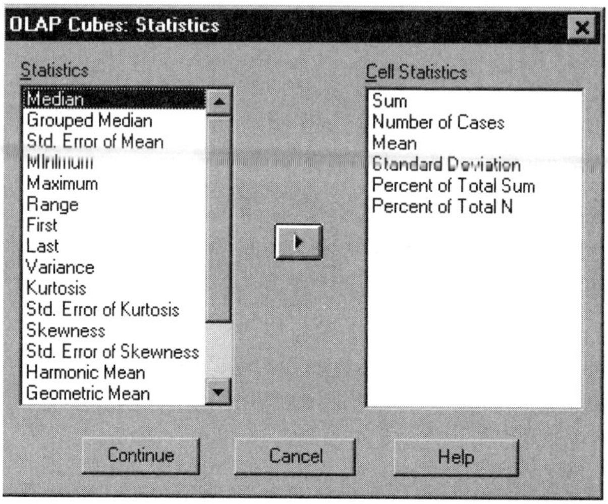


You can choose one or more of the following subgroup statistics for the summary variables within each category of each grouping variable: sum, number of cases, mean, median, grouped median, standard error of the mean, minimum, maximum, range, variable value of the first category of the grouping variable, variable value of the last category of the grouping variable, standard deviation, variance, kurtosis, standard error of kurtosis, skewness, standard error of skewness, percentage of total cases, percentage of total sum, percentage of total cases within grouping variables, percentage of total sum within grouping variables, geometric mean, and harmonic mean.

You can change the order in which the subgroup statistics appear. The order in which the statistics appear in the Cell Statistics list is the order in which they are displayed in the output. Summary statistics are also displayed for each variable across all categories.

## OLAP Cubes Differences

Figure 18-4
*OLAP Cubes Differences dialog box*

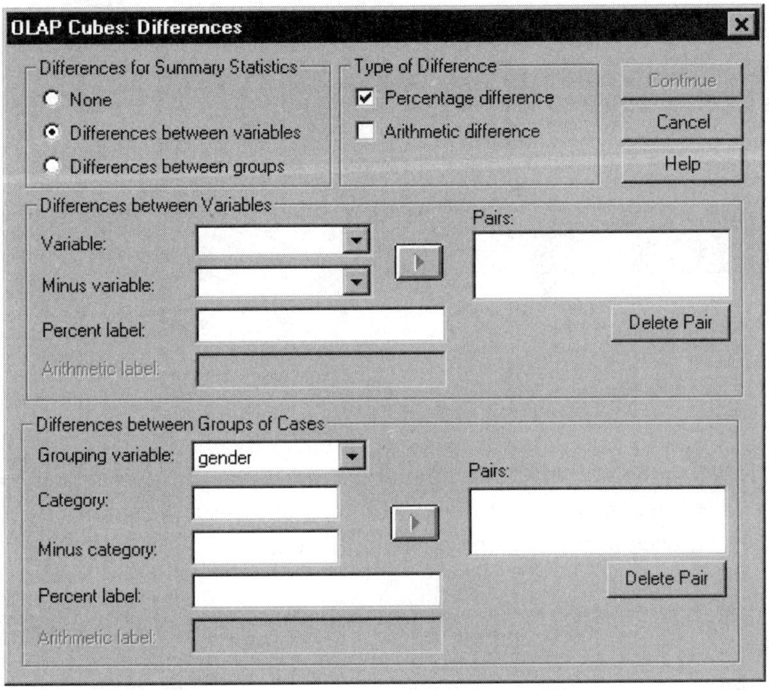


This dialog box allows you to calculate percentage and arithmetic differences between summary variables or between groups defined by a grouping variable. Differences are calculated for all measures selected in the OLAP Cubes Statistics dialog box.

**Differences between Variables.** Calculates differences between pairs of variables. You must select at least two summary variables in the main dialog box before you can specify differences between variables.

**Differences between Groups of Cases.** Calculates differences between pairs of groups defined by a grouping variable. You must select one or more grouping variables in the main dialog box before you can specify differences between groups.

## OLAP Cubes Title

Figure 18-5
*OLAP Cubes Title dialog box*

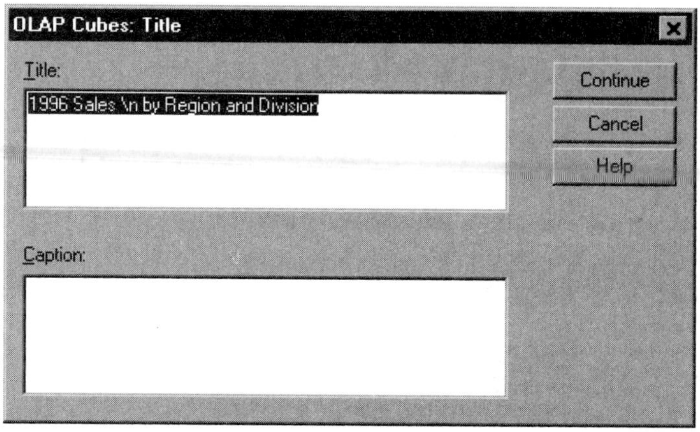


You can change the title of your output or add a caption that will appear below the output table. You can also control line wrapping of titles and captions by typing \n wherever you want to insert a line break in the text.

Chapter

# 19

# T Tests

The Compare Means submenu of the Statistics menu provides three types of *t* tests:

**Independent-samples t test (two-sample t test).** Compares the means of one variable for two groups of cases. Descriptive statistics for each group and Levene's test for equality of variances are provided, as well as both equal- and unequal-variance *t* values and a 95% confidence interval for the difference in means.

**Paired-samples t test (dependent t test).** Compares the means of two variables for a single group. This test is also for matched pairs or case-control study designs. The output includes descriptive statistics for the test variables, the correlation between them, descriptive statistics for the paired differences, the *t* test, and a 95% confidence interval.

**One-sample t test.** Compares the mean of one variable with a known or hypothesized value. Descriptive statistics for the test variables are displayed along with the *t* test. A 95% confidence interval for the difference between the mean of the test variable and the hypothesized test value is part of the default output.

## Independent-Samples T Test

The Independent-Samples T Test procedure compares means for two groups of cases. Ideally, for this test, the subjects should be randomly assigned to two groups, so that any difference in response is due to the treatment (or lack of treatment) and not to other factors. This is not the case if you compare average income for males and females. A person is not randomly assigned to be a male or female. In such situations, you should ensure that differences in other factors are not masking or enhancing a significant difference in means. Differences in average income may be influenced by factors such as education and not by sex alone.

**Example.** Patients with high blood pressure are randomly assigned to a placebo group and a treatment group. The placebo subjects receive an inactive pill and the treatment subjects receive a new drug that is expected to lower blood pressure. After treating the subjects for two months, the two-sample *t* test is used to compare the average blood pressures for the placebo group and the treatment group. Each patient is measured once and belongs to one group.

**Statistics.** For each variable: sample size, mean, standard deviation, and standard error of the mean. For the difference in means: mean, standard error, and confidence interval (you can specify the confidence level). Tests: Levene's test for equality of variances, and both pooled- and separate-variances *t* tests for equality of means.

**Data.** The values of the quantitative variable of interest are in a single column in the data file. The procedure uses a grouping variable with two values to separate the cases into two groups. The grouping variable can be numeric (values such as 1 and 2, or 6.25 and 12.5) or short string (such as *yes* and *no*). As an alternative, you can use a quantitative variable, such as *age,* to split the cases into two groups by specifying a cut point (cut point 21 splits *age* into an under-21 group and a 21-and-over group).

**Assumptions.** For the equal-variance *t* test, the observations should be independent, random samples from normal distributions with the same population variance. For the unequal-variance *t* test, the observations should be independent, random samples from normal distributions. The two-sample *t* test is fairly robust to departures from normality. When checking distributions graphically, look to see that they are symmetric and have no outliers.

## Sample Output

Figure 19-1
*Independent-Samples T Test output*

Group Statistics

| | | | N | Mean | Std. Deviation | Std. Error Mean |
|---|---|---|---|---|---|---|
| Blood pressure | Treatment | placebo | 10 | 142.50 | 17.04 | 5.39 |
| | | new_drug | 10 | 116.40 | 13.62 | 4.31 |

Independent Samples Test

| | | Levene's Test for Equality of Variances | | t-test for Equality of Means | | | | | | |
|---|---|---|---|---|---|---|---|---|---|---|
| | | | | | | | | | 95% Confidence Interval of the Mean | |
| | | F | Significance | t | df | Significance (2-tailed) | Mean Difference | Std. Error Difference | Lower | Upper |
| Blood pressure | Equal variances assumed | .134 | .719 | 3.783 | 18 | .001 | 26.10 | 6.90 | 11.61 | 40.59 |
| | Equal variances not assumed | | | 3.783 | 17.163 | .001 | 26.10 | 6.90 | 11.56 | 40.64 |

# To Obtain an Independent-Samples T Test

▶ From the menus choose:

Analyze
 Compare Means
  Independent-Samples T Test...

Figure 19-2
*Independent-Samples T Test dialog box*

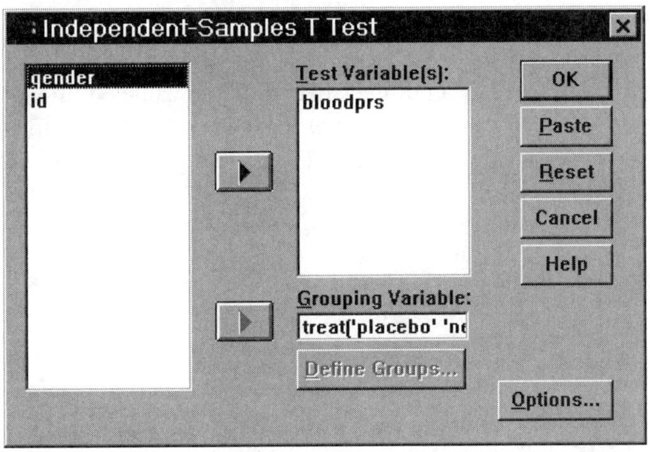


▶ Select one or more quantitative test variables. A separate *t* test is computed for each variable.

▶ Select a single grouping variable, and click Define Groups to specify two codes for the groups that you want to compare.

Optionally, you can click Options to control the treatment of missing data and the level of the confidence interval.

## Independent-Samples T Test Define Groups

Figure 19-3
*Define Groups dialog box for numeric variables*

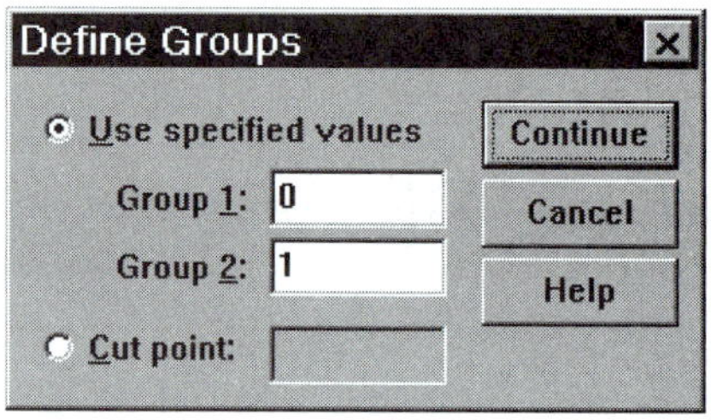


For numeric grouping variables, define the two groups for the *t* test by specifying two values or a cut point:

- **Use specified values.** Enter a value for Group 1 and another for Group 2. Cases with any other values are excluded from the analysis. Numbers need not be integers (for example, 6.25 and 12.5 are valid).
- **Cut point.** Alternatively, enter a number that splits the values of the grouping variable into two sets. All cases with values less than the cut point form one group, and cases with values greater than or equal to the cut point form the other group.

Figure 19-4
*Define Groups dialog box for string variables*

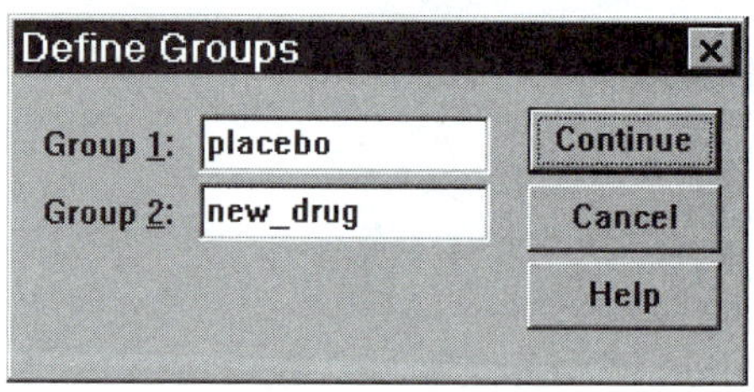


For short string grouping variables, enter a string for Group 1 and another for Group 2, such as *yes* and *no*. Cases with other strings are excluded from the analysis.

## *Independent-Samples T Test Options*

Figure 19-5
*Independent-Samples T Test Options dialog box*

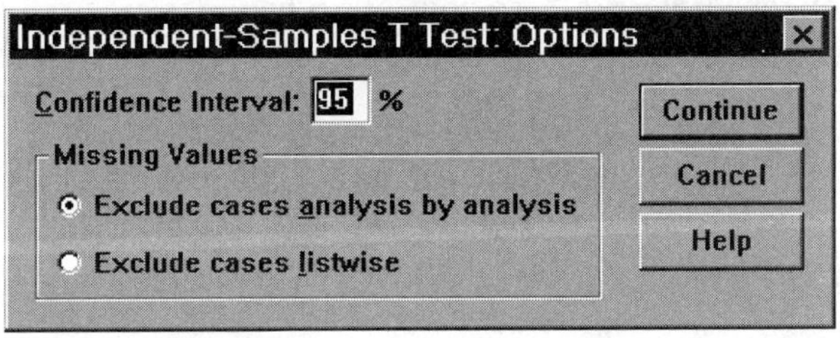


**Confidence Interval.** By default, a 95% confidence interval for the difference in means is displayed. Enter a value between 1 and 99 to request a different confidence level.

**Missing Values.** When you test several variables and data are missing for one or more variables, you can tell the procedure which cases to include (or exclude):

- **Exclude missing data analysis by analysis.** Each *t* test uses all cases that have valid data for the variables tested. Sample sizes may vary from test to test.
- **Exclude cases listwise.** Each *t* test uses only cases that have valid data for all variables used in the requested *t* tests. The sample size is constant across tests.

# *Paired-Samples T Test*

The Paired-Samples T Test procedure compares the means of two variables for a single group. It computes the differences between values of the two variables for each case and tests whether the average differs from 0.

**Example.** In a study on high blood pressure, all patients are measured at the beginning of the study, given a treatment, and measured again. Thus, each subject has two measures, often called *before* and *after* measures. An alternative design for which this test is used is a matched-pairs or case-control study. Here, each record in the data file contains the response for the patient and also for his or her matched control subject. In a blood pressure study, patients and controls might be matched by age (a 75-year-old patient with a 75-year-old control group member).

**Statistics.** For each variable: mean, sample size, standard deviation, and standard error of the mean. For each pair of variables: correlation, average difference in means, *t* test, and confidence interval for mean difference (you can specify the confidence level). Standard deviation and standard error of the mean difference.

**Data.** For each paired test, specify two quantitative variables (interval- or ratio-level of measurement). For a matched-pairs or case-control study, the response for each test subject and its matched control subject must be in the same case in the data file.

**Assumptions.** Observations for each pair should be made under the same conditions. The mean differences should be normally distributed. Variances of each variable can be equal or unequal.

## Sample Output

Figure 19-6
*Paired-Samples T Test output*

Paired Samples Statistics

| | | Mean | N | Std. Deviation | Std. Error Mean |
|---|---|---|---|---|---|
| Pair 1 | After treatment | 116.40 | 10 | 13.62 | 4.31 |
| | Before treatment | 142.50 | 10 | 17.04 | 5.39 |

Paired Samples Test

| | | Paired Differences | | | | | t | df | Significance (2-tailed) |
|---|---|---|---|---|---|---|---|---|---|
| | | Mean | Std. Deviation | Std. Error Mean | 95% Confidence Interval of the Difference | | | | |
| | | | | | Lower | Upper | | | |
| Pair 1 | After treatment - Before treatment | -26.10 | 19.59 | 6.19 | -40.11 | -12.09 | -4.214 | 9 | .002 |

# To Obtain a Paired-Samples T Test

▶ From the menus choose:

Analyze
  Compare Means
    Paired-Samples T Test...

Figure 19-7
*Paired-Samples T Test dialog box*

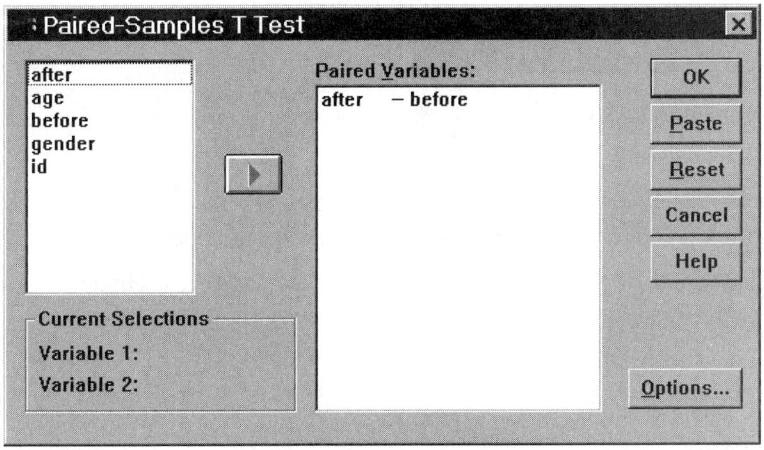


▶ Select a pair of variables, as follows:

- Click each of two variables. The first variable appears in the Current Selections group as *Variable 1*, and the second appears as *Variable 2*.
- After you have selected a pair of variables, click the arrow button to move the pair into the Paired Variables list. You may select more pairs of variables. To remove a pair of variables from the analysis, select a pair in the Paired Variables list and click the arrow button.

Optionally, you can click Options to control treatment of missing data and the level of the confidence interval.

## Paired-Samples T Test Options

Figure 19-8
*Paired-Samples T Test Options dialog box*

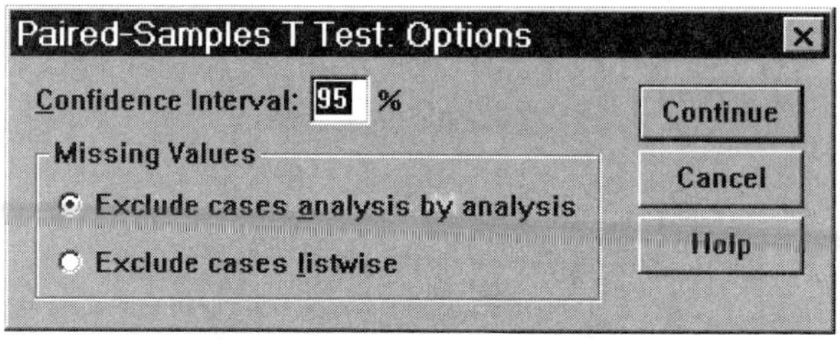


**Confidence Interval.** By default, a 95% confidence interval for the difference in means is displayed. Enter a value between 1 and 99 to request a different confidence level.

**Missing Values.** When you test several variables and data are missing for one or more variables, you can tell the procedure which cases to include (or exclude):

- **Exclude cases analysis by analysis.** Each *t* test uses all cases that have valid data for the pair of variables tested. Sample sizes may vary from test to test.
- **Exclude cases listwise.** Each *t* test uses only cases that have valid data for all pairs of variables tested. The sample size is constant across tests.

# One-Sample T Test

The One-Sample T Test procedure tests whether the mean of a single variable differs from a specified constant.

**Examples.** A researcher might want to test whether the average IQ score for a group of students differs from 100. Or, a cereal manufacturer can take a sample of boxes from the production line and check whether the mean weight of the samples differs from 1.3 pounds at the 95% confidence level.

**Statistics.** For each test variable: mean, standard deviation, and standard error of the mean. The average difference between each data value and the hypothesized test value, a *t* test that tests that this difference is 0, and a confidence interval for this difference (you can specify the confidence level).

**Data.** To test the values of a quantitative variable against a hypothesized test value, choose a quantitative variable and enter a hypothesized test value.

**Assumptions.** This test assumes that the data are normally distributed; however, this test is fairly robust to departures from normality.

# Sample Output

Figure 19-9
*One-Sample T Test output*

One-Sample Statistics

| | IQ |
|---|---|
| N | 15 |
| Mean | 109.33 |
| Std. Deviation | 12.03 |
| Std. Error Mean | 3.11 |

Rows and columns have been transposed.

One-Sample Test

| | Test Value = 100 | | | | | |
|---|---|---|---|---|---|---|
| | | | | | 95% Confidence Interval of the Difference | |
| | t | df | Significance (2-tailed) | Mean Difference | Lower | Upper |
| IQ | 3.005 | 14 | .009 | 9.33 | 2.67 | 15.99 |

## To Obtain a One-Sample T Test

▶ From the menus choose:

Analyze
  Compare Means
    One-Sample T Test...

Figure 19-10
*One-Sample T Test dialog box*

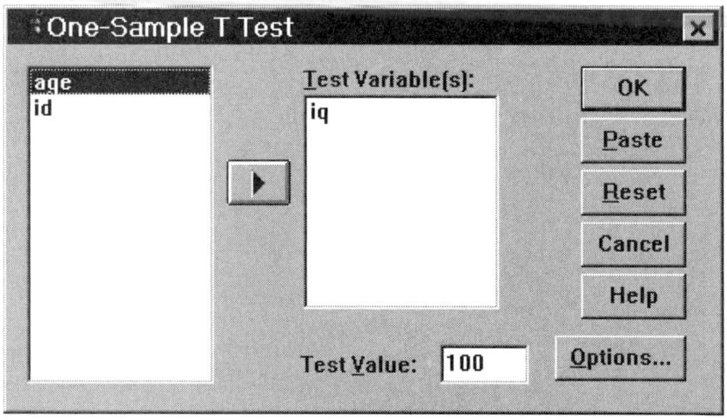


▶ Select one or more variables to be tested against the same hypothesized value.

▶ Enter a numeric test value against which each sample mean is compared.

Optionally, you can click Options to control the treatment of missing data and the level of the confidence interval.

### One-Sample T Test Options

Figure 19-11
*One-Sample T Test Options dialog box*

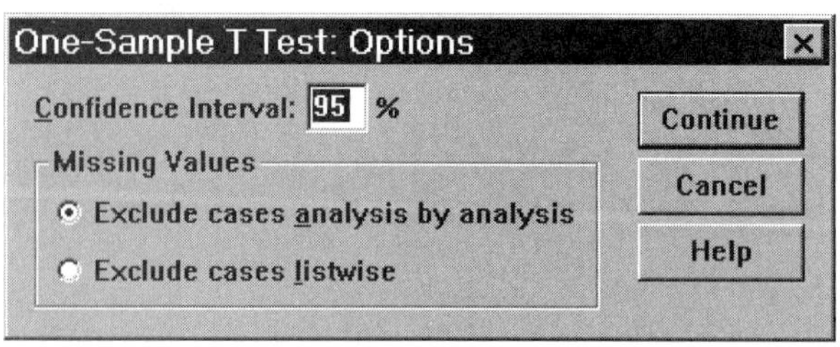

**Confidence Interval.** By default, a 95% confidence interval for the difference between the mean and the hypothesized test value is displayed. Enter a value between 1 and 99 to request a different confidence level.

**Missing Values.** When you test several variables and data are missing for one or more of these variables, you can tell the procedure which cases to include (or exclude).

- **Exclude cases analysis by analysis.** Each *t* test uses all cases that have valid data for the variable tested. Sample sizes may vary from test to test.
- **Exclude cases listwise.** Each *t* test uses only cases that have valid data for all variables used in any of the *t* tests requested. The sample size is constant across tests.

Chapter

# 20

# One-Way Analysis of Variance

The One-Way ANOVA procedure produces a one-way analysis of variance for a quantitative dependent variable by a single factor (independent) variable. Analysis of variance is used to test the hypothesis that several means are equal. This technique is an extension of the two-sample *t* test.

In addition to determining that differences exist among the means, you may want to know which means differ. There are two types of tests for comparing means: *a priori* contrasts and post hoc tests. Contrasts are tests set up *before* running the experiment, and post hoc tests are run *after* the experiment has been conducted. You can also test for trends across categories.

**Example.** Doughnuts absorb fat in various amounts when they are cooked. An experiment is set up involving three types of fat: peanut oil, corn oil, and lard. Peanut oil and corn oil are unsaturated fats, and lard is a saturated fat. Along with determining whether the amount of fat absorbed depends on the type of fat used, you could set up an *a priori* contrast to determine whether the amount of fat absorption differs for saturated and unsaturated fats.

**Statistics.** For each group: number of cases, mean, standard deviation, standard error of the mean, minimum, maximum, and 95% confidence interval for the mean. Levene's test for homogeneity of variance, analysis-of-variance table and robust tests of the equality of means for each dependent variable, user-specified *a priori* contrasts, and post hoc range tests and multiple comparisons: Bonferroni, Sidak, Tukey's honestly significant difference, Hochberg's GT2, Gabriel, Dunnett, Ryan-Einot-Gabriel-Welsch *F* test (R-E-G-W *F*), Ryan-Einot-Gabriel-Welsch range test (R-E-G-W *Q*), Tamhane's T2, Dunnett's T3, Games-Howell, Dunnett's *C*, Duncan's multiple range test, Student-Newman-Keuls (S-N-K), Tukey's *b*, Waller-Duncan, Scheffé, and least-significant difference.

**Data.** Factor variable values should be integers, and the dependent variable should be quantitative (interval level of measurement).

**Assumptions.** Each group is an independent random sample from a normal population. Analysis of variance is robust to departures from normality, although the data should be symmetric. The groups should come from populations with equal variances. To test this assumption, use Levene's homogeneity-of-variance test.

## Sample Output

Figure 20-1
*One-Way ANOVA output*

ANOVA

| | | Sum of Squares | df | Mean Square | F | Significance |
|---|---|---|---|---|---|---|
| Absorbed Grams of Fat | Between Groups | 1596.00 | 2 | 798.00 | 7.824 | .005 |
| | Within Groups | 1530.00 | 15 | 102.00 | | |
| | Total | 3126.00 | 17 | | | |

Descriptives

| | | | | | | | 95% Confidence Interval for Mean | | | |
|---|---|---|---|---|---|---|---|---|---|---|
| | | | N | Mean | Std. Deviation | Std. Error | Lower Bound | Upper Bound | Minimum | Maximum |
| Absorbed Grams of Fat | Type of Oil | Peanut Oil | 6 | 72.00 | 13.34 | 5.45 | 58.00 | 86.00 | 56 | 95 |
| | | Lard | 6 | 85.00 | 7.77 | 3.17 | 76.84 | 93.16 | 77 | 97 |
| | | Corn Oil | 6 | 62.00 | 8.22 | 3.36 | 53.37 | 70.63 | 49 | 70 |
| | | Total | 18 | 73.00 | 13.56 | 3.20 | 66.26 | 79.74 | 49 | 97 |

Contrast Coefficients

| | | Type of Oil | | |
|---|---|---|---|---|
| | | Peanut Oil | Lard | Corn Oil |
| Contrast | 1 | -.5 | 1 | -.5 |

Contrast Tests

| | | | | Value of Contrast | Std. Error | t | df | Significance (2-tailed) |
|---|---|---|---|---|---|---|---|---|
| Absorbed Grams of Fat | Assume equal variances | Contrast | 1 | 18.00 | 5.05 | 3.565 | 15 | .003 |
| | Does not assume equal variances | Contrast | 1 | 18.00 | 4.51 | 3.995 | 12.542 | .002 |

Test of Homogeneity of Variances

| | Levene Statistic | df1 | df2 | Significance |
|---|---|---|---|---|
| Absorbed Grams of Fat | .534 | 2 | 15 | .597 |

# To Obtain a One-Way Analysis of Variance

▶ From the menus choose:

Analyze
  Compare Means
    One-Way ANOVA...

Figure 20-2
*One-Way ANOVA dialog box*

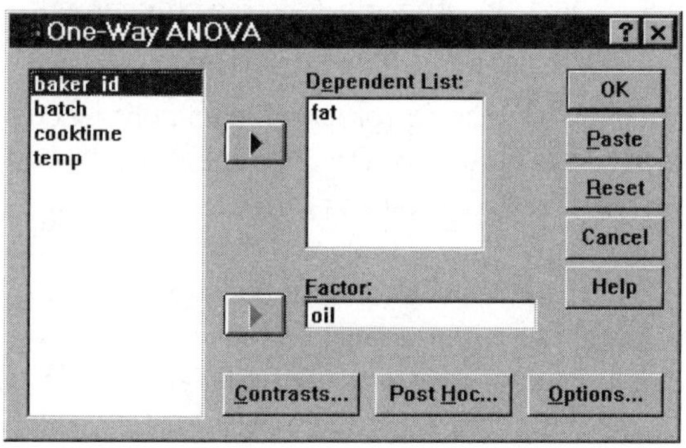


▶ Select one or more dependent variables.

▶ Select a single independent factor variable.

## One-Way ANOVA Contrasts

Figure 20-3
*One-Way ANOVA Contrasts dialog box*

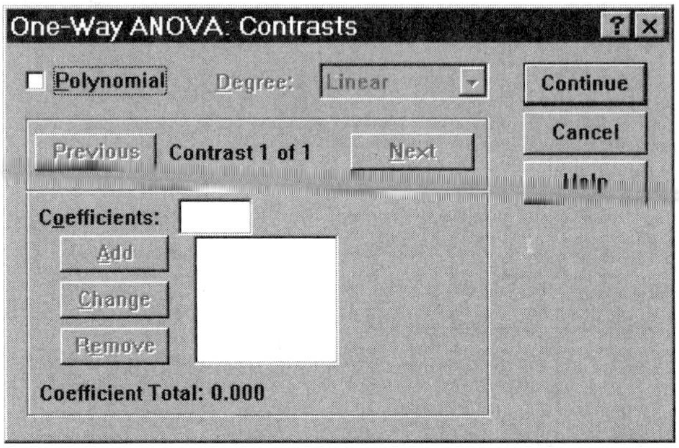


You can partition the between-groups sums of squares into trend components or specify *a priori* contrasts.

**Polynomial.** Partitions the between-groups sums of squares into trend components. You can test for a trend of the dependent variable across the ordered levels of the factor variable. For example, you could test for a linear trend (increasing or decreasing) in salary across the ordered levels of highest degree earned.

- **Degree.** You can choose a $1^{st}$, $2^{nd}$, $3^{rd}$, $4^{th}$, or $5^{th}$ degree polynomial.

**Coefficients.** User-specified *a priori* contrasts to be tested by the *t* statistic. Enter a coefficient for each group (category) of the factor variable and click Add after each entry. Each new value is added to the bottom of the coefficient list. To specify additional sets of contrasts, click Next. Use Next and Previous to move between sets of contrasts.

The order of the coefficients is important because it corresponds to the ascending order of the category values of the factor variable. The first coefficient on the list corresponds to the lowest group value of the factor variable, and the last coefficient corresponds to the highest value. For example, if there are six categories of the factor variable, the coefficients –1, 0, 0, 0, 0.5, and 0.5 contrast the first group with the fifth and sixth groups. For most applications, the coefficients should sum to 0. Sets that do not sum to 0 can also be used, but a warning message is displayed.

## *One-Way ANOVA Post Hoc Tests*

Figure 20-4
*One-Way ANOVA Post Hoc Multiple Comparisons dialog box*

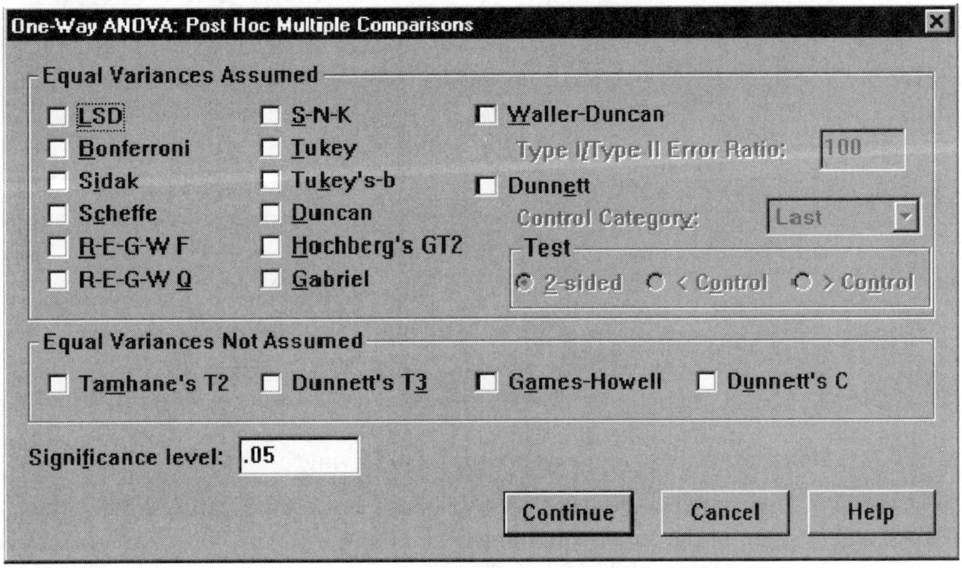


**Tests.** Once you have determined that differences exist among the means, post hoc range tests and pairwise multiple comparisons can determine which means differ. Range tests identify homogeneous subsets of means that are not different from each other. Pairwise multiple comparisons test the difference between each pair of means, and yield a matrix where asterisks indicate significantly different group means at an alpha level of 0.05.

Tukey's honestly significant difference test, Hochberg's GT2, Gabriel's test, and Scheffé's test are multiple comparison tests and range tests. Other available range tests are Tukey's *b*, S-N-K (Student-Newman-Keuls), Duncan, R-E-G-W *F* (Ryan-Einot-Gabriel-Welsch *F* test), R-E-G-W *Q* (Ryan-Einot-Gabriel-Welsch range test), and Waller-Duncan. Available multiple comparison tests are Bonferroni, Tukey's honestly significant difference test, Sidak, Gabriel, Hochberg, Dunnett, Scheffé, and LSD (least significant difference). Multiple comparison tests that do not assume equal variances are Tamhane's T2, Dunnett's T3, Games-Howell, and Dunnett's *C*.

*Note*: You may find it easier to interpret the output from post hoc tests if you deselect Hide Empty Rows and Columns in the Table Properties dialog box (in an activated pivot table, choose Table Properties from the Format menu).

## One-Way ANOVA Options

Figure 20-5
*One-Way ANOVA Options dialog box*

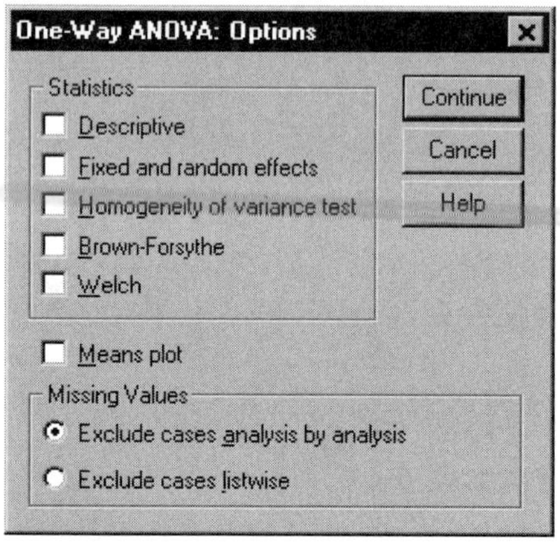


**Statistics.** Choose one or more of the following:

- **Descriptive.** Calculates the number of cases, mean, standard deviation, standard error of the mean, minimum, maximum, and 95% confidence intervals for each dependent variable for each group.
- **Fixed and random effects.** Displays the standard deviation, standard error, and 95% confidence interval for the fixed-effects model and the standard error, 95% confidence interval, and estimate of between-components variance for the random-effects model.
- **Homogeneity of variance tests.** Calculates the Levene statistic to test for the equality of group variances. This test is not dependent on the assumption of normality.
- **Brown-Forsythe.** Calculates the Brown-Forsythe statistic to test for the equality of group means. This statistic is preferable to the *F* statistic when the assumption of equal variances does not hold.
- **Welch.** Calculates the Welch statistic to test for the equality of group means. This statistic is preferable to the *F* statistic when the assumption of equal variances does not hold.

**Means Plot.** Displays a chart that plots the subgroup means (the means for each group defined by values of the factor variable).

**Missing Values.** Controls the treatment of missing values.

- **Exclude cases analysis by analysis.** A case with a missing value for either the dependent or the factor variable for a given analysis is not used in that analysis. Also, a case outside the range specified for the factor variable is not used.
- **Exclude cases listwise.** Cases with missing values for the factor variable or for any dependent variable included on the dependent list in the main dialog box are excluded from all analyses. If you have not specified multiple dependent variables, this has no effect.

Chapter

# 21

# GLM Univariate Analysis

The GLM Univariate procedure provides regression analysis and analysis of variance for one dependent variable by one or more factors and/or variables. The factor variables divide the population into groups. Using this General Linear Model procedure, you can test null hypotheses about the effects of other variables on the means of various groupings of a single dependent variable. You can investigate interactions between factors as well as the effects of individual factors, some of which may be random. In addition, the effects of covariates and covariate interactions with factors can be included. For regression analysis, the independent (predictor) variables are specified as covariates.

Both balanced and unbalanced models can be tested. A design is balanced if each cell in the model contains the same number of cases. In addition to testing hypotheses, GLM Univariate produces estimates of parameters.

Commonly used *a priori* contrasts are available to perform hypothesis testing. Additionally, after an overall *F* test has shown significance, you can use post hoc tests to evaluate differences among specific means. Estimated marginal means give estimates of predicted mean values for the cells in the model, and profile plots (interaction plots) of these means allow you to easily visualize some of the relationships.

Residuals, predicted values, Cook's distance, and leverage values can be saved as new variables in your data file for checking assumptions.

WLS Weight allows you to specify a variable used to give observations different weights for a weighted least-squares (WLS) analysis, perhaps to compensate for a different precision of measurement.

**Example.** Data are gathered for individual runners in the Chicago marathon for several years. The time in which each runner finishes is the dependent variable. Other factors include the weather (cold, pleasant, or hot), number of months of training, number of previous marathons, and gender. Age is considered a covariate. You might find that gender is a significant effect and that the interaction of gender with weather is significant.

**Methods.** Type I, Type II, Type III, and Type IV sums of squares can be used to evaluate different hypotheses. Type III is the default.

**Statistics.** Post hoc range tests and multiple comparisons: least significant difference, Bonferroni, Sidak, Scheffé, Ryan-Einot-Gabriel-Welsch multiple *F*, Ryan-Einot-Gabriel-Welsch multiple range, Student-Newman-Keuls, Tukey's honestly significant difference, Tukey's *b*, Duncan, Hochberg's GT2, Gabriel, Waller Duncan *t* test, Dunnett (one-sided and two-sided), Tamhane's T2, Dunnett's T3, Games-Howell, and Dunnett's *C*. Descriptive statistics: observed means, standard deviations, and counts for all of the dependent variables in all cells. The Levene test for homogeneity of variance.

**Plots.** Spread-versus-level, residual, profile (interaction).

**Data.** The dependent variable is quantitative. Factors are categorical. They can have numeric values or string values of up to eight characters. Covariates are quantitative variables that are related to the dependent variable.

**Assumptions.** The data are a random sample from a normal population; in the population, all cell variances are the same. Analysis of variance is robust to departures from normality, although the data should be symmetric. To check assumptions, you can use homogeneity of variances tests and spread-versus-level plots. You can also examine residuals and residual plots.

# Sample Output

Figure 21-1
*GLM Univariate output*

**Tests of Between-Subjects Effects**

Dependent Variable: SPVOL

| Source | Type III Sum of Squares | df | Mean Square | F | Sig. |
|---|---|---|---|---|---|
| Corrected Model | 22.520[1] | 11 | 2.047 | 12.376 | .000 |
| Intercept | 1016.981 | 1 | 1016.981 | 6147.938 | .000 |
| Flour | 8.691 | 3 | 2.897 | 17.513 | .000 |
| Fat | 10.118 | 2 | 5.059 | 30.583 | .000 |
| Surfactant | .997 | 2 | .499 | 3.014 | .082 |
| Fat*Surfactant | 5.639 | 4 | 1.410 | 8.522 | .001 |
| Error | 2.316 | 14 | .165 | | |
| Total | 1112.960 | 26 | | | |
| Corrected Total | 24.835 | 25 | | | |

1. R Squared = .907 (Adjusted R Squared = .833)

**fat * surfactant**

Dependent Variable: SPVOL

| fat | surfactant | Mean | Std. Error | 95% Confidence Interval | |
|---|---|---|---|---|---|
| | | | | Lower Bound | Upper Bound |
| 1 | 1 | 5.536 | .240 | 5.021 | 6.052 |
| | 2 | 5.891 | .239 | 5.378 | 6.404 |
| | 3 | 6.123 | .241 | 5.605 | 6.641 |
| 2 | 1 | 7.023 | .241 | 6.505 | 7.541 |
| | 2 | 6.708 | .301 | 6.064 | 7.353 |
| | 3 | 6.000 | .203 | 5.564 | 6.436 |
| 3 | 1 | 6.629 | .301 | 5.984 | 7.274 |
| | 2 | 7.200 | .203 | 6.764 | 7.636 |
| | 3 | 8.589 | .300 | 7.945 | 9.233 |

# To Obtain a GLM Univariate Analysis

▶ From the menus choose:

Analyze
  General Linear Model
    Univariate...

Figure 21-2
*Univariate dialog box*

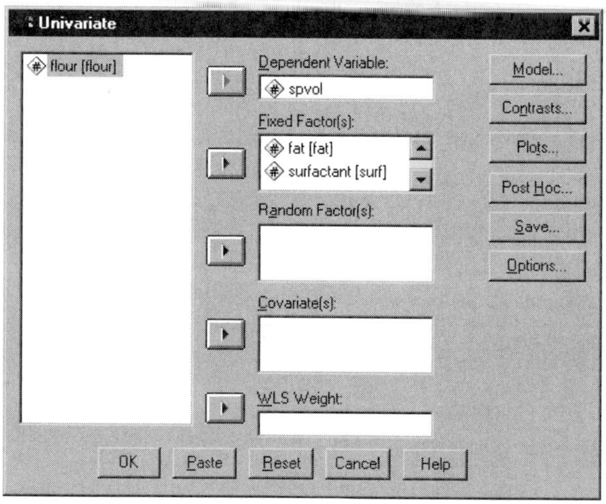


▶ Select a dependent variable.

Select variables for Fixed Factor(s), Random Factor(s), and Covariate(s), as appropriate for your data. For specifying a weight variable, use WLS Weight.

## GLM Univariate Model

Figure 21-3
*Univariate Model dialog box*

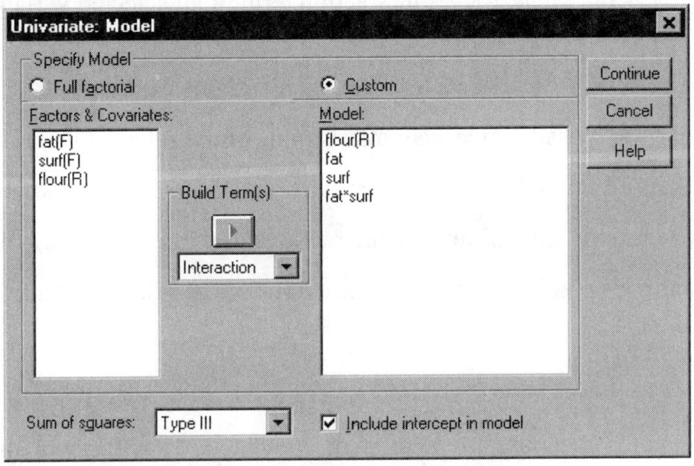


**Specify Model.** A full factorial model contains all factor main effects, all covariate main effects, and all factor-by-factor interactions. It does not contain covariate interactions. Select Custom to specify only a subset of interactions or to specify factor-by-covariate interactions. You must indicate all of the terms to be included in the model.

**Factors and Covariates.** The factors and covariates are listed with (F) for fixed factor and (C) for covariate. In a Univariate analysis, (R) indicates a random factor.

**Model.** The model depends on the nature of your data. After selecting Custom, you can select the main effects and interactions that are of interest in your analysis.

**Sum of squares.** The method of calculating the sums of squares. For balanced or unbalanced models with no missing cells, the Type III sum-of-squares method is most commonly used.

**Include intercept in model.** The intercept is usually included in the model. If you can assume that the data pass through the origin, you can exclude the intercept.

### Build Terms

For the selected factors and covariates:

**Interaction.** Creates the highest-level interaction term of all selected variables. This is the default.

**Main effects.** Creates a main-effects term for each variable selected.

**All 2-way.** Creates all possible two-way interactions of the selected variables.

**All 3-way.** Creates all possible three-way interactions of the selected variables.

**All 4-way.** Creates all possible four-way interactions of the selected variables.

**All 5-way.** Creates all possible five-way interactions of the selected variables.

### Sums of Squares

For the model, you can choose a type of sums of squares. Type III is the most commonly used and is the default.

**Type I.** This method is also known as the hierarchical decomposition of the sum-of-squares method. Each term is adjusted for only the term that precedes it in the model. Type I sums of squares are commonly used for:

- A balanced ANOVA model in which any main effects are specified before any first-order interaction effects, any first-order interaction effects are specified before any second-order interaction effects, and so on.
- A polynomial regression model in which any lower-order terms are specified before any higher-order terms.
- A purely nested model in which the first-specified effect is nested within the second-specified effect, the second-specified effect is nested within the third, and so on. (This form of nesting can be specified only by using syntax.)

**Type II.** This method calculates the sums of squares of an effect in the model adjusted for all other "appropriate" effects. An appropriate effect is one that corresponds to all effects that do not contain the effect being examined. The Type II sum-of-squares method is commonly used for:

- A balanced ANOVA model.
- Any model that has main factor effects only.

- Any regression model.
- A purely nested design. (This form of nesting can be specified by using syntax.)

**Type III.** The default. This method calculates the sums of squares of an effect in the design as the sums of squares adjusted for any other effects that do not contain it and orthogonal to any effects (if any) that contain it. The Type III sums of squares have one major advantage in that they are invariant with respect to the cell frequencies as long as the general form of estimability remains constant. Hence, this type of sums of squares is often considered useful for an unbalanced model with no missing cells. In a factorial design with no missing cells, this method is equivalent to the Yates' weighted-squares-of-means technique. The Type III sum-of-squares method is commonly used for:

- Any models listed in Type I and Type II.
- Any balanced or unbalanced model with no empty cells.

**Type IV.** This method is designed for a situation in which there are missing cells. For any effect *F* in the design, if *F* is not contained in any other effect, the Type IV = Type III = Type II. When *F* is contained in other effects, Type IV distributes the contrasts being made among the parameters in *F* to all higher-level effects equitably. The Type IV sum-of-squares method is commonly used for:

- Any models listed in Type I and Type II.
- Any balanced model or unbalanced model with empty cells.

## GLM Univariate Contrasts

Figure 21-4
*Univariate Contrasts dialog box*

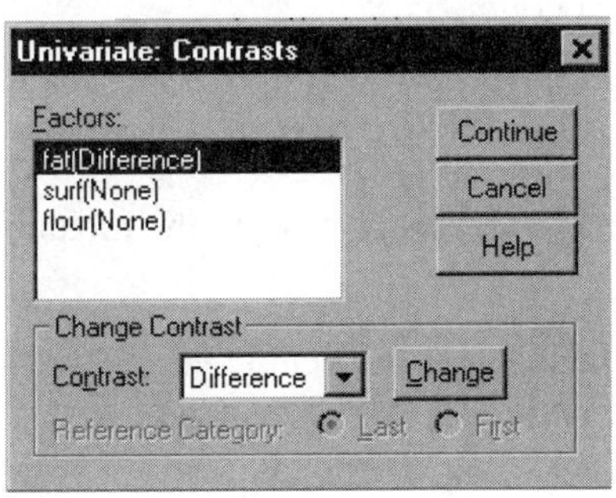

Contrasts are used to test for differences among the levels of a factor. You can specify a contrast for each factor in the model (in a repeated measures model, for each between-subjects factor). Contrasts represent linear combinations of the parameters.

Hypothesis testing is based on the null hypothesis **LB**=0, where **L** is the contrast coefficients matrix and **B** is the parameter vector. When a contrast is specified, SPSS creates an **L** matrix in which the columns corresponding to the factor match the contrast. The remaining columns are adjusted so that the **L** matrix is estimable.

The output includes an *F* statistic for each set of contrasts. Also displayed for the contrast differences are Bonferroni-type simultaneous confidence intervals based on Student's *t* distribution.

### Available Contrasts

Available contrasts are deviation, simple, difference, Helmert, repeated, and polynomial. For deviation contrasts and simple contrasts, you can choose whether the reference category is the last or first category.

### Contrast Types

**Deviation.** Compares the mean of each level (except a reference category) to the mean of all of the levels (grand mean). The levels of the factor can be in any order.

**Simple.** Compares the mean of each level to the mean of a specified level. This type of contrast is useful when there is a control group. You can choose the first or last category as the reference.

**Difference.** Compares the mean of each level (except the first) to the mean of previous levels. (Sometimes called reverse Helmert contrasts.)

**Helmert.** Compares the mean of each level of the factor (except the last) to the mean of subsequent levels.

**Repeated.** Compares the mean of each level (except the last) to the mean of the subsequent level.

**Polynomial.** Compares the linear effect, quadratic effect, cubic effect, and so on. The first degree of freedom contains the linear effect across all categories; the second degree of freedom, the quadratic effect; and so on. These contrasts are often used to estimate polynomial trends.

## GLM Univariate Profile Plots

Figure 21-5
*Univariate Profile Plots dialog box*

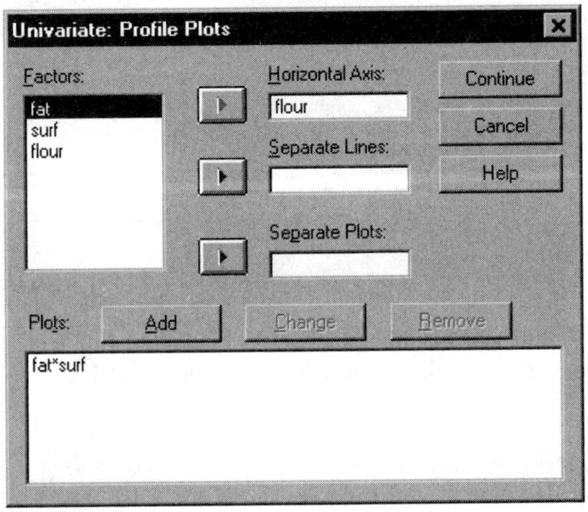


Profile plots (interaction plots) are useful for comparing marginal means in your model. A profile plot is a line plot in which each point indicates the estimated marginal mean of a dependent variable (adjusted for any covariates) at one level of a factor. The levels of a second factor can be used to make separate lines. Each level in a third factor can be used to create a separate plot. All fixed and random factors, if any, are available for plots. For multivariate analyses, profile plots are created for each dependent variable. In a repeated measures analysis, both between-subjects factors and within-subjects factors can be used in profile plots. GLM Multivariate and GLM Repeated Measures are available only if you have the Advanced Models option installed.

A profile plot of one factor shows whether the estimated marginal means are increasing or decreasing across levels. For two or more factors, parallel lines indicate that there is no interaction between factors, which means that you can investigate the levels of only one factor. Nonparallel lines indicate an interaction.

Figure 21-6
*Nonparallel plot (left) and parallel plot (right)*

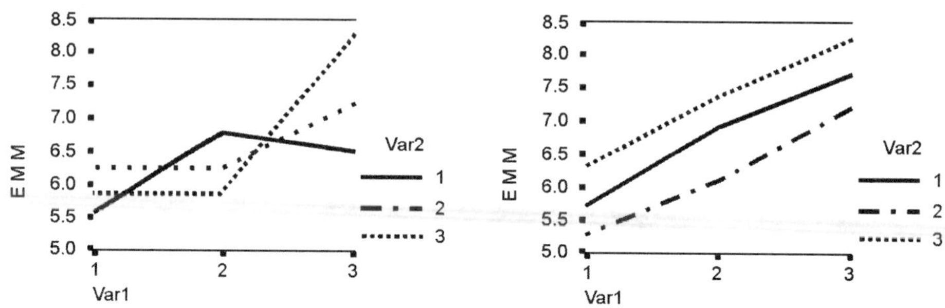


After a plot is specified by selecting factors for the horizontal axis and, optionally, factors for separate lines and separate plots, the plot must be added to the Plots list.

## GLM Univariate Post Hoc Multiple Comparisons for Observed Means

Figure 21-7
*Univariate Post Hoc Multiple Comparisons for Observed Means dialog box*

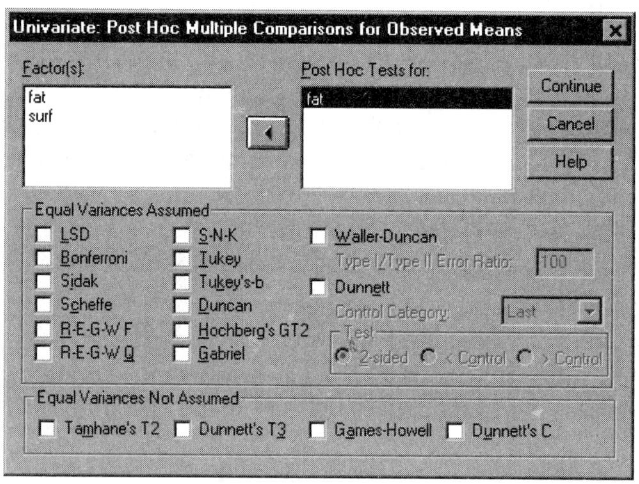


**Post hoc multiple comparison tests.** Once you have determined that differences exist among the means, post hoc range tests and pairwise multiple comparisons can determine which means differ. Comparisons are made on unadjusted values. These tests are used for fixed between-subjects factors only. In GLM Repeated Measures, these tests are not available if there are no between-subjects factors. For GLM Multivariate and GLM Repeated Measures, if there is more than one dependent variable, the post hoc tests are performed for each dependent variable separately. GLM Multivariate and GLM Repeated Measures are available only if you have the Advanced option installed.

The Bonferroni and Tukey's honestly significant difference tests are commonly used multiple comparison tests. The **Bonferroni test**, based on Student's *t* statistic, adjusts the observed significance level for the fact that multiple comparisons are made. **Sidak's *t* test** also adjusts the significance level and provides tighter bounds than the Bonferroni test. **Tukey's honestly significant difference test** uses the Studentized range statistic to make all pairwise comparisons between groups and sets the experimentwise error rate to the error rate for the collection for all pairwise comparisons. When testing a large number of pairs of means, Tukey's honestly significant difference test is more powerful than the Bonferroni test. For a small number of pairs, Bonferroni is more powerful.

**Hochberg's GT2** is similar to Tukey's honestly significant difference test, but the Studentized maximum modulus is used. Usually, Tukey's test is more powerful. **Gabriel's pairwise comparisons test** also uses the Studentized maximum modulus and is generally more powerful than Hochberg's GT2 when the cell sizes are unequal. Gabriel's test may become liberal when the cell sizes vary greatly.

**Dunnett's pairwise multiple comparison *t* test** compares a set of treatments against a single control mean. The last category is the default control category. Alternately, you can choose the first category. You can also choose a two-sided or one-sided test. To test that the mean at any level (except the control category) of the factor is not equal to that of the control category, use a two-sided test. To test whether the mean at any level of the factor is smaller than that of the control category, select < Control. Likewise, to test whether the mean at any level of the factor is larger than that of the control category, select > Control.

Ryan, Einot, Gabriel, and Welsch (R-E-G-W) developed two multiple step-down range tests. Multiple step-down procedures first test whether all means are equal. If all means are not equal, subsets of means are tested for equality. **R-E-G-W *F*** is based on an *F* test and **R-E-G-W *Q*** is based on the Studentized range. These tests are more powerful than Duncan's multiple range test and Student-Newman-Keuls (which are also multiple step-down procedures), but they are not recommended for unequal cell sizes.

When the variances are unequal, use **Tamhane's T2** (conservative pairwise comparisons test based on a *t* test), **Dunnett's T3** (pairwise comparison test based on the Studentized maximum modulus), **Games-Howell pairwise comparison test** (sometimes liberal), or **Dunnett's *C*** (pairwise comparison test based on the Studentized range).

**Duncan's multiple range test**, Student-Newman-Keuls (**S-N-K**), and **Tukey's *b*** are range tests that rank group means and compute a range value. These tests are not used as frequently as the tests previously discussed.

The **Waller-Duncan *t* test** uses a Bayesian approach. This range test uses the harmonic mean of the sample size when the sample sizes are unequal.

The significance level of the **Scheffé test** is designed to allow all possible linear combinations of group means to be tested, not just pairwise comparisons available in this feature. The result is that the Scheffé test is often more conservative than other tests, which means that a larger difference between means is required for significance.

The least significant difference (**LSD**) pairwise multiple comparison test is equivalent to multiple individual *t* tests between all pairs of groups. The disadvantage of this test is that no attempt is made to adjust the observed significance level for multiple comparisons.

**Tests displayed.** Pairwise comparisons are provided for LSD, Sidak, Bonferroni, Games and Howell, Tamhane's T2 and T3, Dunnett's *C*, and Dunnett's T3. Homogeneous subsets for range tests are provided for S-N-K, Tukey's *b*, Duncan, R-E-G-W *F*, R-E-G-W *Q*, and Waller. Tukey's honestly significant difference test, Hochberg's GT2, Gabriel's test, and Scheffé's test are both multiple comparison tests and range tests.

## GLM Univariate Save

Figure 21-8
*Univariate Save dialog box*

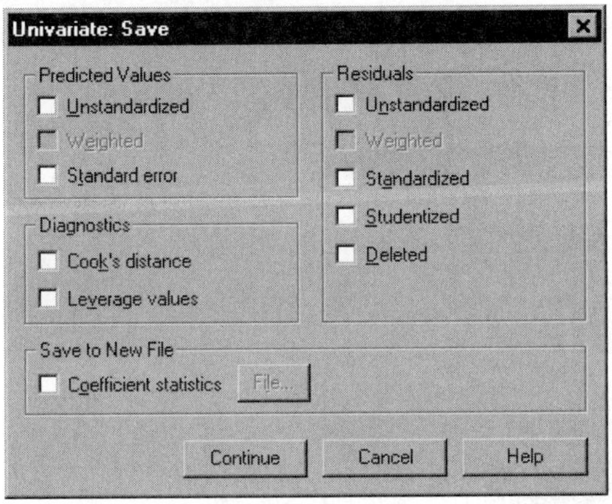


You can save values predicted by the model, residuals, and related measures as new variables in the Data Editor. Many of these variables can be used for examining assumptions about the data. To save the values for use in another SPSS session, you must save the current data file.

**Predicted Values.** The values that the model predicts for each case. Unstandardized predicted values and the standard errors of the predicted values are available. If a WLS variable was chosen, weighted unstandardized predicted values are available.

**Diagnostics.** Measures to identify cases with unusual combinations of values for the independent variables and cases that may have a large impact on the model. Available are Cook's distance and uncentered leverage values.

**Residuals.** An unstandardized residual is the actual value of the dependent variable minus the value predicted by the model. Standardized, Studentized, and deleted residuals are also available. If a WLS variable was chosen, weighted unstandardized residuals are available.

**Save to New File.** Writes an SPSS data file containing a variance-covariance matrix of the parameter estimates in the model. Also, for each dependent variable, there will be a row of parameter estimates, a row of significance values for the *t* statistics corresponding to the parameter estimates, and a row of residual degrees of freedom.

For a multivariate model, there are similar rows for each dependent variable. You can use this matrix file in other procedures that read an SPSS matrix file.

## GLM Univariate Options

Figure 21-9
*Univariate Options dialog box*

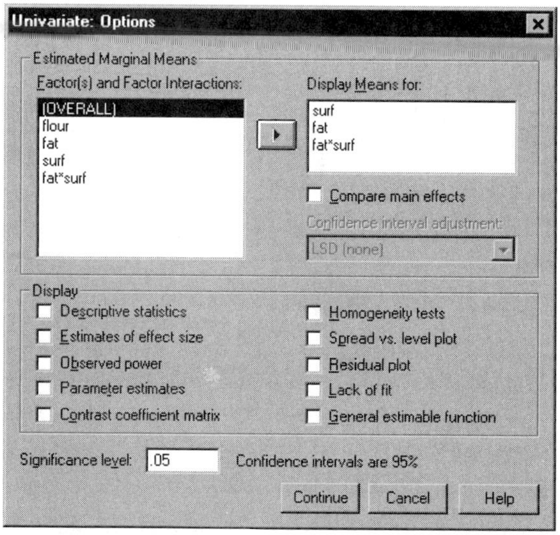


Optional statistics are available from this dialog box. Statistics are calculated using a fixed-effects model.

**Estimated Marginal Means.** Select the factors and interactions for which you want estimates of the population marginal means in the cells. These means are adjusted for the covariates, if any.

- **Compare main effects.** Provides uncorrected pairwise comparisons among estimated marginal means for any main effect in the model, for both between- and within-subjects factors. This item is available only if main effects are selected under the Display Means for list.
- **Confidence interval adjustment.** Select least significant difference (LSD), Bonferroni, or Sidak adjustment to the confidence intervals and significance. This item is available only if Compare main effects is selected.

**Display.** Select Descriptive statistics to produce observed means, standard deviations, and counts for all of the dependent variables in all cells. Estimates of effect size gives a partial eta-squared value for each effect and each parameter estimate. The eta-squared statistic describes the proportion of total variability attributable to a factor. Select Observed power to obtain the power of the test when the alternative hypothesis is set based on the observed value. Select Parameter estimates to produce the parameter estimates, standard errors, *t* tests, confidence intervals, and the observed power for each test. Select Contrast coefficient matrix to obtain the **L** matrix.

Homogeneity tests produces the Levene test of the homogeneity of variance for each dependent variable across all level combinations of the between-subjects factors, for between-subjects factors only. The spread-versus-level and residual plots options are useful for checking assumptions about the data. This item is disabled if there are no factors. Select Residual plots to produce an observed-by-predicted-by-standardized residuals plot for each dependent variable. These plots are useful for investigating the assumption of equal variance. Select Lack of fit to check if the relationship between the dependent variable and the independent variables can be adequately described by the model. General estimable function allows you to construct custom hypothesis tests based on the general estimable function. Rows in any contrast coefficient matrix are linear combinations of the general estimable function.

**Significance level.** You might want to adjust the significance level used in post hoc tests and the confidence level used for constructing confidence intervals. The specified value is also used to calculate the observed power for the test. When you specify a significance level, the associated level of the confidence intervals is displayed in the dialog box.

## UNIANOVA Command Additional Features

The SPSS command language also allows you to:

- Specify nested effects in the design (using the DESIGN subcommand).
- Specify tests of effects versus a linear combination of effects or a value (using the TEST subcommand).
- Specify multiple contrasts (using the CONTRAST subcommand).
- Include user-missing values (using the MISSING subcommand).
- Specify EPS criteria (using the CRITERIA subcommand).

- Construct a custom **L** matrix, **M** matrix, or **K** matrix (using the LMATRIX, MMATRIX, and KMATRIX subcommands).
- For deviation or simple contrasts, specify an intermediate reference category (using the CONTRAST subcommand).
- Specify metrics for polynomial contrasts (using the CONTRAST subcommand).
- Specify error terms for post hoc comparisons (using the POSTHOC subcommand).
- Compute estimated marginal means for any factor or factor interaction among the factors in the factor list (using the EMMEANS subcommand).
- Specify names for temporary variables (using the SAVE subcommand).
- Construct a correlation matrix data file (using the OUTFILE subcommand).
- Construct a matrix data file that contains statistics from the between-subjects ANOVA table (using the OUTFILE subcommand).
- Save the design matrix to a new data file (using the OUTFILE subcommand).

Chapter

22

# Bivariate Correlations

The Bivariate Correlations procedure computes Pearson's correlation coefficient, Spearman's rho, and Kendall's tau-*b* with their significance levels. Correlations measure how variables or rank orders are related. Before calculating a correlation coefficient, screen your data for outliers (which can cause misleading results) and evidence of a linear relationship. Pearson's correlation coefficient is a measure of linear association. Two variables can be perfectly related, but if the relationship is not linear, Pearson's correlation coefficient is not an appropriate statistic for measuring their association.

**Example.** Is the number of games won by a basketball team correlated with the average number of points scored per game? A scatterplot indicates that there is a linear relationship. Analyzing data from the 1994–1995 NBA season yields that Pearson's correlation coefficient (0.581) is significant at the 0.01 level. You might suspect that the more games won per season, the fewer points the opponents scored. These variables are negatively correlated (–0.401), and the correlation is significant at the 0.05 level.

**Statistics.** For each variable: number of cases with nonmissing values, mean, and standard deviation. For each pair of variables: Pearson's correlation coefficient, Spearman's rho, Kendall's tau-*b*, cross-product of deviations, and covariance.

**Data.** Use symmetric quantitative variables for Pearson's correlation coefficient and quantitative variables or variables with ordered categories for Spearman's rho and Kendall's tau-*b*.

**Assumptions.** Pearson's correlation coefficient assumes that each pair of variables is bivariate normal.

# Sample Output

Figure 22-1
*Bivariate Correlations output*

Correlations

| | | Number of Games Won | Scoring Points Per Game | Defense Points Per Game |
|---|---|---|---|---|
| Pearson Correlation | Number of Games Won | 1.000 | .581** | -.401* |
| | Scoring Points Per Game | .581** | 1.000 | .457* |
| | Defense Points Per Game | -.401* | .457* | 1.000 |
| Significance (2-tailed) | Number of Games Won | . | .001 | .038 |
| | Scoring Points Per Game | .001 | . | .017 |
| | Defense Points Per Game | .038 | .017 | . |
| N | Number of Games Won | 27 | 27 | 27 |
| | Scoring Points Per Game | 27 | 27 | 27 |
| | Defense Points Per Game | 27 | 27 | 27 |

**. Correlation at 0.01(2-tailed):...

*. Correlation at 0.05(2-tailed):...

## *To Obtain Bivariate Correlations*

▶ From the menus choose:

Analyze
 Correlate
  Bivariate...

Figure 22-2
*Bivariate Correlations dialog box*

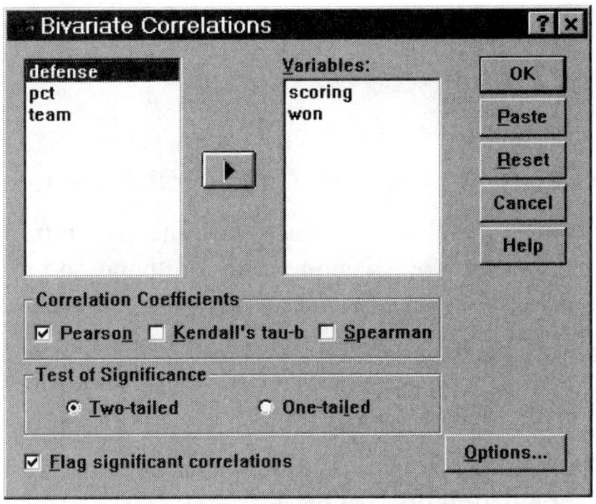


▶ Select two or more numeric variables.

The following options are also available:

- **Correlation Coefficients.** For quantitative, normally distributed variables, choose the Pearson correlation coefficient. If your data are not normally distributed or have ordered categories, choose Kendall's tau-b or Spearman, which measure the association between rank orders. Correlation coefficients range in value from –1 (a perfect negative relationship) and +1 (a perfect positive relationship). A value of 0 indicates no linear relationship. When interpreting your results, be careful not to draw any cause-and-effect conclusions due to a significant correlation.
- **Test of Significance.** You can select two-tailed or one-tailed probabilities. If the direction of association is known in advance, select One-tailed. Otherwise, select Two-tailed.
- **Flag significant correlations.** Correlation coefficients significant at the 0.05 level are identified with a single asterisk, and those significant at the 0.01 level are identified with two asterisks.

## Bivariate Correlations Options

Figure 22-3
*Bivariate Correlations Options dialog box*

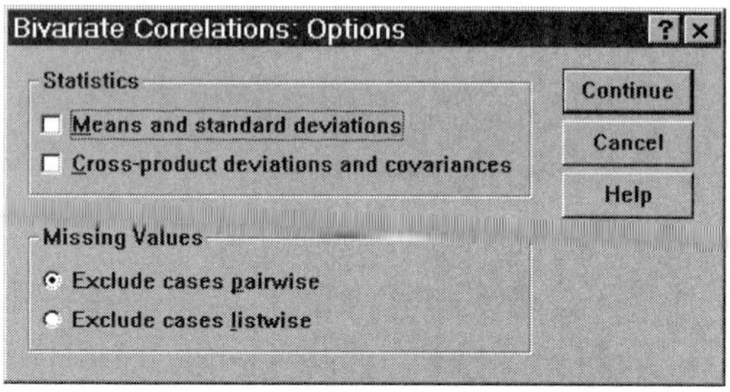


**Statistics.** For Pearson correlations, you can choose one or both of the following:

- **Means and standard deviations.** Displayed for each variable. The number of cases with nonmissing values is also shown. Missing values are handled on a variable-by-variable basis regardless of your missing values setting.
- **Cross-product deviations and covariances.** Displayed for each pair of variables. The cross-product of deviations is equal to the sum of the products of mean-corrected variables. This is the numerator of the Pearson correlation coefficient. The covariance is an unstandardized measure of the relationship between two variables, equal to the cross-product deviation divided by $N$–1.

**Missing Values.** You can choose one of the following:

- **Exclude cases pairwise.** Cases with missing values for one or both of a pair of variables for a correlation coefficient are excluded from the analysis. Since each coefficient is based on all cases that have valid codes on that particular pair of variables, the maximum information available is used in every calculation. This can result in a set of coefficients based on a varying number of cases.
- **Exclude cases listwise.** Cases with missing values for any variable are excluded from all correlations.

## CORRELATIONS and NONPAR CORR Command Additional Features

The SPSS command language also allows you to:

- Write a correlation matrix for Pearson correlations that can be used in place of raw data to obtain other analyses such as factor analysis (with the MATRIX subcommand).
- Obtain correlations of each variable on a list with each variable on a second list (using the keyword WITH on the VARIABLES subcommand).

See the *SPSS Syntax Reference Guide* for complete syntax information.

Chapter

# 23

# Partial Correlations

The Partial Correlations procedure computes partial correlation coefficients that describe the linear relationship between two variables while controlling for the effects of one or more additional variables. Correlations are measures of linear association. Two variables can be perfectly related, but if the relationship is not linear, a correlation coefficient is not an appropriate statistic for measuring their association.

**Example.** Is there a correlation between birth rate and death rate? An ordinary correlation reveals a significant correlation coefficient (0.367) at the 0.01 level. However, when you take into effect (or control for) an economic measure, birth rate and death rate are no longer significantly correlated. The correlation coefficient drops to 0.1003 (with a $p$ value of 0.304).

**Statistics.** For each variable: number of cases with nonmissing values, mean, and standard deviation. Partial and zero-order correlation matrices, with degrees of freedom and significance levels.

**Data.** Use symmetric, quantitative variables.

**Assumptions.** The Partial Correlations procedure assumes that each pair of variables is bivariate normal.

# Sample Output

Figure 23-1
*Partial Correlations output*

```
--- PARTIAL CORRELATION COEFFICIENTS ---

Zero Order Partials

          BIRTH_RT  DEATH_RT  LOG_GDP

BIRTH_RT    1.0000     .3670    -.7674
          (    0)  (  106)  (  106)
          P= .      P= .000   P= .000

DEATH_RT     .3670    1.0000    -.4015
          (  106)  (    0)  (  106)
          P= .000   P= .      P= .000

LOG_GDP     -.7674    -.4015    1.0000
          (  106)  (  106)  (    0)
          P= .000   P= .000   P= .

(Coefficient / (D.F.) / 2-tailed Significance)

" . " is printed if a coefficient cannot be computed


--- PARTIAL CORRELATION COEFFICIENTS ---

Controlling for..  LOG_GDP

          BIRTH_RT  DEATH_RT

BIRTH_RT    1.0000     .1003
          (    0)  (  105)
          P= .      P= .304

DEATH_RT     .1003    1.0000
          (  105)  (    0)
          P= .304   P= .

(Coefficient / (D.F.) / 2-tailed Significance)

" . " is printed if a coefficient cannot be computed
```

# *To Obtain Partial Correlations*

▶ From the menus choose:

Analyze
  Correlate
    Partial...

Figure 23-2
*Partial Correlations dialog box*

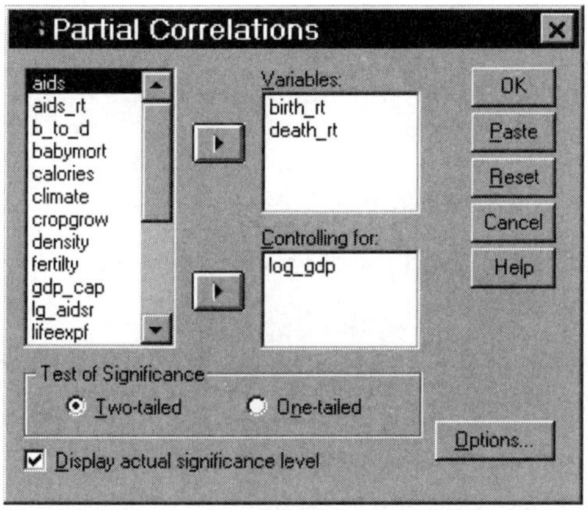


▶ Select two or more numeric variables for which partial correlations are to be computed.

▶ Select one or more numeric control variables.

The following options are also available:

- **Test of Significance.** You can select two-tailed or one-tailed probabilities. If the direction of association is known in advance, select One-tailed. Otherwise, select Two-tailed.
- **Display actual significance level.** By default, the probability and degrees of freedom are shown for each correlation coefficient. If you deselect this item, coefficients significant at the 0.05 level are identified with a single asterisk, coefficients significant at the 0.01 level are identified with a double asterisk, and degrees of freedom are suppressed. This setting affects both partial and zero-order correlation matrices.

## Partial Correlations Options

Figure 23-3
*Partial Correlations Options dialog box*

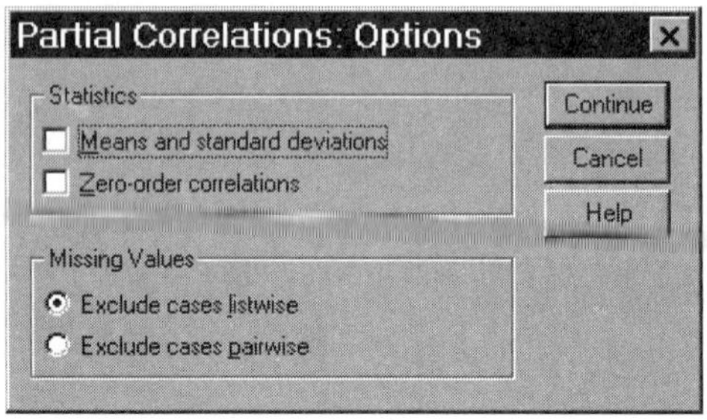


**Statistics.** You can choose one or both of the following:

- **Means and standard deviations.** Displayed for each variable. The number of cases with nonmissing values is also shown.
- **Zero-order correlations.** A matrix of simple correlations between all variables, including control variables, is displayed.

**Missing Values.** You can choose one of the following alternatives:

- **Exclude cases listwise.** Cases having missing values for any variable, including a control variable, are excluded from all computations.
- **Exclude cases pairwise.** For computation of the zero-order correlations on which the partial correlations are based, a case having missing values for both or one of a pair of variables is not used. Pairwise deletion uses as much of the data as possible. However, the number of cases may differ across coefficients. When pairwise deletion is in effect, the degrees of freedom for a particular partial coefficient are based on the smallest number of cases used in the calculation of any of the zero-order correlations.

Chapter

**24**

# Distances

This procedure calculates any of a wide variety of statistics measuring either similarities or dissimilarities (distances), either between pairs of variables or between pairs of cases. These similarity or distance measures can then be used with other procedures, such as factor analysis, cluster analysis, or multidimensional scaling, to help analyze complex data sets.

**Example.** Is it possible to measure similarities between pairs of automobiles based on certain characteristics, such as engine size, MPG, and horsepower? By computing similarities between autos, you can gain a sense of which autos are similar to each other and which are different from each other. For a more formal analysis, you might consider applying a hierarchical cluster analysis or multidimensional scaling to the similarities to explore the underlying structure.

**Statistics.** Dissimilarity (distance) measures for interval data are Euclidean distance, squared Euclidean distance, Chebychev, block, Minkowski, or customized; for count data, chi-square or phi-square; for binary data, Euclidean distance, squared Euclidean distance, size difference, pattern difference, variance, shape, or Lance and Williams. Similarity measures for interval data are Pearson correlation or cosine; for binary data, Russel and Rao, simple matching, Jaccard, dice, Rogers and Tanimoto, Sokal and Sneath 1, Sokal and Sneath 2, Sokal and Sneath 3, Kulczynski 1, Kulczynski 2, Sokal and Sneath 4, Hamann, Lambda, Anderberg's *D*, Yule's *Y*, Yule's *Q*, Ochiai, Sokal and Sneath 5, phi 4-point correlation, or dispersion.

# To Obtain a Distance Matrix

▶ From the menus choose:

Analyze
  Correlate
    Distances...

Figure 24-1
*Distances dialog box*

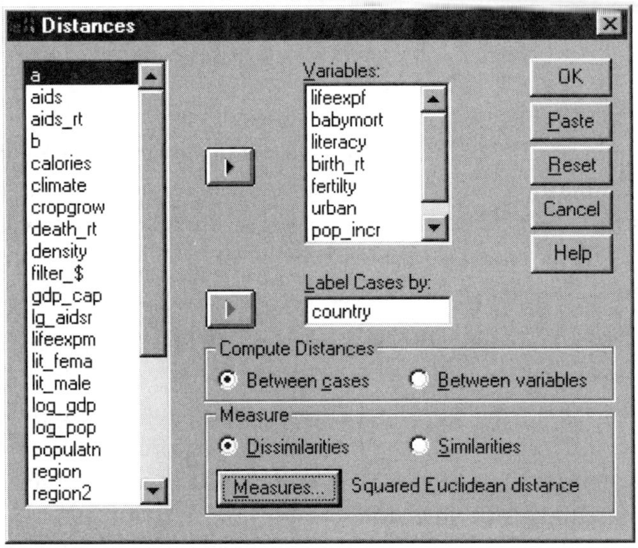


▶ Select at least one numeric variable to compute distances between cases, or select at least two numeric variables to compute distances between variables.

▶ Select an alternative in the Compute Distances group to calculate proximities either between cases or between variables.

# Distances Dissimilarity Measures

Figure 24-2
*Distances Dissimilarity Measures dialog box*

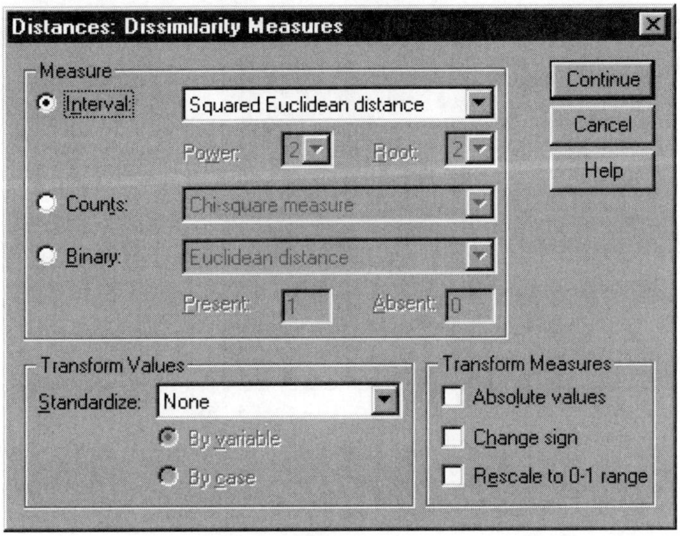


From the Measure group, select the alternative that corresponds to your type of data (interval, count, or binary); then, from the drop-down list, select one of the measures that corresponds to that type of data. Available measures, by data type, are:

- **Interval data.** Euclidean distance, squared Euclidean distance, Chebychev, block, Minkowski, or customized.
- **Count data.** Chi-square measure or phi-square measure.
- **Binary data**. Euclidean distance, squared Euclidean distance, size difference, pattern difference, variance, shape, or Lance and Williams. (Enter values for Present and Absent to specify which two values are meaningful; Distances will ignore all other values.)

The Transform Values group allows you to standardize data values for either cases or variables *before* computing proximities. These transformations are not applicable to binary data. Available standardization methods are *z* scores, range –1 to 1, range 0 to 1, maximum magnitude of 1, mean of 1, or standard deviation of 1.

The Transform Measures group allows you to transform the values generated by the distance measure. They are applied *after* the distance measure has been computed. Available options are absolute values, change sign, and rescale to 0–1 range.

## Distances Similarity Measures

Figure 24-3
*Distances Similarity Measures dialog box*

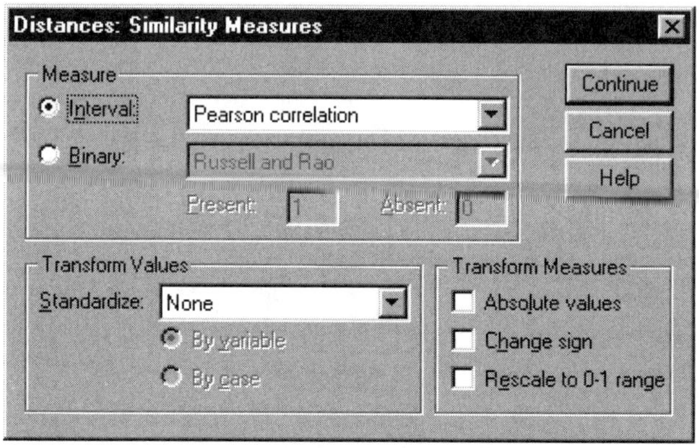


From the Measure group, select the alternative that corresponds to your type of data (interval or binary); then, from the drop-down list, select one of the measures that corresponds to that type of data. Available measures, by data type, are:

- **Interval data.** Pearson correlation or cosine.
- **Binary data**. Russell and Rao, simple matching, Jaccard, Dice, Rogers and Tanimoto, Sokal and Sneath 1, Sokal and Sneath 2, Sokal and Sneath 3, Kulczynski 1, Kulczynski 2, Sokal and Sneath 4, Hamann, Lambda, Anderberg's *D*, Yule's *Y*, Yule's *Q*, Ochiai, Sokal and Sneath 5, phi 4-point correlation, or dispersion. (Enter values for Present and Absent to specify which two values are meaningful; Distances will ignore all other values.)

The Transform Values group allows you to standardize data values for either cases or variables *before* computing proximities. These transformations are not applicable to binary data. Available standardization methods are $z$ scores, range –1 to 1, range 0 to 1, maximum magnitude of 1, mean of 1, and standard deviation of 1.

The Transform Measures group allows you to transform the values generated by the distance measure. They are applied *after* the distance measure has been computed. Available options are absolute values, change sign, and rescale to 0–1 range.

Chapter

# 25

# *Linear Regression*

Linear Regression estimates the coefficients of the linear equation, involving one or more independent variables, that best predict the value of the dependent variable. For example, you can try to predict a salesperson's total yearly sales (the dependent variable) from independent variables such as age, education, and years of experience.

**Example.** Is the number of games won by a basketball team in a season related to the average number of points the team scores per game? A scatterplot indicates that these variables are linearly related. The number of games won and the average number of points scored by the opponent are also linearly related. These variables have a negative relationship. As the number of games won increases, the average number of points scored by the opponent decreases. With linear regression, you can model the relationship of these variables. A good model can be used to predict how many games teams will win.

**Statistics.** For each variable: number of valid cases, mean, and standard deviation. For each model: regression coefficients, correlation matrix, part and partial correlations, multiple $R$, $R^2$, adjusted $R^2$, change in $R^2$, standard error of the estimate, analysis-of-variance table, predicted values, and residuals. Also, 95% confidence intervals for each regression coefficient, variance-covariance matrix, variance inflation factor, tolerance, Durbin-Watson test, distance measures (Mahalanobis, Cook, and leverage values), DfBeta, DfFit, prediction intervals, and casewise diagnostics. Plots: scatterplots, partial plots, histograms, and normal probability plots.

**Data.** The dependent and independent variables should be quantitative. Categorical variables, such as religion, major field of study, or region of residence, need to be recoded to binary (dummy) variables or other types of contrast variables.

**Assumptions.** For each value of the independent variable, the distribution of the dependent variable must be normal. The variance of the distribution of the dependent variable should be constant for all values of the independent variable. The relationship between the dependent variable and each independent variable should be linear, and all observations should be independent.

# Sample Output

Figure 25-1
*Linear Regression output*

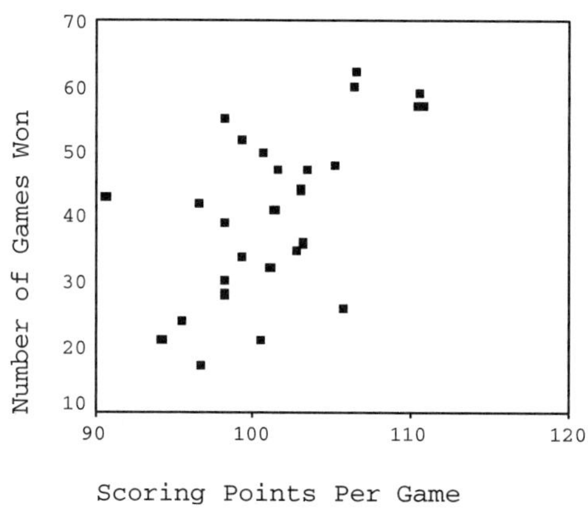


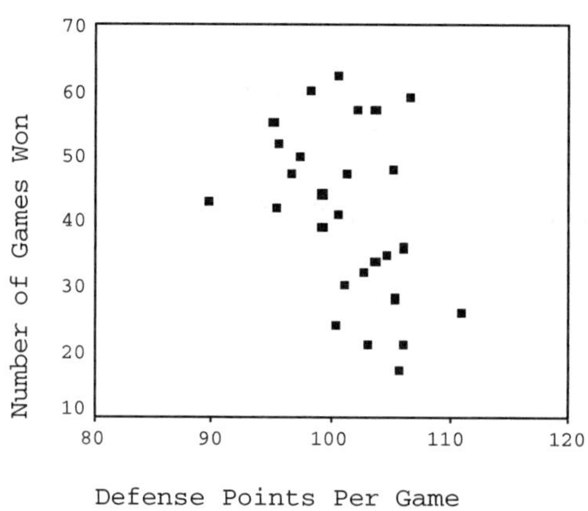

Model Summary[3,4]

| | | Variables | | R | R Square | Adjusted R Square | Std. Error of the Estimate |
|---|---|---|---|---|---|---|---|
| | | Entered | Removed | | | | |
| Model | 1 | Defense Points Per Game, Scoring Points Per Game[1,2] | . | .947 | .898 | .889 | 4.40 |

1. Indep. vars: (constant) Defense Points Per Game, Scoring Points Per Game...
2. All requested variables entered.
3. Dependent Variable: Number of Games Won
4. Method: Enter

ANOVA[2]

| | | | Sum of Squares | df | Mean Square | F | Significance |
|---|---|---|---|---|---|---|---|
| Model | 1 | Regression | 4080.533 | 2 | 2040.266 | 105.198 | .000[1] |
| | | Residual | 465.467 | 24 | 19.394 | | |
| | | Total | 4546.000 | 26 | | | |

1. Indep. vars: (constant) Defense Points Per Game, Scoring Points Per Game...
2. Dependent Variable: Number of Games Won

Coefficients[1]

| Model | | Unstandardized Coefficients | | Standardized Coefficients | t | Sig. |
|---|---|---|---|---|---|---|
| | | B | Std. Error | Beta | | |
| 1 | (Constant) | 28.121 | 21.404 | | 1.314 | .201 |
| | Scoring Points Per Game | 2.539 | .193 | .965 | 13.145 | .000 |
| | Defense Points Per Game | -2.412 | .211 | -.841 | -11.458 | .000 |

1. Dependent Variable: Number of Games Won

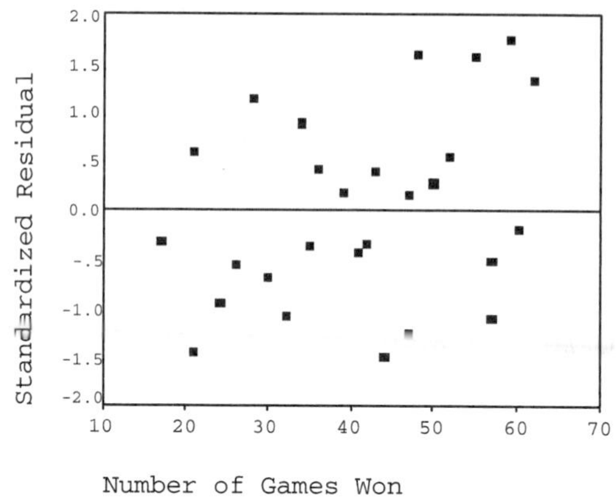


# To Obtain a Linear Regression Analysis

▶ From the menus choose:

Analyze
  Regression
    Linear...

Figure 25-2
*Linear Regression dialog box*

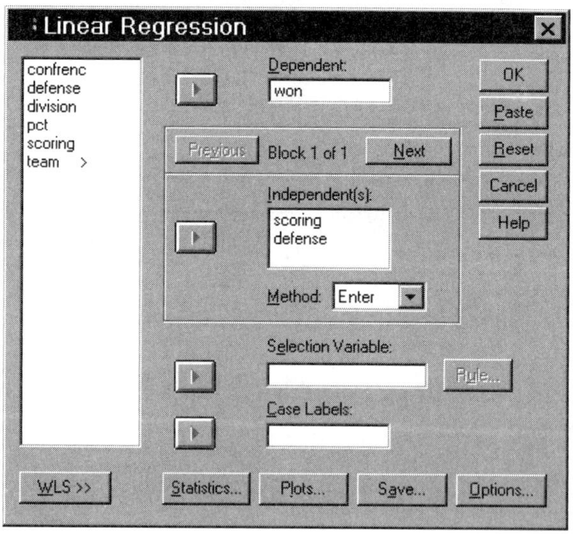

- In the Linear Regression dialog box, select a numeric dependent variable.

- Select one or more numeric independent variables.

Optionally, you can:

- Group independent variables into blocks and specify different entry methods for different subsets of variables.
- Choose a selection variable to limit the analysis to a subset of cases having a particular value(s) for this variable.
- Select a case identification variable for identifying points on plots.
- Click WLS for a weighted least-squares analysis and move a numeric weighting variable into the WLS Weight box.

## Linear Regression Variable Selection Methods

Method selection allows you to specify how independent variables are entered into the analysis. Using different methods, you can construct a variety of regression models from the same set of variables.

To enter the variables in the block in a single step, select Enter. To remove the variables in the block in a single step, select Remove. Forward variable selection enters the variables in the block one at a time based on entry criteria. Backward variable elimination enters all of the variables in the block in a single step and then removes them one at a time based on removal criteria. Stepwise variable entry and removal examines the variables in the block at each step for entry or removal. This is a forward stepwise procedure.

The significance values in your output are based on fitting a single model. Therefore, the significance values are generally invalid when a stepwise method (Stepwise, Forward, or Backward) is used.

All variables must pass the tolerance criterion to be entered in the equation, regardless of the entry method specified. The default tolerance level is 0.0001. Also, a variable is not entered if it would cause the tolerance of another variable already in the model to drop below the tolerance criterion.

All independent variables selected are added to a single regression model. However, you can specify different entry methods for different subsets of variables. For example, you can enter one block of variables into the regression model using stepwise selection and a second block using forward selection. To add a second block of variables to the regression model, click Next.

## Linear Regression Set Rule

Figure 25-3
*Linear Regression Set Rule dialog box*

Cases defined by the selection rule are included in the analysis. For example, if you select a variable, equals, and 5 for the value, then only cases for which the selected variable has a value equal to 5 are included in the analysis. A string value is also permitted.

## Linear Regression Plots

Figure 25-4
*Linear Regression Plots dialog box*

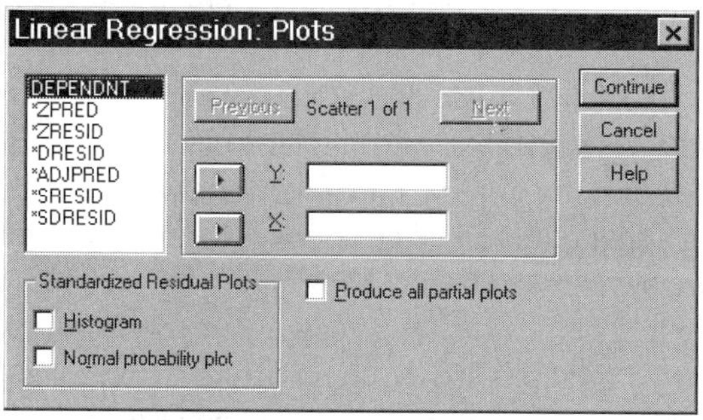


Plots can aid in the validation of the assumptions of normality, linearity, and equality of variances. Plots are also useful for detecting outliers, unusual observations, and influential cases. After saving them as new variables, predicted values, residuals, and other diagnostics are available in the Data Editor for constructing plots with the independent variables. The following plots are available:

**Scatterplots.** You can plot any two of the following: the dependent variable, standardized predicted values, standardized residuals, deleted residuals, adjusted predicted values, Studentized residuals, or Studentized deleted residuals. Plot the standardized residuals against the standardized predicted values to check for linearity and equality of variances.

**Produce all partial plots.** Displays scatterplots of residuals of each independent variable and the residuals of the dependent variable when both variables are regressed separately on the rest of the independent variables. At least two independent variables must be in the equation for a partial plot to be produced.

**Standardized Residual Plots.** You can obtain histograms of standardized residuals and normal probability plots comparing the distribution of standardized residuals to a normal distribution.

If any plots are requested, summary statistics are displayed for standardized predicted values and standardized residuals (*ZPRED and *ZRESID).

## *Linear Regression Save*

Figure 25-5
*Linear Regression Save dialog box*

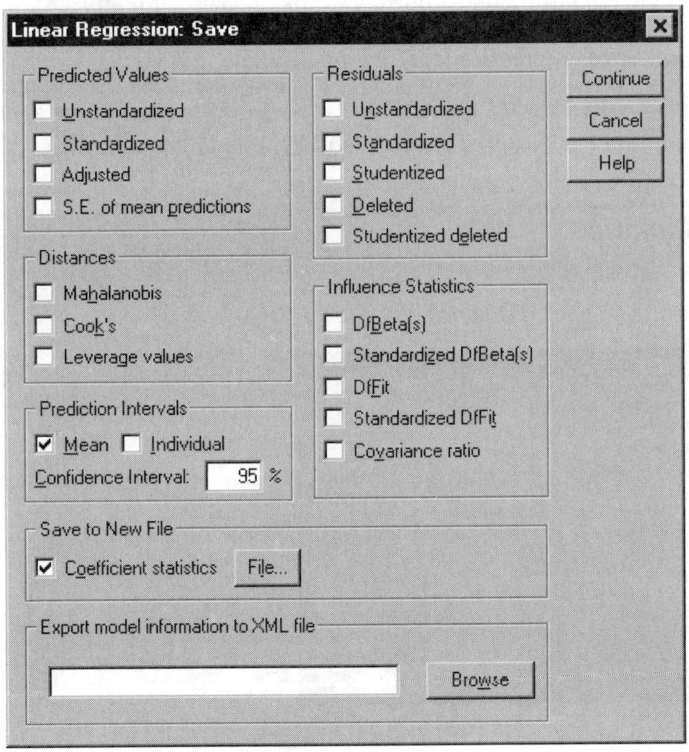

You can save predicted values, residuals, and other statistics useful for diagnostics. Each selection adds one or more new variables to your active data file.

**Predicted Values.** Values that the regression model predicts for each case.

**Distances.** Measures to identify cases with unusual combinations of values for the independent variables and cases that may have a large impact on the regression model.

**Prediction Intervals.** The upper and lower bounds for both mean and individual prediction intervals.

**Residuals.** The actual value of the dependent variable minus the value predicted by the regression equation.

**Influence Statistics.** The change in the regression coefficients (DfBeta(s)) and predicted values (DfFit) that results from the exclusion of a particular case. Standardized DfBetas and DfFit values are also available along with the covariance ratio, which is the ratio of the determinant of the covariance matrix with a particular case excluded to the determinant of the covariance matrix with all cases included.

**Save to New File.** Saves regression coefficients to a file that you specify.

**Export model information to XML file**. Exports model information to the specified file. *SmartScore* and future releases of *WhatIf?* will be able to use this file.

## Linear Regression Statistics

Figure 25-6
*Linear Regression Statistics dialog box*

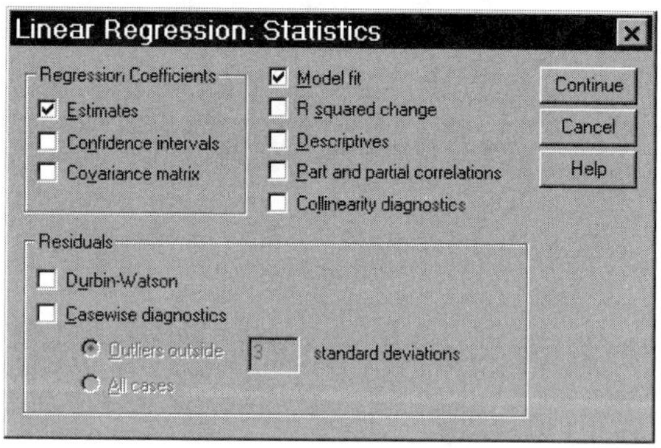

The following statistics are available:

**Regression Coefficients.** Estimates displays Regression coefficient *B*, standard error of *B*, standardized coefficient beta, *t* value for *B*, and two-tailed significance level of *t*. Confidence intervals displays 95% confidence intervals for each regression coefficient, or a covariance matrix. Covariance matrix displays a variance-covariance matrix of regression coefficients with covariances off the diagonal and variances on the diagonal. A correlation matrix is also displayed.

**Model fit.** The variables entered and removed from the model are listed, and the following goodness-of-fit statistics are displayed: multiple *R*, $R^2$ and adjusted $R^2$, standard error of the estimate, and an analysis-of-variance table.

**R squared change.** Displays changes in $R^2$ change, *F* change, and the significance of *F* change.

**Descriptives.** Provides the number of valid cases, the mean, and the standard deviation for each variable in the analysis. A correlation matrix with a one-tailed significance level and the number of cases for each correlation are also displayed.

**Part and partial correlations.** Displays zero-order, part, and partial correlations.

**Collinearity diagnostics.** Eigenvalues of the scaled and uncentered cross-products matrix, condition indices, and variance-decomposition proportions are displayed along with variance inflation factors (VIF) and tolerances for individual variables.

**Residuals.** Displays the Durbin-Watson test for serial correlation of the residuals and casewise diagnostics for the cases meeting the selection criterion (outliers above *n* standard deviations).

## Linear Regression Options

Figure 25-7
*Linear Regression Options dialog box*

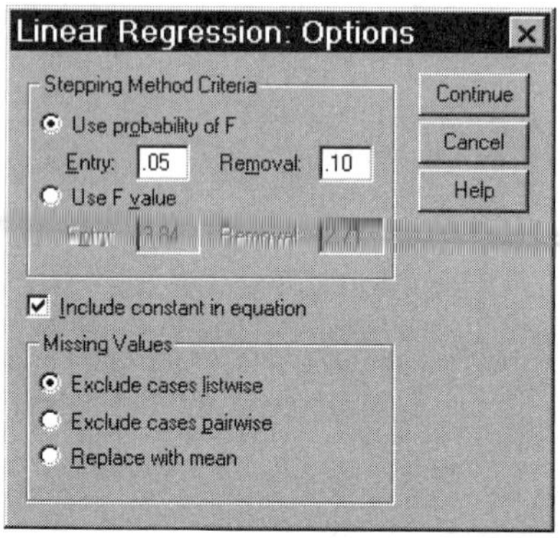


The following options are available:

**Stepping Method Criteria.** These options apply when either the forward, backward, or stepwise variable selection method has been specified. Variables can be entered or removed from the model depending on either the significance (probability) of the *F* value or the *F* value itself.

**Include constant in equation.** By default, the regression model includes a constant term. Deselecting this option forces regression through the origin, which is rarely done. Some results of regression through the origin are not comparable to results of regression that do include a constant. For example, $R^2$ cannot be interpreted in the usual way.

**Missing Values.** You can choose one of the following:

- **Exclude cases listwise.** Only cases with valid values for all variables are included in the analyses.
- **Exclude cases pairwise.** Cases with complete data for the pair of variables being correlated are used to compute the correlation coefficient on which the regression analysis is based. Degrees of freedom are based on the minimum pairwise *N*.
- **Replace with mean.** All cases are used for computations, with the mean of the variable substituted for missing observations.

Chapter

# 26

# Curve Estimation

The Curve Estimation procedure produces curve estimation regression statistics and related plots for 11 different curve estimation regression models. A separate model is produced for each dependent variable. You can also save predicted values, residuals, and prediction intervals as new variables.

**Example.** A fire insurance company conducts a study to relate the amount of damage in serious residential fires to the distance between the closest fire station and the residence. A scatterplot reveals that the relationship between fire damage and distance to the fire station is linear. You might fit a linear model to the data and check the validity of assumptions and the goodness of fit of the model.

**Statistics.** For each model: regression coefficients, multiple $R$, $R^2$, adjusted $R^2$, standard error of the estimate, analysis-of-variance table, predicted values, residuals, and prediction intervals. Models: linear, logarithmic, inverse, quadratic, cubic, power, compound, S-curve, logistic, growth, and exponential.

**Data.** The dependent and independent variables should be quantitative. If you select Time instead of a variable from the working data file as the independent variable, the Curve Estimation procedure generates a time variable where the length of time between cases is uniform. If Time is selected, the dependent variable should be a time-series measure. Time-series analysis requires a data file structure in which each case (row) represents a set of observations at a different time and the length of time between cases is uniform.

**Assumptions.** Screen your data graphically to determine how the independent and dependent variables are related (linearly, exponentially, etc.). The residuals of a good model should be randomly distributed and normal. If a linear model is used, the following assumptions should be met. For each value of the independent variable, the distribution of the dependent variable must be normal. The variance of the distribution of the dependent variable should be constant for all values of the independent variable. The relationship between the dependent variable and the independent variable should be linear, and all observations should be independent.

# Sample Output

Figure 26-1
*Curve Estimation output*

```
MODEL:  MOD_1.


Dependent variable.. DAMAGE           Method.. LINEAR

Listwise Deletion of Missing Data

Multiple R           .96098
R Square             .92348
Adjusted R Square    .91759
Standard Error      2.31635

            Analysis of Variance:

               DF   Sum of Squares      Mean Square

Regression      1        841.76636        841.76636
Residuals      13         69.75098          5.36546

F =      156.88616       Signif F =  .0000

-------------------- Variables in the Equation --------------------

Variable                   B          SE B        Beta          T  Sig T

DISTANCE            4.919331      .392748     .960978     12.525  .0000
(Constant)         10.277929     1.420278                  7.237  .0000

The following new variables are being created:

  Name         Label

  ERR_1        Error for DAMAGE with DISTANCE from CURVEFIT, MOD_1 LINEAR
```

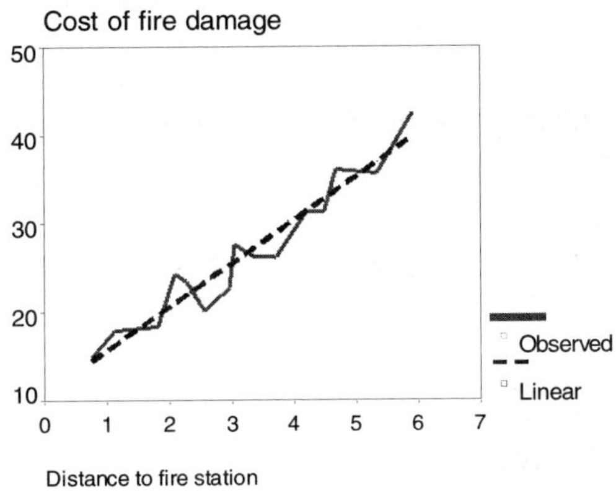


## To Obtain a Curve Estimation

▶ From the menus choose:

Analyze
  Regression
    Curve Estimation...

Figure 26-2
*Curve Estimation dialog box*

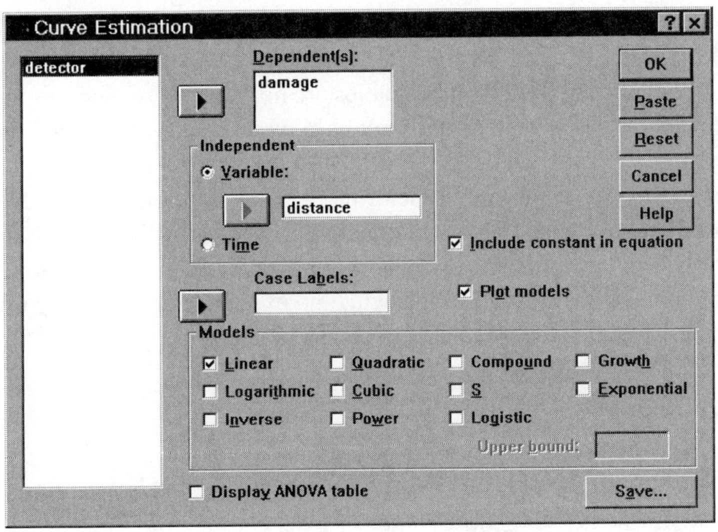

- ▶ Select one or more dependent variables. A separate model is produced for each dependent variable.

- ▶ Select an independent variable (either a variable in the working data file or Time).

Optionally, you can:

- ■ Select a variable for labeling cases in scatterplots. For each point in the scatterplot, you can use the Point Selection tool to display the value of the Case Label variable.
- ■ Click Save to save predicted values, residuals, and prediction intervals as new variables.

The following options are also available:

- ■ **Include constant in equation.** Estimates a constant term in the regression equation. The constant is included by default.
- ■ **Plot models.** Plots the values of the dependent variable and each selected model against the independent variable. A separate chart is produced for each dependent variable.
- ■ **Display ANOVA table.** Displays a summary analysis-of-variance table for each selected model.

## Curve Estimation Models

You can choose one or more curve estimation regression models. To determine which model to use, plot your data. If your variables appear to be related linearly, use a simple linear regression model. When your variables are not linearly related, try transforming your data. When a transformation does not help, you may need a more complicated model. View a scatterplot of your data; if the plot resembles a mathematical function you recognize, fit your data to that type of model. For example, if your data resemble an exponential function, use an exponential model. The following models are available in the Curve Estimation procedure: linear, logarithmic, inverse, quadratic, cubic, power, compound, S-curve, logistic, growth, and exponential. If you are unsure which model best fits your data, try several models and select among them.

## Curve Estimation Save

Figure 26-3
*Curve Estimation Save dialog box*

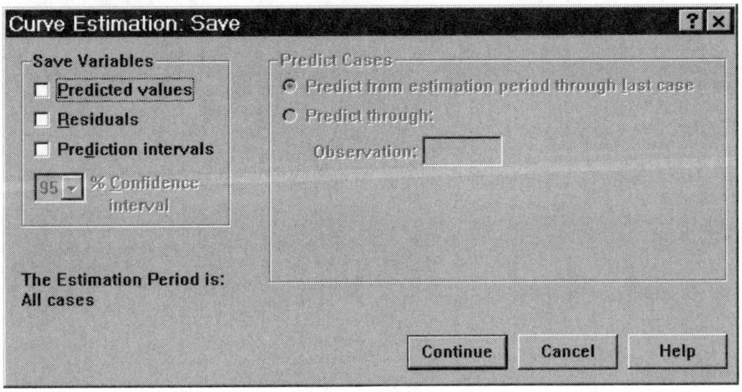


**Save Variables.** For each selected model you can save predicted values, residuals (observed value of the dependent variable minus the model predicted value), and prediction intervals (upper and lower bounds). The new variable names and descriptive labels are displayed in a table in the output window.

**Predict Cases.** If you select Time instead of a variable in the working data file as the independent variable, you can specify a forecast period beyond the end of the time series. You can choose one of the following alternatives:

- **Predict from estimation period through last case.** Predicts values for all cases in the file, based on the cases in the estimation period. The estimation period, displayed at the bottom of the dialog box, is defined with the Range subdialog box of the Select Cases option on the Data menu. If no estimation period has been defined, all cases are used to predict values.
- **Predict through.** Predicts values through the specified date, time, or observation number, based on the cases in the estimation period. This can be used to forecast values beyond the last case in the time series. The available text boxes for specifying the end of the prediction period are dependent on the currently defined date variables. If there are no defined date variables, you can specify the ending observation (case) number.

Use the Define Dates option on the Data menu to create date variables.

Chapter 27

# Discriminant Analysis

Discriminant analysis is useful for situations where you want to build a predictive model of group membership based on observed characteristics of each case. The procedure generates a discriminant function (or, for more than two groups, a set of discriminant functions) based on linear combinations of the predictor variables that provide the best discrimination between the groups. The functions are generated from a sample of cases for which group membership is known; the functions can then be applied to new cases with measurements for the predictor variables but unknown group membership.

*Note:* The grouping variable can have more than two values. The codes for the grouping variable must be integers, however, and you need to specify their minimum and maximum values. Cases with values outside of these bounds are excluded from the analysis.

**Example.** On average, people in temperate zone countries consume more calories per day than those in the tropics, and a greater proportion of the people in the temperate zones are city dwellers. A researcher wants to combine this information in a function to determine how well an individual can discriminate between the two groups of countries. The researcher thinks that population size and economic information may also be important. Discriminant analysis allows you to estimate coefficients of the linear discriminant function, which looks like the right-hand side of a multiple linear regression equation. That is, using coefficients *a*, *b*, *c*, and *d*, the function is:

D = a * climate + b * urban + c * population + d * gross domestic product per capita

If these variables are useful for discriminating between the two climate zones, the values of *D* will differ for the temperate and tropic countries. If you use a stepwise variable selection method, you may find that you do not need to include all four variables in the function.

**Statistics.** For each variable: means, standard deviations, univariate ANOVA. For each analysis: Box's *M*, within-groups correlation matrix, within-groups covariance matrix, separate-groups covariance matrix, total covariance matrix. For each canonical discriminant function: eigenvalue, percentage of variance, canonical correlation, Wilks' lambda, chi-square. For each step: prior probabilities, Fisher's function coefficients, unstandardized function coefficients, Wilks' lambda for each canonical function.

**Data.** The grouping variable must have a limited number of distinct categories, coded as integers. Independent variables that are nominal must be recoded to dummy or contrast variables.

**Assumptions.** Cases should be independent. Predictor variables should have a multivariate normal distribution, and within-group variance-covariance matrices should be equal across groups. Group membership is assumed to be mutually exclusive (that is, no case belongs to more than one group) and collectively exhaustive (that is, all cases are members of a group). The procedure is most effective when group membership is a truly categorical variable; if group membership is based on values of a continuous variable (for example, high IQ versus low IQ), you should consider using linear regression to take advantage of the richer information offered by the continuous variable itself.

## Sample Output

Figure 27-1
*Discriminant analysis output*

**Eigenvalues**

| Function | Eigenvalue | % of Variance | Cumulative % | Canonical Correlation |
|---|---|---|---|---|
| 1 | 1.002 | 100.0 | 100.0 | .707 |

**Wilks' Lambda**

| Test of Function(s) | Wilks' Lambda | Chi-square | df | Sig. |
|---|---|---|---|---|
| 1 | .499 | 31.934 | 4 | .000 |

**Structure Matrix**

| | Function |
|---|---|
| | 1 |
| CALORIES | .986 |
| LOG_GDP | .790 |
| URBAN | .488 |
| LOG_POP | .082 |

**Functions at Group Centroids**

| | Function |
|---|---|
| CLIMATE | 1 |
| tropical | -.869 |
| temperate | 1.107 |

# To Obtain a Discriminant Analysis

▶ From the menus choose:

Analyze
  Classify
    Discriminant...

Figure 27-2
*Discriminant Analysis dialog box*

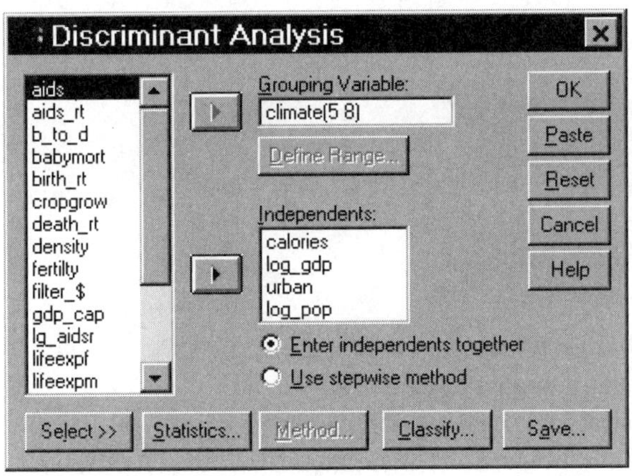


▶ Select an integer-valued grouping variable and click Define Range to specify the categories of interest.

▶ Select the independent, or predictor, variables. (If your grouping variable does not have integer values, Automatic Recode on the Transform menu will create one that does.)

Optionally, you can select cases with a selection variable.

## Discriminant Analysis Define Range

Figure 27-3
*Discriminant Analysis Define Range dialog box*

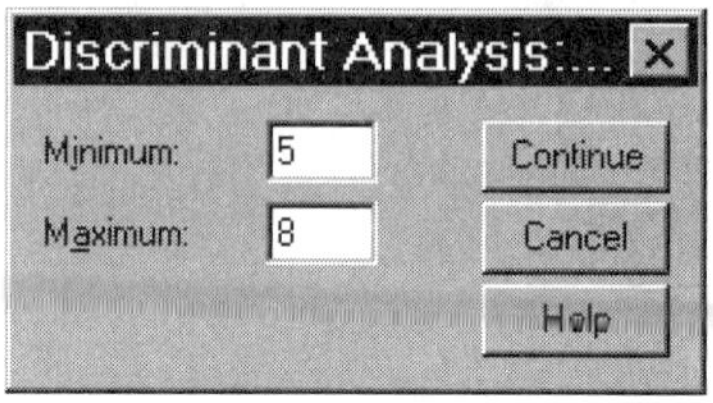


Specify the minimum and maximum value of the grouping value for the analysis. Cases with values outside of this range are not used in the discriminant analysis but are classified into one of the existing groups based on the results of the analysis.

The minimum and maximum must be integers.

## Discriminant Analysis Select Cases

Figure 27-4
*Discriminant Analysis Set Value dialog box*

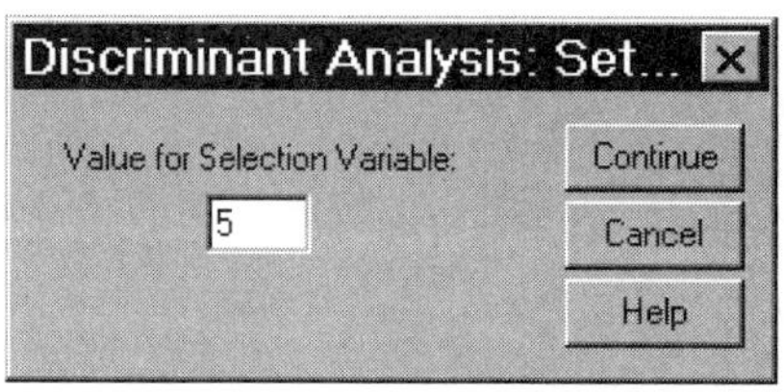


To select cases for your analysis, in the main dialog box click Select, choose a selection variable, and click Value to enter an integer as the selection value. Only cases with that value for the selection variable are used to derive the discriminant functions.

Statistics and classification results are generated for both selected and unselected cases. This provides a mechanism for classifying new cases based on previously existing data or for partitioning your data into training and testing subsets to perform validation on the model generated.

## Discriminant Analysis Statistics

Figure 27-5
*Discriminant Analysis Statistics dialog box*

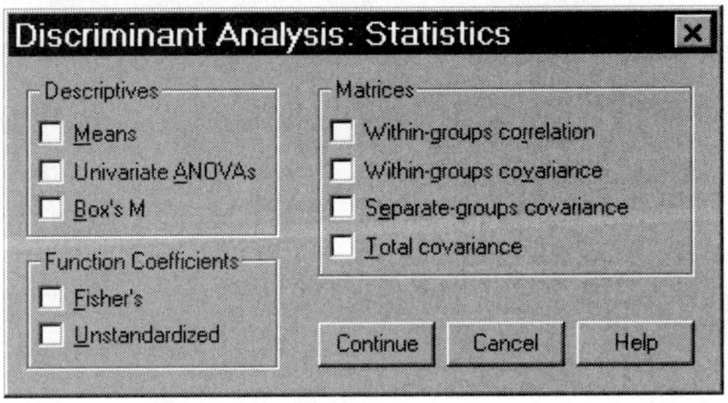


**Descriptives.** Available options are means (including standard deviations), univariate ANOVAs, and Box's *M*.

**Function Coefficients.** Available options are Fisher's classification coefficients and unstandardized coefficients.

**Matrices.** Available matrices of coefficients for independent variables are within-groups correlation matrix, within-groups covariance matrix, separate-groups covariance matrix, and total covariance matrix.

## Discriminant Analysis Stepwise Method

Figure 27-6
*Discriminant Analysis Stepwise Method dialog box*

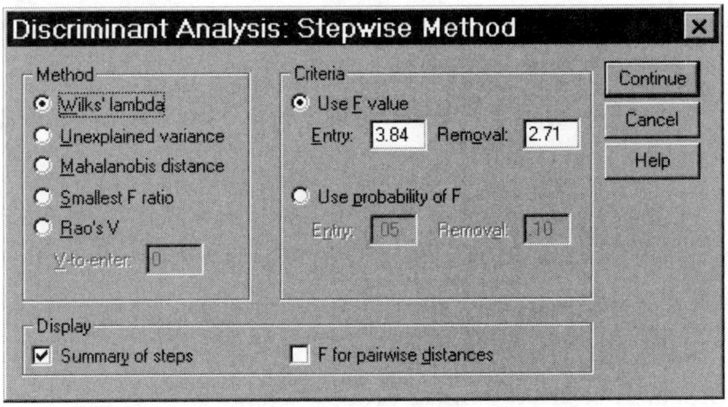

**Method.** Select the statistic to be used for entering or removing new variables. Available alternatives are Wilks' lambda, unexplained variance, Mahalanobis' distance, smallest *F* ratio, and Rao's *V*. With Rao's *V*, you can specify the minimum increase in *V* for a variable to enter.

**Criteria.** Available alternatives are Use F value and Use probability of F. Enter values for entering and removing variables.

**Display.** Summary of steps displays statistics for all variables after each step; F for pairwise distances displays a matrix of pairwise *F* ratios for each pair of groups.

## Discriminant Analysis Classification

Figure 27-7
*Discriminant Analysis Classification dialog box*

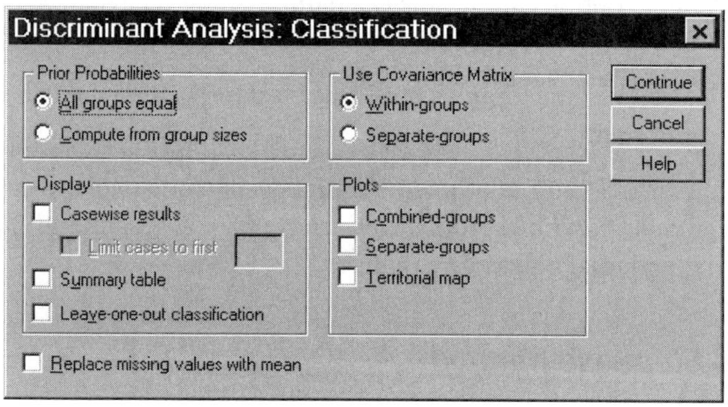


**Prior Probabilities.** These values are used in classification. You can specify equal prior probabilities for all groups, or you can let the observed group sizes in your sample determine the probabilities of group membership.

**Display.** Available display options are casewise results, summary table, and leave-one-out classification.

**Replace missing values with mean.** Select this option to substitute the mean of an independent variable for a missing value *during the classification phase only.*

**Use Covariance Matrix.** You can choose to classify cases using a within-groups covariance matrix or a separate-groups covariance matrix.

**Plots.** Available plot options are combined-groups, separate-groups, and territorial map.

## Discriminant Analysis Save

Figure 27-8
*Discriminant Analysis Save dialog box*

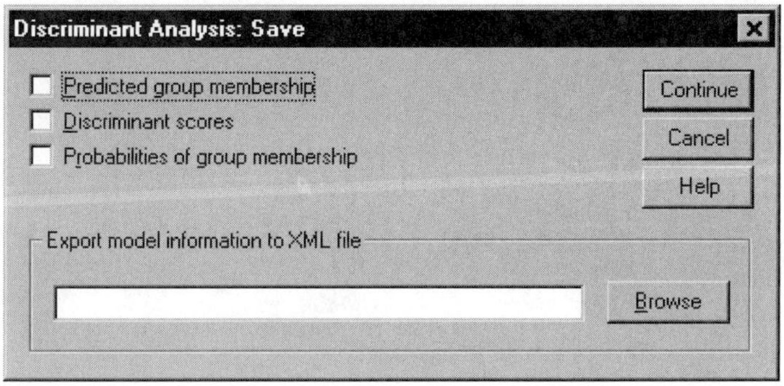


You can add new variables to your active data file. Available options are predicted group membership (a single variable), discriminant scores (one variable for each discriminant function in the solution), and probabilities of group membership given the discriminant scores (one variable for each group).

You can also export model information to an XML file. *SmartScore* and future releases of *WhatIf?* will be able to use this file.

Chapter

**28**

# Factor Analysis

Factor analysis attempts to identify underlying variables, or **factors**, that explain the pattern of correlations within a set of observed variables. Factor analysis is often used in data reduction to identify a small number of factors that explain most of the variance observed in a much larger number of manifest variables. Factor analysis can also be used to generate hypotheses regarding causal mechanisms or to screen variables for subsequent analysis (for example, to identify collinearity prior to performing a linear regression analysis).

The factor analysis procedure offers a high degree of flexibility:

- Seven methods of factor extraction are available.
- Five methods of rotation are available, including direct oblimin and promax for nonorthogonal rotations.
- Three methods of computing factor scores are available, and scores can be saved as variables for further analysis.

**Example.** What underlying attitudes lead people to respond to the questions on a political survey as they do? Examining the correlations among the survey items reveals that there is significant overlap among various subgroups of items—questions about taxes tend to correlate with each other, questions about military issues correlate with each other, and so on. With factor analysis, you can investigate the number of underlying factors and, in many cases, you can identify what the factors represent conceptually. Additionally, you can compute factor scores for each respondent, which can then be used in subsequent analyses. For example, you might build a logistic regression model to predict voting behavior based on factor scores.

**Statistics.** For each variable: number of valid cases, mean, and standard deviation. For each factor analysis: correlation matrix of variables, including significance levels, determinant, and inverse; reproduced correlation matrix, including anti-image; initial solution (communalities, eigenvalues, and percentage of variance explained); Kaiser-Meyer-Olkin measure of sampling adequacy and Bartlett's test of sphericity; unrotated solution, including factor loadings, communalities, and eigenvalues; rotated solution, including rotated pattern matrix and transformation matrix; for oblique rotations: rotated pattern and structure matrices; factor score coefficient matrix and factor covariance matrix. Plots: Scree plot of eigenvalues and loading plot of first two or three factors.

**Data.** The variables should be quantitative at the interval or ratio level. Categorical data (such as religion or country of origin) are not suitable for factor analysis. Data for which Pearson correlation coefficients can sensibly be calculated should be suitable for factor analysis.

**Assumptions.** The data should have a bivariate normal distribution for each pair of variables, and observations should be independent. The factor analysis model specifies that variables are determined by common factors (the factors estimated by the model) and unique factors (which do not overlap between observed variables); the computed estimates are based on the assumption that all unique factors are uncorrelated with each other and with the common factors.

# Sample Output

Figure 28-1
*Factor analysis output*

**Descriptive Statistics**

| | Mean | Std. Deviation | Analysis N |
|---|---|---|---|
| Average female life expectancy | 72.833 | 8.272 | 72 |
| Infant mortality (deaths per 1000 live births) | 35.132 | 32.222 | 72 |
| People who read (%) | 82.472 | 18.625 | 72 |
| Birth rate per 1000 people | 24.375 | 10.552 | 72 |
| Fertility: average number of kids | 3.205 | 1.593 | 72 |
| People living in cities (%) | 62.583 | 22.835 | 72 |
| Log (base 10) of GDP_CAP | 3.504 | .608 | 72 |
| Population increase (% per year)) | 1.697 | 1.156 | 72 |
| Birth to death ratio | 3.577 | 2.313 | 72 |
| Death rate per 1000 people | 8.038 | 3.174 | 72 |
| Log (base 10) of Population | 4.153 | .686 | 72 |

**Communalities**

| | Initial | Extraction |
|---|---|---|
| LIFEEXPF | 1.000 | .953 |
| BABYMORT | 1.000 | .949 |
| LITERACY | 1.000 | .825 |
| BIRTH_RT | 1.000 | .943 |
| FERTILTY | 1.000 | .875 |
| URBAN | 1.000 | .604 |
| LOG_GDP | 1.000 | .738 |
| POP_INCR | 1.000 | .945 |
| B_TO_D | 1.000 | .925 |
| DEATH_RT | 1.000 | .689 |
| LOG_POP | 1.000 | .292 |

Extraction Method: Principal Component Analysis.

**Total Variance Explained**

| | | Initial Eigenvalues | | | Extraction Sums of Squared Loadings | | | Rotation Sums of Squared Loadings | | |
|---|---|---|---|---|---|---|---|---|---|---|
| | | Total | % of Variance | Cumulative % | Total | % of Variance | Cumulative % | Total | % of Variance | Cumulative % |
| Component | 1 | 6.242 | 56.750 | 56.750 | 6.242 | 56.750 | 56.750 | 6.108 | 55.525 | 55.525 |
| | 2 | 2.495 | 22.685 | 79.435 | 2.495 | 22.685 | 79.435 | 2.630 | 23.910 | 79.435 |
| | 3 | .988 | 8.986 | 88.421 | | | | | | |
| | 4 | .591 | 5.372 | 93.793 | | | | | | |
| | 5 | [illegible] | [illegible] | [illegible] | | | | | | |
| | 6 | .172 | 1.561 | 97.496 | | | | | | |
| | 7 | .124 | 1.126 | 98.622 | | | | | | |
| | 8 | 7.0E-02 | .633 | 99.254 | | | | | | |
| | 9 | 4.5E-02 | .405 | 99.660 | | | | | | |
| | 10 | 2.4E-02 | .222 | 99.882 | | | | | | |
| | 11 | 1.3E-02 | .118 | 100.000 | | | | | | |

Extraction Method: Principal Component Analysis.

Scree Plot

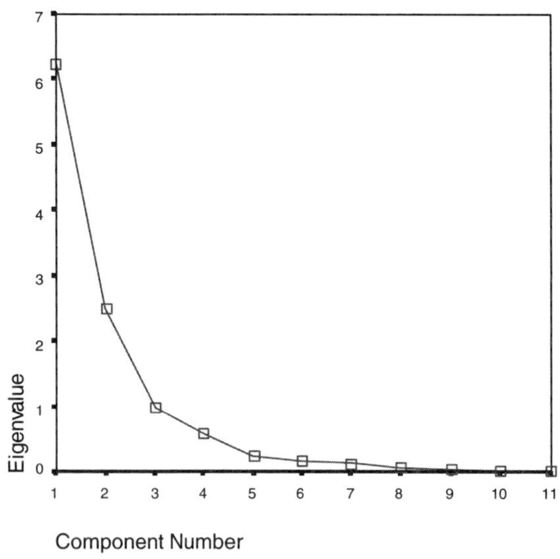

**Rotated Component Matrix**

| | Component | |
|---|---|---|
| | 1 | 2 |
| BIRTH_RT | .969 | |
| FERTILTY | .931 | |
| LITERACY | -.880 | .226 |
| LIFEEXPF | -.856 | .469 |
| BABYMORT | .853 | -.469 |
| POP_INCR | .847 | .476 |
| LOG_GDP | -.794 | .327 |
| URBAN | -.561 | .539 |
| DEATH_RT | | -.827 |
| B_TO_D | .614 | .741 |
| LOG_POP | | -.520 |

Extraction Method: Principal Component Analysis.
Rotation Method: Varimax with Kaiser Normalization.

**Component Transformation Matrix**

| | | 1 | 2 |
|---|---|---|---|
| Component | 1 | .982 | -.190 |
| | 2 | .190 | .982 |

Extraction Method: Principal Component Analysis.
Rotation Method: Varimax with Kaiser Normalization.

Component Plot in Rotated Space

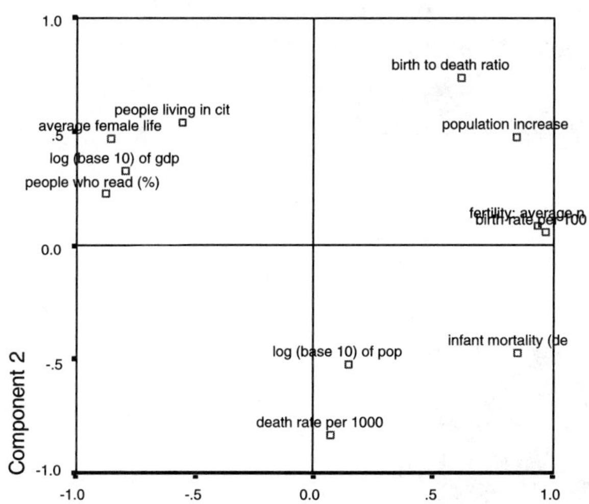


Component 1

# To Obtain a Factor Analysis

▶ From the menus choose:

Analyze
  Data Reduction
    Factor...

▶ Select the variables for the factor analysis.

Figure 28-2
*Factor Analysis dialog box*

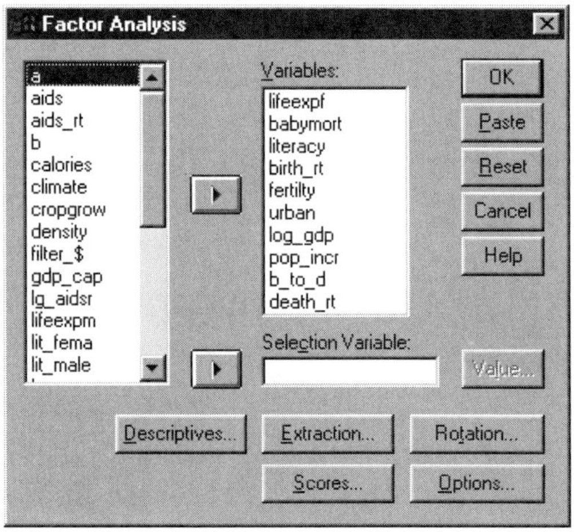


## Factor Analysis Select Cases

Figure 28-3
*Factor Analysis Set Value dialog box*

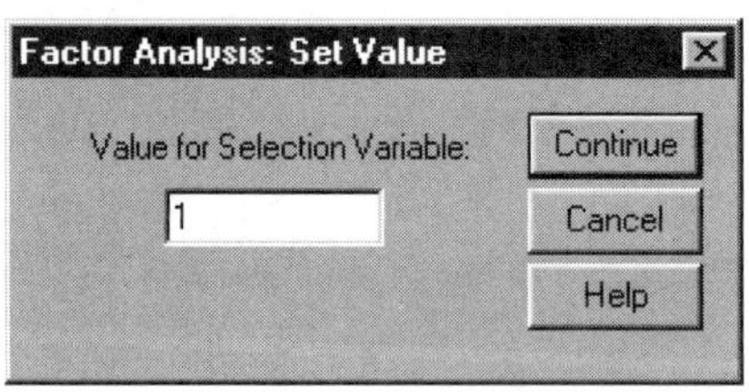

To select cases for your analysis, choose a selection variable and click Value to enter an integer as the selection value. Only cases with that value for the selection variable are used in the factor analysis.

## Factor Analysis Descriptives

Figure 28-4
*Factor Analysis Descriptives dialog box*

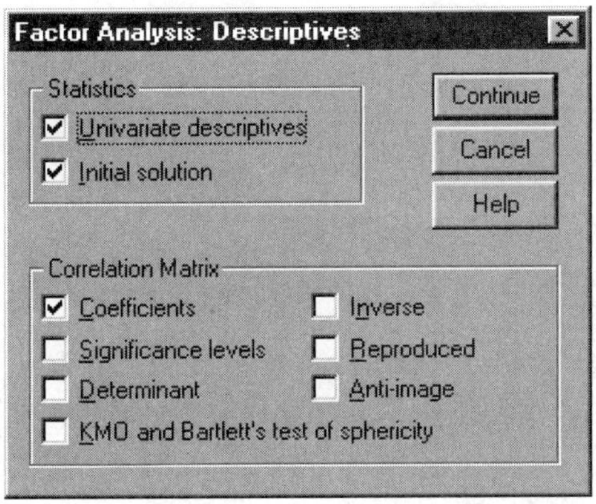


**Statistics.** Univariate statistics include the mean, standard deviation, and number of valid cases for each variable. Initial solution displays initial communalities, eigenvalues, and the percentage of variance explained.

**Correlation Matrix.** The available options are coefficients, significance levels, determinant, KMO and Bartlett's test of sphericity, inverse, reproduced, and anti-image.

# To Specify Descriptive Statistics and Correlation Coefficients

▶ From the menus choose:

Analyze
  Data Reduction
    Factor...

▶ In the Factor Analysis dialog box, click Descriptives.

## Factor Analysis Extraction

Figure 28-5
*Factor Analysis Extraction dialog box*

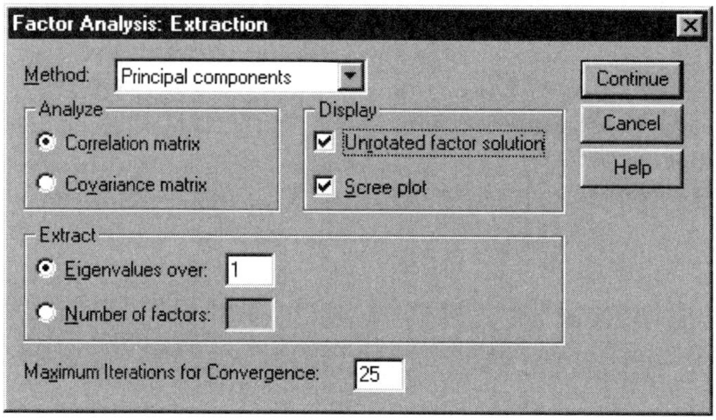


**Method.** Allows you to specify the method of factor extraction. Available methods are principal components, unweighted least squares, generalized least squares, maximum likelihood, principal axis factoring, alpha factoring, and image factoring.

**Analyze.** Allows you to specify either a correlation matrix or a covariance matrix.

**Extract.** You can either retain all factors whose eigenvalues exceed a specified value or retain a specific number of factors.

**Display.** Allows you to request the unrotated factor solution and a scree plot of the eigenvalues.

**Maximum Iterations for Convergence.** Allows you to specify the maximum number of steps the algorithm can take to estimate the solution.

# To Specify Extraction Options

▶ From the menus choose:

Analyze
  Data Reduction
    Factor...

▶ In the Factor Analysis dialog box, click Extraction.

## Factor Analysis Rotation

Figure 28-6
*Factor Analysis Rotation dialog box*

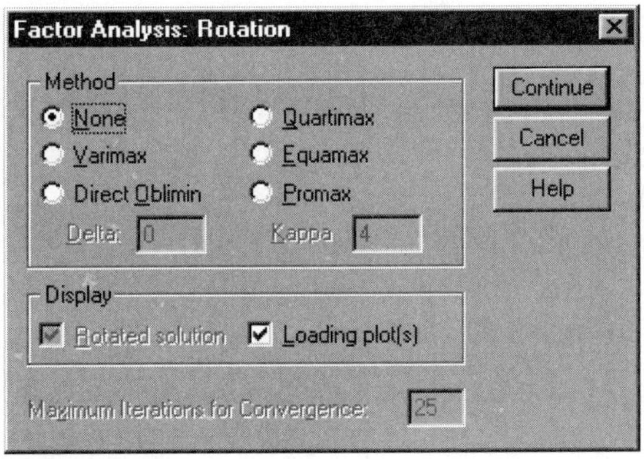


**Method.** Allows you to select the method of factor rotation. Available methods are varimax, direct oblimin, quartimax, equamax, and promax.

**Display.** Allows you to include output on the rotated solution, as well as loading plots for the first two or three factors.

**Maximum Iterations for Convergence.** Allows you to specify the maximum number of steps the algorithm can take to perform the rotation.

# To Specify Rotation Options

- ▶ From the menus choose:

  Analyze
  Data Reduction
  Factor...

- ▶ In the Factor Analysis dialog box, click Rotation.

## Factor Analysis Scores

Figure 28-7
*Factor Analysis Factor Scores dialog box*

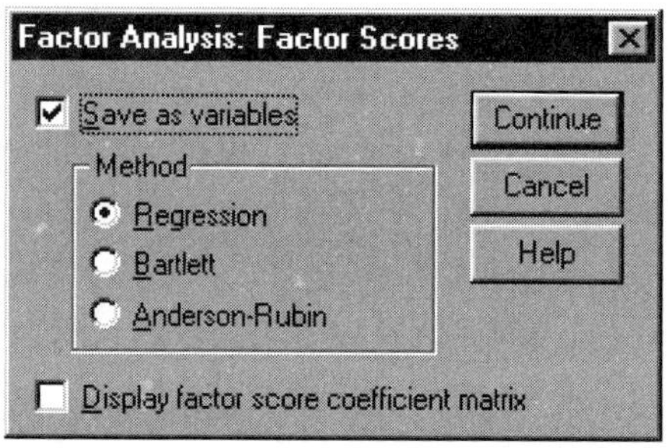


**Save as variables.** Creates one new variable for each factor in the final solution. Select one of the following alternative methods for calculating the factor scores: regression, Bartlett, or Anderson-Rubin.

**Display factor score coefficient matrix.** Shows the coefficients by which variables are multiplied to obtain factor scores. Also shows the correlations between factor scores.

# To Specify Factor Score Options

▶ From the menus choose:

Analyze
 Data Reduction
  Factor...

▶ In the Factor Analysis dialog box, click Scores.

## Factor Analysis Options

Figure 28-8
*Factor Analysis Options dialog box*

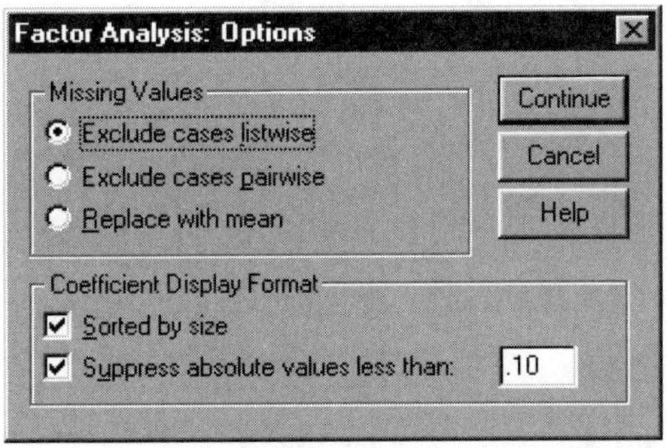


**Missing Values.** Allows you to specify how missing values are handled. The available alternatives are to exclude cases listwise, exclude cases pairwise, or replace with mean.

**Coefficient Display Format.** Allows you to control aspects of the output matrices. You sort coefficients by size and suppress coefficients with absolute values less than the specified value.

# To Specify Factor Analysis Options

- From the menus choose:

  Analyze
    Data Reduction
      Factor...

- In the Factor Analysis dialog box, click Options.

Chapter

# 29

# Hierarchical Cluster Analysis

This procedure attempts to identify relatively homogeneous groups of cases (or variables) based on selected characteristics, using an algorithm that starts with each case (or variable) in a separate cluster and combines clusters until only one is left. You can analyze raw variables or you can choose from a variety of standardizing transformations. Distance or similarity measures are generated by the Proximities procedure. Statistics are displayed at each stage to help you select the best solution.

**Example.** Are there identifiable groups of television shows that attract similar audiences within each group? With hierarchical cluster analysis, you could cluster television shows (cases) into homogeneous groups based on viewer characteristics. This can be used to identify segments for marketing. Or you can cluster cities (cases) into homogeneous groups so that comparable cities can be selected to test various marketing strategies.

**Statistics.** Agglomeration schedule, distance (or similarity) matrix, and cluster membership for a single solution or a range of solutions. Plots: dendrograms and icicle plots.

**Data.** The variables can be quantitative, binary, or count data. Scaling of variables is an important issue—differences in scaling may affect your cluster solution(s). If your variables have large differences in scaling (for example, one variable is measured in dollars and the other is measured in years), you should consider standardizing them (this can be done automatically by the Hierarchical Cluster Analysis procedure).

**Assumptions.** The distance or similarity measures used should be appropriate for the data analyzed (see the Proximities procedure for more information on choices of distance and similarity measures). Also, you should include all relevant variables in your analysis. Omission of influential variables can result in a misleading solution. Because hierarchical cluster analysis is an exploratory method, results should be treated as tentative until they are confirmed with an independent sample.

# Sample Output

Figure 29-1
*Hierarchical cluster analysis output*

**Agglomeration Schedule**

| | | Cluster Combined | | | Stage Cluster First Appears | | |
|---|---|---|---|---|---|---|---|
| | | Cluster 1 | Cluster 2 | Coefficients | Cluster 1 | Cluster 2 | Next Stage |
| Stage | 1 | 11 | 12 | .112 | 0 | 0 | 2 |
| | 2 | 6 | 11 | .132 | 0 | 1 | 4 |
| | 3 | 7 | 9 | .185 | 0 | 0 | 5 |
| | 4 | 6 | 8 | .227 | 2 | 0 | 7 |
| | 5 | 7 | 10 | .274 | 3 | 0 | 7 |
| | 6 | 1 | 3 | .423 | 0 | 0 | 10 |
| | 7 | 6 | 7 | .438 | 4 | 5 | 14 |
| | 8 | 13 | 14 | .484 | 0 | 0 | 15 |
| | 9 | 2 | 5 | .547 | 0 | 0 | 11 |
| | 10 | 1 | 4 | .691 | 6 | 0 | 11 |
| | 11 | 1 | 2 | 1.023 | 10 | 9 | 13 |
| | 12 | 15 | 16 | 1.370 | 0 | 0 | 13 |
| | 13 | 1 | 15 | 1.716 | 11 | 12 | 14 |
| | 14 | 1 | 6 | 2.642 | 13 | 7 | 15 |
| | 15 | 1 | 13 | 4.772 | 14 | 8 | 0 |

**Cluster Membership**

| | | Label | 4 Clusters | 3 Clusters | 2 Clusters |
|---|---|---|---|---|---|
| Case | 1 | Argentina | 1 | 1 | 1 |
| | 2 | Brazil | 1 | 1 | 1 |
| | 3 | Chile | 1 | 1 | 1 |
| | 4 | Domincan R. | 1 | 1 | 1 |
| | 5 | Indonesia | 1 | 1 | 1 |
| | 6 | Austria | 2 | 2 | 1 |
| | 7 | Canada | 2 | 2 | 1 |
| | 8 | Denmark | 2 | 2 | 1 |
| | 9 | Italy | 2 | 2 | 1 |
| | 10 | Japan | 2 | 2 | 1 |
| | 11 | Norway | 2 | 2 | 1 |
| | 12 | Switzerland | 2 | 2 | 1 |
| | 13 | Bangladesh | 3 | 3 | 2 |
| | 14 | India | 3 | 3 | 2 |
| | 15 | Bolivia | 4 | 1 | 1 |
| | 16 | Paraguay | 4 | 1 | 1 |

**Vertical Icicle**

| Number of clusters | 14:India | 14 | 13:Banglade | 13 | 10:Japan | 10 | 9:Italy | 9 | 7:Canada | 7 | 8:Denmark | 8 | 12:Switzerlar | 12 | 11:Norway | 11 | 6:Austria | 6 | 16:Paraquay | 16 | 15:Bolivia | 15 | 5:Indonesia | 5 | 2:Brazil | 2 | 4:Dominican | 4 | 3:Chile | 3 | 1:Argentina |
|---|---|---|---|---|---|---|---|---|---|---|---|---|---|---|---|---|---|---|---|---|---|---|---|---|---|---|---|---|---|---|---|
| 1 | X | X | X | X | X | X | X | X | X | X | X | X | X | X | X | X | X | X | X | X | X | X | X | X | X | X | X | X | X | X | X |
| 2 | X | X | X |  | X | X | X | X | X | X | X | X | X | X | X | X | X | X | X | X | X | X | X | X | X | X | X | X | X | X | X |
| 3 | X | X | X |  | X | X | X | X | X | X | X | X | X | X | X | X | X |  | X | X | X | X | X | X | X | X | X | X | X | X | X |
| 4 | X | X | X |  | X | X | X | X | X | X | X | X | X | X | X | X | X |  | X | X | X |  | X | X | X | X | X | X | X | X | X |
| 5 | X | X | X |  | X | X | X | X | X | X | X | X | X | X | X | X | X |  | X |  | X |  | X | X | X | X | X | X | X | X | X |
| 6 | X | X | X |  | X | X | X | X | X | X | X | X | X | X | X | X | X |  | X |  | X |  | X | X | X |  | X | X | X | X | X |
| 7 | X | X | X |  | X | X | X | X | X | X | X | X | X | X | X | X | X |  | X |  | X |  | X | X | X |  | X |  | X | X | X |
| 8 | X | X | X |  | X | X | X | X | X | X | X | X | X | X | X | X | X |  | X |  | X |  | X |  | X |  | X |  | X | X | X |
| 9 | X |  | X |  | X | X | X | X | X | X | X | X | X | X | X | X | X |  | X |  | X |  | X |  | X |  | X |  | X | X | X |
| 10 | X |  | X |  | X | X | X | X | X |  | X | X | X | X | X | X | X |  | X |  | X |  | X |  | X |  | X |  | X | X | X |
| 11 | X |  | X |  | X | X | X | X | X |  | X | X | X | X | X | X | X |  | X |  | X |  | X |  | X |  | X |  | X |  | X |
| 12 | X |  | X |  | X |  | X | X | X |  | X | X | X | X | X | X | X |  | X |  | X |  | X |  | X |  | X |  | X |  | X |
| 13 | X |  | X |  | X |  | X | X | X |  | X |  | X | X | X | X | X |  | X |  | X |  | X |  | X |  | X |  | X |  | X |
| 14 | X |  | X |  | X |  | X |  | X |  | X |  | X | X | X | X | X |  | X |  | X |  | X |  | X |  | X |  | X |  | X |
| 15 | X |  | X |  | X |  | X |  | X |  | X |  | X | X | X |  | X |  | X |  | X |  | X |  | X |  | X |  | X |  | X |

* * * * * * H I E R A R C H I C A L   C L U S T E R   A N A L Y S I S * * * * * *

Dendrogram using Average Linkage (Between Groups)

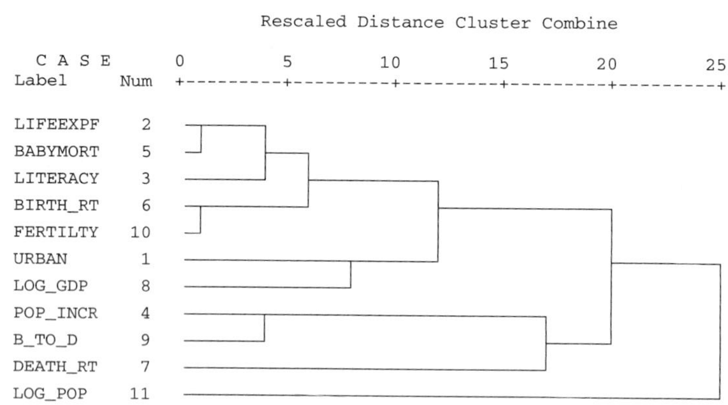

# To Obtain a Hierarchical Cluster Analysis

▶ From the menus choose:

Analyze
  Classify
    Hierarchical Cluster...

Figure 29-2
*Hierarchical Cluster Analysis dialog box*

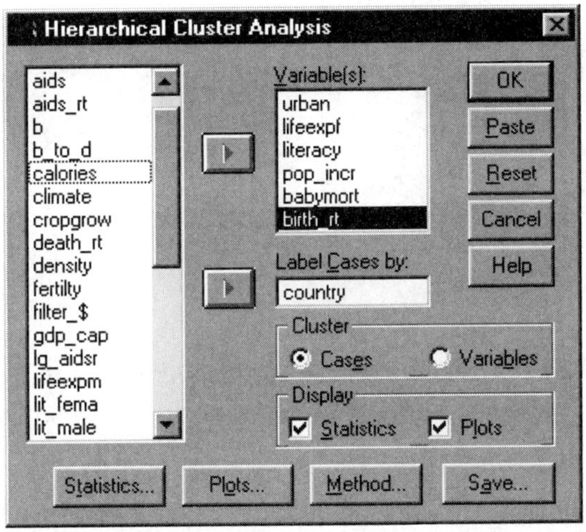


▶ If you are clustering cases, select at least one numeric variable. If you are clustering variables, select at least three numeric variables.

Optionally, you can select an identification variable to label cases.

## Hierarchical Cluster Analysis Method

Figure 29-3
*Hierarchical Cluster Analysis Method dialog box*

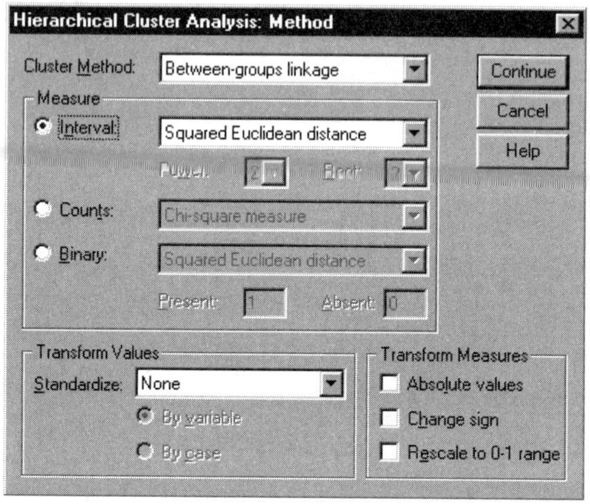


**Cluster Method.** Available alternatives are between-groups linkage, within-groups linkage, nearest neighbor, furthest neighbor, centroid clustering, median clustering, and Ward's method.

**Measure.** Allows you to specify the distance or similarity measure to be used in clustering. Select the type of data and the appropriate distance or similarity measure:

- **Interval data.** Available alternatives are Euclidean distance, squared Euclidean distance, cosine, Pearson correlation, Chebychev, block, Minkowski, and customized.
- **Count data.** Available alternatives are chi-square measure and phi-square measure.
- **Binary data.** Available alternatives are Euclidean distance, squared Euclidean distance, size difference, pattern difference, variance, dispersion, shape, simple matching, phi 4-point correlation, lambda, Anderberg's *D*, dice, Hamann, Jaccard, Kulczynski 1, Kulczynski 2, Lance and Williams, Ochiai, Rogers and Tanimoto, Russel and Rao, Sokal and Sneath 1, Sokal and Sneath 2, Sokal and Sneath 3, Sokal and Sneath 4, Sokal and Sneath 5, Yule's *Y*, and Yule's *Q*.

**Transform Values.** Allows you to standardize data values for either cases or values *before* computing proximities (not available for binary data). Available standardization methods are $z$ scores, range –1 to 1, range 0 to 1, maximum magnitude of 1, mean of 1, and standard deviation of 1.

**Transform Measures.** Allows you to transform the values generated by the distance measure. They are applied *after* the distance measure has been computed. Available alternatives are absolute values, change sign, and rescale to 0–1 range.

## Hierarchical Cluster Analysis Statistics

Figure 29-4
*Hierarchical Cluster Analysis Statistics dialog box*

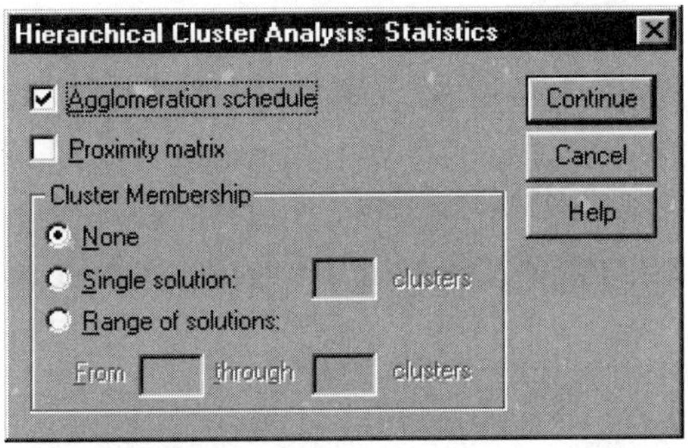


**Agglomeration schedule.** Displays the cases or clusters combined at each stage, the distances between the cases or clusters being combined, and the last cluster level at which a case (or variable) joined the cluster.

**Proximity matrix.** Gives the distances or similarities between items.

**Cluster Membership.** Displays the cluster to which each case is assigned at one or more stages in the combination of clusters. Available options are single solution and range of solutions.

## Hierarchical Cluster Analysis Plots

Figure 29-5
*Hierarchical Cluster Analysis Plots dialog box*

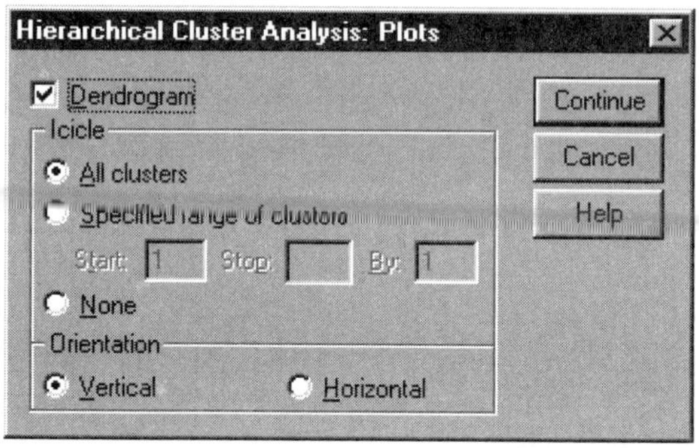


**Dendrogram.** Displays a dendrogram. Dendrograms can be used to assess the cohesiveness of the clusters formed and can provide information about the appropriate number of clusters to keep.

**Icicle.** Displays an icicle plot, including all clusters or a specified range of clusters. Icicle plots display information about how cases are combined into clusters at each iteration of the analysis. Orientation allows you to select a vertical or horizontal plot.

## Hierarchical Cluster Analysis Save New Variables

Figure 29-6
*Hierarchical Cluster Analysis Save dialog box*

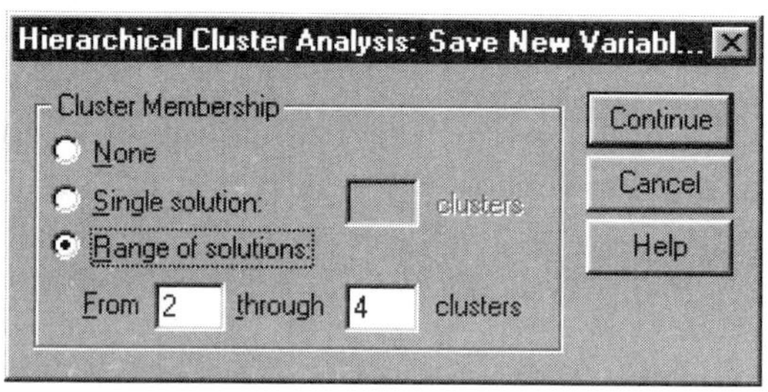


**Cluster Membership.** Allows you to save cluster memberships for a single solution or a range of solutions. Saved variables can then be used in subsequent analyses to explore other differences between groups.

Chapter

# 30

# K-Means Cluster Analysis

This procedure attempts to identify relatively homogeneous groups of cases based on selected characteristics, using an algorithm that can handle large numbers of cases. However, the algorithm requires you to specify the number of clusters. You can specify initial cluster centers if you know this information. You can select one of two methods for classifying cases, either updating cluster centers iteratively or classifying only. You can save cluster membership, distance information, and final cluster centers. Optionally, you can specify a variable whose values are used to label casewise output. You can also request analysis of variance *F* statistics. While these statistics are opportunistic (the procedure tries to form groups that do differ), the relative size of the statistics provides information about each variable's contribution to the separation of the groups.

**Example.** What are some identifiable groups of television shows that attract similar audiences within each group? With *k*-means cluster analysis, you could cluster television shows (cases) into *k* homogeneous groups based on viewer characteristics. This can be used to identify segments for marketing. Or you can cluster cities (cases) into homogeneous groups so that comparable cities can be selected to test various marketing strategies.

**Statistics.** Complete solution: initial cluster centers, ANOVA table. Each case: cluster information, distance from cluster center.

**Data.** Variables should be quantitative at the interval or ratio level. If your variables are binary or counts, use the Hierarchical Cluster Analysis procedure.

**Assumptions.** Distances are computed using simple Euclidean distance. If you want to use another distance or similarity measure, use the Hierarchical Cluster Analysis procedure. Scaling of variables is an important consideration—if your variables are measured on different scales (for example, one variable is expressed in dollars and another is expressed in years), your results may be misleading. In such cases, you should consider standardizing your variables before you perform the *k*-means cluster analysis (this can be done in the Descriptives procedure). The procedure assumes that you have selected the appropriate number of clusters and that you have included all relevant variables. If you have chosen an inappropriate number of clusters or omitted important variables, your results may be misleading.

## Sample Output

Figure 30-1
*K-means cluster analysis output*

**Initial Cluster Centers**

| | Cluster | | | |
|---|---|---|---|---|
| | 1 | 2 | 3 | 4 |
| ZURBAN | -1.88606 | -1.54314 | 1.45741 | .55724 |
| ZLIFEEXP | -3.52581 | -1.69358 | .62725 | .99370 |
| ZLITERAC | -2.89320 | -1.65146 | -.51770 | .88601 |
| ZPOP_INC | .93737 | .16291 | 3.03701 | -1.12785 |
| ZBABYMOR | 4.16813 | 1.38422 | -.69589 | -.88983 |
| ZBIRTH_R | 2.68796 | .42699 | .33278 | -1.08033 |
| ZDEATH_R | 4.41517 | .63185 | -1.89037 | .63185 |
| ZLOG_GDP | -1.99641 | -1.78455 | .53091 | 1.22118 |
| ZB_TO_D | -.52182 | -.31333 | 4.40082 | -.99285 |
| ZFERTILT | 2.24070 | .75481 | .46008 | -.76793 |
| ZLOG_POP | .24626 | 2.65246 | -1.29624 | -.74406 |

**Iteration History**

| | | Change in Cluster Centers | | | |
|---|---|---|---|---|---|
| | | 1 | 2 | 3 | 4 |
| Iteration | 1 | 1.932 | 2.724 | 3.343 | 1.596 |
| | 2 | .000 | .471 | .466 | .314 |
| | 3 | .861 | .414 | .172 | .195 |
| | 4 | .604 | .337 | .000 | .150 |
| | 5 | .000 | .253 | .237 | .167 |
| | 6 | .000 | .199 | .287 | .071 |
| | 7 | .623 | .160 | .000 | .000 |
| | 8 | .000 | .084 | .000 | .074 |
| | 9 | .000 | .080 | .000 | .077 |
| | 10 | .000 | .097 | .185 | .000 |

**Final Cluster Centers**

| | Cluster | | | |
|---|---|---|---|---|
| | 1 | 2 | 3 | 4 |
| ZURBAN | -1.70745 | -.30863 | .16816 | .62767 |
| ZLIFEEXP | -2.52826 | -.15939 | -.28417 | .80611 |
| ZLITERAC | -2.30833 | .13880 | -.81671 | .73368 |
| ZPOP_INC | .59747 | .13400 | 1.45301 | -.95175 |
| ZBABYMOR | 2.43210 | .22286 | .25622 | -.80817 |
| ZBIRTH_R | 1.52607 | .12929 | 1.13716 | -.99285 |
| ZDEATH_R | 2.10314 | -.44640 | -.71414 | .31319 |
| ZLOG_GDP | -1.77704 | -.58745 | -.16871 | .94249 |
| ZB_TO_D | -.29856 | .19154 | 1.45251 | -.84758 |
| ZFERTILT | 1.51003 | -.12150 | 1.27010 | -.87669 |
| ZLOG_POP | .83475 | .34577 | -.49499 | -.22199 |

**Distances between Final Cluster Centers**

| | | 1 | 2 | 3 | 4 |
|---|---|---|---|---|---|
| Cluster | 1 | | 5.627 | 5.640 | 7.924 |
| | 2 | 5.627 | | 2.897 | 3.249 |
| | 3 | 5.640 | 2.897 | | 5.246 |
| | 4 | 7.924 | 3.249 | 5.246 | |

**ANOVA**

| | Cluster | | Error | | F | Sig. |
|---|---|---|---|---|---|---|
| | Mean Square | df | Mean Square | df | | |
| ZURBAN | 10.409 | 3 | .541 | 68 | 19.234 | .000 |
| ZLIFEEXP | 19.410 | 3 | .210 | 68 | 92.614 | .000 |
| ZLITERAC | 18.731 | 3 | .229 | 68 | 81.655 | .000 |
| ZPOP_INC | 18.464 | 3 | .219 | 68 | 84.428 | .000 |
| ZBABYMOR | 18.621 | 3 | .209 | 68 | 77.859 | .000 |
| ZBIRTH_R | 19.599 | 3 | .167 | 68 | 117.339 | .000 |
| ZDEATH_R | 13.628 | 3 | .444 | 68 | 30.676 | .000 |
| ZLOG_GDP | 17.599 | 3 | .287 | 68 | 61.313 | .000 |
| ZB_TO_D | 16.316 | 3 | .288 | 68 | 56.682 | .000 |
| ZFERTILT | 18.829 | 3 | .168 | 68 | 112.273 | .000 |
| ZLOG_POP | 3.907 | 3 | .877 | 68 | 4.457 | .006 |

The F tests should be used only for descriptive purposes because the clusters have been chosen to maximize the differences among cases in different clusters. The observed significance levels are not corrected for this and thus cannot be interpreted as tests of the hypothesis that the cluster means are equal.

# To Obtain a K-Means Cluster Analysis

▶ From the menus choose:

Analyze
  Classify
    K-Means Cluster...

Figure 30-2
*K-Means Cluster Analysis dialog box*

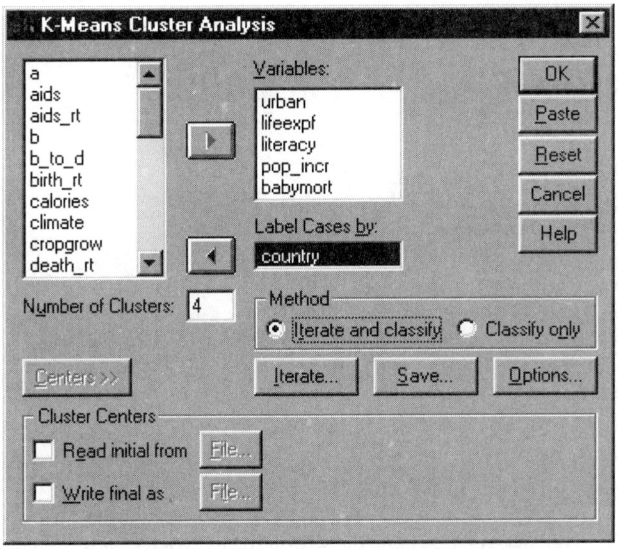


▶ Select the variables to be used in the cluster analysis.

▶ Specify the number of clusters. The number of clusters must be at least two and must not be greater than the number of cases in the data file.

▶ Select either the Iterate and classify method or the Classify only method.

Optionally, you can select an identification variable to label cases.

## K-Means Cluster Analysis Efficiency

The *k*-means cluster analysis command is efficient primarily because it does not compute the distances between all pairs of cases, as do many clustering algorithms, including that used by the hierarchical clustering command.

For maximum efficiency, take a sample of cases and use the Iterate and classify method to determine cluster centers. Click Centers and select Write final as File. Then restore the entire data file, and select Classify only as the method. Click Centers and Read initial from File to classify the entire file using the centers estimated from the sample.

## K-Means Cluster Analysis Iterate

Figure 30-3
*K-Means Cluster Analysis Iterate dialog box*

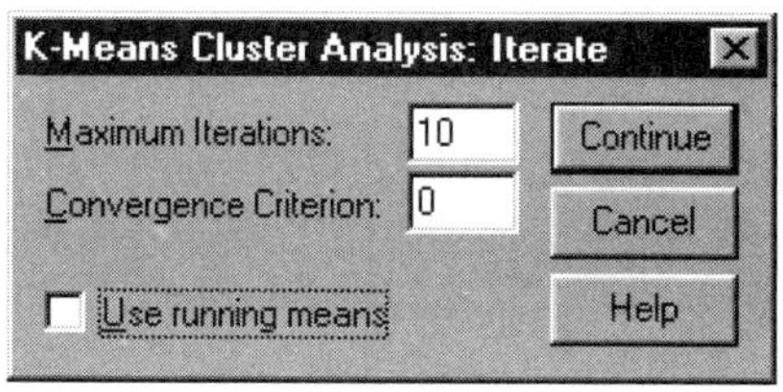


These options are available only if you select the Iterate and Classify method from the main dialog box.

**Maximum iterations.** Limits the number of iterations in the *k*-means algorithm. Iteration stops after this many iterations even if the convergence criterion is not satisfied. This number must be between 1 and 999.

To reproduce the algorithm used by the Quick Cluster command prior to version 5.0, set Maximum iterations to 1.

**Convergence criterion.** Determines when iteration ceases. It represents a proportion of the minimum distance between *initial* cluster centers, so it must be greater than 0 but not greater than 1. If the criterion equals 0.02, for example, iteration ceases when a complete iteration does not move any of the cluster centers by a distance of more than two percent of the smallest distance between any of the initial cluster centers.

**Use running means.** Allows you to request that cluster centers be updated after each case is assigned. If you do not select this option, new cluster centers are calculated after all cases have been assigned.

## K-Means Cluster Analysis Save

Figure 30-4
*K-Means Cluster Analysis Save New Variables dialog box*

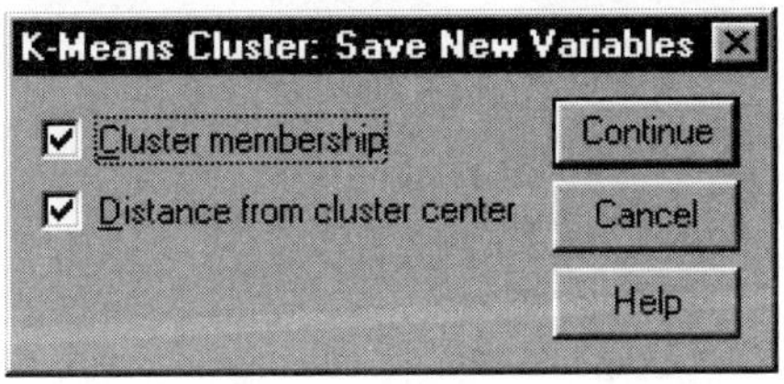


You can save information about the solution as new variables to be used in subsequent analyses:

**Cluster membership.** Creates a new variable indicating the final cluster membership of each case. Values of the new variable range from 1 to the number of clusters.

**Distance from cluster center.** Creates a new variable indicating the Euclidean distance between each case and its classification center.

## K-Means Cluster Analysis Options

Figure 30-5
*K-Means Cluster Analysis Options dialog box*

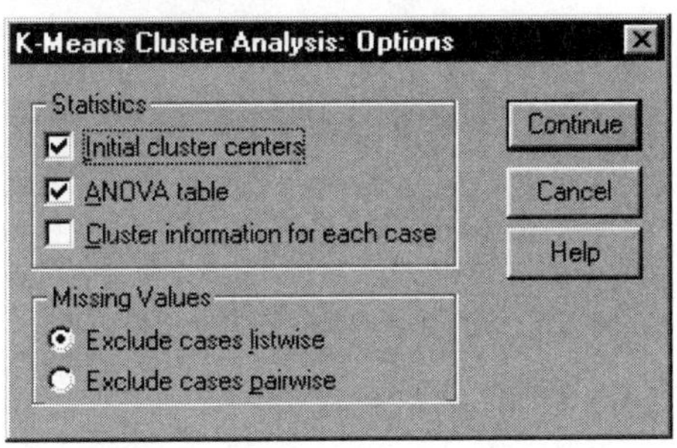


**Statistics.** You can select the following statistics: initial cluster centers, ANOVA table, and cluster information for each case.

**Missing Values.** Available options are Exclude cases listwise or Exclude cases pairwise.

Chapter

# 31

# Nonparametric Tests

The Nonparametric Tests procedure provides several tests that do not require assumptions about the shape of the underlying distribution:

**Chi-Square Test.** Tabulates a variable into categories and computes a chi-square statistic based on the differences between observed and expected frequencies.

**Binomial Test.** Compares the observed frequency in each category of a dichotomous variable with expected frequencies from the binomial distribution.

**Runs Test.** Tests whether the order of occurrence of two values of a variable is random.

**One-Sample Kolmogorov-Smirnov Test.** Compares the observed cumulative distribution function for a variable with a specified theoretical distribution, which may be normal, uniform, or Poisson.

**Two-Independent-Samples Tests.** Compares two groups of cases on one variable. The Mann-Whitney *U* test, the two-sample Kolmogorov-Smirnov test, Moses test of extreme reactions, and the Wald-Wolfowitz runs test are available.

**Tests for Several Independent Samples.** Compares two or more groups of cases on one variable. The Kruskal-Wallis test, the Median test, and the Jonckheere-Terpstra test are available.

**Two-Related-Samples Tests.** Compares the distributions of two variables. The Wilcoxon signed-rank test, the sign test, and the McNemar test are available.

**Tests for Several Related Samples.** Compares the distributions of two or more variables. Friedman's test, Kendall's *W*, and Cochran's *Q* are available.

Quartiles and the mean, standard deviation, minimum, maximum, and number of nonmissing cases are available for all of the above tests.

# Chi-Square Test

The Chi-Square Test procedure tabulates a variable into categories and computes a chi-square statistic. This goodness-of-fit test compares the observed and expected frequencies in each category to test either that all categories contain the same proportion of values or that each category contains a user-specified proportion of values.

**Examples.** The chi-square test could be used to determine if a bag of jelly beans contains equal proportions of blue, brown, green, orange, red, and yellow candies. You could also test to see if a bag of jelly beans contains 5% blue, 30% brown, 10% green, 20% orange, 15% red, and 15% yellow candies.

**Statistics.** Mean, standard deviation, minimum, maximum, and quartiles. The number and the percentage of nonmissing and missing cases, the number of cases observed and expected for each category, residuals, and the chi-square statistic.

**Data.** Use ordered or unordered numeric categorical variables (ordinal or nominal levels of measurement). To convert string variables to numeric variables, use the Automatic Recode procedure, available on the Transform menu.

**Assumptions.** Nonparametric tests do not require assumptions about the shape of the underlying distribution. The data are assumed to be a random sample. The expected frequencies for each category should be at least 1. No more than 20% of the categories should have expected frequencies of less than 5.

# Sample Output

Figure 31-1
*Chi-Square Test output*

Color of Jelly Bean

| | Observed N | Expected N | Residual |
|---|---|---|---|
| Blue | 6 | 18.8 | -12.8 |
| Brown | 33 | 18.8 | 14.2 |
| Green | 9 | 18.8 | -9.8 |
| Yellow | 17 | 18.8 | -1.8 |
| Orange | 22 | 18.8 | 3.2 |
| Red | 26 | 18.8 | 7.2 |
| Total | 113 | | |

Test Statistics

| | Color of Jelly Bean |
|---|---|
| Chi-Square [1] | 27.973 |
| df | 5 |
| Asymptotic Significance | .000 |

1. 0 Cells .0% low freqs 18.8 expected low...

Color of Jelly Bean

| | Observed N | Expected N | Residual |
|---|---|---|---|
| Blue | 6 | 5.7 | .3 |
| Brown | 33 | 33.9 | -.9 |
| Green | 9 | 11.3 | -2.3 |
| Yellow | 17 | 17.0 | .0 |
| Orange | 22 | 22.6 | -.6 |
| Red | 26 | 22.6 | 3.4 |
| Total | 113 | | |

Test Statistics

| | Color of Jelly Bean |
|---|---|
| Chi-Square [1] | 1.041 |
| df | 5 |
| Asymptotic Significance | .959 |

1. 0 Cells .0% low freqs 5.7 expected low...

# To Obtain a Chi-Square Test

▶ From the menus choose:

Analyze
  Nonparametric Tests
    Chi-Square...

Figure 31-2
*Chi-Square Test dialog box*

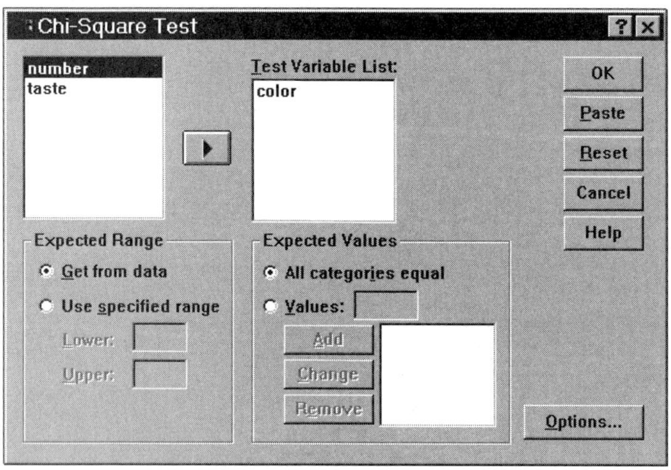


▶ Select one or more test variables. Each variable produces a separate test.

Optionally, you can click Options for descriptive statistics, quartiles, and control of the treatment of missing data.

## Chi-Square Test Expected Range and Expected Values

**Expected range.** By default, each distinct value of the variable is defined as a category. To establish categories within a specific range, click Use specified range and enter integer values for lower and upper bounds. Categories are established for each integer value within the inclusive range, and cases with values outside of the bounds are excluded. For example, if you specify a lowerbound value of 1 and an upperbound value of 4, only the integer values of 1 through 4 are used for the chi-square test.

**Expected values.** By default, all categories have equal expected values. Categories can have user-specified expected proportions. Select Values, enter a value greater than 0 for each category of the test variable, and click Add. Each time you add a value, it appears at the bottom of the value list. The order of the values is important; it corresponds to the ascending order of the category values of the test variable. The first value of the list corresponds to the lowest group value of the test variable, and the last value corresponds to the highest value. Elements of the value list are summed, and then each value is divided by this sum to calculate the proportion of cases expected in the corresponding category. For example, a value list of 3, 4, 5, 4 specifies expected proportions of 3/16, 4/16, 5/16, and 4/16.

## Chi-Square Test Options

Figure 31-3
*Chi-Square Test Options dialog box*

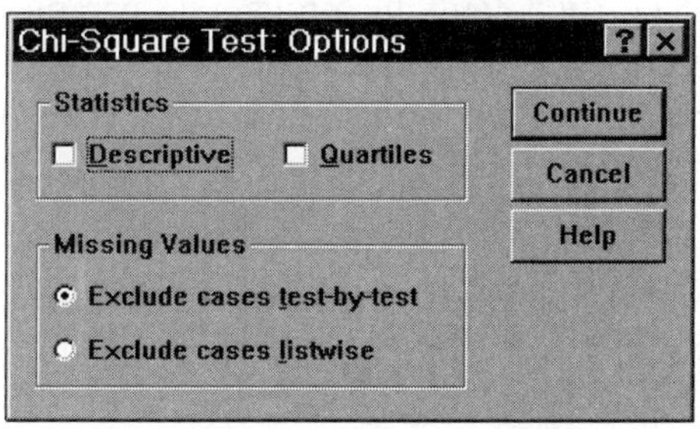


**Statistics.** You can choose one or both of the following summary statistics:

- **Descriptive.** Displays the mean, standard deviation, minimum, maximum, and number of nonmissing cases.

- **Quartiles.** Displays values corresponding to the 25th, 50th, and 75th percentiles.

**Missing Values.** Controls the treatment of missing values.

- **Exclude cases test-by-test.** When several tests are specified, each test is evaluated separately for missing values.
- **Exclude cases listwise.** Cases with missing values for any variable are excluded from all analyses.

### NPAR TESTS Command Additional Features (Chi-Square Test)

The SPSS command language also allows you to:

- Specify different minimum and maximum values or expected frequencies for different variables (with the CHISQUARE subcommand).
- Test the same variable against different expected frequencies or use different ranges (with the EXPECTED subcommand).

See the *SPSS Syntax Reference Guide* for complete syntax information.

## Binomial Test

The Binomial Test procedure compares the observed frequencies of the two categories of a dichotomous variable to the frequencies expected under a binomial distribution with a specified probability parameter. By default, the probability parameter for both groups is 0.5. To change the probabilities, you can enter a test proportion for the first group. The probability for the second group will be 1 minus the specified probability for the first group.

**Example.** When you toss a dime, the probability of a head equals 1/2. Based on this hypothesis, a dime is tossed 40 times, and the outcomes are recorded (heads or tails). From the binomial test, you might find that 3/4 of the tosses were heads and that the observed significance level is small (0.0027). These results indicate that it is not likely that the probability of a head equals 1/2; the coin is probably biased.

**Statistics.** Mean, standard deviation, minimum, maximum, number of nonmissing cases, and quartiles.

**Data.** The variables tested should be numeric and dichotomous. To convert string variables to numeric variables, use the Automatic Recode procedure, available on the Transform menu. A dichotomous variable is a variable that can take on only two possible values: *yes* or *no*, *true* or *false*, 0 or 1, etc. If the variables are not dichotomous, you must specify a cut point. The cut point assigns cases with values greater than the cut point to one group and the rest of the cases to another group.

**Assumptions.** Nonparametric tests do not require assumptions about the shape of the underlying distribution. The data are assumed to be a random sample.

## Sample Output

Figure 31-4
*Binomial Test output*

Binomial Test

| | | Category | N | Observed Proportion | Test Proportion | Asymptotic Significance (2-tailed) |
|---|---|---|---|---|---|---|
| Coin | Group 1 | Head | 30 | .75 | .50 | .003[1] |
| | Group 2 | Tail | 10 | .25 | | |
| | Total | | 40 | 1.00 | | |

1. Based on Z Approximation

# To Obtain a Binomial Test

▶ From the menus choose:

Analyze
  Nonparametric Tests
    Binomial...

Figure 31-5
*Binomial Test dialog box*

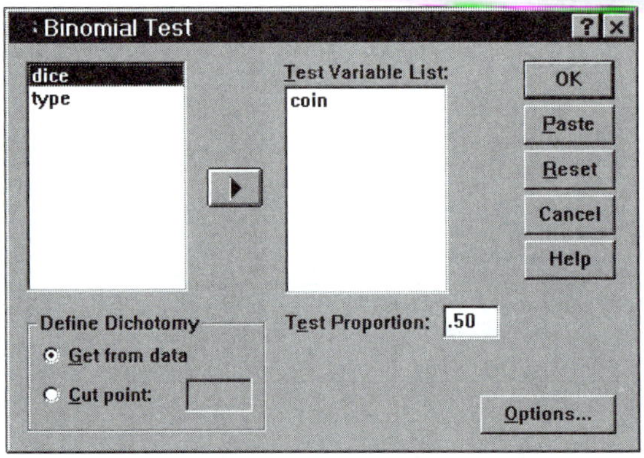


▶ Select one or more numeric test variables.

Optionally, you can click Options for descriptive statistics, quartiles, and control of the treatment of missing data.

## Binomial Test Options

Figure 31-6
*Binomial Test Options dialog box*

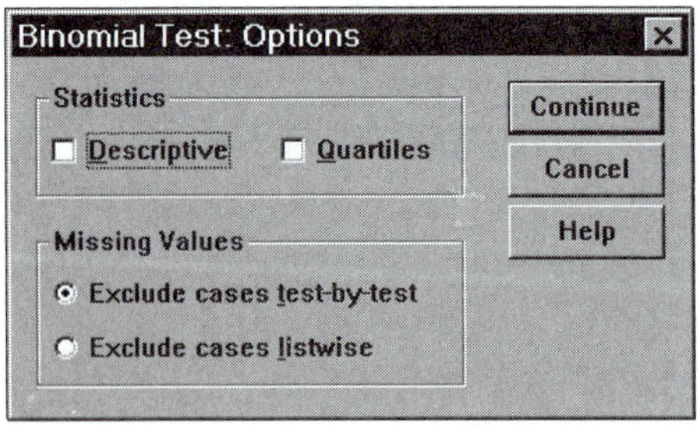

**Statistics.** You can choose one or both of the following summary statistics:

- **Descriptive.** Displays the mean, standard deviation, minimum, maximum, and number of nonmissing cases.
- **Quartiles.** Displays values corresponding to the 25th, 50th, and 75th percentiles.

**Missing Values.** Controls the treatment of missing values.

- **Exclude cases test-by-test.** When several tests are specified, each test is evaluated separately for missing values.
- **Exclude cases listwise.** Cases with missing values for any variable tested are excluded from all analyses.

### NPAR TESTS Command Additional Features (Binomial Test)

The SPSS command language also allows you to:

- Select specific groups (and exclude others) when a variable has more than two categories (with the BINOMIAL subcommand).
- Specify different cut points or probabilities for different variables (with the BINOMIAL subcommand).
- Test the same variable against different cut points or probabilities (with the EXPECTED subcommand).

See the *SPSS Syntax Reference Guide* for complete syntax information.

## Runs Test

The Runs Test procedure tests whether the order of occurrence of two values of a variable is random. A run is a sequence of like observations. A sample with too many or too few runs suggests that the sample is not random.

**Examples.** Suppose that 20 people are polled to find out if they would purchase a product. The assumed randomness of the sample would be seriously questioned if all 20 people were of the same gender. The runs test can be used to determine if the sample was drawn at random.

**Statistics.** Mean, standard deviation, minimum, maximum, number of nonmissing cases, and quartiles.

**Data.** The variables must be numeric. To convert string variables to numeric variables, use the Automatic Recode procedure, available on the Transform menu.

**Assumptions.** Nonparametric tests do not require assumptions about the shape of the underlying distribution. Use samples from continuous probability distributions.

## Sample Output

Figure 31-7
*Runs Test output*

Runs Test

| | Gender |
|---|---|
| Test Value [1] | 1.00 |
| Cases < Test Value | 7 |
| Cases >= Test Value | 13 |
| Total Cases | 20 |
| Number of Runs | 15 |
| Z | 2.234 |
| Asymptotic Significance (2-tailed) | .025 |

1. Median

## To Obtain a Runs Test

▶ From the menus choose:

Analyze
  Nonparametric Tests
    Runs...

Figure 31-8
*Runs Test dialog box*

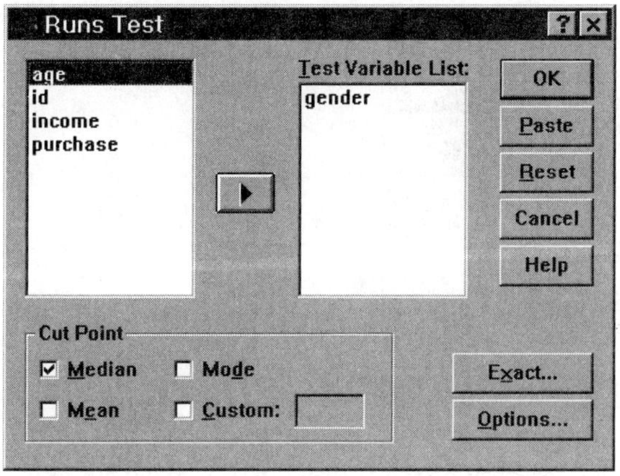


▶ Select one or more numeric test variables.

Optionally, you can click Options for descriptive statistics, quartiles, and control of the treatment of missing data.

## *Runs Test Cut Point*

**Cut Point.** Specifies a cut point to dichotomize the variables you have chosen. You can use either the observed mean, median, or mode, or a specified value as a cut point. Cases with values less than the cut point are assigned to one group, and cases with values greater than or equal to the cut point are assigned to another group. One test is performed for each cut point chosen.

## Runs Test Options

Figure 31-9
*Runs Test Options dialog box*

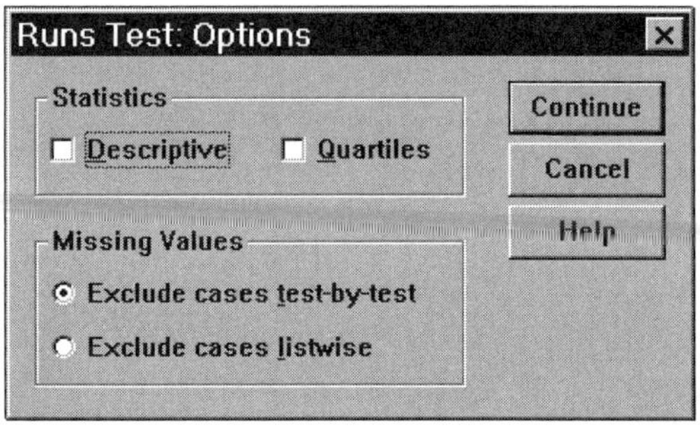


**Statistics.** You can choose one or both of the following summary statistics:

- **Descriptive.** Displays the mean, standard deviation, minimum, maximum, and number of nonmissing cases.
- **Quartiles.** Displays values corresponding to the 25th, 50th, and 75th percentiles.

**Missing Values.** Controls the treatment of missing values.

- **Exclude cases test-by-test.** When several tests are specified, each test is evaluated separately for missing values.
- **Exclude cases listwise.** Cases with missing values for any variable are excluded from all analyses.

## NPAR TESTS Command Additional Features (Runs Test)

The SPSS command language also allows you to:

- Specify different cut points for different variables (with the RUNS subcommand).
- Test the same variable against different custom cut points (with the RUNS subcommand).

See the *SPSS Syntax Reference Guide* for complete syntax information.

# One-Sample Kolmogorov-Smirnov Test

The One-Sample Kolmogorov-Smirnov Test procedure compares the observed cumulative distribution function for a variable with a specified theoretical distribution, which may be normal, uniform, Poisson, or exponential. The Kolmogorov-Smirnov *Z* is computed from the largest difference (in absolute value) between the observed and theoretical cumulative distribution functions. This goodness-of-fit test tests whether the observations could reasonably have come from the specified distribution.

**Example.** Many parametric tests require normally distributed variables. The one-sample Kolmogorov-Smirnov test can be used to test that a variable, say *income,* is normally distributed.

**Statistics.** Mean, standard deviation, minimum, maximum, number of nonmissing cases, and quartiles.

**Data.** Use quantitative variables (interval or ratio level of measurement).

**Assumptions.** The Kolmogorov-Smirnov test assumes that the parameters of the test distribution are specified in advance. This procedure estimates the parameters from the sample. The sample mean and sample standard deviation are the parameters for a normal distribution, the sample minimum and maximum values define the range of the uniform distribution, the sample mean is the parameter for the Poisson distribution, and the sample mean is the parameter for the exponential distribution.

# Sample Output

Figure 31-10
*One-Sample Kolmogorov-Smirnov Test output*

One-Sample Kolmogorov-Smirnov Test

| | | Income |
|---|---|---|
| N | | 20 |
| Normal Parameters [1,2] | Mean | 56250.00 |
| | Std. Deviation | 45146.40 |
| Most Extreme Differences | Absolute | .170 |
| | Positive | .170 |
| | Negative | -.164 |
| Kolmogorov-Smirnov Z | | .760 |
| Asymptotic Significance (2-tailed) | | .611 |

1. Test Distribution is Normal
2. Calculated from data

# To Obtain a One-Sample Kolmogorov-Smirnov Test

▶ From the menus choose:

Analyze
  Nonparametric Tests
    1-Sample K-S...

Figure 31-11
*One-Sample Kolmogorov-Smirnov Test dialog box*

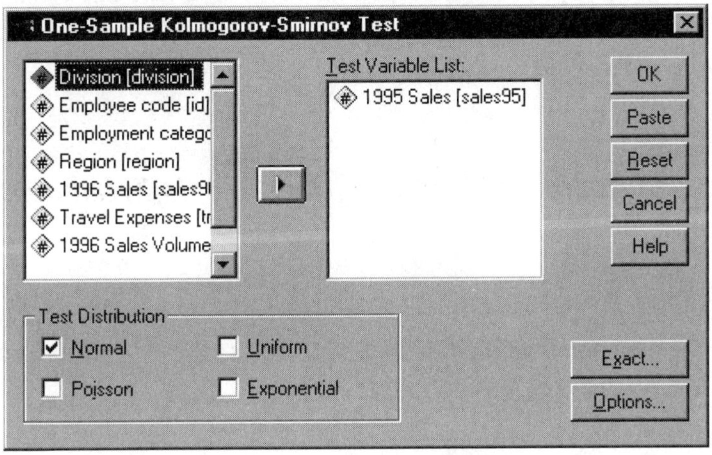


▶ Select one or more numeric test variables. Each variable produces a separate test.

Optionally, you can click Options for descriptive statistics, quartiles, and control of the treatment of missing data.

## One-Sample Kolmogorov-Smirnov Test Options

Figure 31-12
*One-Sample K-S Options dialog box*

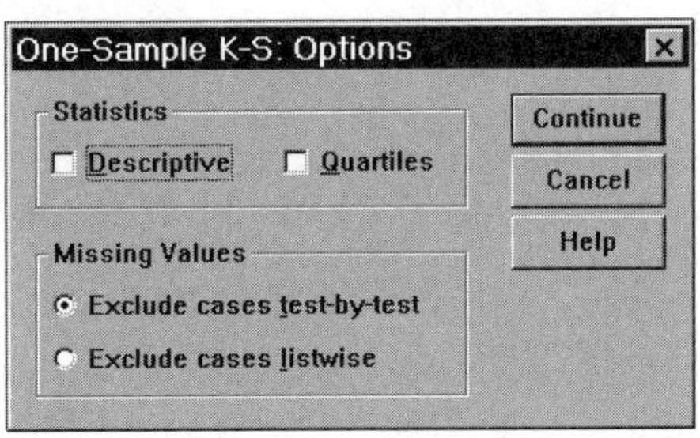


**Statistics.** You can choose one or both of the following summary statistics:

- **Descriptive.** Displays the mean, standard deviation, minimum, maximum, and number of nonmissing cases.
- **Quartiles.** Displays values corresponding to the 25th, 50th, and 75th percentiles.

**Missing Values.** Controls the treatment of missing values.

- **Exclude cases test-by-test.** When several tests are specified, each test is evaluated separately for missing values.
- **Exclude cases listwise.** Cases with missing values for any variable are excluded from all analyses.

### NPAR TESTS Command Additional Features (One-Sample Kolmogorov-Smirnov Test)

The SPSS command language also allows you to:

- Specify the parameters of the test distribution (with the K-S subcommand).

See the *SPSS Syntax Reference Guide* for complete syntax information.

## Two-Independent-Samples Tests

The Two-Independent-Samples Tests procedure compares two groups of cases on one variable.

**Example.** New dental braces have been developed that are intended to be more comfortable, to look better, and to provide more rapid progress in realigning teeth. To find out if the new braces have to be worn as long as the old braces, 10 children are randomly chosen to wear the old braces, and another 10 are chosen to wear the new braces. From the Mann-Whitney $U$ test, you might find that, on average, those with the new braces did not have to wear the braces as long as those with the old braces.

**Statistics.** Mean, standard deviation, minimum, maximum, number of nonmissing cases, and quartiles. Tests: Mann-Whitney $U$, Moses extreme reactions, Kolmogorov-Smirnov $Z$, Wald-Wolfowitz runs.

**Data.** Use numeric variables that can be ordered.

**Assumptions.** Use independent, random samples. The Mann-Whitney $U$ test requires that the two samples tested be similar in shape.

# Sample Output

Figure 31-13
*Two-Independent-Samples output*

Ranks

| | | | N | Mean Rank | Sum of Ranks |
|---|---|---|---|---|---|
| Time Worn in Days | Type of Braces | Old Braces | 10 | 14.10 | 141.00 |
| | | New Braces | 10 | 6.90 | 69.00 |
| | | Total | 20 | | |

Test Statistics [2]

| | Time Worn in Days |
|---|---|
| Mann-Whitney U | 14.000 |
| Wilcoxon W | 69.000 |
| Z | -2.721 |
| Asymptotic Significance (2-tailed) | .007 |
| Exact Significance [2*(1-tailed Sig.)] | .005[1] |

1. Not corrected for ties.
2. Grouping Variable: Type of Braces

# To Obtain Two-Independent-Samples Tests

From the menus choose:

Analyze
  Nonparametric Tests
    2 Independent Samples...

Figure 31-14
*Two-Independent-Samples Tests dialog box*

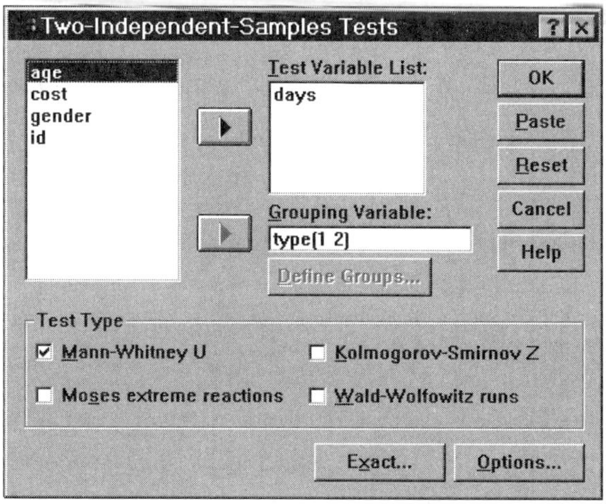


- ▶ Select one or more numeric variables.
- ▶ Select a grouping variable and click Define Groups to split the file into two groups or samples.

## Two-Independent-Samples Test Types

**Test Type.** Four tests are available to test whether two independent samples (groups) come from the same population.

The **Mann-Whitney *U* test** is the most popular of the two-independent-samples tests. It is equivalent to the Wilcoxon rank sum test and the Kruskal-Wallis test for two groups. Mann-Whitney tests that two sampled populations are equivalent in location. The observations from both groups are combined and ranked, with the average rank assigned in the case of ties. The number of ties should be small relative to the total number of observations. If the populations are identical in location, the ranks should be randomly mixed between the two samples. The number of times a score from group 1 precedes a score from group 2 and the number of times a score from group 2 precedes a score from group 1 are calculated. The Mann-Whitney *U* statistic is the smaller of these two numbers. The Wilcoxon rank sum *W* statistic, also displayed, is the rank sum of the smaller sample. If both samples have the same number of observations, *W* is the rank sum of the group named first in the Two-Independent-Samples Define Groups dialog box.

The **Kolmogorov-Smirnov Z test** and the **Wald-Wolfowitz runs test** are more general tests that detect differences in both the locations and the shapes of the distributions. The Kolmogorov-Smirnov test is based on the maximum absolute difference between the observed cumulative distribution functions for both samples. When this difference is significantly large, the two distributions are considered different. The Wald-Wolfowitz runs test combines and ranks the observations from both groups. If the two samples are from the same population, the two groups should be randomly scattered throughout the ranking.

The **Moses extreme reactions test** assumes that the experimental variable will affect some subjects in one direction and other subjects in the opposite direction. It tests for extreme responses compared to a control group. This test focuses on the span of the control group and is a measure of how much extreme values in the experimental group influence the span when combined with the control group. The control group is defined by the group 1 value in the Two-Independent-Samples Define Groups dialog box. Observations from both groups are combined and ranked. The span of the control group is computed as the difference between the ranks of the largest and smallest values in the control group plus 1. Because chance outliers can easily distort the range of the span, 5% of the control cases are trimmed automatically from each end.

## Two-Independent-Samples Tests Define Groups

Figure 31-15
*Two-Independent-Samples Define Groups dialog box*

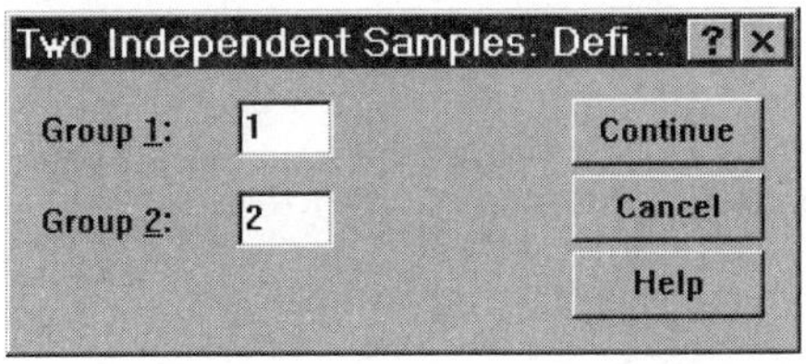

To split the file into two groups or samples, enter an integer value for Group 1 and another for Group 2. Cases with other values are excluded from the analysis.

## Two-Independent-Samples Tests Options

Figure 31-16
*Two-Independent-Samples Options dialog box*

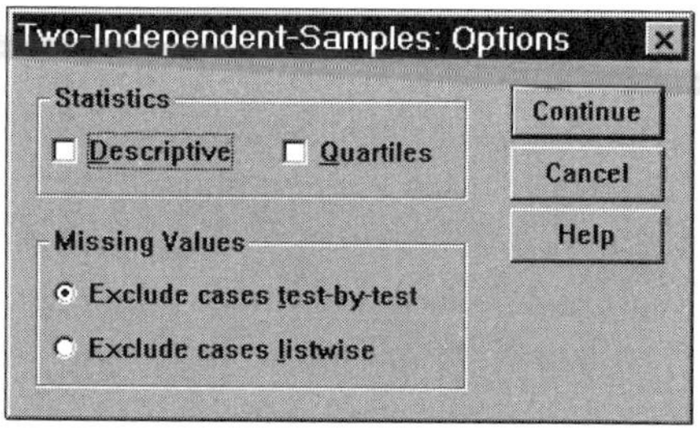


**Statistics.** You can choose one or both of the following summary statistics:

- **Descriptive.** Displays the mean, standard deviation, minimum, maximum, and the number of nonmissing cases.
- **Quartiles.** Displays values corresponding to the 25th, 50th, and 75th percentiles.

**Missing Values.** Controls the treatment of missing values.

- **Exclude cases test-by-test.** When several tests are specified, each test is evaluated separately for missing values.
- **Exclude cases listwise.** Cases with missing values for any variable are excluded from all analyses.

## NPAR TESTS Command Additional Features (Two Independent Samples)

The SPSS command language also allows you to:

- Specify the number of cases to be trimmed for the Moses test (with the MOSES subcommand).

See the *SPSS Syntax Reference Guide* for complete syntax information.

# Tests for Several Independent Samples

The Tests for Several Independent Samples procedure compares two or more groups of cases on one variable.

**Example.** Do three brands of 100-watt lightbulbs differ in the average time the bulbs will burn? From the Kruskal-Wallis one-way analysis of variance, you might learn that the three brands do differ in average lifetime.

**Statistics.** Mean, standard deviation, minimum, maximum, number of nonmissing cases, and quartiles. Tests: Kruskal-Wallis *H*, median.

**Data.** Use numeric variables that can be ordered.

**Assumptions.** Use independent, random samples. The Kruskal-Wallis *H* test requires that the samples tested be similar in shape.

# Sample Output

Figure 31-17
*Tests for Several Independent Samples output*

Ranks

| | | | N | Mean Rank |
|---|---|---|---|---|
| Hours | Brand | Brand A | 10 | 15.20 |
| | | Brand B | 10 | 25.50 |
| | | Brand C | 10 | 5.80 |
| | | Total | 30 | |

Test Statistics [1,2]

| | Hours |
|---|---|
| Chi-Square | 25.061 |
| df | 2 |
| Asymptotic Significance | .000 |

1. Kruskal Wallis Test
2. Grouping Variable: Brand

# To Obtain Tests for Several Independent Samples

From the menus choose:

Analyze
  Nonparametric Tests
    K Independent Samples...

Figure 31-18
*Tests for Several Independent Samples dialog box*

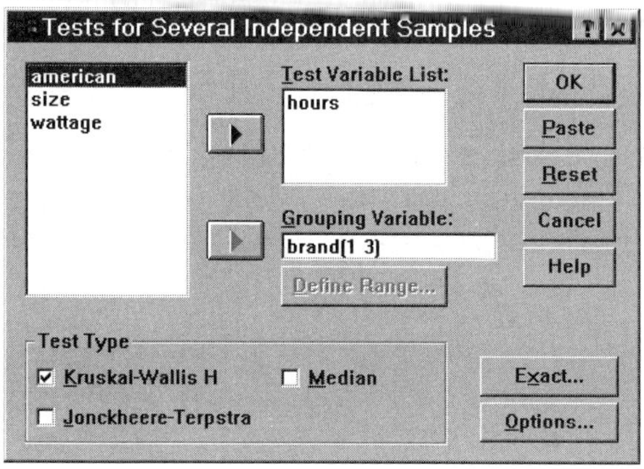


▶ Select one or more numeric variables.

▶ Select a grouping variable and click Define Range to specify minimum and maximum integer values for the grouping variable.

## Several-Independent-Samples Test Types

**Test Type.** Three tests are available to determine if several independent samples come from the same population.

The Kruskal-Wallis *H* test, the median test, and the Jonckheere-Terpstra test all test whether several independent samples are from the same population. The **Kruskal-Wallis *H* test**, an extension of the Mann-Whitney *U* test, is the nonparametric analog of one-way analysis of variance and detects differences in distribution location. The **median test**, which is a more general test but not as powerful, detects distributional differences in location and shape. The Kruskal-Wallis *H* test and the median test assume there is no *a priori* ordering of the *k* populations from which the samples are drawn. When there *is* a natural *a priori* ordering (ascending or descending) of the *k* populations, the **Jonckheere-Terpstra test** is more powerful. For example, the *k* populations might represent *k* increasing temperatures. The hypothesis that different temperatures produce the same response distribution is tested against the alternative that as the temperature increases, the magnitude of the response increases. Here the alternative hypothesis is ordered; therefore, Jonckheere-Terpstra is the most appropriate test to use. The Jonckheere-Terpstra test is available only if you have installed SPSS Exact Tests.

## Tests for Several Independent Samples Define Range

Figure 31-19
*Several Independent Samples Define dialog box*

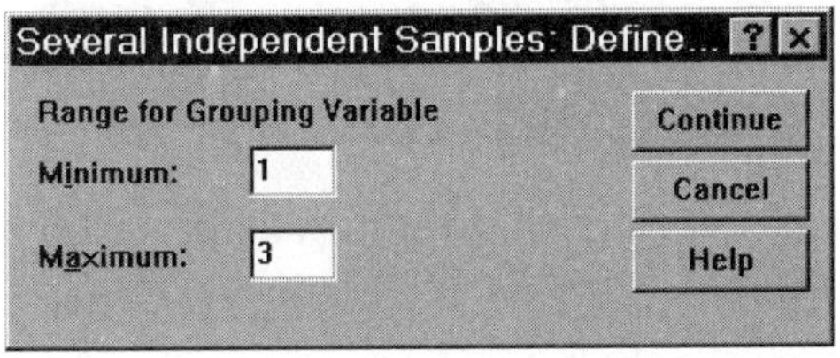


To define the range, enter integer values for minimum and maximum that correspond to the lowest and highest categories of the grouping variable. Cases with values outside of the bounds are excluded. For example, if you specify a minimum value of 1 and a maximum value of 3, only the integer values of 1 through 3 are used. The minimum value must be less than the maximum value, and both values must be specified.

## Tests for Several Independent Samples Options

Figure 31-20
*Several Independent Samples Options dialog box*

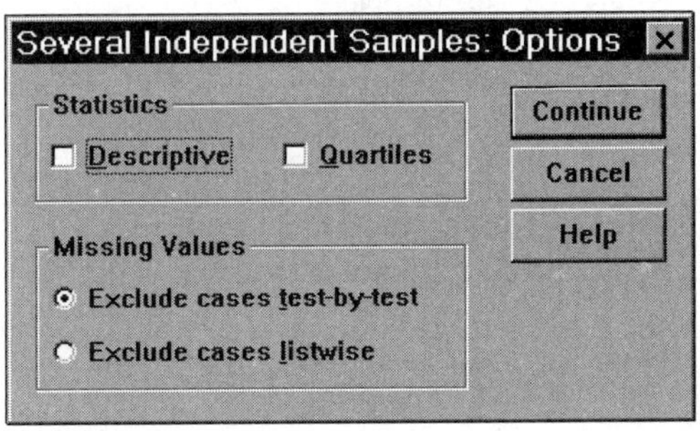

**Statistics.** You can choose one or both of the following summary statistics.

- **Descriptive.** Displays the mean, standard deviation, minimum, maximum, and the number of nonmissing cases.
- **Quartiles.** Displays values corresponding to the 25th, 50th, and 75th percentiles.

**Missing Values.** Controls the treatment of missing values.

- **Exclude cases test-by-test.** When several tests are specified, each test is evaluated separately for missing values.
- **Exclude cases listwise.** Cases with missing values for any variable are excluded from all analyses.

### NPAR TESTS Command Additional Features (K Independent Samples)

The SPSS command language also allows you to:

- Specify a value other than the observed median for the median test (with the MEDIAN subcommand).

See the *SPSS Syntax Reference Guide* for complete syntax information.

## Two-Related-Samples Tests

The Two-Related-Samples Tests procedure compares the distributions of two variables.

**Example.** In general, do families receive the asking price when they sell their homes? By applying the Wilcoxon signed-rank test to data for 10 homes, you might learn that seven families receive less than the asking price, one family receives more than the asking price, and two families receive the asking price.

**Statistics.** Mean, standard deviation, minimum, maximum, number of nonmissing cases, and quartiles. Tests: Wilcoxon signed rank, sign, McNemar.

**Data.** Use numeric variables that can be ordered.

**Assumptions.** Although no particular distributions are assumed for the two variables, the population distribution of the paired differences is assumed to be symmetric.

# Sample Output

Figure 31-21
*Two-Related-Samples output*

Ranks

| | | N | Mean Rank | Sum of Ranks |
|---|---|---|---|---|
| Asking Price - Sale Price | Negative Ranks | 7[1] | 4.93 | 34.50 |
| | Positive Ranks | 1[2] | 1.50 | 1.50 |
| | Ties | 2[3] | | |
| | Total | 10 | | |

1. Asking Price < Sale Price
2. Asking Price > Sale Price
3. Asking Price = Sale Price

Test Statistics [2]

| | Asking Price - Sale Price |
|---|---|
| Z | -2.313[1] |
| Asymptotic Significance (2-tailed) | .021 |

1. Based on positive ranks
2. Wilcoxon Signed Ranks Test

## To Obtain Two-Related-Samples Tests

From the menus choose:

Analyze
  Nonparametric Tests
    2 Related Samples...

Figure 31-22
*Two-Related-Samples Tests dialog box*

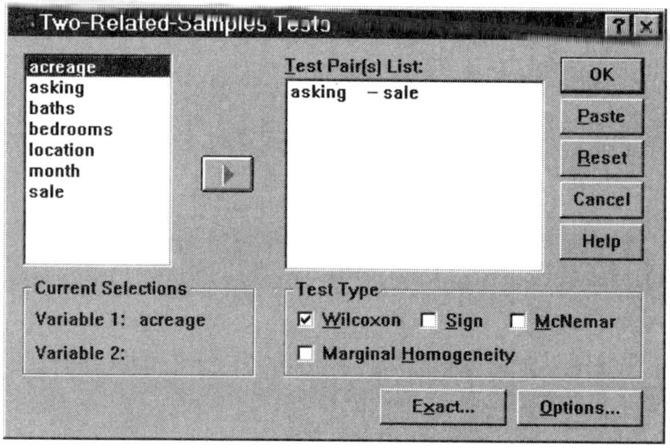


▶ Select one or more pairs of variables, as follows:

- Click each of two variables. The first variable appears in the Current Selections group as *Variable 1*, and the second appears as *Variable 2*.
- After you have selected a pair of variables, click the arrow button to move the pair into the Test Pair(s) list. You may select more pairs of variables. To remove a pair of variables from the analysis, select a pair in the Test Pair(s) list and click the arrow button.

### Two-Related-Samples Test Types

**Test Type.** The tests in this section compare the distributions of two related variables. The appropriate test to use depends on the type of data.

If your data are continuous, use the sign test or the Wilcoxon signed-rank test. The **sign test** computes the differences between the two variables for all cases and classifies the differences as either positive, negative, or tied. If the two variables are similarly distributed, the number of positive and negative differences will not differ significantly. The **Wilcoxon signed-rank test** considers information about both the sign of the differences and the magnitude of the differences between pairs. Because the Wilcoxon signed-rank test incorporates more information about the data, it is more powerful than the sign test.

If your data are binary, use the **McNemar test**. This test is typically used in a repeated measures situation, in which each subject's response is elicited twice, once before and once after a specified event occurs. The McNemar test determines whether the initial response rate (before the event) equals the final response rate (after the event). This test is useful for detecting changes in responses due to experimental intervention in before-and-after designs.

If your data are categorical, use the **marginal homogeneity test**. This is an extension of the McNemar test from binary response to multinomial response. It tests for changes in response using the chi-square distribution and is useful for detecting response changes due to experimental intervention in before-and-after designs. The marginal homogeneity test is available only if you have installed Exact Tests.

## Two-Related-Samples Tests Options

Figure 31-23
*Two-Related-Samples Options dialog box*

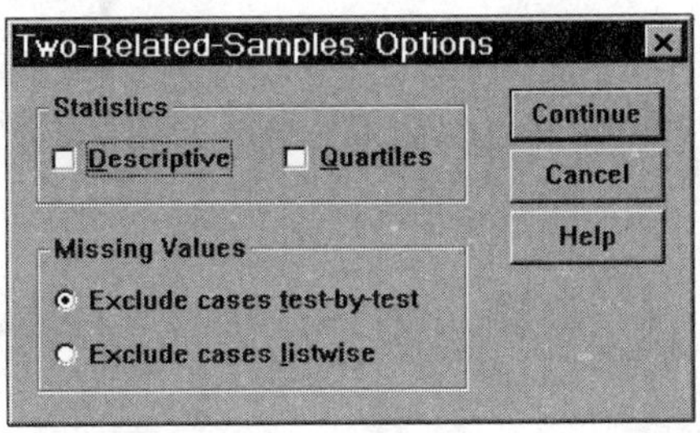


**Statistics.** You can choose one or both of the following summary statistics:

- **Descriptive.** Displays the mean, standard deviation, minimum, maximum, and the number of nonmissing cases.
- **Quartiles.** Displays values corresponding to the 25th, 50th, and 75th percentiles.

**Missing Values.** Controls the treatment of missing values.

- **Exclude cases test-by-test.** When several tests are specified, each test is evaluated separately for missing values.
- **Exclude cases listwise.** Cases with missing values for any variable are excluded from all analyses.

## NPAR TESTS Command Additional Features (Two Related Samples)

The SPSS command language also allows you to:

- Test a variable with each variable on a list.

See the *SPSS Syntax Reference Guide* for complete syntax information.

# Tests for Several Related Samples

The Tests for Several Related Samples procedure compares the distributions of two or more variables.

**Example.** Does the public associate different amounts of prestige with a doctor, a lawyer, a police officer, and a teacher? Ten people are asked to rank these four occupations in order of prestige. Friedman's test indicates that the public does in fact associate different amounts of prestige with these four professions.

**Statistics.** Mean, standard deviation, minimum, maximum, number of nonmissing cases, and quartiles. Tests: Friedman, Kendall's *W*, and Cochran's *Q*.

**Data.** Use numeric variables that can be ordered.

**Assumptions.** Nonparametric tests do not require assumptions about the shape of the underlying distribution. Use dependent, random samples.

# Sample Output

Figure 31-24
*Tests for Several Related Samples output*

Ranks

| | Mean Rank |
|---|---|
| Doctor | 1.50 |
| Lawyer | 2.50 |
| Police | 3.40 |
| Teacher | 2.60 |

Test Statistics [1]

| | |
|---|---|
| N | 10 |
| Chi-Square | 10.920 |
| df | 3 |
| Asymptotic Significance | .012 |

1. Friedman Test

## To Obtain Tests for Several Related Samples

From the menus choose:

Analyze
  Nonparametric Tests
    K Related Samples...

Figure 31-25
*Tests for Several Related Samples dialog box*

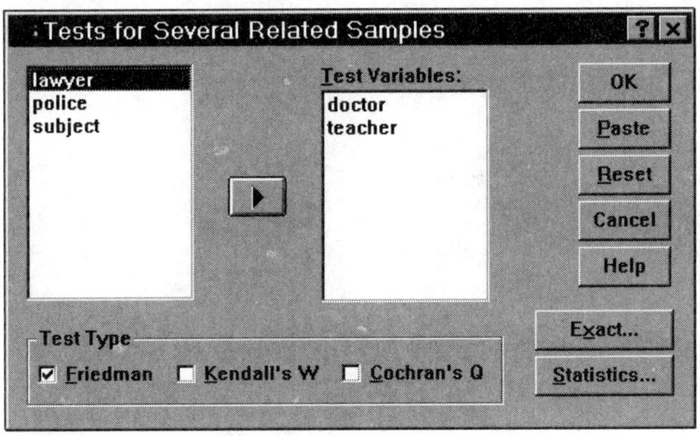


▶ Select two or more numeric test variables.

## Tests for Several Related Samples Test Types

**Test Type.** Three tests are available to compare the distributions of several related variables.

The **Friedman test** is the nonparametric equivalent of a one-sample repeated measures design or a two-way analysis of variance with one observation per cell. Friedman tests the null hypothesis that *k* related variables come from the same population. For each case, the *k* variables are ranked from 1 to *k*. The test statistic is based on these ranks. **Kendall's *W*** is a normalization of the Friedman statistic. Kendall's *W* is interpretable as the coefficient of concordance, which is a measure of agreement among raters. Each case is a judge or rater and each variable is an item or person being judged. For each variable, the sum of ranks is computed. Kendall's *W* ranges between 0 (no agreement) and 1 (complete agreement). **Cochran's *Q*** is identical to the Friedman test but is applicable when all responses are binary. It is an extension of the McNemar test to the *k*-sample situation. Cochran's *Q* tests the hypothesis that several related dichotomous variables have the same mean. The variables are measured on the same individual or on matched individuals.

## Tests for Several Related Samples Statistics

Figure 31-26
*Several Related Samples Statistics dialog box*

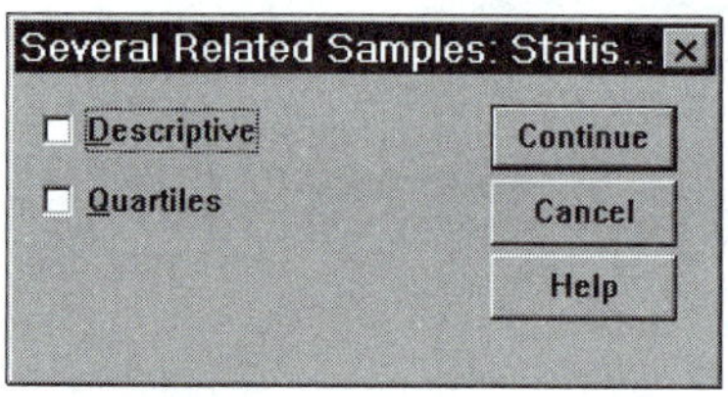


- **Descriptive.** Displays the mean, standard deviation, minimum, maximum, and the number of nonmissing cases.
- **Quartiles.** Displays values corresponding to the 25th, 50th, and 75th percentiles.

## NPAR TESTS Command Additional Features (K Related Samples)

See the *SPSS Syntax Reference Guide* for complete syntax information.

Chapter

# 32

# *Multiple Response Analysis*

Two procedures are available for analyzing multiple dichotomy and multiple category sets. The Multiple Response Frequencies procedure displays frequency tables. The Multiple Response Crosstabs procedure displays two- and three-dimensional crosstabulations. Before using either procedure, you must define multiple response sets.

**Example.** This example illustrates the use of multiple response items in a market research survey. The data are fictitious and should not be interpreted as real. An airline might survey passengers flying a particular route to evaluate competing carriers. In this example, American Airlines wants to know about its passengers' use of other airlines on the Chicago-New York route and the relative importance of schedule and service in selecting an airline. The flight attendant hands each passenger a brief questionnaire upon boarding. The first question reads: Circle all airlines you have flown at least once in the last six months on this route—American, United, TWA, USAir, Other. This is a multiple response question, since the passenger can circle more than one response. However, this question cannot be coded directly because a variable can have only one value for each case. You must use several variables to map responses to each question. There are two ways to do this. One is to define a variable corresponding to each of the choices (for example, American, United, TWA, USAir, and Other). If the passenger circles United, the variable *united* is assigned a code of 1, otherwise 0. This is a **multiple dichotomy method** of mapping variables. The other way to map responses is the **multiple category method**, in which you estimate the maximum number of possible responses to the question and set up the same number of variables, with codes used to specify the airline flown. By perusing a sample of questionnaires, you might discover that no user has flown more than three different airlines on this route in the last six months. Further, you find that due to the deregulation of airlines, 10 other airlines are named in the Other category. Using the multiple response method, you would define three variables, each coded as 1 = *american*, 2 = *united*, 3 = *twa*, 4 = *usair*, 5 = *delta*, and so on. If a given passenger circles American and TWA, the first variable has a code of 1, the second has a code of 3, and the third has a missing-value code. Another passenger might have circled American and entered Delta. Thus, the first variable has a code of 1, the second has a code of 5, and the third a missing-value code. If you use the multiple dichotomy method, on the other hand, you end up with 14 separate variables. Although either method of mapping is feasible for this survey, the method you choose depends on the distribution of responses.

## Multiple Response Define Sets

The Define Multiple Response Sets procedure groups elementary variables into multiple dichotomy and multiple category sets, for which you can obtain frequency tables and crosstabulations. You can define up to 20 multiple response sets. Each set must have a unique name. To remove a set, highlight it on the list of multiple response sets and click Remove. To change a set, highlight it on the list, modify any set definition characteristics, and click Change.

You can code your elementary variables as dichotomies or categories. To use dichotomous variables, select Dichotomies to create a multiple dichotomy set. Enter an integer value for Counted value. Each variable having at least one occurrence of the counted value becomes a category of the multiple dichotomy set. Select Categories to create a multiple category set having the same range of values as the component variables. Enter integer values for the minimum and maximum values of the range for categories of the multiple category set. The procedure totals each distinct integer value in the inclusive range across all component variables. Empty categories are not tabulated.

Each multiple response set must be assigned a unique name of up to seven characters. The procedure prefixes a dollar sign ($) to the name you assign. You cannot use the following reserved names: *casenum*, *sysmis*, *jdate*, *date*, *time*, *length*, and *width*. The name of the multiple response set exists only for use in multiple response procedures. You cannot refer to multiple response set names in other procedures. Optionally, you can enter a descriptive variable label for the multiple response set. The label can be up to 40 characters long.

## To Define Multiple Response Sets

▶ From the menus choose:

Analyze
  Multiple Response
    Define Sets...

Figure 32-1
*Define Multiple Response Sets dialog box*

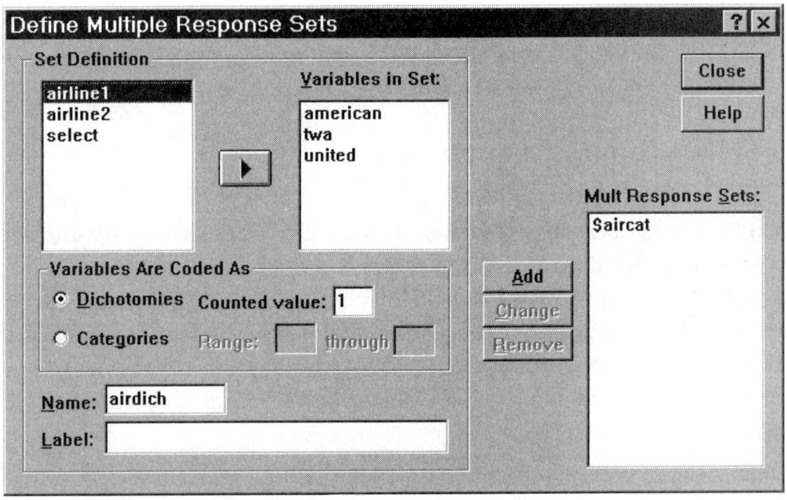


▶ Select two or more variables.

▶ If your variables are coded as dichotomies, indicate which value you want to have counted. If your variables are coded as categories, define the range of the categories.

▶ Enter a unique name for each multiple response set.

▶ Click Add to add the multiple response set to the list of defined sets.

# Multiple Response Frequencies

The Multiple Response Frequencies procedure produces frequency tables for multiple response sets. You must first define one or more multiple response sets (see "Multiple Response Define Sets" on p. 410).

For multiple dichotomy sets, category names shown in the output come from variable labels defined for elementary variables in the group. If the variable labels are not defined, variable names are used as labels. For multiple category sets, category labels come from the value labels of the first variable in the group. If categories missing for the first variable are present for other variables in the group, define a value label for the missing categories.

**Missing Values.** Cases with missing values are excluded on a table-by-table basis. Alternatively, you can choose one or both of the following:

- **Exclude cases listwise within dichotomies.** Excludes cases with missing values for any variable from the tabulation of the multiple dichotomy set. This applies only to multiple response sets defined as dichotomy sets. By default, a case is considered missing for a multiple dichotomy set if none of its component variables contains the counted value. Cases with missing values for some (but not all) variables are included in the tabulations of the group if at least one variable contains the counted value.
- **Exclude cases listwise within categories.** Excludes cases with missing values for any variable from tabulation of the multiple category set. This applies only to multiple response sets defined as category sets. By default, a case is considered missing for a multiple category set only if none of its components has valid values within the defined range.

**Example.** Each variable created from a survey question is an elementary variable. To analyze a multiple response item, you must combine the variables into one of two types of multiple response sets: a multiple dichotomy set or a multiple category set. For example, if an airline survey asked which of three airlines (American, United, TWA) you have flown in the last six months and you used dichotomous variables and defined a **multiple dichotomy set**, each of the three variables in the set would become a category of the group variable. The counts and percentages for the three airlines are displayed in one frequency table. If you discover that no respondent mentioned more than two airlines, you could create two variables, each having three codes, one for each airline. If you define a **multiple category set**, the values are tabulated by adding the same codes in the elementary variables together. The resulting set of values is the same as those for each of the elementary variables. For example, 30 responses for United are the sum of the 5 United responses for airline 1 and the 25 United responses for airline 2. The counts and percentages for the three airlines are displayed in one frequency table.

**Statistics.** Frequency tables displaying counts, percentages of responses, percentages of cases, number of valid cases, and number of missing cases.

**Data.** Use multiple response sets.

**Assumptions.** The counts and percentages provide a useful description for data from any distribution.

**Related procedures.** The Multiple Response Define Sets procedure allows you to define multiple response sets.

## Sample Output

Figure 32-2
*Multiple Response Frequencies output*

```
Group $AIRDICH
     (Value tabulated = 1)

                                                              Pct of  Pct of
Dichotomy label                        Name          Count  Responses  Cases

American                               AMERICAN        75      67.6     92.6
TWA                                    TWA              6       5.4      7.4
United                                 UNITED          30      27.0     37.0
                                                    -------    -----    -----
                               Total responses        111     100.0    137.0

19 missing cases;  81 valid cases
```

## To Obtain Multiple Response Frequencies

▶ From the menus choose:

Analyze
  Multiple Response
    Frequencies...

Figure 32-3
*Multiple Response Frequencies dialog box*

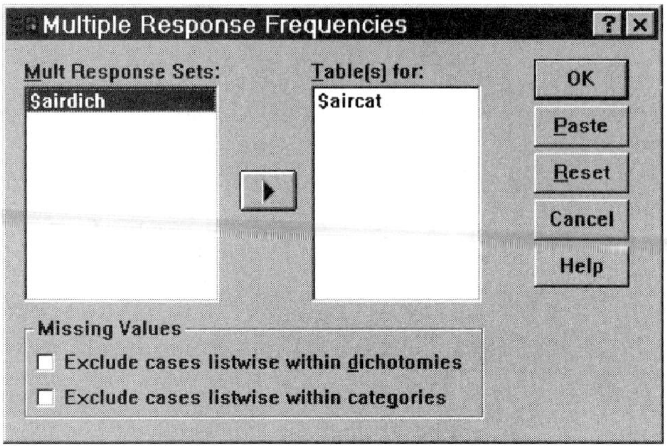


▶ Select one or more multiple response sets.

## Multiple Response Crosstabs

The Multiple Response Crosstabs procedure crosstabulates defined multiple response sets, elementary variables, or a combination. You can also obtain cell percentages based on cases or responses, modify the handling of missing values, or get paired crosstabulations. You must first define one or more multiple response sets (see "To Define Multiple Response Sets" on p. 411).

For multiple dichotomy sets, category names shown in the output come from variable labels defined for elementary variables in the group. If the variable labels are not defined, variable names are used as labels. For multiple category sets, category labels come from the value labels of the first variable in the group. If categories missing for the first variable are present for other variables in the group, define a value label for the missing categories. The procedure displays category labels for columns on three lines, with up to eight characters per line. To avoid splitting words, you can reverse row and column items or redefine labels.

**Example.** Both multiple dichotomy and multiple category sets can be crosstabulated with other variables in this procedure. An airline passenger survey asks passengers for the following information: "Circle all of the following airlines you have flown at least once in the last six months (American, United, TWA). Which is more important in selecting a flight—schedule or service? Select only one." After entering the data as dichotomies or multiple categories and combining them into a set, you can crosstabulate the airline choices with the question involving service or schedule.

**Statistics.** Crosstabulation with cell, row, column, and total counts, and cell, row, column, and total percentages. The cell percentages can be based on cases or responses.

**Data.** Use multiple response sets or numeric categorical variables.

**Assumptions.** The counts and percentages provide a useful description of data from any distribution.

**Related procedures.** The Multiple Response Define Sets procedure allows you to define multiple response sets.

## Sample Output

Figure 32-4
*Multiple Response Crosstabs output*

```
                 * * *  C R O S S T A B U L A T I O N  * * *

  $AIRCAT (group)
by SELECT  Select


                    SELECT

               Count  |Schedule Service
                      |                 Row
                      |                 Total
                      |     0  |     1  |
$AIRCAT       --------+--------+--------+
                   1  |    41  |    34  |    75
  American            |        |        |  92.6
                      +--------+--------+
                   2  |    27  |     3  |    30
  United              |        |        |  37.0
                      +--------+--------+
                   3  |     3  |     3  |     6
  TWA                 |        |        |   7.4
                      +--------+--------+
              Column       44       37      81
               Total     54.3     45.7   100.0
```

# To Obtain Multiple Response Crosstabs

▶ From the menus choose:

Analyze
  Multiple Response
    Crosstabs...

Figure 32-5
*Multiple Response Crosstabs dialog box*

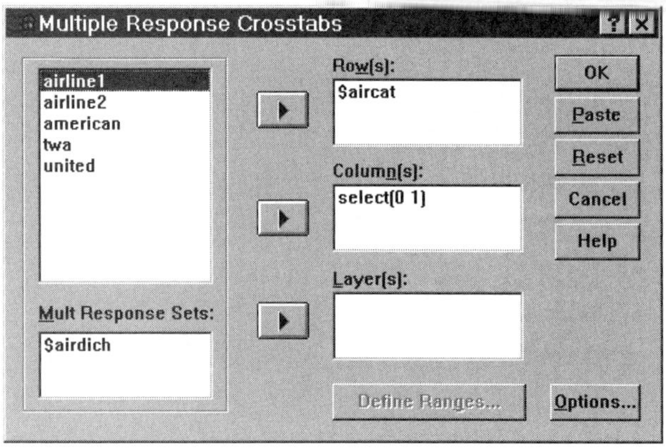


▶ Select one or more numeric variables or multiple response sets for each dimension of the crosstabulation.

▶ Define the range of each elementary variable.

Optionally, you can obtain a two-way crosstabulation for each category of a control variable or multiple response set. Select one or more items for the Layer(s) list.

## Multiple Response Crosstabs Define Variable Ranges

Figure 32-6
*Multiple Response Crosstabs Define Variable Range dialog box*

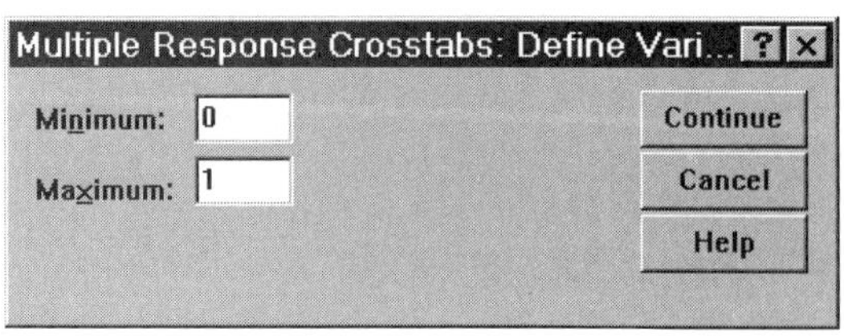

Value ranges must be defined for any elementary variable in the crosstabulation. Enter the integer minimum and maximum category values that you want to tabulate. Categories outside the range are excluded from analysis. Values within the inclusive range are assumed to be integers (non-integers are truncated).

## Multiple Response Crosstabs Options

Figure 32-7
*Multiple Response Crosstabs Options dialog box*

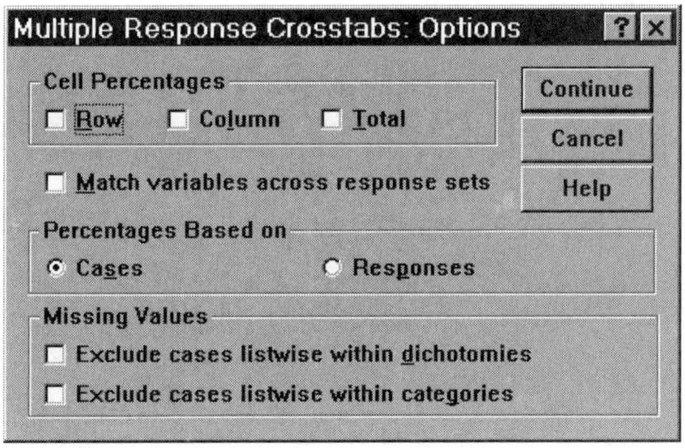


**Cell Percentages.** Cell counts are always displayed. You can choose to display row percentages, column percentages, and two-way table (total) percentages.

**Percentages Based on.** You can base cell percentages on cases (or respondents). This is not available if you select matching of variables across multiple category sets. You can also base cell percentages on responses. For multiple dichotomy sets, the number of responses is equal to the number of counted values across cases. For multiple category sets, the number of responses is the number of values in the defined range.

**Missing Values.** You can choose one or both of the following:

- **Exclude cases listwise within dichotomies.** Excludes cases with missing values for any variable from the tabulation of the multiple dichotomy set. This applies only to multiple response sets defined as dichotomy sets. By default, a case is considered missing for a multiple dichotomy set if none of its component variables contains the counted value. Cases with missing values for some, but not all, variables are included in the tabulations of the group if at least one variable contains the counted value.

- **Exclude cases listwise within categories.** Excludes cases with missing values for any variable from tabulation of the multiple category set. This applies only to multiple response sets defined as category sets. By default, a case is considered missing for a multiple category set only if none of its components has valid values within the defined range.

By default, when crosstabulating two multiple category sets, the procedure tabulates each variable in the first group with each variable in the second group and sums the counts for each cell; therefore, some responses can appear more than once in a table. You can choose the following option:

**Match variables across response sets.** Pairs the first variable in the first group with the first variable in the second group, and so on. If you select this option, the procedure bases cell percentages on responses rather than respondents. Pairing is not available for multiple dichotomy sets or elementary variables.

## MULT RESPONSE Command Additional Features

The SPSS command language also allows you to:

- Obtain crosstabulation tables with up to five dimensions (with the BY subcommand).
- Change output formatting options, including suppression of value labels (with the FORMAT subcommand).

See the *SPSS Syntax Reference Guide* for complete syntax information.

Chapter 33

# Reporting Results

Case listings and descriptive statistics are basic tools for studying and presenting data. You can obtain case listings with the Data Editor or the Summarize procedure, frequency counts and descriptive statistics with the Frequencies procedure, and subpopulation statistics with the Means procedure. Each of these uses a format designed to make information clear. If you want to display the information in a different format, Report Summaries in Rows and Report Summaries in Columns give you the control you need over data presentation.

## Report Summaries in Rows

Report Summaries in Rows produces reports in which different summary statistics are laid out in rows. Case listings are also available, with or without summary statistics.

**Example.** A company with a chain of retail stores keeps records of employee information, including salary, job tenure, and the store and division in which each employee works. You could generate a report that provides individual employee information (listing) broken down by store and division (break variables), with summary statistics (for example, mean salary) for each store, division, and division within each store.

**Data Columns.** Lists the report variables for which you want case listings or summary statistics and controls the display format of data columns.

**Break Columns.** Lists optional break variables that divide the report into groups and controls the summary statistics and display formats of break columns. For multiple break variables, there will be a separate group for each category of each break variable within categories of the preceding break variable in the list. Break variables should be discrete categorical variables that divide cases into a limited number of meaningful categories. Individual values of each break variable appear, sorted, in a separate column to the left of all data columns.

**Report**. Controls overall report characteristics, including overall summary statistics, display of missing values, page numbering, and titles.

**Display cases**. Displays the actual values (or value labels) of the data-column variables for every case. This produces a listing report, which can be much longer than a summary report.

**Preview**. Displays only the first page of the report. This option is useful for previewing the format of your report without processing the whole report.

**Data are already sorted**. For reports with break variables, the data file must be sorted by break variable values before generating the report. If your data file is already sorted by values of the break variables, you can save processing time by selecting this option. This option is particularly useful after running a preview report.

## Sample Output

Figure 33-1
*Combined report with case listings and summary statistics*

| Division | Age | Tenure in Company | Tenure in Grade | Salary--Annual |
|---|---|---|---|---|
| Carpeting | 27.00 | 3.67 | 2.17 | $9,200 |
| | 22.00 | 3.92 | 3.08 | $10,900 |
| | 23.00 | 3.92 | 3.08 | $10,900 |
| | 24.00 | 4.00 | 3.25 | $10,000 |
| | 30.00 | 4.08 | 3.08 | $10,000 |
| | 27.00 | 4.33 | 3.17 | $10,000 |
| | 33.00 | 2.67 | 2.67 | $9,335 |
| | 33.00 | 3.75 | 3.25 | $10,000 |
| | 44.00 | 4.83 | 4.33 | $15,690 |
| | 36.00 | 3.83 | 3.25 | $10,000 |
| | 35.00 | 3.50 | 3.00 | $15,520 |
| | 35.00 | 6.00 | 5.33 | $19,500 |
| Mean | 30.75 | 4.04 | 3.31 | $11,754 |
| Appliances | 21.00 | 2.67 | 2.67 | $8,700 |
| | 26.00 | 2.92 | 2.08 | $8,000 |
| | 32.00 | 2.92 | 2.92 | $8,900 |
| | 33.00 | 3.42 | 2.92 | $8,900 |
| | 34.00 | 5.08 | 4.50 | $15,300 |
| | 24.00 | 3.17 | 3.17 | $8,975 |
| | 42.00 | 6.50 | 6.50 | $18,000 |
| | 30.00 | 2.67 | 2.67 | $7,500 |
| | 38.00 | 5.00 | 4.42 | $28,300 |
| Mean | 31.11 | 3.81 | 3.54 | $12,508 |

## To Obtain a Summary Report: Summaries in Rows

- From the menus choose:

  Analyze
  Reports
  Report Summaries in Rows...

- Select one or more variables for Data Columns. One column in the report is generated for each variable selected.
- For reports sorted and displayed by subgroups, select one or more variables for Break Columns.
- For reports with summary statistics for subgroups defined by break variables, select the break variable in the Break Columns list and click Summary in the Break Columns group to specify the summary measure(s).
- For reports with overall summary statistics, click Summary in the Report group to specify the summary measure(s).

Figure 33-2
*Report Summaries in Rows dialog box*

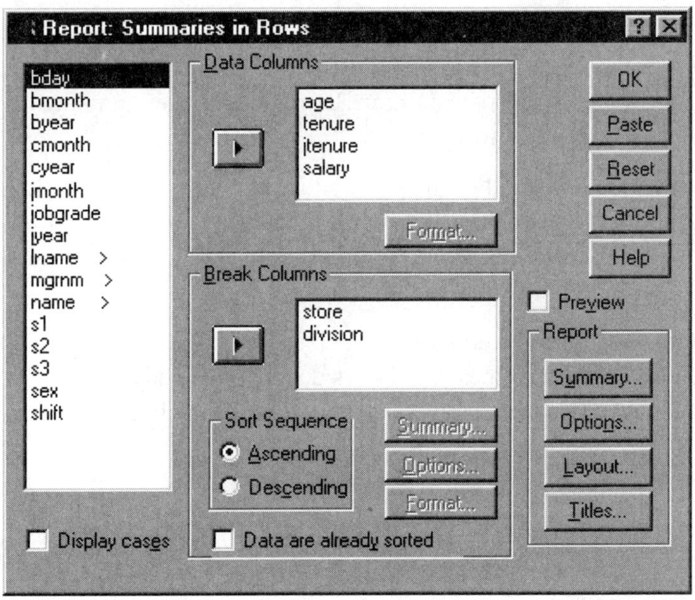

## Report Column Format

The Format dialog boxes control column titles, column width, text alignment, and the display of data values or value labels. Data Column Format controls the format of data columns on the right side of the report page. Break Format controls the format of break columns on the left side.

Figure 33-3
*Report Data Column Format dialog box*

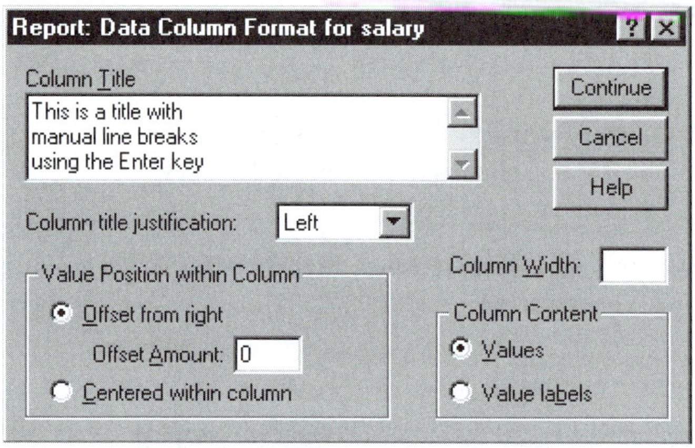


**Column Title**. For the selected variable, controls the column title. Long titles are automatically wrapped within the column. Use the Enter key to manually insert line breaks where you want titles to wrap.

**Value Position within Column**. For the selected variable, controls the alignment of data values or value labels within the column. Alignment of values or labels does not affect alignment of column headings. You can either indent the column contents by a specified number of characters or center the contents.

**Column Content**. For the selected variable, controls the display of either data values or defined value labels. Data values are always displayed for any values that do not have defined value labels. (Not available for data columns in column summary reports.)

## Report Summary Lines

The two Summary Lines dialog boxes control the display of summary statistics for break groups and for the entire report. Summary Lines controls subgroup statistics for each category defined by the break variable(s). Final Summary Lines controls overall statistics, displayed at the end of the report.

Figure 33-4
*Report Summary Lines dialog box*

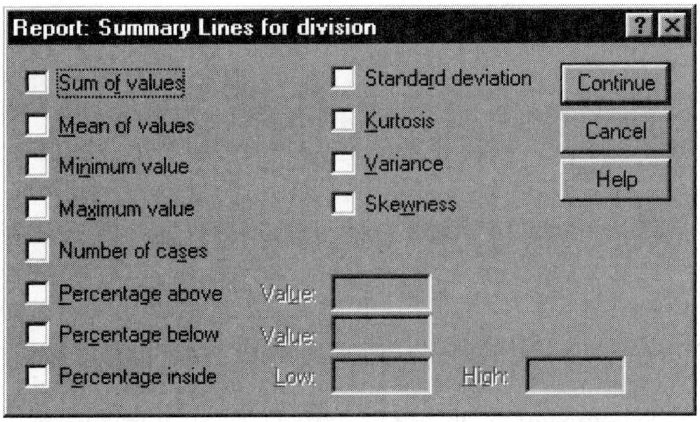


Available summary statistics are sum, mean, minimum, maximum, number of cases, percentage of case above or below a specified value, percentage of cases within a specified range of values, standard deviation, kurtosis, variance, and skewness.

## Report Break Options

Break Options controls spacing and pagination of break category information.

Figure 33-5
*Report Break Options dialog box*

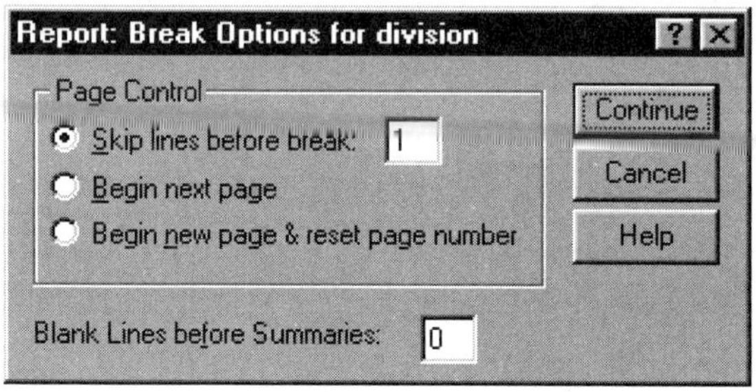


**Page Control.** Controls spacing and pagination for categories of the selected break variable. You can specify a number of blank lines between break categories or start each break category on a new page.

**Blank Lines before Summaries.** Controls the number of blank lines between break category labels or data and summary statistics. This is particularly useful for combined reports that include both individual case listings and summary statistics for break categories; in these reports, you can insert space between the case listings and the summary statistics.

## Report Options

Report Options controls the treatment and display of missing values and report page numbering.

Figure 33-6
*Report Options dialog box*

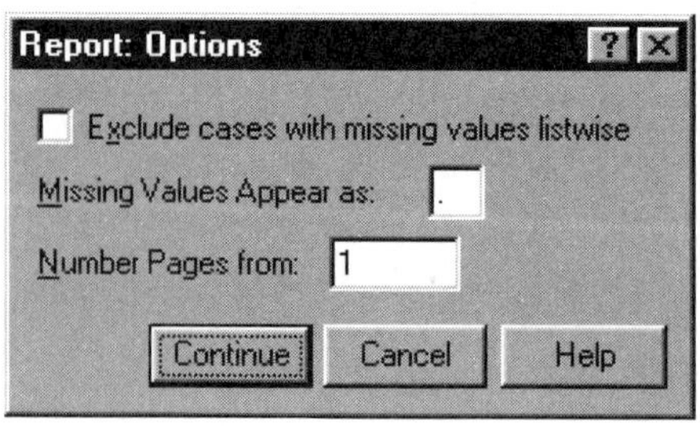

**Exclude cases with missing values listwise.** Eliminates (from the report) any case with missing values for any of the report variables.

**Missing Values Appear as.** Allows you to specify the symbol that represents missing values in the data file. The symbol can be only one character and is used to represent both system-missing and user-missing values.

**Number Pages from**. Allows you to specify a page number for the first page of the report.

## Report Layout

Report Layout controls the width and length of each report page, placement of the report on the page, and the insertion of blank lines and labels.

Figure 33-7
*Report Layout dialog box*

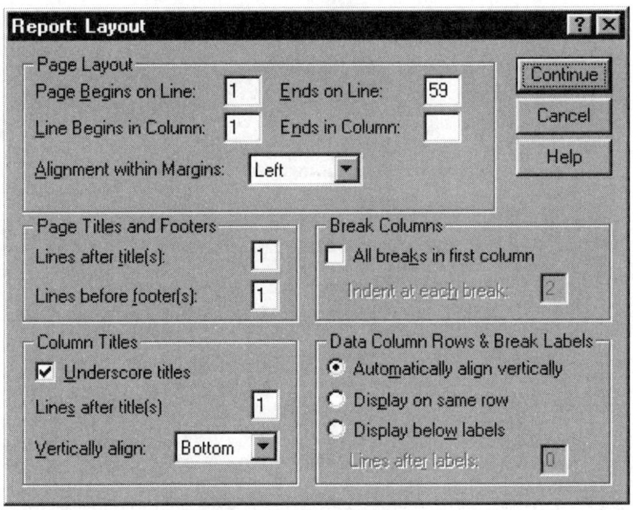


**Page Layout**. Controls the page margins expressed in lines (top and bottom) and characters (left and right) and report alignment within the margins.

**Page Titles and Footers**. Controls the number of lines that separate page titles and footers from the body of the report.

**Break Columns**. Controls the display of break columns. If multiple break variables are specified, they can be in separate columns or in the first column. Placing all break variables in the first column produces a narrower report.

**Column Titles**. Controls the display of column titles, including title underlining, space between titles and the body of the report, and vertical alignment of column titles.

**Data Column Rows & Break Labels.** Controls the placement of data column information (data values and/or summary statistics) in relation to the break labels at the start of each break category. The first row of data column information can start either on the same line as break category label or on a specified number of lines after the break category label. (Not available for columns summary reports.)

## Report Titles

Report Titles controls the content and placement of report titles and footers. You can specify up to 10 lines of page titles and up to 10 lines of page footers, with left-justified, centered, and right-justified components on each line.

Figure 33-8
*Report Titles dialog box*

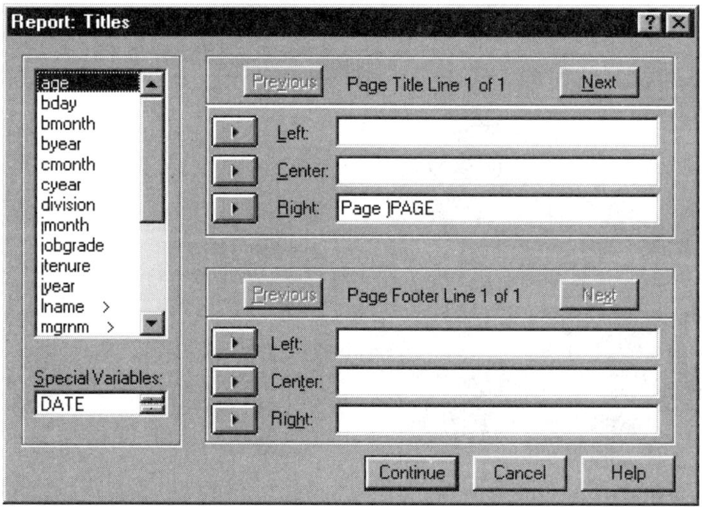


If you insert variables into titles or footers, the current value label or value of the variable is displayed in the title or footer. In titles, the value label corresponding to the value of the variable at the beginning of the page is displayed. In footers, the value label corresponding to the value of the variable at the end of the page is displayed. If there is no value label, the actual value is displayed.

**Special Variables**. The special variables *DATE* and *PAGE* allow you to insert the current date or the page number into any line of a report header or footer. If your data file contains variables named *DATE* or *PAGE*, you cannot use these variables in report titles or footers.

## Report Summaries in Columns

Report Summaries in Columns produces summary reports in which different summary statistics appear in separate columns.

**Example.** A company with a chain of retail stores keeps records of employee information, including salary, job tenure, and the division in which each employee works. You could generate a report that provides summary salary statistics (for example, mean, minimum, maximum) for each division.

**Data Columns**. Lists the report variables for which you want summary statistics and controls the display format and summary statistics displayed for each variable.

**Break Columns**. Lists optional break variables that divide the report into groups and controls the display formats of break columns. For multiple break variables, there will be a separate group for each category of each break variable within categories of the preceding break variable in the list. Break variables should be discrete categorical variables that divide cases into a limited number of meaningful categories.

**Report**. Controls overall report characteristics, including display of missing values, page numbering, and titles.

**Preview**. Displays only the first page of the report. This option is useful for previewing the format of your report without processing the whole report.

**Data are already sorted**. For reports with break variables, the data file must be sorted by break variable values before generating the report. If your data file is already sorted by values of the break variables, you can save processing time by selecting this option. This option is particularly useful after running a preview report.

## Sample Output

Figure 33-9
*Summary report with summary statistics in columns*

| | | | Mean | Minimum | Maximum |
|---|---|---|---|---|---|
| | | Annual | Annual | Annual | |
| Division | Mean Age | Salary | Salary | Salary | |
| Carpeting | 30.75 | $11,764 | $9,200 | $19,500 | |
| Appliances | 31.11 | $12,508 | $7,500 | $28,300 | |
| Furniture | 36.87 | $13,255 | $8,975 | $17,050 | |
| Hardware | 36.20 | $17,580 | $7,450 | $22,500 | |

## To Obtain a Summary Report: Summaries in Columns

▶ From the menus choose:

Analyze
 Reports
  Report Summaries in Columns...

▶ Select one or more variables for Data Columns. One column in the report is generated for each variable selected.

▶ To change the summary measure for a variable, select the variable in the Data Columns list and click Summary.

▶ To obtain more than one summary measure for a variable, select the variable in the source list and move it into the Data Columns list multiple times, one for each summary measure you want.

▶ To display a column containing the sum, mean, ratio, or other function of existing columns, click Insert Total. This places a variable called *total* into the Data Columns list.

▶ For reports sorted and displayed by subgroups, select one or more variables for Break Columns.

Figure 33-10
*Report Summaries in Columns dialog box*

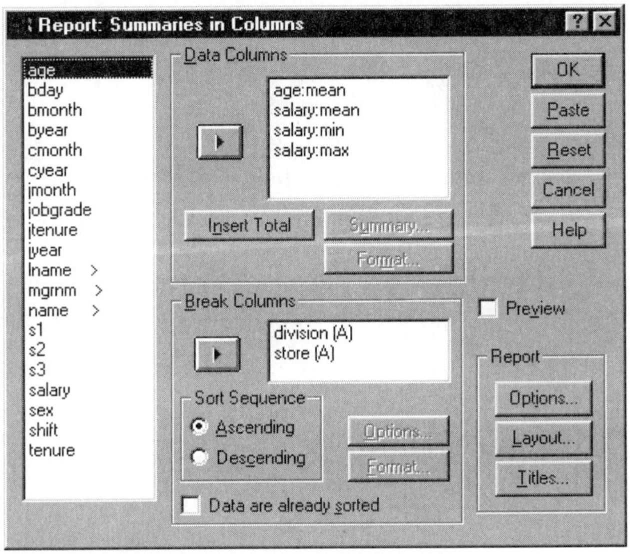


## Report Summary Lines

Summary Lines controls the summary statistic displayed for the selected data column variable.

Figure 33-11
*Report Summary Lines dialog box*

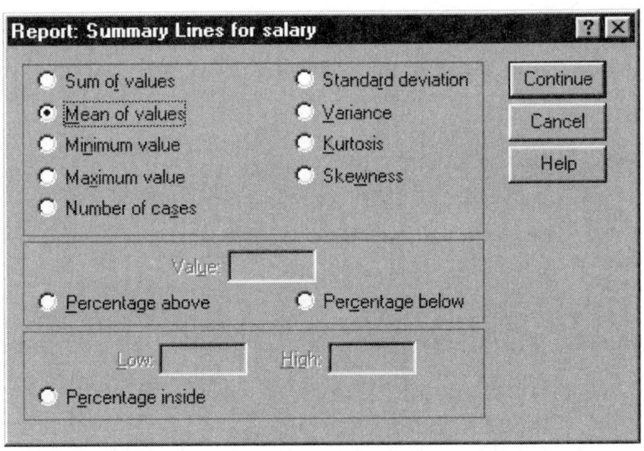

Available summary statistics are sum, mean, minimum, maximum, number of cases, percentage of case above or below a specified value, percentage of cases within a specified range of values, standard deviation, variance, kurtosis, and skewness.

## Total Summary Column

Summary Column controls the total summary statistics that summarize two or more data columns.

Available total summary statistics are sum of columns, mean of columns, minimum, maximum, difference between values in two columns, quotient of values in one column divided by values in another column, and product of columns values multiplied together.

Figure 33-12
*Report Summary Column dialog box*

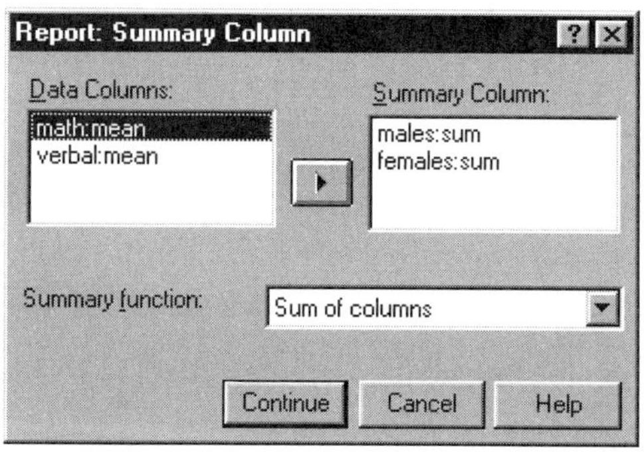


**Sum of columns.** The *total* column is the sum of the columns in the Summary Column list.

**Mean of columns**. The *total* column is the average of the columns in the Summary Column list.

**Minimum of columns**. The *total* column is the minimum of the columns in the Summary Column list.

**Maximum of columns**. The *total* column is the maximum of the columns in the Summary Column list.

**1st column – 2nd column**. The *total* column is the difference of the columns in the Summary Column list. The Summary Column list must contain exactly two columns.

**1st column / 2nd column**. The *total* column is the quotient of the columns in the Summary Column list. The Summary Column list must contain exactly two columns.

**% 1st column / 2nd column**. The *total* column is the first column's percentage of the second column in the Summary Column list. The Summary Column list must contain exactly two columns.

**Product of columns**. The *total* column is the product of the columns in the Summary Column list.

## Report Column Format

Data and break column formatting options for Report Summaries in Columns are the same as those described for Report Summaries in Rows.

## Report Break Options for Summaries in Columns

Break Options controls subtotal display, spacing, and pagination for break categories.

Figure 33-13
*Report Break Options dialog box*

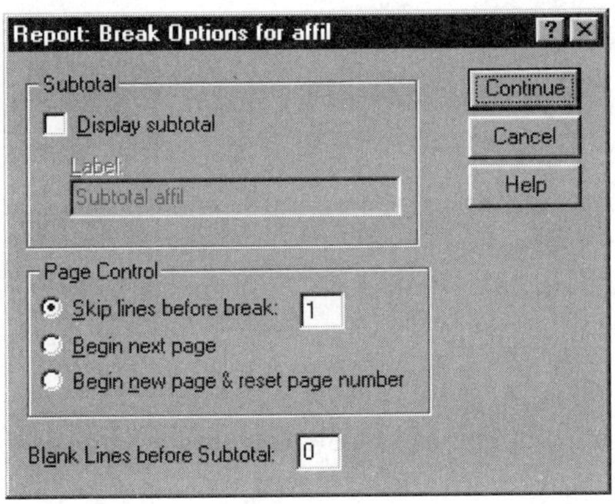


**Subtotal**. Controls the display subtotals for break categories.

**Page Control**. Controls spacing and pagination for categories of the selected break variable. You can specify a number of blank lines between break categories or start each break category on a new page.

**Blank Lines before Subtotal**. Controls the number of blank lines between break category data and subtotals.

## Report Options for Summaries in Columns

Options controls the display of grand totals, the display of missing values, and pagination in column summary reports.

Figure 33-14
*Report Options dialog box*

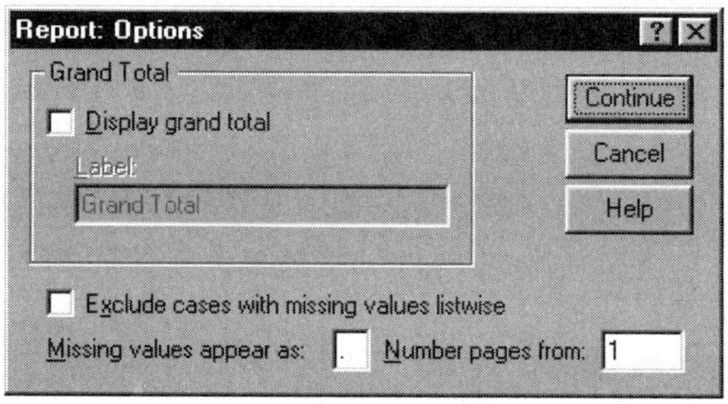


**Grand Total**. Displays and labels a grand total for each column; displayed at the bottom of the column.

**Missing values.** You can exclude missing values from the report or select a single character to indicate missing values in the report.

## Report Layout for Summaries in Columns

Report layout options for Report Summaries in Columns are the same as those described for Report Summaries in Rows.

## REPORT Command Additional Features

The SPSS command language also allows you to:

- Display different summary functions in the columns of a single summary line.
- Insert summary lines into data columns for variables other than the data column variable, or for various combinations (composite functions) of summary functions.
- Use Median, Mode, Frequency, and Percent as summary functions.
- Control more precisely the display format of summary statistics.
- Insert blank lines at various points in reports.
- Insert blank lines after every *n*th case in listing reports.

Because of the complexity of the REPORT syntax, you may find it useful, when building a new report with syntax, to approximate the report generated from the dialog boxes, copy and paste the corresponding syntax, and refine that syntax to yield the exact report that you want.

See the *SPSS Syntax Reference Guide* for complete syntax information.

Chapter

# 34

# *Reliability Analysis*

Reliability analysis allows you to study the properties of measurement scales and the items that make them up. The Reliability Analysis procedure calculates a number of commonly used measures of scale reliability and also provides information about the relationships between individual items in the scale. Intraclass correlation coefficients can be used to compute interrater reliability estimates.

**Example.** Does my questionnaire measure customer satisfaction in a useful way? Using reliability analysis, you can determine the extent to which the items in your questionnaire are related to each other, you can get an overall index of the repeatability or internal consistency of the scale as a whole, and you can identify problem items that should be excluded from the scale.

**Statistics.** Descriptives for each variable and for the scale, summary statistics across items, inter-item correlations and covariances, reliability estimates, ANOVA table, intraclass correlation coefficients, Hotelling's $T^2$, and Tukey's test of additivity.

**Models.** The following models of reliability are available:

- **Alpha (Cronbach).** This is a model of internal consistency, based on the average inter-item correlation.
- **Split-half.** This model splits the scale into two parts and examines the correlation between the parts.
- **Guttman.** This model computes Guttman's lower bounds for true reliability.
- **Parallel.** This model assumes that all items have equal variances and equal error variances across replications.
- **Strict parallel.** This model makes the assumptions of the parallel model and also assumes equal means across items.

**Data.** Data can be dichotomous, ordinal, or interval, but they should be coded numerically.

**Assumptions.** Observations should be independent, and errors should be uncorrelated between items. Each pair of items should have a bivariate normal distribution. Scales should be additive, so that each item is linearly related to the total score.

**Related procedures.** If you want to explore the dimensionality of your scale items (to see if more than one construct is needed to account for the pattern of item scores), use Factor Analysis or Multidimensional Scaling. To identify homogeneous groups of variables, you can use Hierarchical Cluster Analysis to cluster variables.

## Sample Output

Figure 34-1
*Reliability output*

```
                        Mean        Std Dev        Cases

  1.     ANY            .4868         .5001        906.0
  2.     BORED          .5022         .5003        906.0
  3.     CRITICS        .5033         .5003        906.0
  4.     PEERS          .5287         .4995        906.0


                    Correlation Matrix

                ANY         BORED        CRITICS      PEERS

ANY            1.0000
BORED           .8150       1.0000
CRITICS         .8128        .8256       1.0000
PEERS           .7823        .8068        .8045       1.0000



Reliability Coefficients      4 items

Alpha =    .9439          Standardized item alpha =    .9439
```

# To Obtain a Reliability Analysis

▶ From the menus choose:

Analyze
  Scale
    Reliability Analysis...

Figure 34-2
*Reliability Analysis dialog box*

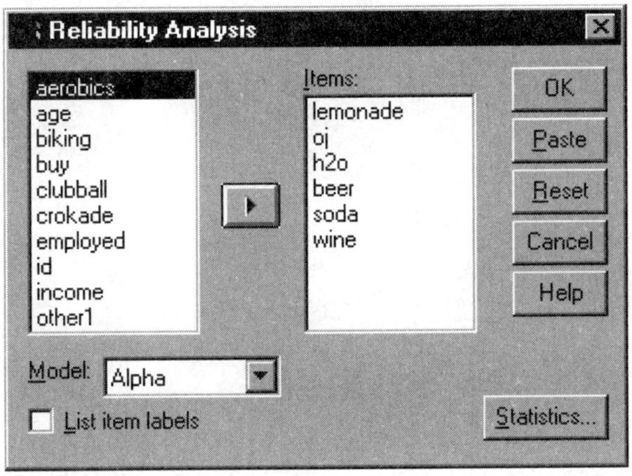


▶ Select two or more variables as potential components of an additive scale.

▶ Choose a model from the Model drop-down list.

## Reliability Analysis Statistics

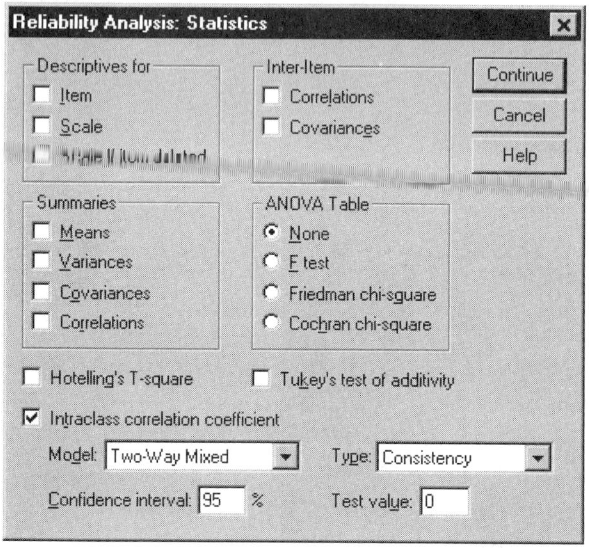


Figure 34-3
*Reliability Analysis Statistics dialog box*

You can select various statistics describing your scale and items. Statistics reported by default include the number of cases, the number of items, and reliability estimates as follows:

- Alpha models: Coefficient alpha. For dichotomous data, this is equivalent to the Kuder-Richardson 20 (KR20) coefficient.
- Split-half models: Correlation between forms, Guttman split-half reliability, Spearman-Brown reliability (equal and unequal length), and coefficient alpha for each half.
- Guttman models: Reliability coefficients lambda 1 through lambda 6.
- Parallel and Strictly parallel models: Test for goodness-of-fit of model, estimates of error variance, common variance, and true variance, estimated common inter-item correlation, estimated reliability, and unbiased estimate of reliability.

**Descriptives for.** Produces descriptive statistics for scales or items across cases. Available options are Item, Scale, and Scale if item deleted.

**Summaries.** Provides descriptive statistics of item distributions across all items in the scale. Available options are Means, Variances, Covariances, and Correlations.

**Inter-item.** Produces matrices of correlations or covariances between items.

**ANOVA Table.** Produces tests of equal means. Available alternatives are None, *F* test, Friedman chi-square, or Cochran chi-square.

**Hotelling's T-square.** Produces a multivariate test of the null hypothesis that all items on the scale have the same mean.

**Tukey's test of additivity.** Produces a test of the assumption that there is no multiplicative interaction among the items.

**Intraclass correlation coefficient.** Produces measures of consistency or agreement of values within cases.

- **Model.** Select the model for calculating the intraclass correlation coefficient. Available models are Two-way mixed, Two-way random, and One-way random.
- **Type.** Select the type of index. Available types are Consistency and Absolute Agreement.
- **Confidence interval.** Specify the level for the confidence interval. Default is 95%.
- **Test value.** Specify the hypothesized value of the coefficient for the hypothesis test. This is the value to which the observed value is compared. Default value is 0.

## RELIABILITY Command Additional Features

The SPSS command language also allows you to:

- Read and analyze a correlation matrix.
- Write a correlation matrix for later analysis.
- Specify splits other than equal halves for the split-half method.

Chapter

# 35

# Multidimensional Scaling

Multidimensional scaling attempts to find the structure in a set of distance measures between objects or cases. This is accomplished by assigning observations to specific locations in a conceptual space (usually two- or three-dimensional) such that the distances between points in the space match the given dissimilarities as closely as possible. In many cases, the dimensions of this conceptual space can be interpreted and used to further understand your data. If you have objectively measured variables, you can use multidimensional scaling as a data reduction technique (the Multidimensional Scaling procedure will compute distances from multivariate data for you, if necessary). Multidimensional scaling can also be applied to subjective ratings of dissimilarity between objects or concepts. Additionally, the Multidimensional Scaling procedure can handle dissimilarity data from multiple sources, as you might have with multiple raters or questionnaire respondents.

**Example.** How do people perceive relationships between different cars? If you have data from respondents indicating similarity ratings between different makes and models of cars, multidimensional scaling can be used to identify dimensions that describe consumers' perceptions. You might find, for example, that the price and size of a vehicle define a two-dimensional space, which accounts for the similarities reported by your respondents.

**Statistics.** For each model: data matrix, optimally scaled data matrix, S-stress (Young's), stress (Kruskal's), RSQ, stimulus coordinates, average stress and RSQ for each stimulus (RMDS models). For individual difference (INDSCAL) models: subject weights and weirdness index for each subject. For each matrix in replicated multidimensional scaling models: stress and RSQ for each stimulus. Plots: stimulus coordinates (two- or three-dimensional), scatterplot of disparities versus distances.

**Data.** If your data are dissimilarity data, all dissimilarities should be quantitative and should be measured in the same metric. If your data are multivariate data, variables can be quantitative, binary, or count data. Scaling of variables is an important issue—

differences in scaling may affect your solution. If your variables have large differences in scaling (for example, one variable is measured in dollars and the other is measured in years), you should consider standardizing them (this can be done automatically by the Multidimensional Scaling procedure).

**Assumptions.** The Multidimensional Scaling procedure is relatively free of distributional assumptions. Be sure to select the appropriate measurement level (ordinal, interval, or ratio) under Options to be sure that the results are computed correctly.

**Related procedures.** If your goal is data reduction, an alternative method to consider is factor analysis, particularly if your variables are quantitative. If you want to identify groups of similar cases, consider supplementing your multidimensional scaling analysis with a hierarchical or *k*-means cluster analysis.

## To Obtain a Multidimensional Scaling Analysis

▶ From the menus choose:

Analyze
  Scale
    Multidimensional Scaling...

Figure 35-1
*Multidimensional Scaling dialog box*

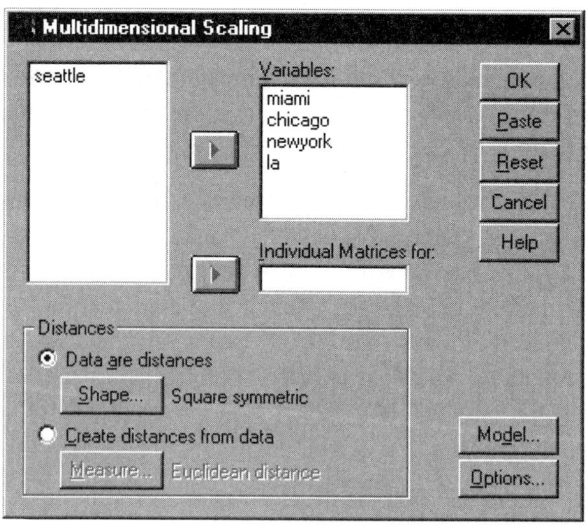

- In Distances, select either Data are distances or Create distances from data.
- If your data are distances, you must select at least four numeric variables for analysis, and you can click Shape to indicate the shape of the distance matrix.
- If you want SPSS to create the distances before analyzing them, you must select at least one numeric variable, and you can click Measure to specify the type of distance measure you want. You can create separate matrices for each category of a grouping variable (which can be either numeric or string) by moving that variable into the Individual Matrices For list.

## Multidimensional Scaling Shape of Data

Figure 35-2
*Multidimensional Scaling Shape of Data dialog box*

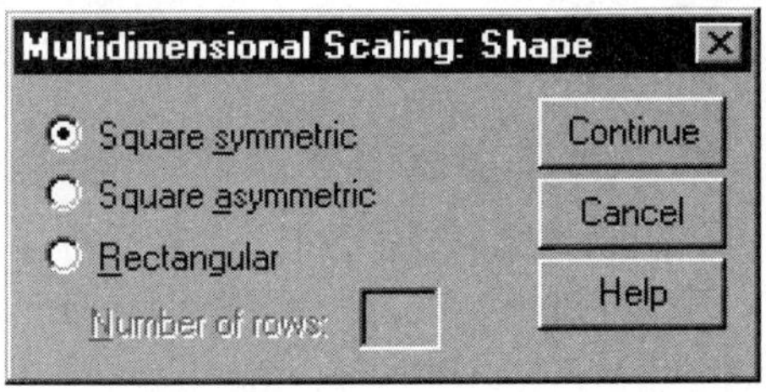


If your working data file represents distances among a set of objects, or distances between two sets of objects, you must specify the shape of your data matrix in order to get the correct results. Choose an alternative: Square symmetric, Square asymmetric, or Rectangular. *Note:* You cannot select Square symmetric if the Model dialog box specifies row conditionality.

## Multidimensional Scaling Create Measure

Figure 35-3
*Multidimensional Scaling Create Measure from Data dialog box*

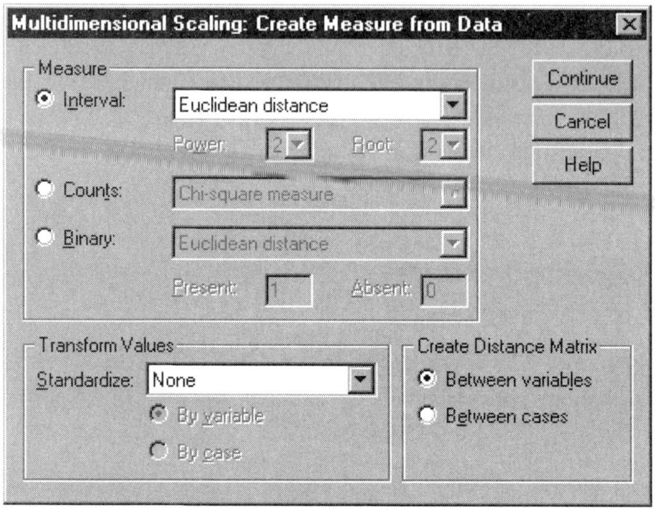


Multidimensional scaling uses dissimilarity data to create a scaling solution. If your data are multivariate data (values of measured variables), you must create dissimilarity data in order to compute a multidimensional scaling solution. You can specify the details of creating dissimilarity measures from your data.

**Measure.** Allows you to specify the dissimilarity measure for your analysis. Select one alternative from the Measure group corresponding to your type of data, and then select one of the measures from the drop-down list corresponding to that type of measure. Available alternatives are:

- **Interval**. Euclidean distance, squared Euclidean distance, Chebychev, Block, Minkowski, or Customized.
- **Count**. Chi-square measure or Phi-square measure.
- **Binary**. Euclidean distance, Squared Euclidean distance, Size difference, Pattern difference, Variance, or Lance and Williams.

**Create Distance Matrix.** Allows you to choose the unit of analysis. Alternatives are Between variables or Between cases.

**Transform Values.** In certain cases, such as when variables are measured on very different scales, you may want to standardize values before computing proximities (not applicable to binary data). Select a standardization method from the Standardize drop-down list (if no standardization is required, select None).

## Multidimensional Scaling Model

Figure 35-4
*Multidimensional Scaling Model dialog box*

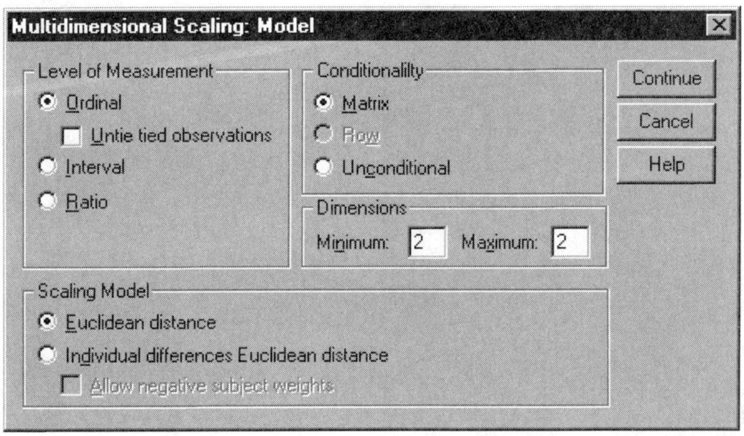


Correct estimation of a multidimensional scaling model depends on aspects of the data and the model itself.

**Level of measurement.** Allows you to specify the level of your data. Alternatives are Ordinal, Interval, or Ratio. If your variables are ordinal, selecting Untie tied observations requests that they be treated as continuous variables, so that ties (equal values for different cases) are resolved optimally.

**Conditionality.** Allows you to specify which comparisons are meaningful. Alternatives are Matrix, Row, or Unconditional.

**Dimensions.** Allows you to specify the dimensionality of the scaling solution(s). One solution is calculated for each number in the range. Specify integers between 1 and 6; a minimum of 1 is allowed only if you select Euclidean distance as the scaling model. For a single solution, specify the same number as minimum and maximum.

**Scaling Model.** Allows you to specify the assumptions by which the scaling is performed. Available alternatives are Euclidean distance or Individual differences Euclidean distance (also known as INDSCAL). For the Individual differences Euclidean distance model, you can select Allow negative subject weights, if appropriate for your data.

## Multidimensional Scaling Options

Figure 35-5
*Multidimensional Scaling Options dialog box*

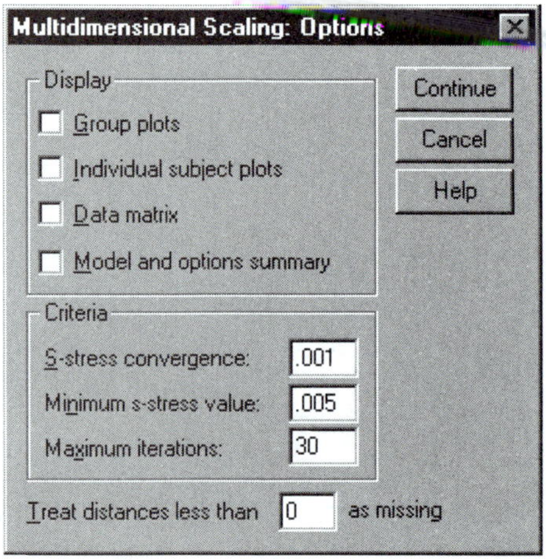


You can specify options for your multidimensional scaling analysis:

**Display.** Allows you to select various types of output. Available options are Group plots, Individual subject plots, Data matrix, and Model and options summary.

**Criteria.** Allows you to determine when iteration should stop. To change the defaults, enter values for S-stress convergence, Minimum S-stress value, and Maximum iterations.

**Treat distances less than n as missing.** Distances less than this value are excluded from the analysis.

## Multidimensional Scaling Command Additional Features

The SPSS command language also allows you to:

- Use three additional model types, known as ASCAL, AINDS, and GEMSCAL in the literature on multidimensional scaling.
- Carry out polynomial transformations on interval and ratio data.
- Analyze similarities (rather than distances) with ordinal data.
- Analyze nominal data.
- Save various coordinate and weight matrices into files and read them back in for analysis.
- Constrain multidimensional unfolding.

Chapter
36

# Ratio Statistics

The Ratio Statistics procedure provides a comprehensive list of summary statistics for describing the ratio between two scale variables.

You can sort the output by values of a grouping variable in ascending or descending order. The ratio statistics report can be suppressed in the output and the results saved to an external file.

**Example.** Is there good uniformity in the ratio between the appraisal price and sale price of homes in each of five counties? From the output, you might learn that the distribution of ratios varies considerably from county to county.

**Statistics.** Median, mean, weighted mean, confidence intervals, coefficient of dispersion (COD), median-centered coefficient of variation, mean-centered coefficient of variation, price-related differential (PRD), standard deviation, average absolute deviation (AAD), range, minimum and maximum values, and the concentration index computed for a user-specified range or percentage within the median ratio.

**Data.** Use numeric codes or short strings to code grouping variables (nominal or ordinal level measurements).

**Assumptions.** The variables that define the numerator and denominator of the ratio should be scale variables that take positive values.

# To Obtain Ratio Statistics

▶ From the menus choose:

Analyze
  Descriptive Statistics
    Ratio...

Figure 36-1
*Ratio Statistics dialog box*

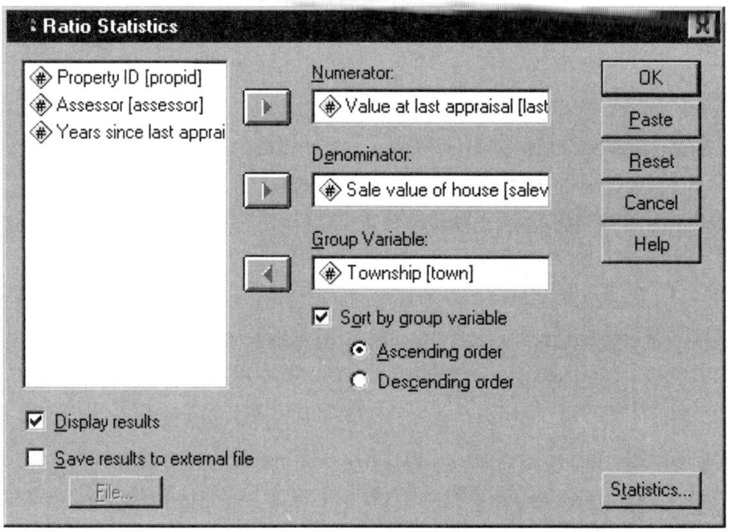


▶ Select a numerator variable.

▶ Select a denominator variable.

Optionally, you can:

- Select a grouping variable and specify the ordering of the groups in the results.
- Choose whether or not to display the results in the Output Viewer.
- Choose whether or not to save the results to an external file for later use, and specify the name of the file to which the results are saved.

## Ratio Statistics

Figure 36-2
*Statistics dialog box*

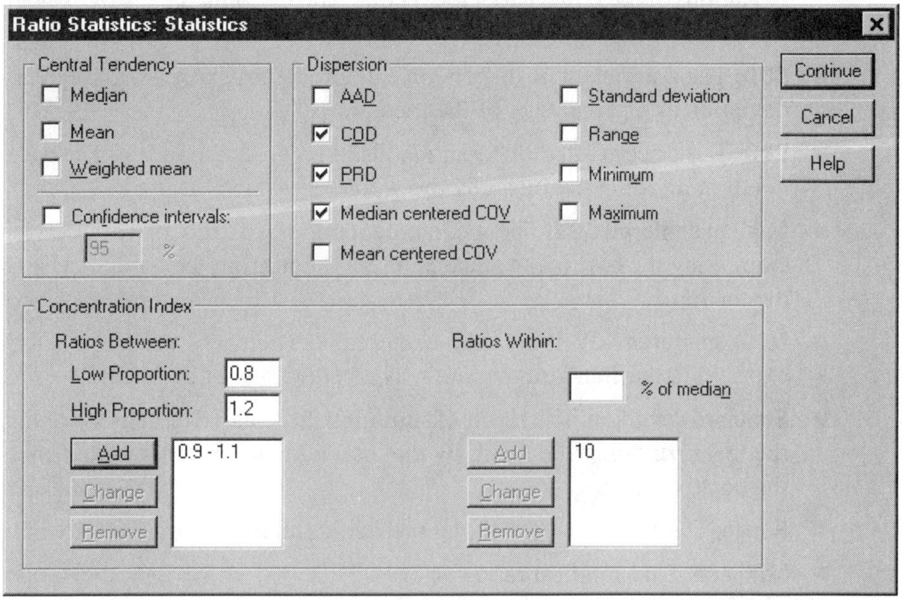


**Central Tendency.** Measures of central tendency are statistics that describe the distribution of ratios.

- **Median.** The value such that the number of ratios less than this value and the number of ratios greater than this value are the same.
- **Mean.** The result of summing the ratios and dividing the result by the total number of ratios.
- **Weighted mean.** The result of dividing the mean of the numerator by the mean of the denominator. It is also the mean of the ratios weighted by the denominator.
- **Confidence intervals.** This displays confidence intervals for the mean, the median, and the weighted mean (if requested). Specify a value greater than or equal to 0 and less than 100 as the confidence level.

**Dispersion.** These are statistics that measure the amount of variation, or spread, in the observed values.

- **AAD.** The average absolute deviation is the result of summing the absolute deviations of the ratios about the median and dividing the result by the total number of ratios.
- **COD.** The coefficient of dispersion is the result of expressing the average absolute deviation as a percentage of the median.
- **PRD.** The price-related differential, also known as the index of regressivity, is the result of dividing the mean by the weighted mean.
- **Median centered COV.** The median-centered coefficient of variation is the result of expressing the root mean squares of deviation from the median as a percentage of the median.
- **Mean centered COV.** The mean-centered coefficient of variation is the result of expressing the standard deviation as a percentage of the mean.
- **Standard deviation.** The result of summing the squared deviations of the ratios about the mean, dividing the result by the total number of ratios minus one, and taking the positive square root.
- **Range.** The result of subtracting the minimum ratio from the maximum ratio.
- **Minimum.** The smallest ratio.
- **Maximum.** The largest ratio.

**Concentration Index.** The coefficient of concentration measures the percentage of ratios that fall within an interval. It can be computed in two different ways:

- **Ratios Between.** Here the interval is defined explicitly by specifying the low and high values of the interval. Enter values for the low and high proportions and click Add to obtain an interval.
- **Ratios Within.** Here the interval is defined implicitly by specifying the percentage of the median. Enter a value between 0 and 100 and click Add. The lower end of the interval is equal to $(1 - 0.01 \times \text{value}) \times \text{median}$, and the upper end is equal to $(1 + 0.01 \times \text{value}) \times \text{median}$.

Chapter

# 37

# Overview of the Chart Facility

High-resolution charts and plots are created by the procedures on the Graphs menu and by many of the procedures on the Analyze menu. This chapter provides an overview of the chart facility. Interactive charts, available on the Interactive submenu of the Graphs menu are covered in a separate book, *SPSS Interactive Graphics.*

## How to Create and Modify a Chart

Before you can create a chart, you need to get your data into the Data Editor. You can enter the data directly into the Data Editor, open a previously saved data file, or read a spreadsheet, tab-delimited data file, or database file. The Tutorial menu selection on the Help menu has online examples of creating and modifying a chart, and the online Help system provides information on how to create and modify all chart types.

### Creating the Chart

After you get your data into the Data Editor, you can create a chart by selecting a chart type from the Graphs menu. This opens a chart dialog box, as shown in Figure 37-1.

Figure 37-1
*Chart dialog box*

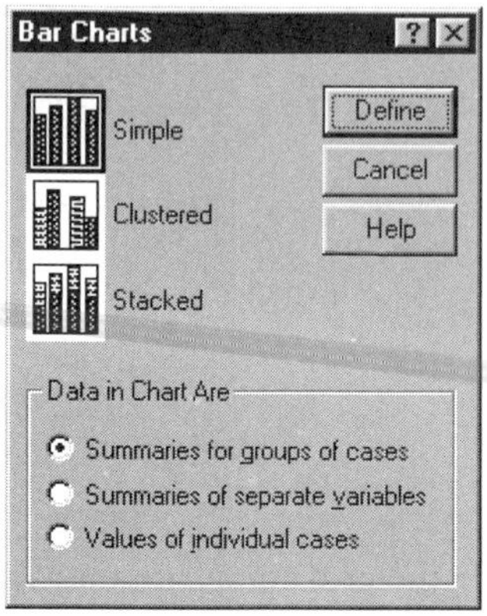


The dialog box contains icons for various types of charts and a list of data structures. Click Define to open a chart definition dialog box such as the following one.

Figure 37-2
*Chart definition dialog box*

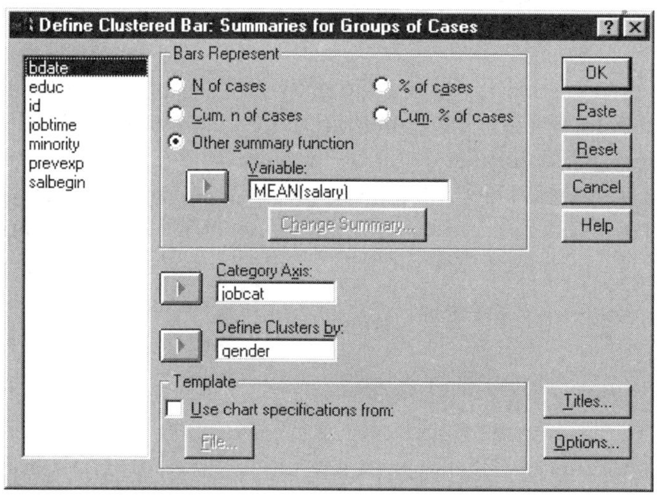


In this dialog box, you can select the variables appropriate for the chart and choose the options you want. For information about the various choices, click Help.

The chart is displayed in the Viewer, as shown in Figure 37-3.

**Figure 37-3**
*Chart in Viewer*

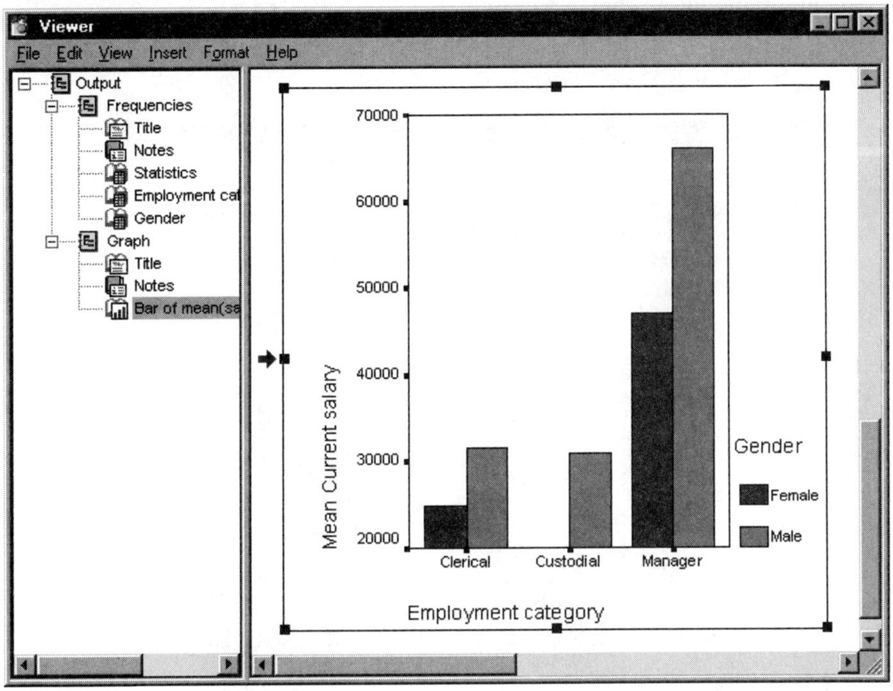

## Modifying the Chart

To modify a chart, double-click anywhere on the chart. This displays the chart in a chart window, as shown in Figure 37-4.

Figure 37-4
*Original chart in chart window*

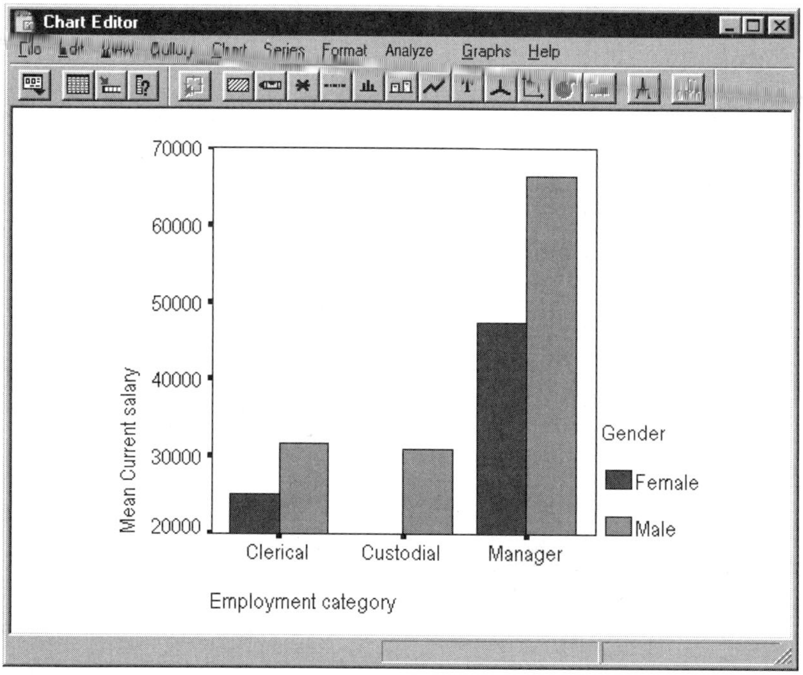


You can modify any part of the chart or use the gallery to change to another type of chart illustrating the same data. Some typical modifications include the following:

- Edit axis titles and labels.
- Edit the legend, which identifies the colors or patterns of the bars.
- Add a title.
- Change the location of the bar origin line.
- Add annotation.
- Add an outer frame.

Figure 37-5 shows a modified chart.

Figure 37-5
*Modified chart*

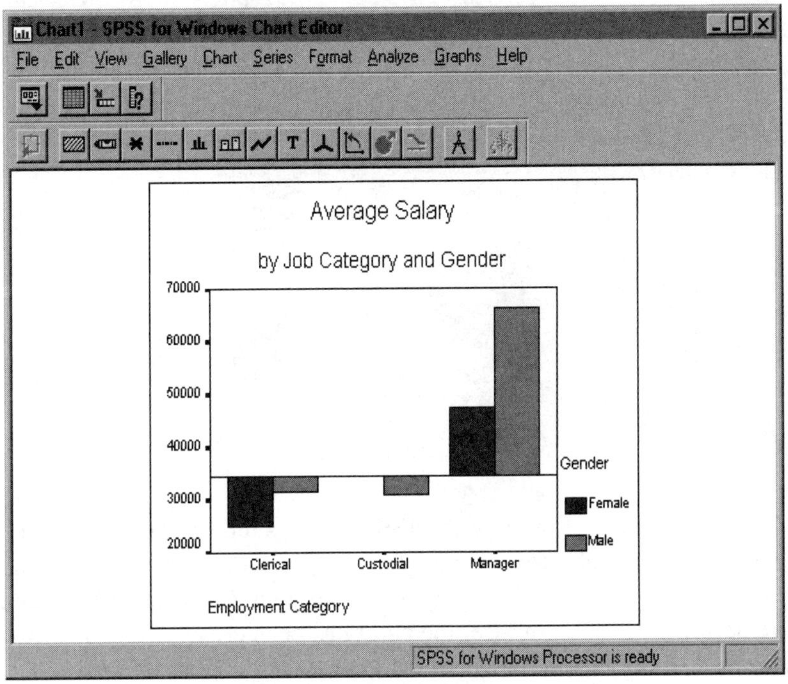


Chart modifications are saved when you close the chart window, and the modified chart is displayed in the Viewer.

# Chart Definition Global Options

When you are defining a chart, the specific chart definition dialog box usually contains the pushbuttons Titles and Options and a Template group, as shown in Figure 37-6. These global options are available for most charts, regardless of type. They are not available for P-P plots, Q-Q plots, sequence charts, or time series charts.

Figure 37-6
*A chart definition dialog box*

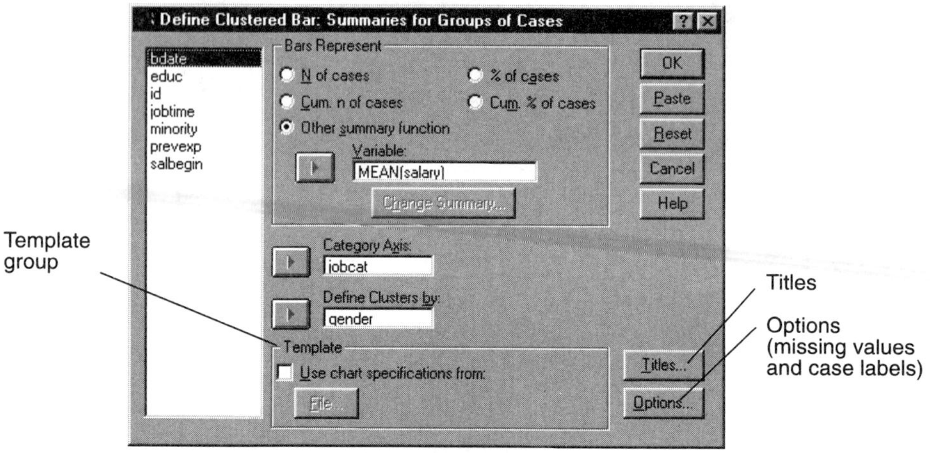


The Titles dialog box allows you to specify titles, subtitles, and footnotes. You can click Options to control the treatment of missing values for most charts and case labels for scatterplots. You can apply a template of previously selected attributes either when you are defining the chart or after the chart has been created. The next few sections describe how to define these characteristics at the time you define the chart.

## Titles, Subtitles, and Footnotes

In any chart, you can define two title lines, one subtitle line, and two footnote lines as part of your original chart definition. To specify titles or footnotes while defining a chart, click Titles in the chart definition dialog box (see Figure 37-6). This opens the Titles dialog box, as shown in Figure 37-7.

Figure 37-7
*Titles dialog box*

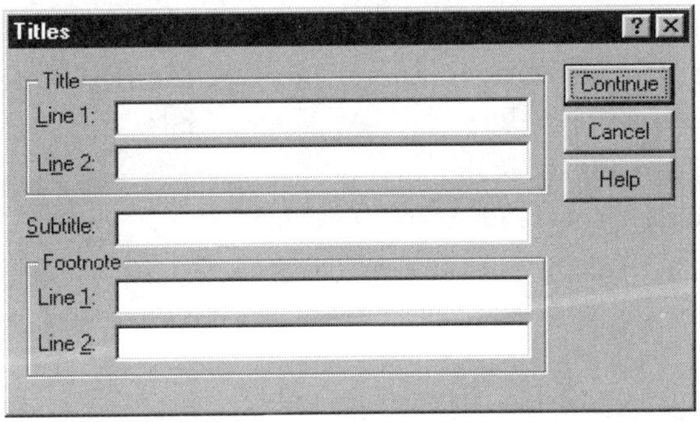


Each line can be up to 72 characters long. The number of characters that will actually fit in the chart depends upon the font and size. Most titles are left-justified by default and, if too long, are cropped on the right. Pie chart titles, by default, are center-justified and, if too long, are cropped at both ends.

You can also add, delete, or revise text lines, as well as change their font, size, and justification, within the Chart Editor.

## Options

The Options dialog box provides options for treatment of missing values and display of case labels, as shown in Figure 37-8. This dialog box is available from the chart definition dialog box (see Figure 37-6).

Figure 37-8
*Options dialog box*

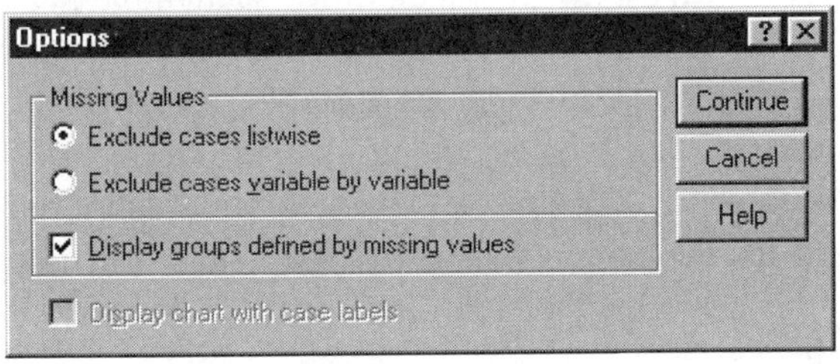


The availability of each option depends on your previous choices. Missing-value options are not available for charts using values of individual cases or for histograms.

The case-labels display option is available only for a scatterplot that has a variable selected for case labels.

**Missing Values.** If you selected summaries of separate variables for a categorical chart or if you are creating a scatterplot, you can choose one of the following alternatives for exclusion of cases having missing values:

- **Exclude cases listwise.** If any of the variables in the chart has a missing value for a given case, the whole case is excluded from the chart.
- **Exclude cases variable by variable.** If a selected variable has any missing values, the cases having those missing values are excluded when the variable is analyzed.

The following option is also available for missing values:

- **Display groups defined by missing values.** If there are missing values in the data for variables used to define categories or subgroups, user-missing values (values identified as missing by the user) and system-missing values are included together in a category labeled *Missing*. The "missing" category is displayed on the category axis or in the legend, adding, for example, an extra bar, a slice to a pie chart, or an extra box to a boxplot. In a scatterplot, missing values add a "missing" category to the set of markers. If there are no missing values, the "missing" category is not displayed.

  This option is selected by default. If you want to suppress display after the chart is drawn, select Displayed from the Series menu and move the categories you want suppressed to the Omit group.

  This option is not available for an overlay scatterplot or for single-series charts in which the data are summarized by separate variables.

To see the difference between listwise and variable-by-variable exclusion of missing values, consider Figure 37-9, which shows a bar chart for each of the two options. The charts were created from a version of the *bank.sav* employee data file that was edited to have some system-missing (blank) values in the variables for current salary and job category. In some other cases of the job category variable, the value 9 was entered and defined as missing. For both charts, the option Display groups defined by missing values is selected, which adds the category *Missing* to the other job categories displayed. In each chart, the values of the summary function, *Number of cases*, are displayed in the bar labels.

Figure 37-9
*Examples of missing-data treatment in charts*

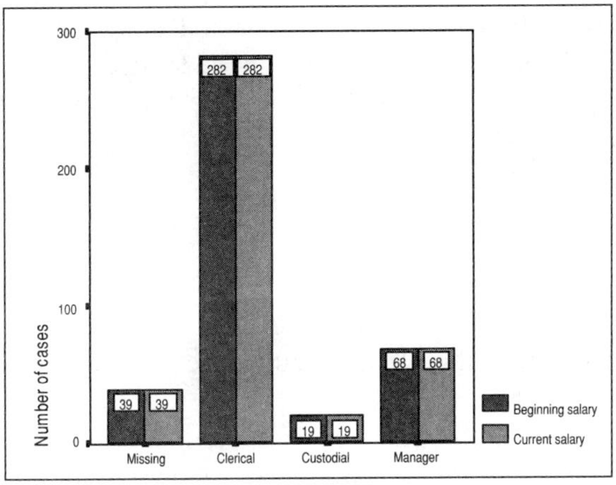


Listwise exclusion of missing values

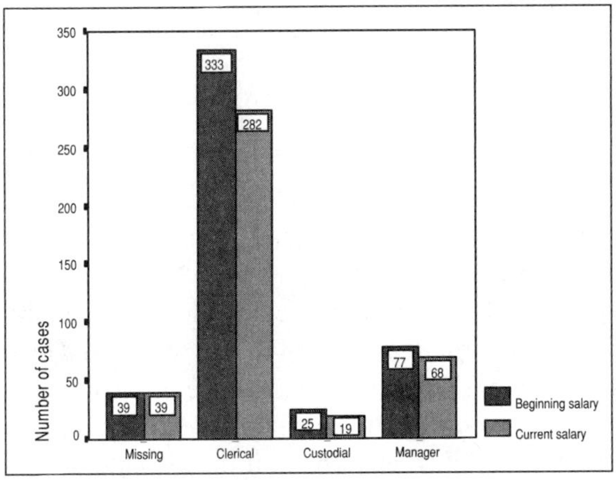


Variable-by-variable exclusion of missing values

In both charts, 26 cases have a system-missing value for the job category and 13 cases have the user-missing value (9). In the listwise chart, the number of cases is the same for both variables in each bar cluster because whenever a value was missing, the case was excluded for all variables. In the variable-by-variable chart, the number of nonmissing cases for each variable in a category is plotted without regard to missing values in other variables.

The final selection in the Options dialog box controls the status of case labels when a scatterplot is first displayed.

- **Display chart with case labels.** When this option is selected, all case labels are displayed when a scatterplot is created. By default, it is deselected—that is, the default scatterplot is displayed without labels. If you select this option, case labels may overlap.

## Chart Templates

You can apply many of the attributes and text elements from one chart to another. This allows you to modify one chart, save that chart, and then use it as a template to create a number of other similar charts.

To use a template when creating a chart, select Use chart specifications from (in the Template group in the chart definition dialog box shown in Figure 37-6) and click File. This opens a standard file selection dialog box.

To apply a template to a chart already in a chart window, from the menus choose:

File
  Apply Chart Template...

This opens a standard file selection dialog box. Select a file to use as a template. If you are creating a new chart, the filename you select is displayed in the Template group when you return to the chart definition dialog box.

A template is used to borrow the format from one chart and apply it to the new chart you are generating. In general, any formatting information from the old chart that can apply to the new chart will automatically apply. For example, if the old chart is a clustered bar chart with bar colors modified to yellow and green and the new chart is a multiple line chart, the lines will be yellow and green. If the old chart is a simple bar chart with drop shadows and the new chart is a simple line chart, the lines will not have drop shadows because drop shadows don't apply to line charts. If there are titles in the template chart but not in the new chart, you will get the titles from the template chart. If there are titles defined in the new chart, they will override the titles in the template chart.

- **Apply title and footnote text.** Applies the text of the title and footnotes of the template to the current chart, overriding any text defined in the Titles dialog box in the current chart. The attributes of the title and footnotes (font, size, and color) are applied whether or not this item is selected. This check box appears only if you are applying the template in a chart window, not when creating a new chart.

### Creating Chart Templates

To create a chart template:

- ▶ Create a chart.
- ▶ Edit the chart to contain the attributes you want to save in a template.
- ▶ From the chart window menus choose:

File
  Save Chart Template...

Chapter

# 38

# ROC Curves

This procedure is a useful way to evaluate the performance of classification schemes in which there is one variable with two categories by which subjects are classified.

**Example.** It is in a bank's interest to correctly classify customers into those who will and will not default on their loans, so special methods are developed for making these decisions. ROC curves can be used to evaluate how well these methods perform.

**Statistics.** Area under the ROC curve with confidence interval and coordinate points of the ROC curve. Plots: ROC curve.

**Methods.** The estimate of the area under the ROC curve can be computed either nonparametrically or parametrically using a binegative exponential model.

**Data.** Test variables are quantitative. They are often composed of probabilities from discriminant analysis or logistic regression or scores on an arbitrary scale indicating a rater's "strength of conviction" that a subject falls into one category or another. The state variable can be of any type and indicates the true category to which a subject belongs. The value of the state variable indicates which category should be considered *positive*.

**Assumptions.** It is assumed that increasing numbers on the rater scale represent the increasing belief that the subject belongs to one category, while decreasing numbers on the scale represent the increasing belief that the subject belongs to the other category. The user must choose which direction is *positive*. It is also assumed that the *true* category to which each subject belongs is known.

# Sample Output

Figure 38-1
*ROC Curve output*

**Case Processing Summary**

| ACTUAL | Valid N (listwise) |
|---|---|
| Positive[1] | 74 |
| Negative | 76 |

Larger values of the test result variable(s) indicate stronger evidence for a positive actual state.

1. The positive actual state is 1.00.

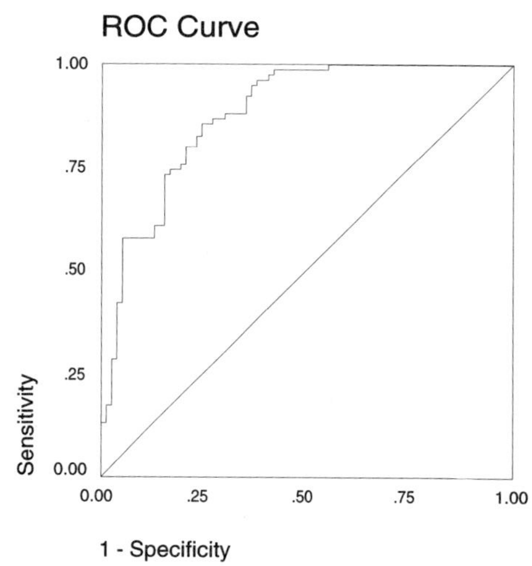


**Area Under the Curve**

Test Result Variable(s): PROBS

| Area | Std. Error[1] | Asymptotic Sig.[2] | Asymptotic 95% Confidence Interval | |
|---|---|---|---|---|
| | | | Lower Bound | Upper Bound |
| .877 | .028 | .000 | .823 | .931 |

1. Under the nonparametric assumption

2. Null hypothesis: true area = 0.5

# How to Obtain an ROC Curve

▶ From the menus choose:

Graphs
 ROC Curve...

Figure 38-2
*ROC Curve dialog box*

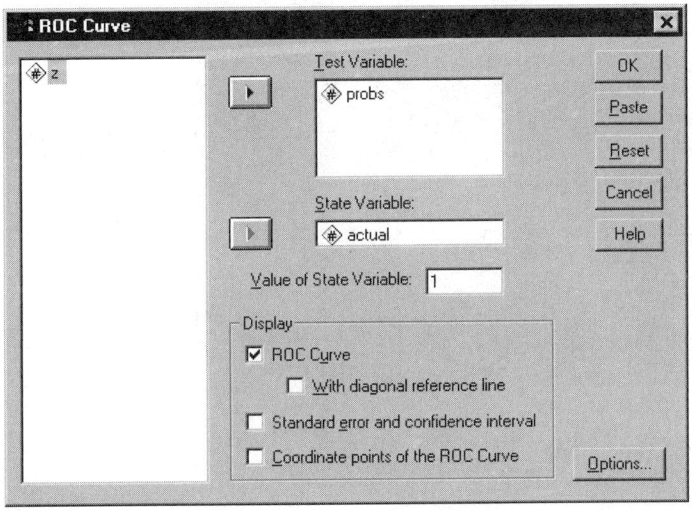


▶ Select one or more test probability variables.

▶ Select one state variable.

▶ Identify the *positive* value for the state variable.

## ROC Curve Options

Figure 38-3
*ROC Curve Options dialog box*

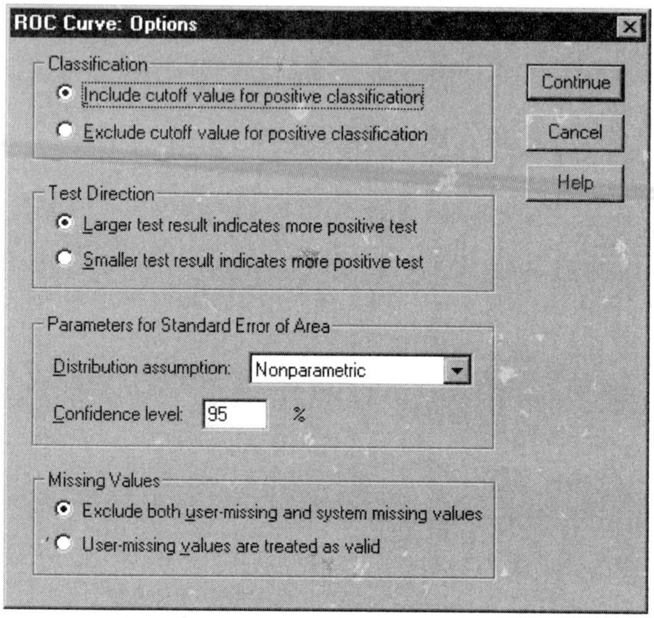


You can specify the following options for your ROC analysis:

**Classification.** Allows you to specify whether the cutoff value should be included or excluded when making a *positive* classification. This currently has no effect on the output.

**Test Direction.** Allows you to specify the direction of the scale in relation to the *positive* category.

**Parameters for Standard Error of Area.** Allows you to specify the method of estimating the standard error of the area under the curve. Available methods are nonparametric and binegative exponential. Also allows you to set the level for the confidence interval. The available range is 50% to 100%.

**Missing Values.** Allows you to specify how missing values are handled.

Chapter

**39**

# Utilities

This chapter describes the functions found on the Utilities menu and the ability to reorder target variable lists using the Windows system menus.

## Variable Information

The Variables dialog box displays variable definition information for the currently selected variable, including:

- Data format
- Variable label
- User-missing values
- Value labels

Figure 39-1
*Variables dialog box*

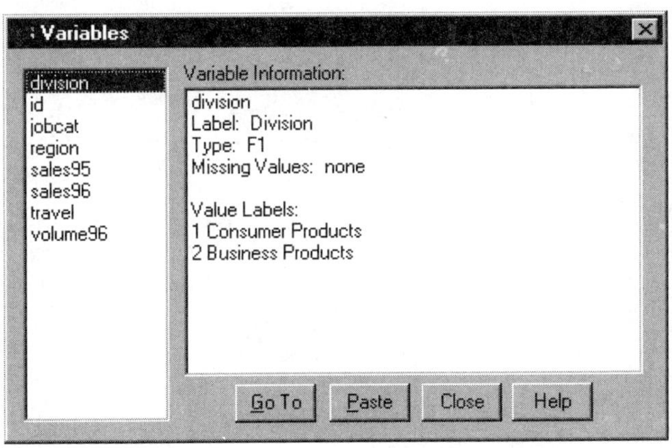

**Go To.** Goes to the selected variable in the Data Editor window.

**Paste.** Pastes the selected variables into the designated syntax window at the cursor location. (Not available in the Student version.)

To modify variable definitions, use Define Variable on the Data menu.

### To Obtain Variable Information

- From the menus choose:

  Utilities
  Variables...

- Select the variable for which you want to display variable definition information.

## Variable Sets

You can restrict the variables that appear on dialog box source variable lists by defining and using variable sets. This is particularly useful for data files with a large number of variables. Small variable sets make it easier to find and select the variables for your analysis and can also enhance performance. If your data file has a large number of variables and dialog boxes that open slowly, restricting dialog box source lists to smaller subsets of variables should reduce the amount of time it takes to open dialog boxes.

## Define Variable Sets

Define Variable Sets creates subsets of variables to display in dialog box source lists.

Figure 39-2
*Define Variable Sets dialog box*

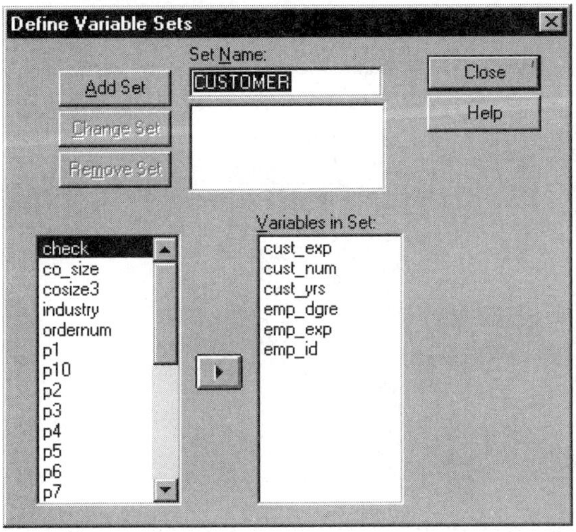


**Set Name.** Set names can be up to 12 characters long. Any characters, including blanks, can be used. Set names are not case sensitive.

**Variables in Set.** Any combination of numeric, short string, and long string variables can be included in a set. The order of variables in the set has no effect on the display order of the variables on dialog box source lists. A variable can belong to multiple sets.

### To Define Variable Sets

▶ From the menus choose:

Utilities
  Define Sets...

▶ Select the variables you want to include in the set.

▶ Enter a name for the set (up to 12 characters).

▶ Click Add Set.

## Use Sets

Use Sets restricts the variables displayed in dialog box source lists to the selected sets you have defined.

Figure 39-3
*Use Sets dialog box*

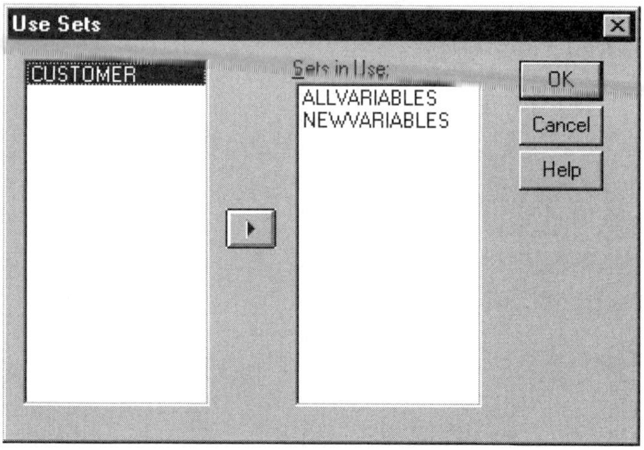


**Sets in Use.** Displays the sets used to produce the source variable lists in dialog boxes. Variables appear on the source lists in alphabetical or file order. The order of sets and the order of variables within a set have no effect on source list variable order. By default, two system-defined sets are in use:

**ALLVARIABLES.** This set contains all variables in the data file, including new variables created during a session.

**NEWVARIABLES.** This set contains only new variables created during the session.

You can remove these sets from the list and select others, but there must be at least one set on the list. If you don't remove the *ALLVARIABLES* set from the Sets in Use list, any other sets you include are irrelevant.

### To Restrict Dialog Box Source Lists to Defined Variable Sets

▶ From the menus choose:

Utilities
 Use Sets...

▶ Select the defined variable sets that contain the variables you want to appear in dialog box source lists.

## Reordering Target Variable Lists

Variables appear on dialog box target lists in the order in which they are selected from the source list. If you want to change the order of variables on a target list—but you don't want to deselect all the variables and reselect them in the new order—you can move variables up and down on the target list using the system menu in the upper left corner of the dialog box (accessed by clicking the left side of the dialog box title bar).

Figure 39-4
*Windows system menu with target list reordering*

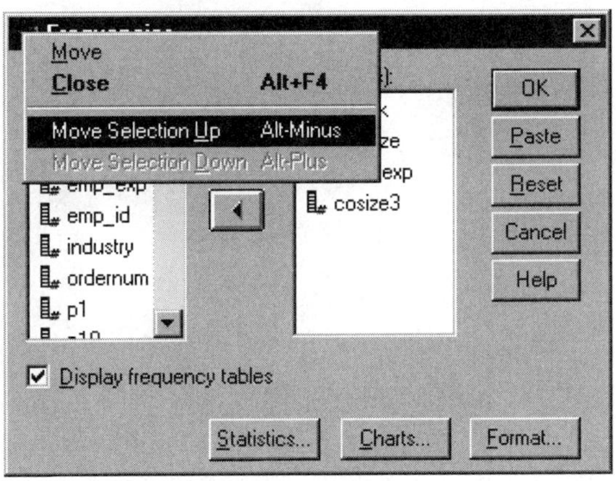


**Move Selection Up.** Moves the selected variable(s) up one position on the target list.

**Move Selection Down.** Moves the selected variable(s) down one position on the target list.

You can move multiple variables simultaneously if they are contiguous (grouped together). You cannot move noncontiguous groups of variables.

Chapter

# 40

# Options

Options control a wide variety of settings, including:

- Session journal, which keeps a record of all commands run in every session.
- Display order for variables in dialog box source lists.
- Items displayed and hidden in new output results.
- TableLook for new pivot tables and ChartLook for new interactive charts.
- Custom currency formats.
- Autoscript files and autoscript functions to customize output.

### To Change Options Settings

▶ From the menus choose:

Edit
  Options...

▶ Click the tabs for the settings that you want to change.

▶ Change the settings.

▶ Click OK or Apply.

# General Options

Figure 40-1
*Options General tab*

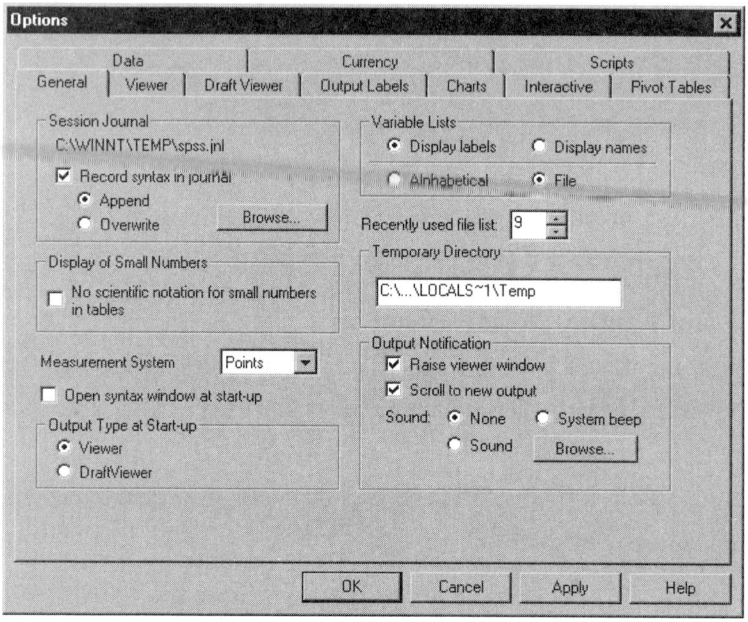


**Session Journal.** Journal file of all commands run in a session. This includes commands entered and run in syntax windows and commands generated by dialog box choices. You can edit the journal file and use the commands again in other sessions. You can turn journaling off and on, append or overwrite the journal file, and select the journal filename and location. You can copy command syntax from the journal file and save it in a syntax file for use with the automated production facility. (Command syntax and automatic production are not available in the Student version.)

**Display of Small Numbers.** Suppresses the display of scientific notation for small decimal values in output. Very small decimal values will be displayed as 0 (or 0.000).

**Measurement System.** Measurement system used (points, inches, or centimeters) for specifying attributes such as pivot table cell margins, cell widths, and space between tables for printing.

**Open syntax window at start-up.** Syntax windows are text file windows used to enter, edit, and run commands. If you frequently work with command syntax, select this option to automatically open a syntax window at the beginning of each session. This is useful primarily for experienced users who prefer to work with command syntax instead of dialog boxes. (Not available with Student version.)

**Variable Lists.** Controls display of variables in dialog box list boxes. You can display variable names or variable labels. Names or labels can be displayed in alphabetical order or in file order, which is the order in which they actually occur in the data file (and are displayed in the Data Editor window). A change in variable list display takes effect the next time that you open a data file. Display order affects only source variable lists. Target variable lists always reflect the order in which variables were selected.

*Note*: Interactive graphics (Graphs menu, Interactive) dialog boxes and dialog boxes in the Map option are not affected by variable list options. Variable lists in those dialog boxes can be changed by right-clicking the source variable list and selecting display options from the pop-up context menu.

**Recently used file list.** Controls the number of recently used files that appear on the File menu.

**Temporary Directory.** Controls the location of temporary files created during a session. In distributed mode (available with the server version), this does not affect the location of temporary data files. In distributed mode, the location of temporary data files is controlled by the environment variable SPSSTMPDIR, which can be set only on the computer running the server version of the software. If you need to change the location of the temporary directory, contact your system administrator.

**Output Type at Start-up.** Controls the type of Viewer used and output format. The Viewer produces interactive pivot tables and interactive charts. The Draft Viewer converts pivot tables to text output and charts to metafiles.

**Output Notification.** Controls the manner in which the program notifies you that it has finished running a procedure and that the results are available in the Viewer.

# Viewer Options

Viewer output display options affect only new output produced after you change the settings. Output already displayed in the Viewer is not affected by changes in these settings.

Figure 40-2
*Options Viewer tab*

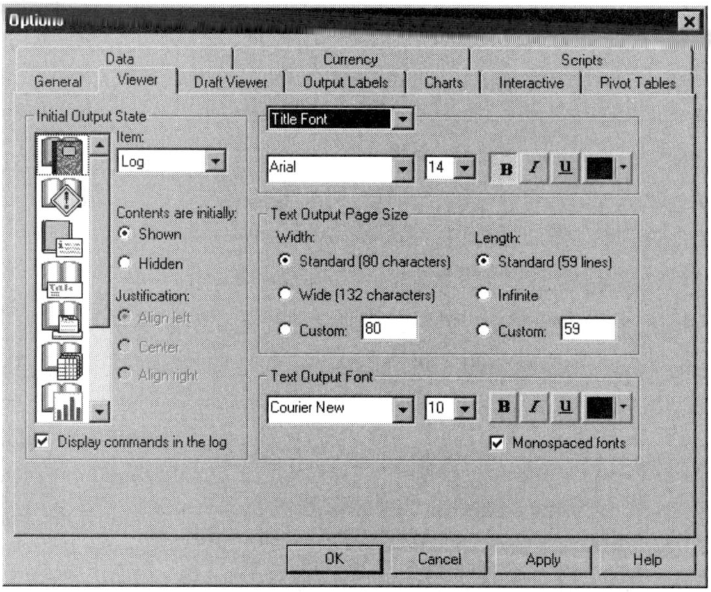


**Initial Output State.** Controls which items are automatically displayed or hidden each time you run a procedure and how items are initially aligned. You can control the display of the following items: log, warnings, notes, titles, pivot tables, charts, and text output (output not displayed in pivot tables). You can also turn the display of commands in the log on or off. You can copy command syntax from the log and save it in a syntax file for use with the automated production facility. (Command syntax and automatic production are not available in the Student version.)

*Note*: All output items are displayed left-aligned in the Viewer. Only the alignment of printed output is affected by the justification settings. Centered and right-aligned items are identified by a small symbol above and to the left of the item.

**Title Font.** Controls the font style, size, and color for new output titles.

**Page Title Font.** Controls the font style, size, and color for new page titles and page titles generated by TITLE and SUBTITLE command syntax or created by New Page Title on the Insert menu.

**Text Output Page Size.** For text output, controls the page width (expressed in number of characters) and page length (expressed in number of lines). For some procedures, some statistics are displayed only in wide format.

**Text Output Font.** Font used for text output. Text output is designed for use with a monospaced (fixed-pitch) font. If you select a nonmonospaced font, tabular output will not align properly.

## *Draft Viewer Options*

Draft Viewer output display options affect only new output produced after you change the settings. Output already displayed in the Draft Viewer is not affected by changes in these settings.

Figure 40-3
*Options Draft Viewer tab*

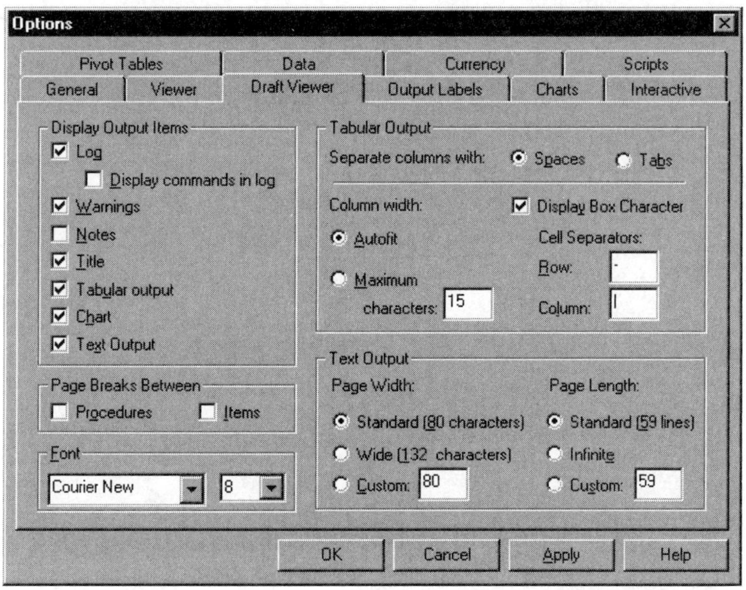

**Display Output Items.** Controls which items are automatically displayed each time that you run a procedure. You can control the display of the following items: log, warnings, notes, titles, tabular output (pivot tables converted to text output), charts, and text output (space-separated output). You can also turn on or off the display of commands in the log. You can copy command syntax from the log and save it in a syntax file for use with the automated production facility. (Command syntax and automatic production are not available in the Student version.)

**Page Breaks Between.** Inserts page breaks between output from different procedures and/or between individual output items.

**Font.** Font used for new output. Only fixed-pitch (monospaced) fonts are available because space-separated text output will not align properly with a proportional font.

**Tabular Output.** Controls settings for pivot table output converted to tabular text output. Column width and column separator specifications are available only if you select Spaces for the column separator. For space-separated tabular output, by default all line wrapping is removed and each column is set to the width of the longest label or value in the column. To limit the width of columns and wrap long labels, specify a number of characters for the column width.

*Note*: Tab-separated tabular output will not align properly in the Draft Viewer. This format is useful for copying and pasting results to word processing applications where you can use any font that you want (not just fixed-pitch fonts) and set the tabs to align output properly.

**Text Output.** For text output other than converted pivot table output, controls the page width (expressed in number of characters) and page length (expressed in number of lines). For some procedures, some statistics are displayed only in wide format.

# Output Label Options

Output Label options control the display of variable and data value information in the outline and pivot tables. You can display variable names, defined variable labels and actual data values, defined value labels, or a combination.

Descriptive variable and value labels (Variable view in the Data Editor, *Label* and *Values* columns) often make it easier to interpret your results. However, long labels can be awkward in some tables.

Figure 40-4
*Options Output Label tab*

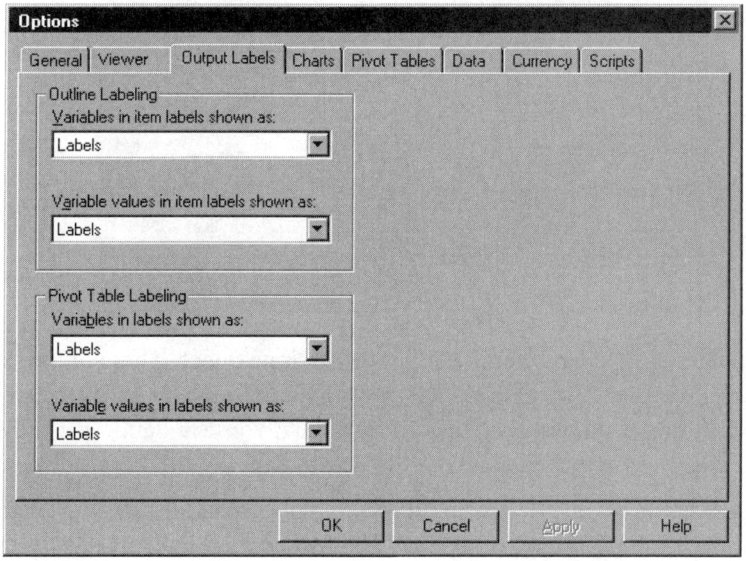


Output label options affect only new output produced after you change the settings. Output already displayed in the Viewer is not affected by changes in these settings. These settings affect only pivot table output. Text output is not affected by these settings.

## Chart Options

Figure 40-5
*Options Charts tab*

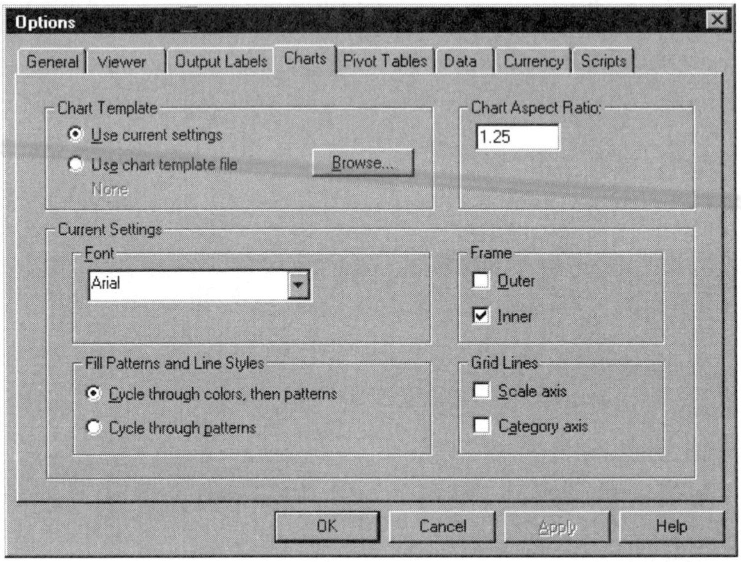


**Chart Template.** New charts can use either the settings selected here or the settings from a chart template file. Click Browse to select a chart template file. To create a chart template file, create a chart with the attributes that you want and save it as a template (choose Save Chart Template from the File menu).

**Chart Aspect Ratio.** The width-to-height ratio of the outer frame of new charts. You can specify a width-to-height ratio from 0.1 to 10.0. Values below 1 make charts that are taller than they are wide. Values over 1 make charts that are wider than they are tall. A value of 1 produces a square chart. Once a chart is created, its aspect ratio cannot be changed.

**Font.** Font used for all text in new charts.

**Fill Patterns and Line Styles.** The initial assignment of colors and patterns for new charts. Cycle through colors, then patterns uses the default palette of 14 colors and then adds patterns to colors if necessary. Cycle through patterns uses only patterns to differentiate chart elements and does not use color.

**Frame.** Controls the display of inner and outer frames on new charts.

**Grid Lines.** Controls the display of scale and category axis grid lines on new charts.

*Note*: These settings have no effect on interactive charts (the Graphs menu's Interactive submenu).

# Interactive Chart Options

Figure 40-6
*Options Interactive tab*

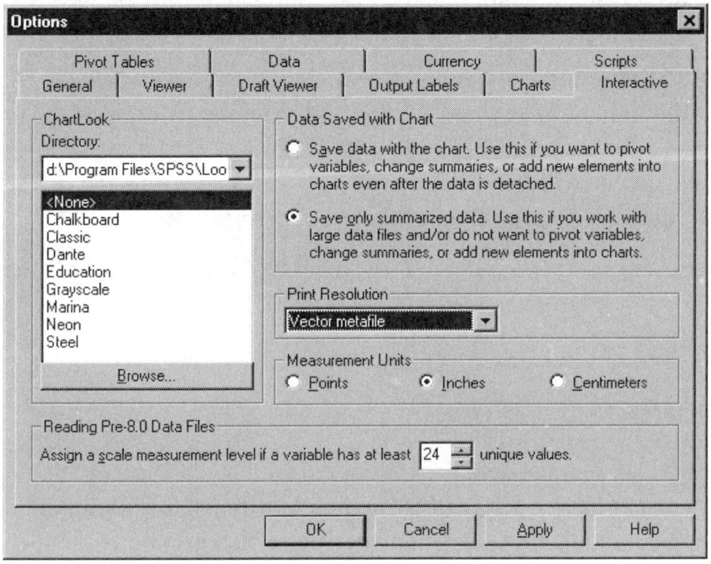


For interactive charts (Graphs menu, Interactive submenu), the following options are available:

**ChartLook.** Select a ChartLook from the list of files and click OK or Apply. By default, the list displays the ChartLooks saved in the *Looks* directory of the directory in which the program is installed. You can use one of the ChartLooks provided with the program, or you can create your own in the Interactive Graphics Editor (in an activated chart, choose ChartLooks from the Format menu).

- **Directory.** Allows you to select a ChartLook directory. Use Browse to add directories to the list.
- **Browse.** Allows you to select a ChartLook from another directory.

**Measurement Units.** Measurement system used (points, inches, or centimeters) for specifying attributes such as the size of the data region in a chart.

**Data Saved with Chart.** Controls information saved with interactive charts once the charts are no longer attached to the data file that created them (for example, if you open a Viewer file saved in a previous session). Saving data with the chart enables you to perform most of the interactive functions available for charts attached to the data file that created them (except adding variables that weren't included in the original chart).

However, this can substantially increase the size of Viewer files, particularly for large data files.

**Print Resolution.** Controls the print resolution of interactive charts. In most cases, Vector metafile will print faster and provide the best results. For bitmaps, lower resolution charts print faster; higher resolution charts look better.

**Reading Pre-8.0 Data Files**. For data files created in previous versions of SPSS, you can specify the minimum number of data values for a numeric variable used to classify the variable as scale or categorical. Variables with fewer than the specified number of unique values are classified as categorical. Any variable with defined value labels is classified as categorical, regardless of the number of unique values.

*Note*: These settings affect only interactive charts (the Graphs menu's Interactive submenu).

## Pivot Table Options

Pivot Table options sets the default TableLook used for new pivot table output. TableLooks can control a variety of pivot table attributes, including the display and width of grid lines; font style, size, and color; and background colors.

Figure 40-7
*Options Pivot Tables tab*

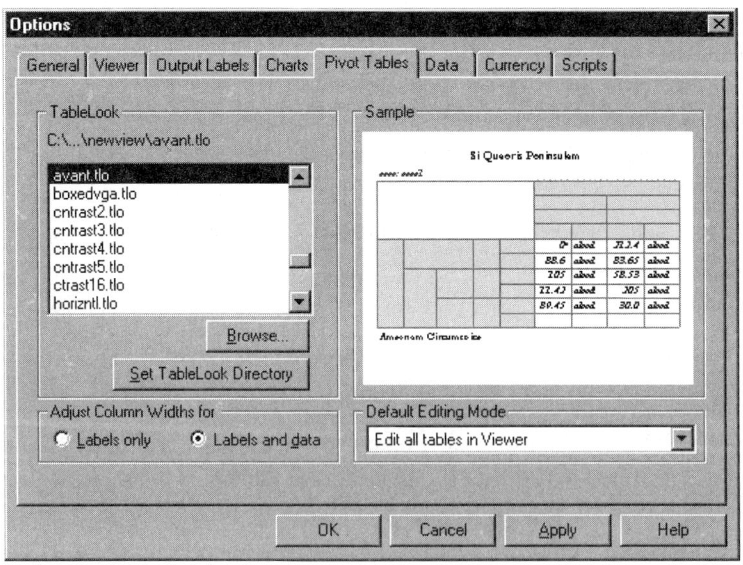

**TableLook.** Select a TableLook from the list of files and click OK or Apply. By default, the list displays the TableLooks saved in the *Looks* directory of the directory in which the program is installed. You can use one of the TableLooks provided with the program, or you can create your own in the Pivot Table Editor (choose TableLooks from the Format menu).

- **Browse.** Allows you to select a TableLook from another directory.
- **Set TableLook Directory.** Allows you to change the default TableLook directory.

**Adjust Column Widths for.** Controls the automatic adjustment of column widths in pivot tables.

- **Labels only.** Adjusts column width to the width of the column label. This produces more compact tables, but data values wider than the label will not be displayed (asterisks indicate values too wide to be displayed).
- **Labels and data.** Adjusts column width to whichever is larger, the column label or the largest data value. This produces wider tables, but it ensures that all values will be displayed.

**Default Editing Mode.** Controls activation of pivot tables in the Viewer window or in a separate window. By default, double-clicking a pivot table activates the table in the Viewer window. You can choose to activate pivot tables in a separate window or select a size setting that will open smaller pivot tables in the Viewer window and larger pivot tables in a separate window.

# Data Options

Figure 40-8
*Options Data tab*

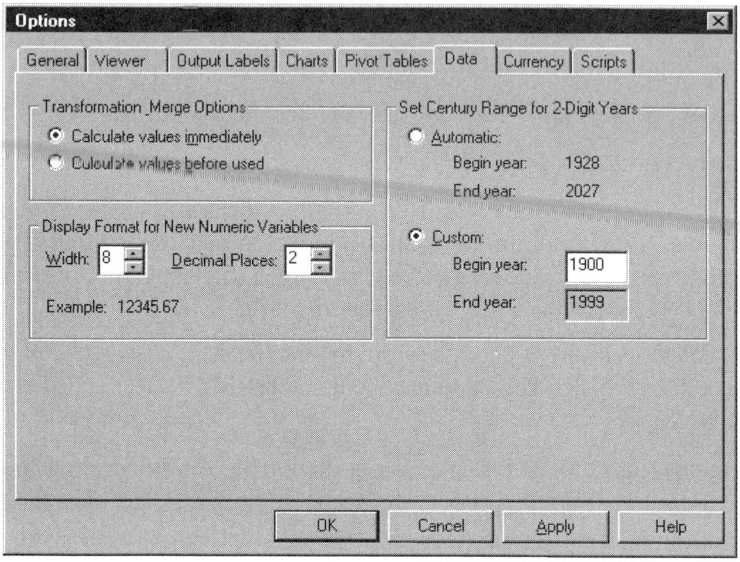


**Transformation and Merge Options.** Each time the program executes a command, it reads the data file. Some data transformations (such as Compute and Recode) and file transformations (such as Add Variables and Add Cases) do not require a separate pass of the data, and execution of these commands can be delayed until the program reads the data to execute another command, such as a statistical procedure. For large data files, select Calculate values before used to delay execution and save processing time.

**Display Format for New Numeric Variables.** Controls the default display width and number of decimal places for new numeric variables. There is no default display format for new string variables. If a value is too large for the specified display format, first decimal places are rounded and then values are converted to scientific notation. Display formats do not affect internal data values. For example, the value 123456.78 may be rounded to 123457 for display, but the original unrounded value is used in any calculations.

**Set Century Range for 2-Digit Years**. Defines the range of years for date-format variables entered and/or displayed with a two-digit year (for example, 10/28/86, 29-OCT-87). The automatic range setting is based on the current year, beginning 69 years prior to and ending 30 years after the current year (adding the current year makes a total range of 100 years). For a custom range, the ending year is automatically determined based on the value that you enter for the beginning year.

# Currency Options

You can create up to five custom currency display formats that can include special prefix and suffix characters and special treatment for negative values.

The five custom currency format names are CCA, CCB, CCC, CCD, and CCE. You cannot change the format names or add new ones. To modify a custom currency format, select the format name from the source list and make the changes that you want.

Figure 40-9
*Options Currency tab*

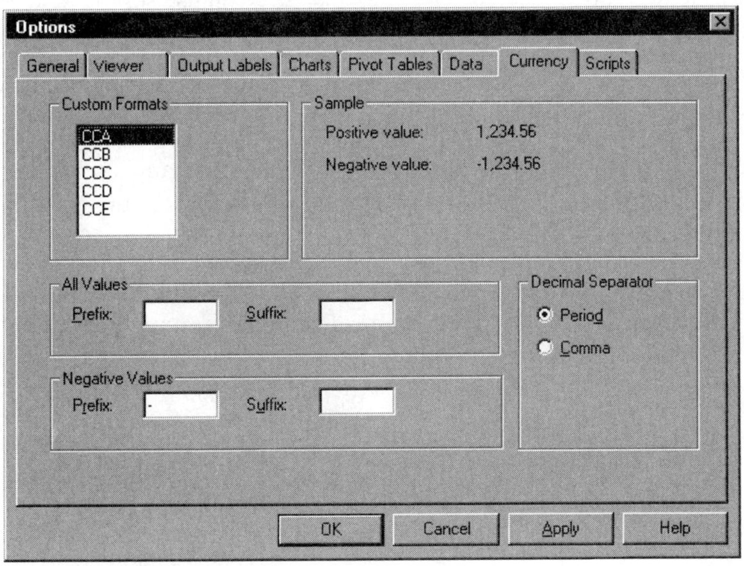


Prefixes, suffixes, and decimal indicators defined for custom currency formats are for display purposes only. You cannot enter values in the Data Editor using custom currency characters.

### To Create Custom Currency Formats

- Click the Currency tab.
- Select one of the currency formats from the list (CCA, CCB, CCC, CCD, CCE).
- Enter the prefix, suffix, and decimal indicator values.
- Click OK or Apply.

## Script Options

Use the Scripts tab to specify your global procedures file and autoscript file, and select the autoscript subroutines that you want to use. You can use scripts to automate many functions, including customizing pivot tables.

**Global Procedures.** A global procedures file is a library of script subroutines and functions that can be called by script files, including autoscript files.

*Note:* The global procedures file that comes with the program is selected by default. Many of the available scripts use functions and subroutines in this global procedures file and will not work if you specify a different global procedures file.

**Autoscripts.** An autoscript file is a collection of script subroutines that run automatically each time you run procedures that create certain types of output objects.

Figure 40-10
*Options Scripts tab*

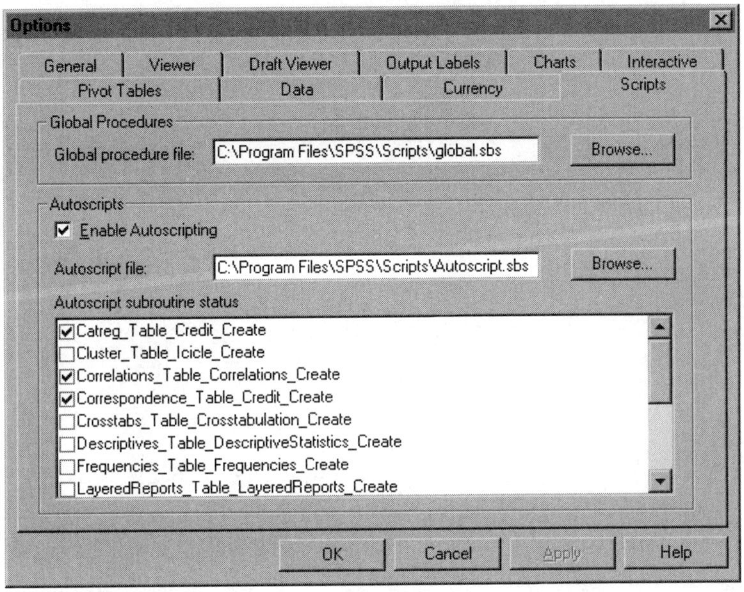


All of the subroutines in the current autoscript file are displayed, allowing you to enable and disable individual subroutines.

### To Specify Options for Autoscripts and Global Procedures

▶ Click the Scripts tab.

▶ Select Enable Autoscripting.

▶ Select the autoscript subroutines that you want to enable.

You can also specify a different autoscript file or global procedure file.

Chapter

# 41

# Customizing Menus and Toolbars

## Menu Editor

You can use the Menu Editor to customize your menus. With the Menu Editor you can:

- Add menu items that run customized scripts.
- Add menu items that run command syntax files.
- Add menu items that launch other applications and automatically send data to other applications.

You can send data to other applications in the following formats: SPSS, Excel 4.0, Lotus 1-2-3 release 3, SYLK, tab-delimited, and dBASE IV.

### To Add Items to the Menus

▶ From the menus choose:

Utilities
  Menu Editor...

▶ In the Menu Editor dialog box, double-click the menu to which you want to add a new item.

▶ Select the menu item above which you want the new item to appear.

▶ Click Insert Item to insert a new menu item.

- ▶ Select the file type for the new item (script file, command syntax file, or external application).
- ▶ Click Browse to select a file to attach to the menu item.

Figure 41-1
*Menu Editor dialog box*

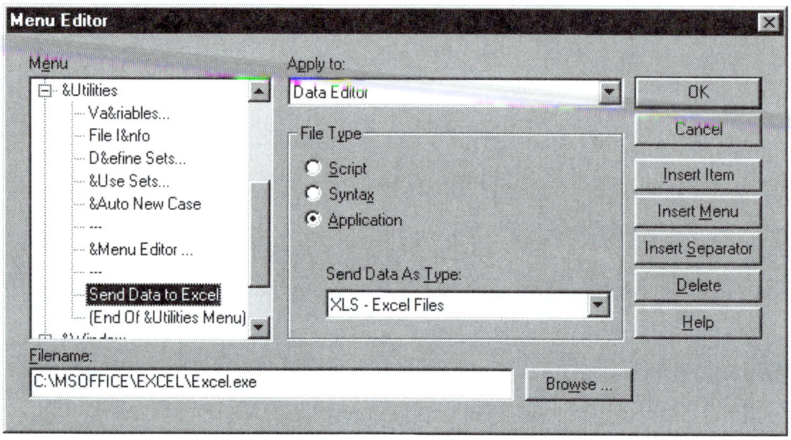


You can also add entirely new menus and separators between menu items.

Optionally, you can automatically send the contents of the Data Editor to another application when you select that application on the menus.

# Customizing Toolbars

You can customize toolbars and create new toolbars. Toolbars can contain any of the available tools, including tools for all menu actions. They can also contain custom tools that launch other applications, run command syntax files, or run script files.

## Show Toolbars

Use Show Toolbars to show or hide toolbars, customize toolbars, and create new toolbars. Toolbars can contain any of the available tools, including tools for all menu actions. They can also contain custom tools that launch other applications, run command syntax files, or run script files.

Figure 41-2
*Show Toolbars dialog box*

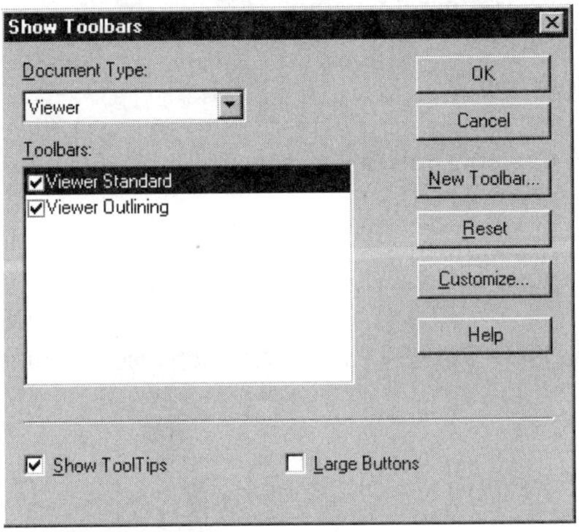


## To Customize Toolbars

- From the menus choose:

  View
  Toolbars...

- Select the toolbar you want to customize and click Customize, or click New Toolbar to create a new toolbar.

- For new toolbars, enter a name for the toolbar, select the windows in which you want the toolbar to appear, and click Customize.

- Select an item in the Categories list to display available tools in that category.

- Drag and drop the tools you want onto the toolbar displayed in the dialog box.

- To remove a tool from the toolbar, drag it anywhere off the toolbar displayed in the dialog box.

To create a custom tool to open a file, run a command syntax file, or run a script:

- ▶ Click New Tool in the Customize Toolbar dialog box.
- ▶ Enter a descriptive label for the tool.
- ▶ Select the action you want for the tool (open a file, run a command syntax file, or run a script).
- ▶ Click Browse to select a file or application to associate with the tool.

New tools are displayed in the User-Defined category, which also contains user-defined menu items.

### Toolbar Properties

Use Toolbar Properties to select the window types in which you want the selected toolbar to appear. This dialog box is also used for creating names for new toolbars.

Figure 41-3
*Toolbar Properties dialog box*

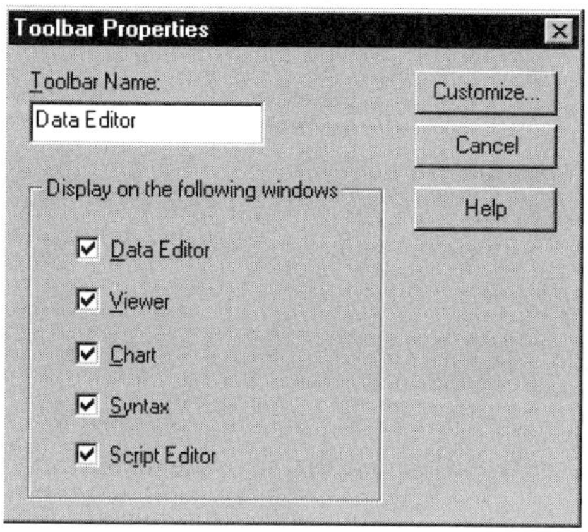

### To Set Toolbar Properties

- ▶ From the menus choose:

  View
   Toolbars...

- ▶ For existing toolbars, click Customize, and then click Properties in the Customize Toolbar dialog box.

- ▶ For new toolbars, click New Tool.

- ▶ Select the window types in which you want the toolbar to appear. For new toolbars, also enter a toolbar name.

### Customize Toolbar

Use the Customize Toolbar dialog box to customize existing toolbars and create new toolbars. Toolbars can contain any of the available tools, including tools for all menu actions. They can also contain custom tools that launch other applications, run command syntax files, or run script files.

Figure 41-4
*Customize Toolbar dialog box*

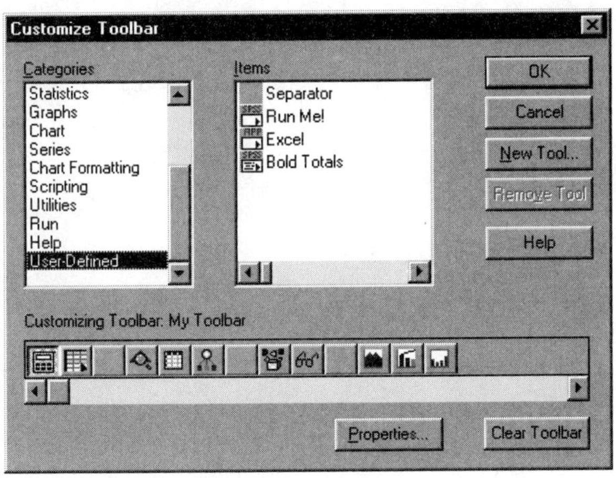

### Create New Tool

Use the Create New Tool dialog box to create custom tools to launch other applications, run command syntax files, and run script files.

Figure 41-5
*Create New Tool dialog box*

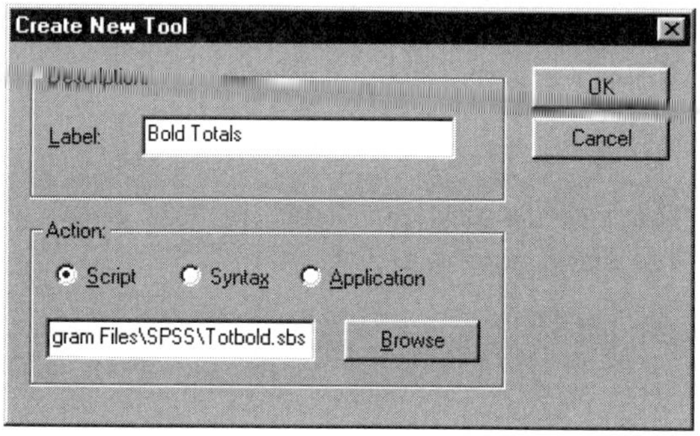


### Bitmap Editor

Use the Bitmap Editor to create custom icons for toolbar buttons. This is particularly useful for custom tools you create to run scripts, syntax, and other applications.

Figure 41-6
*Bitmap Editor*

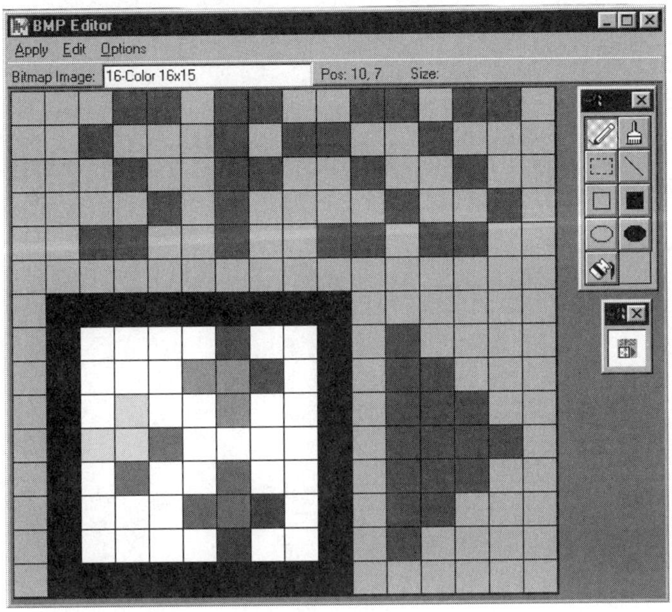


### *To Edit Toolbar Bitmaps*

- From the menus choose:

  View
   Toolbars...

- Select the toolbar you want to customize and click Customize.

- Click the tool with the bitmap icon you want to edit on the example toolbar.

- Click Edit Tool.

- Use the toolbox and the color palette to modify the bitmap or create a new bitmap icon.

Chapter

# 42

# Production Facility

The Production Facility provides the ability to run the program in an automated fashion. The program runs unattended and terminates after executing the last command, so you can perform other tasks while it runs. Production mode is useful if you often run the same set of time-consuming analyses, such as weekly reports.

The Production Facility uses command syntax files to tell the program what to do. A command syntax file is a simple text file containing command syntax. You can use any text editor to create the file. You can also generate command syntax by pasting dialog box selections into a syntax window or by editing the journal file.

After you create syntax files and include them in a production job, you can view and edit them from the Production Facility.

Figure 42-1
*Production Facility*

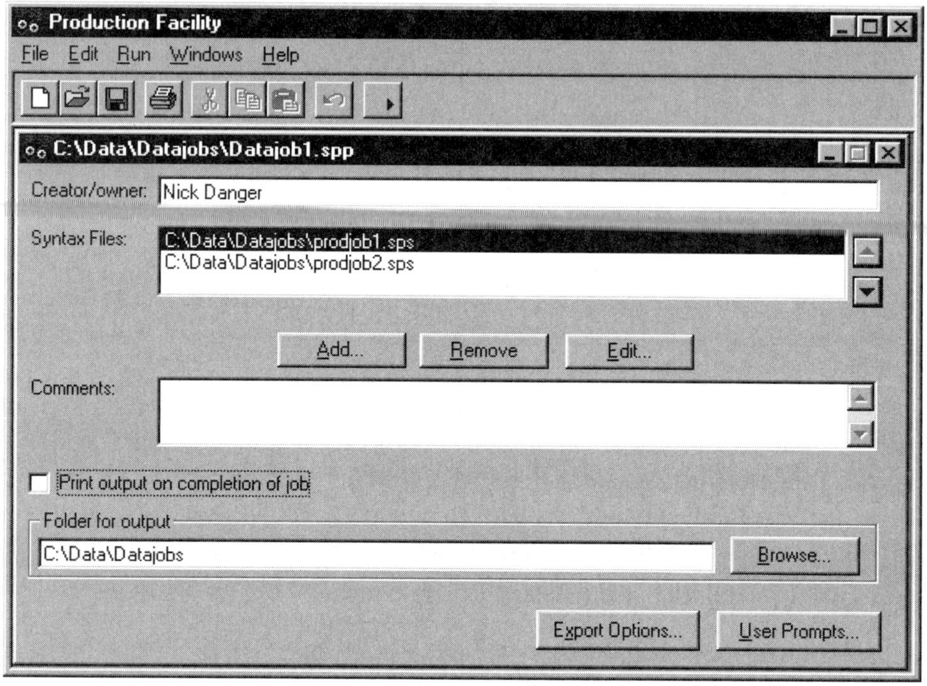


**Production job results.** Each production run creates an output file with the same name as the production job and the extension *.spo*. For example, a production job file named *prodjob.spp* creates an output file named *prodjob.spo*. The output file is a Viewer document.

**Output type.** Viewer output produces pivot tables and high-resolution, interactive charts. Draft Viewer output produces text output and metafile pictures of charts. Text output can be edited in the Draft Viewer, but charts cannot be edited in the Draft Viewer.

### *To Run a Production Job*

- ▶ Create a command syntax file.
- ▶ Start the Production Facility, available on the Start menu.
- ▶ Specify the syntax files that you want to use in the production job. Click Add to select the syntax files.
- ▶ Save the production job file.
- ▶ Run the production job file. Click the Run button on the toolbar, or from the menus choose:

  Run
   Production Job

## *Syntax Rules for the Production Facility*

Syntax rules for command syntax files used in the Production Facility are the same as the rules for Include files:

- Each command must begin in the first column of a new line.
- Continuation lines must be indented at least one space.
- The period at the end of the command is optional.

If you generate command syntax by pasting dialog box choices into a syntax window, the format of the commands is suitable for the Production Facility.

**UNC path names.** Relative path specifications for data files are relative to the current server in distributed analysis mode, not relative to your local computer. If you have network access to the remote server version of SPSS, we recommend that you use UNC (universal naming convention) path names to specify the location of data files in your command syntax files, as in:

```
GET FILE = '\\hqdev01\public\july\sales.sav'.
```

Figure 42-2
*Command syntax pasted from dialog box selections*

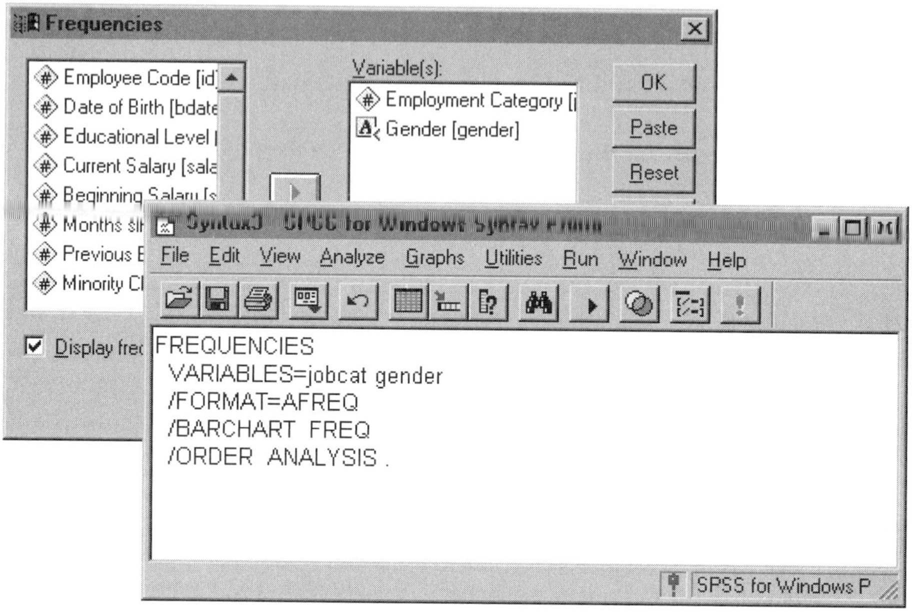


## Production Export Options

Export Options saves pivot tables and text output in HTML and text formats, and it saves charts in a variety of common formats used by other applications. You can export all output, pivot tables, and text output without charts, or charts without other output.

Figure 42-3
*Export Options dialog box*

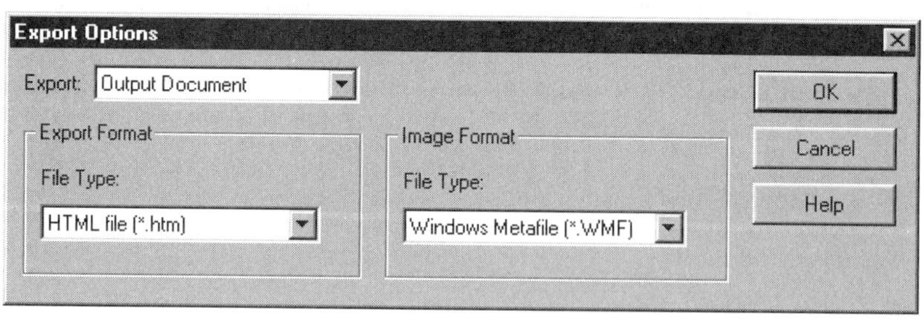

**Export Format.** Controls the export format for output documents. For HTML document format, charts are embedded by reference, and you should export charts in a suitable format for inclusion in HTML documents. For text document format, a line is inserted in the text file for each chart, indicating the filename of the exported chart.

- Pivot tables can be exported as HTML tables (HTML 3.0 or later), as tab-separated text, or as space-separated text.
- Text output can be exported as preformatted HTML or space-separated text. A fixed-pitch (monospaced) font is required for proper alignment of space-separated text output. (By default, most Web browsers use a fixed-pitch font for preformatted text.)
- Exported chart names are based on the production job filename, a sequential number, and the extension of the selected format. For example, if the production job *prodjob.spp* exports charts in Windows metafile format, the chart names would be *prodjob1.wmf, prodjob2.wmf, prodjob3.wmf,* and so on.

**Image Format.** Controls the export format for charts. Charts can be exported in the following formats: Windows metafile, Windows bitmap, encapsulated PostScript, JPEG, TIFF, CGM, PNG, or Macintosh PICT.

Text export options (for example, tab-separated or space-separated) and chart export options (for example, color settings, size, and resolution) are set in SPSS and cannot be changed in the Production Facility. Use Export on the File menu in SPSS to change text and chart export options.

The only Export option available for Draft Viewer output is to export the output in simple text format. Charts for Draft Viewer output cannot be exported.

# User Prompts

Macro symbols defined in a production job file and used in a command syntax file simplify tasks such as running the same analysis for different data files or running the same set of commands for different sets of variables. For example, you could define the macro symbol *@datfile* to prompt you for a data filename each time you run a production job that uses the string *@datfile* in place of a filename.

Figure 42-4
*User Prompts dialog box*

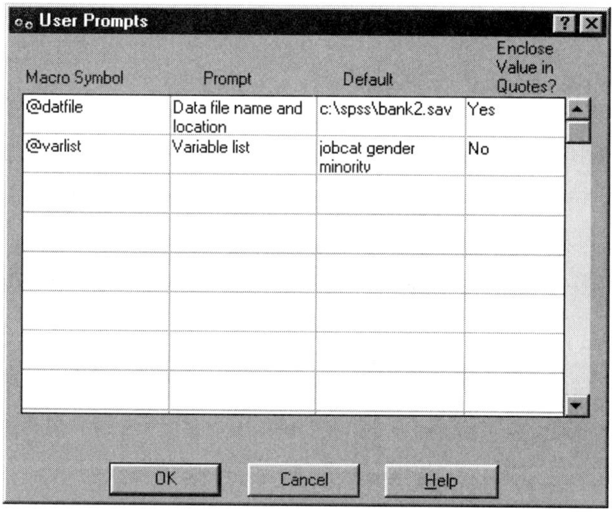


**Macro Symbol.** The macro name used in the command syntax file to invoke the macro that prompts the user to enter information. The macro symbol name must begin with an @ and cannot exceed eight characters.

**Prompt.** The descriptive label that is displayed when the production job prompts you to enter information. For example, you could use the phrase "What data file do you want to use?" to identify a field that requires a data filename.

**Default.** The value that the production job supplies by default if you don't enter a different value. This value is displayed when the production job prompts you for information. You can replace or modify the value at runtime.

**Enclose Value in Quotes?** Enter Y or Yes if you want the value enclosed in quotes. Otherwise, leave the field blank or enter N or No. For example, you should enter Yes for a filename specification because filename specifications should be enclosed in quotes.

Figure 42-5
*Macro prompts in a command syntax file*

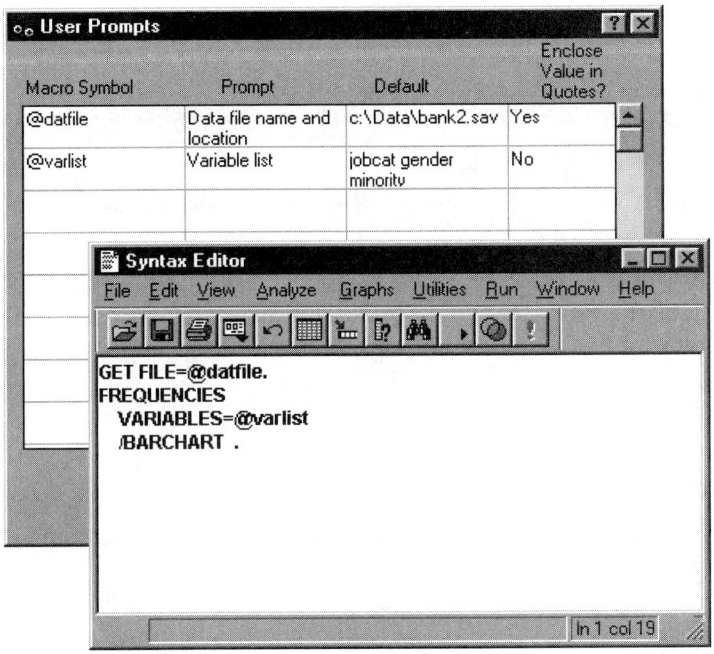

# Production Macro Prompting

The Production Facility prompts you for values whenever you run a production job that contains defined macro symbols. You can replace or modify the default values that are displayed. Those values are then substituted for the macro symbols in all command syntax files associated with the production job.

Figure 42-6
*Production macro prompting dialog box*

# Production Options

Production Options enable you to:

- Specify a default text editor for syntax files accessed with the Edit button in the main dialog box.
- Run the production job as an invisible background process or display the results it generates as the job runs.
- Specify a remote server, domain name, user ID, and password for distributed analysis (applicable only if you have network access to the server version of SPSS). If you don't specify these settings, the default settings in the SPSS Server Login dialog box are used. You can select only remote servers that you have previously defined in the Add Server dialog box in SPSS (File menu, Switch Server, Add).

Figure 42-7
*Options dialog box*

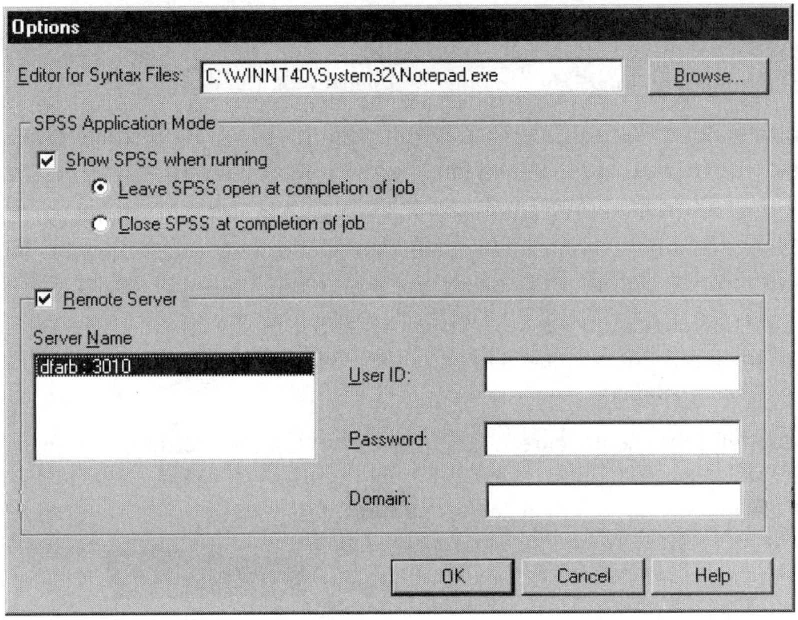


### *To Change Production Options*

From the Production Facility menus choose:

Edit
  Options...

# *Format Control for Production Jobs*

There are a number of settings in SPSS that can help ensure the best format for pivot tables created in production jobs:

**TableLooks.** By editing and saving TableLooks (Format menu in an activated pivot table), you can control many pivot table attributes. You can specify font sizes and styles, colors, and borders. To ensure that wide tables do not split across pages, select Rescale wide table to fit page on the Table Properties General tab.

**Output labels.** Output Label options (Edit menu, Options, Output Labels tab) control the display of variable and data value information in pivot tables. You can display variable names and/or defined variable labels, actual data values and/or defined value labels. Descriptive variable and value labels often make it easier to interpret your results; however, long labels can be awkward in some tables.

**Column width.** Pivot Table options (Edit menu, Options, Pivot Table tab) control the default TableLook and the automatic adjustment of column widths in pivot tables.

- Labels only adjusts the column width to the width of the column label. This produces more compact tables, but data values wider than the label will not be displayed (asterisks indicate values too wide to be displayed).
- Labels and data adjusts the column width to whichever is larger, the column label or the largest data value. This produces wider tables, but it ensures that all values will be displayed.

Production jobs use the current TableLook and Options settings in effect. You can set the TableLook and Options settings before running your production job, or you can use SET commands in your syntax files to control them. Using SET commands in syntax files enables you to use multiple TableLooks and Options settings in the same job.

### To Create a Custom Default TableLook

▶ Activate a pivot table (double-click anywhere in the table).

▶ From the menus choose:

Format
  TableLook...

▶ Select a TableLook from the list and click Edit Look.

▶ Adjust the table properties for the attributes that you want.

▶ Click Save Look or Save As to save the TableLook and click OK.

▶ From the menus choose:

Edit
  Options...

▶ Click the Pivot Tables tab.

▶ Select the TableLook from the list and click OK.

### To Set Options for Production Jobs

- ▶ From the menus choose:

  Edit
   Options...

- ▶ Select the options that you want.

- ▶ Click OK.

You can set the default TableLook, output label settings, and automatic column width adjustment with Options. Options settings are saved with the program. When you run a production job, the Options settings in effect the last time you ran the program are applied to the production job.

## Controlling Pivot Table Format with Command Syntax

**SET TLOOK.** Controls the default TableLook for new pivot tables, as in:

- SET TLOOK = 'c:\prodjobs\mytable.tlo'.

**SET TVARS.** Controls the display of variable names and labels in new pivot tables:

- SET TVARS = LABELS displays variable labels.
- SET TVARS = NAMES displays variable names.
- SET TVARS = BOTH displays both variable names and labels.

**SET ONUMBER.** Controls the display of data values or value labels in new pivot tables:

- SET ONUMBER = LABELS displays value labels.
- SET ONUMBER = VALUES displays data values.
- SET ONUMBER = BOTH displays data values and value labels.

**SET TFIT.** Controls automatic column width adjustment for new pivot tables:

- SET TFIT = LABELS adjusts column width to the width of the column label.
- SET TFIT = BOTH adjusts column width to the width of the column label or the largest data value, whichever is wider.

## Running Production Jobs from a Command Line

Command line switches enable you to schedule production jobs to run at certain times with scheduling utilities like the one available in Microsoft Plus!. You can run production jobs from a command line with the following switches:

**-r.** Runs the production job. If the production job contains any user prompts, you must supply the requested information before the production job will run.

**-s.** Runs the production job and suppresses any user prompts or alerts. The default user prompt values are used automatically.

**Distributed analysis.** If you have network access to the server version of SPSS, you can also use the following switches to run the Production Facility in distributed analysis mode:

**-x.** Name or IP address of the remote server.

**-n.** Port number.

**-d.** Domain name.

**-u.** User ID for remote server access.

**-p.** Password for remote server access.

If you specify any of the command lines switches for distributed analysis, you must specify all of the distributed analysis command line switches (-x, -n, -d, -u, and -p).

You should provide the full path for both the Production Facility (*spssprod.exe*) and the production job, and both should be enclosed in quotes, as in:

```
"c:\program files\spss\spssprod.exe" "c:\spss\datajobs\prodjob.spp" -s -r
```

For command line switches that require additional specifications, the switch must be followed by an equals sign followed immediately by the specification. If the specification contains spaces (such as a two-word server name), enclose the value in quotes or apostrophes, as in:

```
-x="HAL 9000" -u="secret word"
```

**Default server.** If you have network access to the server version of SPSS, the default server and related information (if not specified in command line switches) is the default server specified the SPSS Server Login dialog box. If no default is specified there, the job runs in local mode.

If you want to run a production job in local mode but your local computer is not your default server, specify null quoted strings for all of the distributed analysis command line switches, as in:

```
"c:\program files\spss\spssprod.exe" "c:\spss\datajobs\prodjob.spp" -x="" -n="" -d="" -u="" -p=""
```

## Publish to Web

Publish to Web exports output for publishing to SmartViewer Web Server. Tables and reports published in SmartViewer can be viewed and manipulated over the Web, in real time, using a standard browser.

- Pivot tables are published as dynamic tables that can be manipulated over the Web to obtain different views of the data.
- Charts are published as JPEG or PNG graphic files.
- Text output is published as preformatted HTML. (By default, most Web browsers use a fixed-pitch font for preformatted text.)

**Publish.** Allows you to specify the output that you want to publish:

- **Output Document.** Publishes the entire output document, including hidden or collapsed items.
- **Output Document (No Notes).** Publishes everything but the Notes tables that are automatically produced for each procedure.
- **Tables Only.** Excludes charts. All pivot tables and all text tables are published.
- **Tables Only (No Notes).** Excludes charts and Notes tables.
- **Charts Only.** Only publishes the charts in the document.
- **Nothing.** Turns off publishing to the Web. Since all settings are saved with the production job (*.spp* file), results will be published every time you run the production job unless you select Nothing. This turns off publishing while still generating other types of output (Viewer files, HTML files) specified in the production job.

**Publish Tables as.** Controls how pivot tables are published:

- **Interactive.** Tables are dynamic objects that can be manipulated over the Web to obtain different views of the data.
- **Static.** Tables are static and cannot be manipulated after publishing.

**Configure.** Opens the SmartViewer Web Server *Configure Automated Publishing* page in a browser window. This is required when you create a new production job to publish to the Web.

A user ID and password are also required to access the SmartViewer Web Server. When you create a new production job to publish to the Web, you will be prompted for your user ID and password. This information is stored in the production job in encrypted format.

*Note*: Publish to Web is available only for sites with SmartViewer Web Server installed and requires a plug-in to activate the publishing feature. Contact your system administrator or Webmaster for instructions on downloading the plug-in. If SmartViewer is unavailable at your site, use Export Output to save output in HTML format.

## SmartViewer Web Server Login

Publishing to SmartViewer Web Server requires a valid SmartViewer Web Server user name (user ID) and password. Contact your system administrator or Webmaster for more information.

Chapter

# 43

# Scripting Facility

The scripting facility allows you to automate tasks, including:

- Automatically customize output in the Viewer.
- Open and save data files.
- Display and manipulate dialog boxes.
- Run data transformations and statistical procedures using command syntax.
- Export charts as graphic files in a number of formats.

A number of scripts are included with the software, including autoscripts that run automatically every time a specific type of output is produced. You can use these scripts as they are or you can customize them to your needs. If you want to create your own scripts, you can begin by choosing from a number of starter scripts.

# To Run a Script

▶ From the menus choose:

Utilities
 Run Script...

Figure 43-1
*Run Script dialog box*

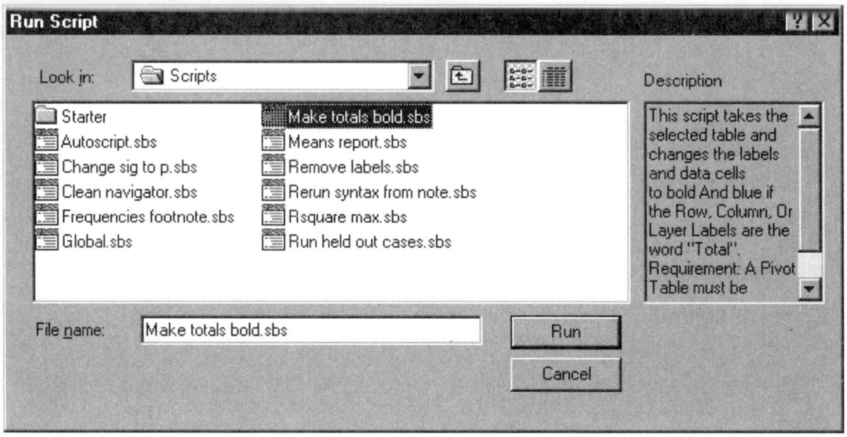


▶ Select the *Scripts* folder.

▶ Select the script you want.

For instructions on running a script from a menu or toolbar, see Chapter 41.

The following scripts are included with the program:

**Analyze held out cases.** Repeats a Factor or Discriminant analysis using cases not selected in a previous analysis. A Notes table produced by a previous run of Factor or Discriminant must be selected before running the script.

**Change significance to p.** Change *Sig.* to *p*= in the column labels of any pivot table. The table must be selected before running the script.

**Clean navigator.** Delete all Notes tables from an output document. The document must be open in the designated Viewer window before running the script.

**Frequencies footnote.** Insert statistics displayed in a Frequencies Statistics table as footnotes in the corresponding frequency table for each variable. The Frequencies Statistics table must be selected before running the script.

**Make totals bold.** Apply the bold format and blue color to any row, column, or layer of data labeled *Total* in a pivot table. The table must be selected before running the script.

**Means report.** Extract information from a Means table and write results to several output ASCII files. The Means table must be selected before running the script.

**Remove labels.** Delete all row and column labels from the selected pivot table. The table must be selected before running the script.

**Rerun syntax from note.** Resubmit the command found in the selected Notes table using the active data file. If no data file is open, the script attempts to read the data file used originally. The Notes table must be selected before running the script.

**Rsquare max.** In a Regression Model Summary table, apply the bold format and blue color to the row corresponding to the model that maximizes adjusted $R^2$. The Model Summary table must be selected before running the script.

*Note*: This list may not be complete.

## Autoscripts

Autoscripts run automatically when triggered by the creation of a specific piece of output by a given procedure. For example, there is an autoscript that automatically removes the upper diagonal and highlights correlation coefficients below a certain significance whenever a Correlations table is produced by the Bivariate Correlations procedure.

The Scripts tab of the Options dialog box (Edit menu) displays the autoscripts that are available on your system and allows you to enable or disable individual scripts.

Figure 43-2
*Scripts tab of Options dialog box*

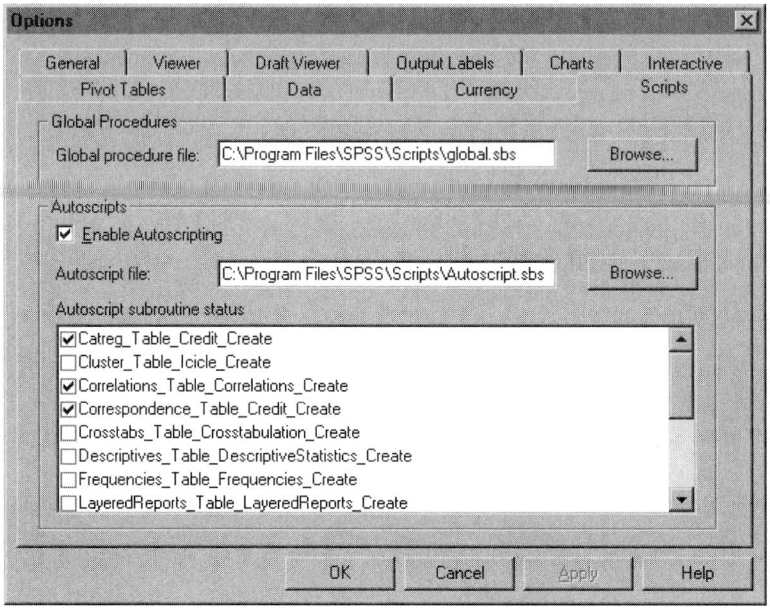


Autoscripts are specific to a given procedure and output type. An autoscript that formats the ANOVA tables produced by One-Way ANOVA is not triggered by ANOVA tables produced by other statistical procedures (although you could use global procedures to create separate autoscripts for these other ANOVA tables that shared much of the same code). However, you can have a separate autoscript for each type of output produced by the same procedure. For example, Frequencies produces both a frequency table and a table of statistics, and you can have a different autoscript for each.

# Creating and Editing Scripts

You can customize many of the scripts included with the software for your specific needs. For example, there is a script that removes all Notes tables from the designated output document. You can easily modify this script to remove output items of any type and label you want.

Figure 43-3
*Modifying a script in the Script Editor*

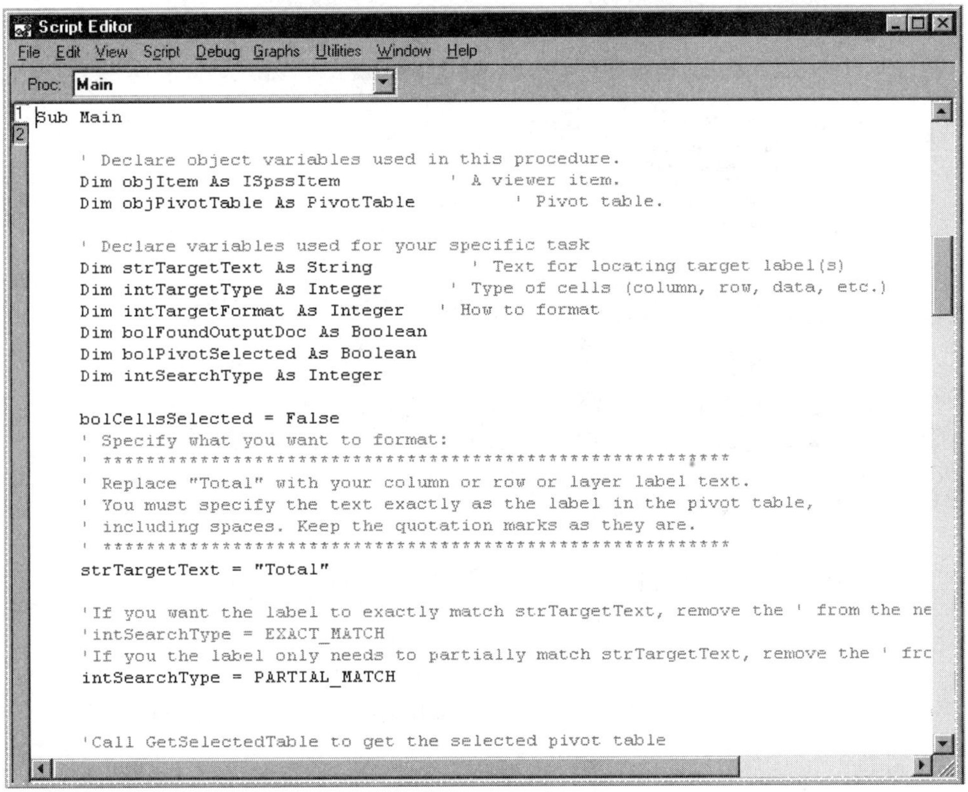


If you prefer to create your own scripts, you can begin by choosing from a number of starter scripts.

## To Edit a Script

▶ From the menus choose:

File
  Open
    Script

Figure 43-4
*Opening a script file*

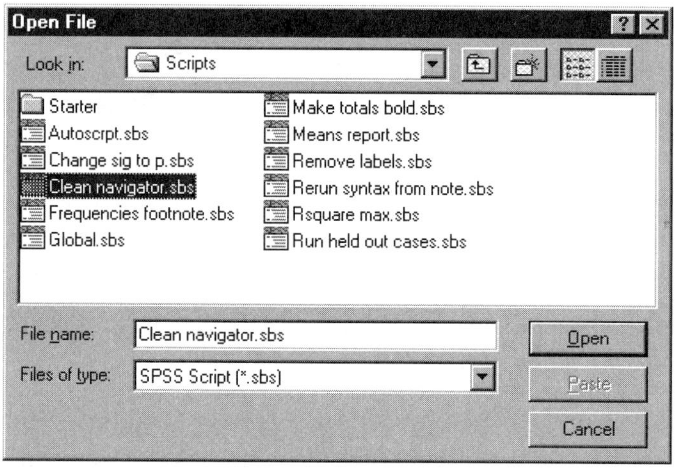


▶ Select the *Scripts* folder.

▶ Under Files of Type, select SPSS Script (*.sbs).

▶ Select the script you want.

If you open more than one script, each opens in its own window.

## Script Window

The script window is a fully featured programming environment that uses the Sax BASIC language and includes a dialog box editor, object browser, debugging features, and context-sensitive Help.

Figure 43-5
*Script window*

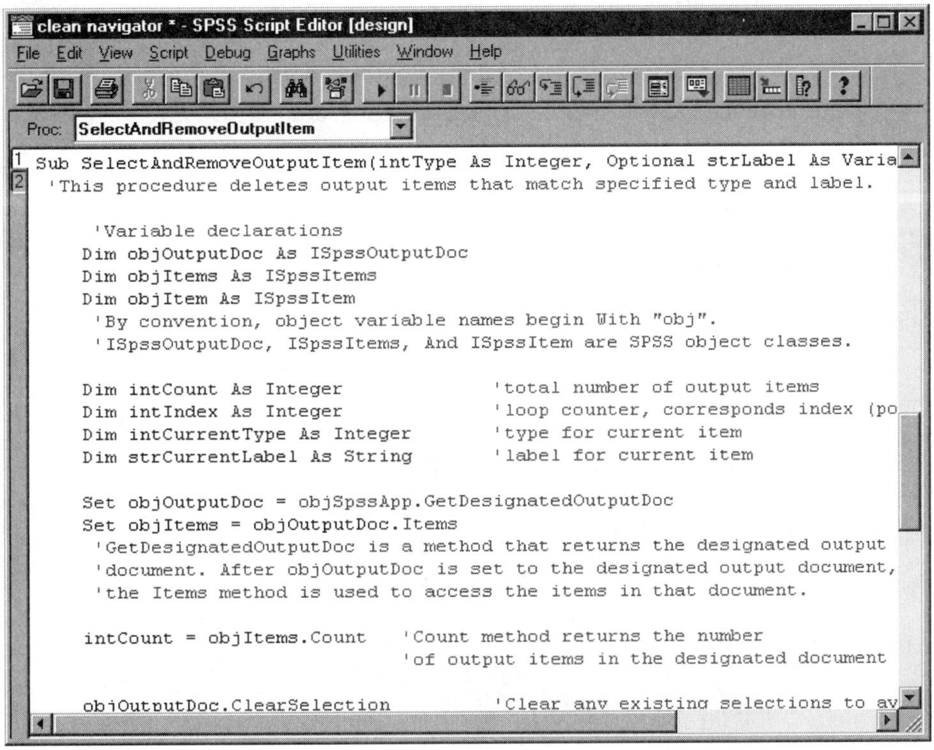


- As you move the cursor, the name of the current procedure is displayed at the top of the window.
- Terms colored blue are reserved words in BASIC (for example Sub, End Sub, and Dim). You can access context-sensitive Help on these terms by clicking them and pressing F1.
- Terms colored magenta are objects, properties, or methods. You can also click these terms and press F1 for Help, but only where they appear in valid statements and are colored magenta. (Clicking the name of an object in a comment will not work because it brings up Help on the Sax BASIC language rather than on SPSS objects.)
- Comments are displayed in green.
- Press F2 at any time to display the object browser, which displays objects, properties, and methods.

### Script Editor Properties

Code elements in the script window are color-coded to make them easier to distinguish. By default, comments are green, Sax BASIC terms are blue, and names of valid objects, properties, and methods are magenta. You can specify different colors for these elements and change the size and font for all text.

### To Set Script Window Properties

▶ From the menus choose:

Script
  Editor Properties...

Figure 43-6
*Editor Properties dialog box*

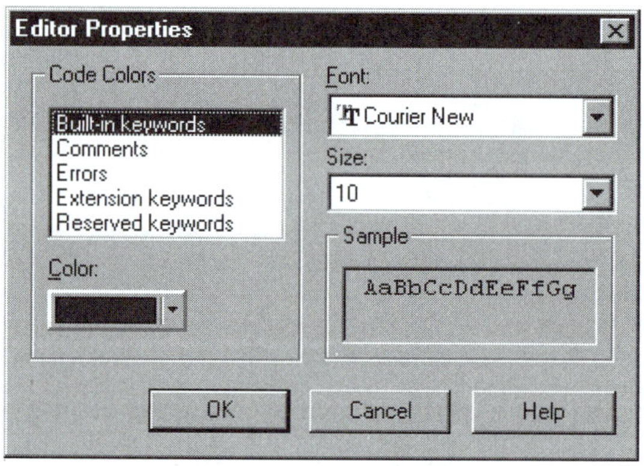


▶ To change the color of a code element type, select the element and choose a color from the drop-down palette.

## Starter Scripts

When you create a new script, you can begin by choosing from a number of starter scripts.

Figure 43-7
*Use Starter Script dialog box*

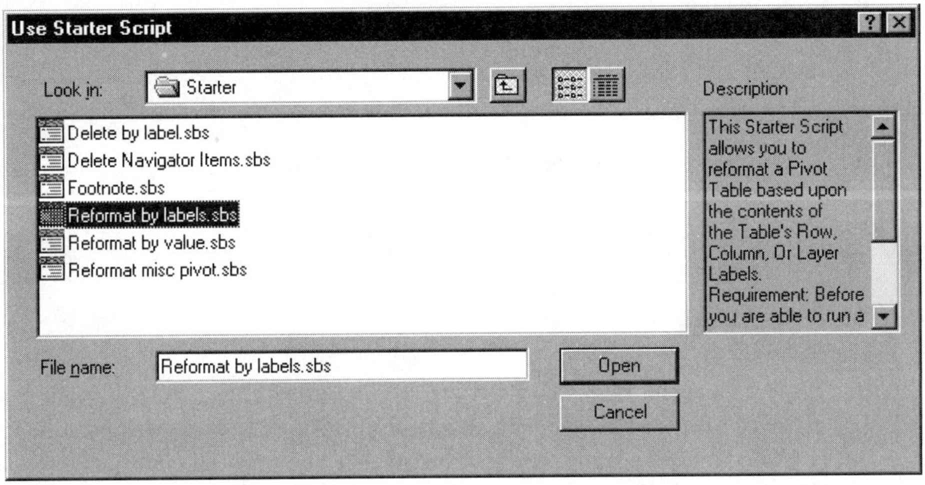


Each starter script supplies code for one or more common procedures and is commented with hints on how to customize the script to your particular needs.

**Delete by label.** Delete rows or columns in a pivot table based on the contents of the RowLabels or ColumnLabels. In order for this script to work, the Hide empty rows and columns option must be selected in the Table Properties dialog box.

**Delete navigator items.** Delete items from the Viewer based on a number of different criteria.

**Footnote.** Reformat a pivot table footnote, change the text in a footnote, or add a footnote.

**Reformat by labels.** Reformat a pivot table based upon the row, column, or layer labels.

**Reformat by value.** Reformat a pivot table based upon the value of data cells or a combination of data cells and labels.

**Reformat misc pivot.** Reformat or change the text in a pivot table title, corner text, or caption.

In addition, you can use any of the other available scripts as starter scripts, although they may not be as easy to customize. Just open the script and save it with a different filename.

### To Create a Script

▶ From the menus choose:

File
 New
  Script...

▶ Select a starter script if you want to begin with one.

▶ If you do not want to use a starter script, click Cancel.

## Creating Autoscripts

You create an autoscript by starting with the output object that you want to serve as the trigger. For example, to create an autoscript that runs whenever a frequency table is produced, create a frequency table in the usual manner and single-click the table in the Viewer to select it. You can then right-click or use the Utilities menu to create a new autoscript triggered whenever that type of table is produced.

Figure 43-8
*Creating a new autoscript*

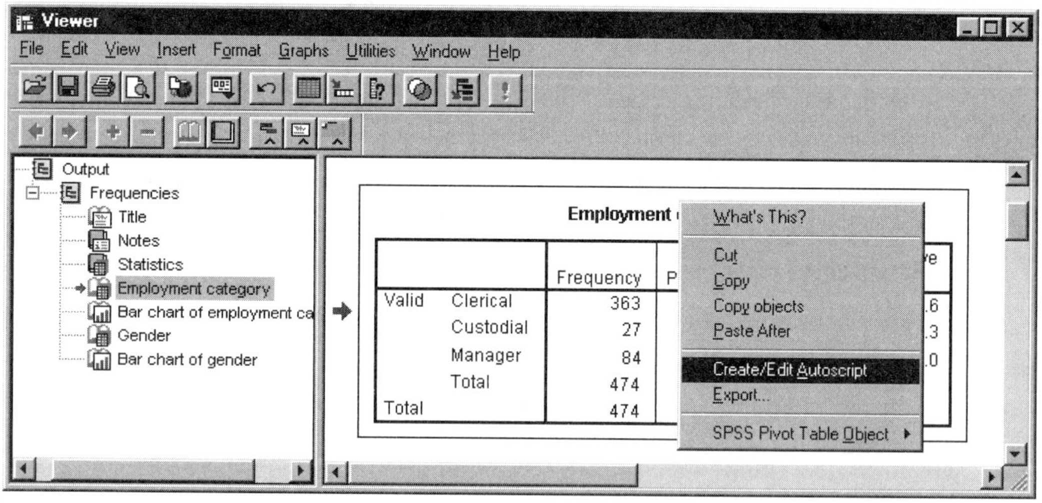


Each autoscript you create is added to the current autoscript file (*autscript.sbs*, by default) as a new procedure. The name of the procedure references the event that serves as the trigger. For example, if you create an autoscript triggered whenever Explore creates a Descriptives table, the name of the autoscript subroutine would be Explore_Table_Descriptives_Create.

Figure 43-9
*New autoscript procedure displayed in script window*

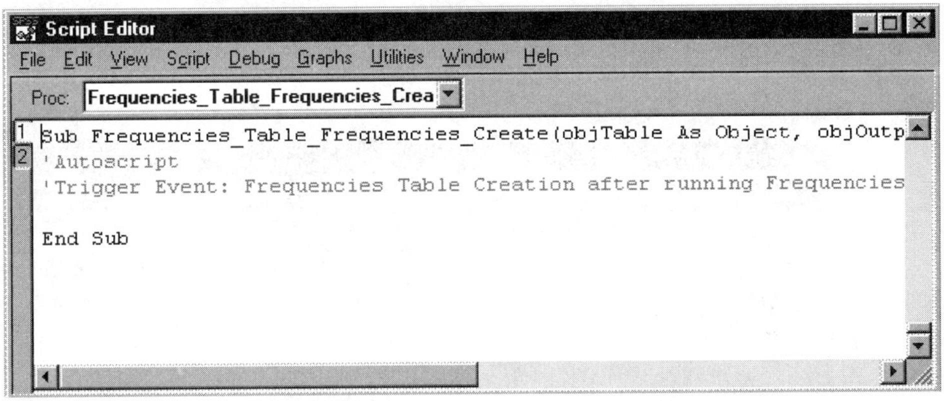


This makes autoscripts easier to develop because you do not need to write code to get the object you want to operate on, but it requires that autoscripts are specific to a given piece of output and statistical procedure.

### *To Create an Autoscript*

▶ Select the object you want to serve as a trigger in the Viewer.

▶ From the menus choose:

Utilities
  Create/Edit Autoscript...

If no autoscript exists for the selected object, a new autoscript is created. If an autoscript already exists, the existing script is displayed.

▶ Type the code.

▶ From the Edit menu, choose Options to enable or disable the autoscript.

### Events That Trigger Autoscripts

The name of the autoscript procedure references the event that serves as the trigger. The following events can trigger autoscripts:

**Creation of pivot table.** The name of the procedure references both the table type and the procedure that created it—for example, Correlations_Table_Correlations_Create.

Figure 43-10
*Autoscript procedure for Correlations table*

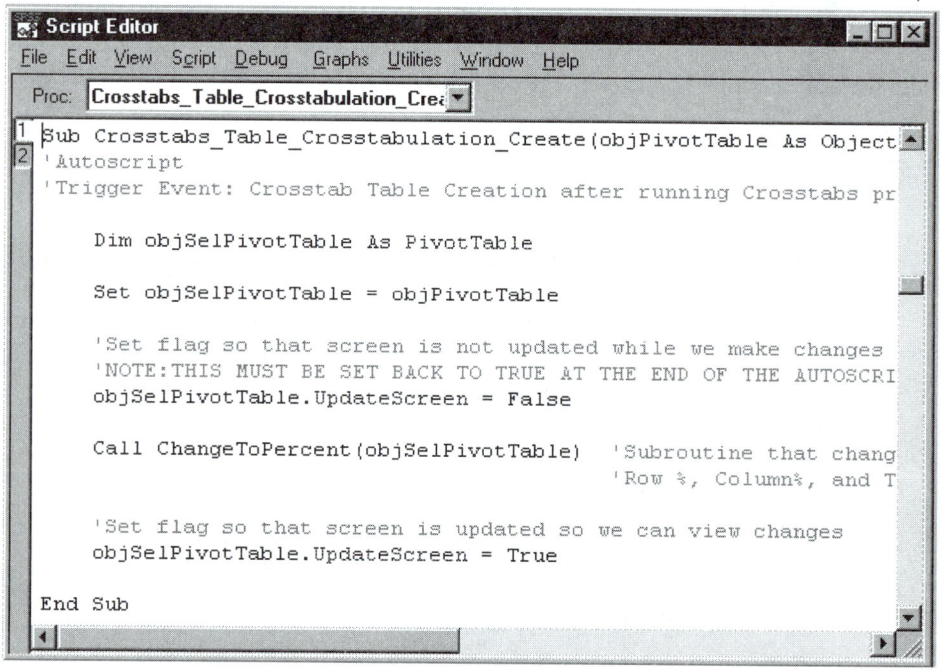


**Creation of title.** Referenced to the statistical procedure that created it: Correlations_Title_Create.

**Creation of notes.** Referenced to the procedure that created it: Correlations_Notes_Create.

**Creation of warnings.** Referenced by the procedure that created it.

You can also use a script to trigger an autoscript indirectly. For example, you could write a script that invokes the Correlations procedure, which in turn triggers the autoscript registered to the resulting Correlations table.

### The Autoscript File

All autoscripts are saved in a single file (unlike other scripts, each of which is saved in a separate file). Any new autoscripts you create are also added to this file. The name of the current autoscript file is displayed in the Scripts tab of the Options dialog box (Edit menu).

Figure 43-11
*Autoscript subroutines displayed in Options dialog box*

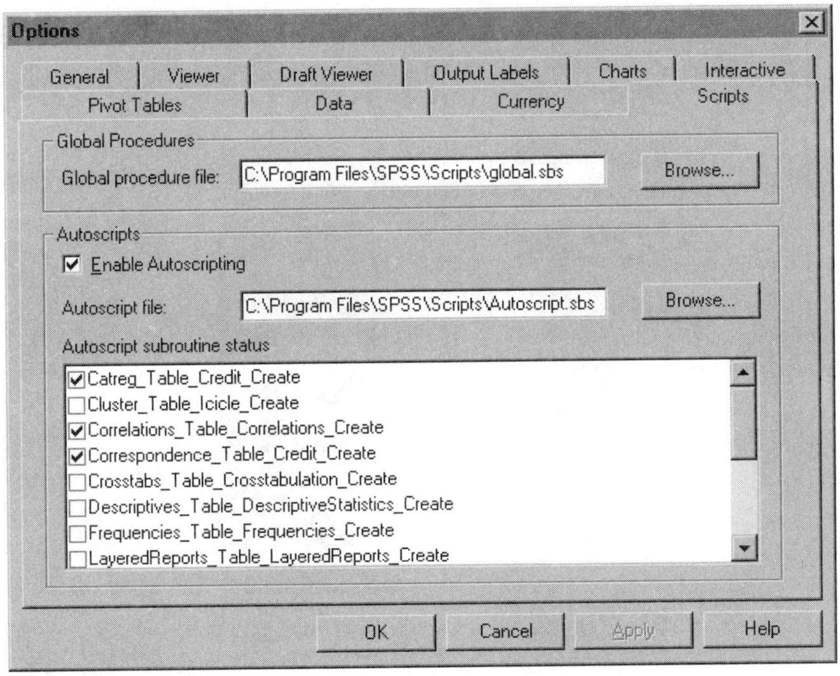


The Options dialog box also displays all of the autoscripts in the currently selected autoscript file, allowing you to enable and disable individual scripts.

The default autoscript file is *autscript.sbs*. You can specify a different autoscript file, but only one can be active at any one time.

# How Scripts Work

Scripts work by manipulating objects using properties and methods. For example, pivot tables are a class of objects. With objects of this class, you can use the SelectTable method to select all of the elements in the table, and you can use the TextColor property to change the color of selected text. Each object class has specific properties and methods associated with it. The collection of all object classes (or types) is called the type library.

Figure 43-12
*Tree view of object hierarchy*

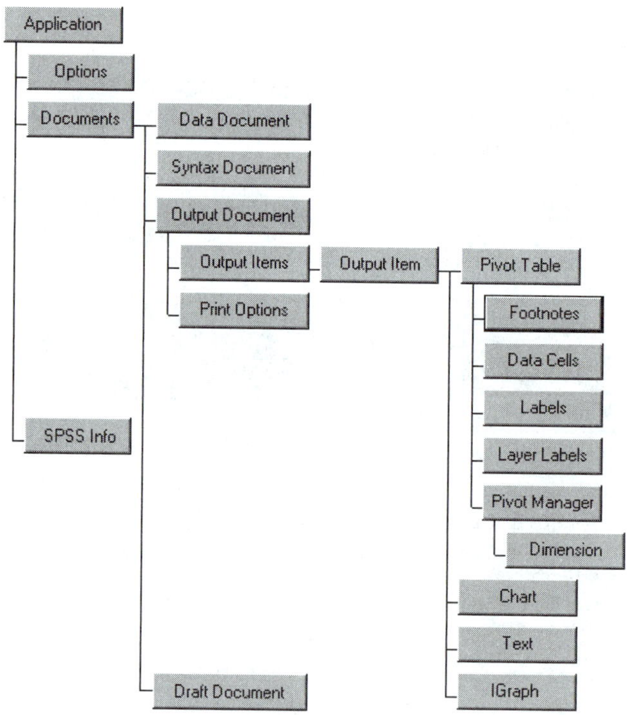


Using objects is a two-step process. First, you create a reference to the object (called *getting* the object). Then, you use properties and methods to do something. You get objects by navigating the hierarchy of objects, at each step using properties or methods of objects higher in the hierarchy to get at the objects beneath. For example, to get a pivot table object, you have to first get the output document that contains the pivot table and then get the items in that output document.

Each object that you get is stored in a variable. (Remember that all you are really storing in the variable is a reference to the object.) One of the first steps in creating a script is often to declare variables for the objects that you need.

*Tip*: It is difficult to understand how scripts work if you do not understand how the program works. Before writing a script, use the mouse to perform the task several times as you normally would. At each step, consider what objects you are manipulating and what properties of each object you are changing.

## Declaring Variables

Although not always required, it is a good idea to declare all variables before using them. This is most often done using Dim declaration statements:

```
Dim objOutputDoc As ISpssOutputDoc
Dim objPivotTable As PivotTable
Dim intType As Integer
Dim strLabel As String
```

Each declaration specifies the variable name and type. For example, the first declaration above creates an object variable named objOutputDoc and assigns this variable to the ISpssOutputDoc object class. The variable does not yet have a value because it has not been set to a particular output document. All the statement does is declare that the variable exists. (This process has been referred to as "renaming the objects you want to use.")

**Variable naming conventions.** By convention, the name of each variable indicates its type. Object variable names begin with obj, integer variables begin with int, and string variables begin with str. These are only conventions—you can name your variables anything you want—but following them makes it much easier to understand your code.

**SPSS object classes.** ISpssOutputDoc and PivotTable are names of SPSS object classes. Each class represents a type of object that the program can create, such as an output document or pivot table. Each object class has specific properties and methods associated with it. The collection of all SPSS object classes (or types) is referred to as the type library.

The following variable names are used in the sample scripts included with the software and are recommended for all scripts. Notice that with the exception of pivot tables, object classes have names beginning with ISpss.

| Object | Type or Class | Variable Name |
|---|---|---|
| SPSS application | IspssApp | objSpssApp—variable is global and does not require declaration |
| SPSS options | ISpssOptions | objSpssOptions |
| SPSS file information | ISpssInfo | objSpssInfo |
| Documents | ISpssDocuments | objDocuments |
| Data document | ISpssDataDoc | objDataDoc |
| Syntax document | ISpssSyntaxDoc | objSyntaxDoc |
| Viewer document | ISpssOutputDoc | objOutputDoc |
| Print options | ISpssPrintOptions | objPrintOptions |
| Output items collection | ISpssItems | objOutputItems |
| Output item | ISpssItem | objOutputItem |
| Chart | ISpssChart | objSPSSChart |
| Text | ISpssRtf | objSPSSText |
| Pivot table | PivotTable | objPivotTable |
| Footnotes | ISpssFootnotes | objFootnotes |
| Data cells | ISpssDataCells | objDataCells |
| Layer labels | ISpssLayerLabels | objLayerLabels |
| Column labels | ISpssLabels | objColumnLabels |
| Row labels | ISpssLabels | objRowLabels |
| Pivot manager | ISpssPivotMgr | objPivotMgr |
| Dimension | ISpssDimension | objDimension |

## Getting Automation Objects

To *get* an object means to create a reference to the object so that you can use properties and methods to do something. Each object reference that you get is stored in a variable. To get an object, first declare an object variable of the appropriate class, then set the variable to the specific object. For example, to get the designated output document:

```
Dim objOutputDoc As ISpssOutputDoc
Set objOutputDoc = objSpssApp.GetDesignatedOutputDoc
```

you use properties and methods of objects higher in the object hierarchy to get at the objects beneath. The second statement above gets the designated output document using GetDesignatedOutputDoc, a method associated with the application object, which is the highest-level object. Similarly, to get a pivot table object, you first get the output document that contains the pivot table, and then get the collection of items in that output document, and so on.

### Example: Getting an Output Item

This script gets the third output item in the designated output document and activates it. If that item is not an OLE object, the script produces an error.

See below for another example that activates the first pivot table in the designated output document.

```
Sub Main

Dim objOutputDoc As ISpssOutputDoc'declare object variables
Dim objOutputItems As ISpssItems
Dim objOutputItem As ISpssItem

Set objOutputDoc = objSpssApp.GetDesignatedOutputDoc 'get reference to designated output doc
Set objOutputItems = objOutputDoc.Items() 'get collection of items in doc
Set objOutputItem = objOutputItems.GetItem(2) 'get third output item
'(item numbers start at 0 so "2" gets third)

objOutputItem.Activate 'activate output item

End sub
```

### Example: Getting the First Pivot Table

This script gets the first pivot table in the designated output document and activates it.

```
Sub Main

Dim objOutputDoc As ISpssOutputDoc 'declare object variables
Dim objOutputItems As ISpssItems
Dim objOutputItem As ISpssItem
Dim objPivotTable As PivotTable

Set objOutputDoc = objSpssApp.GetDesignatedOutputDoc'get reference to designated output doc
Set objOutputItems = objOutputDoc.Items()'get collection of items in doc
```

```
Dim intItemCount As Integer'number of output items
Dim intItemType As Integer'type of item (defined by SpssType property)

intItemCount = objOutputItems.Count()'get number of output items
  For index = 0 To intItemCount'loop through output items
  Set objOutputItem = objOutputItems.GetItem(index)'get current item
  intItemType = objOutputItem.SPSSType()'get type of current item
  If intItemType = SPSSPivot Then
    Set objPivotTable = objOutputItem.Activate()'if item is a pivot table, activate it
    Exit For
  End If
Next index

End sub
```

Examples are also available in the online Help. You can try them yourself by pasting the code from Help into the script window.

## Properties and Methods

Like real world objects, OLE automation objects have features and uses. In programming terminology, the features are referred to as properties, and the uses are referred to as methods. Each object class has specific methods and properties that determine what you can do with that object.

| Object | Property | Method |
|---|---|---|
| Pencil (real world) | Hardness<br>Color | Write<br>Erase |
| Pivot table (SPSS) | TextFont<br>DataCellWidths<br>CaptionText | SelectTable<br>ClearSelection<br>HideFootnotes |

### Using Properties

Properties set or return attributes of objects, such as color or cell width. When a property appears to the left side of an equals sign, you are writing to it. For example, to set the caption for an activated pivot table (objPivotTable) to "Anita's results":

```
objPivotTable.CaptionText = "Anita's results"
```

When a property appears on the right side, you are reading from it. For example, to get the caption of the activated pivot table and save it in a variable:

```
strFontName = objPivotTable.CaptionText
```

### Using Methods

Methods perform actions on objects, such as selecting all the elements in a table:

```
objPivotTable.SelectTable
```

or removing a selection:

```
objPivotTable.ClearSelection
```

Some methods return another object. Such methods are extremely important for navigating the object hierarchy. For example, the GetDesignatedOutputDoc method returns the designated output document, allowing you to access the items in that output document:

```
Set objOutputDoc = objSpssApp.GetDesignatedOutputDoc
Set objItems = objOutputDoc.Items
```

## The Object Browser

The object browser displays all object classes and the methods and properties associated with each. You can also access Help on individual properties and methods and paste selected properties and methods into your script.

Figure 43-13
*Object browser*

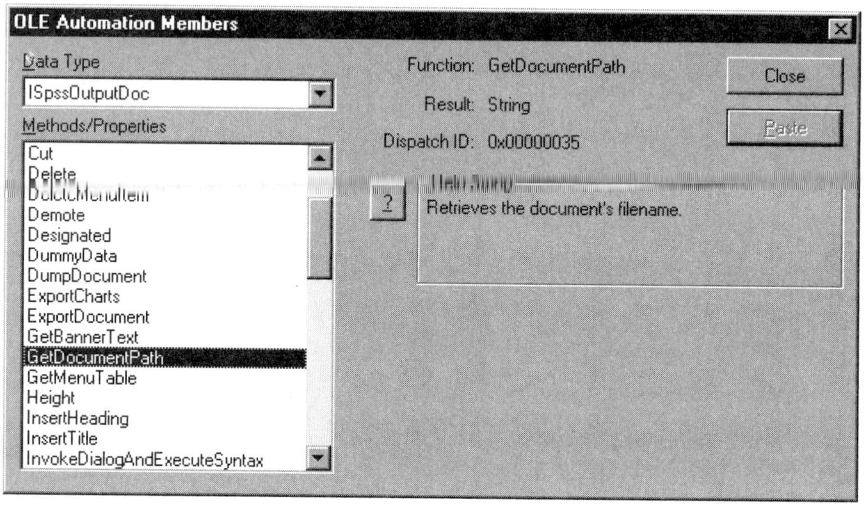


- From the script window menus choose:

  Debug
  Object Browser...

- Select an object class from the Data Type list to display the methods and properties for that class.

- Select properties and methods for context-sensitive Help or to paste them into your script.

# Procedures

A procedure is a named sequence of statements that are executed as a unit. Organizing code in procedures makes it easier to manage and reuse pieces of code. Scripts must have at least one procedure (the Main subroutine) and often they have several. The Main procedure may contain few statements, aside from calls to subroutines that do most of the work.

Figure 43-14
*New Procedure dialog box*

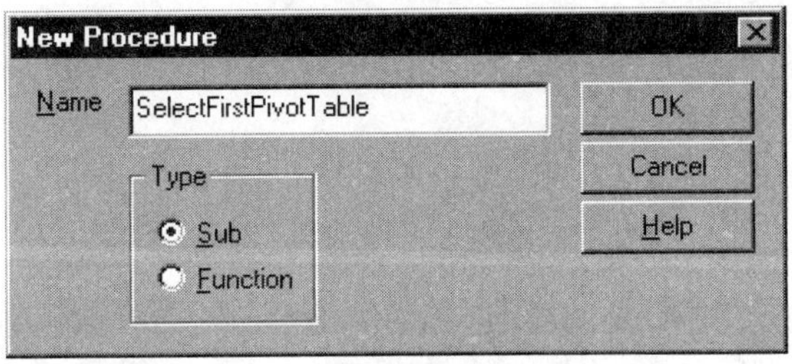


Procedures can be subroutines or functions. A procedure begins with a statement that specifies the type of procedure and the name (for example, Sub Main or Function DialogMonitor( )) and concludes with the appropriate End statement (End Sub or End Function).

As you scroll through the script window, the name of the current procedure is displayed at the top of the script window. Within a script, you can call any procedure as many times as you want. You can also call any procedure in the global script file, which makes it possible to share procedures between scripts.

## To Add a New Procedure in a Script

- From the menus choose:

  Script
   New Procedure...

- Type a name for the procedure.

- Select Subroutine or Function.

  Alternatively, you can create a new procedure by typing the statements that define the procedure directly in the script.

## Global Procedures

If you have a procedure or function that you want to use in a number of different scripts, you can add it to the global script file. Procedures in the global script file can be called by all other scripts.

Figure 43-15
*Global script file*

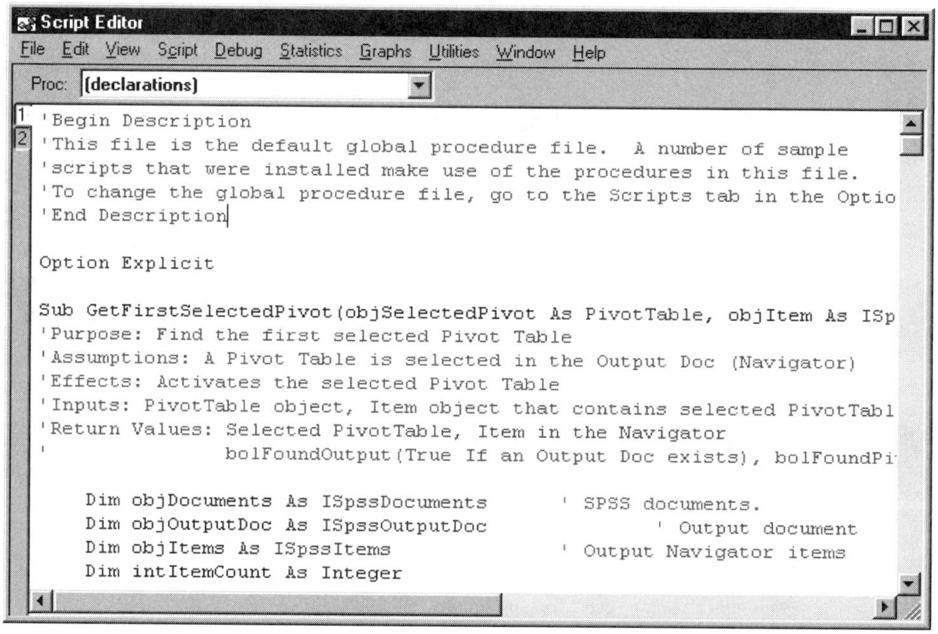


The default global script file is *global.sbs*. You can freely add procedures to this file. You can also specify a different global file on the Scripts tab in the Options dialog box (Edit menu), but only one file can be active as the global file at any given time. That means that if you create a new global file and specify it as the global file, the procedures and functions in *global.sbs* are no longer available.

You can view the global script file in any script window (click the #2 tab on the left side of the window just below the toolbar), but you can edit it in only one window at a time.

Global procedures must be called by other script procedures. You cannot run a global script directly from the Utilities menu or a script window.

## Adding a Description to a Script

You can add a description to be displayed in the Run Script and Use Starter Script dialog boxes. Just add a comment on the first line of the script that starts with Begin Description, followed by the desired comment (one or more lines), followed by End Description. For example:

```
'Begin Description
'This script changes "Sig." to "p=" in the column labels of any pivot table.
'Requirement: The Pivot Table that you want to change must be selected.
'End Description
```

The description must be formatted as a comment (each line beginning with an apostrophe).

## Scripting Custom Dialog Boxes

There are two steps to implementing a custom dialog box: first create the dialog box using the UserDialog Editor, and then create a dialog monitor function (DialogFunc) that monitors the dialog box and defines its behavior.

The dialog box itself is defined by a Begin Dialog...End Dialog block. You do not need to type this code directly—the UserDialog Editor provides an easy, graphical way to define the dialog box.

Figure 43-16
*Creating a dialog box in the UserDialog Editor*

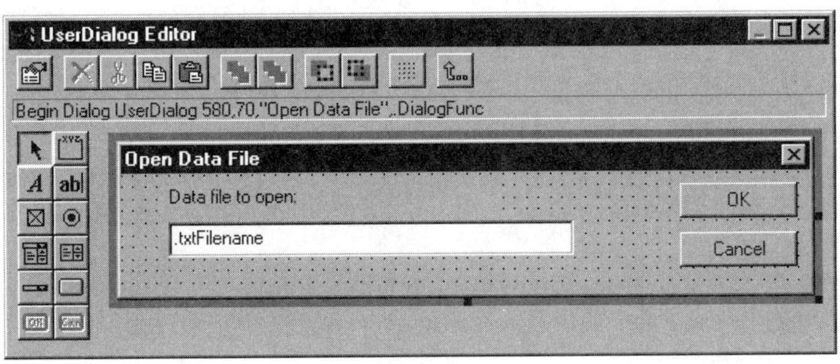

The Editor initially displays a blank dialog box form. You can add controls, such as radio buttons and check boxes, by selecting the appropriate tool and dragging with the mouse. (Hold the mouse over each tool for a description.) You can also drag the sides and corners to resize the dialog box. After adding a control, right-click the control to set properties for that control.

**Dialog monitor function.** To create the dialog monitor function, right-click the dialog box form (make sure no control is selected on the form) and enter a name for the function in the DialogFunc field. The statements that define the function are added to your script, although you will have to edit the function manually to define the behavior for each action.

When finished, click the Save and Exit icon (far right on the toolbar) to add the code for the dialog box to your script.

## To Create a Custom Dialog Box

▶ In the script window, click the cursor in the script where you want to insert the code for the dialog box.

▶ From the menus choose:

Script
  Dialog Editor...

▶ Select tools from the palette and drag in the new dialog box form to add controls, such as buttons and check boxes.

▶ Resize the dialog box by dragging the handles on the sides and corners.

▶ Right-click the form (with no control selected) and enter a name for the dialog monitor function in the DialogFunc field.

▶ Click the Save and Exit icon (far right on the toolbar) when you are finished.

You have to edit your dialog monitor function manually to define the behavior of the dialog box.

## Dialog Monitor Functions (DialogFunc)

A dialog monitor function defines the behavior of a dialog box for each of a number of specified cases. The function takes the following (generic) form:

```
Function DialogFunc(strDlgItem as String, intAction as Integer, intSuppValue as Integer)
  Select Case intAction
    Case 1 ' dialog box initialization
    ...  'statements to execute when dialog box is initialized
    Case 2 ' value changing or button pressed
    ...  'statements...
    Case 3 ' TextBox or ComboBox text changed ...
    Case 4 ' focus changed ...
    Case 5 ' idle ...
  End Select
End Function
```

**Parameters.** The function must be able to pass three parameters: one string (strDlgItem) and two integers (intAction and intSuppValue). The parameters are values passed between the function and the dialog box, depending on what action is taken.

For example, when a user clicks a control in the dialog box, the name of the control is passed to the function as strDlgItem (the field name is specified in the dialog box definition). The second parameter (intAction) is a numeric value that indicates what action took place in the dialog box. The third parameter is used for additional information in some cases. You must include all three parameters in the function definition even if you do not use all of them.

**Select Case intAction.** The value of intAction indicates what action took place in the dialog box. For example, when the dialog box initializes, intAction = 1. If the user presses a button, intAction changes to 2, and so on. There are five possible actions, and you can specify statements that execute for each action as indicated below. You do not need to specify all five possible cases—only the ones that apply. For example, if you do not want any statements to execute on initialization, omit Case 1.

- **Case intAction = 1.** Specify statements to execute when the dialog box is initialized. For example, you could disable one or more controls or add a beep. The string strDlgItem is a null string; intSuppValue is 0.

- **Case 2.** Executes when a button is pushed or when a value changes in a CheckBox, DropListBox, ListBox or OptionGroup control. If a button is pushed, strDlgItem is the button, intSuppValue is meaningless, and you must set DialogFunc = True to prevent the dialog from closing. If a value changes, strDlgItem is the item whose value has changed, and intSuppValue is the new value.
- **Case 3.** Executes when a value changes in a TextBox or ComboBox control. The string strDlgItem is the control whose text changed and is losing focus; intSuppValue is the number of characters.
- **Case 4.** Executes when the focus changes in the dialog box. The string strDlgItem is gaining focus, and intSuppValue is the item that is losing focus (the first item is 0, second is 1, and so on).
- **Case 5.** Idle processing. The string strDlgItem is a null string; intSuppValue is 0. Set DialogFunc = True to continue receiving idle actions.

For more information, see the examples and the DialogFunc prototype in the Sax BASIC Language Reference Help file.

### *Example: Scripting a Simple Dialog Box*

This script creates a simple dialog box that opens a data file. See related sections for explanations of the BuildDialog subroutine and dialog monitor function.

Figure 43-17
*Open Data File dialog box created by script*

```
Sub Main
  Call BuildDialog
End Sub

'define dialog box
Sub BuildDialog
  Begin Dialog UserDialog 580,70,"Open Data File",.DialogFunc
    Text 40,7,280,21,"Data file to open:",.txtDialogTitle
    TextBox 40,28,340,21,.txtFilename
    OKButton 470,7,100,21,.cmdOK
    CancelButton 470,35,100,21,.cmdCancel
  End Dialog
  Dim dlg As UserDialog
  Dialog dlg
End Sub

 'define function that determines behavior of dialog box
Function DialogFunc(strDlgItem As String, intAction As Integer, intSuppValue As Integer) As Boolean
  Select Case intAction
    Case 1 ' beep when dialog is initialized
      Beep
    Case 2 ' value changing or button pressed
      Select Case strDlgItem
      Case "cmdOK" 'if user clicks OK, open data file with specified filename
      strFilename = DlgText("txtFilename")
      Call OpenDataFile(strFilename)
      DialogFunc = False
      Case "cmdCancel"'If user clicks Cancel, close dialog
      DialogFunc = False
      End Select
  End Select
End Function

Sub OpenDataFile(strFilename As Variant) 'Open data file with specified filename
  Dim objDataDoc As ISpssDataDoc
  Set objDataDoc = objSpssApp.OpenDataDoc(strFilename)
End Sub
```

Examples are also available in the online Help. You can try them yourself by pasting the code from Help into the script window.

# Debugging Scripts

The Debug menu allows you to step through your code, executing one line or subroutine at a time and viewing the result. You can also insert a break point in the script to pause the execution at the line that contains the break point.

To debug an autoscript, open the autoscript file in a script window, insert break points in the procedure that you want to debug, and then run the statistical procedure that triggers the autoscript.

**Step Into.** Execute the current line. If the current line is a subroutine or function call, stop on the first line of that subroutine or function.

**Step Over.** Execute to the next line. If the current line is a subroutine or function call, execute the subroutine or function completely.

**Step Out.** Step out of the current subroutine or function call.

**Step to Cursor.** Execute to the current line.

**Toggle Break.** Insert or remove a break point. The script pauses at the break point, and the debugging pane is displayed.

**Quick Watch.** Display the value of the current expression.

**Add Watch.** Add the current expression to the watch window.

**Object Browser.** Display the object browser.

**Set Next Statement.** Set the next statement to be executed. Only statements in the current subroutine/function can be selected.

**Show Next Statement.** Display the next statement to be executed.

## To Step through a Script

▶ From the Debug menu, choose any of the Step options to execute code, one line or subroutine at a time.

The Immediate, Watch, Stack, and Loaded tabs are displayed in the script window, along with the debugging toolbar.

▶ Use the toolbar (or hot keys) to continue stepping through the script.

▶ Alternatively, select Toggle Break to insert a break point at the current line.

The script pauses at the break point.

## The Debugging Pane

When you step through code, the Immediate, Watch, Stack, and Loaded tabs are displayed.

Figure 43-18
*Debugging pane displayed in script window*

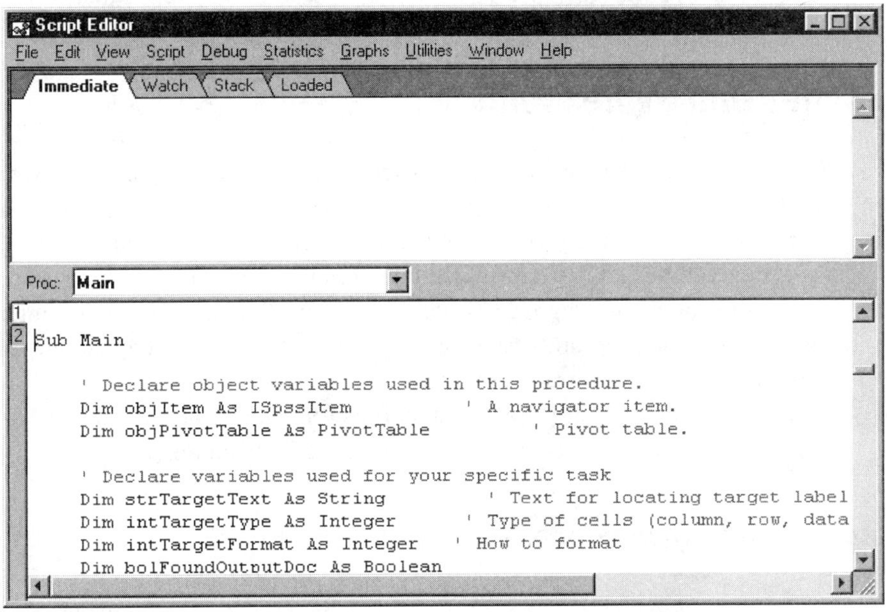


**Immediate tab.** Click the name of any variable and click the eyeglass icon to display the current value of the variable. You can also evaluate an expression, assign a variable, or call a subroutine.

- Type ?expr and press Enter to show the value of *expr*.
- Type var = expr and press Enter to change the value of *var*.
- Type subname args and press Enter to call a subroutine or built-in instruction.

- Type Trace and press Enter to toggle trace mode. Trace mode prints each statement in the immediate window when a script is running.

**Watch tab.** To display a variable, function, or expression, click it and choose Add Watch from the Debug menu. Displayed values are updated each time execution pauses. You can edit the expression to the left of ->. Press Enter to update all the values immediately. Press Ctrl-Y to delete the line.

**Stack tab.** Displays the lines that called the current statement. The first line is the current statement, the second line is the one that called the first, and so on. Click any line to highlight that line in the edit window.

**Loaded tab.** List the currently active scripts. Click a line to view that script.

## Script Files and Syntax Files

Syntax files (**.sps*) are not the same as script files (**.sbs*). Syntax files have commands written in the command language that allows you to run statistical procedures and data transformations. While scripts allow you to manipulate output and automate other tasks that you normally perform using the graphical interface of menus and dialog boxes, the command language provides an alternative method for communicating directly with the program's back end, the part of the system that handles statistical computations and data transformations.

You can combine scripts and syntax files for even greater flexibility, by running a script from within command syntax, or by embedding command syntax within a script.

### Running Command Syntax from a Script

You can run command syntax from within an automation script using the ExecuteCommands method. Command syntax allows you to run data transformations and statistical procedures and to produce charts. Much of this functionality cannot be automated directly from command scripts.

The easiest way to build a command syntax file is to make selections in dialog boxes and paste the syntax for the selections into the script window.

Figure 43-19
*Pasting command syntax into a script*

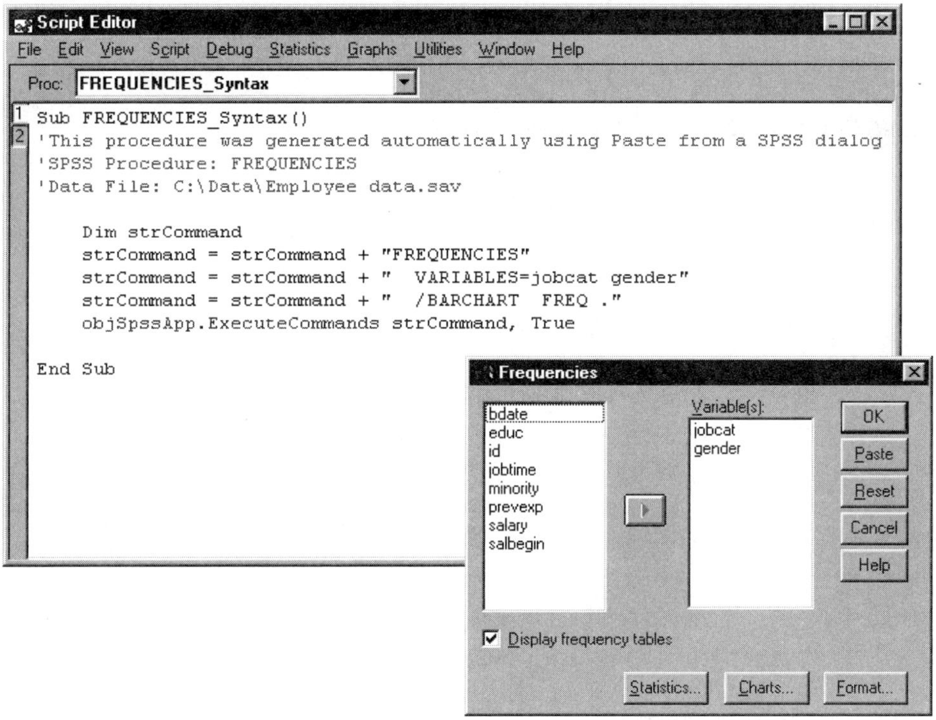


When you open dialog boxes using the script window menus, the Paste button pastes all of the code needed to run commands from within a script.

*Note*: You must use the script window menus to open the dialog box; otherwise, commands will be pasted to a syntax window rather than the scripting window.

## To Paste Command Syntax into a Script

▶ From the script window menus, choose commands from the Statistics, Graphs, and Utilities menus to open dialog boxes.

▶ Make selections in the dialog box.

▶ Click Paste.

*Note*: You must use the script window menus to open the dialog box; otherwise, commands will be pasted to a syntax window rather than the scripting window.

## *Running a Script from Command Syntax*

You can use the SCRIPT command to run a script from within command syntax. Specify the name of the script you want to run, with the filename enclosed in quotes, as follows:

```
SCRIPT 'C:\PROGRAM FILES\SPSS\CLEAN NAVIGATOR.SBS'.
```

Appendix

# A

# *Database Access Administrator*

The Database Access Administrator is a utility designed to simplify large or confusing data sources for use with the Database Wizard. It allows users and administrators to customize their data source in the following ways:

- Create aliases for database tables and fields.
- Create variable names for fields.
- Hide extraneous tables and fields.

The Database Access Administrator does not actually change your database. Instead, it generates files that hold all of your information, which act as database "views."

You can use the Database Access Administrator to specify up to three different views per database: Enterprise level, Department level, and Personal level. Both the Database Access Administrator and the Database Wizard recognize these files by the following names:

- Enterprise level: *dba01.inf*
- Department level: *dba02.inf*
- Personal level: *dba03.inf*

Each file contains level-specific information about any number of data sources. For example, your *dba03.inf* file could contain personal view information for a corporate accounts database, your company's hourlog database, and a database that you use to keep track of your CD collection.

When you open the Database Access Administrator, it will search your system's path for these files and automatically display information for all three views of any data source you have configured.

**Inheritance and priorities**. Whenever you use the Database Wizard, it presents the lowest-level view of your data source that it can find on your system's path, where the levels are, from highest to lowest, Enterprise, Department, and Personal. Each level's file holds information about all of your data sources for that level. For example, your marketing department will have one file, *dba02.inf*, that contains the aliasing information for all of the database views established for the marketing department. Each person in the marketing department will have a file, *dba03.inf*, that contains customized views of all of the databases that he or she uses.

In the Database Access Administrator, Aliases, Variable Names, and Hide Orders are inherited from the top down.

**Example.** If the Regions table is hidden at the Enterprise level, it is invisible at both the Department and Personal levels. This table would not be displayed in the Database Wizard.

**Example.** The field JOBCAT in the EmployeeSales table is not aliased at the Enterprise level, but it is aliased as Job Categories at the Department level. It appears as Job Categories at the Personal level. Additionally, if the Employee Sales table is aliased as Employee Information at the Personal level, the original field (EmployeeSales.JOBCAT) would appear in the Database Wizard as 'Employee Information'.'Job Categories'.

To start the Database Access Administrator, run the file *spssdbca.exe*, which is installed in your SPSS directory. For more information about the Database Access Administrator, refer to its online Help.

Appendix

# B

# Customizing HTML Documents

You can automatically add customized HTML code to documents exported in HTML format, including:

- HTML document titles
- Document type specification
- Meta tags and script code (for example, JavaScript)
- Text displayed before and after exported output

## To Add Customized HTML Code to Exported Output Documents

▶ Open the file *htmlfram.txt* (located in the directory in which SPSS is installed) in a text editor.

▶ Replace the comments in the "fields" on the lines between the double open brackets (<<) with the text or HTML code you want to insert in your exported HTML documents.

▶ Save the file as a text file.

*Note:* If you change the name or location of the text file, you have to modify the system registry to use the file to customize your exported HTML output.

## Content and Format of the Text File for Customized HTML

The HTML code that you want to add automatically to your HTML documents must be specified in a simple text file that contains six fields, each delimited by two open angle brackets on the preceding line (<<):

<<
Text or code that you want to insert at the top of the document before the <HTML> specification (for example, comments that include document type specifications)

<<
Text used as the document title (displayed in the title bar)

<<
Meta tags or script code (for example, JavaScript code)

<<
HTML code that modifies the <BODY> tag (for example, code that specifies background color)

<<
Text and/or HTML code that is inserted after the exported output (for example, copyright notice)

<<
Text and/or HTML code that is inserted before the exported output (for example, company name, logo, etc.)

## To Use a Different File or Location for Custom HTML Code

If you change the name or location of *htmlfram.txt*, you must modify the system registry to use the file in customized HTML output.

▶ From the Windows Start menu choose Run, type regedit, and click OK.

▶ In the left pane of the Registry Editor, choose:

```
HHKEY_CURRENT_USER
 Software
  SPSS
   SPSS for Windows
    10.0
     Spsswin
```

- In the right pane, double-click the string HTMLFormatFile.
- For Value data, enter the full path and name of the text file containing the custom HTML specifications (for example, *c:\myfiles\htmlstuf.txt*).

### Sample Text File for Customized HTML

```
<<
<!DOCTYPE HTML PUBLIC "-//W3C//DTD HTML 3.2//EN">
<<
NVI, Inc.
<<
<META NAME="keywords" CONTENT="gizmos, gadgets, gimcracks">
<<
bgcolor="#FFFFFF"
<<
<H4 align=center>This page made possible by...
<br><br>
<IMG SRC="spss2.gif" align=center></H4>
<<
<h2 align=center>NVI Sales</h2>
<h3 align=center>Regional Data</h3>
```

### Sample HTML Source for Customized HTML

```
<!DOCTYPE HTML PUBLIC "-//W3C//DTD HTML 3.2//EN">
<HTML>
<HEAD>
<TITLE>
NVI Sales, Inc.
</TITLE>
<META NAME="keywords" CONTENT="gizmos, gadgets, gimcracks">
```

```
</HEAD>
<BODY bgcolor="#FFFFFF">
<h2 align=center>NVI Sales</h2>
<h3 align=center>Regional Data</h3>
```

[Exported output]

```
<H4 align=center>This page made possible by...
<br><br>
<IMG SRC="spss2.gif" align=center></H4>
</BODY>
</HTML>
```

# Index

# *SPSS® Interactive Graphics 10.0*

SPSS

For more information about SPSS® software products, please visit our WWW site at *http://www.spss.com* or contact

Marketing Department
SPSS Inc.
233 South Wacker Drive, 11th Floor
Chicago, IL 60606-6307
Tel: (312) 651-3000
Fax: (312) 651-3668



3 4 5 6 7 8 9 0    03 02 01

ISBN 0-13-017903-5

# Preface

SPSS® 10.0 is a comprehensive system for analyzing data. This manual, *SPSS Interactive Graphics 10.0,* documents **interactive charts,** an important feature in the SPSS Base:

- In the Viewer, start with a blank interactive chart, assign variables to the axes and legends, and specify which graphical elements (bars, lines, a cloud of points, etc.) you want. As soon as you choose each graphical element, it is added to the chart.
- From the Graphs menu, choose Interactive, and then choose a chart type (Bar, Line, Scatterplot, etc.). A dialog box, in which you can assign variables to the axes and legends, specify summary functions, and change appearance attributes before the chart is created, is displayed.

Once you have created a chart, you can make many modifications dynamically. For example, you can insert or delete graphical elements, change colors and textures, rotate 3-D graphs smoothly, and adjust fit lines and surfaces.

This manual is to be used along with the *SPSS Base 10.0 User's Guide,* which documents the graphical user interface of SPSS for Windows. The User's Guide contains complete information about statistical procedures and the original graphics system (which can be used for types of charts not available in interactive graphics). A companion book, the *SPSS Base 10.0 Applications Guide*, provides examples of statistical procedures and related data transformations, with advice on screening data, using appropriate procedures, and interpreting the output. Beneath the menus and dialog boxes, SPSS uses a command language that can be used to create and run production jobs. Dialog boxes can "paste" commands into a syntax window, where they can be modified and saved; a few features of the system can be accessed only via command syntax. Complete command syntax is documented in the *SPSS Syntax Reference Guide Release 10,* which is included on the CD version of the software and is available for purchase separately in print. The Help system contains brief syntax diagrams in addition to full help on the graphical user interface.

## SPSS Options

The SPSS family of products includes add-on enhancements to the SPSS Base system, which are available on several computer platforms. Contact your local SPSS office or sales representative about availability of the following options:

- **SPSS Regression Models™** provides techniques for analyzing data that do not fit traditional linear statistical models. It includes procedures for probit analysis, logistic regression, weight estimation, two-stage least-squares regression, and general nonlinear regression.
- **SPSS Advanced Models™** focuses on techniques often used in sophisticated experimental and biomedical research. It includes procedures for general linear models (GLM), variance components analysis, loglinear analysis, actuarial life tables, Kaplan-Meier survival analysis, and basic and extended Cox regression.
- **SPSS Tables™** creates a variety of presentation-quality tabular reports, including complex stub-and-banner tables and displays of multiple response data.
- **SPSS Trends™** performs comprehensive forecasting and time series analyses with multiple curve-fitting models, smoothing models, and methods for estimating autoregressive functions.
- **SPSS Categories®** performs optimal scaling procedures, including correspondence analysis.
- **SPSS Conjoint™** performs conjoint analysis.
- **SPSS Exact Tests™** calculates exact *p* values for statistical tests when small or very unevenly distributed samples could make the usual tests inaccurate.
- **SPSS Missing Value Analysis™** describes patterns of missing data, estimates means and other statistics, and imputes values for missing observations.
- **SPSS Maps™** turns your geographically distributed data into high-quality maps with symbols, colors, bar charts, pie charts, and combinations of themes to present not only what is happening but where it is happening.

The SPSS family of products also includes applications for data entry, text analysis, classification, neural networks, and flowcharting.

## *Compatibility*

The SPSS Base 10.0 system is designed to operate on computer systems running Windows 95, Windows 98, or Windows NT 4.0.

## *Serial Numbers*

Your serial number is your identification number with SPSS Inc. You will need this serial number when you call SPSS Inc. for information regarding support, payment, or an upgraded system. The serial number was provided with your Base system. Before using the system, please copy this number to the registration card.

## *Registration Card*

Don't put it off: *fill out and send us your registration card.* Until we receive your registration card, you have an unregistered system. Even if you have previously sent a card to us, please fill out and return the card enclosed in your Base system package. Registering your system entitles you to:

- Technical support services
- New product announcements and upgrade announcements

## *Customer Service*

If you have any questions concerning your shipment or account, contact your local office, listed on page vii. Please have your serial number ready for identification when calling.

## *Training Seminars*

SPSS Inc. provides both public and onsite training seminars for SPSS. All seminars feature hands-on workshops. SPSS seminars will be offered in major U.S. and European cities on a regular basis. For more information on these seminars, call your local office, listed on page vii.

### Technical Support

The services of SPSS Technical Support are available to registered customers of SPSS. Customers may contact Technical Support for assistance in using SPSS products or for installation help for one of the supported hardware environments. To reach Technical Support, see the SPSS home page on the World Wide Web at *http://www.spss.com*, or call your local office, listed on page vii. Be prepared to identify yourself, your organization, and the serial number of your system.

### Additional Publications

Individuals worldwide can order manuals directly from the SPSS World Wide Web site at *http://www.spss.com/Pubs*. For telephone orders in the United States and Canada, call SPSS Inc. at 1-800-253-2565. For telephone orders outside of North America, contact your local SPSS office, listed on page vii.

Individuals in the United States can also order these manuals by calling Prentice Hall at 1-800-947-7700. If you represent a bookstore or have a Prentice Hall account, call 1-800-382-3419. In Canada, call 1-800-567-3800.

### Tell Us Your Thoughts

Your comments are important. Please send us a letter and let us know about your experiences with SPSS products. We especially like to hear about new and interesting applications using the SPSS system. Write to SPSS Inc. Marketing Department, Attn: Director of Product Planning, 233 South Wacker Drive, 11th Floor, Chicago, IL 60606-6307.

### Contacting SPSS

If you would like to be on our mailing list, contact one of our offices, listed on page vii, or visit our WWW site at *http://www.spss.com*. We will send you a copy of our newsletter and let you know about SPSS Inc. activities in your area.

**SPSS Inc.**
Chicago, Illinois, U.S.A.
Tel: 1.312.651.3000
www.spss.com/corpinfo
**Customer Service:**
1.800.521.1337
**Sales:**
1.800.543.2185
sales@spss.com
**Training:**
1.800.543.6607
**Technical Support:**
1.312.651.3410
support@spss.com

**SPSS Federal Systems**
Tel: 1.703.527.6777
www.spss.com

**SPSS Argentina srl**
Tel: +5411.4814.5030
www.spss.com

**SPSS Asia Pacific Pte. Ltd.**
Tel: +65.245.9110
www.spss.com

**SPSS Australasia Pty. Ltd.**
Tel: +61.2.9954.5660
www.spss.com

**SPSS Belgium**
Tel: +32.162.389.82
www.spss.com

**SPSS Benelux BV**
Tel: +31.183.651777
www.spss.nl

**SPSS Brasil Ltda**
Tel: +55.11.5505.3644
www.spss.com

**SPSS Czech Republic**
Tel: +420.2.24813839
www.spss.cz

**SPSS Danmark A/S**
Tel: +45.45.46.02.00
www.spss.com

**SPSS Finland Oy**
Tel: +358.9.524.801
www.spss.com

**SPSS France SARL**
Tel: +01.55.35.27.00 x03
www.spss.com

**SPSS Germany**
Tel: +49.89.4890740
www.spss.com

**SPSS Hellas SA**
Tel: +30.1.72.51.925/72.51.950
www.spss.com

**SPSS Hispanoportuguesa S.L.**
Tel: +34.91.447.37.00
www.spss.com

**SPSS Hong Kong Ltd.**
Tel: +852.2.811.9662
www.spss.com

**SPSS India**
Tel: +91.80.225.0260
www.spss.com

**SPSS Ireland**
Tel: +353.1.496.9007
www.spss.com

**SPSS Israel Ltd.**
Tel: +972.9.9526700
www.spss.com

**SPSS Italia srl**
Tel: +39.51.252573
www.spss.it

**SPSS Japan Inc.**
Tel: +81.3.5466.5511
www.spss.com

**SPSS Kenya Limited**
Tel: +254.2.577.262/3
www.spss.com

**SPSS Korea KIC Co., Ltd.**
Tel: +82.2.3446.7651
www.spss.co.kr

**SPSS Latin America**
Tel: +1.312.651.3539
www.spss.com

**SPSS Malaysia Sdn Bhd**
Tel: +60.3.7873.6477
www.spss.com

**SPSS Mexico SA de CV**
Tel: +52.5.682.87.68
www.spss.com

**SPSS Norway**
Tel: +47.22.40.20.60
www.spss.com

**SPSS Polska**
Tel: +48.12.6369680
www.spss.pl

**SPSS Russia**
Tel: +7.095.125.0069
www.spss.com

**SPSS Schweiz AG**
Tel: +41.1.266.90.30
www.spss.com

**SPSS Sweden AB**
Tel: +46.8.506.105.68
www.spss.com

**SPSS BI (Singapore) Pte. Ltd.**
Tel: +65.324.5150
www.spss.com

**SPSS South Africa**
Tel: +27.11.807.3189
www.spss.com

**SPSS Taiwan Corp.**
Taipei, Republic of China
Tel: +886.2.25771100
www.sinter.com.tw/spss/

**SPSS (Thailand) Co., Ltd.**
Tel: +66.2.260.7070, +66.2.260.7080
www.spss.com

**SPSS UK Ltd.**
Tel: +44.1483.719200
www.spss.com

# Contents

# 3 *Area Charts* *37*



# 4 *Bar Charts* *53*

## 5 *Boxplots* 71



## 6 *Error Bars* 85

## 7 *Histograms* 99



## 8 *Line, Dot, and Ribbon Charts* 111

# 9 *Pie Charts* *129*



# 10 *Scatterplots* *147*

## 11 *Fit Lines, Surfaces, and Spikes* *161*



## 12 *Modifying Interactive Charts* *171*

Chapter

# 1

# Introduction to Interactive Charts

An interactive chart is dynamic. Not only can you change its cosmetic appearance, but you can also change the assignment of variables having various roles in the chart. Variables can be moved between axes, between axes and legends, and between axes (or legends) and panels. Changes to interactive charts are evident in the Viewer as soon as the variables are reassigned. The interactive chart can go from 2-D to 3-D and back again as you watch. Dragging the mouse and clicking the right-mouse button are keys to easy chart manipulation.

Interactive charts can be created in the following ways:

- Starting with a chart type from the Interactive submenu of the Graphs menu
- Starting with a blank chart from the Insert menu

This chapter provides an introduction to creating interactive charts by starting from the Graphs menu. It includes facilities that are common to many types of charts. Later, each type of chart is described in a separate chapter. Another way to create a chart interactively is to start with the Insert menu, as described in Chapter 2. Modification of existing charts is described in Chapter 12.

Before you can create a chart, you need to have data in the Data Editor. You can enter the data directly into the Data Editor, open a previously saved data file, or read a spreadsheet, tab-delimited data file, or database file. A tutorial (available from the Help menu) has online examples of creating interactive charts.

The chart examples provided in the online tutorial and the examples presented in this book represent only a few of many charts possible with interactive graphics.

# Interactive versus Standard Charts

In addition to the new interactive charts, SPSS also produces many other charts. Interactive charts are available only from the Interactive submenu of the Graphs menu. All other charts on the Graphs menu, as well as charts created by statistical procedures, are standard, high-resolution charts. Like interactive charts, standard charts are presentation-quality graphics that can be edited in many ways. The main difference is that standard charts lack interactive features such as the ability to change the charted variables and update the chart on the fly, change summary functions after creating a chart, or insert additional chart elements.

The interface for creating and modifying standard charts differs from the interface for interactive charts in a number of ways, including:

- Drag-and-drop variable selection is available for interactive charts only; variable selection in standard chart dialog boxes is the same as variable selection in statistical dialog boxes.
- You can toggle between display of variable names and variable labels in interactive chart dialog boxes by using a context menu that appears when you right-click a variable list. For standard chart dialog boxes, display of variable names or labels is controlled by General Options (Edit menu, Options, General tab) and doesn't take effect until the next time you open a data file.
- Variable lists in interactive chart dialog boxes have icons that identify variables as built-in, scale, or categorical, and you can change the classification of scale and categorical variables with right-mouse context menus. In standard chart dialog boxes, icons identify variables as either numeric or string (alphanumeric), and this classification is based on the variable type as defined in the Data Editor.
- Right-mouse button "What's This?" help is available for controls in standard chart dialog boxes; this feature is not available in interactive chart dialog boxes.
- Right-mouse button variable information is available in variable lists in standard chart dialog boxes. This feature is not available in interactive chart dialog boxes. (The Variables item on the Utilities menu provides similar information.)
- Interactive charts are edited in the Viewer window; standard charts are edited in a separate window.
- Interactive charts can be modified to insert additional variables, elements, summary functions, and so on. Standard chart modification features are largely limited to changing attributes of the elements that were present in the chart when it was created.

- Interactive charts can be embedded in other applications as fully interactive ActiveX objects or pasted as bitmaps. Standard charts cannot be embedded in other applications; they can be pasted as metafiles (pictures) or bitmaps.

### When to Use Standard Charts instead of Interactive Charts

Interactive charts are ideal for exploratory analysis of small data files or subsets of larger data files. There are, however, certain chart types that aren't available in interactive format, and there are situations in which the use of interactive charts may be unsuitable.

- Pareto, control, sequence, normal probability, and time-series charts are available only as standard charts.
- Standard charts may take significantly less time to create than interactive charts with large data files.
- Standard charts may require significantly less memory to create and less disk space to save than interactive charts, particularly for production jobs that produce large numbers of charts.
- Standard charts may be more efficient when using distributed analysis mode with a remote server (available only with the server version).

## Creating Interactive Charts from the Graphs Menu

By using the procedures listed on the Interactive submenu on the Graphs menu, you can specify variables and chart options before a chart is created. Later, the chart can be modified in the Viewer. When you choose a chart type from the Interactive submenu on the Graphs menu, the corresponding dialog box is displayed with its Assign Variables tab selected.

Figure 1-1
*Assign Variables tab for bar charts*

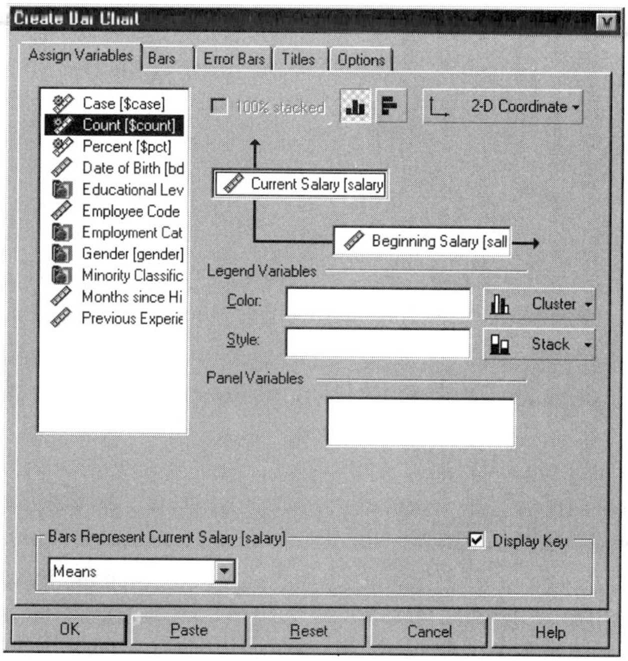


To create a chart, you need only to assign variables, but you can visit other tabs if you want to customize your chart.

**Source list.** Variables available for the chart type are in the source list. You can change the order in which variables are listed by right-clicking a variable and from the context menu choosing Sort By Name, Sort By File Order, or Sort By Type. You can also choose Display Variable Labels or Display Variable Names. On the context menu, these entries and data dimensions take the place of What's This? and Variable Information found in other dialog boxes in the system.

**Assigning variables.** Axis variables are assigned by dragging them from the source list and dropping them on the axis targets. You can also drag variables from one target to another. If a variable is dropped on a target that already has a variable assigned, the variables swap places. You can also assign multiple variables to each axis using the Ctrl-click method.

**Summary functions.** A scale variable that has been assigned to a dependent axis may have a summary function for many types of charts. For example, the summary function *Means* would often be appropriate for the variable *Salary*. The summary function for a scale variable can be specified by selecting from a list of summary functions near the bottom of this dialog box.

**Completing the chart.** As soon as a minimum number of variables are assigned, a chart can be created and displayed in the Viewer. OK is always enabled. If you click OK and the program determines that you need to specify more information, an alert box gives information on what is needed. Before clicking OK, you may want to refine the chart by selecting from the options available on the other tabs of the dialog box.

Figure 1-2
*Chart in the Viewer*

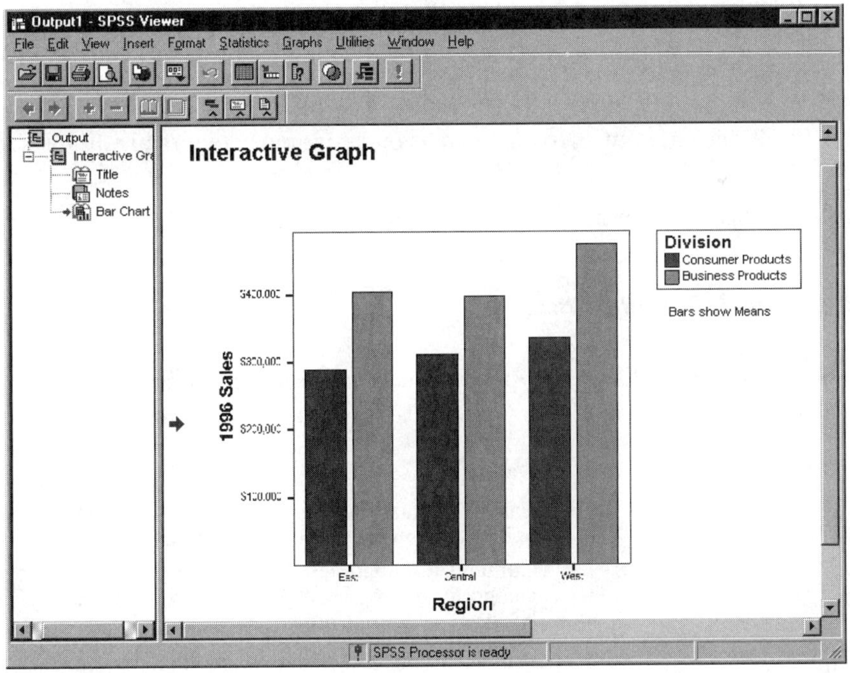

### To Assign Variables in a New Interactive Chart

▶ From the menus choose:

Graphs
 Interactive

▶ Choose a chart type.

▶ Drag one or more variables to each axis target. (Use the Ctrl-click method to select and drag multiple variables).

Optionally, you can:

- Split the chart element into categories by assigning categorical variables to Color, Style, and Size, where appropriate for the chart type.
- Assign colors to the chart objects by assigning a scale variable to Color.
- Assign sizes to the chart objects by assigning a scale variable to Size.
- Split the chart into separate panels by assigning categorical variables to Panel Variables.
- Change the summary function for the dependent variable.

## Data Dimension Types in Charts

In an interactive chart, the types of data dimensions are indicated by an icon for each type (scale, categorical, and scale built-ins) in the chart variable list.

| Dimension | Icon | Description |
|---|---|---|
| Scale |  | Values can fall anywhere along a scale. Distance along the axis encodes values. All values are available. |
| Categorical |  | Contains a limited number of discrete values. Along an axis, categories are represented by evenly spaced ticks. Values between categories are not used. |
| Built-in |  | Produces a chart of counts or percentages, or a casewise chart. |

You can define a variable as scale, ordinal, or nominal in the Define Variable dialog box in the Data Editor. A change in level of measurement in the Define Variable dialog box applies to all charts created after the change. (Changing the level in a chart creation dialog box or in an interactive chart applies only to the current chart.) In interactive charts, ordinal and nominal variables are both treated as categorical data dimensions.

**Changing data dimensions in a chart.** The data dimension of a variable in a variable list can be changed by right-clicking the variable and choosing Scale or Categorical from the context menu. This change applies only to the current chart.

**Summary built-in dimensions.** The summary built-in dimensions are *Count* and *Percent*. For example, in a bar chart, the bars could represent the number of employees (count) in each job category or the percentage of employees in each job category.

**Case.** The built-in dimension *Case* indicates that each case in the data file is represented on the axis.

### To Change the Measurement Level of a Variable in a Chart

▶ From the menus choose:

Graphs
  Interactive

▶ Choose a chart type.

▶ On the Assign Variables tab, right-click a variable in one of the lists.

▶ Choose Scale or Categorical.

This choice affects only the current chart.

After the chart is created, you can also change the dimension in the variable list in the Assign Graph Variables dialog box.

## Legend Variables

Categorical legend variables split the elements in the chart into categories. Scale legend variables apply color or size to the elements based on the value or summary value of the legend variable.

**Categorical variables.** If a legend variable is categorical, the colors or styles are assigned according to the discrete categories of the variable. For example, in a bar chart, if *Region* is assigned to Color, the bars for the East, Central, and West divisions are different colors. In a scatterplot, if *Year* is assigned to Style, the markers are a different shape for each year.

Figure 1-3
*Scatterplot with a style legend*

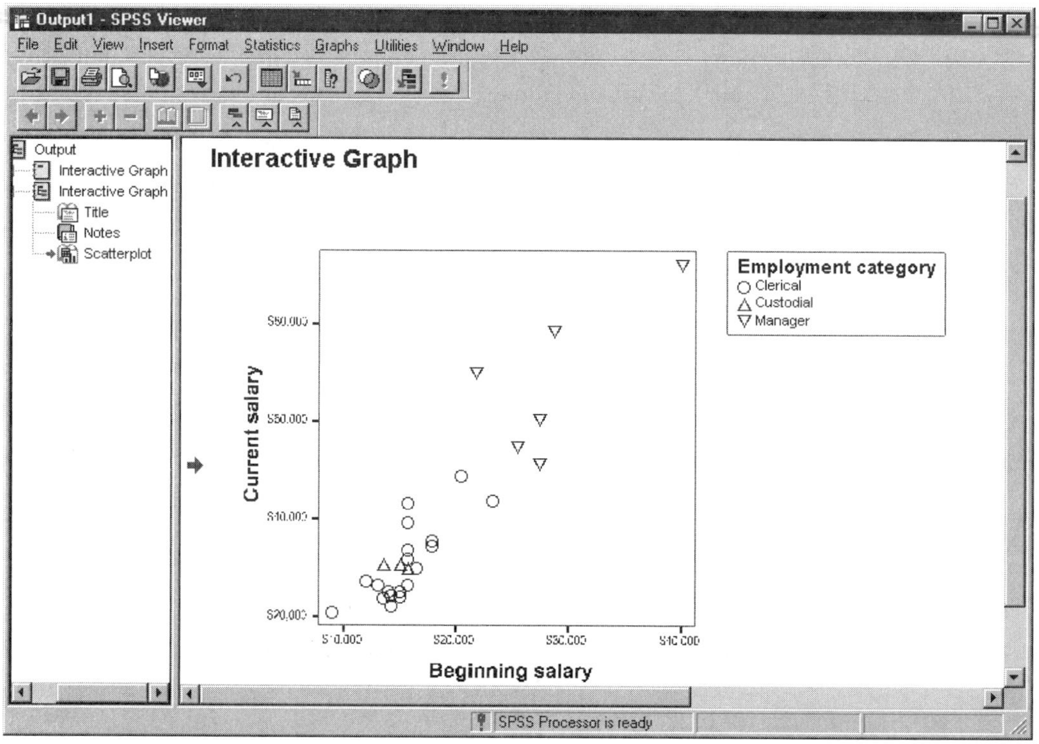


**Scale variables.** If a scale variable is assigned to Color in a scatterplot, symbols take colors from a continuous scale. For example, if the color variable is *Age,* each symbol is colored according to the value of the age variable for the case. A scale variable can also be assigned to Size. The symbols are sized according to the values of the scale variable.

If a scale variable is assigned to Color in a summary chart, the colors of the chart objects are based on a function of the scale variable. For example, if the color variable is *Age*, the colors of the elements vary along a gradient as the *mean age* of the group increases. In a bar chart, the color of each bar would be determined by the mean age of the cases represented in the bar.

## *Panel Variables*

Panel variables divide the chart into small panels, each representing a different set of cases. Only categorical variables can be assigned as panel variables. For a single panel variable, each category is represented in one panel. For multiple panel variables, each combination of categories across variables is represented in a panel. For example, if one of two panel variables has three categories and the other has two, the total number of panels is six.

Figure 1-4
*Panels for the categorical variable Region*

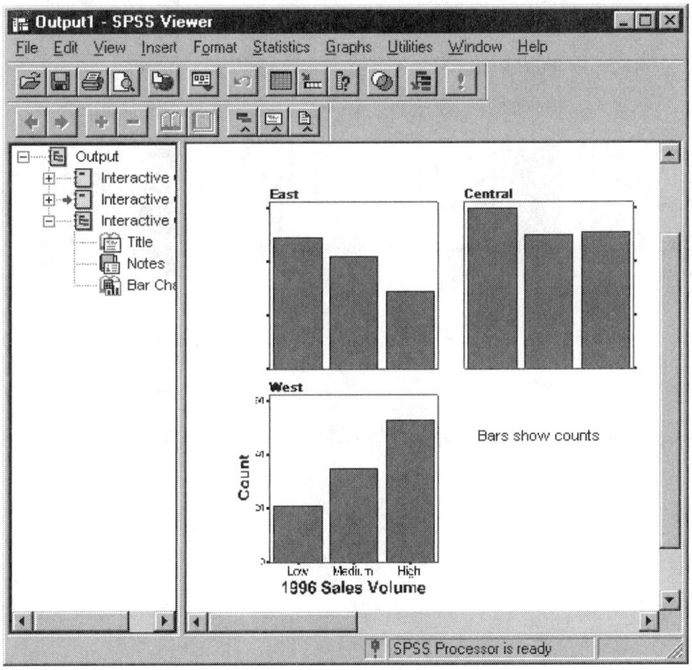

## Summarizing Multiple Variables

Depending on how your data are organized, you may want to create charts that summarize and compare multiple variables. For example, if sales data for each year are recorded in a separate variable, you can create a single chart that summarizes sales data for each year in a separate bar.

Figure 1-5
*Bar charts summarizing two variables*

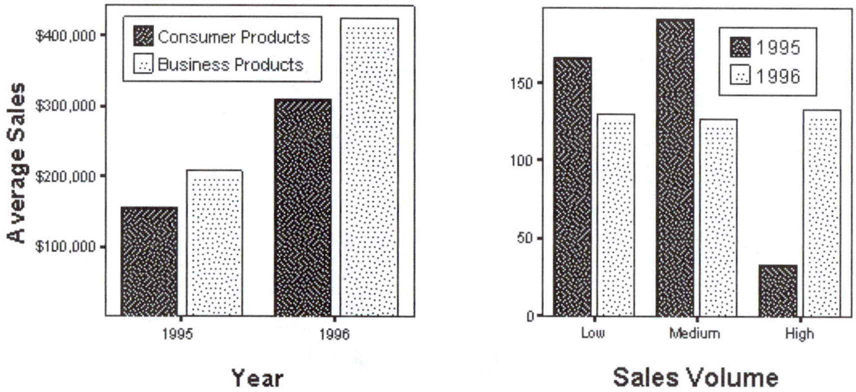


## To Create a Chart Summarizing Multiple Variables

▶ From the menus choose:

Graphs
  Interactive

▶ Choose a chart type.

▶ On the Assign Variables tab, use the Ctrl-click method to select multiple variables in the source list.

▶ Drag the variables to one of the axes.

Optionally, you can specify category and value axis labels as well as modify value labels for categories in the Specify Labels dialog box.

This creates two temporary variables that are used in the procedure:

**Category** (or the label you specify for categories). A categorical variable in which each "category" is one of the selected variables. For categorical variables, you can use this variable as a color, style, or panel variable to identify each variable.

**Value** (or the label you specify for values). For scale variables, a variable that contains the summary values for each category. For categorical variables, a variable that contains the category values of each variable.

You can use these variables when you edit the chart and when you create the same type of chart again, but they are not available for any other interactive graphics procedures, and you cannot save them with the data file.

### Specify Labels

Figure 1-6
*Specify Labels dialog box*

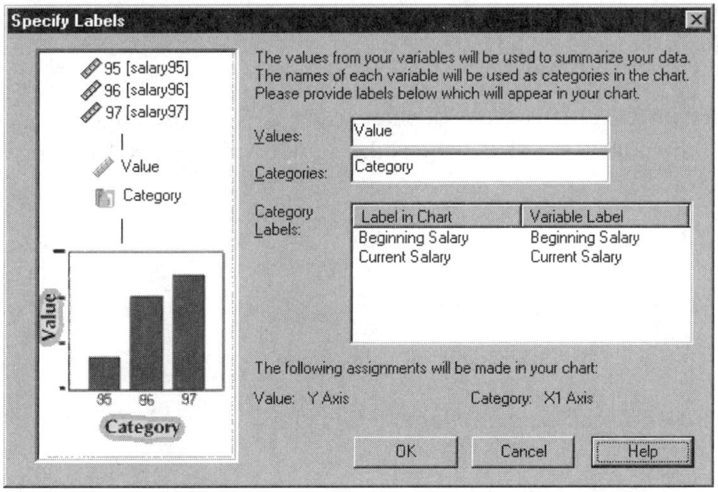


This dialog box provides options for labeling charts of multiple variables.

**Values**. Label for the values axis. For scale variables, the values axis represents the values of the summary function displayed in the chart. For categorical variables, the values axis represents the different categories of each variable. This label is also used to identify the temporary variable associated with the values axis.

**Categories**. Label for the category axis. The category axis represents the different variables displayed in the chart.

**Category Labels**. Labels used to identify each variable displayed in the chart. By default, the defined variable labels are used. For variables without defined variable labels, variable names are used.

# To Create a Chart from a Pivot Table

- ▶ Double-click the pivot table to activate it.
- ▶ Select the rows, columns, or cells you want to display in the chart.
- ▶ Right-click anywhere in the selected area.
- ▶ Choose Create Graph from the context menu and select a chart type.

## Coordinate System

**Number of dimensions**. Many types of charts can be 2-D or 3-D. Selecting a coordinate system from the drop-down list changes the number of axes available for assigning variables.

**2-D** **3-D**

Another choice, 3-D Effect, gives depth to the graph objects in a 2-D chart.

## Chart Orientation

Whenever a chart type can have either horizontal or vertical orientation, orientation icons are available on the Assign Variables tab of the chart creation dialog box. The icons vary according to chart type. The following are examples of bar chart orientation icons:

| **Vertical** | **Horizontal** |
|---|---|
|  |  |

Horizontal orientation is available for 2-D charts only.

Orientation can be changed after a chart has been created by activating the chart and clicking the vertical or horizontal icon on the toolbar. This changes the location of the axis targets.

| **Vertical** | **Horizontal** |
|---|---|
|  |  |

## Create Chart: Titles

Text for titles, subtitles, and captions can be specified on the Titles tab of chart creation dialog boxes.

Figure 1-7
*Titles tab*

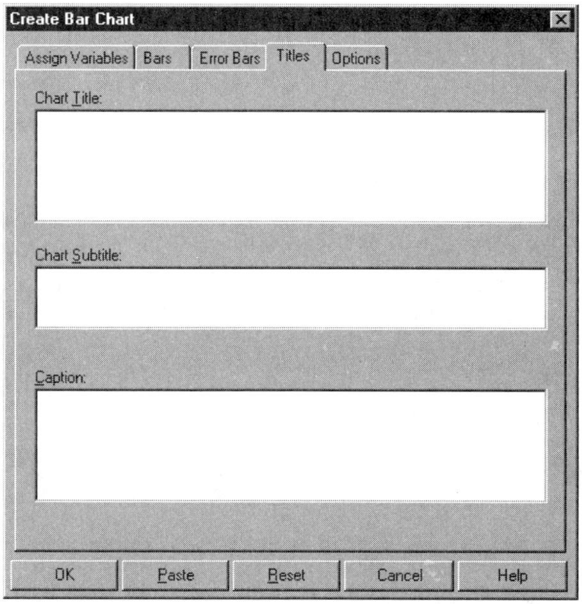


To specify the initial font, point size, color, alignment of titles, subtitles, and captions, use a ChartLook.

## *Create Chart: Options*

Figure 1-8
*Options tab*

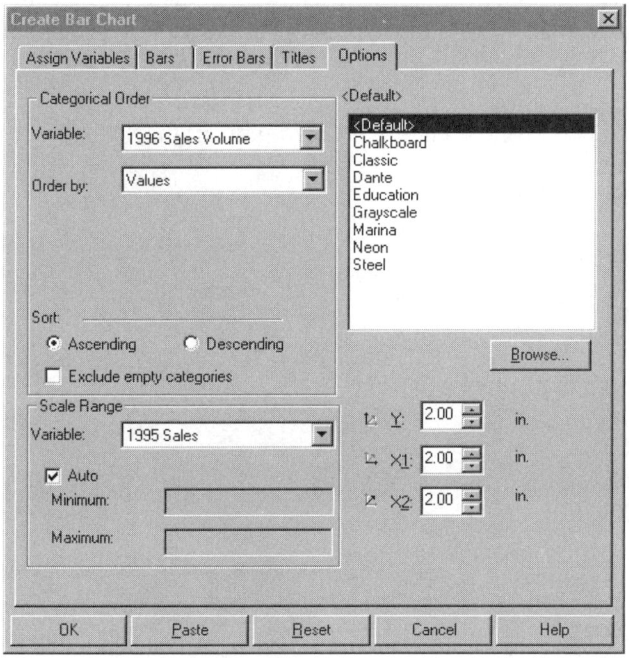


The Options tab for each type of interactive chart offers additional ways to customize your output. You can determine the order of categorical variables as well as the range for scale variables. You can also select a ChartLook and the size of the data region.

**Categorical Order.** Categorical variables can be ordered in several ways. You can order a variable by a property (such as values, label, occurrence, and counts*)*, or you can order the variable by the summary function of another variable. Optionally, you can determine if the order will be ascending or descending, and you can exclude categories that have no data.

**Scale Range.** Minimum and maximum values can be set for all for scale variables. You can use the default values from the data set, or you can create a custom range.

**ChartLook.** This list contains the ChartLooks stored in the *Looks* directory (or the default directory selected from Options on the Edit menu). A ChartLook controls the initial visual properties of the chart, such as colors and symbols. To find ChartLooks that are stored in other directories, click Browse.

**Size.** The size of the data region is determined by the length of each axis. The units of measurement are specified in Options (Interactive tab) on the Edit menu in the Viewer. If you assign a panel variable, the *y* and *x1* lengths are used to determine the aspect ratios of the panels.

*Y*, *x1*, and *x2* are assigned as shown in the following diagrams:

**Vertical**

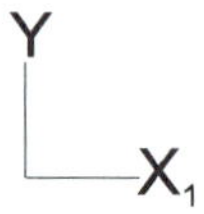


**Horizontal**

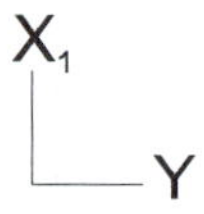


For 3-D charts, *y* is the dependent axis.

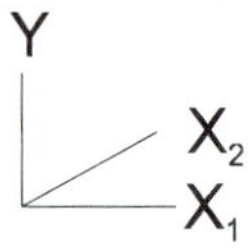


### Persistence in Dialog Boxes

Selections made in a dialog box for creating a chart persist; that is, the next time the same chart creation dialog box is opened, the program *remembers* the previous selections. For example, a triangle shape selected for a previous scatterplot is still selected when you open the dialog box to create another scatterplot.

To clear all selections and reset to default values, click Reset. Clicking Reset once sets default values for all tabs in a dialog box.

## Missing Values in Interactive Charts

Cases are excluded listwise for all interactive charts. That is, a case with a missing value for any variable used in the chart is excluded.

If you want the cases to be included in a chart, in the Data Editor remove any variable definitions of user-missing values. Also, assign values where there are system-missing values. You may want to save a duplicate data file before changing the missing value designations.

## Summary Functions in Charts

Summary functions apply to scale variables selected for a dependent axis or a slice summary. Percentages are based on the specified percent base. For a slice summary, only summary functions appropriate for the type of chart are available.

**First Values.** The value found in the first case for each category in the data file at the time the summary function was assigned.

**Kurtosis.** A measure of the extent to which observations cluster around a central point. For a normal distribution, the value of the kurtosis statistic is 0. Positive kurtosis indicates that the observations cluster more and have longer tails than those in the normal distribution, and negative kurtosis indicates that the observations cluster less and have shorter tails.

**Last Values.** The value found in the last case for each category in the data file that created it.

**Maximum Values.** The largest value for each category.

**Means.** The arithmetic average for each category.

**Medians.** The value below which half of the cases fall in each category. If there is an even number of cases, the median is the average of the two middle cases when they are sorted in ascending or descending order.

**Minimum Values.** The smallest value within the category.

**Modes.** The most frequently occurring value within each category. If multiple modes exist, the smallest value is used.

**Number of Cases Above (N of Cases >).** The number of cases having values above the specified value.

**Number of Cases Between (N Between).** The number of cases between two specified values.

**Number of Cases Equal to (N of Cases =).** The number of cases equal to the specified value.

**Number of Cases Greater Than or Equal to (N of Cases >=).** The number of cases having values above or equal to the specified value.

**Number of Cases Less Than (N of Cases <).** The number of cases below the specified value.

**Number of Cases Less Than or Equal to (N of Cases <=).** The number of cases below or equal to the specified value.

**Percentage of Cases Above (% of Cases >).** The percentage of cases having values above the specified value.

**Percentage of Cases Between (N Between).** The percentage of cases between two specified values.

**Percentage of Cases Between (% Between).** The percentage of cases having values between two specified values.

**Percentage of Cases Equal to (% of Cases =).** The percentage of cases equal to the specified value.

**Percentage of Cases Greater Than or Equal to (% of Cases >=).** The percentage of cases having values above or equal to the specified value.

**Percentage of Cases Less Than (% of Cases <).** The percentage of cases having values below the specified value.

**Percentage of Cases Less Than or Equal to (% of Cases <=).** The percentage of cases having values below or equal to the specified value.

**Percentiles.** The data value below which the specified percentage of values fall within each category.

**Skewness.** A measure of the asymmetry of a distribution. The normal distribution is symmetric and has a skewness value of 0. A distribution with a significant positive skewness has a long right tail. A distribution with a significant negative skewness has a long left tail.

**Standard Deviations (SD).** A measure of dispersion around the mean, expressed in the same unit of measurement as the observations, equal to the square root of the variance. In a normal distribution, 68% of cases fall within one standard deviation of the mean and 95% of cases fall within two standard deviations.

**Standard Errors of Kurtosis (S.E. of Kurtosis).** The ratio of kurtosis to its standard error can be used as a test of normality (that is, you can reject normality if the ratio is less than –2 or greater than +2). A large positive value for kurtosis indicates that the tails of the distribution are longer than those of a normal distribution; a negative value for kurtosis indicates shorter tails (becoming like those of a box-shaped uniform distribution).

**Standard Errors of the Mean (S.E. of the Mean).** A measure of how much the value of the mean may vary among samples taken from the same distribution. It can be used to roughly compare the observed mean to a hypothesized value (that is, you can conclude the two values are different if the ratio of the difference to the standard error is less than –2 or greater than +2).

**Standard Errors of Skewness (S.E. of Skewness).** The ratio of skewness to its standard error can be used as a test of normality (that is, you can reject normality if the ratio is less than –2 or greater than +2). A large positive value for skewness indicates a long right tail; an extreme negative value indicates a long left tail.

**Sums.** The sums of the values within each category.

**Sums of Absolute Values.** The sums of the absolute values within each category.

**Sums of Squares.** The sums of the squares of the values within each category.

**Variances.** A measure of how much observations vary from the mean, expressed in squared units.

Chapter

# 2

# Working with Charts Interactively

Starting with a blank interactive chart or with an interactive chart already created, you can add and delete various chart elements and objects and change the data summary function until you have exactly the right combination to illustrate the characteristics of your data. With interactive charts, you don't have to make a new chart to add data or change the role of a variable—you can simply change the variable assignments.

This chapter discusses elements and text that can be inserted into a chart. See Chapter 12 for information about how to modify elements and objects that have already been inserted into a chart and how to rearrange them.

## Creating an Interactive Chart

Charts can be created interactively, starting with a blank chart and adding one or more chart elements simply by clicking buttons and dragging variables.

**Example.** A blank 2-D chart is inserted, and variables are assigned to the *x* and *y* axes. A scatterplot cloud is inserted from the drop-down list obtained by clicking the Insert Element tool. Following each mouse action, changes in the chart are immediately displayed.

Figure 2-1
*Blank 2-D chart and variable assignments*

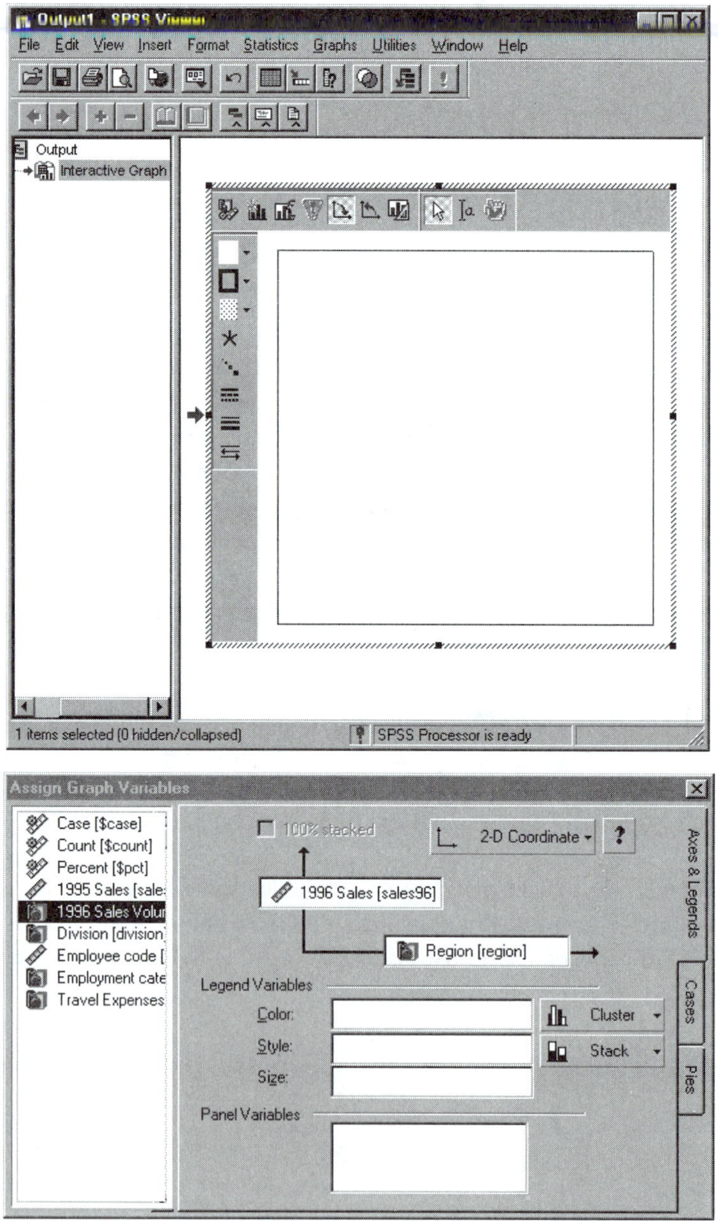

Figure 2-2
*Scatterplot cloud added*

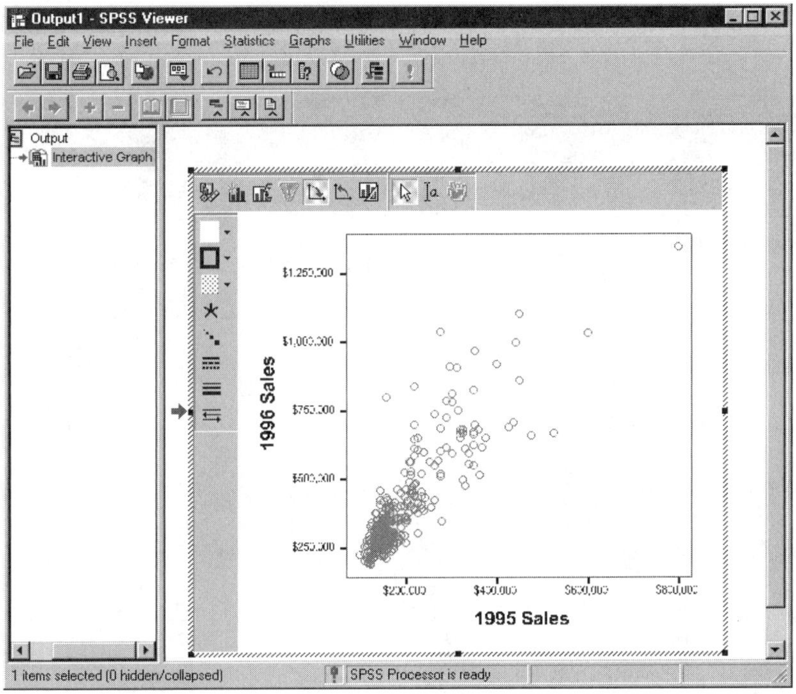

Next, to group the symbols by style, a categorical variable is assigned to Legend Variables Style.

Figure 2-3
*Scatterplot grouped by a variable assigned to Legend Variables Style*

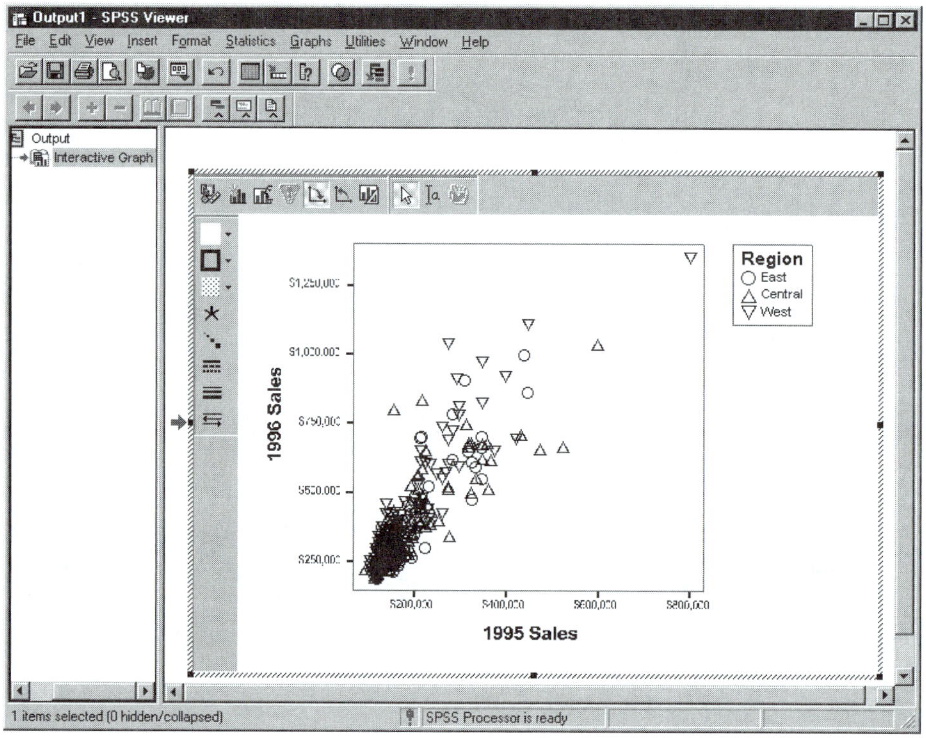

Finally, a smoother (LLR fit line) is added for the total group of points.

Figure 2-4
*Scatterplot with smoother added*

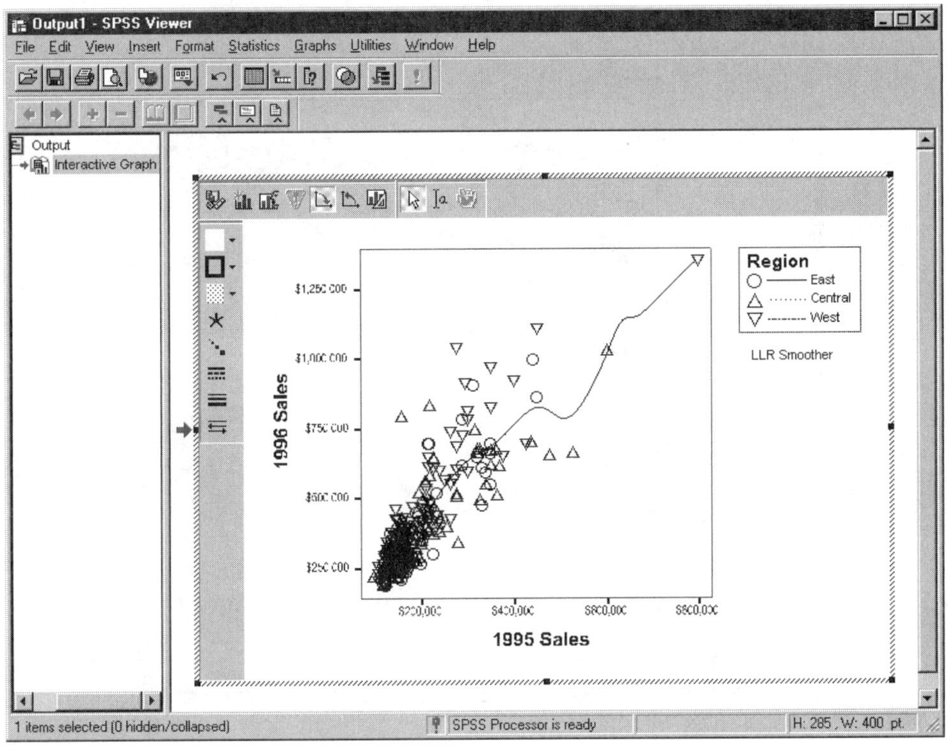


**Adding more elements.** Other elements can be added to the chart. Smoothers can be added for the subgroups assigned in the legend. In a bar chart, a line element could be added; error bars might be added to a bar chart or a line chart. Each additional chart element responds to the same assignment of variables.

### To Create a 2-D Chart Interactively

▶ From the Viewer menus choose:

Insert
  Interactive 2-D Graph

This produces an activated blank 2-D chart, with interactive graph menus displayed at the top of the Viewer.

Figure 2-5
*Blank 2-D chart*

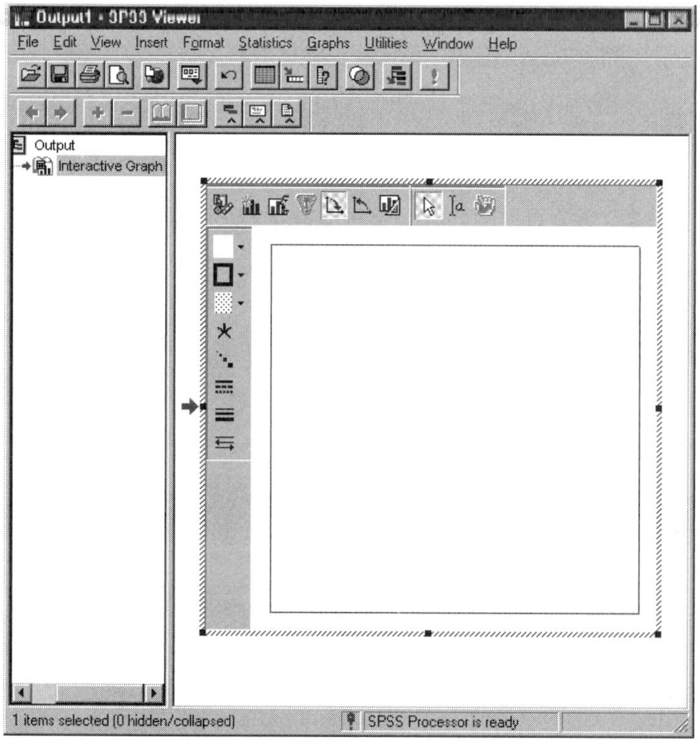


- From the menus choose:

  Insert

  *or*

- Click the Insert Element tool on the chart toolbar.

- Select a graphical element, such as Bar or Cloud.

▶ From the menus choose:

Edit
 Assign Variables

*or*

▶ Click the Assign Graph Variables tool on the chart toolbar.

▶ Drag variables from the source list to the appropriate targets: axes, legend, or panel.

The chart changes as you assign each variable.

You can add more than one element to the chart. The variable assignments apply to all elements. If you pay attention to the current assignment of variables before assigning new elements, you can avoid charts containing a multitude of elements (for example, hundreds of plotted pies because of a scale variable assigned to an axis).

### To Create a 3-D Chart Interactively

▶ From the Viewer menus choose:

Insert
  Interactive 3-D Graph

This produces an activated blank 3-D chart, with interactive graph menus displayed.

Figure 2-6
*Blank 3-D chart*

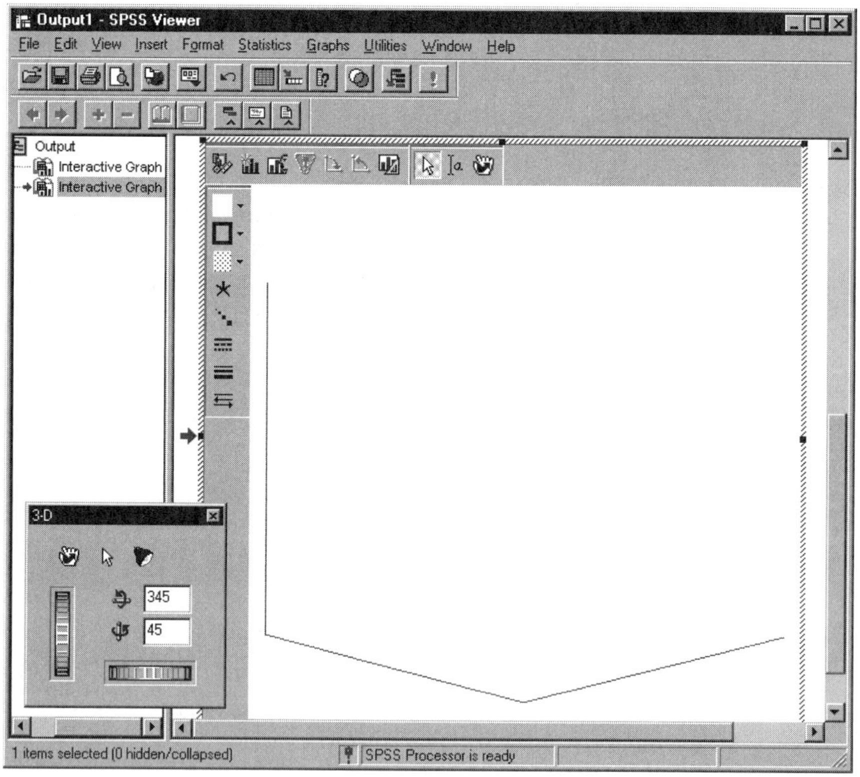

- From the menus choose:

  Insert

  *or*

- Click the Insert Element tool.

- Select a graphical element, such as Bar or Cloud.

- From the menus choose:

  Edit
  Assign Variables

  *or*

- Click the Assign Graph Variables tool.

- Drag variables from the source list to the appropriate targets: axes, legend, or panel.

  The chart changes as you assign each variable.

You can add more than one element to the chart. The variable assignments apply to all elements. If you pay attention to the current assignment of variables before inserting new elements, you can avoid charts containing a multitude of elements (for example, hundreds of plotted pies because of a scale variable assigned to an axis).

## Assign Graph Variables: Axes and Legends

In the Assign Graph Variables dialog box, you can assign variables to various roles in a chart. The chart changes as soon as you drag the variables to their new targets. On the Axes & Legends tab, variables can be assigned to axes, to color, style, and size legends, or to panels.

Figure 2-7
*Assign Graph Variables dialog boxes for 2-D and 3-D charts*

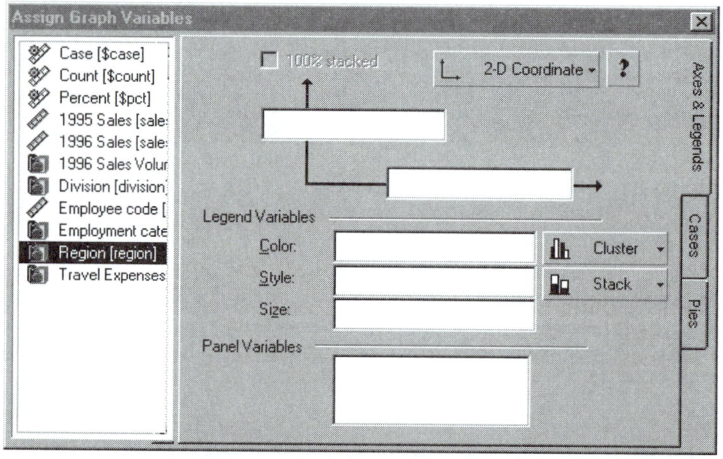


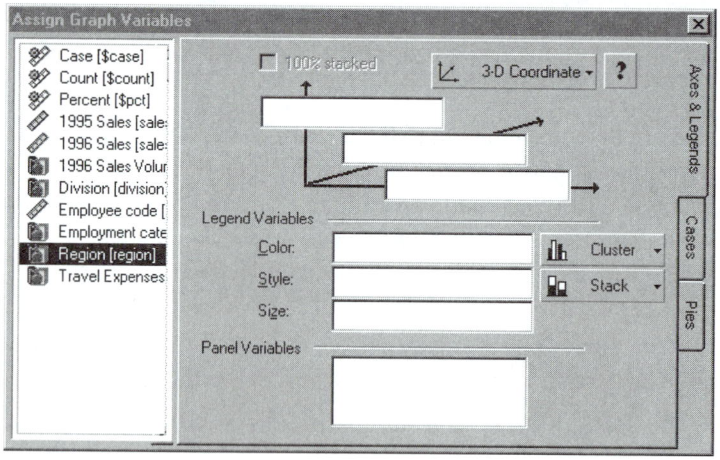

**Coordinate systems.** Choosing a 2-D or 3-D coordinate system determines the number of axis targets available. Selecting 3-D Effect displays each 2-D element in the chart as a three-dimensional solid object, but no variable is assigned to the third axis.

**Variables.** The variable list contains scale variables, categorical variables, and built-in variables, distinguishable by their icons. You can switch a scale variable to a categorical variable and vice versa by using the context menu (right-click on the variable and select Categorical or Scale). Reassigning the variable type applies only to the current chart.

Be careful when assigning variables with a large number of distinct values. You could get such a large number of bars, for example, that you couldn't distinguish them. If you add a pie element when a scale variable is assigned to one of the axes, a large number of tiny plotted pies may be generated. If the chart is not what you expected, try looking at the Chart Manager to see what elements are actually in the chart and what warnings have been posted.

**Summary Functions.** If a scale variable is assigned to the dependent axis, the summary function (means, medians, sums, etc.) is determined by the graphical element inserted into the chart. For example, bars could represent means and lines could represent maximum values in the same chart.

**Legend Variables.** In the legend, color, style, and size can be used to show group membership by assigning categorical variables. Color and Style are the targets used to split categories in various charts or to slice pies. Also, scale variables can be assigned to Color or Size. With a scale variable assigned in a chart with a summary function (for example, bars represent means), the legend displays a gradient that represents means of the scale variable.

The Color and Style legends can be set to Cluster or Stack. Stacking applies only to bar or area elements. Other types of elements ignore it. If a stacked element is present, it can be stacked as percentages with the 100% stacked option.

**Panel Variables.** For easy comparison of groups, you can create separate panel charts for each category or combination of categories by assigning one or more categorical variables to Panel Variables.

This dialog box can remain open while you change element and object properties.

### To Assign Graph Variables

- ▶ Activate a chart or insert a new 2-D or 3-D chart.
- ▶ From the menus choose:

  Edit
   Assign Variables

  *or*

- ▶ Click the Assign Graph Variables tool.

- ▶ Drag the desired variables to the appropriate targets. Use the Shift-click method to drag more than one variable.
- ▶ If you want a stacked element, select Stack from the drop-down list for Color or Style.
- ▶ If you want a paneled chart, drag one or more variables to the Panel Variables box.

  If you drag a variable to a target that already has a variable assigned, the variables swap places.

## Assign Graph Variables: Cases

Figure 2-8
*Assign Graph Variables: Cases tab*

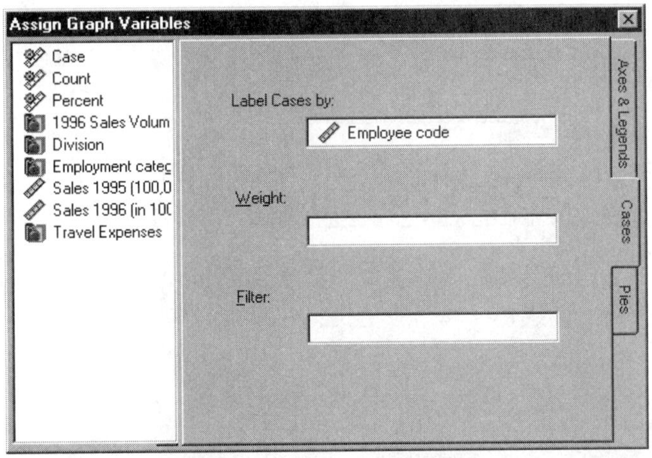


**Label Cases by.** Labels can be assigned for individual points or for cases plotted along an axis. The values of a variable assigned to Identify Points by are used to label plotted points in scatterplots and boxplots.

When a variable is assigned to Label Cases by, the values are used to label the ticks along an axis to which the built-in variable *$case* has been assigned. These values are ignored if the *$case* variable is not assigned.

**Weight.** The weight variable should represent the number of observations represented by each case. In any calculations, each case value is multiplied by the value in the weight variable for the case. A scale or categorical variable can be used.

**Filter.** If a case has a value of 0 for the filter variable, that case is not used in the chart. A scale or categorical variable can be used.

## Assign Graph Variables: Pies

Figure 2-9
*Assign Graph Variables: Pies tab*

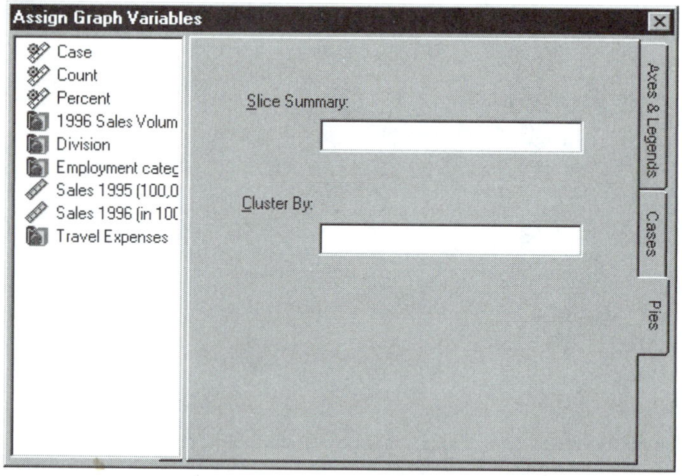


Variables can be assigned or changed for pie charts through this dialog box. These changes affect all pie elements in the chart. Pie slices can be changed on the Axes & Legends tab of this dialog box.

**Slice Summary.** One of the built-in variables (*$count* or *$pct*) or a scale variable can be assigned to the Slice Summary target. For a scale variable, the default summary function is *Sums*.

**Cluster By.** Only categorical variables can be assigned to Cluster By. In a clustered pie stack, each category is represented by one pie.

## Inserting a Chart Title

A title, subtitle, or caption can be inserted into the chart. The text of the inserted object can then be edited. A title, subtitle, or caption cannot be inserted if the object already exists.

### To Insert a Title, Subtitle, or Caption into a Chart

▶ Activate the chart.

▶ From the menus choose:

Insert
  Title

*or*

Insert
  Subtitle

*or*

Insert
  Caption

A title, subtitle, or caption is inserted into the chart.

▶ Double-click to edit the title, subtitle, or caption in place.

Optionally, you can drag the title, subtitle, or caption to a new position.

## Inserting Text into a Chart

Using the Insert menu, you can add text to a chart and then drag it to another position. Another way to insert text is to click the Text tool and then click the chart at the position at which you want the text to be placed. You can later drag the text to a new position in the chart.

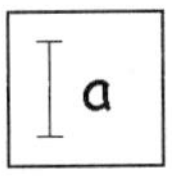

### To Insert Text into a Chart

- ▶ Activate the chart (double-click it).
- ▶ From the menus choose:

  Insert
    Text

  *or*

- ▶ Click the Text tool.
- ▶ Click where you want the text to start.

  A text object is placed on the chart.

- ▶ Enter the desired text.

Optionally, you can drag the text to a new position in the chart.

## Editing Text in a Chart

You can edit text in a chart, including titles, subtitles, captions, axis titles, legend titles, labels, and text added to the chart after creation.

### To Edit Text in a Chart

- ▶ Activate the chart (double-click it).
- ▶ Use the Arrow pointer to select the text object that you want to edit.
- ▶ Click once to get an insertion point, and then enter or edit the text.

Optionally, you can select part of the text and delete or replace the selection.

Chapter

# 3

# Area Charts

A simple area chart is like a line chart with the space below the line filled in. Areas for several categories can be stacked on top of one another, with data values additive from one category to the next. A stacked area chart emphasizes the categories as components of the whole. If you want to show how the percentage contribution of each category changes, as opposed to how the sum of values changes, you can create a chart showing a total of 100% for each value along the independent axis.

Another way to represent categories is with a clustered area chart in which the areas for all categories of the legend variable have the same baseline. This representation is most useful in 3-D.

## Sample Output

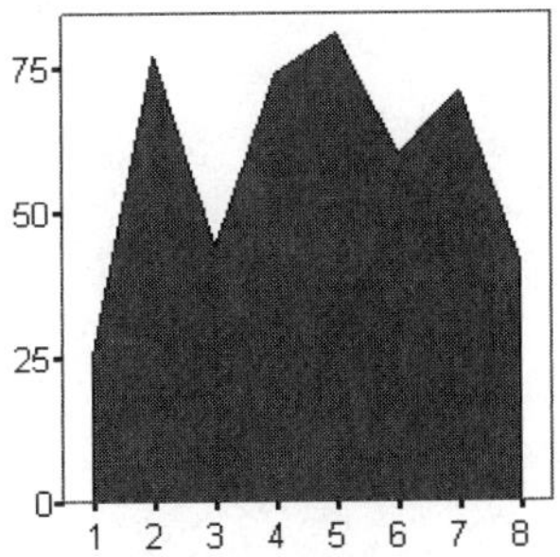


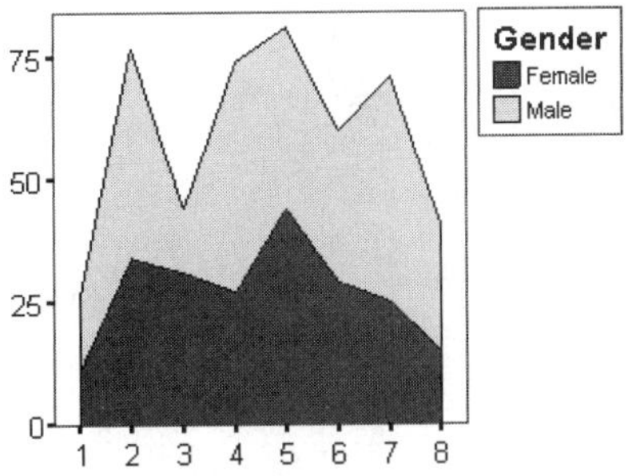

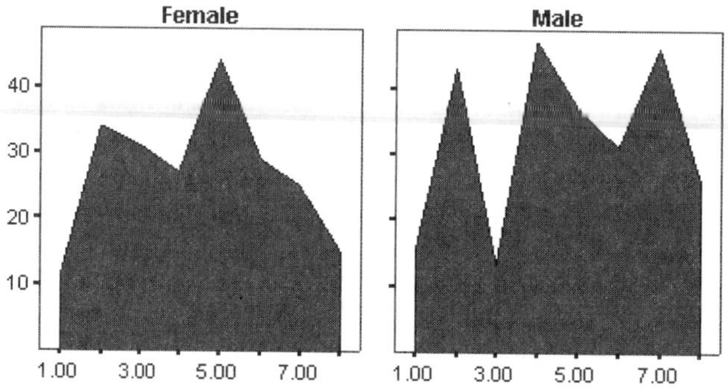


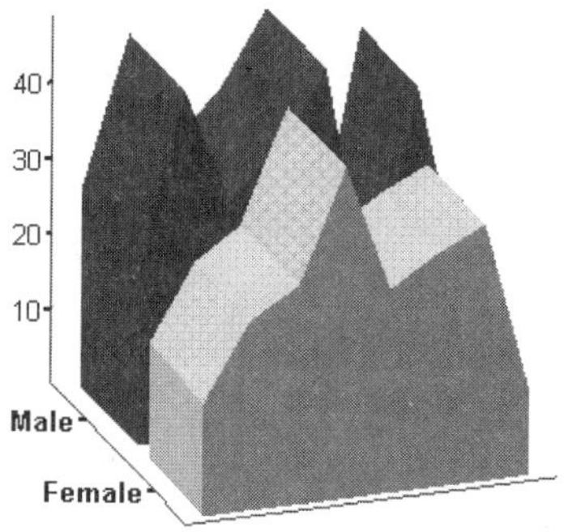


# To Create an Interactive Area Chart

▶ From the menus choose:

Graphs
 Interactive
  Area...

## Create Area Chart: Assign Variables

Figure 3-1
*Create Area Chart: Assign Variables tab*

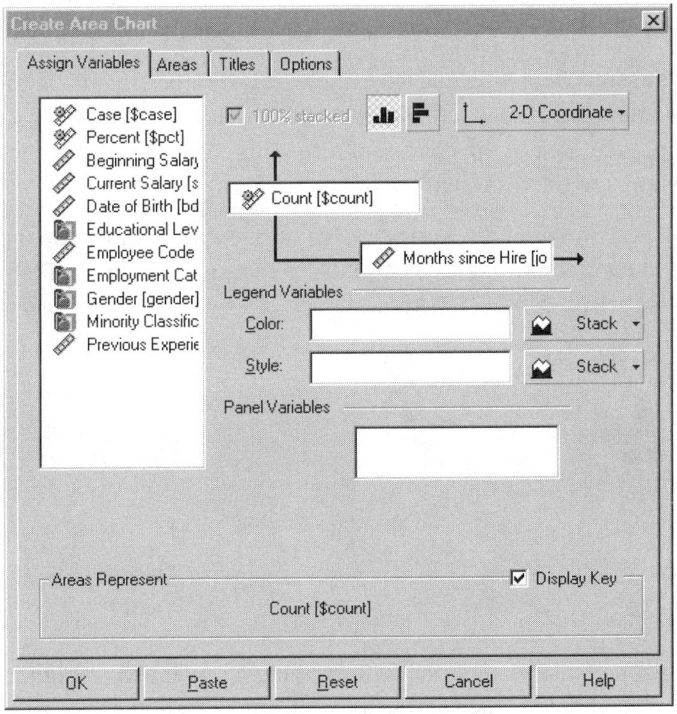


In a simple area chart, the points are plotted and joined with lines, and the area is filled in between the data line and the baseline. One common use is to show the continuity of a summary variable (dependent) through time (independent variable). The summary function can be changed near the bottom of the dialog box, and a key can be displayed to identify the function. Legend categories define stacked or clustered area charts.

**Stacked area charts.** Areas for categories can be stacked. The top of the previous category forms the base for the next category. This type of chart emphasizes the sum of the categories and the flow along the independent axis. However, in this representation, specific values of individual categories cannot be easily determined.

**100% stacked area charts.** If an area chart is stacked, you can change the dependent axis to represent 100%. The areas show the percentage contributed by each category of the legend variable, but, in contrast to a regular stacked area chart, the 100% stacked chart does not indicate increases or decreases in the totals.

**Clustered area charts.** The categories of a color or style variable divide a clustered chart into areas that have a common baseline. This choice works best when used with 3-D coordinates or 3-D effect. (Clustering may hide some of the areas behind other areas.)

**Number of dimensions.** Selecting 2-D Coordinate or 3-D Coordinate from the drop-down list changes the number of axis targets for variable selection. Selecting 3-D Effect displays each plotted area in the chart as a three-dimensional solid object, but no variable is assigned to the third axis.

**Orientation.** Clicking an orientation (vertical or horizontal) icon sets up the appropriate axis targets, as shown, for variable selection. Orientation icons are available only when 2-D Coordinate is selected.

**Vertical** **Horizontal**

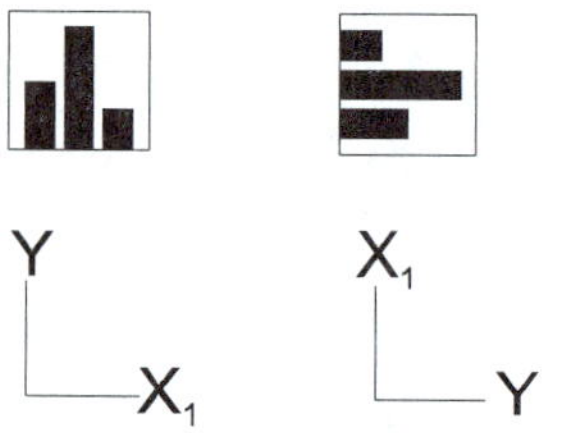


**Case Variable.** If the built-in variable *Case* is assigned to an axis, another target becomes available where you can assign a variable for labeling cases. For example, the labels might be days of the week or months.

Many of the charts shown below are vertical. To create a horizontal chart, click the horizontal icon before or after dragging variables.

### *To Create a Simple Area Chart*

- ▶ Drag one or more variables (usually categorical) to the *x1* axis. This will be the base of the areas.

- ▶ Drag *Count* or a scale variable to the *y* axis (if not there by default).

  For another summary chart, you can use the built-in variable *Percent*.

  Optionally, you can:

  - Swap the axes by clicking the orientation icon. Currently assigned variables swap along with the axes.
  - Change the area baseline on the Areas tab.

#### *To Create an Area Chart Summarizing a Scale Variable*

- ▶ Drag a variable (usually categorical) to the *x1* axis.

- ▶ Drag a scale variable to the *y* axis.

  By default, the data points represent the mean of the scale variable.

  Optionally, you can:

  - Select another summary function from the Areas Represent drop-down list near the bottom of the dialog box.

#### *To Create a Stacked or Clustered Area Chart*

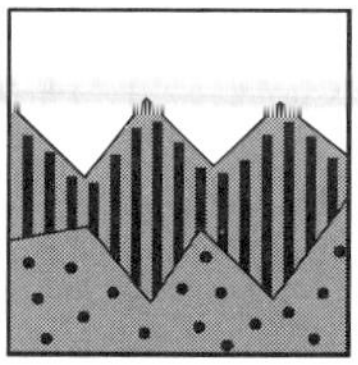

- ▶ Drag a variable (usually categorical) to the *x1* axis.
- ▶ Drag a scale variable to the *y* axis.
- ▶ Drag a categorical variable to Color or Style and select Stack or Cluster from the drop-down list.

  In a stacked chart, the top of one category forms the base for the next category. In a clustered area chart, all areas have the same baseline.

  Optionally, you can:

  - Swap the axes by clicking the orientation icon. Currently assigned variables swap along with the axes.

#### *To Create a 100% Stacked Area Chart*

- ▶ Drag a variable (usually categorical) to the *x1* axis.
- ▶ Drag a scale variable to the *y* axis.
- ▶ Drag a categorical variable to Color or Style and select Stack from the drop-down list.

  This enables the 100% Stacked check box.

▶ Select 100% Stacked.

Optionally, you can:

- Swap the axes by clicking the orientation icon. Currently assigned variables swap along with the axes.

### To Create an Area Chart with Colors Assigned by a Summary of a Scale Variable

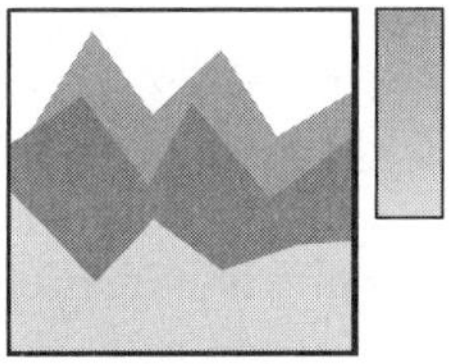

▶ Drag a variable (usually categorical) to the *x1* axis.

▶ Drag a scale variable to the *y* axis.

▶ Drag a scale variable to Color.

The color of each area indicates the mean of the color variable for the category represented by the area.

### To Create Area Chart Panels for Categories

▶ Drag a variable (usually categorical) to the *x1* axis.

▶ Drag a scale variable to the *y* axis.

▶ Drag one or more categorical variables to Panel Variables.

### To Create a 3-D Effect Clustered Area Chart

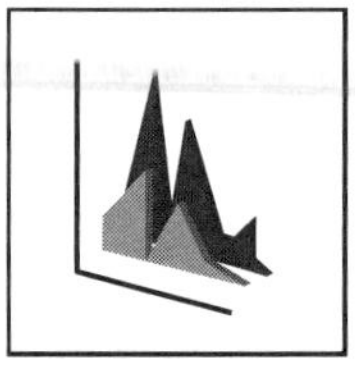

- Drag a variable (usually categorical) to the *x1* axis.
- Drag a scale variable to the *y* axis.
- Drag a categorical variable to Color or Style and select Cluster from the drop-down list.
- Select 3-D Effect from the dimensions drop-down list.

### To Create a 3-D Area Chart

- Select 3-D Coordinate from the dimensions drop-down list.

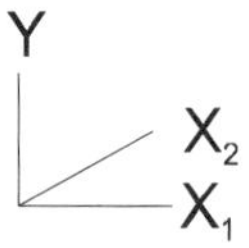


- Drag a scale variable to the *y* axis.
- Drag variables (usually categorical) to the *x1* and *x2* axes.

## Create Area Chart: Areas

Figure 3-2
*Create Area Chart: Areas tab*

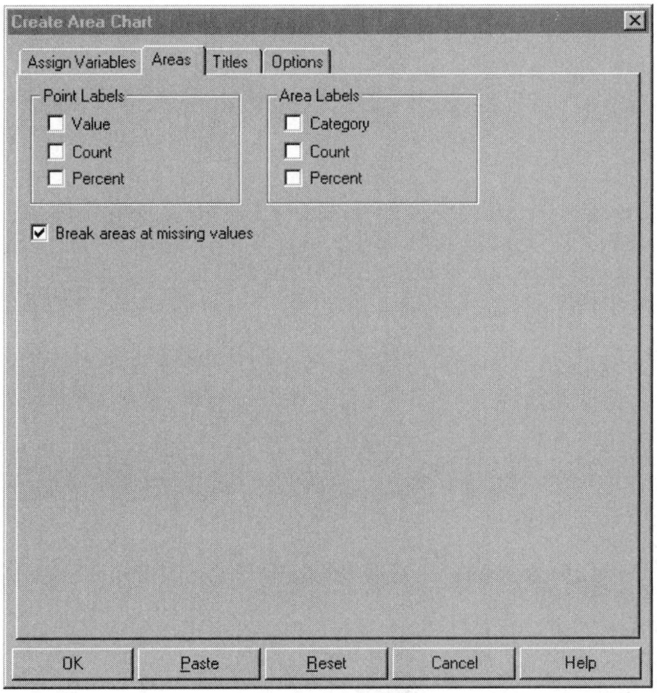


Several options are available to enhance areas.

**Point Labels.** The data points that define the edge of the area polygon can be labeled. Values, counts, and percentages are available. Any combination of these is allowed.

**Area Labels.** The area polygons can be labeled with the category name, the percentage of total cases, and the number of cases included in each area. Any combination is allowed.

**Break areas at missing values.** When this item is selected, the area is interrupted at any point along the independent axis where there is a missing value. If this item is deselected, the edge of the area is interpolated through the missing value and the area is filled in.

# Modifying Areas

To modify the area element (all areas) in an existing chart:

- ▶ Activate the chart (double-click it).
- ▶ From the menus choose:

Format
  Graph Elements
    Area

*or*

- ▶ Right-click an area and from the context menu choose:

Areas...

- ▶ Select the desired changes.

## Areas: Area Options

Figure 3-3
*Areas: Area Options tab*

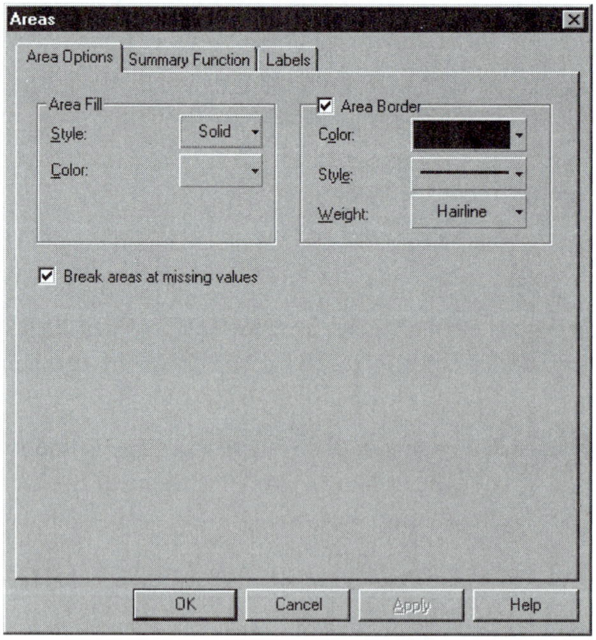

Several options are available to enhance areas.

**Area Fill.** Fills all areas in the chart with the selected style and color. If style or color is controlled by the data, it cannot be changed.

**Area Border.** Sets the border style, color, and weight for all areas in the chart. This option is available only for 2-D charts.

**Break areas at missing values.** When this item is selected, the area is interrupted when there is a missing value along the independent axis. If this item is deselected, the edge of the area is interpolated through the missing value and the area is filled in.

## *Areas: Summary Function*

Figure 3-4
*Areas: Summary Function tab*

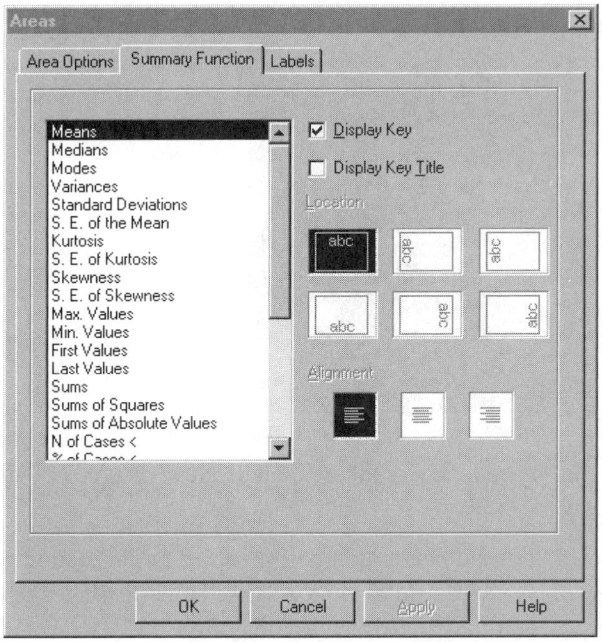


For an existing chart, if there is a scale variable on the dependent axis, you can change the summary function. For example, if the original areas represent the *means* of a variable, you can change to the *maximum values* of the same variable.

**Key display options.** These selections change the way summary information is displayed in the chart. You can display the key and determine the alignment and location of the key title.

## Areas: Labels

Figure 3-5
*Areas: Labels tab*

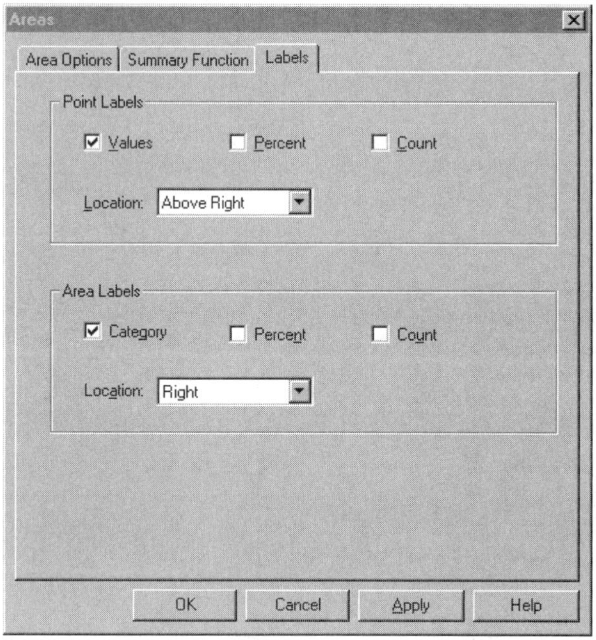


These controls apply to all point labels or all area labels. Several types of labels can be displayed simultaneously.

**Point Labels.** Labels on each of the points that define the edge of the area polygon. Values, counts, and percentages are available. A percent label displays the percentage of all cases in the area polygon that contribute to the point.

**Area Labels.** The area polygons can be labeled with the category name, the percentage of cases, and the number of cases included in each area. A percent label displays the percentage that contributes to the area out of the total number of cases.

### Areas: Area Width

Figure 3-6
*Areas: Area Width tab*

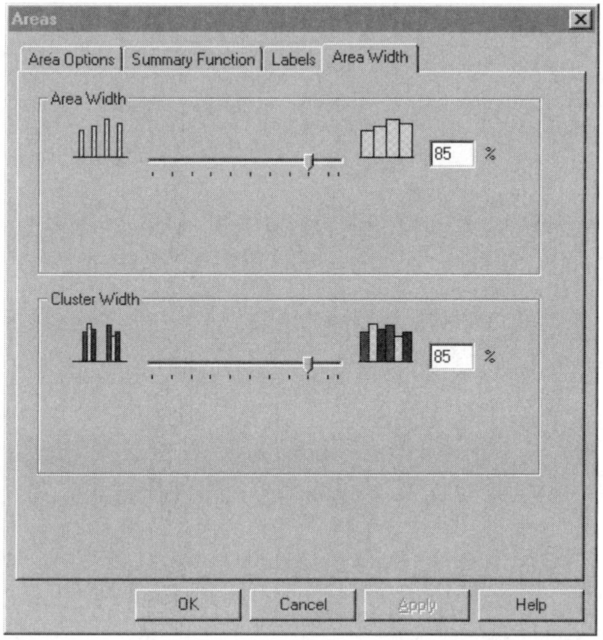


For 3-D or 3-D Effect area charts, you can change the width of the areas or the width of clusters of areas by dragging a slider. The cluster-width slider is available only if the chart is clustered.

## Changing Area Properties

Individual areas or a selection of several areas have the properties Fill, Border, and Labels, which can be changed if the property is not controlled by assigned variables. However, in a stacked area chart in which color is used to distinguish categories, the color of a group of areas in one category can be changed only for the whole group (using the legend).

In addition to selecting the areas in the display, you can also select labels.

### To Change Area Properties

▶ Activate the chart (double-click it).

▶ Select one or more areas.

▶ From the menus choose:

Edit
 Area Properties...

*or*

▶ Right-click an area or selected group of areas and choose Properties.

Optionally, you can:

- Change the fill and border.
- Turn labels on or off for points or areas.

## Area Properties

Figure 3-7
*Area Properties dialog box*

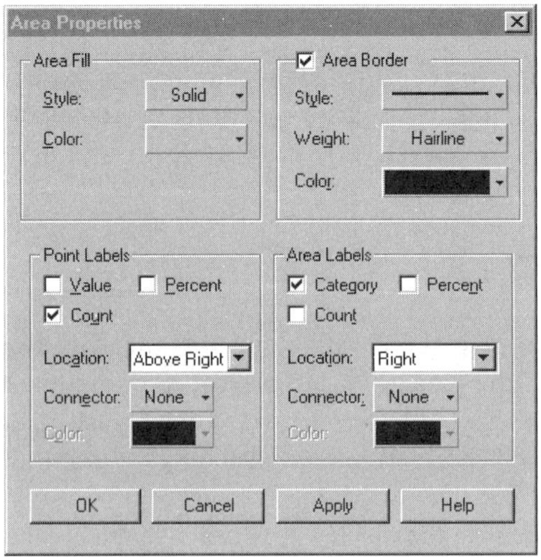

The properties apply only to currently selected areas.

**Area Fill.** The style and color of the selected areas can be changed, if not controlled by the data.

**Area Border.** If borders are on (selected), you can change the style, color, or weight.

**Point Labels.** Labels on each of the points that define the edge of the area polygon. Values, counts, and percentages are available. A percent label displays the percentage of all cases in the area polygon that contributes to the point.

**Area Labels.** An area polygon can be labeled with the category name, a percentage, and the number of cases included in each area. A percent label displays the percentage of cases that contributes to the area out of the total number of cases.

## *Point Label Properties*

Figure 3-8
*Point Label Properties dialog box*

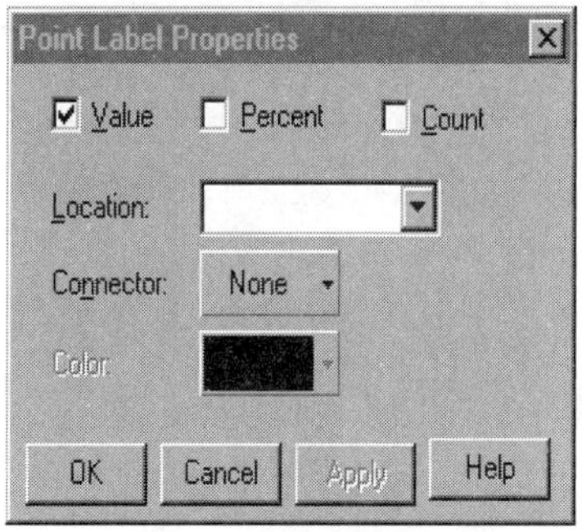


The properties apply only to currently selected point labels.

A data point can be labeled with the value represented, the percentage of cases in the area that contribute to the point, and the count of cases in the area that contribute to the point. You can control the location of a label with respect to the data point, the style of connector, and its color.

## Area Label Properties

Figure 3-9
*Area Label Properties dialog box*

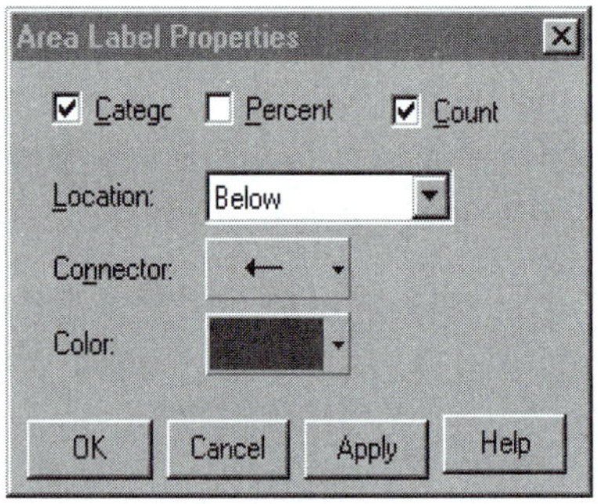


The properties apply only to currently selected area labels.

An area can be labeled with the category name, the percentage of all cases that contribute to the area, and the count (number of cases) represented in the area. You can control the location of a label with respect to the data point, the style of connector, and its color.

Chapter

# 4

# Bar Charts

A simple bar chart presents a summary variable divided into discrete categories, making it easy to compare categories visually. A glance at a bar chart tells you the relative sizes of the quantities represented by the bars, which can be drawn vertically or horizontally. Bars can be subdivided into clusters by a category variable and further subdivided by placing another category variable in the third dimension. Categories can also be stacked. Many other variations are possible.

## Sample Output

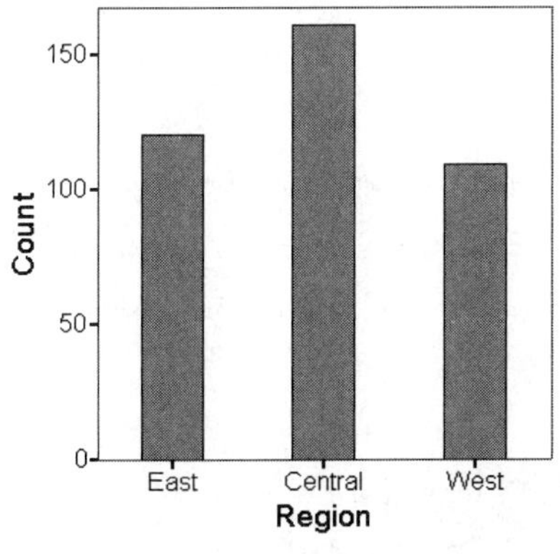


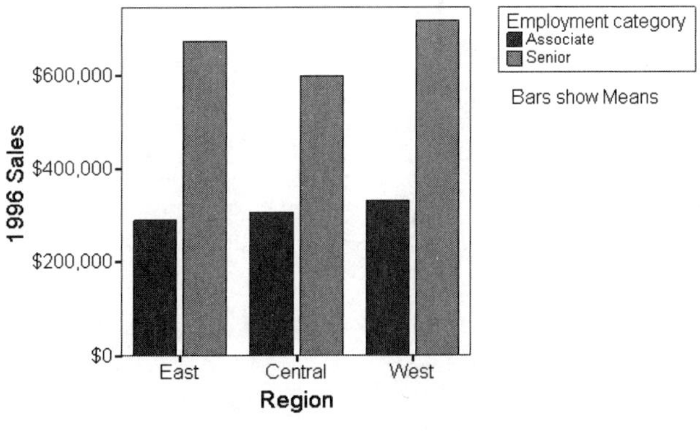

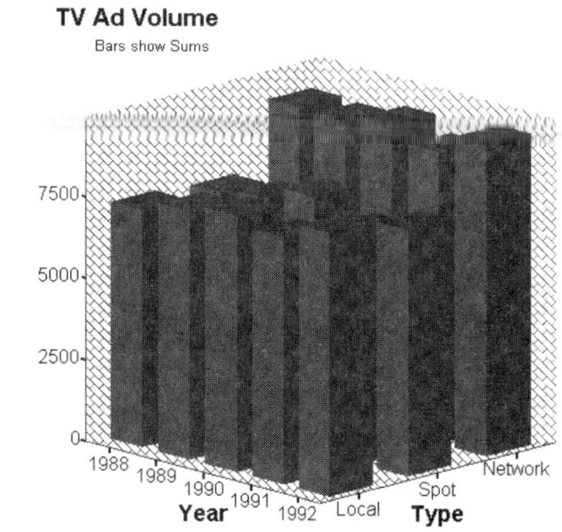
TV Ad Volume
Bars show Sums
7500
5000
2500
0
1988
1989
1990
1991
1992
Year
Local
Spot
Network
Type

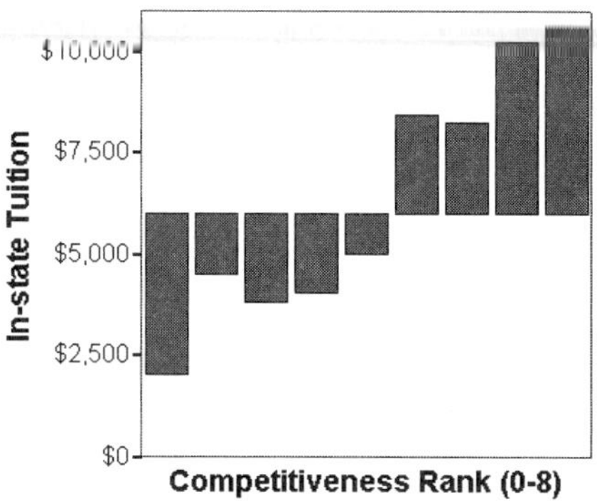
$10,000
$7,500
$5,000
$2,500
$0
In-state Tuition
Competitiveness Rank (0-8)

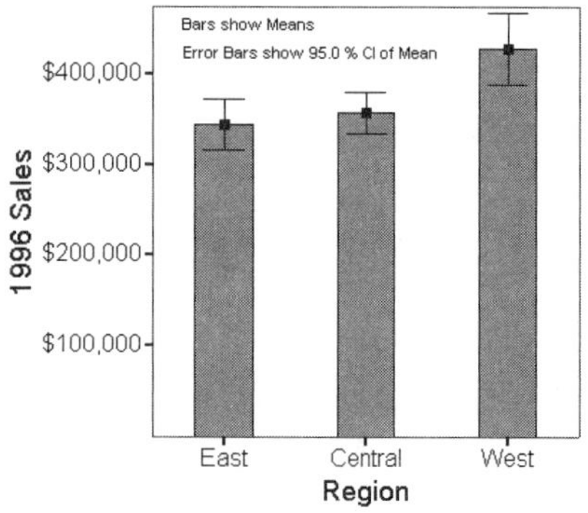
Bars show Means
Error Bars show 95.0 % CI of Mean
$400,000
$300,000
$200,000
$100,000
1996 Sales
East
Central
West
Region

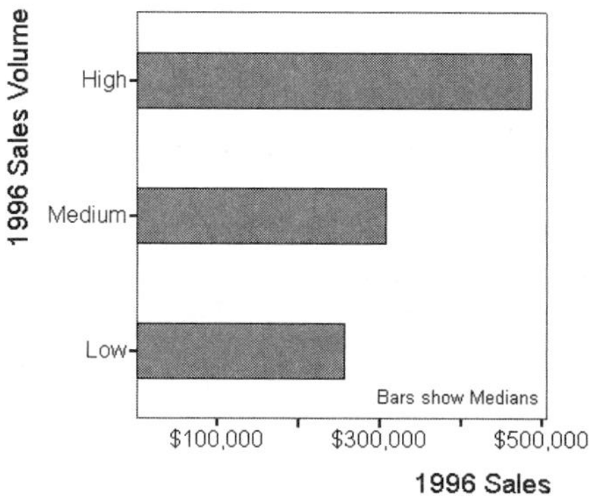
High
Medium
Low
1996 Sales Volume
Bars show Medians
$100,000
$300,000
$500,000
1996 Sales

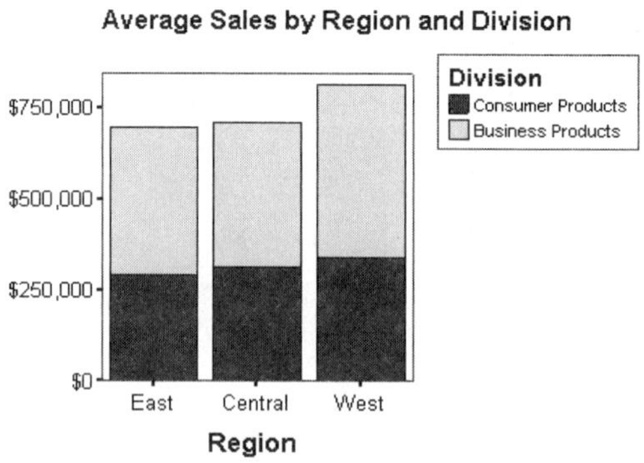
Average Sales by Region and Division
Division
Consumer Products
Business Products
$750,000
$500,000
$250,000
$0
East
Central
West
Region

# To Create a Bar Chart

▶ From the menus choose:

Graphs
 Interactive
  Bar...

## Create Bar Chart: Assign Variables

Figure 4-1
*Create Bar Chart: Assign Variables tab*

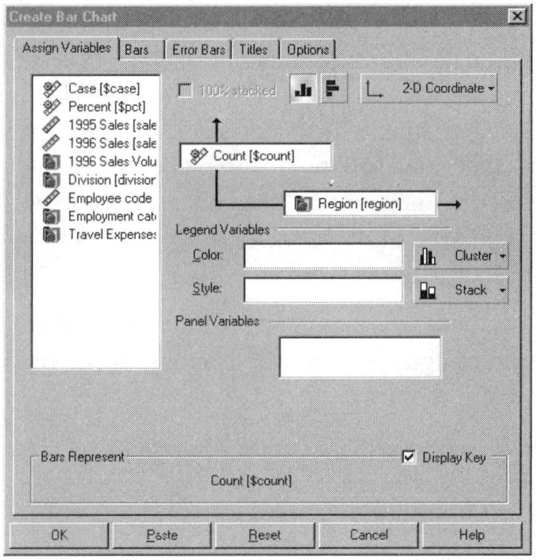


A bar chart presents summary statistics for one or more variables, most often within groups defined by one or two categorical variables. Bar length commonly represents a count of cases for each category, a percentage of the total number of cases, or a function of another variable (for example, the mean value for each category). The function can be changed near the bottom of the dialog box, and you can display a key that identifies the function.

**Number of dimensions.** Selecting 2-D Coordinate or 3-D Coordinate changes the number of axis targets for variable selection. Selecting 3-D Effect specifies that the bars are three-dimensional objects, lined up along one axis.

**Orientation.** Clicking the vertical or horizontal orientation icon sets up the appropriate axis targets for variable selection. Orientation icons are available only when 2-D Coordinate is selected.

**Vertical**

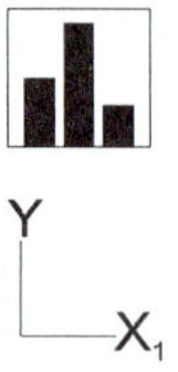


**Horizontal**

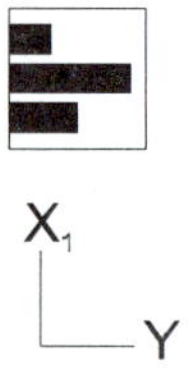


**Clustered and Stacked Bars.** If a categorical variable is assigned to Color or Style, the bars for categories can be clustered next to one another or stacked. In a stacked bar, the categories of the legend variable are stacked on top of one another. The top of one segment forms the base for the next segment. Because this type of chart emphasizes the sum of the categories, only functions appropriate for summation should be selected for stacking in Bars Represent. If a color or style stack legend has been selected, you can change the dependent axis to represent 100%. The segments then represent the percentage contributed by each category.

**Case Variable.** If the built-in variable *Case* is assigned to an axis, another target becomes available where you can assign a variable for labeling cases. For example, the labels might be days of the week or months.

Most of the charts shown below are vertical. To create a horizontal chart, click the horizontal orientation icon before or after dragging variables.

### *To Create a Simple Bar Chart*

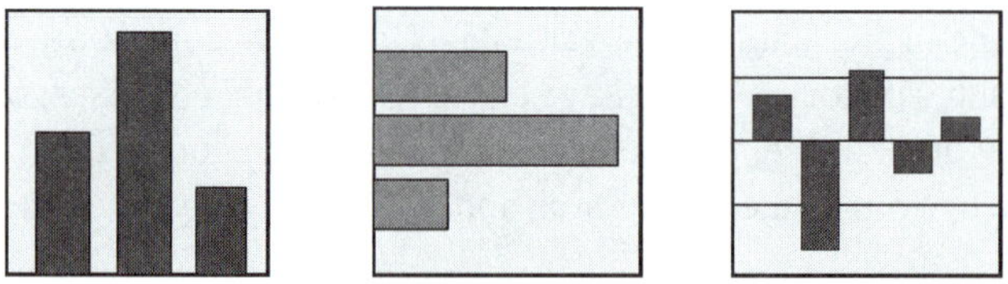

- Drag a variable (usually categorical) to the *x1* axis. This will be the base of the bars.
- Drag *Count* or a scale variable to the *y* axis (if one is not already there by default).

For another summary chart, you can use the built-in variable *Percent*.

Optionally, you can:

- Assign multiple variables to each axis by Shift-clicking.
- Swap the axes by clicking the orientation icon. The currently assigned variables swap with the axes.
- Change the bar baseline on the Bars tab.

### To Create a Bar Chart Summarizing a Scale Variable

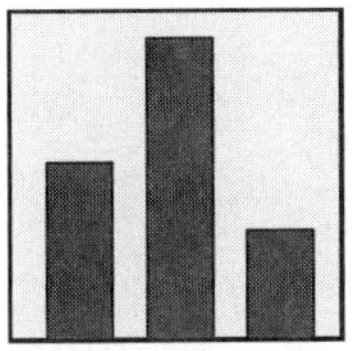

- ▶ Drag a variable (usually categorical) to the *x1* axis.
- ▶ Drag a scale variable to the *y* axis.

By default, the bars represent the mean of the scale variable.

Optionally, you can:

- Select another summary function from the Bars Represent drop-down list near the bottom of the dialog box.
- Choose whether to display the key. The key displays the name of the summary function on the chart.

### To Create a Clustered Bar Chart

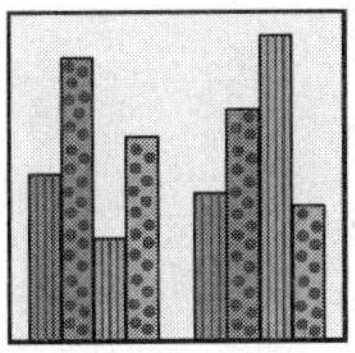

- ▶ Drag a variable (usually categorical) to the *x1* axis.
- ▶ Drag another variable to the *y* axis.
- ▶ Drag a categorical variable to Color or Style.

### To Create a 3-D Bar Chart

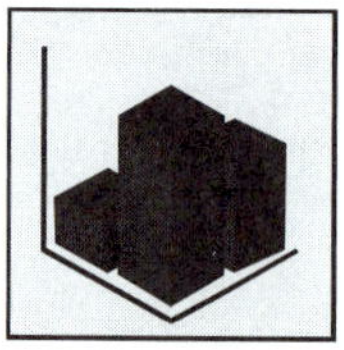

- ▶ Select 3-D Coordinate from the drop-down list.

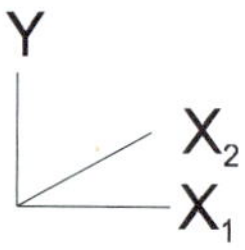


- ▶ Drag *Count* or another variable to the *y* axis.
- ▶ Drag variables (usually categorical) to the *x1* and *x2* axes. Assigning a scale variable to the *x1* or *x2* axis can result in a large number of bars.

### To Create a Bar Chart of Individual Cases

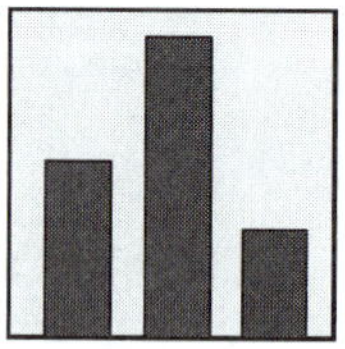

- ▶ Drag *Case* to the *x1* axis. The number of bars is equal to the number of cases.
- ▶ Right-click on *Case* and select Categorical (to avoid overlapping bars).

▶ Drag a variable (usually a scale variable) to the *y* axis.

Optionally, you can:

- Swap the axes by clicking the orientation icon. The currently assigned variables swap with the axes.
- Assign a variable for case labels.

*Note*: Bar charts that display values for individual cases are meaningful only if you select a summary variable for the dependent (*y*) axis. Summary functions such as mean, median, or mode will result in bars that display the value of the summary variable for each case. Counts, percentages, and summary functions that represent the number of cases or percentage of cases above or below a specified value will not reveal any particularly useful information when charting cases, since every case has a count of exactly 1.

### To Create Bar Chart Panels for Categories

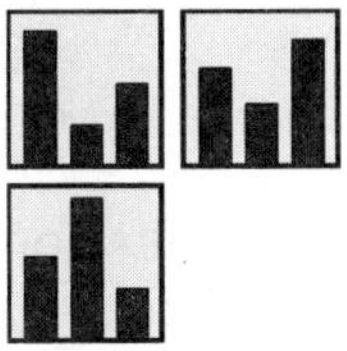

▶ Drag a variable (usually categorical) to the *x1* axis.

▶ Drag a scale variable or a built-in variable to the *y* axis.

▶ Drag one or more categorical variables to Panel Variables.

### To Create a Bar Chart with Colors Assigned by a Scale Variable

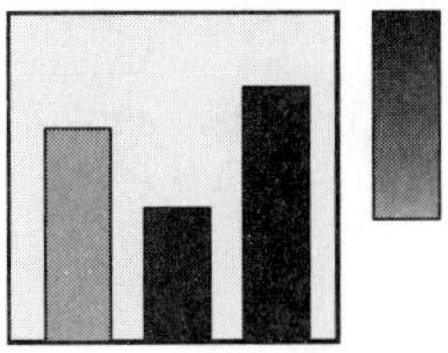

- Drag a variable (usually categorical) to the *x1* axis.
- Drag a scale variable or a built-in variable to the *y* axis.
- Drag a scale variable to Color.

  The color of each bar indicates the mean of the legend color variable for the category represented by the bar.

#### To Create a Bar Chart with a Scale Variable on the Independent Axis

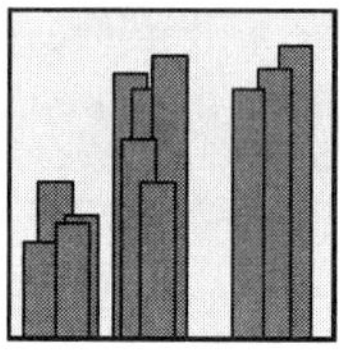

- Drag a scale variable to the *x1* axis.
- Drag a scale variable or a built-in variable to the *y* axis.

  The bars are spaced along the independent axis according to the values of the scale variable.

#### To Create a Bar Chart with Error Bars

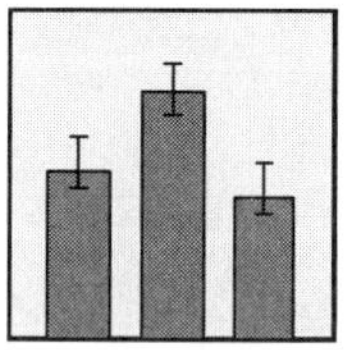

- Drag a categorical variable to the *x1* axis.
- Drag a scale variable to the *y* axis.
- Select Means as the summary function.

- Click the Error Bars tab and select Display Error Bars.
- Specify the properties of the error bars.

  Optionally, you can:

  - Specify a confidence interval or the number of standard deviations or the number of standard errors of the mean.
  - Specify the direction in relation to the bars in the chart.
  - Specify the look of the error bars.

### To Create a Stacked Bar Chart

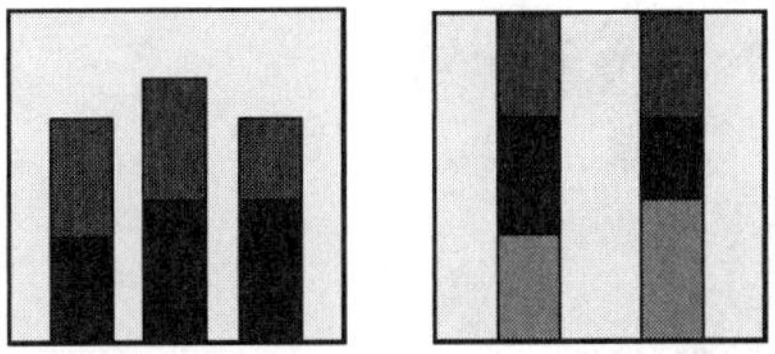

- Drag a categorical variable to the *x1* axis.
- Drag a scale variable to the *y* axis.
- Select Sums or another appropriate summary function.
- Drag a categorical variable to Color or Style and select Stack from the corresponding drop-down list.

  Optionally, you can display bar segments as percentages by selecting 100% Stacked.

### To Create a Bar Chart with 3-D Effect

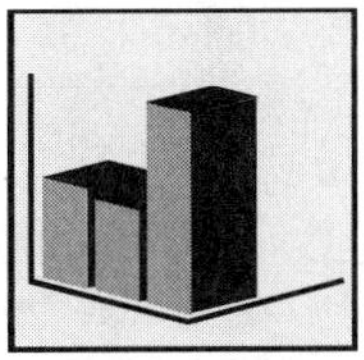

- Select the vertical orientation icon.
- Select 3-D Effect from the orientation drop-down list.
- Drag a categorical variable to the *x1* axis.
- Drag a built-in or scale variable to the *y* axis.

Optionally, you can activate the chart and rotate the axes.

## Create Bar Chart: Bars

Figure 4-2
*Create Bar Chart: Bars tab*

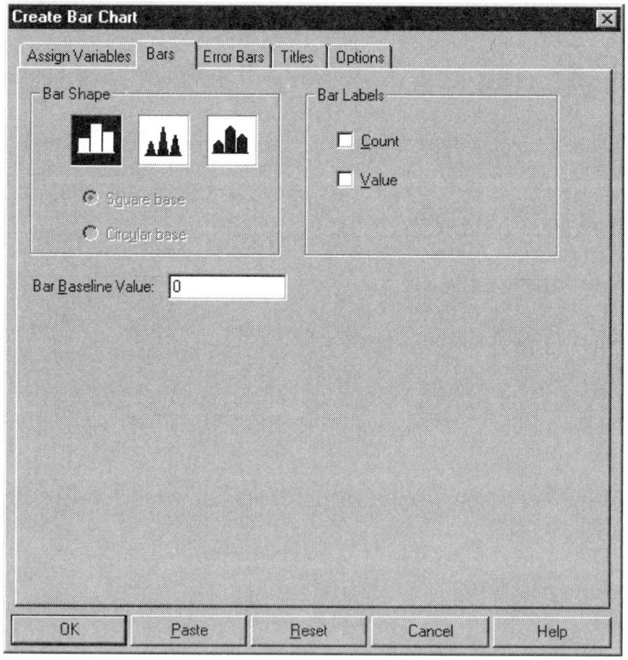


Several options are available to enhance bar charts.

**Bar Shape.** Displays rectangles, pyramids, or monuments. For 3-D bars, the shape of the base can be round or square.

**Bar Labels.** Displays labels giving the count (number of cases) and the value represented by the length of the bar.

**Bar Baseline Value.** Sets the location of the baseline from which bars will hang (vertical bars) or extend (horizontal bars). The baseline emphasizes the differences between the groups below and above the baseline.

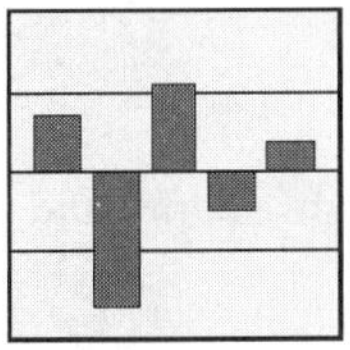

## Create Bar Chart: Error Bars

Figure 4-3
*Create Bar Chart: Error Bars tab*

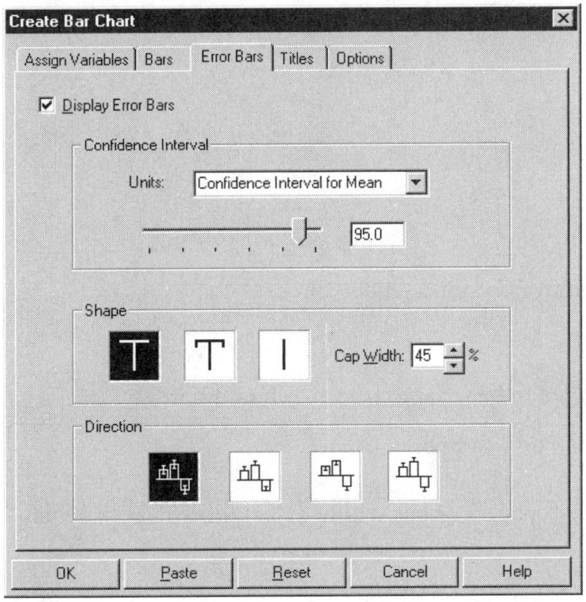


**Error bars**, indicating the variability of the measure displayed, are available when the dependent variable is a scale variable and bars or lines represent the summary function *Means*. The length of an error bar represents the amount of variability. The length of the error bars is displayed as the lower and upper limits of a confidence interval (at a specified percentage level) or in standard deviations or standard errors of the mean.

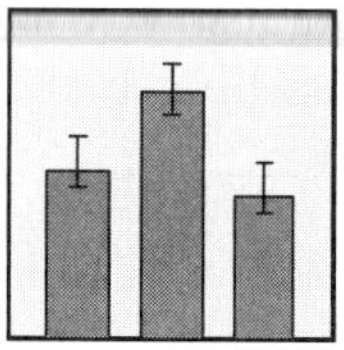

You can specify the confidence interval's level, direction, and shape, and change the appearance of error bars.

## Modifying Bars

To modify the bar element (all bars) in an existing chart:

- ▶ Activate the chart by clicking it.

- ▶ From the menus choose:

  Format
    Graph Elements
      Bars

  *or*

- ▶ Right-click a bar and from the context menu choose:

  Bars...

- ▶ Select the desired changes in bar shape, labels, fill, and borders.

  You can also change the bar baseline.

To change the summary function or bar width, select the appropriate tabs in the Bars dialog box.

## Bars: Bar Options

Figure 4-4
*Bars: Bar Options tab*

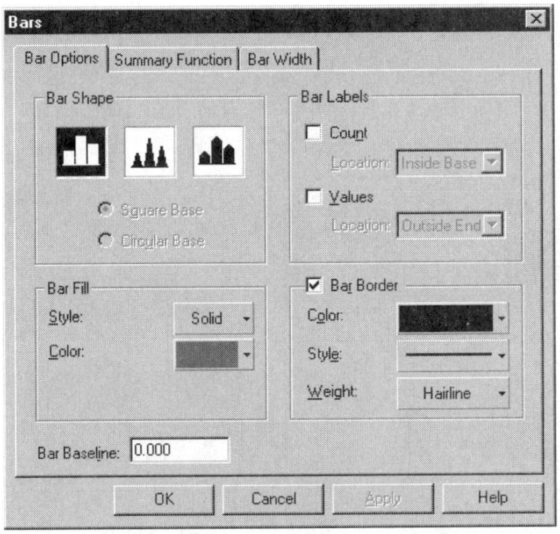


Several options are available to enhance bar charts.

**Bar Shape.** Displays rectangles, pyramids, or monuments. For 3-D bars, the shape of the base can be round or square.

**Bar Labels.** Displays labels giving the number of cases or the value represented by the length of each bar.

**Bar Fill.** Fills all bars in the chart with the selected style and color. Style or color that is controlled by the data is not available for change.

**Bar Border.** Sets the border style, color, and weight for all bars in the chart.

**Bar Baseline.** Sets the location of the baseline from which bars will hang (vertical bars) or extend (horizontal bars). The baseline emphasizes the differences between the groups below and above the baseline.

## Bars: Summary Function

Figure 4-5
*Bars: Summary Function tab*

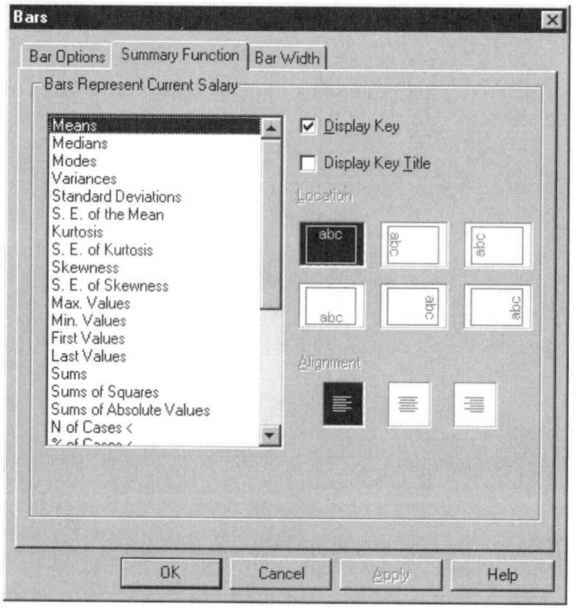


For an existing chart, if there is a scale variable on the dependent axis, you can change the summary function. For example, if the original bars represent the *means* of a variable, you can change to the *maximum values* of the same variable.

**Key display options**. These selections change the way summary information is displayed in the chart. You can display the key and determine the alignment and location of the key title.

### Bars: Bar Width

Figure 4-6
*Bars: Bar Width tab*

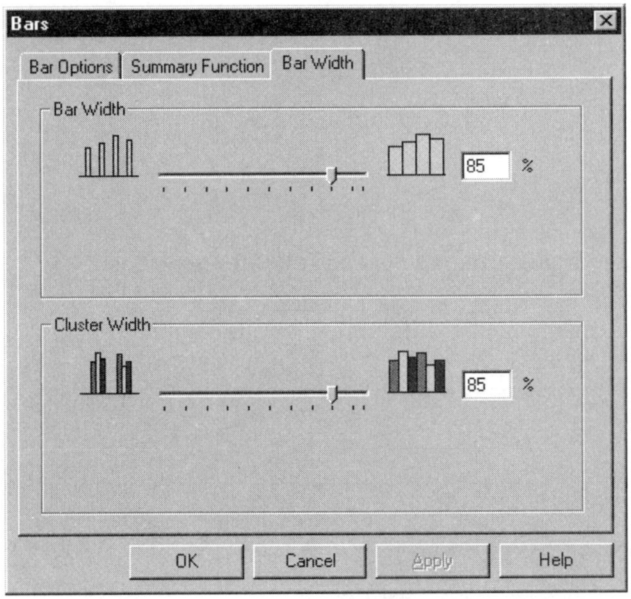


After bars are created, you can change the width of the bars or of clusters by dragging the appropriate slider.

## Changing Individual Bar Properties

Individual bars or a selection of several bars have the properties Fill, Border, and Labels, which can be changed as long as the property is not controlled by the data. For example, in a simple bar chart, you can change the color of each bar. However, in a clustered bar chart in which color is used to distinguish categories, the color of a group of bars in one category can be changed only for the whole group in the legend.

### To Change Bar Properties

- ▶ Activate the chart by clicking it.
- ▶ Select one or more bars in a bar chart.
- ▶ From the menus choose:

  Edit
  Bar Properties...

  *or*

- ▶ Right-click a bar or selected group of bars and choose Properties.

Optionally, you can change the bar fill, border, or labels.

## Bar Properties

Figure 4-7
*Bar Properties dialog box*

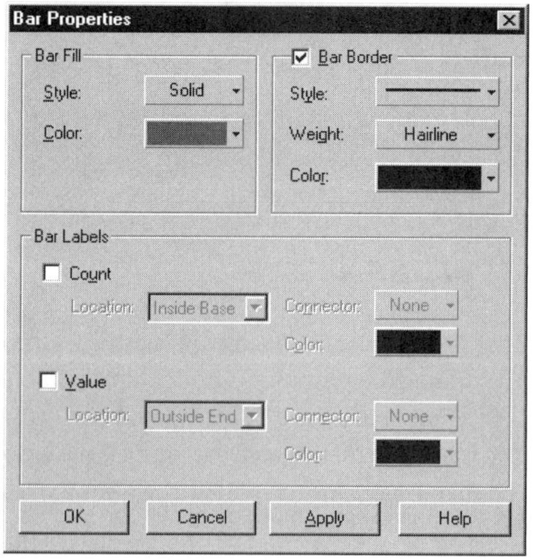


Changes to the properties apply only to currently selected bars.

**Bar Fill.** The style and color of the selected bars can be changed, if they are not controlled by the data assignments.

**Bar Border.** If borders are on (selected), you can change the style, color, or weight.

**Bar Labels.** Labels can show the number of cases (count) used to calculate the value for each bar and the value represented by each bar. For each type of label, the location, type of connector, and connector color can be set.

Chapter

# 5

# Boxplots

A boxplot characterizes the distribution and dispersion of a variable, displaying its median and quartiles. Special symbols identify the position of outliers and extreme values, if any. Simple boxplots display boxes for a single scale variable. The cases can be grouped by the values of a categorical variable. Clustered boxplots display a cluster of boxes for each value of another categorical variable.

## Sample Output

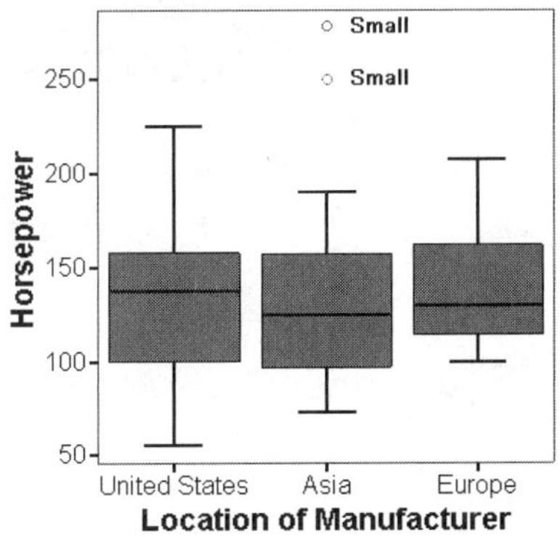


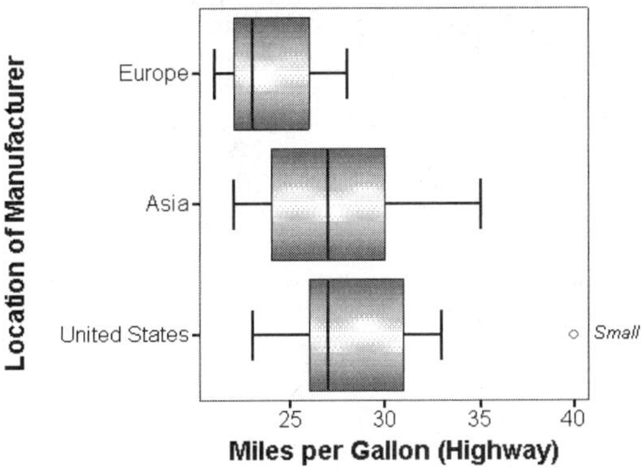

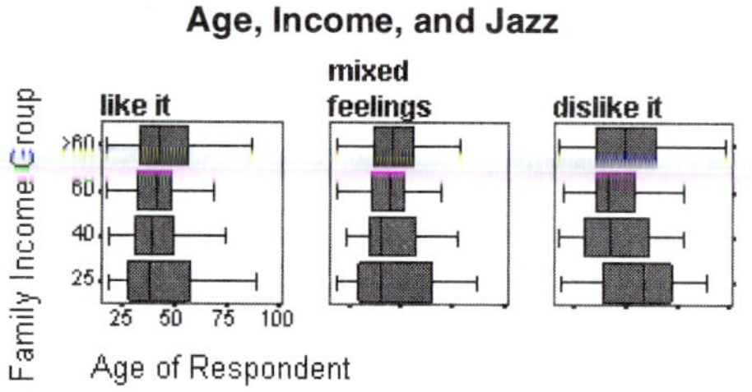
Age, Income, and Jazz
like it
mixed feelings
dislike it
Family Income Group
>60
60
40
25
25
50
75
100
Age of Respondent

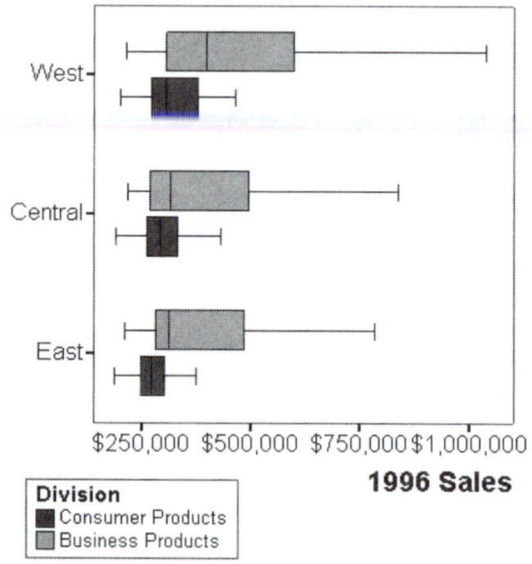
West
Central
East
$250,000
$500,000
$750,000
$1,000,000
1996 Sales
Division
Consumer Products
Business Products

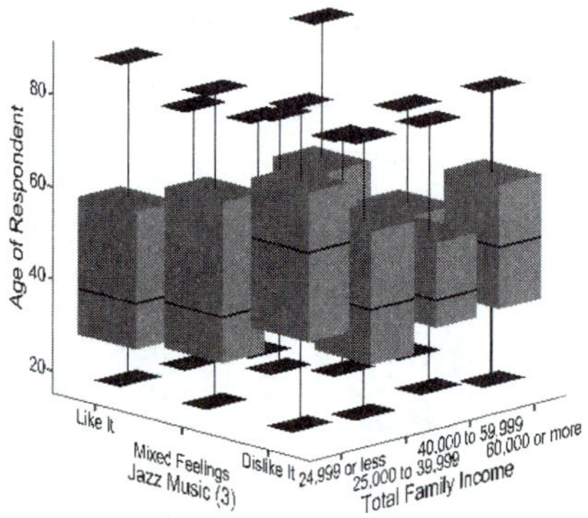
Age of Respondent
80
60
40
20
Like It
Mixed Feelings
Dislike It
Jazz Music (3)
24,999 or less
25,000 to 39,999
40,000 to 59,999
60,000 or more
Total Family Income

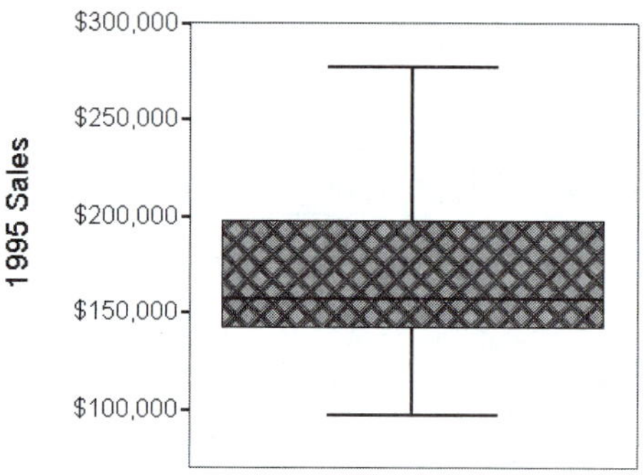
1995 Sales
$300,000
$250,000
$200,000
$150,000
$100,000

# To Create an Interactive Boxplot

▶ From the menus choose:

Graphs
 Interactive
  Boxplot...

## Create Boxplot: Assign Variables

Figure 5-1
*Create Boxplot: Assign Variables tab*

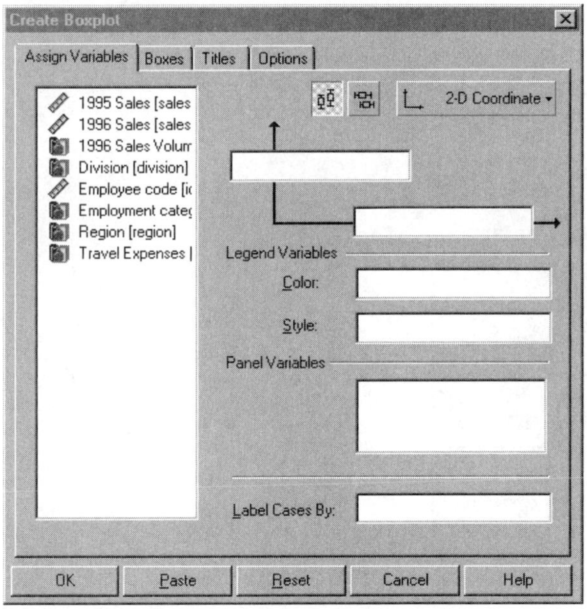


A boxplot, sometimes called a box-and-whiskers plot, shows the median, quartiles, and outlier and extreme values for a scale variable. It can be split into categories and clusters.

**Number of dimensions.** Selecting 2-D Coordinate or 3-D Coordinate changes the number of axis targets for variable selection. Selecting 3-D Effect specifies that the boxes are three-dimensional objects, lined up along one axis.

**Orientation.** Clicking an orientation (vertical or horizontal) icon sets up the appropriate axis targets, as shown, for variable selection. Orientation icons are available only when 2-D Coordinate is selected.

Many of the charts shown below are horizontal. To create a vertical chart, click the vertical icon before or after dragging variables.

**Vertical**

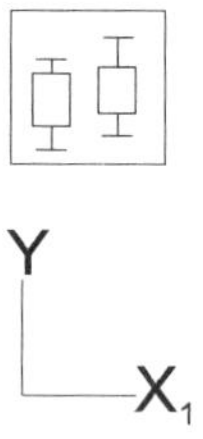


**Horizontal**

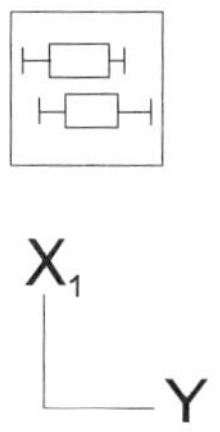


### *To Create a Simple Boxplot*

**Vertical**

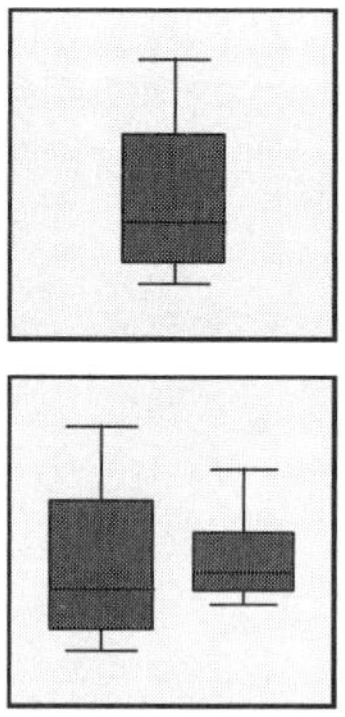

**Horizontal**

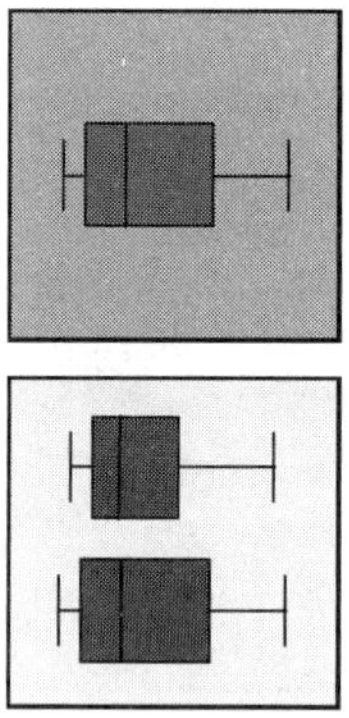

▶ Drag a scale variable to the *y* axis. This is sufficient to draw a boxplot of a single variable.

▶ To display boxes for separate categories, drag a categorical variable to the *x1* axis.

Optionally, you can:

- Drag a variable to Label Cases By, for identifying the outliers and extremes.

- Swap the axes by clicking the orientation icon. Currently assigned variables swap, along with the axes.
- Use a scale variable on the *x1* axis, although this assignment can create a large number of boxes.

### To Create a Clustered Boxplot

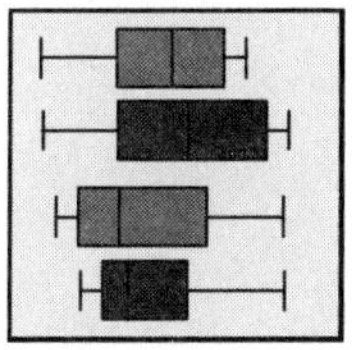

▶ Drag a variable (usually categorical) to the *x1* axis.

▶ Drag a scale variable to the *y* axis.

▶ Drag a categorical variable to Color or Style (or both).

Optionally, you can:

- Swap the axes by clicking the orientation icon. Currently assigned variables swap, along with the axes.

### To Create a 3-D Boxplot

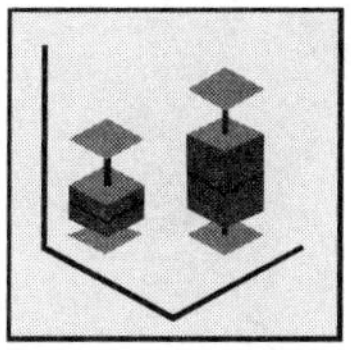

▶ Select 3-D Coordinate from the drop-down list.

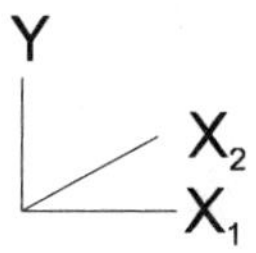

- Drag a scale variable to the *y* axis.
- Drag variables (usually categorical) to the *x1* and *x2* axes.

#### To Create Boxplot Panels for Categories

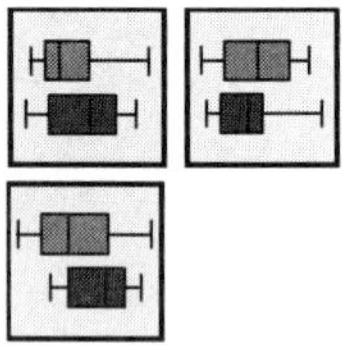

- Drag a variable (usually categorical) to the *x1* axis.
- Drag a scale variable to the *y* axis.
- Drag one or more categorical variables to Panel Variables.

#### To Create a Boxplot with Colors Assigned by a Summary of a Scale Variable

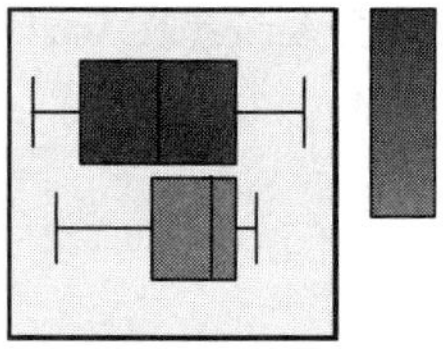

- Drag a variable (usually categorical) to the *x1* axis.
- Drag a scale variable to the *y* axis.
- Drag a scale variable to Color.

  The color of each box indicates the mean of the color variable for the category represented by the box.

## Create Boxplot: Boxes

Figure 5-2
*Create Boxplot: Boxes tab*

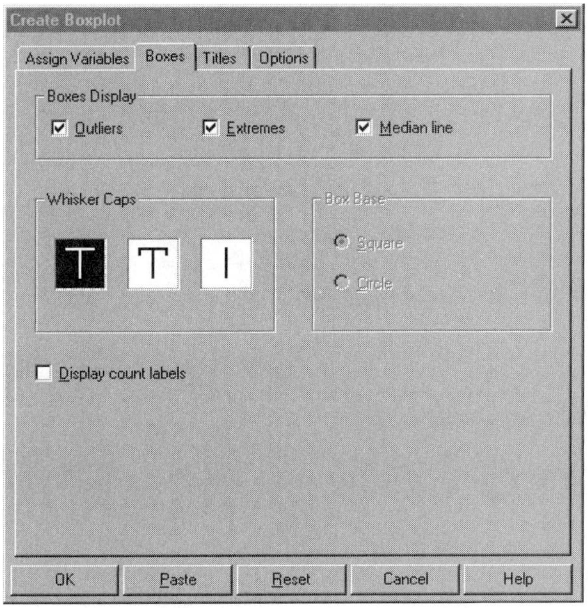


Several options are available to enhance boxplots.

**Boxes Display.** Outliers, extremes, and the median line can be displayed for each box. Outliers are between 1.5 box lengths and 3 box lengths from the end of the box. Extremes are more than 3 box lengths from the end of the box.

**Whisker Caps.** Several shapes are available for the cap at the end of each whisker in a 2-D boxplot.

**Box Base.** The bases of 3-D boxes can be square or circular.

**Display count labels.** When selected, the number of cases included in each category is displayed.

# Modifying Boxes

To modify the box element (all boxes) in an existing chart:

- ▶ Activate the chart (double-click it).
- ▶ From the menus choose:

Format
  Graph Elements
    Box

*or*

- ▶ Right-click a box and from the context menu choose:

Boxes...

- ▶ Select the desired changes.

## Boxes: Box Options

Figure 5-3
*Boxes: Box Options tab*

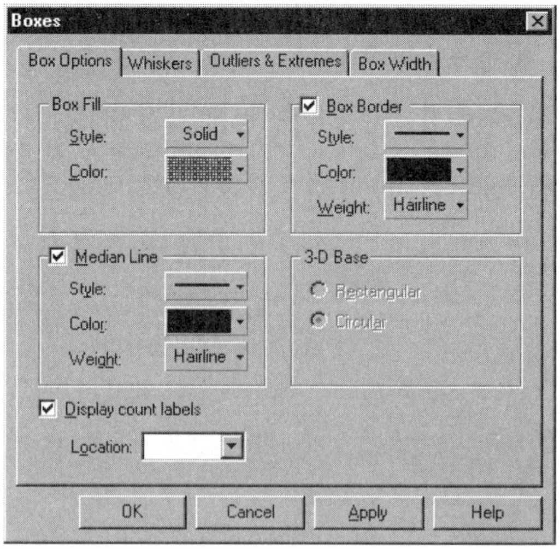


Several options are available to enhance boxes.

**Box Fill.** Fills all boxes in the chart with the selected style and color. If style or color is controlled by the data, it cannot be changed.

**Box Border.** Sets the border style, color, and weight for all boxes in the chart. This option is available only for 2-D charts.

**Median Line.** Displays the median line in each box. You can change style, weight, and color.

**Display count labels.** Count labels show how many cases contribute to each box. If count labels have been dragged to another position, you can use the location to bring them back to the base.

**3-D Base.** The base for 3-D boxes can be rectangular or circular.

## *Boxes: Whiskers*

Figure 5-4
*Boxes: Whiskers tab*

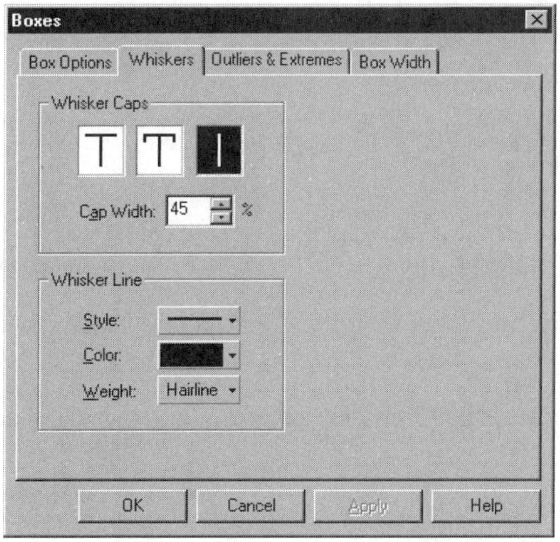


Whiskers at the ends of the box show the distance from the end of the box to the largest and smallest observed values that are less than 1.5 box lengths from either end of the box.

**Whisker Caps.** The whisker caps can have different shapes. The width of the cap is set as a percentage of the width of a box.

**Whisker Line.** The line extending from the end of each box can have style, color, and weight assigned.

## Boxes: Outliers and Extremes

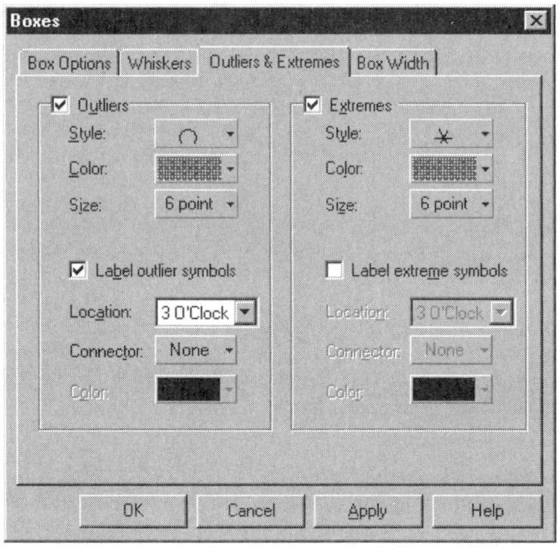


Figure 5-5
*Boxes: Outliers & Extremes tab*

Cases far from the box on either end can be displayed or suppressed. Also, their styles, labels, and label connectors can be changed.

**Outliers.** Cases with values that are between 1.5 and 3 box lengths from either end of the box.

**Extremes.** Cases with values more than 3 box lengths from either end of the box.

### *Boxes: Box Width*

Figure 5-6
*Boxes: Box Width tab*

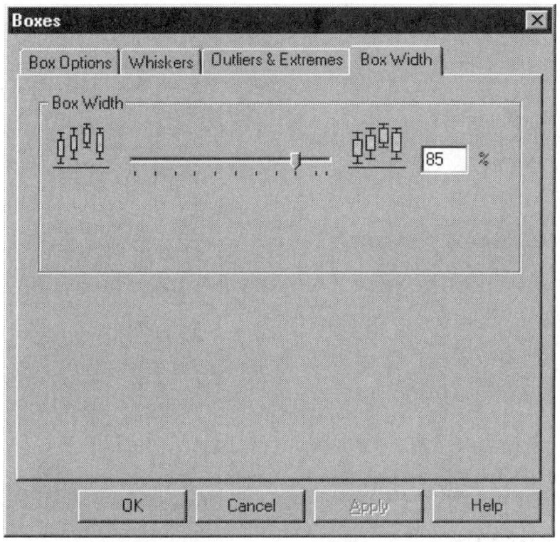


After boxes are created, you can change the width of the boxes or the width of clusters of boxes by dragging a slider.

## *Changing Individual Box Properties*

Individual boxes or a selection of several boxes have the properties Fill, Border, and Median Line, which can be changed if the property is not controlled by the data. For example, in a simple boxplot, you can change the color of each individual box. However, in a clustered boxplot in which color is used to distinguish categories, the color of a group of boxes in one category can be changed only for the whole group in the legend.

In addition to selecting the boxes in the display, you can also select whiskers of a box, the confidence interval, or individual outlier or extreme symbols. Boxes are unique elements in that their individual parts can be selected, but a box, whiskers, and median cannot be selected by using Shift-click. You can select several whiskers, several extremes, several boxes, or several medians.

### To Change Box Properties

▶ Activate the chart (double-click it).

▶ Select one or more boxes, medians, or whiskers.

▶ From the menus choose:

Edit
  Box Properties

*or*

▶ Right-click a box or selected group of boxes or whiskers or medians, and choose Properties.

Depending on which part is selected, you can:

- Change the fill, border, or median line, or display count labels.
- Change the whisker style, color, or weight.
- Change the symbol label properties.

## Box Properties

Figure 5-7
*Box Properties dialog box*

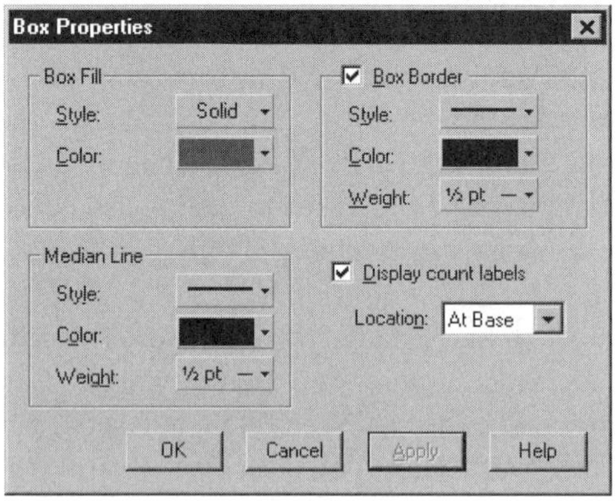


The properties apply only to currently selected boxes or median lines.

**Box Fill.** The style and color of the selected boxes can be changed, if not controlled by the data.

**Box Border.** If borders are on (selected), you can change the style, color, or weight.

**Median Line.** The style, color, and weight of the median lines can be changed.

**Display count labels.** Labels can show the number of cases for each box.

## *Box Symbol Properties*

Figure 5-8
*Box Symbol Properties dialog box*

The properties apply only to currently selected extremes and outliers.

**Display Symbol Label.** Symbols are labeled with values of the label variable (assigned when the chart was created). If no variable was specified, the extremes and outliers are labeled with case numbers.

**Changing the label variable.** If the chart is live (still connected to the original data), the label variable can be changed in Assign Variables.

## Box Whisker Properties

Figure 5-9
*Box Whisker Properties dialog box*

The properties apply only to currently selected whiskers.

**Whisker Line.** You can change the style, color, or weight of the lines that make up the whiskers.

Chapter

# 6

# Error Bars

Error bars indicate the variability of the measure displayed. Error bars can be built around the mean. They are often used in conjunction with other elements—for example, an error bar element can be added to a bar chart.

## Sample Output

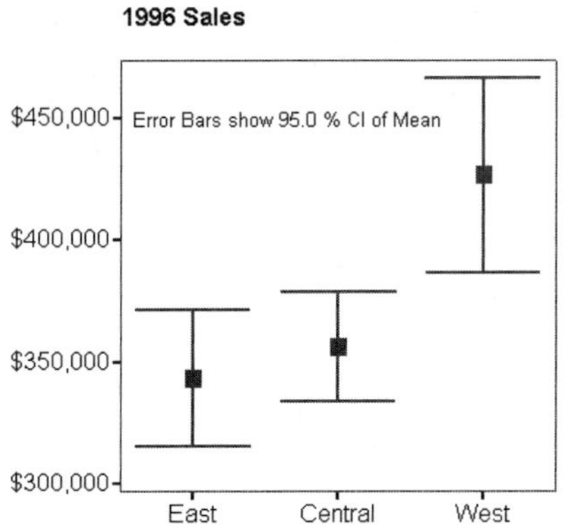


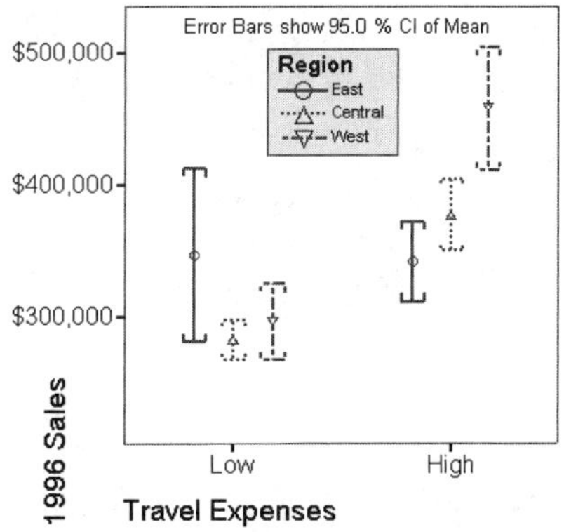

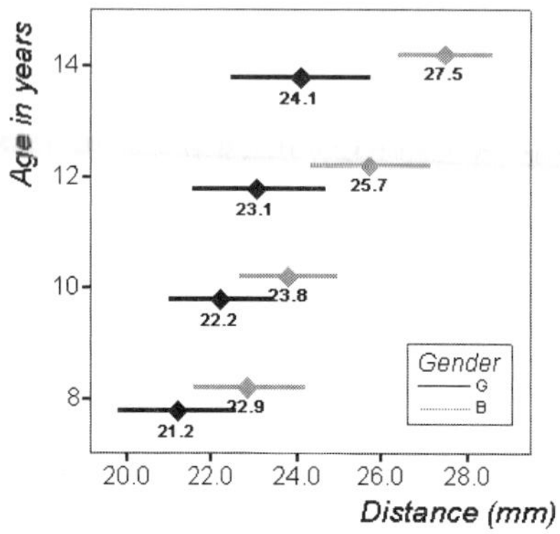


## Error Bar Charts with Other Graph Elements

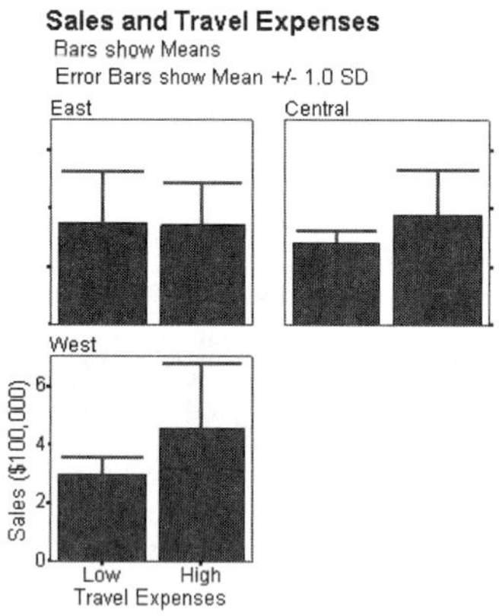


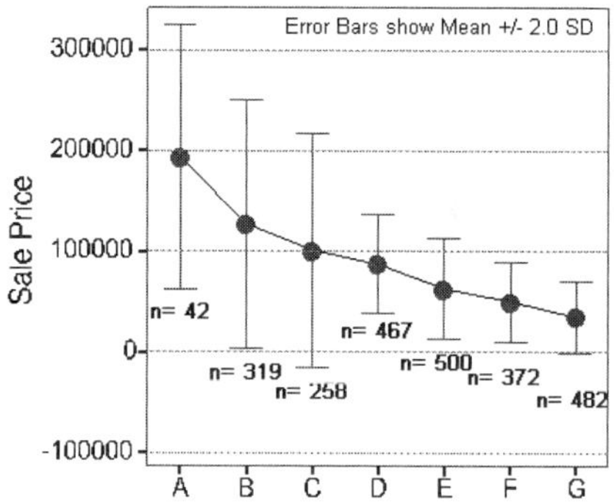


# To Create an Error Bar Chart

▶ From the menus choose:

Graphs
 Interactive
  Error Bar...

## *Create Error Bar Chart: Assign Variables*

Figure 6-1
*Create Error Bar Chart: Assign Variables tab*

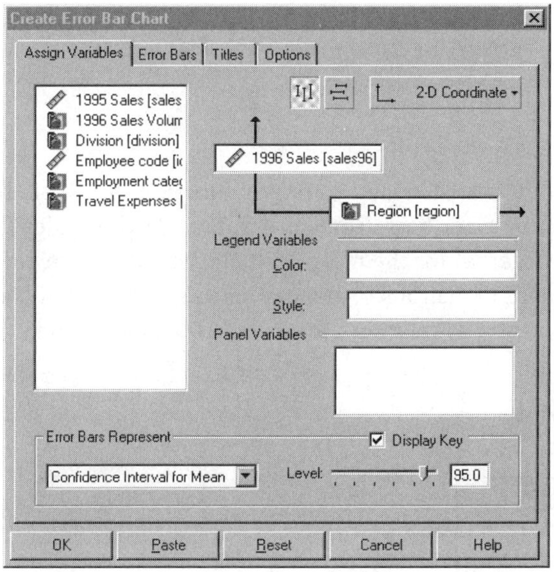


Error bars help you visualize distributions and dispersion by indicating the variability of the measure being displayed. The mean of a scale variable is plotted for a set of categories, and the length of an error bar on either side of the mean value indicates a confidence interval or a specified number of standard errors or standard deviations. Error bars can extend in one direction or both directions from the mean.

Error bars are sometimes displayed in the same chart with other chart elements such as bars or lines.

**Number of dimensions.** Selecting 2-D Coordinate or 3-D Coordinate changes the number of axis targets for variable selection. Selecting 3-D Effect specifies that the error bars are three-dimensional objects, displayed in a row.

**Orientation.** Clicking an orientation (vertical or horizontal) icon sets up the appropriate axis targets for variable selection. Orientation icons are available only when 2-D Coordinate is selected.

**Vertical** **Horizontal**

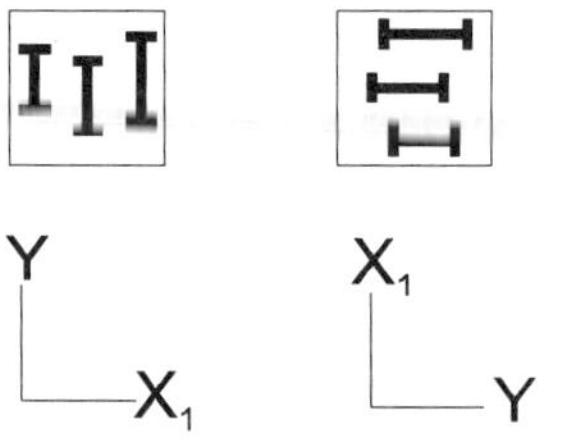


**Error Bars Represent.** Lists the statistics and summary functions available for determining the lengths of the error bars. You can display a key that identifies the function. On a confidence interval for the mean, you can specify a percentage for the level. The number of standard deviations or standard errors represented is determined by the multiplier, which can be any number greater than 0 and less than or equal to 6.

### *To Create a Simple Error Bar Chart*

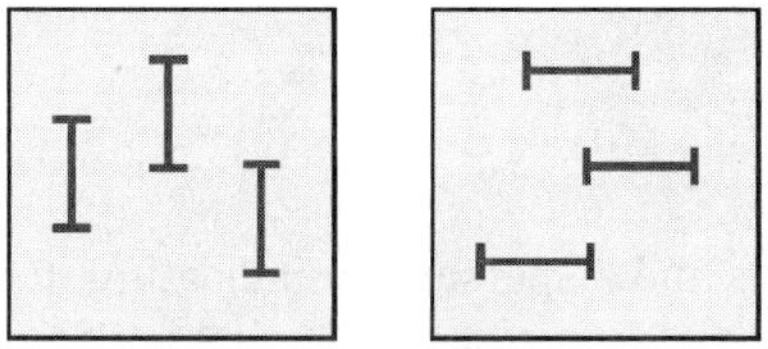

- Drag a variable (usually categorical) to the *x1* axis.
- Drag a scale variable to the *y* axis.

  By default, the length of the error bars represents the confidence interval around the mean.

  Optionally, you can:

  - Change the statistic used to determine the length of the error bars.
  - Change the multiplier for standard deviation or standard error.
  - Change the percentage level of the confidence interval.
  - Swap the axes by clicking the orientation icon. Previously assigned variables swap, along with the axes.

### To Create a Clustered Error Bar Chart

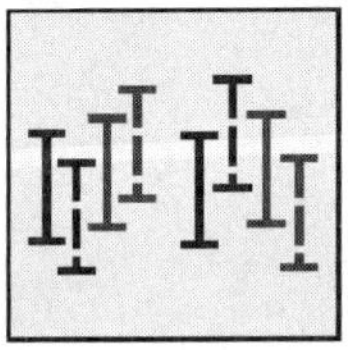

- Drag a categorical variable to the *x1* axis.
- Drag a scale variable to the *y* axis.
- Drag categorical variables to Color, Style, or both.

### To Create a 3-D Error Bar Chart

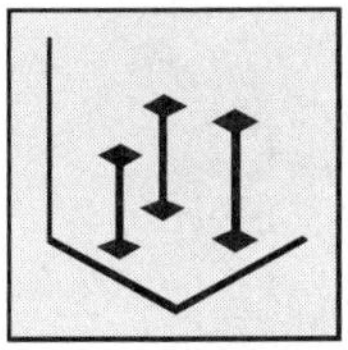

- Select 3-D Coordinate from the drop-down list.

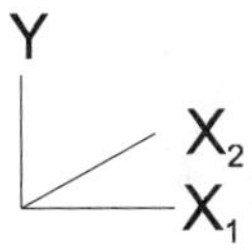


- Drag a scale variable to the *y* axis.
- Drag categorical variables to the *x1* and *x2* axes.

### To Create an Error Bar Chart with Colors Assigned by a Summary of a Scale Variable

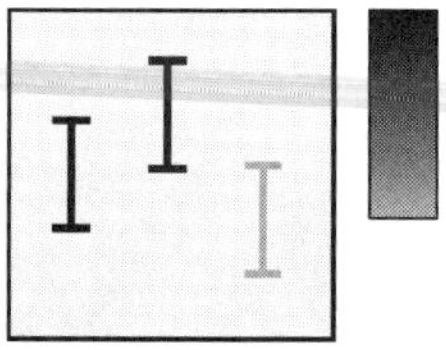

- Drag a categorical variable to the *x1* axis.
- Drag a scale variable to the *y* axis.
- Drag a scale variable to Color.

  The color of each error bar indicates the mean of the legend color variable for the category represented by the error bar.

### To Create Error Bar Panels for Categories

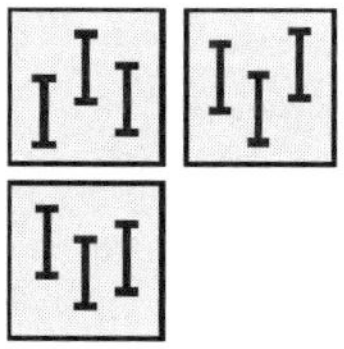

- Drag a variable to the *x1* axis.
- Drag a scale variable to the *y* axis.
- Drag one or more categorical variables to Panel Variables.

## Create Error Bar Chart: Error Bars

Figure 6-2
*Create Error Bar Chart: Error Bars tab*

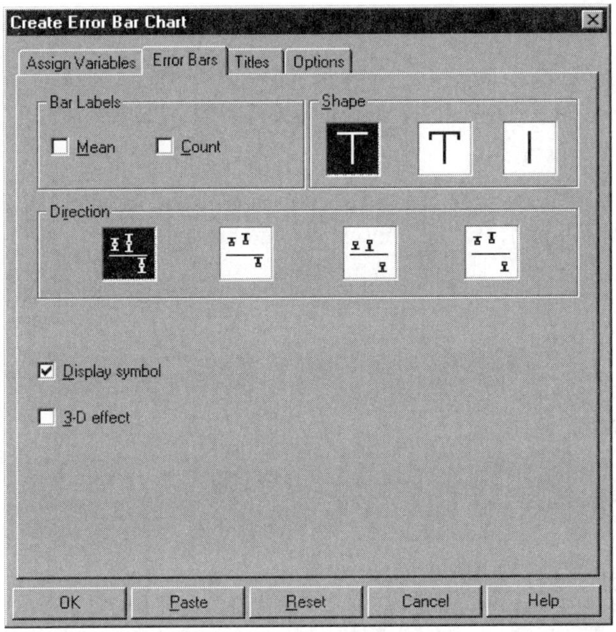


Several options are available to enhance error bar charts.

**Bar Labels.** The number of cases (count) and the value of the mean can be displayed.

**Direction.** Arranges the error bars. Error bars can show the part above the mean, the part below the mean, or both. Error bars can also be based on values above or below the baseline.

**Shape.** Various shapes are available for the caps at the ends of the error bars.

**Display symbol.** Determines whether a marker is displayed at the mean value for each error bar.

# Modifying Error Bars

To modify the error bar element (all error bars) in an existing chart:

▶ From the menus choose:

Format
  Graph Elements
    Error Bar

*or*

▶ Right-click an error bar and from the context menu choose:

Error Bars...

▶ Select the desired changes.

## Error Bar: Error Bar Options

Figure 6-3
*Error Bar: Error Bar Options tab*

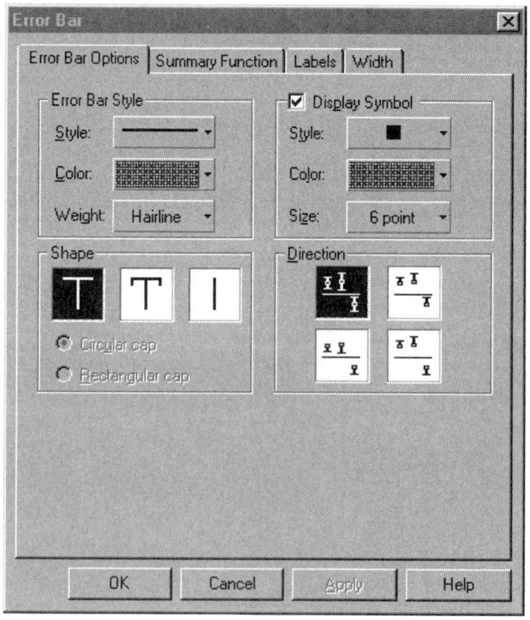

Several options are available to enhance error bars.

**Error Bar Style.** Changes the style, color, or weight for all error bars in the chart. If the color or style is controlled by the data, you cannot change them with this option.

**Display Symbol.** Changes the symbol marker, color, and size of the symbols at the mean values. If the color or style is controlled by the data, you cannot change them with this option.

**Shape.** Various shapes are available for the caps on the ends of the error bars.

**Direction.** Arranges the error bars. Error bars can show the part above the mean, the part below the mean, or both. Error bars can also be based on values above or below the baseline.

## *Error Bar: Summary Function*

Figure 6-4
*Error Bar: Summary Function tab*

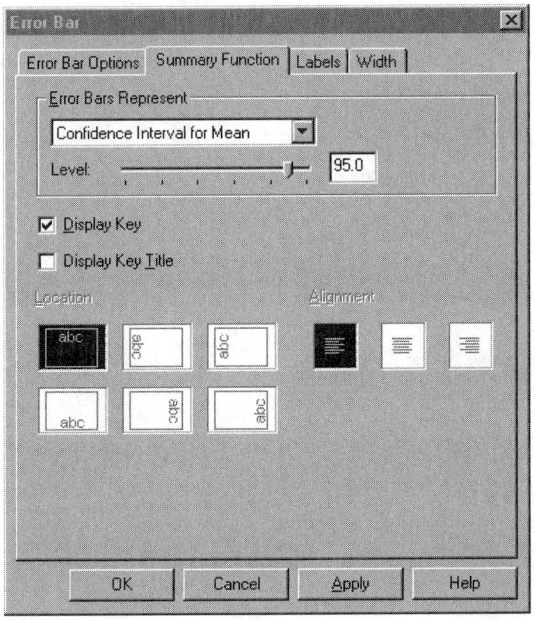


**Error Bars Represent.** Lists the statistics available for determining the lengths of the error bars. On a confidence interval for the mean, you can specify a percentage for the level. The number of standard deviations or standard errors represented is determined by the multiplier, which can be any number greater than 0 and less than or equal to 6.

**Display key options.** These selections change the way summary information is displayed in the chart. You can display the key and determine the alignment and location of the key title.

## Error Bar: Labels

Figure 6-5
*Error Bar: Labels tab*

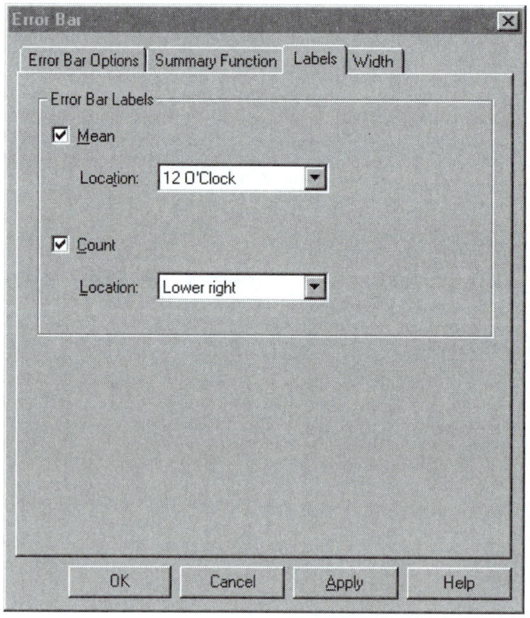


Labels can be displayed that show the values of the count or mean for each category. Each type of label can have its own location within the chart.

## Error Bar: Width

Figure 6-6
*Error Bar: Width tab*

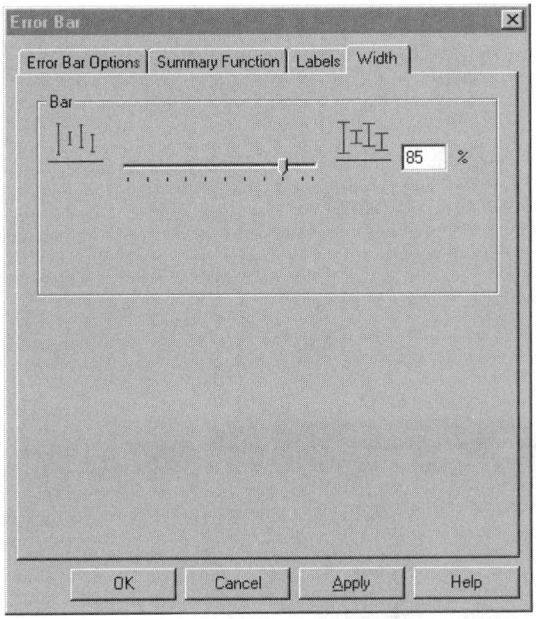


After error bars are created, you can change the width of the bar caps or the width of clusters by dragging the slider.

# Changing Error Bar Properties

Individual error bars or a selection of several error bars have a style, symbol, and labels that can be changed as long as the property is not controlled by the data.

### To Change Error Bar Properties

▶ Select one or more error bars.

▶ From the menus choose:

Format
  Properties...

*or*

▶ Right-click an error bar or selected group of error bars and choose Properties.

Optionally, you can:

- Change the line style or symbol.
- Turn labels and their connectors on or off.

## Error Bar Properties

Figure 6-7
*Error Bar Properties dialog box*

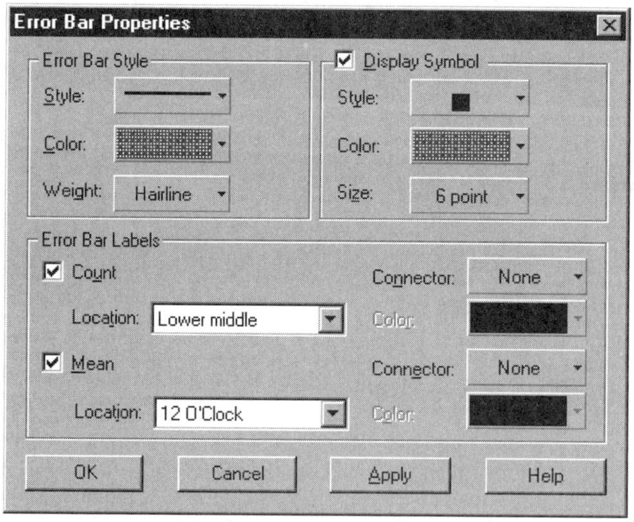


The properties apply only to currently selected error bars.

**Error Bar Style.** The style, color, and weight of the selected error bars can be changed, if they are not controlled by the data.

**Display Symbol.** A symbol style can be selected and its color and size specified. This symbol is at the mean value.

**Error Bar Labels.** Bar labels can be turned on or off and their locations specified. For each type of label, the connector style and color can be specified.

Chapter

**7**

# Histograms

Often, an investigator wants to know how data are distributed across a range of values. A **histogram** shows the distribution of values in a quantitative variable by dividing the range into equally spaced intervals and plotting the count of cases in each interval as a bar. Instead of the count of cases, you can also plot the percentage. A cumulative option is also available.

## Sample Output

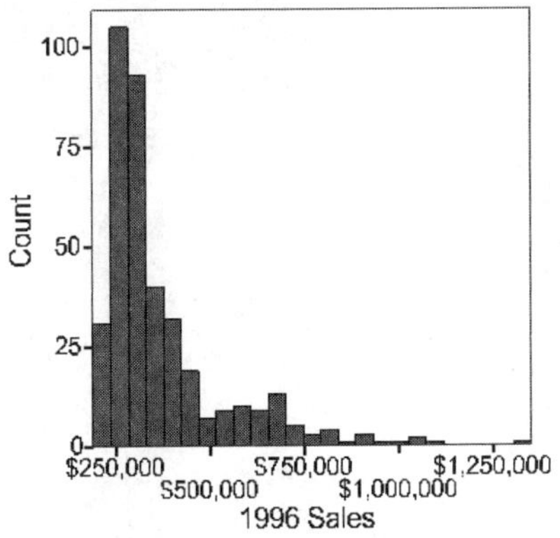


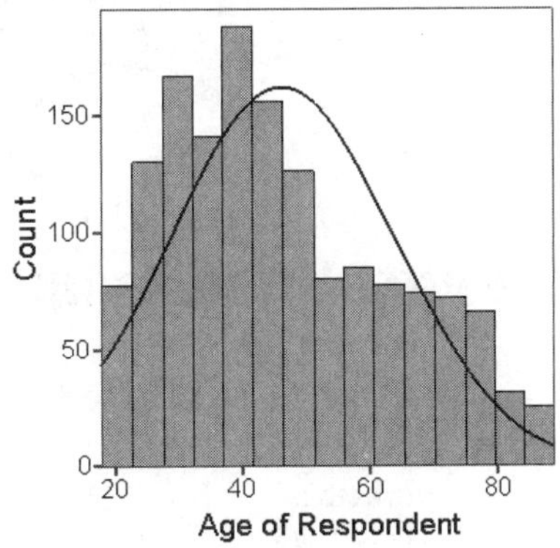

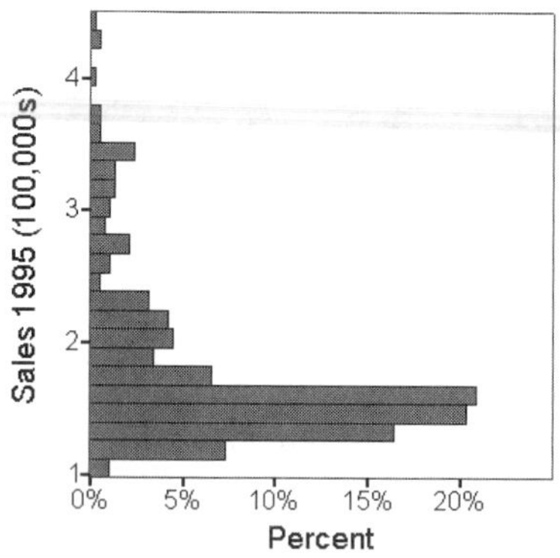


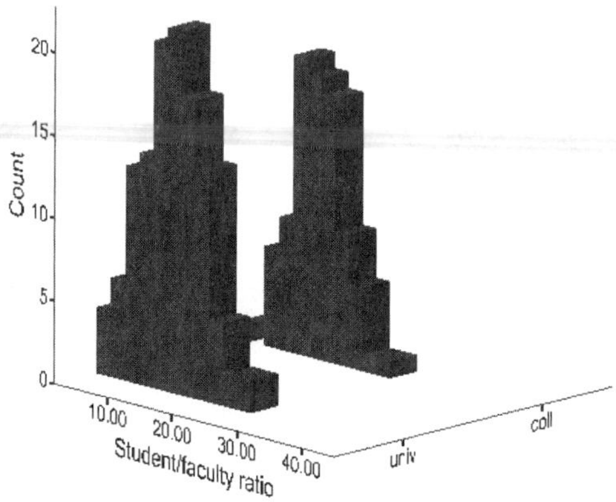


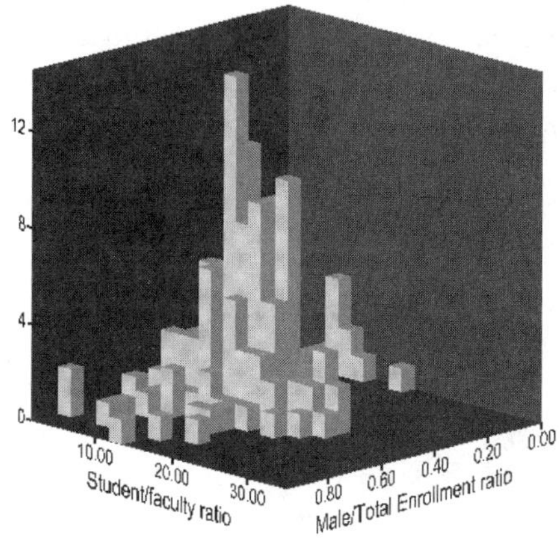


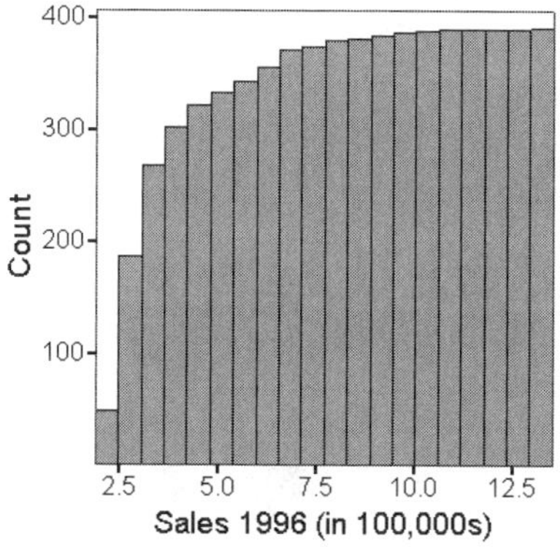


# To Create a Histogram

► From the menus choose:

Graphs
  Interactive
    Histogram...

## *Create Histogram: Assign Variables*

Figure 7-1
*Create Histogram: Assign Variables tab*

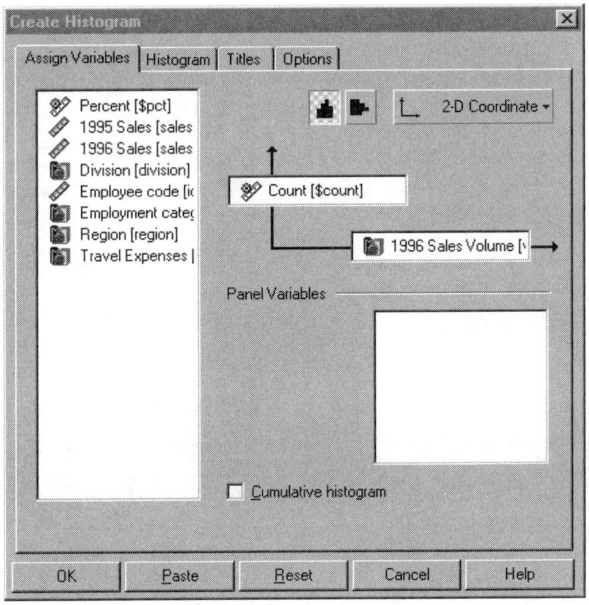


A histogram groups the values of a variable into evenly spaced groups (intervals or bins) and plots a count of the number of cases in each group. The count can be expressed as a percentage. Percentages are useful for comparing data sets of different sizes. The count or percentage can also be accumulated across the groups.

A histogram can indicate outliers and deviations from symmetry. Such deviations can indicate that a variable is unsuitable for analysis by a procedure that assumes a normal distribution.

**Number of dimensions.** Selecting 2-D Coordinate or 3-D Coordinate changes the number of axis targets for variable selection. Selecting 3-D Effect specifies that the histograms are three-dimensional objects.

**Orientation.** Clicking an orientation (vertical or horizontal) icon sets up the appropriate axis targets for variable selection. Orientation icons are available only when 2-D Coordinate is selected.

**Vertical**

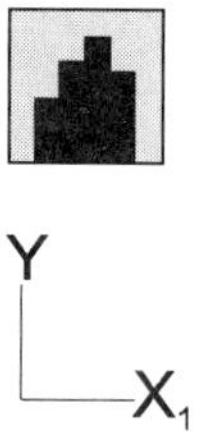


**Horizontal**

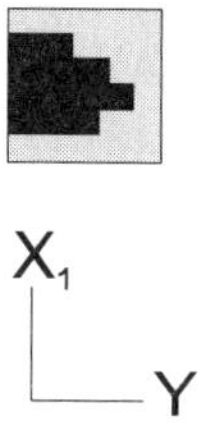


**Variables.** Only *Count* or *Percent* can be assigned to the *y* axis. For the *x1* axis, assign a scale variable.

**Cumulative histogram.** In a cumulative histogram, each bar represents the sum of the previous intervals plus the current interval.

### *To Create a Simple Histogram*

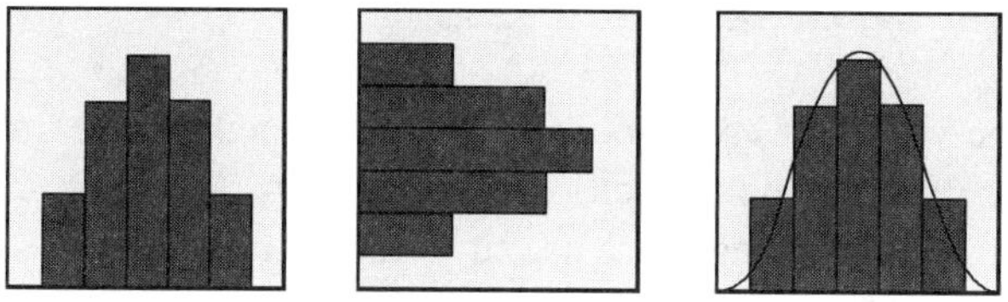

- ▶ Select the vertical or horizontal orientation icon.
- ▶ Drag *Count* to the *y* axis (if it is not there by default).
- ▶ Drag a scale variable to the *x1* axis.

Optionally, you can:

- Add a normal curve (Histogram tab).
- Swap the axes by clicking the orientation icon. Previously assigned variables swap, along with the axes.

- Use the built-in variable *Percent*.
- Create a cumulative histogram.

#### To Create a Categorical 3-D Histogram

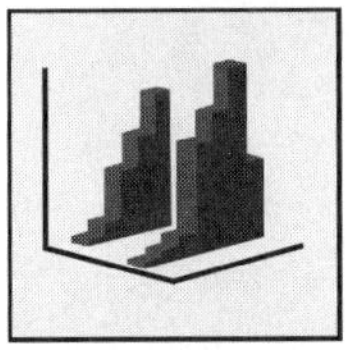

▶ Select 3-D Coordinate from the drop-down list.

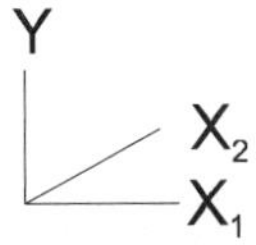


▶ Drag *Count* or *Percent* to the *y* axis.

▶ Drag a scale variable to the *x2* axis.

▶ Drag a categorical variable to the *x1* axis.

Optionally, you can:

- Assign a scale variable to *x1* and a categorical variable to *x2*.

#### To Create a Bivariate Histogram

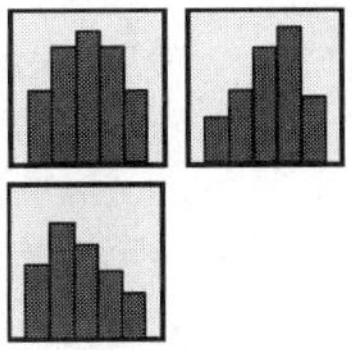

- Select 3-D Coordinate from the drop-down list.

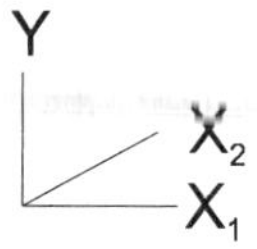


- Drag *Count* or *Percent* to the *y* axis.

- Drag scale variables to the *x1* and *x2* axes.

### To Create a Cumulative Histogram

- Drag *Count* or *Percent* to the *y* axis.

- Drag a scale variable to the *x1* axis.

- Select Cumulative histogram.

### To Create Histogram Panels for Categories

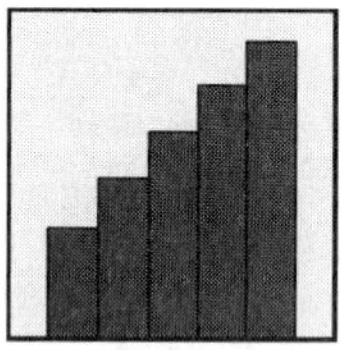

- Drag a scale variable to the *x1* axis.

- Drag *Count* or *Percent* to the *y* axis.

▶ Drag one or more categorical variables to Panel Variables.

## Create Histogram: Histogram

Figure 7-2
*Histogram tab*

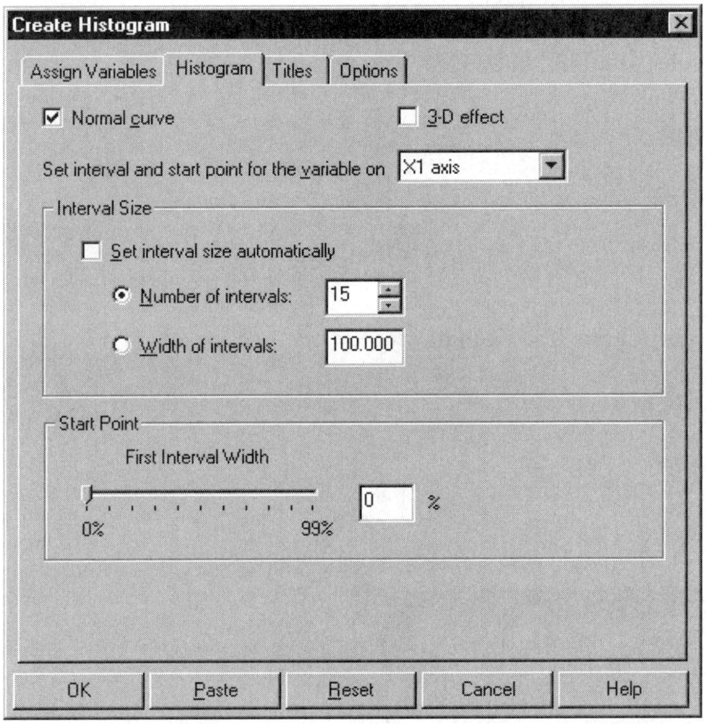


Several options are available to enhance histograms.

**Normal curve.** A normal curve can be superimposed onto the histogram, with the same mean and variance as the data. The normal curve is available only for a 2-D histogram.

**Set interval and start point for the variable.** This choice determines the axis for which you are setting the interval size and start point. If the chart is not 3-D, the settings for a second axis are ignored.

**Interval Size.** To set either the number of intervals or the width of intervals, deselect Set interval size automatically and enter the number. The maximum number of intervals is 250.

**Start Point.** The start point of the first interval can be set anywhere from the minimum scale value up to the minimum value plus the width of one interval.

# Modifying a Histogram

To modify an existing histogram element:

- ▶ Activate the chart (double-click it).
- ▶ From the menus choose:

Format
  Graph Elements
    Histogram

*or*

- ▶ Right-click a histogram and from the context menu choose:

Histogram...

## Histogram: Histogram

Figure 7-3
*Histogram tab*

Several options are available to enhance histograms.

**Fill.** The style and color of the inside of the histogram.

**Border.** (2-D only.) The appearance of the borders of the bars that make up the histogram, including the base line.

**Cumulative Histogram.** In a cumulative histogram, each bar represents the sum of the previous intervals plus the current interval.

**Normal Curve.** (2-D only.) Displays a normal curve based on the mean and variance of your data. The style, color, and weight of the normal curve can be changed.

**Interval Tool.** Changes the interval size, number, and start point for a histogram.

## *Histogram: 3-D Depth*

Figure 7-4
*Histogram 3-D Depth tab*

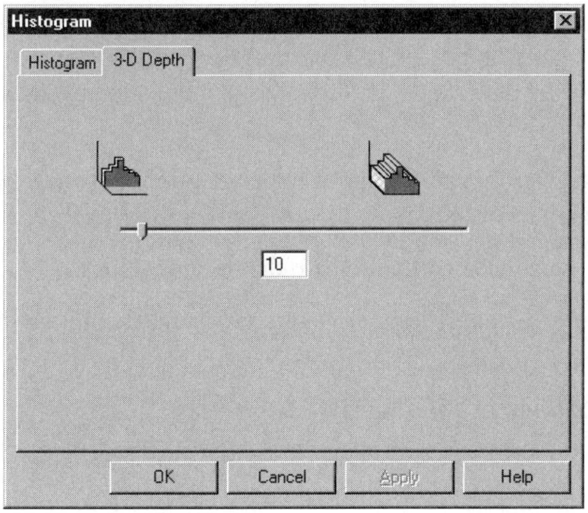


The slider controls the depth of 3-D histograms in the chart.

## Histogram: Interval Tool

Figure 7-5
*Interval Tool dialog box*

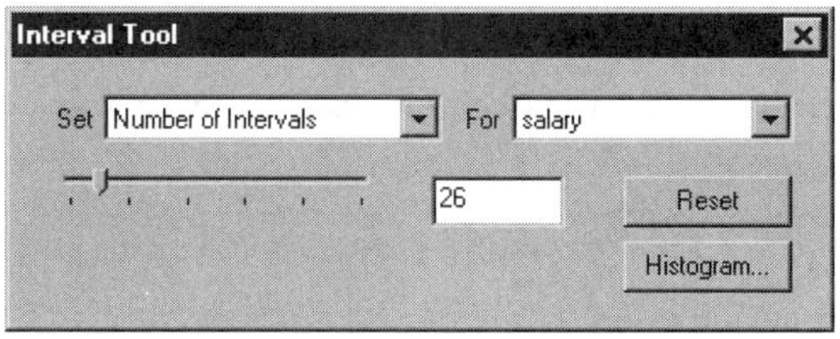


The Interval Tool dialog box is used to dynamically change the size of intervals in a histogram. You can either use the slider or enter a number. To view changes, press Enter on your keyboard.

**Set.** Using the Set drop-down list, you can specify options for the number of intervals, the interval size, and the start point of the first interval. The start point ranges from the scale minimum to the scale minimum plus the width of one interval.

You can specify from 1 to 250 intervals. If a specified interval size is not evenly divisible into the current data range, the last (partial) bar of the histogram is not displayed. If you change the data range for the interval axis, interval sizes are recomputed.

**For.** In a bivariate histogram, you can change the specifications for each axis independently by choosing a variable from the drop-down list.

**Reset.** The Reset button sets the specifications to the default values.

**Histogram.** Closes the Interval Tool dialog box and opens the Histogram dialog box.

### To Change Interval Specifications in a Histogram

- Activate the chart.

- From the menus choose:

  Edit
   Interval...

  *or*

- Right-click the histogram and choose Interval Tool.

▶ Select a variable from the For drop-down list.

▶ Choose a type of specification from the Set drop-down list.

Optionally, you can:

- Change the number of intervals.
- Change the interval size.
- Change the start point.

Press Enter to apply the new specifications.

## Changing Histogram Properties

For selected histograms you can change the fill, border, and normal curve.

### To Change Histogram Properties

▶ Select a histogram.

▶ From the menus choose:

Format
  Graph Elements
    Histogram

*or*

▶ Right-click a histogram and choose Properties.

Optionally, you can:

- Change the fill, border, or normal curve.

## Histogram Properties

Figure 7-6
*Histogram Properties dialog box*

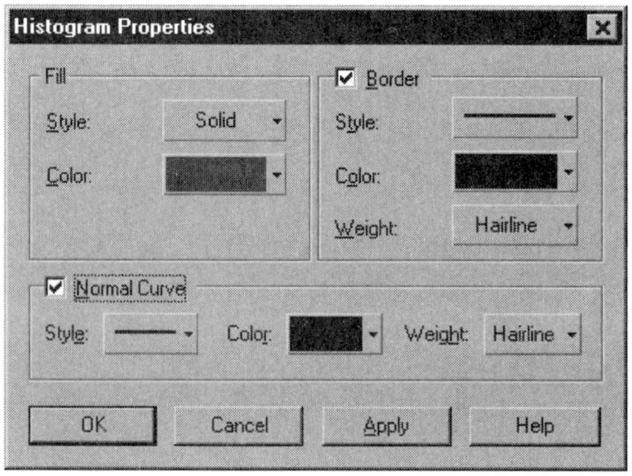


The properties listed apply only to the currently selected histogram. Single bars in the histogram cannot be selected individually.

**Fill.** The style and color of the histogram can be changed if not encoded by the data.

**Border.** The border is around the whole histogram. It can be turned on or off, and the style, weight, and color can be changed.

**Normal Curve.** If the normal curve is turned on, you can change the style, color, or weight.

Chapter

**8**

# Line, Dot, and Ribbon Charts

A dot or line chart usually presents a summary function plotted against a categorical variable. A point is plotted for each value of the category variable. In a line chart, the points are connected by lines. A line chart is often used when the category axis is defined by an ordered series, although the points can represent any set of values.

The data can be connected with lines (ribbons in 3-D), and dot symbols can be displayed at the plotted points. Multiple-line charts can have drop lines connecting the categories. In a drop-line chart, the dots in each category are connected by a line.

## Sample Output

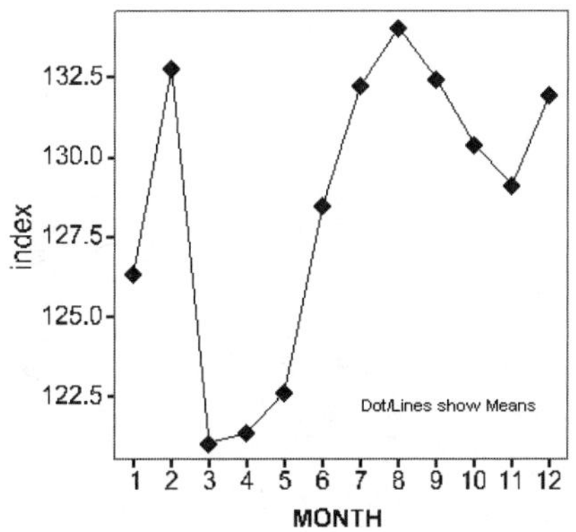


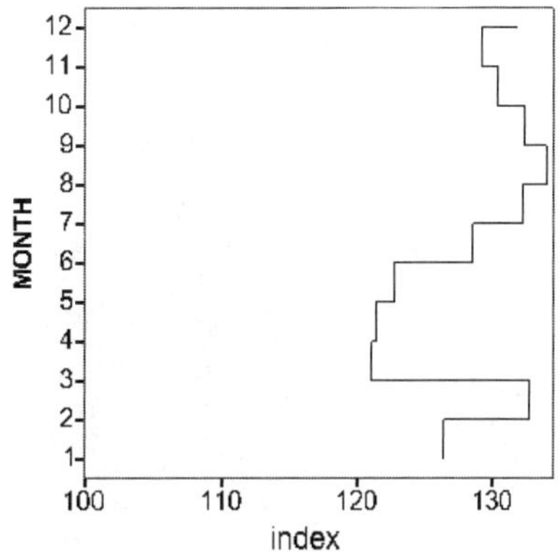

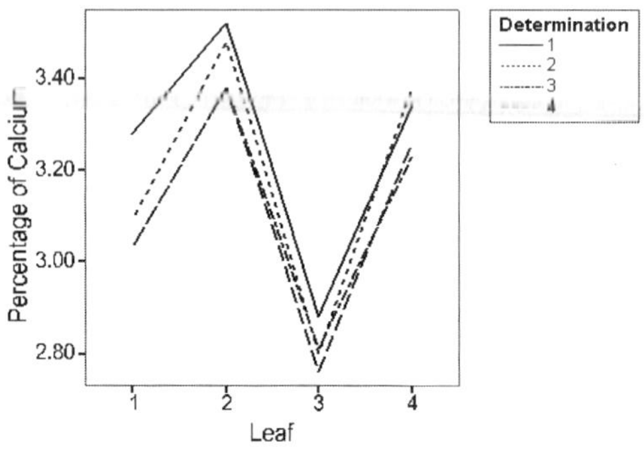
Determination
1
2
3
4
Percentage of Calcium
Leaf

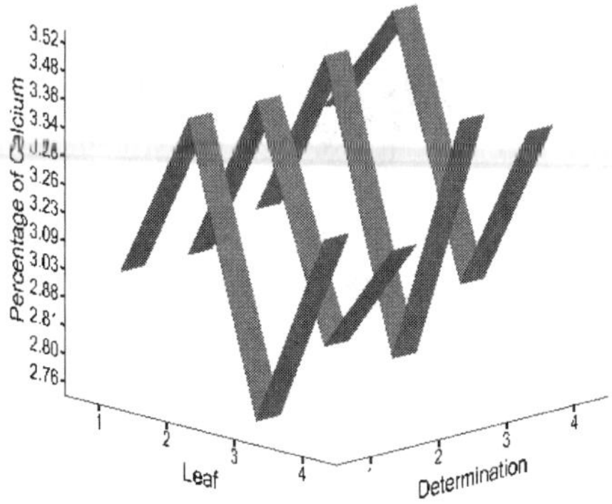
Percentage of Calcium
Leaf
Determination

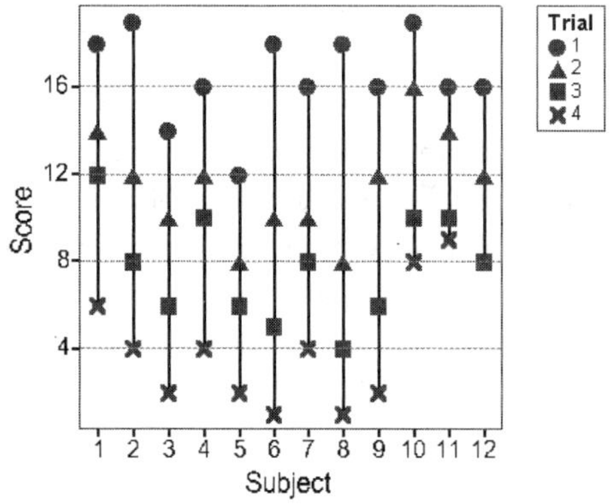
Trial
1
2
3
4
Score
Subject

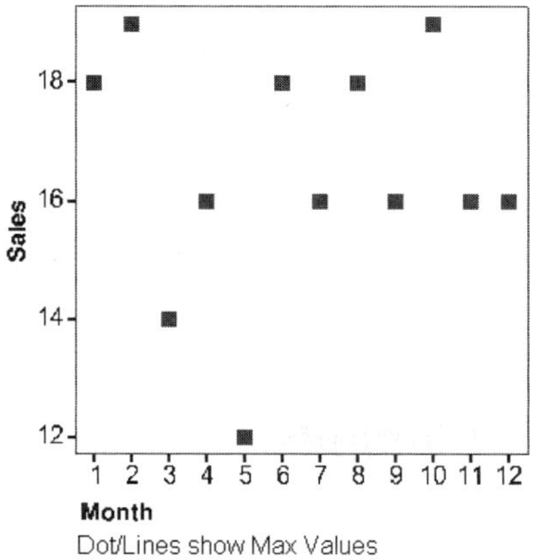
Sales
Month
Dot/Lines show Max Values

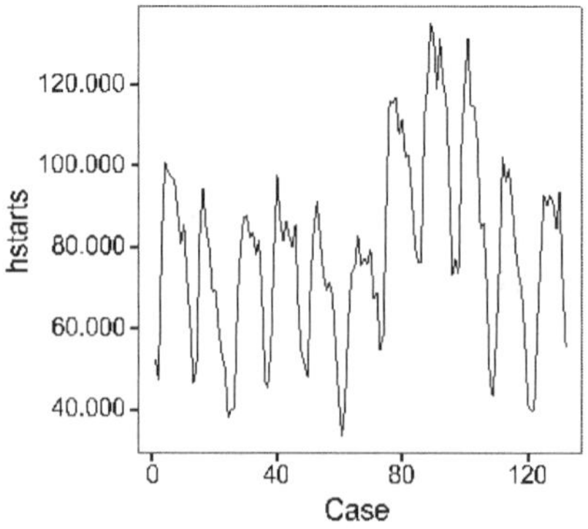
hstarts
Case

# To Create a Line or Dot Chart

▶ From the menus choose:

Graphs
 Interactive
  Line...

Related options include Dot, Ribbon, and Drop-Line.

# Create Dots, Lines, Ribbons, or Drop Lines: Assign Variables

Figure 8-1
*Create Lines: Assign Variables tab*

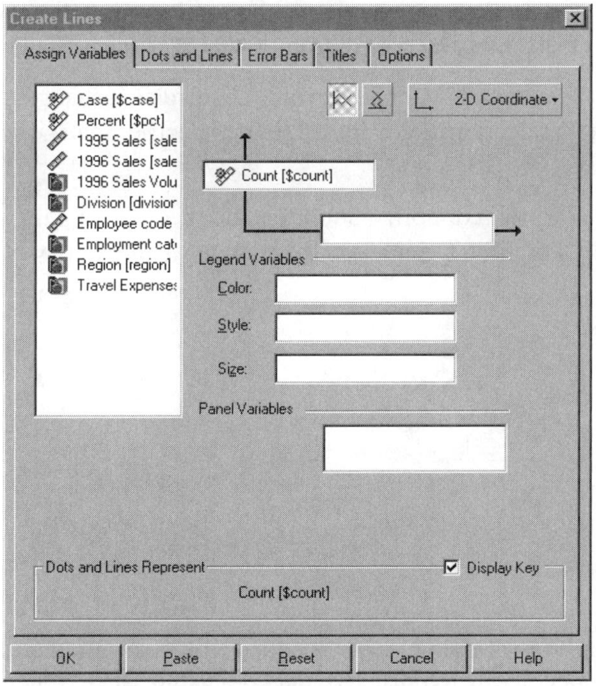


Dot charts, line charts, ribbon charts, and drop-line charts are all created by similar methods.

**Lines.** A line chart summarizes categories of one or more variables. Line charts tend to emphasize flow or movement instead of individual values. They are commonly used to display data over time and therefore can be used to give a good sense of trends. Line charts are especially effective for presenting a large number of values in a compact space. Dots can be displayed at the data points.

**Dots.** The display can show dots at the data points, lines connecting the points, or both dots and lines.

**Ribbons.** A ribbon chart is similar to a line chart, with the lines displayed as ribbons in a third dimension. Ribbon charts can be two-dimensional (displayed with a 3-D effect) or three-dimensional.

**Drop Lines.** For multiple-line or dot charts, where a category variable is assigned to Color or Style, drop lines are available between color or style dots in the same axis category.

**Summary function.** For a dependent scale variable, the summary function can be changed from the Dots and Lines Represent drop-down list.

**Number of dimensions.** Selecting 2-D Coordinate or 3-D Coordinate changes the number of axis targets for variable selection. Selecting 3-D Effect specifies that the lines become ribbons.

**Orientation.** Clicking the vertical or horizontal orientation icon sets up the appropriate axis targets for variable selection. Orientation icons are available only when 2-D Coordinate is selected.

**Vertical**

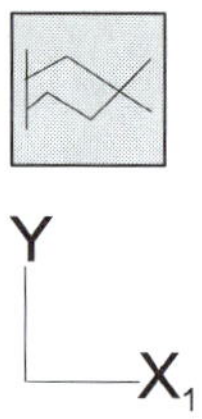


**Horizontal**

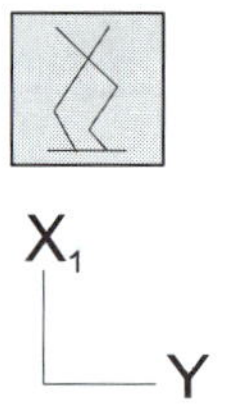


**Case Variable.** If the built-in variable *Case* is assigned to an axis, another target becomes available where you can assign a variable for labeling cases. For example, the labels might be days of the week or months.

### *To Create a Simple Line or Dot Chart*

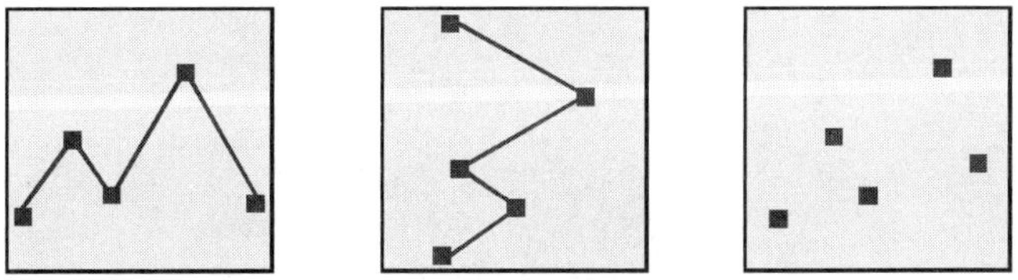

- ▶ Drag a variable (often categorical) to the *x1* axis.

- ▶ Drag *Count, Percent,* or a scale variable to the *y* axis (if one is not already there by default).

  Optionally, you can:

  - Swap the axes by clicking the orientation icon. The currently assigned variables swap with the axes.
  - Display dots or lines or both (in the Dots and Lines tab).

### *To Create a Line Chart Summarizing a Scale Variable*

- ▶ Drag a scale variable to the *y* axis.

- ▶ Drag a variable (often categorical) to the *x1* axis.

  By default, the points represent the mean of the scale variable. Optionally, you can select another summary function in the Dots and Lines Represent drop-down list.

### To Create a Multiple-Line Chart

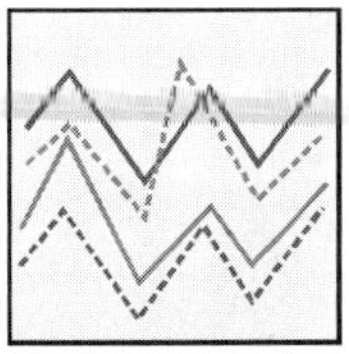

- Drag a variable (often categorical) to the *x1* axis.
- Drag another variable to the *y* axis.
- Drag a categorical variable to Color or Style or Size.

  Size can apply to symbol size for dots or line weight for lines.

### To Create a Line or Dot Chart of Individual Cases

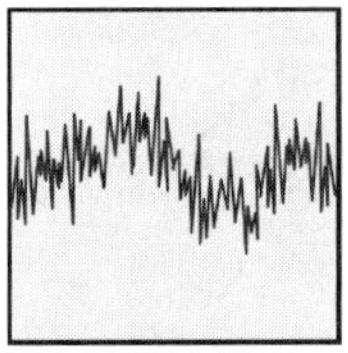

- Drag *Cases* to the *x1* axis.
- Drag a variable (usually a scale variable) to the *y* axis.

  *Note*: Charts that display values for individual cases are meaningful only if you select a summary variable for the dependent (*y*) axis. Summary functions such as mean, median, or mode will result in dots or points on a line that display the value of the summary variable for each case. Counts, percentages, and summary functions that represent the number of cases or percentage of cases above or below a specified value will not reveal any particularly useful information when charting cases, since every case has a count of exactly 1.

### *To Create a Drop-Line Chart*

▶ From the menus choose:

Graphs
  Interactive
    Drop-Line...

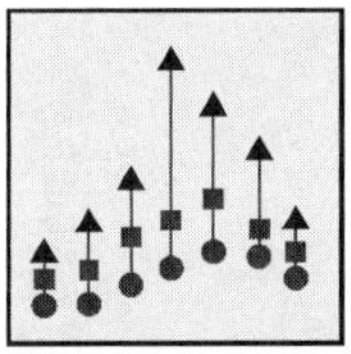

▶ Drag a variable (often categorical) to the *x1* axis.

▶ Drag *Count*, *Percent*, or a scale variable to the *y* axis (if one is not already there by default).

▶ Drag a categorical variable to Color, Style, or Size.

▶ On the Dots and Lines tab, select Drop Lines.

### *To Create a 2-D Ribbon Chart*

▶ From the menus choose:

Graphs
  Interactive
    Ribbon...

▶ Drag a variable (usually categorical) to the *x1* axis.

▶ Drag *Count, Percent,* or a scale variable to the *y* axis (if one is not already there by default).

Optionally, you can:

- Swap the axes by clicking the orientation icon. The currently assigned variables swap with the axes.
- Display dots (Ribbons tab).
- Change the interpolation style (Ribbons tab).

#### To Create a 3-D Ribbon Chart

- From the menus choose:

  Graphs
    Interactive
      Ribbon...

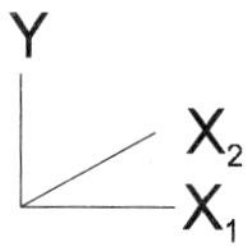


- Select 3-D Coordinate from the drop-down list.
- Drag variables to the *x1* and *x2* axes.
- Drag *Count* or another variable to the *y* axis (if one is not already there by default).

#### To Create Line or Dot Chart Panels for Categories

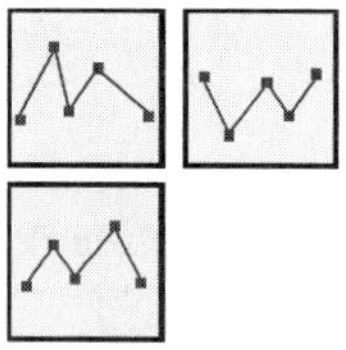

- Drag a categorical variable to the *x1* axis.
- Drag a scale variable or a built-in variable to the *y* axis.
- Drag one or more categorical variables to Panel Variables.

## Dots and Lines

Figure 8-2
*Create Lines: Dots and Lines tab*

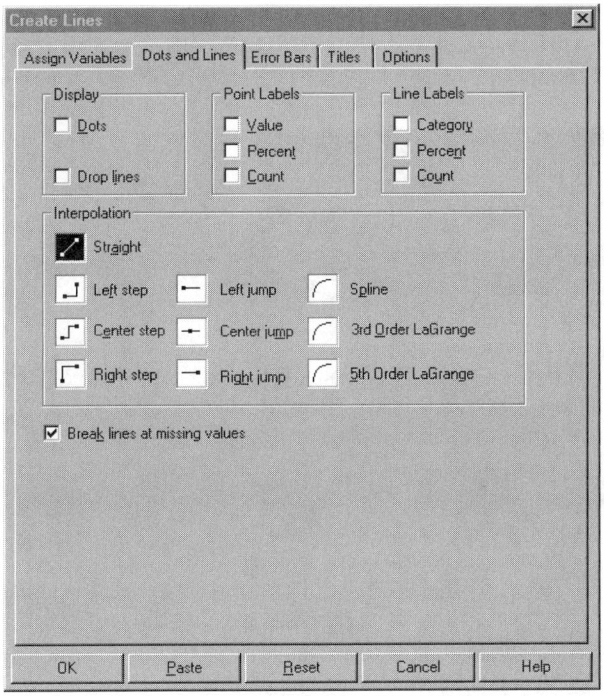


Several options are available to enhance dot, line, and ribbon charts.

**Display.** Dots, lines, or both can be displayed. The choices depend on the type of chart. Drop lines join the points in a single category on a multiple-line chart.

**Point Labels and Line Labels.** Point labels display the number of cases, percentage of cases, or the value represented by the distance of the point from the axis. Labels for each line are also available, showing the category, percentage, or count.

**Interpolation.** Controls how the lines are drawn between data points. Choices include straight lines; left, center, and right steps (horizontal lines through the points, with risers); and left, center, and right jumps (no risers). Also available are spline, 3$^{rd}$ order LaGrange, and 5$^{th}$ order LaGrange lines.

**Break lines at missing values.** With this option selected, lines are not drawn through categories that have no values.

## Create Line Chart: Error Bars

Figure 8-3
*Create Line Chart: Error Bars tab*

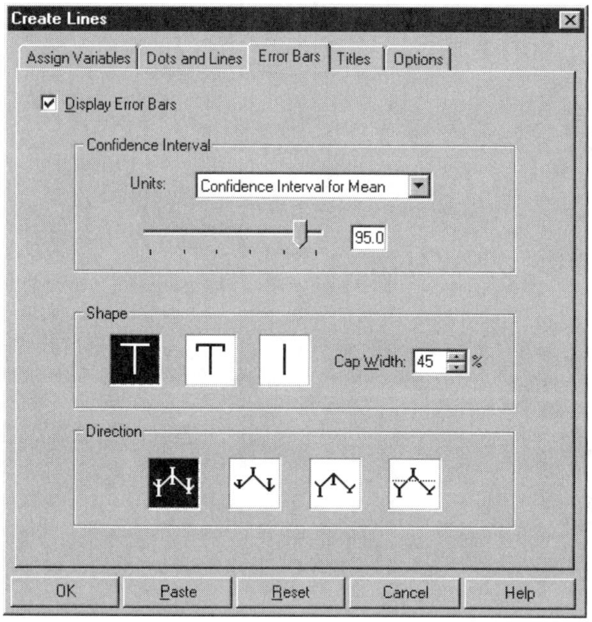


**Error bars**, indicating the variability of the measure displayed, are available when the dependent variable is a scale variable, and bars or lines represent the summary function *Means*. The length of an error bar represents the amount of variability. The length of the error bars is displayed as the lower and upper limits of a confidence interval (at a specified percentage level) or in standard deviations or standard errors of the mean.

You can specify the confidence interval's level, direction, and shape, and change the appearance of error bars.

# Modifying Dots, Lines, and Ribbons

To modify the lines and dots element (all lines, dots, and ribbons) in an existing chart:

- Activate the chart (double-click it).
- From the menus choose:

  Format
  Graph Elements
  Line

  *or*

- Right-click a line or dot, and from the context menu choose:

  Dots and Lines...

- Select the desired options.

## Dots and Lines: Options

Figure 8-4
*Dots and Lines: Options tab*

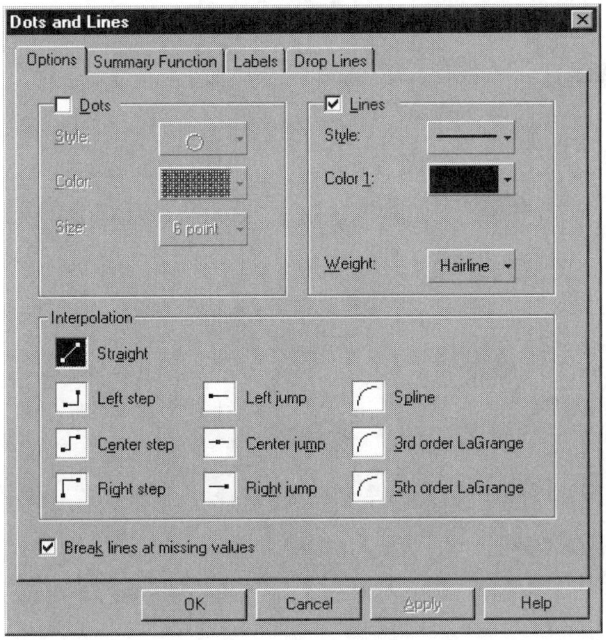

Several options are available for lines, dots, and ribbons.

**Dots.** The dots can be turned on or off. The style, color, and size can be changed if they have not been locked by variable assignments.

**Lines.** The lines can be turned on or off. The style, color, and weight can be changed if they have not been locked by variable assignments.

**Interpolation.** Controls how the lines are drawn between data points. Choices include straight lines; left, center, and right steps (horizontal lines through the points, with risers); and left, center, and right jumps (no risers). Also available are spline, 3$^{rd}$ order LaGrange, and 5$^{th}$ order LaGrange lines.

**Break lines at missing values.** With this option selected, lines are not drawn through categories that have no values.

## Dots and Lines: Summary Function

Figure 8-5
*Dots and Lines: Summary Function tab*

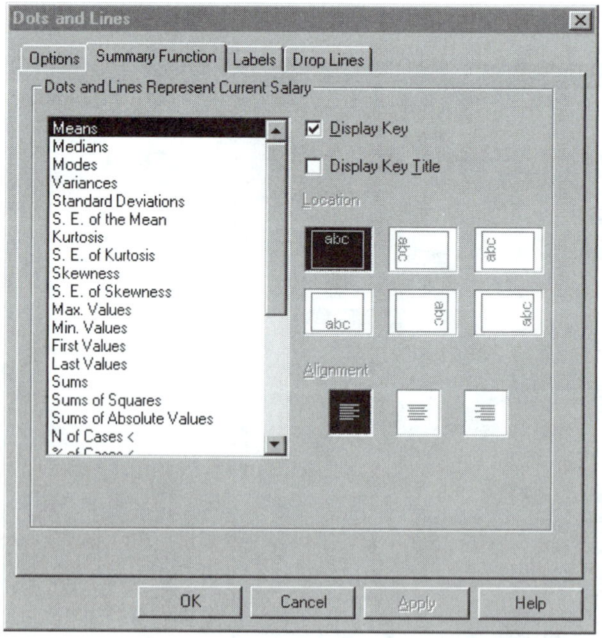

For an existing chart, if there is a scale variable on the dependent axis, you can change the summary function. For example, if the original lines represent the *Means* of a variable, you can change to the *Maximum values* of the same variable.

**Display key options**. These selections change the way summary information is displayed in the chart. You can display the key and determine the alignment and location of the key title.

## Dots and Lines: Labels

Figure 8-6
*Dots and Lines: Labels tab*

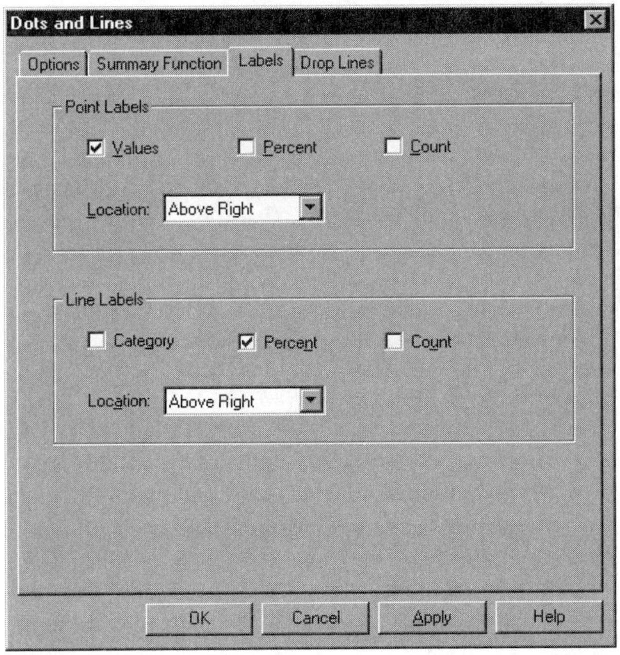


**Point Labels.** Value, percentage, and count labels can be displayed for data points.

**Line Labels.** Category, percentage, and count labels can be displayed for lines.

You can specify the position of the labels with respect to the points or lines.

## Dots and Lines: Drop Lines

Figure 8-7
*Dots and Lines: Drop Lines tab*

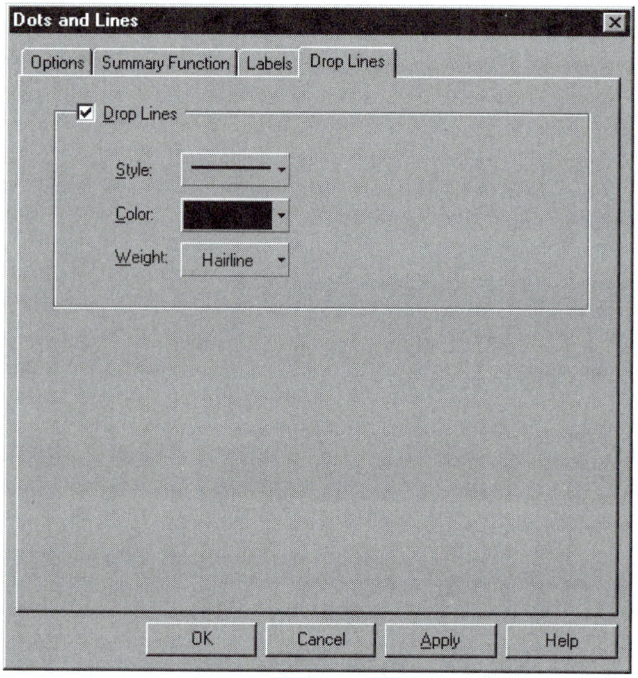


On a multiple-line chart, drop lines connect the points in each category across lines. Drop lines can be displayed or hidden. The style, color, and weight can be specified. Drop lines are not available when a scale variable is on the independent axis.

## Dots and Lines: Ribbon Width

Figure 8-8
*Dots and Lines: Ribbon Width tab*

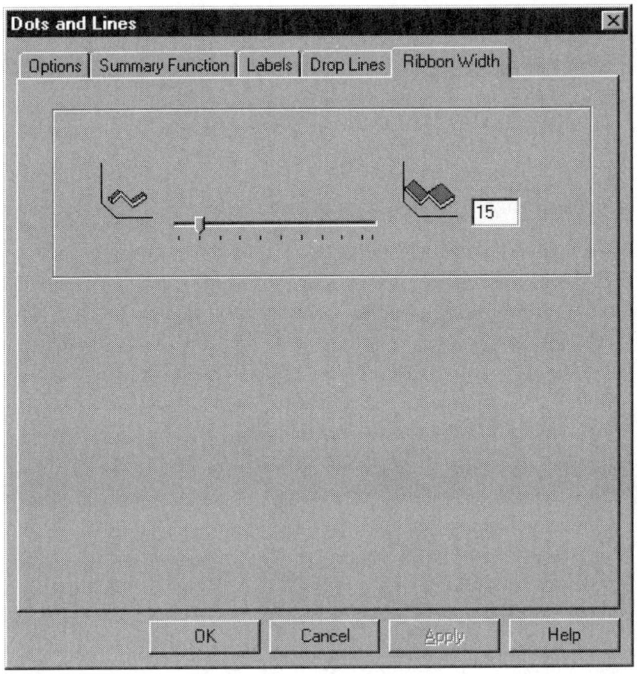


For three-dimensional line or ribbon charts, you can change the width of the ribbons.

### To Change Line, Dot, or Ribbon Properties

A line or ribbon or dot set, or a selection of several lines or ribbons and dot sets, have properties that can be changed, as long as the property is not controlled by the data.

▶ Select one or more lines, ribbons, or dot sets in a line, ribbon, or dot chart.

▶ From the menus choose:

Edit
 Line Properties

*or*

▶ Right-click a line, dot, or ribbon (or selected group), and choose Properties from the context menu.

Optionally, you can:

- Change the line appearance and dot appearance.
- Change line labels and dot labels.

## Dot and Line Properties

Figure 8-9
*Dot and Line Properties dialog box*

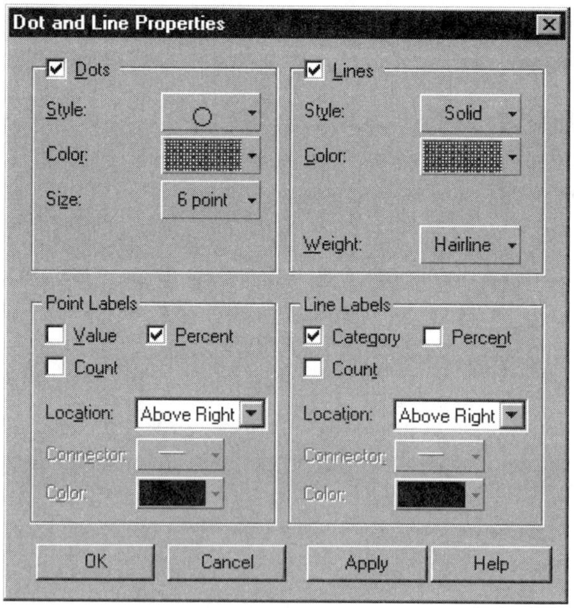

The properties listed here apply only to the lines, ribbons, or dot sets that are currently selected. A dot set consists of all of the dots that fall on the same line, whether or not the line is displayed.

**Dots.** Changes the style, color, and size of selected dot sets.

**Lines.** Changes the style, color, and weight of selected lines.

**Point Labels.** Displays the value represented by each data point. Also, labels can be displayed that show the number of cases used to calculate the value for each point or the percentage.

**Line Labels.** Displays the percentage or count of cases represented by the line, as well as the category.

## To Change Point Label Properties

▶ Select one or more dot labels.

▶ From the menus choose:

Edit
  Line Properties

*or*

▶ Right-click a dot label and select Properties from the context menu.

Optionally, you can:

- Change the labels displayed.
- Change the location, connector, and color of the labels.

## Point Label Properties

Figure 8-10
*Point Label Properties dialog box*

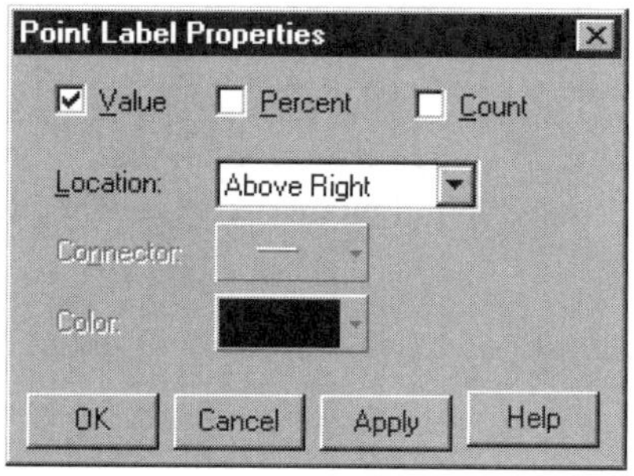


The properties listed here apply only to dot labels that are currently selected.

**Value, Percent, Count.** The display of three different labels can be selected or deselected.

**Location.** The location can be changed with respect to the selected dots.

**Connector.** The style of connector can be selected from the drop-down list.

**Color.** The color of the selected labels can be changed.

Chapter

# 9

# Pie Charts

What proportion does each group contribute to the total? A pie chart demonstrates the contribution of parts to a whole. Each slice of the pie belongs to a group defined by a category of a variable. The size of a slice is proportional to the frequency (count) of its group or to a function of a summary variable. For example, one pie chart shows the number of employees in each department, making it easy to compare relative department sizes. In another pie, each slice shows the sum of sales for individuals in a group.

To compare separate categories, pie charts can be displayed separately in **panels** or stacked in a **cluster**. In a cluster, pies of different diameters are stacked to make comparison of slices easy. In another type of display, **plotted pies,** you can plot pies for subgroups defined by combinations of categories, using Cartesian coordinates ($x$ and $y$ axes) with a pie at each intersection of categories.

## Sample Output

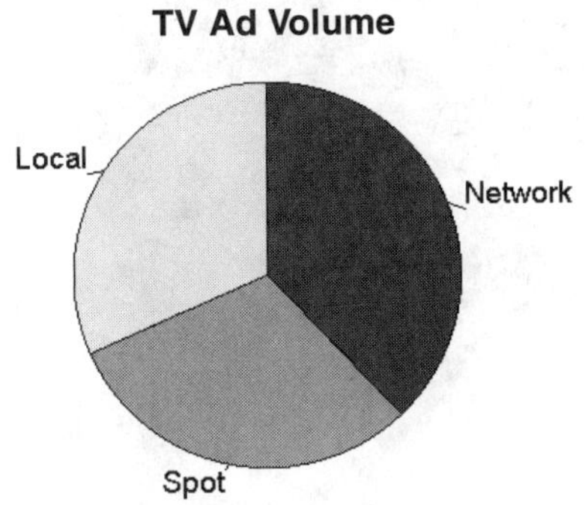


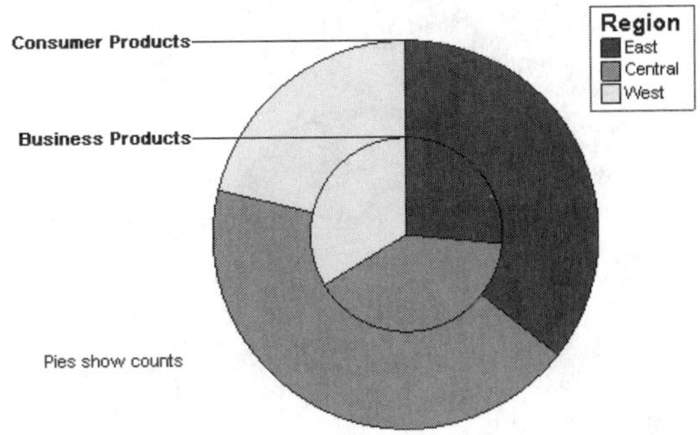

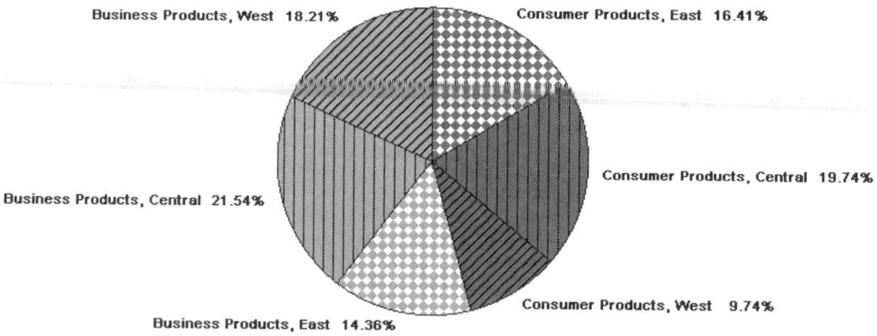
Business Products, West 18.21%
Consumer Products, East 16.41%
Consumer Products, Central 19.74%
Business Products, Central 21.54%
Consumer Products, West 9.74%
Business Products, East 14.36%

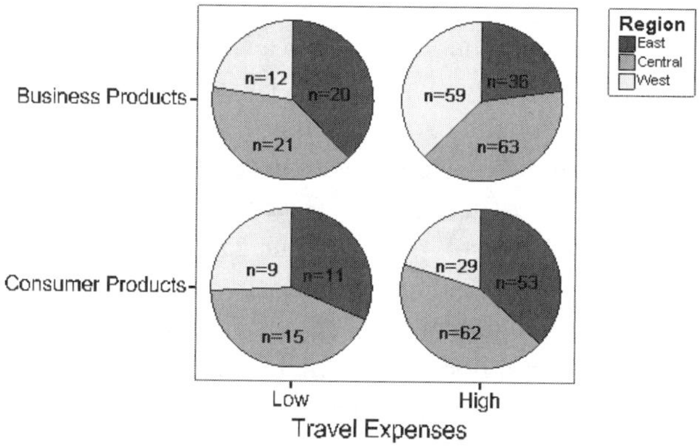
Region
East
Central
West
Business Products
n=12
n=20
n=21
n=59
n=36
n=63
Consumer Products
n=9
n=11
n=15
n=29
n=53
n=62
Low
High
Travel Expenses

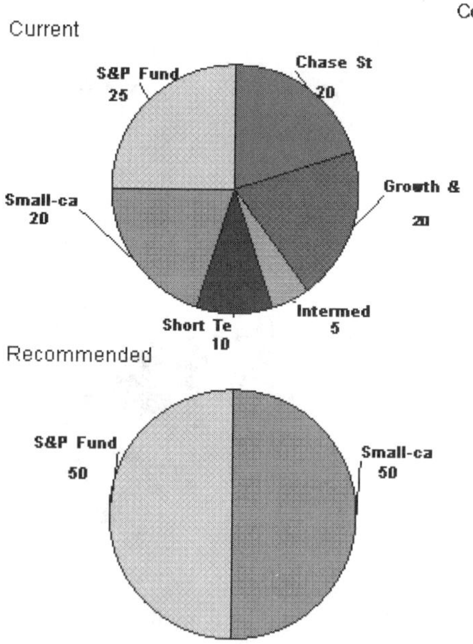
Current
S&P Fund
25
Chase St
20
Growth &
20
Small-ca
20
Short Te
10
Intermed
5
Recommended
S&P Fund
50
Small-ca
50

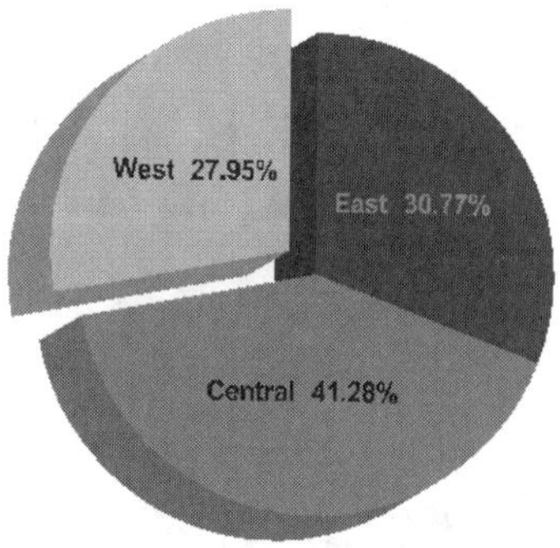
West 27.95%
East 30.77%
Central 41.28%

# To Create a Pie Chart

▶ From the menus choose:

Graphs
 Interactive
  Pie
   Simple... *or* Clustered... *or* Plotted...

## Create Simple Pie Chart: Assign Variables

Figure 9-1
*Create Simple Pie Chart: Assign Variables tab*

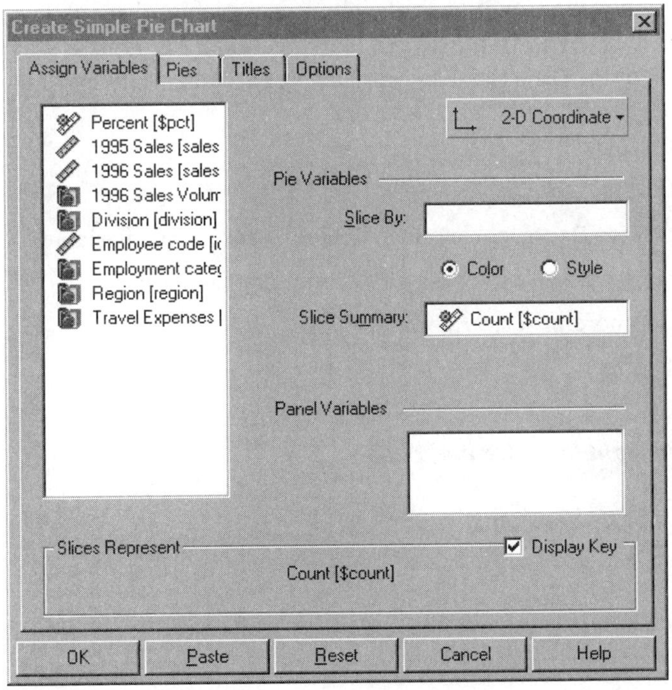


A simple pie chart summarizes categories defined by a single variable or by a group of related variables. For each category, the size of each slice represents the count, the percentage, or a summary function of a variable. You can display a key to identify the built-in or summary function. You can also create a paneled pie chart.

**3-D Effect.** Selecting this effect from the drop-down list gives the pie depth.

### To Create a Simple Pie Chart Sliced by a Categorical Variable

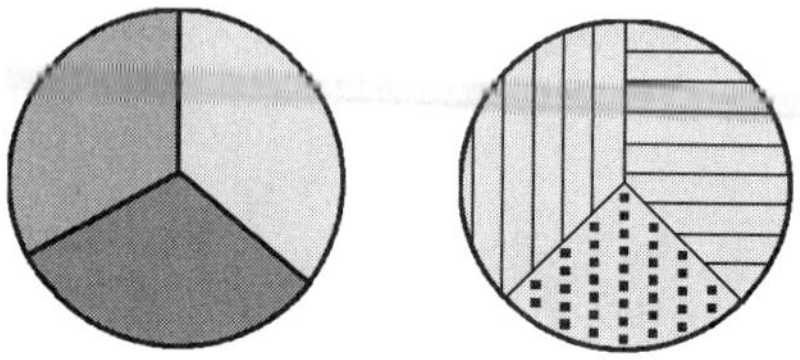

▶ Drag a categorical variable to Slice By.

▶ Drag *Count*, *Percent*, or a scale variable to Slice Summary (if it is not there by default).

In the Slice Summary, the *Count* or *Percent* built-in variables display the number of cases in each slice category or the percentage of cases. By default, a scale variable displays the sum of the Slice Summary variable in each slice category.

Optionally, you can:

- Slice by either Style or Color.
- Change the Slices Represent summary function for a scale variable.
- Display a key to identify the built-in or summary function.
- Assign one or more panel variables.
- Apply a 3-D effect.

### To Create a Pie Chart Split by Color and Style

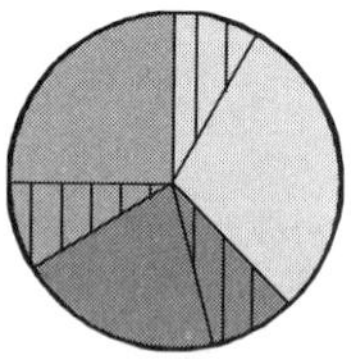

▶ Drag a category variable to Slice By and select Color.

▶ Click OK, and in the Viewer activate the pie chart (double-click it).

▶ From the menus choose:

Edit
 Assign Variables

*or*

▶ Click the Assign Graph Variables tool.

▶ Drag a categorical variable to Style.

When a pie chart is split by both color and style, the primary split is always by color. That is, the pie is first divided by color, and then each color is divided by style.

### To Create a Pie Chart Using a Scale Variable to Color Slices

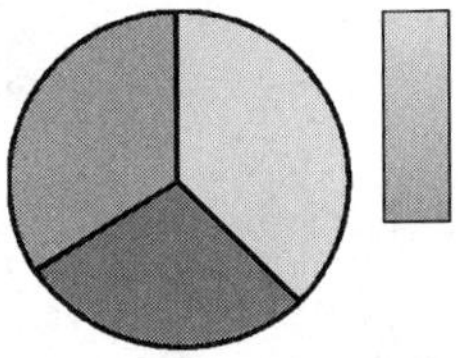

▶ Drag a categorical variable to Slice By.

▶ Select Style.

▶ Drag *Count*, *Percent*, or a scale variable to Slice Summary (if it is not there by default) and click OK.

▶ In the Viewer, activate the chart (double-click it).

▶ From the menus choose:

Edit
 Assign Variables

*or*

▶ Click the Assign Graph Variables tool.

▶ Drag a scale variable to Color.

The colors are assigned by a summary function of the scale variable (the default is *Means*).

### To Create Pie Chart Panels for Categories

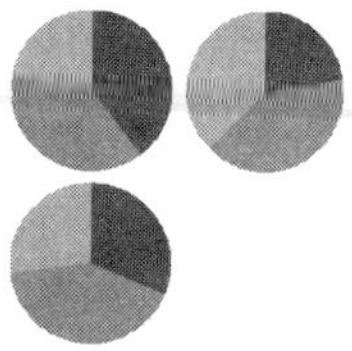

- Drag a categorical variable to Slice By.
- Drag *Count*, *Percent*, or a scale variable to Slice Summary (if it is not there by default).
- Drag one or more categorical variables to Panel Variables.

## Create Simple Pie Chart: Pies

Figure 9-2
*Create Simple Pie Chart: Pies tab*

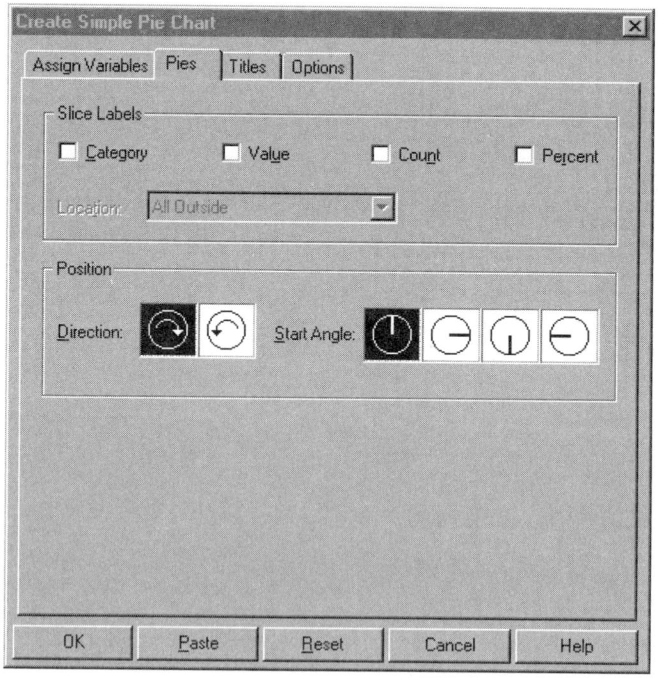

**Slice Labels.** Slices can have up to four types of labels. The initial appearance of labels is controlled in the ChartLook.

**Position.** Slices start at a position specified by a clock position: 12:00, 3:00, 6:00, or 9:00. After the first slice, the direction the slices follow is either clockwise or counterclockwise.

### *To Specify Enhancements for a New Simple Pie Chart*

- ▶ Click the Pies tab.
- ▶ Select slice labels or position.

## *Create Clustered Pie Chart: Assign Variables*

Figure 9-3
*Create Clustered Pie Chart: Assign Variables tab*

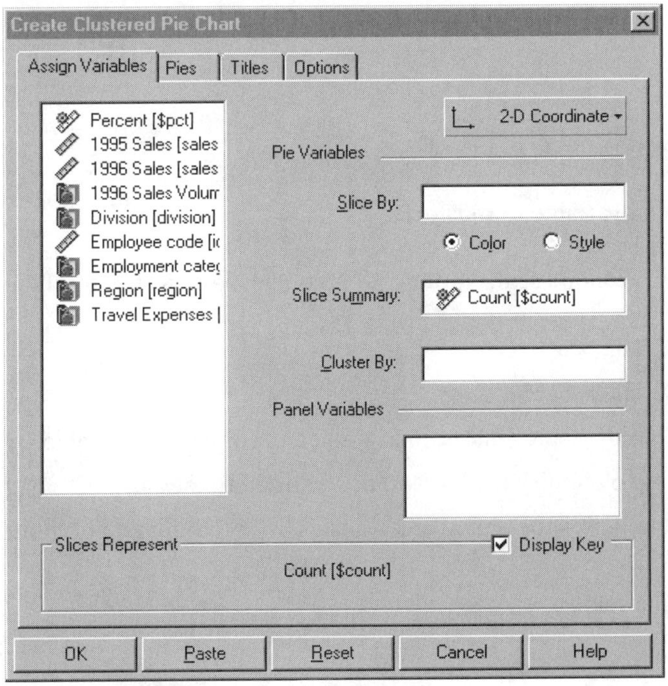

A clustered pie chart contains a cluster of simple pies, all of which are stacked into categories by the same variable. The pies are of different sizes and appear to be stacked on top of one another. The cluster contains as many pies as there are categories in the cluster variable.

The size of a slice represents the count or percentage in a category of the slice variable, or a summary function of a scale variable. You can display a key to identify the built-in or summary function. The size of slices in different pies can be compared by observing their respective angles.

**3-D Effect.** Selecting this effect from the drop-down list gives the pie depth.

▶ From the menus choose:

Graphs
 Interactive
  Pie
   Clustered...

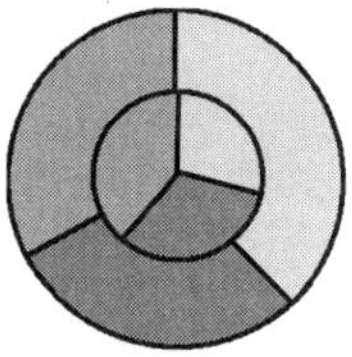

▶ Drag a categorical variable to Slice By.

▶ Drag a categorical variable to Cluster By.

▶ Drag *Count*, *Percent*, or a scale variable to Slice Summary (if it is not there by default).

Optionally, you can:

- Switch between Color and Style.
- Change the Slices Represent summary function for a scale variable.
- Display a key to identify the built-in or summary function.
- Create clustered pies for separate categories by assigning one or more categorical Panel Variables.
- Apply a 3-D effect.

# Clustered and Plotted Pie Enhancements

Figure 9-4
*Create Clustered Pie Chart: Pies tab*

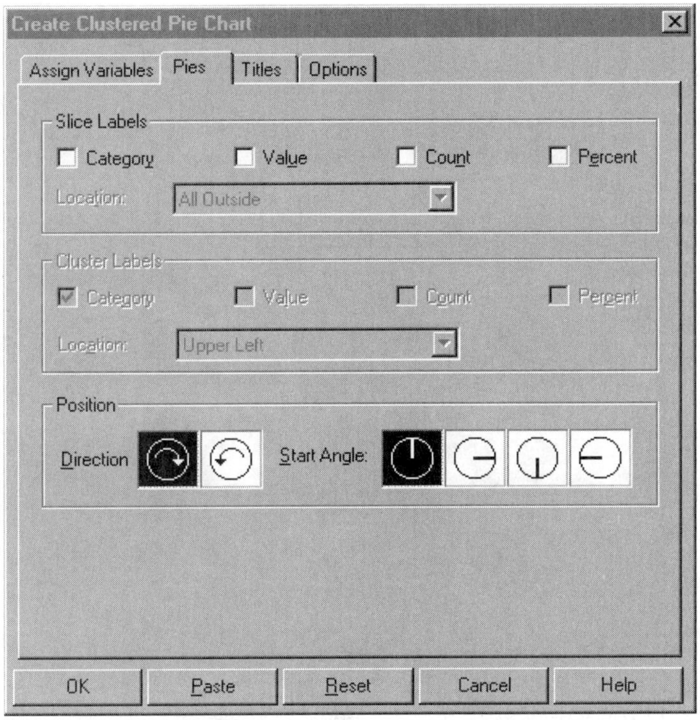


**Slice Labels.** Slices can have up to four types of labels. The initial appearance of labels is controlled in the ChartLook.

**Cluster Labels.** Labels available for each pie in a cluster include category labels, category percentage, number of cases, and category value.

**Position.** Slices start at a position specified by a clock position: 12:00, 3:00, 6:00, or 9:00. After the first slice, the direction the slices follow is either clockwise or counterclockwise.

## Create Plotted Pie Chart: Assign Variables

Figure 9-5
*Create Plotted Pie Chart: Assign Variables tab*

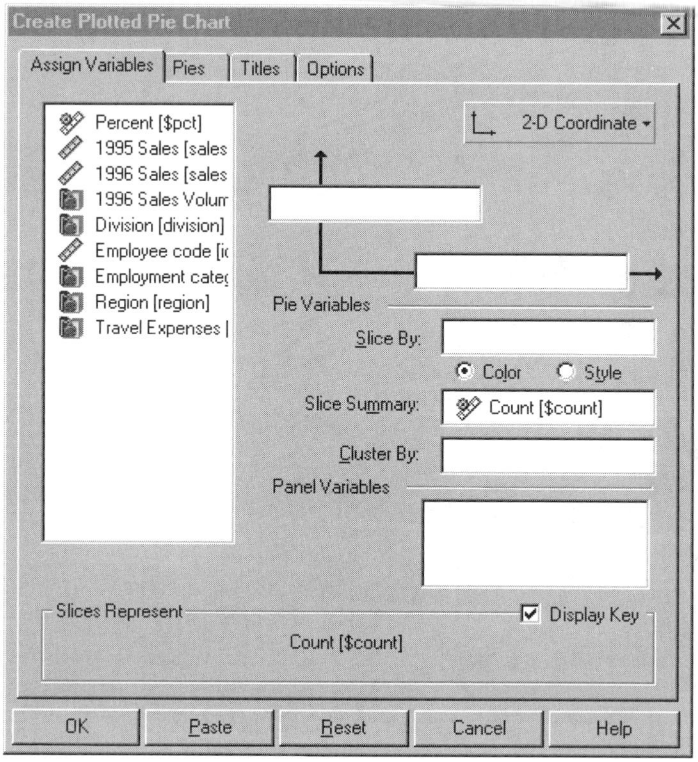


A plotted pie chart contains a set of pies placed at the points defined by rectangular coordinates. It is similar to a scatterplot with pie markers. The pies are all sliced by the same categorical variable.

The size of a slice represents the count or percentage in a category of the slice variable, or a summary function of a scale variable. You can display a key to identify the built-in or summary function.

Scale variables on one or both axes can produce a large number of very small pies.

**Number of dimensions.** Selecting 2-D Coordinate or 3-D coordinate changes the number of axis targets for variable selection. Selecting 3-D Effect specifies that the pies are three-dimensional objects.

For Plotted Pie Options, see "Clustered and Plotted Pie Enhancements" on p. 137.

### To Create a Plotted Pie Chart

▶ From the menus choose:

Graphs
 Interactive
  Pie
   Plotted...

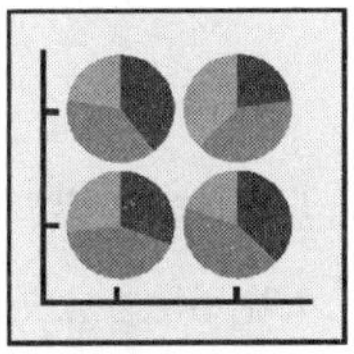

▶ Select 2-D Coordinate for a two-dimensional chart.

▶ To define the pie slices for all pies, drag a categorical variable to Slice By.

▶ To define the subgroups of the pies, drag variables (usually categorical) to the *x1* and *y* axes.

▶ Drag *Count*, *Percent*, or a scale variable to Slice Summary (if it is not there by default).

Optionally, you can:

- Switch between Color and Style.
- Change the Slices Represent summary function for a scale variable.
- Display a key to identify the built-in or summary function.
- Assign a categorical variable for clustering pies.
- Create plotted pie charts for separate categories by assigning one or more categorical Panel Variables.
- Select 3-D Coordinate for a three-dimensional chart.
- Select 3-D Effect to give depth to the pies.

# Modifying Pies

To modify the pie elements (all pies) in an existing chart:

▶ From the menus choose:

Format
  Graph Elements
    Pies

*or*

▶ Right-click a pie and from the context menu choose:

Pies...

▶ Select the desired changes in Pie Options, Summary Function, Labels, or Pie Size.

In the Pies dialog box, you can choose a tab to modify the pie fill, pie border, position, and summary function. You can also change the labels and the size of pies.

## Pies: Pie Options

Figure 9-6
*Pies: Pie Options tab*

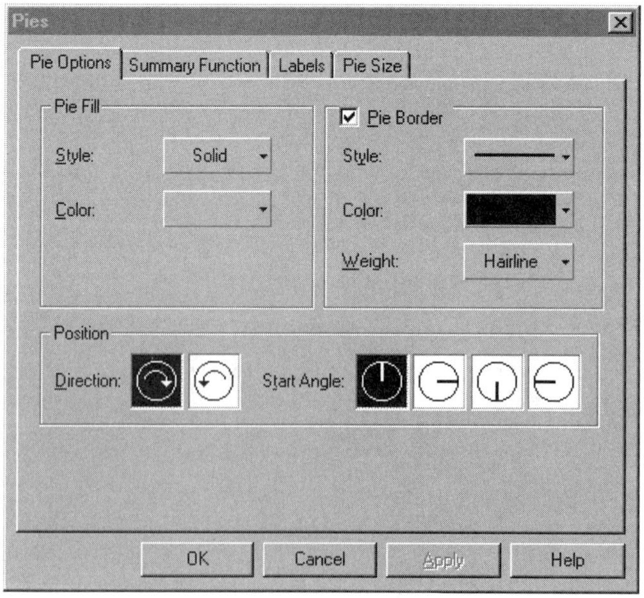

After pies are created, you can change their appearance. These options affect all pies in the chart.

**Pie Fill.** Color or style not controlled by data can be changed.

**Pie Border.** Style, color, and weight of the pie border can be changed. This applies to the border of the whole pie in 2-D. In a 3-D pie, there are no borders.

**Position.** Slices start at a position specified by a clock position: 12:00, 3:00, 6:00, or 9:00. After the first slice, the direction the slices follow is either clockwise or counterclockwise.

## Pies: Summary Function

Figure 9-7
*Pies: Summary Function tab*

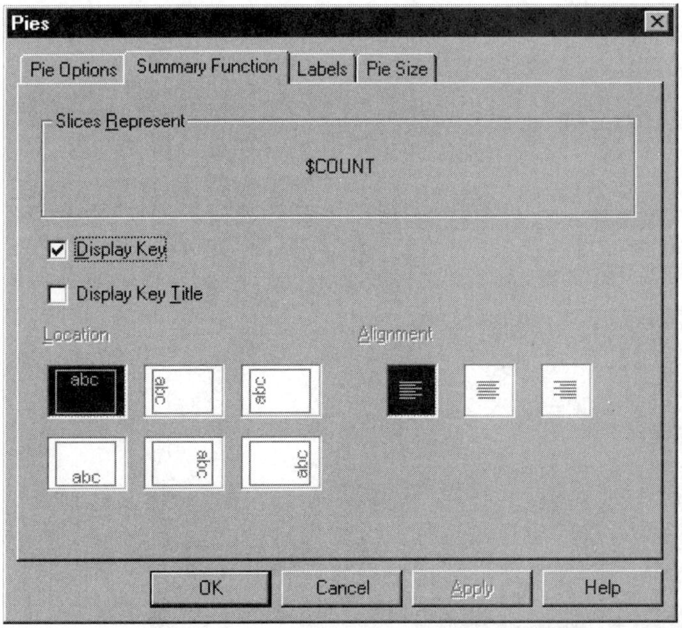


**Slices Represent.** For an existing chart that was created using a summary function of a data variable, you can change the summary function. For example, if the original slices represent the *sum* of a variable, you can change to the *sums of squares* of the same variable. If *Count* or *Percent* is assigned, it is listed here.

**Display key options**. These selections change the way summary information is displayed in the chart. You can display the key and determine the alignment and location of the key title.

### *To Change Pie Chart Summary Function*

- Click the Summary Function tab.
- Select the desired options for summary function and key display.

## *Pies: Labels*

Figure 9-8
*Pies: Labels tab*

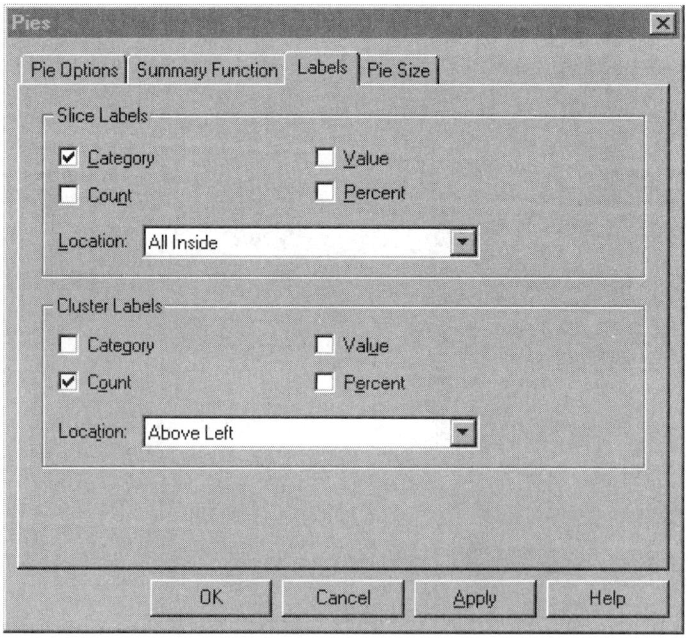


Value labels can have a numeric format. The location of the labels and lines connecting them to the slices or pies can be specified.

**Slice Labels.** Several text and numeric labels are available for slices derived from a categorical variable assigned to Color or Style. You can also specify the location of the labels in relation to the pie.

**Cluster Labels.** Labels can be applied to individual pies when the pies are stacked in a cluster. You can also specify the location of the labels outside the pies.

### *To Change the Labels for a Pie Chart*

- Click the Labels tab.
- Enter changes.

## *Pies: Pie Size*

Figure 9-9
*Pies: Pie Size tab*

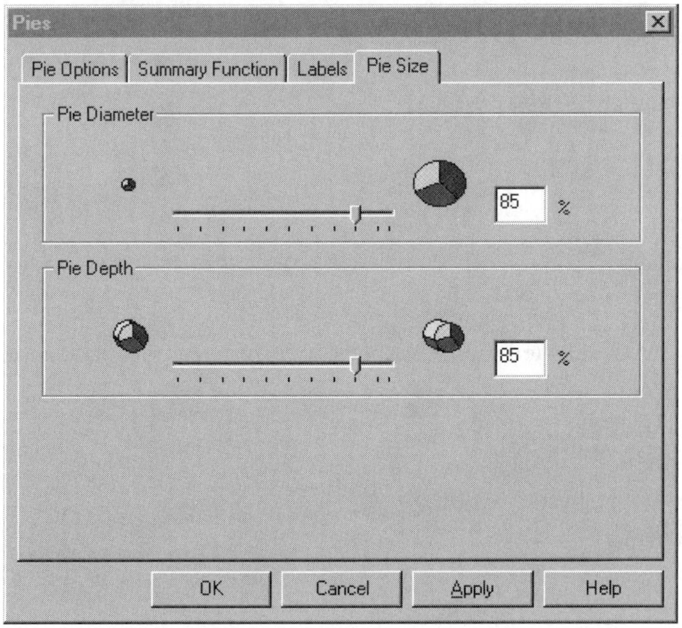

After pie charts are created, you can make the pie smaller or larger, up to a maximum determined by the size of the data region.

If the 3-D effect is turned on, you can specify a depth for the thickness of the pies.

### To Change the Size of Pies

▶ Click the Pie Size tab.

▶ Drag the slider or enter a percentage.

## Changing Pie Slice Properties

Individual slices or a selection of several slices have the properties Fill and Border that can be changed as long as the property is not controlled by the data. Individual labels can be turned on or off, and slices can be exploded out from the center.

### To Change Pie Slice Properties

▶ Select one or more slices in a pie chart.

▶ From the menus choose:

Edit
  Pie Properties

*or*

▶ Right-click a slice or selected group of slices, and from the context menu choose Properties.

Optionally, you can:

- Change the labels, border, or fill.
- Explode the slice.

## Slice Properties

Figure 9-10
*Slice Properties dialog box*

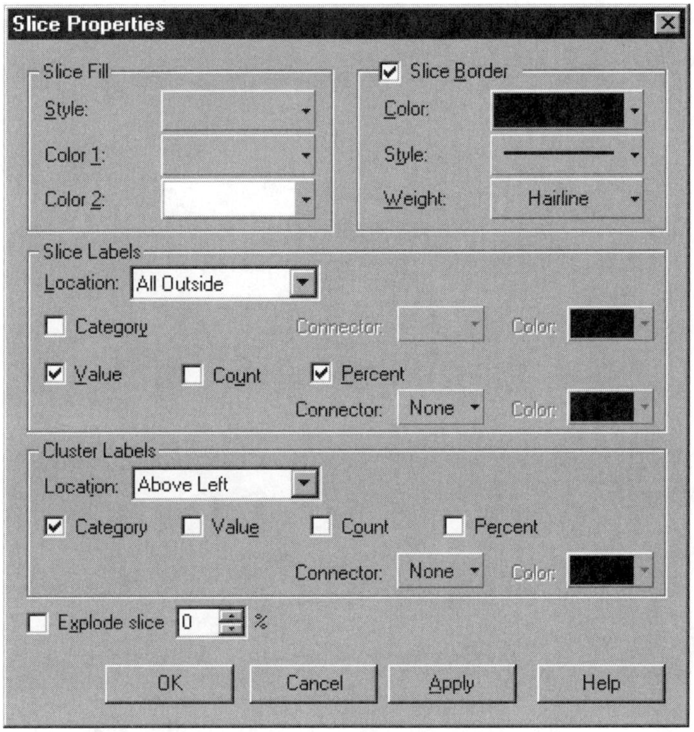


These properties apply only to the selected slice or slices.

**Slice Fill** and **Slice Border.** The attributes of the fill can be changed if they are not controlled by data. The border color, style, and weight can be changed.

**Labels.** The labels for the selected slice can be turned on or off, as can the labels for a pie in a clustered pie chart.

**Explode slice.** The selected slice can be exploded (moved out along a radius) by the percentage entered.

Chapter

# 10

# Scatterplots

In a scatterplot, the actual values of two or three variables are plotted along two or three axes. The resulting cloud of points helps you visualize the relationship between the variables. You can observe whether the points fall near a line or a well-defined curve. In three dimensions, the points may fall near a surface. If a legend variable is used, the characteristics of subgroups become evident.

Study of the plot can help you develop a mathematical model of the relationship. Points that do not fit the relationship stand out in the plot and signal that you should investigate them further.

## Sample Output

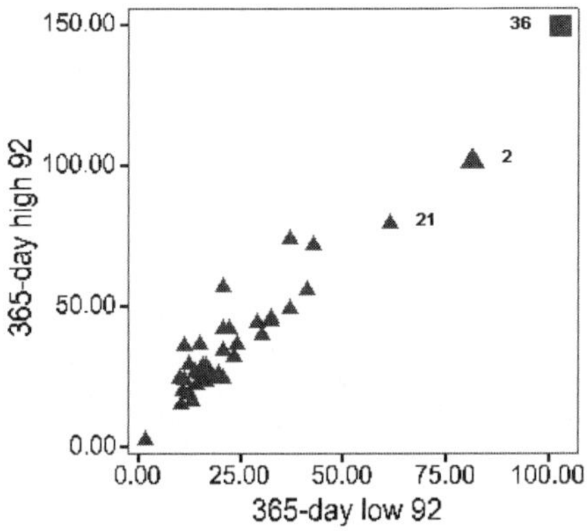


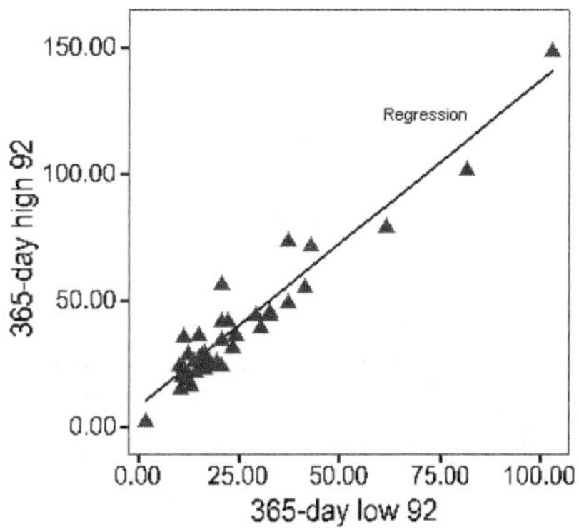

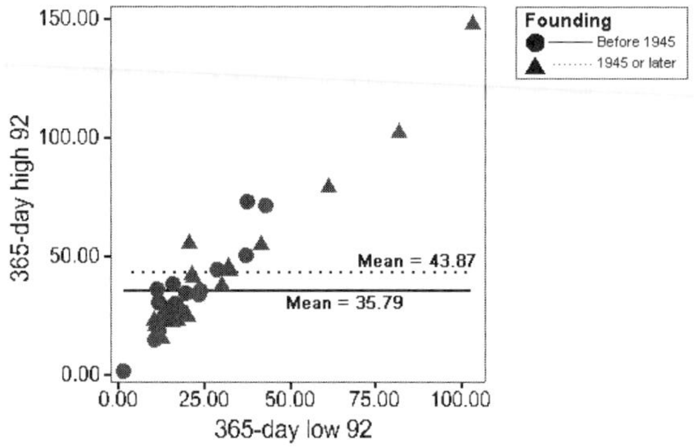
150.00
100.00
50.00
0.00
365-day high 92
0.00
25.00
50.00
75.00
100.00
365-day low 92
Mean = 43.87
Mean = 35.79
Founding
Before 1945
1945 or later

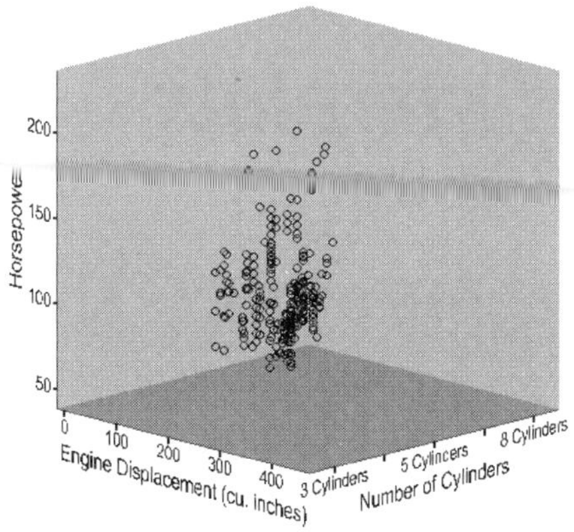
200
150
100
50
Horsepower
0
100
200
300
400
Engine Displacement (cu. inches)
3 Cylinders
5 Cylinders
8 Cylinders
Number of Cylinders

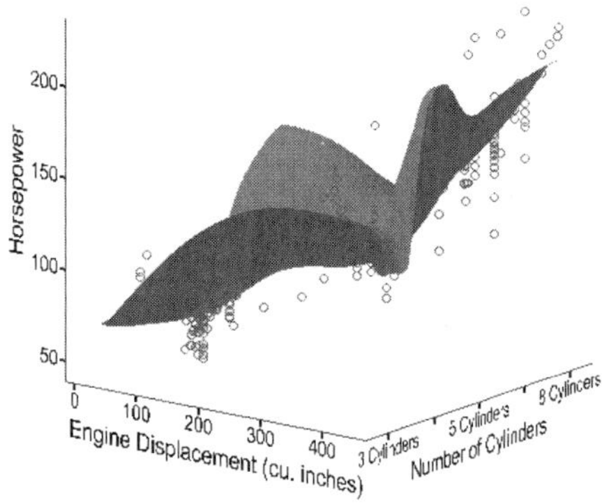
200
150
100
50
Horsepower
0
100
200
300
400
Engine Displacement (cu. inches)
3 Cylinders
5 Cylinders
8 Cylinders
Number of Cylinders

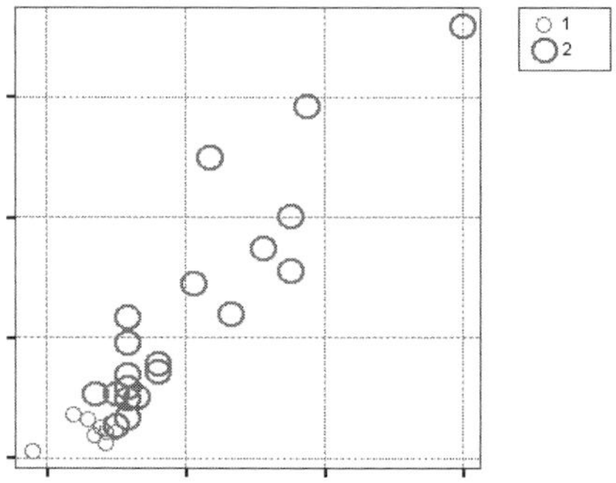
1
2

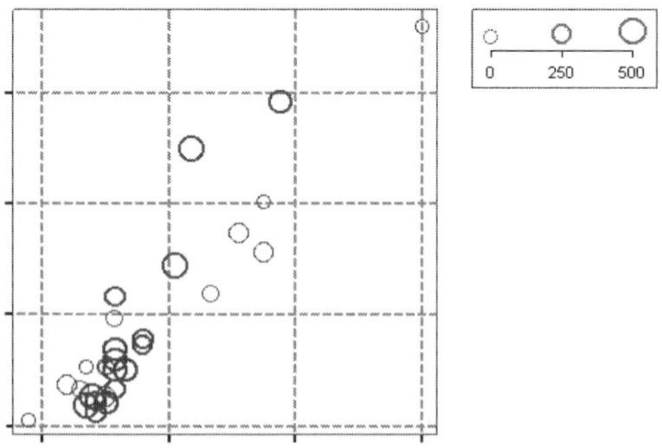
0
250
500

Female
Male
80
60
40
20
Beginning Salary ($1000s)
25
50
75
100
125
Current Salary ($1000s)

# To Create a Scatterplot

▶ From the menus choose:

Graphs
 Interactive
  Scatterplot...

## Create Scatterplot: Assign Variables

Figure 10-1
*Create Scatterplot: Assign Variables tab*

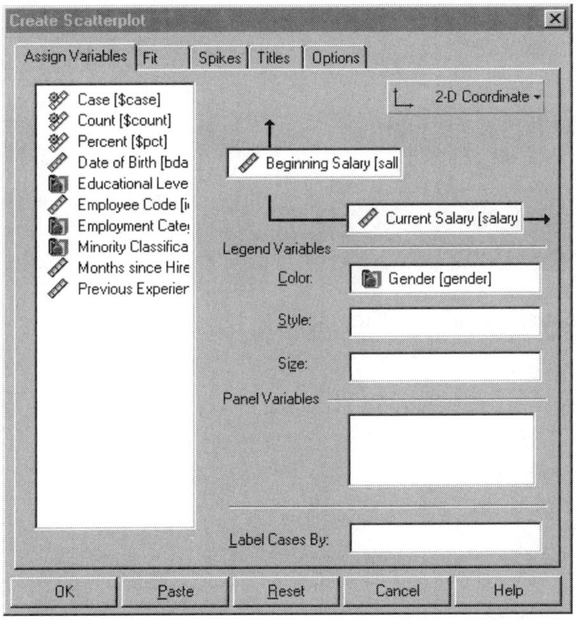


Scatterplots highlight the relationship between two or three quantitative variables by plotting the actual values along two or three axes. They often allow you to see relationships, such as a curvilinear pattern, that descriptive statistics do not reveal, and they can uncover bivariate outliers (for example, a low-priced house with 47 rooms).

Characteristics of subgroups can be studied if you assign a legend variable.

**Number of dimensions.** Selecting 2-D Coordinate or 3-D Coordinate changes the number of axis targets for variable selection.

**2-D**

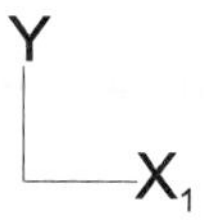


**3-D**

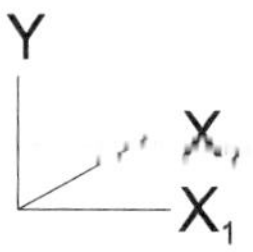


**Label Cases By.** The values of a variable can be used to label points. If no variable is specified, case numbers will be used when labels are displayed.

### *To Create a Simple Scatterplot*

▶ Drag a variable (usually scale) to the *x1* axis.

▶ Drag another variable (usually scale) to the *y* axis.

Optionally, you can:

- Assign a variable for point labels.
- Add fit lines or surfaces (on the Fit tab).

### *To Create a Scatterplot Ordered by Case Number*

▶ Drag a scale variable to the *y* axis.

▶ Drag the built-in variable *Case* to the *x1* axis.

To label the cases with the values of another variable, drag a variable to Label Cases By.

### To Create a Scatterplot Split by Categories

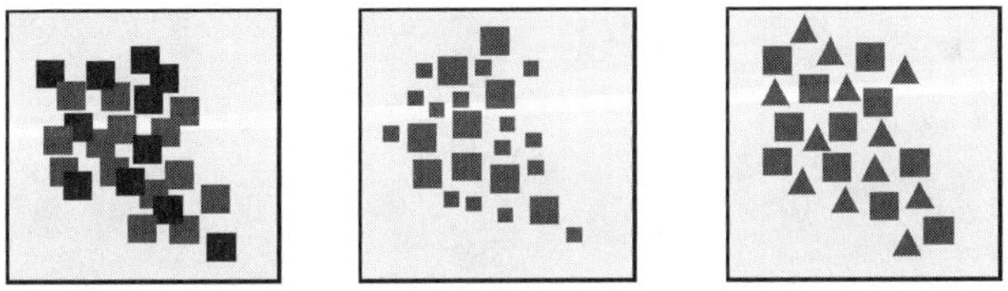

- Drag a scale variable to the *y* axis.
- Drag a variable (usually scale) to the *x1* axis.
- Drag a categorical variable to Color, Style, or Size.

  Optionally, you can drag variables to more than one of the legend targets.

### To Create a Scatterplot with Colors or Sizes Assigned by a Summary of a Scale Variable

- Drag a variable to the *x1* axis.
- Drag a scale variable to the *y* axis.
- Drag a scale variable to Color or Size.

  The color or size of each symbol indicates its value in relation to the color or size scale in the legend.

### To Create a 3-D Scatterplot

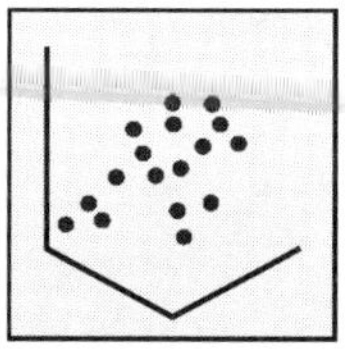

▶ Select 3-D Coordinate from the drop-down list.

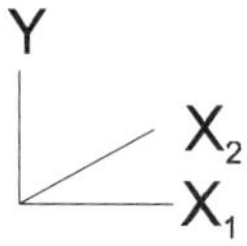


▶ Drag a scale or built-in variable to the *y* axis (dependent axis).

▶ Drag variables to the *x1* and *x2* axes.

### To Create Scatterplot Panels for Categories

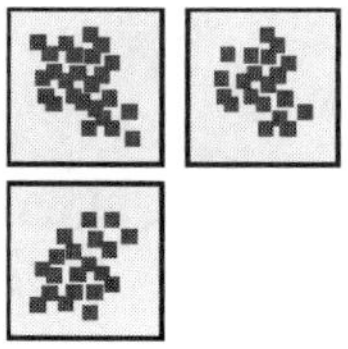

▶ Drag a variable to the *x1* axis.

▶ Drag a scale variable or a built-in variable to the *y* axis.

▶ Drag one or more categorical variables to Panel Variables.

Optionally, you can drag variables to the legend targets.

## Create Scatterplot: Fit

Figure 10-2
*Create Scatterplot: Fit tab*

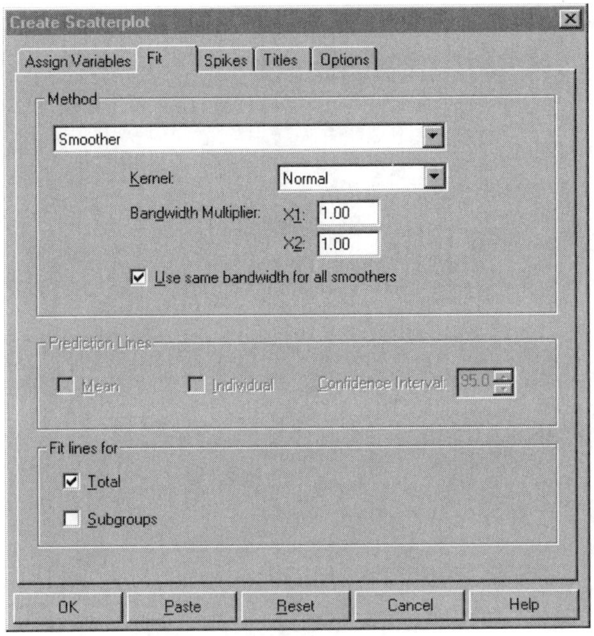


Several methods are available to fit lines to the points in a scatterplot.

**Method.** Fit lines show the best fit according to the method selected. Available methods for scatterplots are None, Regression, Mean, and Smoother. When Regression is selected, you can specify whether or not to have a constant in the equation. With no constant, the line goes through the origin.

When Smoother (local linear regression) is selected, you can specify the type of kernel, the bandwidth multipliers, and whether to use the same bandwidth for all smoothers. The same bandwidth can be useful for subgroups or panels.

**Prediction Lines.** When a mean or regression method is used, a mean prediction line or individual prediction lines are available that illustrate a specified confidence level.

**Fit lines for.** In addition to a fit line for the total cloud, if there is a categorical split, you can select fit lines for subgroups. If you add a fit line, be sure that at least one of these options is selected.

## Create Scatterplot: Spikes

Figure 10-3
*Create Scatterplot: Spikes tab*

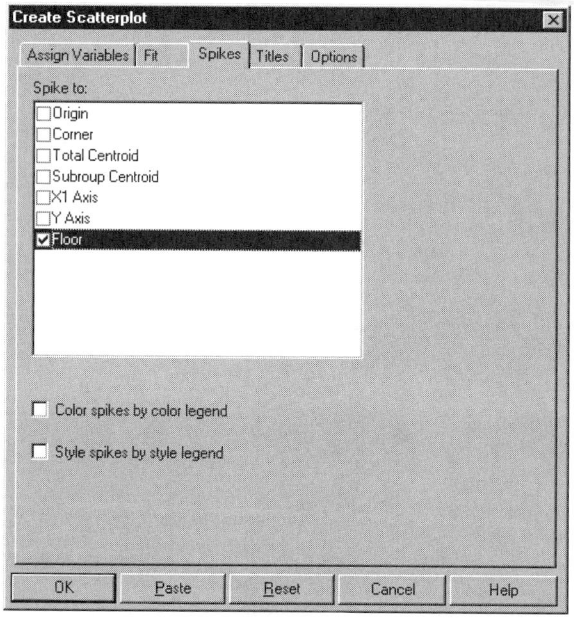


Spikes are lines drawn from cloud symbols to a point, axis, line, or surface. Spikes can help you read values from the axis or compare distances using line length. When drawn to the horizontal axis, spikes are sometimes called drop lines.

**Spike to.** Spike lines can be drawn to axes, reference lines, mean fit lines, and regression fit lines.

**Color spikes by color legend.** Matches spike color to the color legend for categorical variables.

**Style spikes by style legend.** Matches spike style to the style legend for categorical variables.

# Modifying a Cloud

To modify a cloud of symbols in an existing scatterplot:

▶ From the menus choose:

Format
  Graph Elements
    Cloud...

*or*

▶ Right-click a symbol and from the context menu choose:

Cloud...

In the Cloud dialog box, you can choose tabs to modify symbols, labels, or the jittering of points. You can also change the attributes of the whole cloud of symbols.

## Cloud: Symbols

Figure 10-4
*Cloud: Symbols tab*

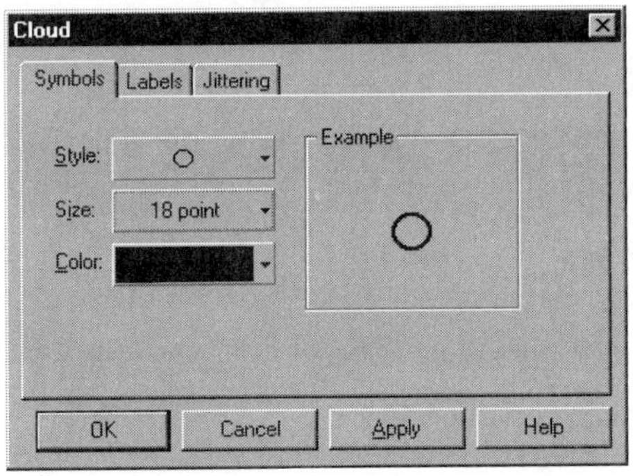


The style, size, and color of the cloud of symbols can be changed, if these attributes are not locked by the data. For example, suppose a variable *Group* is assigned to the color legend, making Group 1 red and Group 2 green. The Color option for the cloud on the Symbols tab is locked in this case, but you can change size and style.

## Cloud: Labels

Figure 10-5
*Cloud: Labels tab*

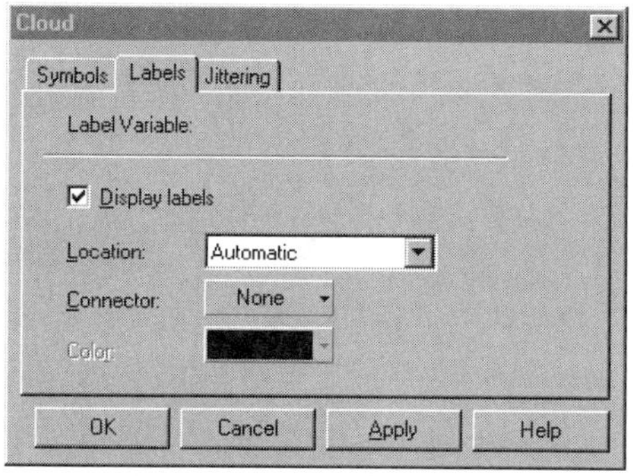


**Label Variable.** Indicates whether a label variable has been selected. If not, case numbers are used as labels. A label variable can be assigned in the Assign Graph Variables dialog box.

**Display labels.** Turns all labels on or off.

**Location.** Labels can be located at various positions around a circle, as times on a clock, or each label can be centered on the symbol.

**Connector.** Specifies the type of connector between the label and its corresponding symbol.

**Color.** Changes the color of connectors.

## Cloud: Jittering

Figure 10-6
*Cloud: Jittering tab*

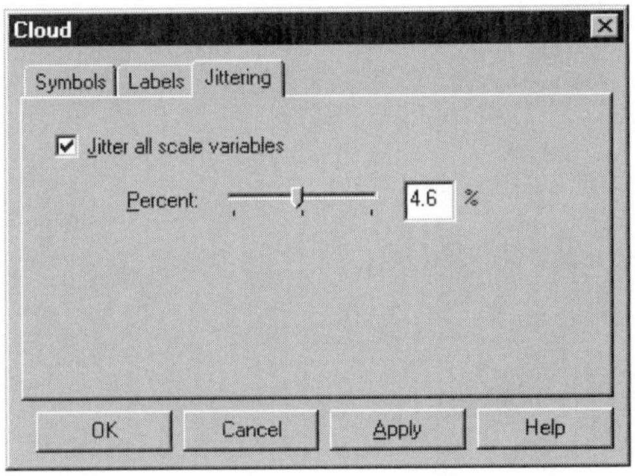


Jittering adjusts the display of points that would fall exactly on top of one another if no adjustment were made.

**Jitter all scale variables.** Adds a small amount of random noise to any scale data, whether or not the points are coincident. Categorical data are not jittered.

# Changing Selected Symbol Properties

You can set the style, size, color, and label of individual symbols or a selection of several symbols.

### To Change Individual Symbols in a Scatterplot

- ▶ Activate the chart by clicking it.
- ▶ Select one or more symbols in the chart.
- ▶ Right-click a symbol and from the menus choose:

  Properties

Optionally, you can change the appearance or labels of the selected symbols.

## *Symbol Properties: Appearance*

Figure 10-7
*Symbol properties: Appearance tab*

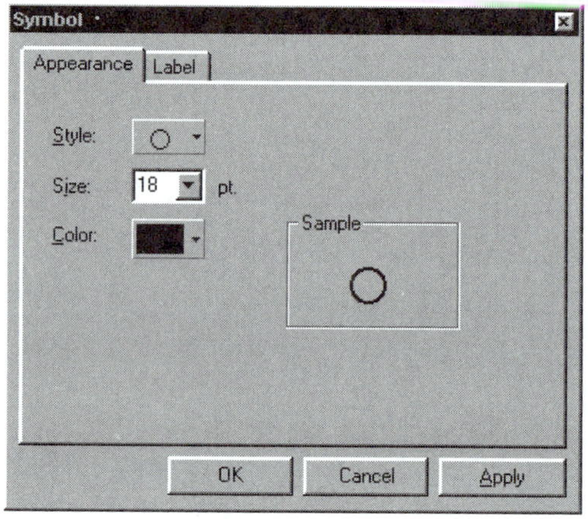


Individual symbols or a selected group of symbols can be changed if they are not controlled by the data. Choices are reflected in the Sample box.

**Style.** You can use symbols from the software's built-in symbol font or from other fonts installed on your system.

**Size.** Symbols can vary in size. A particular symbol or group of symbols could be larger for emphasis.

**Color.** Symbols can vary in color. A group of symbols might be a bright color to call attention to them.

## Symbol Properties: Label

Figure 10-8
*Symbol properties: Label tab*

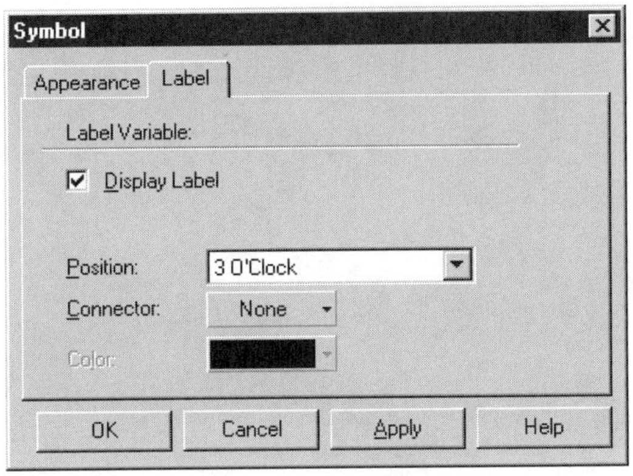


Case labels can be displayed for individual symbols or a selected group of symbols. You can change the format, position, or connector.

Chapter

# 11

# Fit Lines, Surfaces, and Spikes

A fit line or surface can be added to a scatterplot to help you discern the relationship shown in the plot. The following are available for scatterplots:

**Mean.** For a 2-D chart, a line is drawn at the mean of the dependent (*y*) variable. For a 3-D chart, a plane is displayed.

**Regression.** Ordinary least squares are used to calculate the regression line or surface.

**Smoother.** A local linear regression (LLR) curve (or a surface for 3-D) is added to the plot. If the data appear to have many fluctuations, a smoother can help you see underlying patterns.

**Groups.** When the cloud is split into more than one group, you can show a fit line for all of the points in the cloud or lines for each subgroup.

**Spikes.** A line is drawn from the cloud symbols to a point, axis, line, or surface. Spikes can help you read values from the axis or compare distances using line length. When drawn to a horizontal axis, spikes are sometimes called **drop lines**.

## To Add a Mean Fit Line to an Existing Scatterplot

▶ Create a scatterplot (cloud).

▶ Activate the chart (double-click it).

▶ From the menus choose:

Insert
  Fit Line
    Mean

### To Add a Regression Fit Line to an Existing Scatterplot

- ▶ Create a scatterplot (cloud).
- ▶ Activate the chart (double-click it).
- ▶ From the menus choose:

  Insert
  Fit Line
  Regression

### To Add a Smoother to an Existing Scatterplot

- ▶ Create a scatterplot (cloud).
- ▶ Activate the chart (double-click it).
- ▶ From the menus choose:

  Insert
  Fit Line
  Smoother

## To Adjust a Fit Line or Surface

- ▶ Activate the chart (double-click it).
- ▶ Select a fit line.
- ▶ From the menus choose:

  Edit
  Parameters

  *or*

- ▶ Right-click the fit line and from the context menu choose Parameters.
- ▶ Adjust the desired parameters.

## Mean Parameters

Figure 11-1
*Mean Parameters palette*

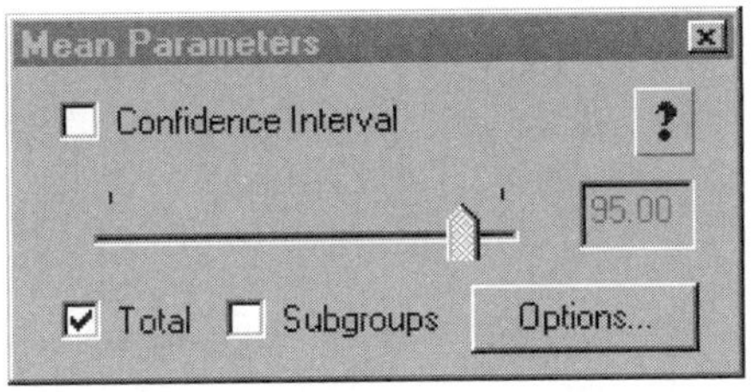


This palette controls the parameters for a mean fit line. You can display a confidence interval around the fit line at a level between 50% and 100%, and this percentage level can be changed.

**Total.** Display a line for the complete set of points.

**Subgroups.** If the data points are split into subgroups by a legend variable, you can display a line for each subgroup.

## Regression Parameters

Figure 11-2
*Regression Parameters palette*

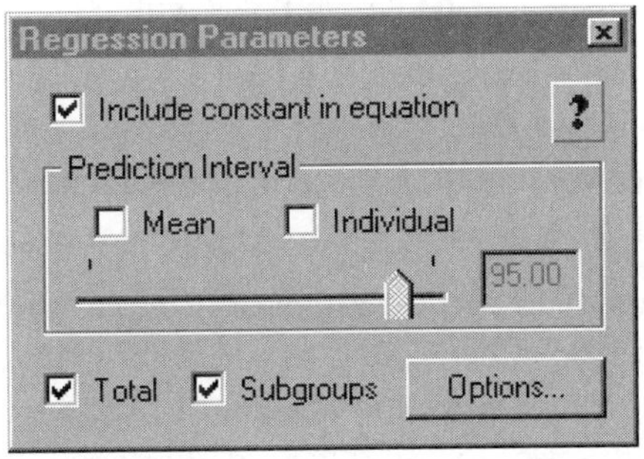


This palette controls the parameters for a regression fit line.

**Include constant in equation.** Deselect this item to display a regression line through the origin.

**Prediction Interval.** You can display a confidence interval around the fit line at a level between 50% and 100%. Both Mean and Individual prediction lines are available.

**Total.** Display a line for the complete set of points.

**Subgroups.** If the data points are split into subgroups by a legend variable, you can display a line for each subgroup.

## Smoother Parameters

Figure 11-3
*Smoother Parameters palette*

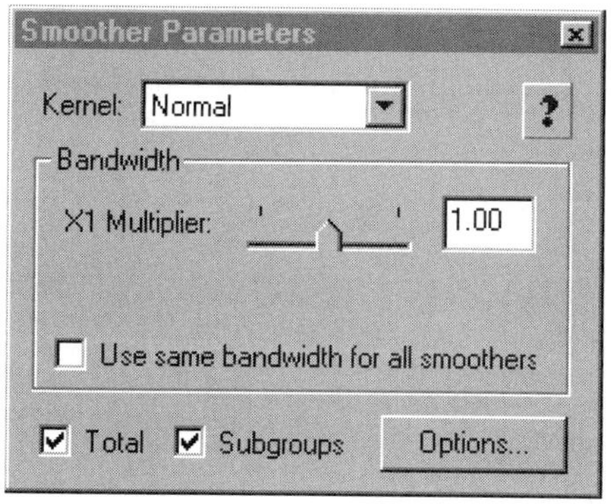


This palette controls the parameters for a smoother (local linear regression). If you change the parameters, you will see the chart change on the screen.

**Kernel.** From the drop-down list, you can choose the kernel to be used. A normal kernel is the default. With an Epanechnikov kernel, the curve is not as smooth as with a normal kernel but is smoother than with a uniform kernel. (For more information, see Simonoff, Jeffrey S., *Smoothing Methods in Statistics*, 1996, New York: Springer-Verlag.)

**Bandwidth.** The bandwidth multiplier changes the amount of data that is included in each calculation of a small part of the smoother. The program determines the default size of the bandwidth that is designated as having a multiplier of 1. The multiplier can be adjusted to emphasize specific features of the plot that are of interest. Any positive multiplier (including fractions) is allowed. The larger the multiplier, the smoother the curve. The range between 0 and 10 should suffice in most applications. For 3-D plots, you can specify a multiplier for each independent axis, (*x1* and *x2*).

You can select Use same bandwidth for all smoothers when you want the same bandwidth for different subgroups or panels.

**Total.** Displays a line for the complete set of points.

**Subgroups.** If the data points are split into subgroups by a legend variable, you can display a line for each subgroup.

For more information on local linear regression, see Fan and Marron, Fast Implementations of Nonparametric Curve Estimators, *Journal of Computational and Graphical Statistics*, 3: 35–56, 1994.

# Changing Fit Line Properties

Fit line appearance and labels can be changed from the Options dialog boxes.

## Mean and Regression Properties

Figure 11-4
*Mean Options dialog box*

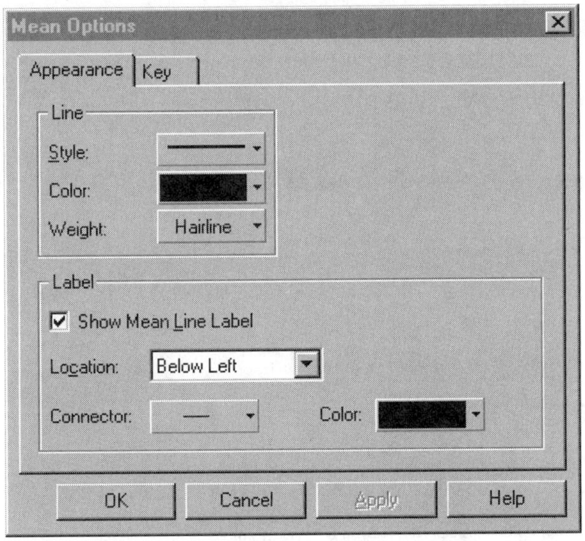

Figure 11-5
*Regression Options dialog box*

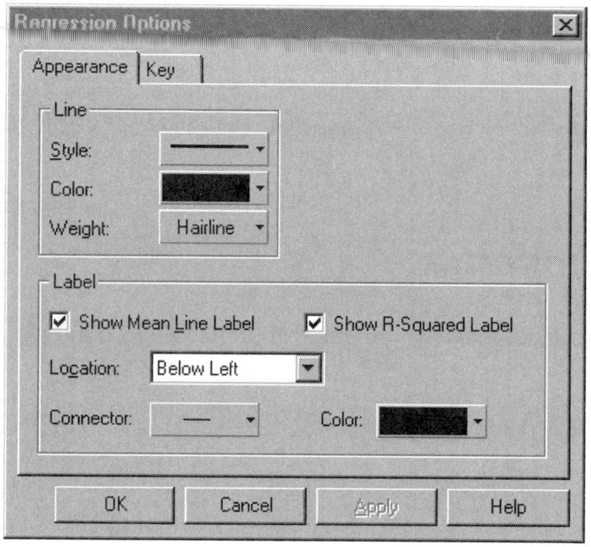


For a selected mean or regression fit line, you can change the style, color, weight, and label. For a regression fit line, you can also choose Show R-Squared Label.

### To Change Mean and Regression Fit Line Properties

- Activate the chart (double-click it).
- Select a fit line.
- From the menus choose:

  Edit
  Properties...

  *or*

- Right-click the fit line and from the context menu choose Options.

Optionally, you can change the style, weight, color, and labels.

## Smoother Properties

Figure 11-6
*Smoother Options dialog box*

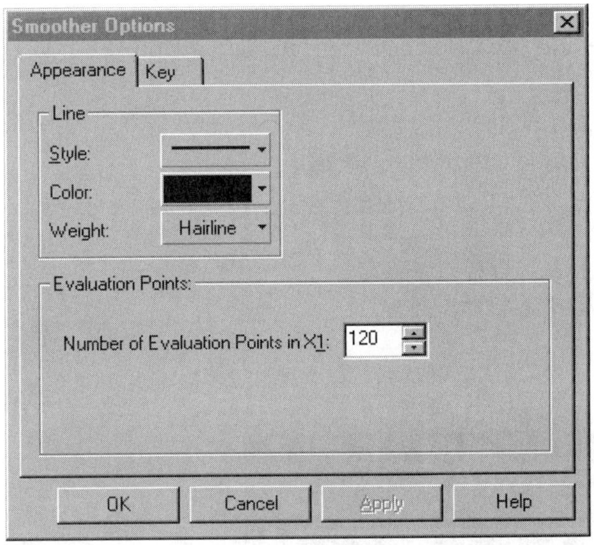


For a selected mean fit line, you can change the style, color, weight, and label.

**Evaluation Points** govern the number of points used in the evenly spaced grid on which the smoother will be evaluated. The default for a 2-D smoother is 120, while for the 3-D smoother, it is 30 by 30. The larger the number of evaluation points, the finer will be the rendering of the smoother; however, it is also more expensive computationally. Particularly in the three-dimensional case, the evaluation time for smoothers increases rapidly with the number of evaluation points. If you change the number of evaluation points, you should try to choose a number slightly less than the nearest power of 2 because the convolution algorithm is used. For example, it is better to choose 15 (which is 2 to the 4th power minus 1) rather than to choose 17.

### To Change Smoother Properties

- ▶ Activate the chart (double-click it).
- ▶ Select a mean fit line.

▶ From the menus choose:

Edit
 Properties...

or

▶ Right-click the fit line and from the context menu choose Options.

Optionally, you can:

- Change the style, weight, color, and labels.
- Change the number of evaluation points for the *x1* and *x2* axes.

# Adding Spikes to a Scatterplot

Figure 11-7
*Spikes dialog box*

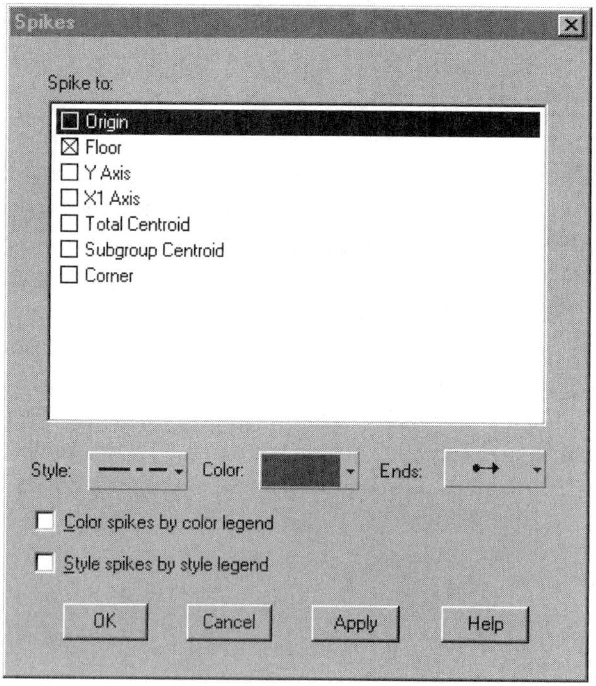

Spikes are lines drawn from cloud symbols to a point, axis, line, or surface. Spikes can help you read values from the axis or compare distances using line length. When drawn to a horizontal axis, spikes are sometimes called **drop lines**.

**Spike to**. Spike lines can be drawn to origins, the floor, axes, reference lines, and mean or regression fit lines. You can choose style, color, and ends options for spike lines.

**Color spikes by color legend.** Matches spike color to the color legend for categorical variables.

**Style spikes by style legend.** Matches spike style to the style legend for categorical variables.

### *To Add Spikes to an Existing Scatterplot*

▶ Create a scatterplot (cloud).

▶ Activate the chart (double-click it).

▶ From the menus choose:

Insert
  Spikes...

▶ Spike to floor, axes, origins, reference lines, and mean or regression fit lines.

▶ Choose color and style options.

## *Changing Spike Properties*

Spikes can be changed from the Properties dialog boxes.

## Spike Properties

Figure 11-8
*Spike Properties dialog box*

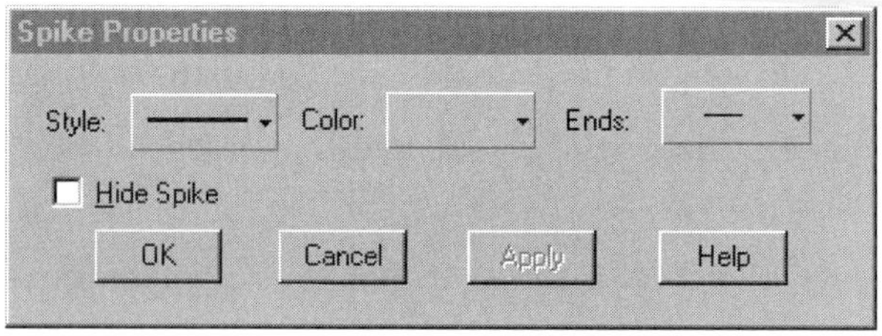


For a selected spike line, you can change the style, color, and ends. Selected spikes can also be hidden.

### To Change Spike Properties

▶ Activate the chart (double-click it).

▶ Select a spike line.

▶ From the menus choose:

Edit
  Properties...

*or*

▶ Right-click the spike line and from the context menu choose Properties.

Optionally, you can:

- Change the style, color, and ends for spike lines.
- Hide the selected spike lines.

Chapter

# 12

# Modifying Interactive Charts

After creating a chart, you may wish to modify it, either to obtain more information about the data or to enhance the chart for presentation. Dynamic chart modification capabilities described in this chapter allow you to:

- Change labeling.
- Adjust each axis.
- Modify panels.
- Change legends and keys.
- Change the size and fill of the data region.
- Use the Chart Manager to edit or delete chart objects.
- Rearrange chart objects.
- Edit and apply ChartLooks.
- Change colors and styles of chart objects.

In addition, you can make the following modifications by using information in previous chapters:

- Change variable assignments.
- Add or delete graphic elements.
- Change summary functions.
- Add fit lines, reference lines, or surfaces.

### To Activate a Chart in the Viewer

▶ Double-click anywhere in the chart.

*or*

▶ Select the chart and from the menus choose:

Edit
  SPSS Interactive Graph Object
    Edit *or* Open

The menus change to Interactive Graphics Editor menus, and the chart has its own movable toolbars.

## Selection of Chart Objects to Modify

Objects in the chart can be selected separately or in groups and then modified.

**Examples**:

- Select one bar in a simple bar chart and change its color.
- Select the set of red bars and apply a texture.
- Select two pie slices and explode them.
- Select an axis and change the scale and the line style.

**Context menu.** A right-click on most objects displays a context menu. At the bottom of the context menu for a chart element (bars, cloud, pie, etc.) are two items: the name of the element and Properties (for example, Bars and Properties).

- To modify the whole element (for example, all the bars in a chart), choose the name of the element.
- To modify only the selected object or objects, choose Properties.

Figure 12-1
*Context menu*

**Example:**

Right-click one bar in a simple bar chart with no legend. To change the color of only the selected bar, choose Properties from the context menu. To change the color of all the bars simultaneously (the bar element), choose Bars from the context menu.

**Changing a whole category.** If you want to apply properties to a category of objects, you should select the category in the legend, not the set of individual objects within the category.

### *To Select and Modify a Chart Object*

- Activate the chart (double-click it).
- Right-click the object to be modified.

  The object is selected and a context menu is displayed. You can choose an action or a dialog box from the context menu.

  *or*

- Click the object to be modified.

▶ Select a command from the menus at the top of the Viewer.

*or*

▶ Double-click the object to be modified.

This displays a dialog box for editing the object you clicked. Double-clicking a graphical element displays the dialog box for that element. For example, double-clicking a bar displays the Bars dialog box.

### To Select a Category of Objects

▶ Click the category swatch in the legend. For example, to select the red bars in a chart, click the red swatch in the legend.

### To Move a Chart Object

▶ Activate the chart (double-click it).

▶ Drag an object (such as a legend or title) to a new position.

Titles, captions, legends, keys, and axis titles can be moved. As you make other changes, the object retains its position relative to the data region.

## Interactive, Interactive (Detached), and Static Charts

An interactive chart has access to the variables used to create it. Using the Assign Graph Variables dialog box, you can change variable assignments whenever the chart is activated.

- If the data file that was used to create the chart is still open and nothing has changed in the Data Editor since the chart was created, the chart is labeled **Interactive** in the status bar of the Viewer. You can change any of the variable assignments for interactive charts, using all of the variables available in the active data file. These charts use the Interactive Chart Editor.
- If Save data with the chart is selected on the Interactive tab of Options and the data file has been changed or a new data file has been opened, the chart is detached from the data file and is labeled **Interactive (detached)** in the status bar of the Viewer. For a detached chart, you can still change variable assignments; however, only

variables used while the chart was actively connected to the open data file are now available. The Assign Graph Variables dialog box contains a message about available variables.

- All interactive charts become static charts if Save only summarized data is selected on the Interactive tab of Options (Edit menu of the Viewer). In a **static** chart, only the summarized data is saved, and you cannot change variable assignments, although you can change attributes such as color, fill, and symbol size. You can turn an interactive chart into a static chart by right-clicking and choosing Save only summarized data from the context menu. A static chart cannot be changed to an interactive chart.
- Non-interactive charts and charts created in previous versions of the software are not interactive. The chart objects can be edited for attributes such as color, but the variable assignments cannot be changed. These charts use the Chart Editor window.

*Note*: In the SmartViewer, all charts are either Interactive (detached) or Static charts.

Figure 12-2
*Assign Graph Variables dialog boxes for an Interactive chart and an Interactive (detached) chart*

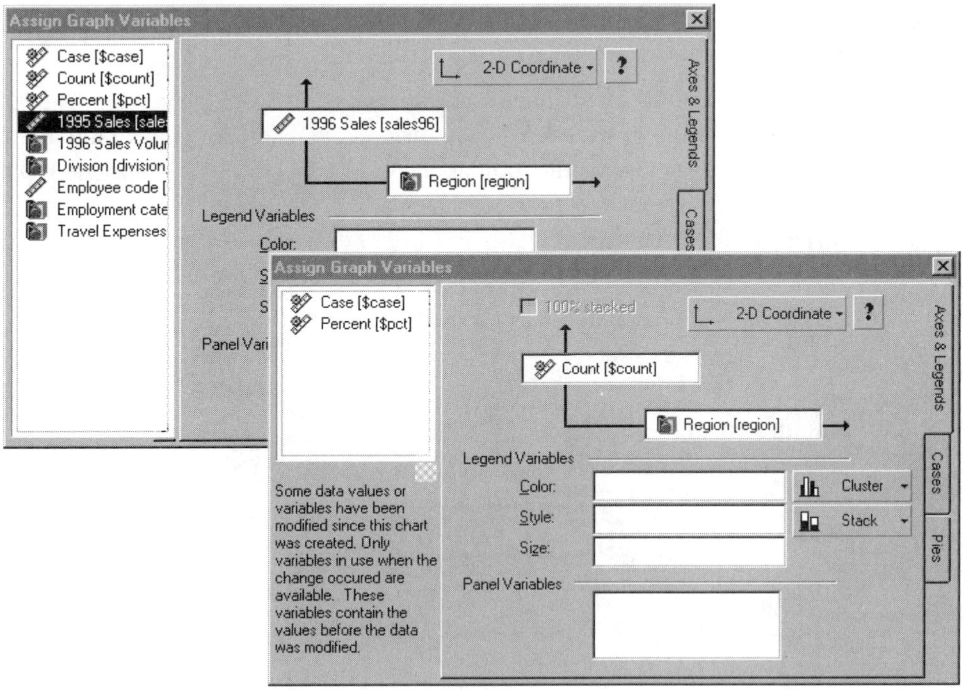

## To Change the Assignments of Variables

- ▶ Activate the chart (double-click it).
- ▶ From the menus choose:

  Edit
    Assign Variables

  *or*

- ▶ Click the Assign Variables tool on the chart toolbar.
- ▶ Drag the desired variables to their new targets.

  The chart changes immediately.

There is no need to drag the previous variables out of a variable target before dragging another variable to the target. The variables pivot (exchange positions) when you drag and drop one variable on top of another.

## Modifying 3-D Charts

Three-dimensional charts have some special controls displayed on the 3-D palette when the chart is activated. You can turn on the palette or change the lighting by clicking the 3-D tool on the toolbar. The 3-D tool is available only in 3-D charts.

**3-D Tool** 

**Light Source** 

**Rotation Hand** 

**Rotation Dial** 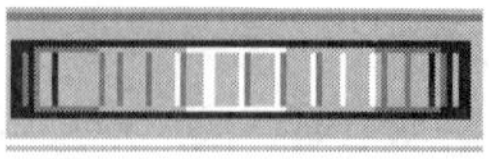

**Light Source.** The position of the light source can be changed. This changes the shading of various surfaces and helps the objects appear more realistic. The position of the light source can direct the observer's attention to important features of the chart.

**Rotation.** Three-dimensional charts can be rotated both horizontally and vertically. Rotation facilitates seeing what is behind the objects that are in the front area of the chart. It is also useful for visually spotting patterns in the data. Two types of tools are available for rotating the chart: the rotation hand and the dials.

### To Rotate a 3-D Chart

▶ If the 3-D palette is not displayed, click the 3-D tool on the toolbar and select 3-D Palette.

There are two dials in the 3-D tool palette, one horizontal and one vertical.

▶ Drag either dial with the mouse.

The chart rotates when the dial is turned by the mouse. The number of degrees of rotation is indicated in a text box. Another way to set the rotation amount is to enter the number of degrees in the text box.

▶ To reset the rotation in either direction to its default value, click the Vertical Reset tool or the Horizontal Reset tool (the rotating arrow icons next to the text boxes).

Optionally, you can click the rotation hand and then drag within the chart itself.

### To Display the 3-D Palette

▶ Activate a 3-D chart (double-click it).

▶ If the 3-D palette is not displayed, click the 3-D tool on the toolbar and select 3-D Palette.

*or*

▶ From the menus choose:

View
 3-D Palette

### To Change the Direction of Light

- ▶ Activate a 3-D chart (double-click it).
- ▶ On the 3-D palette, click the Light Source tool.
- ▶ Select the direction of the light source.

*or*

- ▶ Click the 3-D tool on the toolbar to change the lighting or activate the palette.

## Chart Manager

Figure 12-3
*Chart Manager dialog box*

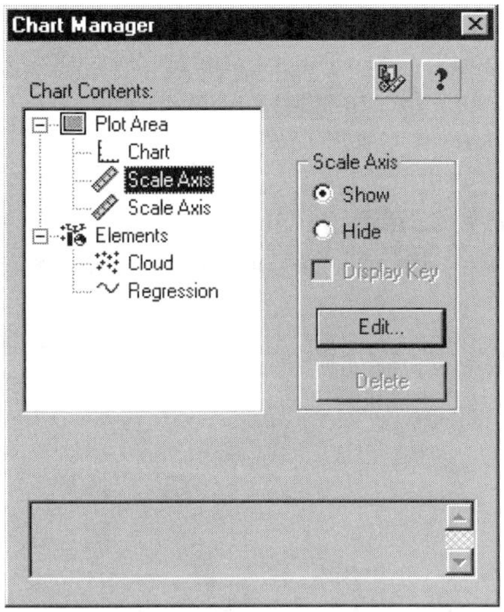


The Chart Manager gives easy access to all of the separate components that make up a chart. They can be selected individually on the list, and then edited, deleted, or hidden. Keys can be displayed for chart elements such as clouds and fit lines.

The Chart Manager also gives information or warnings about individual components of the chart. For example, if the selected component is Bar, the Chart Manager displays the summary function currently in use for bars in the chart. Warnings are preceded by an exclamation point.

### *To Use the Chart Manager*

▶ Activate the chart (double-click it).

▶ From the menus choose:

Edit
  Chart Manager...

*or*

▶ Click the Chart Manager tool.

▶ Select an item in the Chart Contents list.

▶ Read any information about the item that appears under the list.

Optionally, you can:

- Show or hide the selected item.
- Display a key associated with the selected item, if available.
- Edit the selected item, if available.
- Delete the selected item from the chart.
- Click the Assign Graph Variables tool to open the Assign Graph Variables dialog box.

# Inserting Additional Elements

You can add elements to an interactive chart to convey additional information. For example:

- Add scatterplot clouds or error bars to a bar chart of means to show the distribution of data.
- Add error bars to bar or line charts of means to show confidence intervals for the mean values.
- Add additional lines to a line chart to display lines for different summary functions (for example, mean and median).
- Add fit lines to scatterplots to show trends and patterns.

Inserted elements often require additional modification for adequate display. The default color of many inserted elements is often the same as the color of existing elements in the chart, making it difficult to distinguish separate elements (for example, a red line displayed on a red bar is essentially invisible). Also, when inserting an element of the same type as an element that already exists in the chart, it may appear as if nothing has happened because the new element is exactly the same as the original element. For example, if you want to insert a line that displays median values in a line chart that displays mean values, the default inserted line also shows means, making the two lines indistinguishable.

The easiest way to change the attributes of an inserted element that is difficult to see or select is to select the element in the Chart Manager.

### To Insert Additional Elements in a Chart

▶ Activate the chart (double-click it).

▶ From the menus choose:

Insert
  [element type]

*or*

▶ Click the Insert Element tool on the chart toolbar.

▶ Select an element type from the list.

Any element you select is inserted in the chart. However, only elements that are compatible with the information already displayed in the chart are displayed. For example, error bars will be displayed on a bar chart that displays mean values of a scale variable but not on a bar chart of simple counts. In many cases, the Chart Manager contains information that explains why an element is not displayed.

Figure 12-4
*Element information in the Chart Manager*

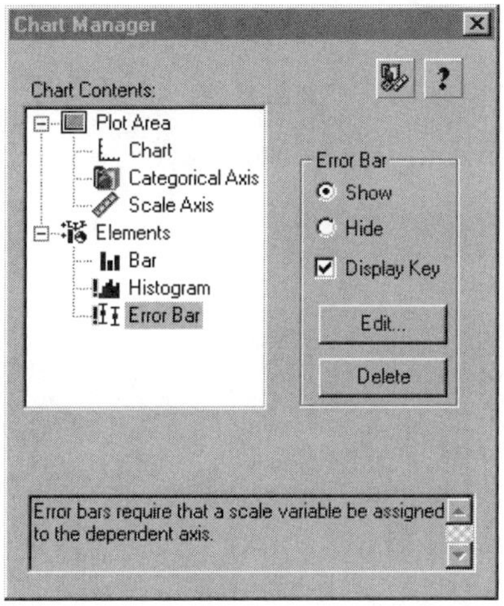


## Keys

Each element in a chart can have a key. The key shows summary information about the element. You cannot edit the text of a key, but you can change the key display properties in the chart modifications dialog box. If you change the summary function for an element, the key changes accordingly.

**Dragging.** A key can be dragged with the mouse to a new position in the chart.

### To Show or Hide a Key

▶ Activate the chart (double-click it).

▶ From the menus choose:

Edit
  Chart Manager...

▶ Select an element in the list.

▶ Select or deselect Display Key.

*or*

▶ If the key is displayed, right-click the key and choose Hide Key.

## Key Properties

Figure 12-5
*Key display properties on the Summary Function tab*

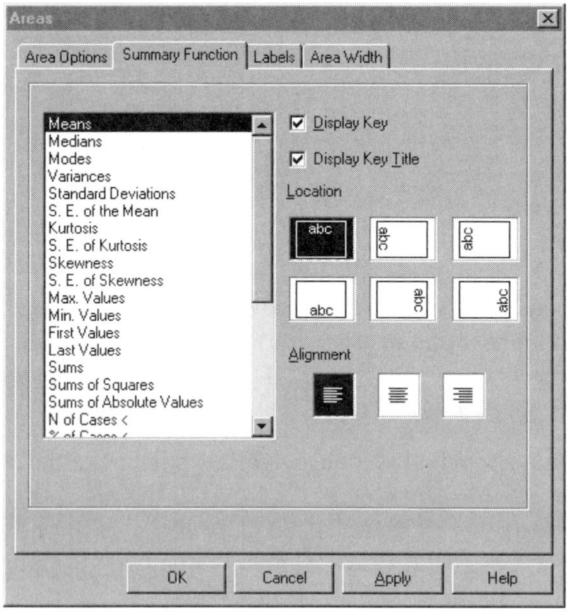

A key shows summary information about a chart element. For all chart elements, the following options can be changed:

**Display Key.** Deselect this item to hide the key.

**Display Key Title.** The title for a key can be on or off.

**Location.** The title can be in various positions with respect to the text of the key.

**Alignment.** The title can be at either edge or centered.

### *To Change Key Properties*

- Activate the chart (double-click it).
- From the menus choose:

  Format
  Key
  [element name]

  *or*

- Right-click the key, and from the context menu choose Properties.
- Select the desired options.

# Data Region

Figure 12-6
*2-D and 3-D Data Region dialog boxes*

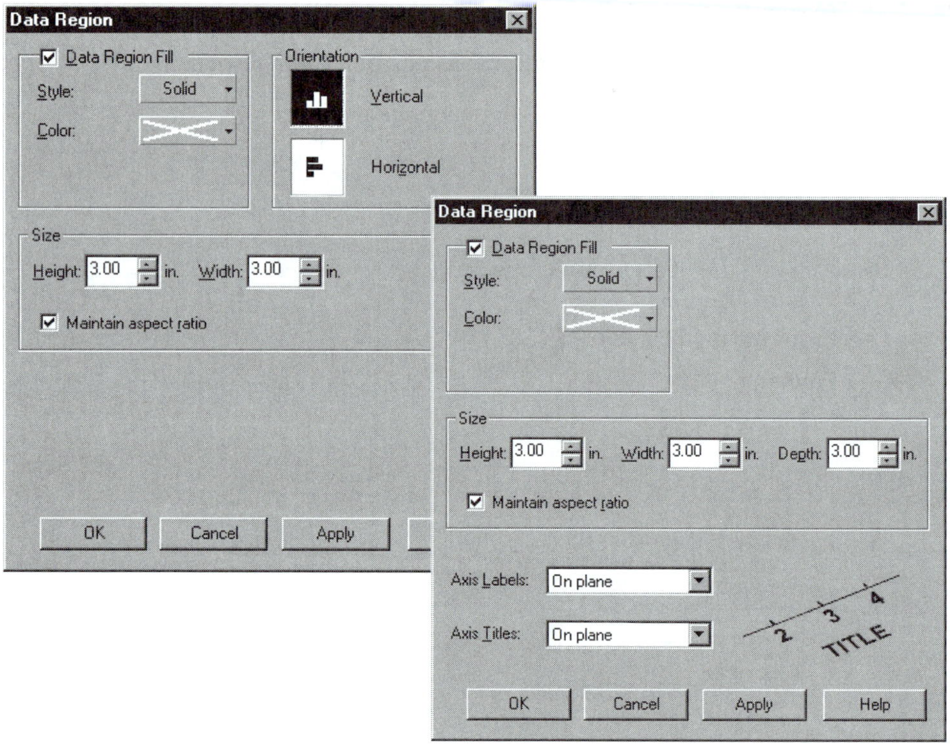


A 2-D data region is the area where the data are plotted, initially defined by the position of the axes. A 3-D data region is the volume where the data are plotted, initially defined by the position of the axes. Other objects in the chart are located with respect to the data region.

**Data Region Fill.** The background of the data region can have a fill or be turned off. In a 3-D chart, the fill is shaded according to the location of the light source.

**Orientation (2-D only).** The dependent (*y*) axis can be either vertical or horizontal. Changing orientation swaps the axes, along with their assigned variables.

**Size.** The size of the data region can be specified. This area or volume does not include axis labels or axis titles. If Maintain aspect ratio is selected, entering a height, width, or depth automatically changes the other two so that the ratio is maintained. Units are determined from the Interactive tab of the Options dialog box (Edit menu in the Viewer).

**Axis Labels (3-D only).** Labels can face the front of the chart or lie on the plane formed by two intersecting axes.

**Axis Titles (3-D only).** Titles can face the front of the chart or lie on the plane formed by two intersecting axes. Labels and titles can have different orientations.

### *To Change the Appearance of the 2-D Data Region*

▶ Activate a 2-D chart.

▶ From the menus choose:

Format
  Data Region...

*or*

▶ Click the Chart Manager tool, select Chart, and click Edit.

▶ Select the desired characteristics.

Optionally, you can:

- Change the fill.
- Change the size.
- Change the orientation.

### *To Change the Appearance of the 3-D Data Region*

▶ Activate a 3-D chart.

▶ From the menus choose:

Format
  Data Region...

*or*

▶ Click the Chart Manager tool, select Chart, and click Edit.

▶ Select the desired characteristics.

Optionally, you can:

- Change the fill.
- Change the size.
- Change label and title orientation.

# Panels

Panels are a means of incorporating more data dimensions in a chart. Each panel contains a chart for a different set of cases, determined by categories of a variable or a combination of categories.

## To Change a Panel Data Region

▶ Activate a paneled chart (double-click it).

▶ From the menus choose:

Format
  Data Region...

▶ Click a tab (Size, Categories, Appearance, Arrangement, or Titles).

▶ Select the desired options.

▶ Click OK to apply the new options and close the dialog box, or click Apply to apply the new options and leave the dialog box open.

## Panel Data Region: Size

Figure 12-7
*Panel Data Region: Size tab*

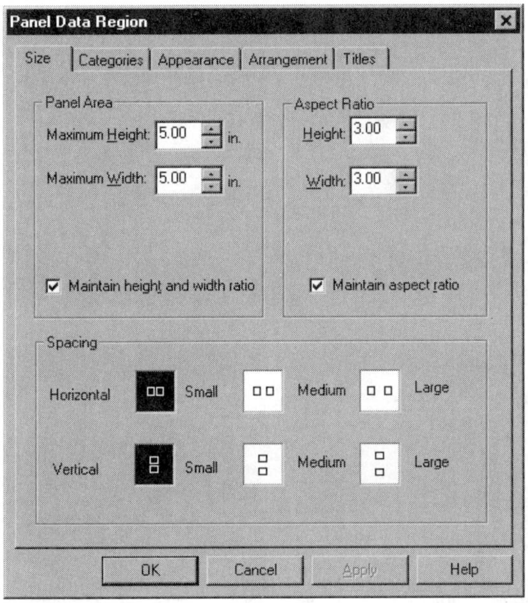


**Panel Area.** Specifies the size, in inches, of the panel area. The default size is $5 \times 5$. The height and width ratio is maintained by default.

**Aspect Ratio.** Changes the ratio of lengths for panels. Values for height, width, and depth (3-D chart only) represent a ratio, not actual lengths. To make panels larger or smaller, change the panel area values. The aspect ratio is maintained by default.

**Spacing.** Allows you to customize the orientation and spacing of panels in the panel area.

### To Change Panel Data Region Size

- ▶ Click the Size tab.
- ▶ Deselect Maintain height and width ratio and Maintain aspect ratio to change panel size ratios.
- ▶ Select the desired options.

## Panel Data Region: Appearance

Figure 12-8
*Panel Data Region: Appearance tab for 2-D and 3-D*

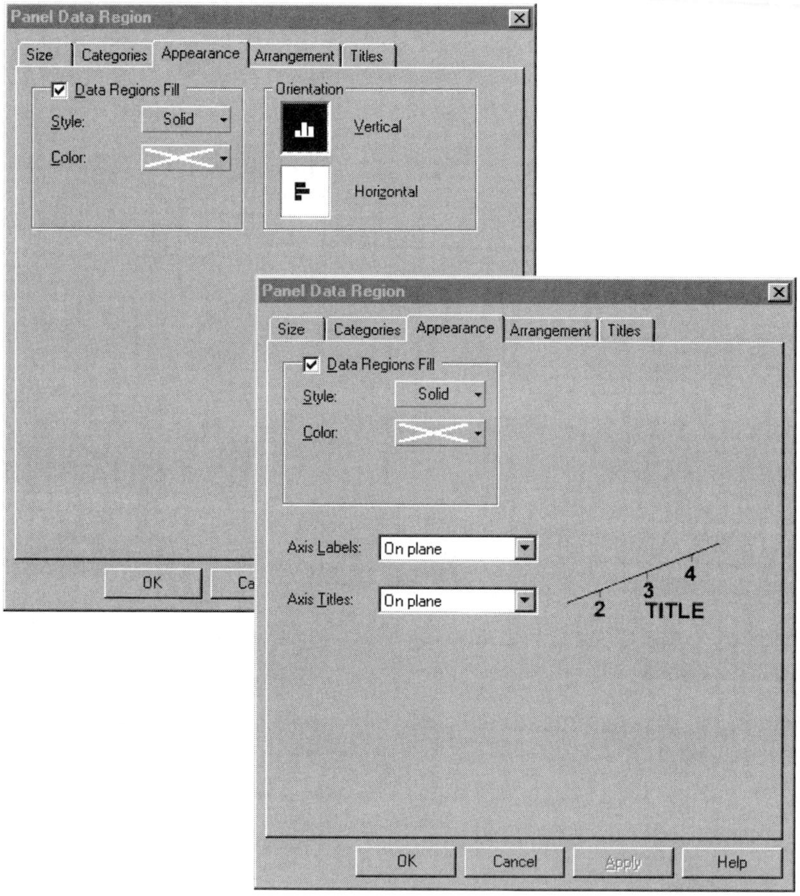


**Data Region Fill.** The fill of the data region is the background behind the elements. Style and color of the data region can be changed.

**Orientation (2-D only).** Changing the orientation of the data region here has the same effect as changing the orientation on the Assign Variables dialog box. The variables are switched, along with the axes.

**Axis Labels (3-D only).** Labels can face the front of the chart or lie on the plane formed by two intersecting axes.

**Axis Titles (3-D only).** Titles can face the front of the chart or lie on the plane formed by two intersecting axes. Labels and titles can have different orientations.

### *To Modify Panel Data Region Appearance*

- Click the Appearance tab.
- Select the desired options.

## *Panel Data Region: Arrangement*

If panels are based on only one variable, you can adjust the arrangement of panels.

Figure 12-9
*Panel Data Region: Arrangement tab*

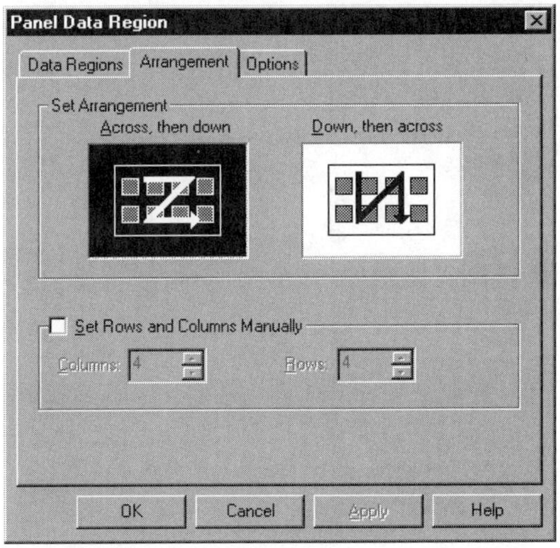


**Set Arrangement.** Across, then down means that the first row is filled by categories, then the second row, and so on. The other choice, Down, then across, means that the first column is filled, then the second column, the third, and so on.

**Set Rows and Columns Manually.** If you have both rows and columns, they can be arranged automatically, or you can select this item and specify either the number of rows or the number of columns, depending on which arrangement is selected.

### To Change the Arrangement of Panels

▶ Click the Arrangement tab.

▶ Select the desired options.

## Panel Data Region: Titles

Figure 12-10
*Panel Data Region: Titles tab*

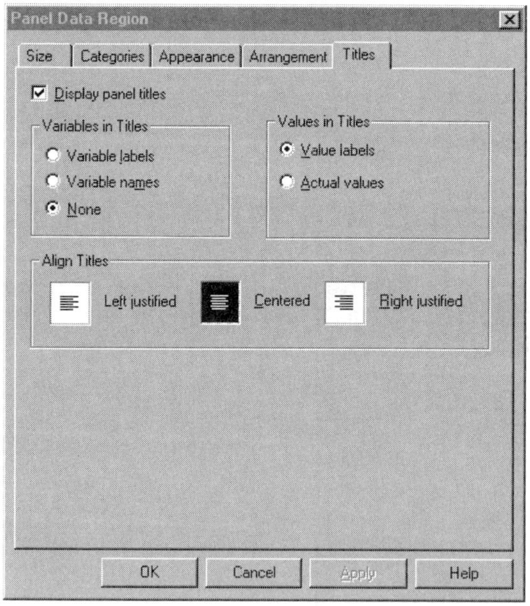


**Display Panel Titles.** Titles for each panel can be displayed or hidden.

**Variables in Titles.** Specifies whether panel titles will feature variable labels such as *Employment Category* or variable names such as *jobcat*.

**Values in Titles.** Specifies whether panel titles will feature value labels, such as *Managerial,* or actual values, such as *jobcat 3.*

**Align Titles.** Positions panel titles as centered or left- or right-justified.

### To Change Panel Data Region Titles

- Click the Titles tab.
- Select the desired options.

## Layout

Objects in a chart can have various arrangements in and around the data region. These objects include the title, subtitle, caption, legend, and key.

Figure 12-11
*Default layout*

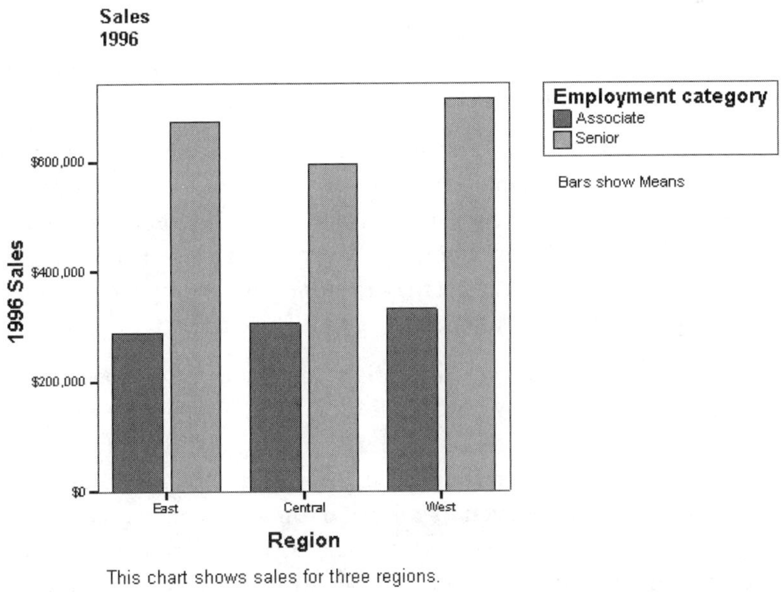


After the chart is made, you can drag the chart objects to new positions.

### To Arrange Chart Objects

- ▶ Activate the chart.
- ▶ From the menus choose:

  Format
  Arrange All

The title, subtitle, caption, legends, and keys are arranged around the data region of the chart in default positions. You can drag them to new positions.

## Legend Modification

Color, size, and style are often used to encode independent data dimensions visually in a chart. For example, red bars or lines could represent domestic sales, while green bars or lines might represent international sales. Similarly, small symbols and large symbols can be used to distinguish categories, as can different styles of symbols or different styles of fill. You can make distinctions in color or size on a continuous scale as well as on discrete categories.

A legend shows how to decode color, size, or style in a chart. You can assign variables to a legend on the Assign Variables tab when creating a chart or later when modifying a chart. A legend has many properties that are subject to change.

**Categorical legends.** When a categorical variable is assigned to a legend target, each category in the legend variable is assigned a color, style, or size as determined by the ChartLook. When a categorical variable is assigned, the elements in the chart are split or divided into groups. The assignment is displayed in a legend on the chart. Up to three legend variables can be assigned at the same time, depending on the type of chart. Each of these assignments creates a separate legend. Thus, a chart can have multiple legends.

**Scale legends.** In the legend, a scale variable can be assigned to Color or Size, when those targets are available. When a scale variable is assigned to a legend, the existing elements take on the color or size defined by the legend. By default, the scale for categories is determined according to the mean of the variable. For example, suppose that the variable *age* is assigned to color and (on a continuous scale) the mean age ranges from light red (20 years) to dark red (95 years). An object in the chart that represents a summary of values for 25 cases would be colored according to the mean age of those 25 cases.

**Position and display.** A legend can be dragged to a new position. It can also be hidden.

### To Change Legend Properties

▶ Activate the chart (double-click it).

▶ From the menus choose:

Format
  Legend

▶ Choose Color Legend, Style Legend, or Size Legend.

*or*

▶ Double-click the legend to be modified.

*or*

▶ Open the Chart Manager, select the legend, and click Edit.

▶ Click a tab.

▶ Select the desired options.

If you click Apply, the new properties are applied to the selected legend and the dialog box remains open. If you click OK, the properties are applied to the legend and the dialog box closes.

### To Change the Position of a Legend

▶ Activate the chart (double-click it).

▶ Use the mouse to drag the legend to a new position.

### To Show or Hide a Legend

▶ Activate the chart (double-click it).

▶ From the menus choose:

Edit
  Chart Manager...

*or*

▶ Click the Chart Manager icon.

▶ Select the legend of interest in the Chart Contents. This enables the Show and Hide radio buttons.

▶ Select Show or Hide.

*or*

If the legend is displayed, right-click the legend and choose Hide Legend from the context menu.

## Legend: Title

Figure 12-12
*Legend: Title tab*

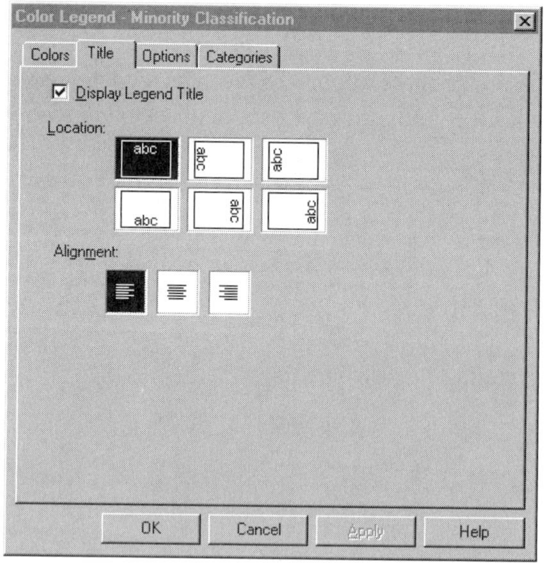

Legend titles can be displayed or turned off.

**Location.** The title can be located with respect to the edges of the legend. When the title is vertical on either side of the legend box, the title orientation can be either up or down.

**Alignment.** Alignment places the title at either edge or in the center of the legend box.

### To Change a Legend Title

▶ Click the Title tab.

Optionally, you can:

- Turn the legend title on or off.
- Change the alignment and location of the legend title.

To change text in the legend, double-click the text to be changed or use the Text tool.

## Categorical Legend: Options

Figure 12-13
*Categorical Legend: Options tab*

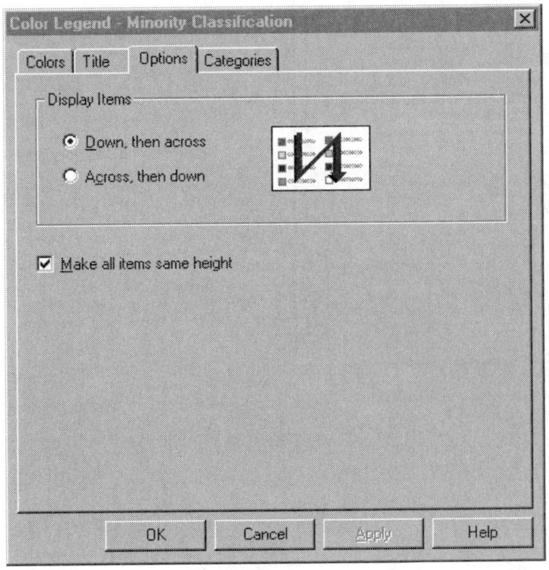

For a categorical legend having more than one column, items can be ordered in rows (across, then down) or columns (down, then across). Also, all items can be assigned the height of the tallest item. This feature is useful for a legend that has more than one column.

### To Change the Display Arrangement of a Categorical Legend

- ▶ Click the Options tab.
- ▶ Select the desired display formats.

## Categorical Legend: Categories

Figure 12-14
*Color or Size Legend (Categorical): Categories tab*

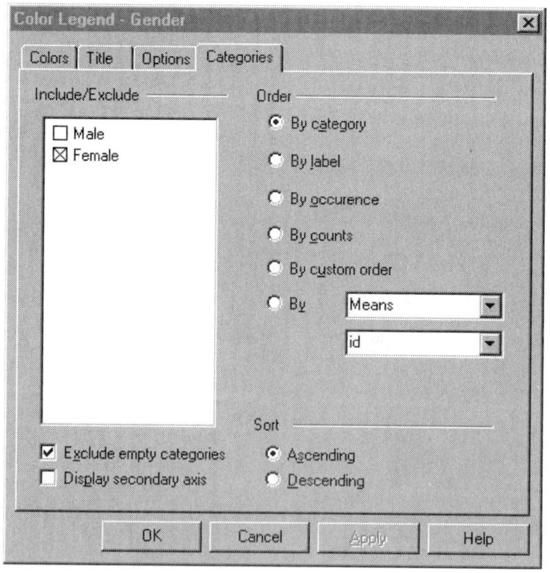


Through the Categorical Legend dialog box, you can reorder categories for display in your chart. You can change the order, sort and type of categories included.

**Panel Variable.** Selects which variable to reorder for charts with panel variables.

**Include/Exclude.** Controls which categories are displayed in the chart.

**Exclude empty categories.** Hides categories with no data.

**Order.** Reorders categories manually by drag and drop. Standard order uses properties such as Label, Occurrence, and Counts.

**Sort**. Displays categories in ascending or descending order.

**Display secondary axis**. Displays a second axis in the chart that mirrors the primary axis. (*Note:* Secondary axes are not displayed for 3-D or paneled charts.)

### To Modify Legend Categories

▶ Click the Categories tab.

▶ Reorder categories for display in your chart.

Optionally, you can:

- Reorder the variables in the list by dragging and dropping them.
- Exclude empty categories.
- Display a secondary axis.
- Sort categories by ascending or descending order.

## Color Legends

In color legends, if a categorical variable is assigned, each category is assigned a distinct color. If a scale variable is assigned to a color legend, a continuous color gradient is used to indicate the values along a scale. For summary elements, the scale is determined by a summary function.

## Color Legend (Categorical): Colors

Figure 12-15
*Color Legend (Categorical): Colors tab*

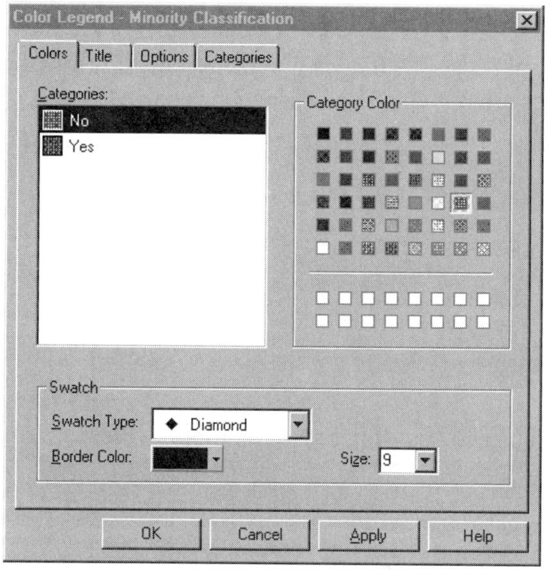


You can select categories individually to change colors. You can also change the swatch in the legend, as well as the size and the color of the border around the swatch.

### To Change Colors in a Category Legend

- Click the Colors tab.
- Select a category.
- Select the desired color for that category.

Optionally, you can modify the swatch in the legend.

### *To Add Custom Colors to a Color Legend*

- Click the Colors tab.
- Double-click one of the 16 custom color swatches at the bottom of the palette.
- Define a custom color.

  You can assign the custom color to any category in the list.

## *Color Legend (Scale): Colors*

Figure 12-16
*Color Legend (Scale): Colors tab*

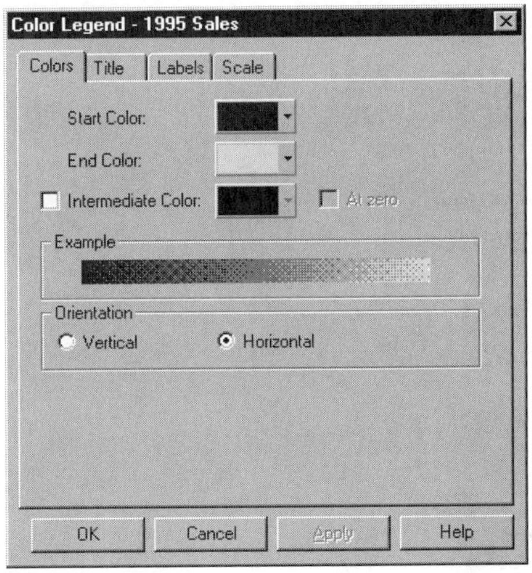


When a scale variable has been assigned to the Color target on the Assign Variables dialog box, colors are assigned to categories according to the value of a summary function. Colors are assigned to symbols by their values along the scale. For example, in a bar chart, the color of each bar can indicate the mean age of persons in a category. In a scatterplot, the color of a symbol can indicate the age for each case, if the scale variable *age* is assigned to Color. In this dialog box, you can customize the color gradient.

**Start Color.** Assigned to the smallest value in the data range.

**End Color.** Assigned to the largest value in the data range.

**Intermediate Color.** If you want a three-color gradient, an intermediate color can be selected. It will be placed halfway between the smallest and largest values in the data range.

**Intermediate Color At zero.** If a three-color gradient is selected, the intermediate color value can be assigned to the location of the value 0 in the data range. If there is no 0 in the data range, the intermediate color is not used.

**Orientation.** The gradient can be displayed in the legend either horizontally or vertically.

### *To Modify Colors in a Scale Legend*

- ▶ Click the Colors tab.
- ▶ Select starting and ending colors.

Optionally, you can:

- Change the orientation of the gradient in the legend.
- Select an intermediate color.

## *Color or Size Legend (Scale): Scale*

Figure 12-17
*Color or Size Legend (Scale): Scale tab*

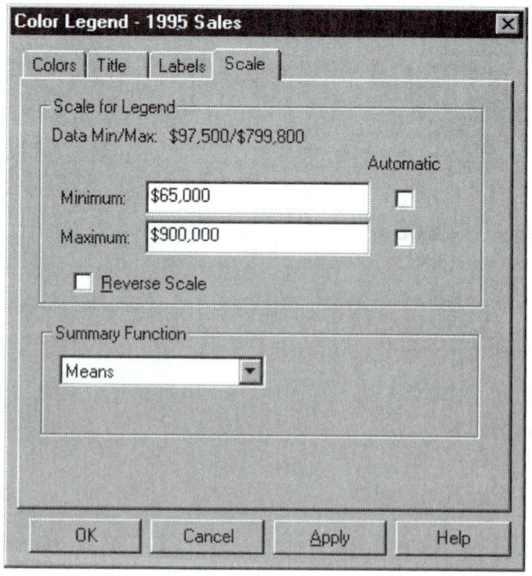

In a color scale legend, you can specify the minimum and maximum values to be associated with the colors at the ends of the scale. For example, suppose a scale represents mean ages with a gradient from red (minimum) to blue (maximum). Assuming that the cases represent adults, you could associate red with age 20 and blue with age 95. The colors in the spectrum between red and blue represent the ages between 20 and 95. Similarly, in a size scale legend, you can specify the minimum and maximum values for symbol sizes at either end of the scale.

By default, the minimum and maximum data points are used at the ends of the scale. You can specify other values for the minimum and maximum. You can also reverse the scale.

**Summary Function.** The values of the summary function of the scale variable are represented by colors in the strip. The default summary function is Means.

### To Modify a Legend Scale

▶ Click the Scale tab.

▶ To specify minimum and maximum values, deselect Automatic and enter values.

Optionally, you can:

- Reverse the scale.
- Change the summary function.

## Color or Style Legend (Scale): Labels

Figure 12-18
*Color or Style Scale Legend: Labels tab*

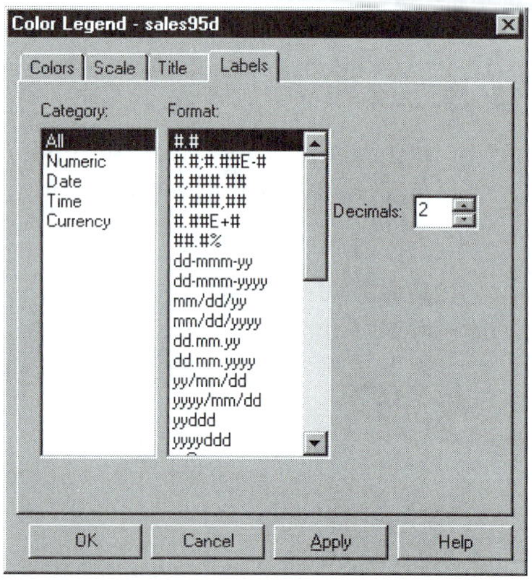


You can change the print format of the scale value labels on legends.

**Category.** The categories define various groups of formats listed in the next column.

**Format.** You can use formats to suppress or add percentage signs and dollar signs and to switch between scientific notation and regular numeric display.

**Decimals.** This sets the number of decimals displayed in the legend labels.

### To Change Labels on a Scale Legend

- ▶ Click the Labels tab.
- ▶ Select the desired options.

## Style Legends

Style is interpreted differently by various chart elements. A bar has a fill style, a line can be made up of dashes or dots, and a symbol in a scatterplot or other chart can have a shape.

## Style Legend (Categorical): Symbol

Figure 12-19
*Style Legend (Categorical): Symbol tab*

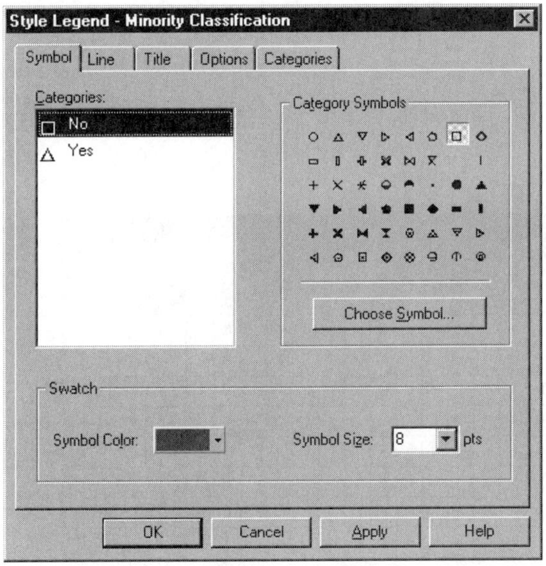


Symbols can be assigned to represent categories in a cloud of points or in a dot chart. The list of currently available symbols is displayed in this dialog box. To use a symbol from a font that is not displayed here, click Choose Symbol.

The color and size of the symbol can be changed if they are not assigned in other legends.

### To Change the Symbol for a Category

- ▶ Click the Symbol tab.
- ▶ Select a category in the list.
- ▶ Choose the desired symbol for the selected category.

Optionally, you can:

- Click Choose Symbol and select a different font for symbols.
- Change color and size if they are not controlled by the data.

### Symbol

Figure 12-20
*Choose Symbol dialog box*

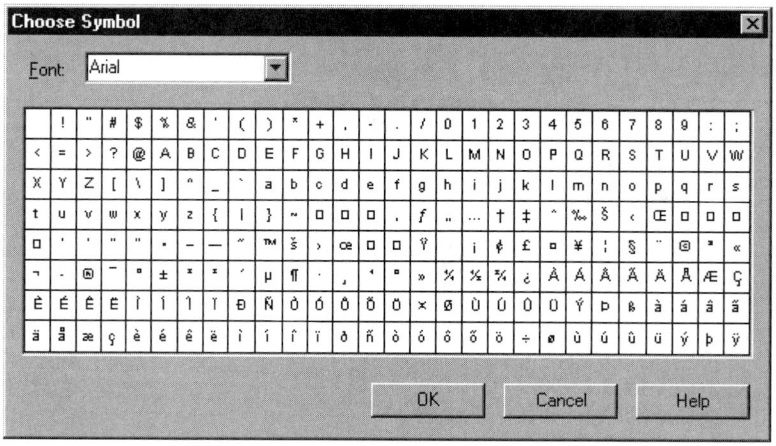


For interactive charts, you can select a symbol from any font stored on your system.

### To Select a Legend Symbol from a Font

- ▶ Click the Symbol tab.
- ▶ Click Choose Symbol.

- Select a font for symbols.
- Double-click a symbol.

## Style Legend (Categorical): Fill

Figure 12-21
*Style Legend (Categorical): Fill tab*

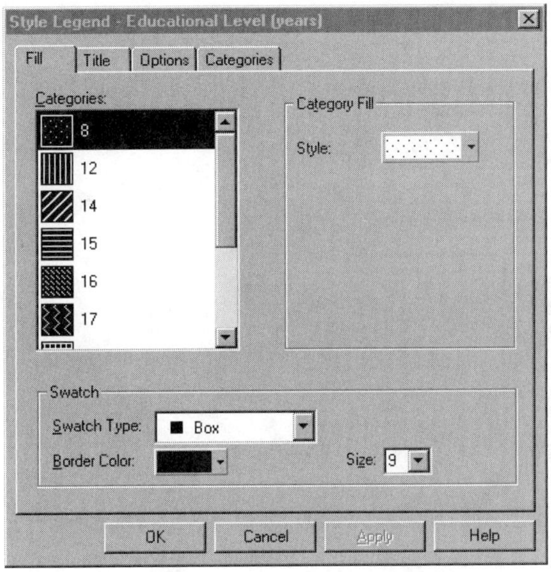


Fill styles can be assigned to distinguish categories in some chart elements. For example, one category might use cross-hatching and another might use vertical lines.

### To Change Category Fill Styles

- Click the Fill tab.
- Select a category in the list.
- Select the desired fill style and color for the selected category.

Optionally, you can change the shape, color, and size of the swatch if these characteristics are not controlled by the data.

## Style Legend (Categorical): Line

Figure 12-22
*Style Legend (Categorical): Line tab*

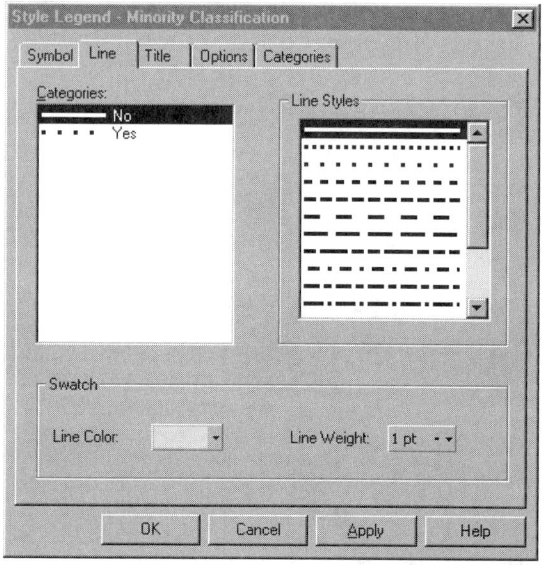


Line styles can be assigned to distinguish categories in some chart elements. For example, one category might use a solid line, and another, a dashed line.

### To Change Line Styles for Categories

- Click the Line tab.
- Select a category in the list.
- Select the desired line style for the selected category.

Optionally, you can change the color and weight of the swatch line if these characteristics are not controlled by the data.

## Size Legends

Size is interpreted according to the type of element. For symbols, the height is measured; for lines, the weight of the line is measured.

## Size Legend (Categorical): Symbol

Figure 12-23
*Size Legend (Categorical): Symbol tab*

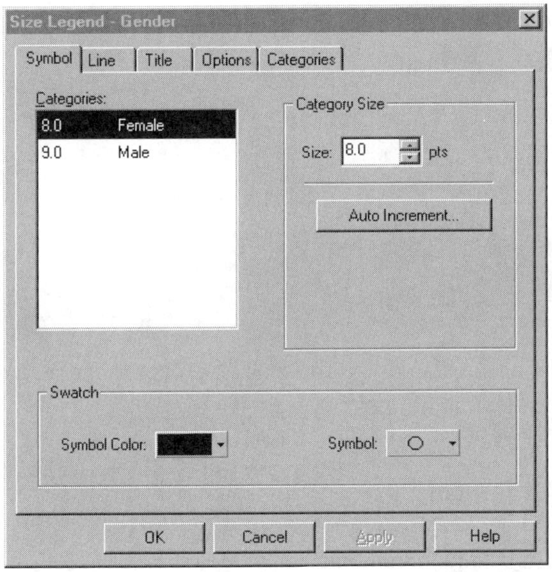


Each category can have an individual size assigned. Sizes can be assigned automatically with a specified starting size and an increment.

### To Change the Sizes for Categories

- ▶ Click the Symbol tab.
- ▶ Select a category in the list.
- ▶ Enter the desired size for the selected category.

Optionally, you can:

- Assign automatic increments in size, with a specified starting size and an increment (percentage or fixed amount).
- Change the color and shape of the swatch if these characteristics are not controlled by the data.

### Auto Increment

Figure 12-24
*Auto Increment dialog box*

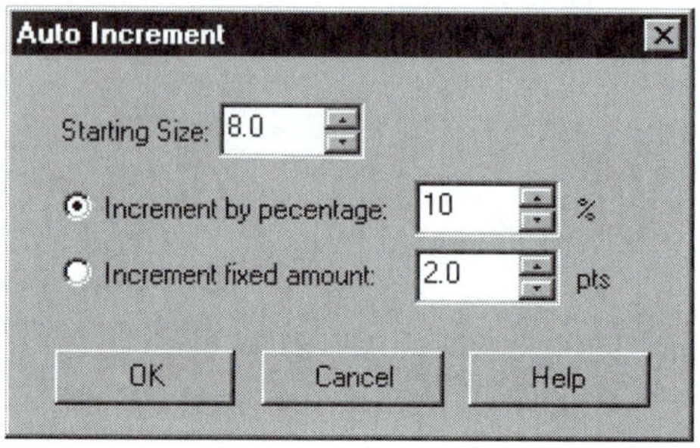


You can specify increments in the size of symbols as a percentage or a fixed amount. The starting size for the smallest symbol can be specified.

### To Set Automatic Increments for Symbols

- ▶ Click the Symbol tab and click Auto Increment.
- ▶ Select a starting size.
- ▶ Select increments.

## Size Legend (Categorical): Line

Figure 12-25
*Size Legend: Line tab*

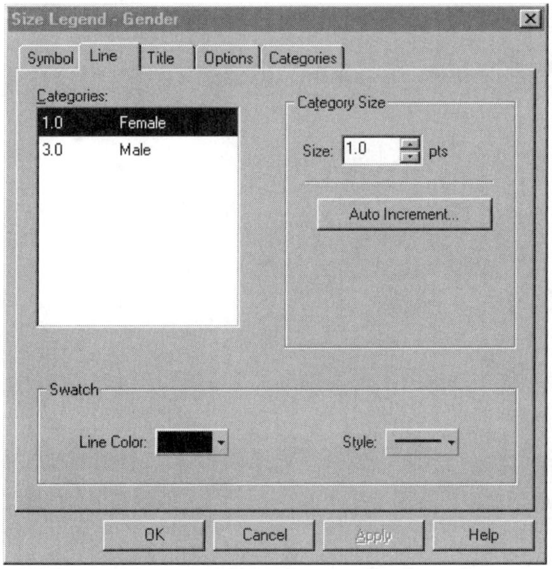


If a categorical variable is assigned to a size legend, lines corresponding to the categories can have different weights.

**Weight.** Weights can be specified for each category (to one decimal place).

**Auto Increment.** To resize all lines at once, click Auto Increment.

**Swatch.** The swatch in the legend can have a color and style if these characteristics are not controlled by the variable assignments.

### To Change Line Weights Assigned to Categories

- Click the Line tab.
- Select a category.
- Enter a size.

Optionally, you can assign automatic increments.

## Size Legend (Scale): Symbol

Figure 12-26
*Size Legend: Symbol tab*

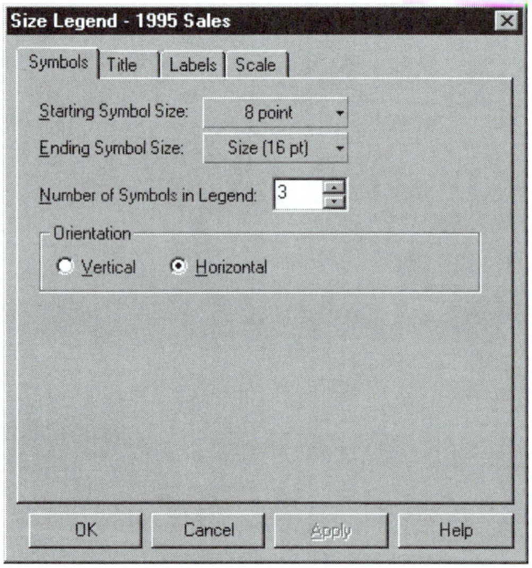


If a scale variable is assigned to a size legend, you can adjust the size range of the symbols and the type of display in the legend.

This feature is commonly used to make a bubble plot (with empty symbols such as circles), where a scale variable is assigned to the size legend. The plot is examined to see if the large and small bubbles form a pattern within any other patterns. Another use for a scale size legend is to create an influence plot, assigning DfBeta values or covariance ratios (from regression calculations) to the size legend.

### To Change a Scale Size Legend

- ▶ Click the Symbol tab.
- ▶ Specify starting and ending sizes.
- ▶ Select the type of legend display.

Optionally, you can:

- Select the type of legend display.
- Select the orientation.

# Frame Properties

Legends and keys can have frames. For these frames, you can select properties for the border, margins, and fill.

Figure 12-27
*Frame properties dialog box*

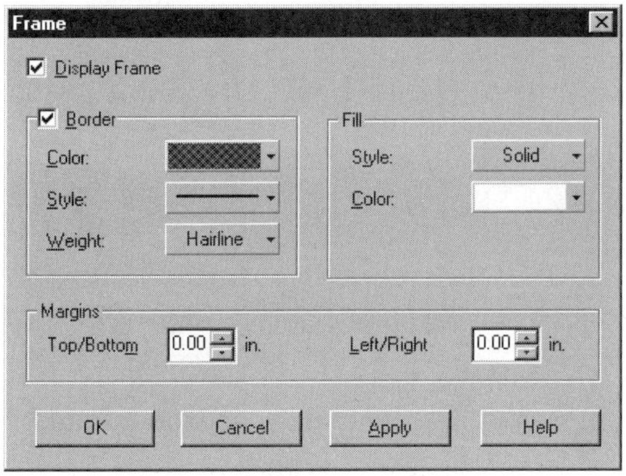


For margins, the units are determined from settings defined on the Interactive tab of Options (Edit menu).

## To Change Frame Properties

▶ Activate the chart (double-click it).

▶ Select a legend or a key.

▶ From the menus choose:

Format
 Frame...

*or*

▶ Right-click the legend or key and choose Frame.

▶ Select the desired frame options.

Optionally, you can:

- Display a frame for the object.
- Change the border.
- Change the fill style and colors.
- Set margins.

# Axis Modification

The axis properties of interactive graphs can be changed in the Scale Axis or Category Axis dialog box. Using the tabs on one of these dialog boxes, you can:

- Change the tick format and range.
- Control the appearance of major ticks, minor ticks, and the axis line.
- Determine the frequency, placement, and formatting of axis labels.
- Specify text and alignment of axis titles.
- Determine placement and appearance of grid lines.
- Determine placement and appearance of reference lines.
- Display a secondary axis for 2-D charts (not available for paneled charts).

### To Change Axis Properties

▶ Activate the chart by clicking it.

▶ Double-click an axis or its labels.

*or*

- From the menus choose:

  Format
  Axis
  [axis name]

  *or*

- Open the Chart Manager, select an axis, and click Edit.

- Click a tab (Scale, Appearance, Labels, Title, Grid Lines, or Reference Lines).

- Select the desired options.

- Click OK (which closes the dialog box) or Apply (which leaves the dialog box open).

## Scale Axis: Title

Figure 12-28
*Scale Axis: Title tab*

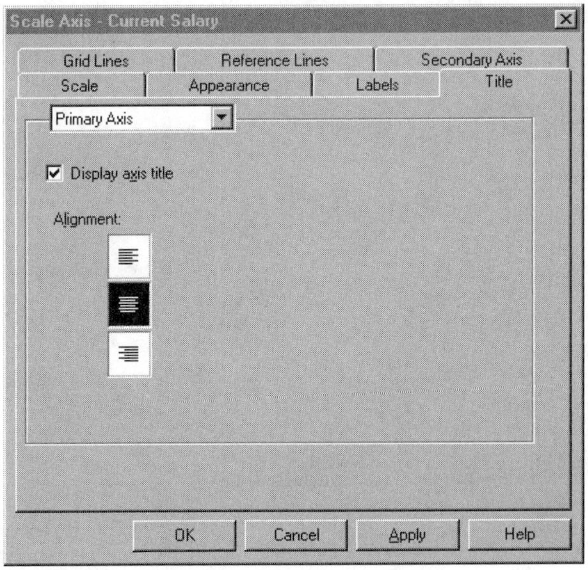


You can change titles for both the primary and secondary axes.

**Display axis title.** To suppress the axis title, deselect Display axis title.

**Alignment.** The text can be aligned with either end of the axis or in the middle. You can also drag it to a new position.

### To Modify an Axis Title

- Click the Title tab.
- Select the desired options.

To edit the axis title, double-click it or use the Text tool.

## Scale Axis: Scale

Figure 12-29
*Scale Axis: Scale tab*

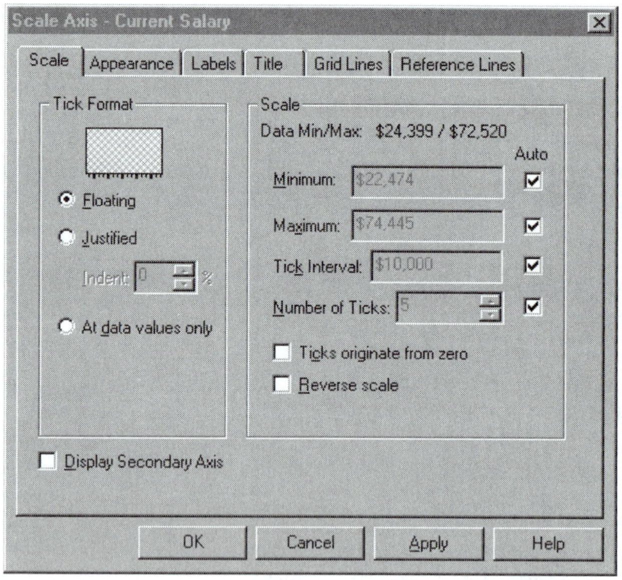


**Tick Format.** Determines how major ticks are positioned on the axis. The illustration at the top of this group changes as you make a new selection. To place ticks only at the ends of the axis, select Justified and specify Number of ticks = 2.

**Scale.** Adjustments to the scale can help you emphasize specific characteristics of a chart.

**Minimum.** With Auto selected, the program chooses the minimum value of the scale. You can deselect Auto and enter a value.

**Maximum.** With Auto selected, the program chooses the maximum value of the scale. You can deselect Auto and enter a value.

**Tick Interval.** The distance between ticks. You can deselect Auto and enter a value. This item is linked to the number of ticks.

**Number of Ticks.** You can choose Auto or enter a number. This item is linked to the tick interval.

**Ticks originate from zero.** The first tick is at the 0 point.

**Reverse scale.** The scale is switched between ascending and descending.

**Display Secondary Axis.** Creates a secondary axis. Click the Secondary Axis tab to specify options. *Note:* Secondary axes are not displayed for 3-D or paneled charts.

### *To Modify the Scale on a Scale Axis*

▶ Click the Scale tab.

▶ Select a tick format.

Optionally, you can:

- Deselect Auto and enter a value for Minimum, Maximum, or Tick Interval.
- Deselect Auto and change the Number of Ticks.
- Set the origin for ticks at zero.
- Reverse the scale.
- Select or deselect Display Secondary Axis.

## Scale Axis: Appearance

Figure 12-30
*Scale Axis: Appearance tab*

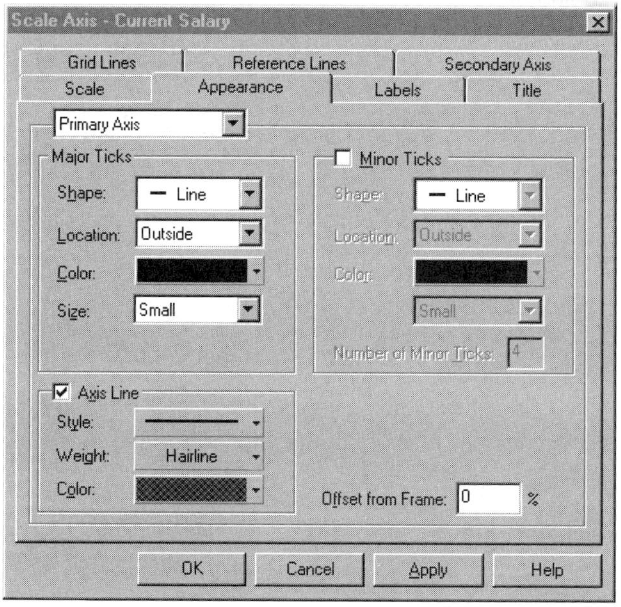


For both the primary and the secondary axes, the appearance of ticks and of the axis line can be changed.

**Primary Axis/Secondary Axis.** Specifies an axis to modify.

**Major Ticks** and **Minor Ticks.** You can change the shape, location relative to the axis, color, and size of either kind of ticks. Minor ticks can be turned off, or you can specify the number of minor ticks between adjacent major ticks.

**Axis Line.** The style, weight, and color of the axis line can be changed, or the line can be turned off.

**Jitter.** Adds a small amount of random noise to any scale data, whether or not the points are coincident. Categorical data are not jittered.

**Offset from Frame.** The axis can be moved away from the data region by a percentage of the size of the data region.

### To Modify the Appearance of a Scale Axis

- Click the Appearance tab.
- Select the desired options.

## Scale Axis: Labels

Figure 12-31
*Scale Axis: Labels tab*

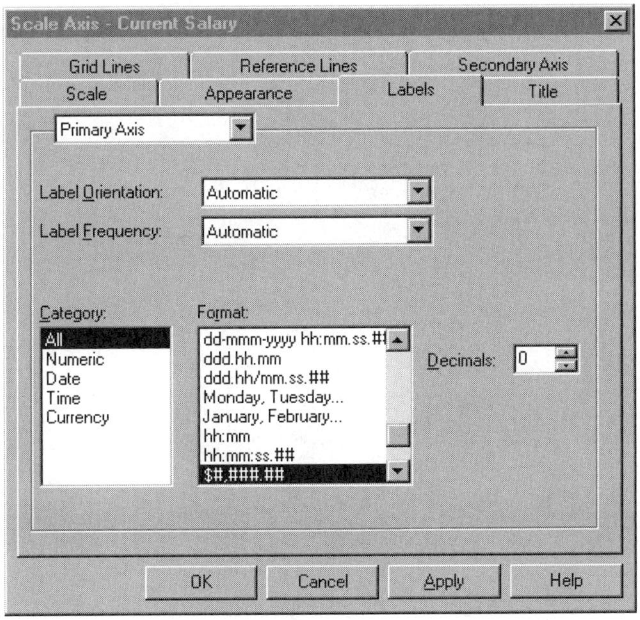


The properties of axis labels include their orientation and frequency. When automatic settings are selected, the program chooses an orientation and frequency that avoid overlap. You can select label properties for both the primary and the secondary axes.

**Label Orientation**. Controls the orientation of the labels in relation to the axis.

**Label Frequency**. Determines how many major ticks are labeled.

**Format.** You can select a label format and the number of decimal places. The Category box lists groups of data formats shown in the Format box. To view all possible formats, select All. To view a smaller group of formats, select one of the categories.

### To Modify Scale Axis Labels

- Click the Labels tab.
- Select the desired options.

## Scale Axis: Grid Lines

Figure 12-32
*Scale Axis: Grid Lines tab*

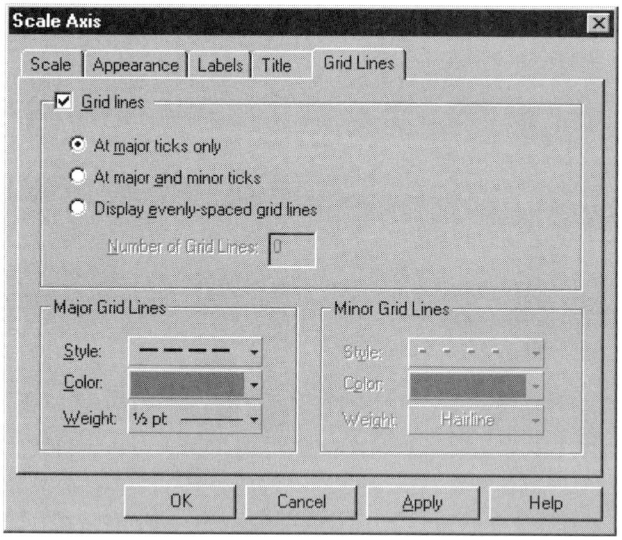


Grid lines, drawn at major and minor ticks along an axis, can be turned on or off. You can also enter a specific number for grid lines spaced evenly along the axis. The style, color, and weight can be specified for both major and minor grid lines.

### To Modify Scale Axis Grid Lines

- Click the Grid Lines tab.
- Select the desired options.

## Scale Axis: Reference Lines

Figure 12-33
*Scale Axis: Reference Lines tab*

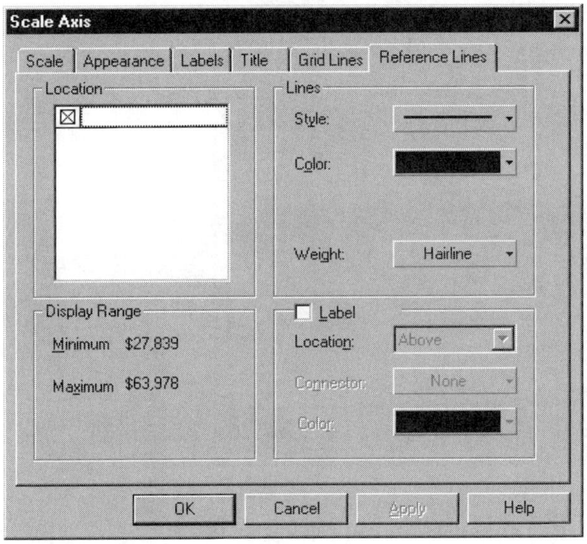


Reference lines are optional lines drawn on a bar chart, line chart, or scatterplot to emphasize a particular value on a scale or category axis.

Reference lines are positioned at values on the scale axis. Labels and connectors can be displayed. The style, color, and weight can be specified for each line.

### To Create Scale Axis Reference Lines

- Click the Reference Lines tab.
- Select an item in the Location box and enter a value within the display range.

- Select options such as labels, line style, color, and weight.

## Scale Axis: Secondary Axis

Figure 12-34
*Scale Axis: Secondary Axis tab*

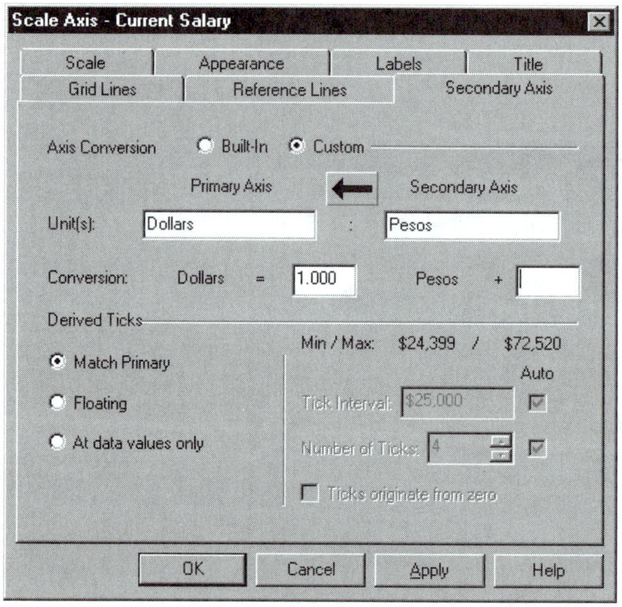


Displaying a secondary axis creates two frames of reference for the same variable. For example, data can be referenced in both dollars and francs. *Note:* Secondary axes are not displayed for 3-D or paneled charts.

**Axis Conversion.** Options include a standard built-in conversion or a custom conversion.

**Units**. Provides a unit list for built-in conversions. When custom conversion is selected, you can create new units by typing in the field. The arrow control transforms the direction of the algebraic expression.

**Conversion.** Illustrates the algebraic expression for a conversion. You can customize a conversion by entering new data values for each unit.

**Derived Ticks.** Displays options for major ticks on the secondary axis (minor ticks are chosen on the Appearance tab). Ticks can match the primary axis ticks or appear only at data values. Interval and number can be specified for floating ticks.

### To Create a Secondary Axis

- Select Display Secondary Axis.
- Click the Secondary Axis tab.
- Select Built-in or Custom.
- Select a unit type. For custom conversions, enter a name for the units on the primary and secondary axes.
- Select options for derived ticks.

  *Note*: Secondary axes are not displayed for 3-D or paneled charts.

## Category Axis: Categories

Figure 12-35
*Categorical Axis: Categories tab*

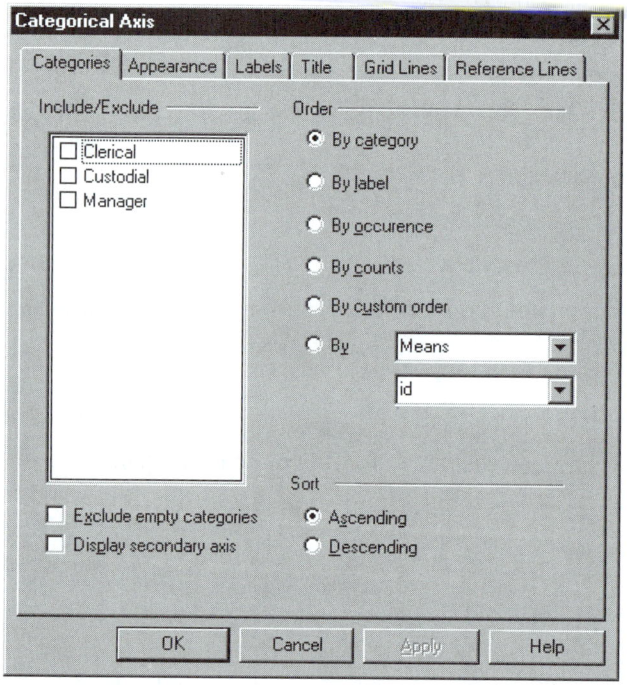


Reordering and excluding categories allows you to create a customized chart. You can change the order, sort, and type of categories.

**Panel Variable.** Selects which variable to reorder for charts with panel variables.

**Include/Exclude.** Controls which categories are displayed in the chart.

**Exclude empty categories.** Hides categories with no data. Empty categories are excluded by default. A category is defined as any value with a defined value label.

**Order.** Reorders categories manually by drag and drop. Standard order uses properties such as label, occurrence, and counts.

**Sort.** Displays categories in ascending or descending order.

**Display secondary axis**. Displays a second axis in the chart that mirrors the primary axis. *Note*: Secondary axes are not displayed for 3-D or paneled charts.

### To Modify Categories

▶ Click the Categories tab.

▶ Select categories to exclude (deselect to include).

▶ Select a built-in category order such as Category, Label, Occurrence, or Counts.

*or*

▶ Select Custom Order. You can reorder categories by dragging and dropping them.

*or*

Order categories by the summary function of another variable:

▶ Select a summary function from the drop-down list.

▶ Select a variable from the drop-down list.

Optionally, you can:

- Exclude empty categories (default).
- Display a secondary axis (not available for 3-D or paneled charts).
- Sort categories in ascending or descending order.

## Changing Category Order

Categories can be reordered or omitted for display in your chart. There are three ways to reorder categories.

**Order by Property Type.** Each categorical variable can be ordered by properties such as Values, Label, Occurrence, and Counts.

**Order by Function of Another Variable.** Reorder categories by the summary function of another variable. Certain functions, such as Means, require a scale variable. Properties such as N of Cases or Percentiles require you to define the property value.

**Create a Custom Order.** Categorical variables can also be reordered manually. Drag and drop the categories to create a new order for the chart display.

## Category Axis: Appearance

Figure 12-36
*Categorical Axis: Appearance tab*

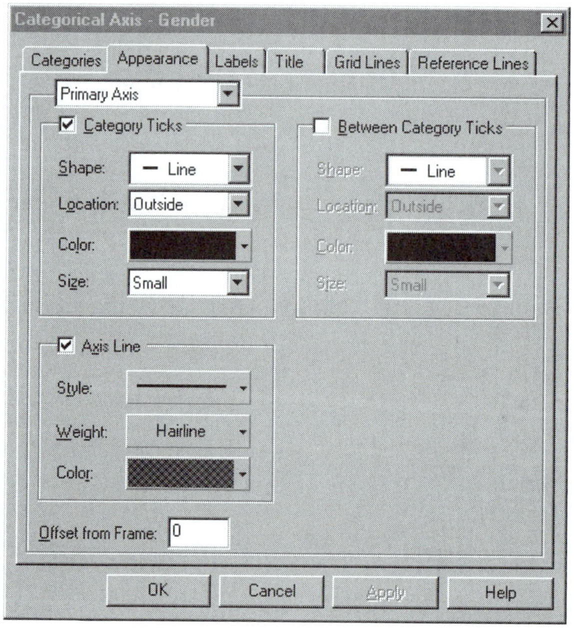


For both the primary and secondary axes, the appearance of ticks and of the axis line can be changed.

**Category Ticks** and **Between Category Ticks.** Changes the shape, location, color, and size of ticks. Select Between Category Ticks to place ticks halfway between adjacent category ticks.

**Axis Line.** The style, weight, and appearance of the axis line can be changed.

**Offset from Frame.** The axis can be moved away from the data region by a percentage of the size of the data region.

### To Modify the Appearance of a Category Axis

- Click the Appearance tab.
- Select the desired options.

## Category Axis: Labels

Figure 12-37
*Categorical Axis: Labels tab*

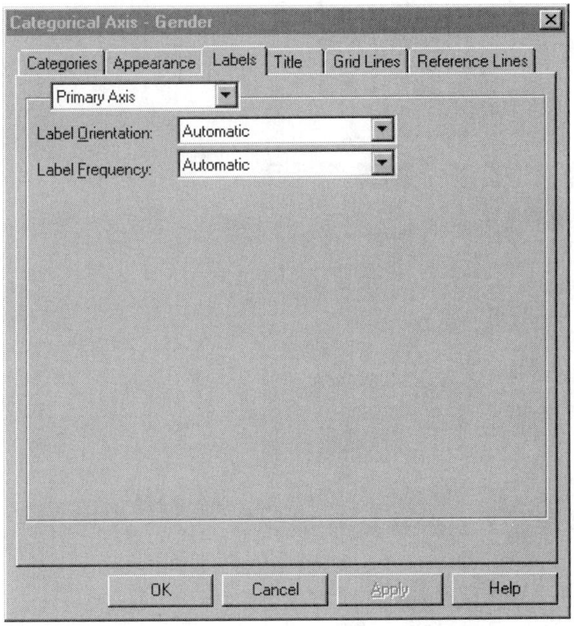


You can select label properties for both the primary and secondary axes.

**Label Orientation.** Labels are oriented with respect to the axis. Automatic lets the program choose an orientation with minimum overlap for the specified frequency. Other choices include Horizontal, Parallel to axis, Staggered in 2 rows, Staggered in 3 rows, Rotated 90 degrees, and Rotated 270 degrees.

**Label Frequency.** The number of labels is specified in relation to the category ticks. Choices include Automatic, No labels, All categories, Every other category, and Every third category.

### To Modify Category Axis Labels

- ▶ Click the Labels tab.
- ▶ Select the desired options.

## Category Axis: Grid Lines

Figure 12-38
*Categorical Axis: Grid Lines tab*

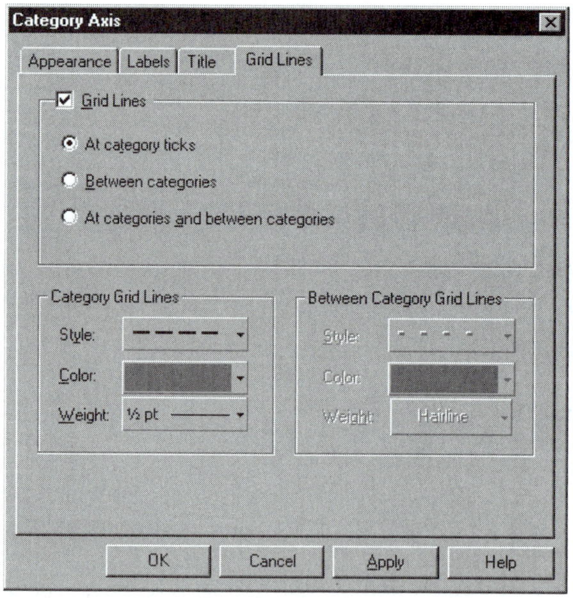


Grid lines, drawn at category ticks and between-category ticks along an axis, can be turned on or off. You can also enter a specific number for grid lines spaced evenly along the axis. The style, color, and weight can be specified for both category and between-category grid lines.

#### To Modify Category Axis Grid Lines

- Click the Grid Lines tab.
- Select the desired options.

### Category Axis: Reference Lines

Reference lines are optional lines drawn on a bar chart, line chart, or scatterplot to emphasize a particular value on a scale or category axis.

For each reference line, determine the position of the line by selecting one or more categories. You can also choose to display labels and connectors. The style, color, and weight can be specified for reference lines.

#### To Create Category Axis Reference Lines

- Click the Reference Lines tab.
- Select a category to include or exclude reference lines.
- Select options such as labels, line style, color, and weight.

### Grid Lines

Grid lines can be displayed or hidden, perpendicular to each axis. You can modify grid lines for each axis by modifying the axis, or you can access a dialog box that shows the features of grid lines for all axes. This dialog box has a tab for each axis.

Figure 12-39
*Grid Lines dialog box*

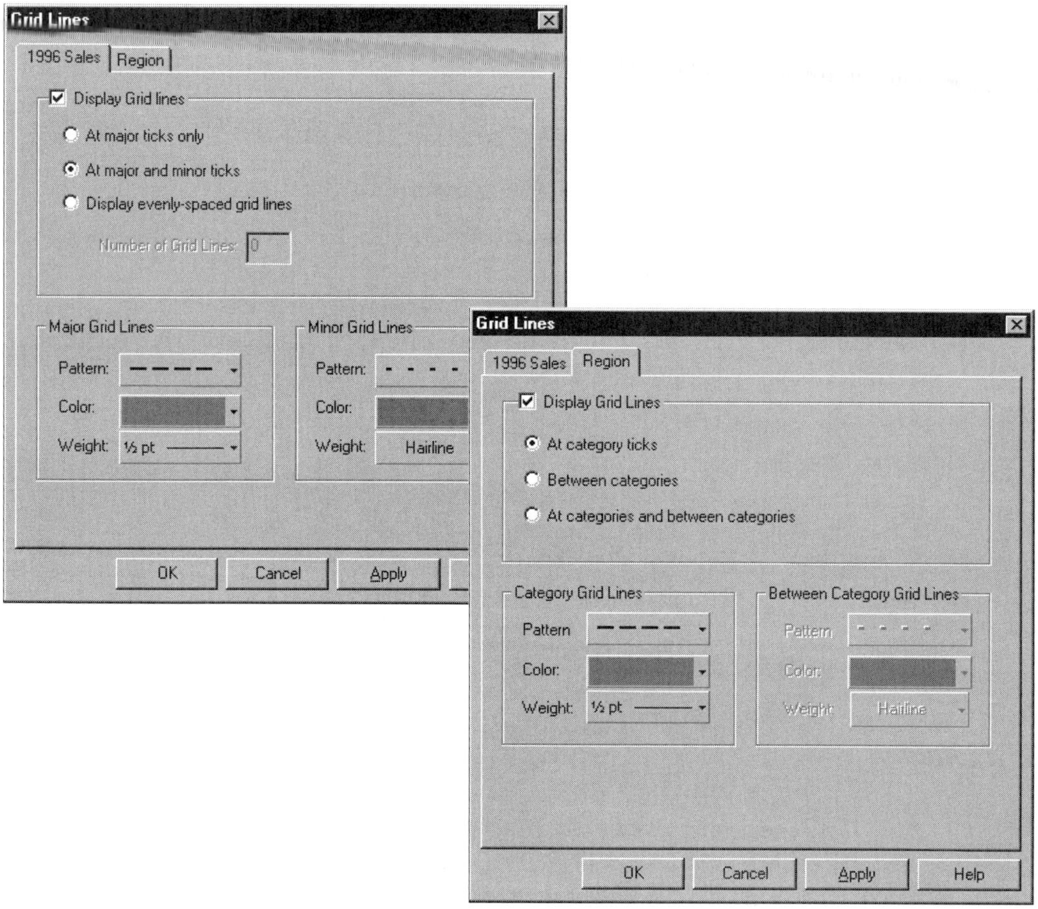


**Display Grid lines.** If grid lines are turned on for a scale axis, they can be at major ticks (scale axis), at both major and minor ticks, or evenly spaced in the data region. For a category axis, grid lines can be at category ticks, between category ticks, or both.

**Major** or **Category Grid Lines.** The pattern, color, and weight of major grid lines can be changed.

**Minor** or **Between Category Grid Lines.** The pattern, color, and weight of minor grid lines can be changed.

### To Modify Grid Lines

- ▶ Activate the chart (double-click it).
- ▶ From the menus choose:

  Format
    Grid Lines...

- ▶ Select the features you want for grid lines associated with each axis.

## Reference Line Properties

Figure 12-40
*Reference Lines dialog box*

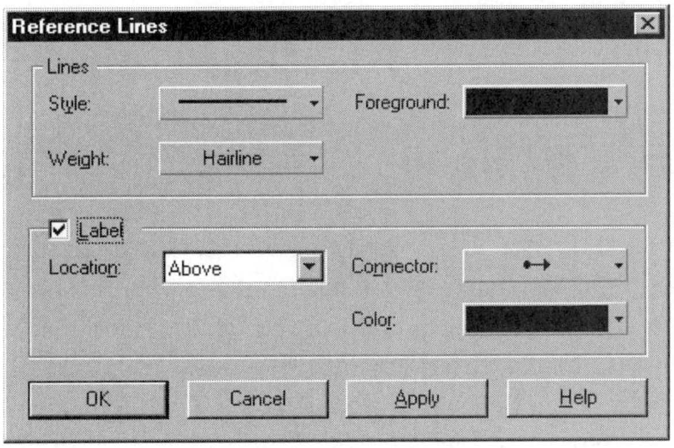


Reference lines are optional lines drawn on a bar chart, line chart, or scatterplot to emphasize a particular value on a scale or category axis. You can change the properties of each reference line in order to customize the appearance of your chart. Line style, weight, color, connectors, and label options can be specified.

### To Modify Reference Line Properties

▶ Activate the chart (double-click it).

▶ From the menus choose:

Edit
  Reference Line Properties

or

▶ Right-click over the reference line.

▶ Select Properties from the menu.

Optionally, you can:

- Specify line style, weight, color, and foreground.
- Specify label location, connector, and color.

## Changing the Appearance of Charts

You can change the appearance of a chart by editing an individual chart, by changing chart properties, or by applying a ChartLook. ChartLooks are similar to TableLooks. Each ChartLook consists of a collection of chart properties, including specifications for colors, styles, sizes, text objects, filled objects, lines and symbols, and axes. With a ChartLook, you can apply the collection of properties to a chart all at once. You can select from a list of preset ChartLooks, or you can create and save a custom ChartLook.

## ChartLook

Figure 12-41
*ChartLook dialog box*

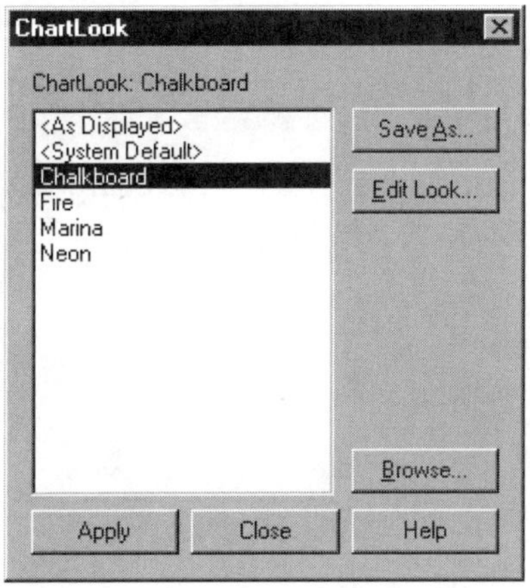


A ChartLook is a set of properties that defines the appearance of an interactive chart. You can select a previously defined ChartLook or create your own. When you create an interactive chart from the Graphs menu, you can choose a ChartLook from the list on the Options tab.

ChartLooks are stored in files with the extension *.clo* (if file extensions are displayed), making it easy to copy the file and give a ChartLook to other members of a group.

**Default ChartLook for new interactive charts.** You can use any defined ChartLook as the default ChartLook for new interactive charts. The default ChartLook is set on the Interactive tab of the Options dialog box. (You can access this dialog box from the Edit menu of the Viewer.)

### To Apply a ChartLook to an Interactive Chart

- Activate the chart (double-click it).
- From the menus choose:

Format
  ChartLooks...

- Select a ChartLook from the list of files. To select a file from another directory, click Browse.

- Click Apply to apply the ChartLook to the activated chart.

  *or*

- Double-click the ChartLook you want to apply.

  All of the properties defined in the ChartLook are applied to the chart, regardless of any previous changes made to the chart.

### To Edit or Create a ChartLook

- Activate a chart (double-click it).

- From the menus choose:

  Format
    ChartLooks...

- Select a ChartLook that is similar to the look you want to create.

- Click Edit Look.

- Adjust the chart properties for the attributes you want and click OK.

- Click Save As to save it as a new ChartLook.

- Select a directory and enter a filename.

  Editing a ChartLook affects only the selected chart. An edited ChartLook is not applied to any other charts that use that ChartLook unless you select those charts and reapply the ChartLook.

### To Create a New ChartLook from a Chart

- Activate a chart that has a look you want to save (double-click it).

▶ From the menus choose:

Format
 ChartLook...

▶ Select <As Displayed> from the list.

▶ Click Save As.

▶ Select a directory and enter a filename.

### To Delete a ChartLook

The original directory where ChartLooks are stored is *Looks*, a subdirectory of the directory where the program is installed. ChartLooks can be stored in any directory.

▶ Find the directory where the ChartLook is stored.

▶ Delete the ChartLook file (*filename.clo*).

The <System Default> ChartLook cannot be deleted.

## Interactive Chart Properties

The Chart Properties dialog box allows you to set various properties of an interactive chart and save a set of those properties as a ChartLook. Using the tabs on this dialog box, you can set:

- The color sequence for a categorical legend or color range for a scale legend
- The fill, symbol, and line sequences for categorical legends
- Sizes of symbols and lines for categorical and scale legends
- Text properties for objects such as titles and labels
- Fill and borders for chart objects such as bars and pie slices
- The look of axes and ticks along the axes
- Properties of lines, symbols, and connectors

### To Change Interactive Chart Properties

- ▶ Activate the chart (double-click it).
- ▶ From the menus choose:

  Format
   Chart Properties...
- ▶ Click a tab (Colors, Styles, Sizes, Text, Filled Objects, Lines & Symbols, or Axes).
- ▶ Select the options you want.
- ▶ Click OK or Apply.

  The new properties are applied to the selected chart. To apply new chart properties to a ChartLook instead of just the selected chart, edit the ChartLook (Format menu, ChartLooks).

## Chart Properties: Colors

Figure 12-42
*Chart Properties: Colors tab*

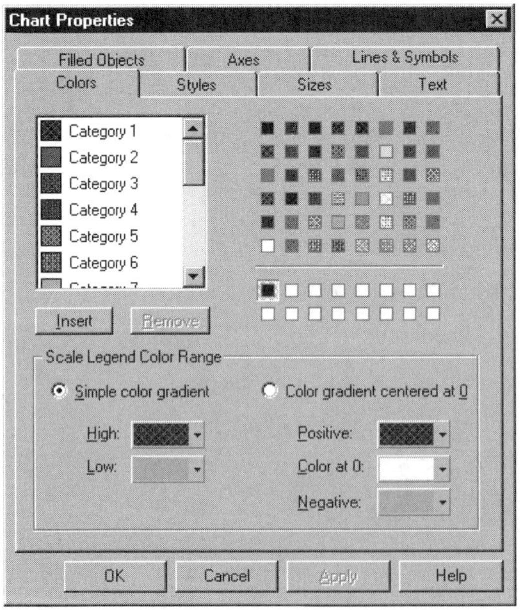

The sequence of colors in a categorical legend or the range of colors in a scale legend can be specified. If a variable has more categories than the list, the sequence is repeated.

**Categorical sequence.** The list of numbered categories displays the sequence of colors for categories. When the ChartLook is applied to a chart with a color category legend, colors are assigned to the categories in the order listed here. From this dialog box, you can rearrange the list or assign a new color to any category.

**Scale Legend Color Range.** When the chart properties are applied to a chart with a scale variable assigned to the Legend Color target, the color gradient is used. A simple gradient ranges between two colors for high and low values.

**Intermediate Color.** If you want a three-color gradient, you can select an intermediate color. This color will be placed halfway between the smallest and largest values in the data range.

**Intermediate color at zero.** If you select a three-color gradient, the intermediate color value can be assigned to the location of the value 0 in the data range. If there is no 0 in the data range, the intermediate color is not used.

### *To Change the Color Sequence for Categories*

▶ Activate a chart (double-click it).

▶ From the menus choose:

Format
  Chart Properties...

▶ Click the Colors tab.

▶ To change a category color assignment, select a category and then select a color for that category from the palette.

Optionally, you can:

- Insert a new category above the selected category.
- Remove a selected category.

### To Change the Scale Legend Color Range

- Activate a chart (double-click it).
- From the menus choose:

  Format
  Chart Properties...

- Select Simple color gradient or Color gradient centered at 0.
- Select colors for the various positions in the gradient.

### To Add Custom Colors to a ChartLook Palette

- Activate a chart (double-click it).
- From the menus choose:

  Format
  Chart Properties...

- Double-click one of the 16 custom color swatches at the bottom of the palette.
- Define a custom color.

  You can assign the custom color to any category in the list.

## Chart Properties: Styles

Figure 12-43
*Chart Properties: Styles tab*

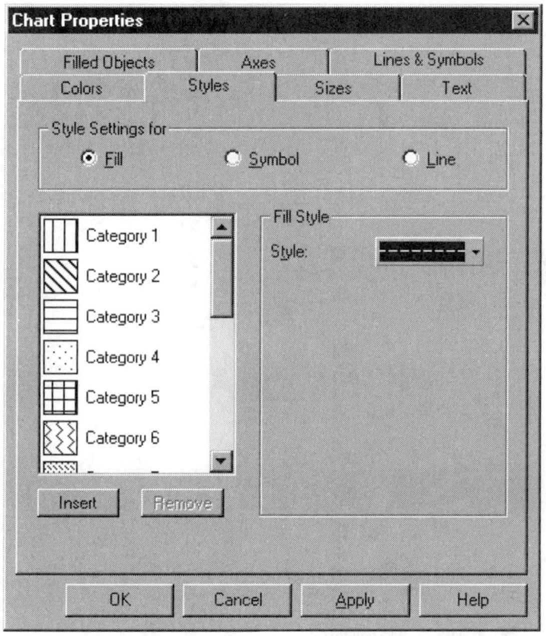


The sequence of styles in a categorical legend can be specified. The list displays the sequence in which styles will be assigned whenever there is a style legend.

Different lists are displayed, depending on whether Fill, Symbol, or Line is selected. A chart uses whichever sequences are applicable. For example, if a chart has both bars and error bars, the Fill sequence is used for the bars and the Line sequence is used for the error bars.

### To Change Chart Properties: Styles

- Click Fill, Symbol, or Line.
- Click a category.
- Select a style for that category.

▶ Select each style you want to change and change it.

Optionally, you can:

- Insert a new category below the selected category.
- Remove a selected category.

## Chart Properties: Sizes

Figure 12-44
*Chart Properties: Sizes tab*

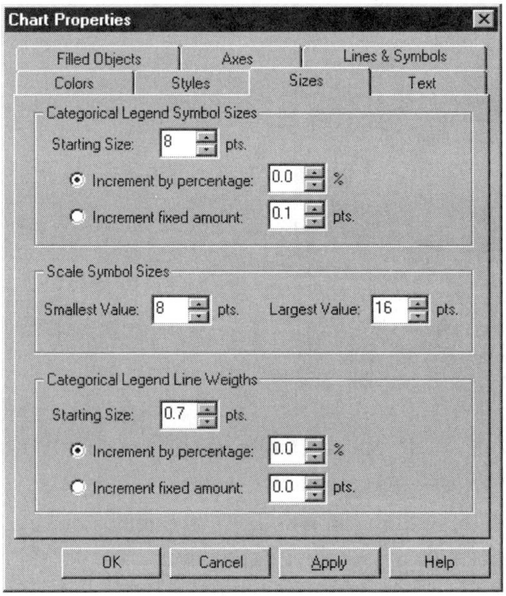


The settings on this tab determine the sequence of symbol sizes or line weight specifications to be applied whenever there is a size legend.

**Categorical Legend Symbol Sizes.** If a categorical variable is assigned to the Legend Size target, symbols in the chart will be different sizes, according to the starting size (size of the symbol attached to the first category) and the increment for each successive category symbol, by percentage or by a fixed amount.

**Scale Symbol Sizes.** If a scale variable is assigned to the Legend Size target, this specification controls the size of the smallest and largest symbol used for the scale. The program interpolates for in-between values.

**Categorical Legend Line Weights.** If a categorical variable is assigned to the Legend Size target, lines that represent the categories will be different weights, according to the starting size and the increment specified.

### To Change Chart Properties: Sizes

▶ Click the Sizes tab.

▶ Enter any changes.

Optionally, you can:

- Change the starting size and increment for categorical symbol sequences.
- Change the smallest and largest values for scale symbol sizes.
- Change the starting size and increment for categorical line weight sequences.

## Chart Properties: Text

Figure 12-45
*Chart Properties: Text tab*

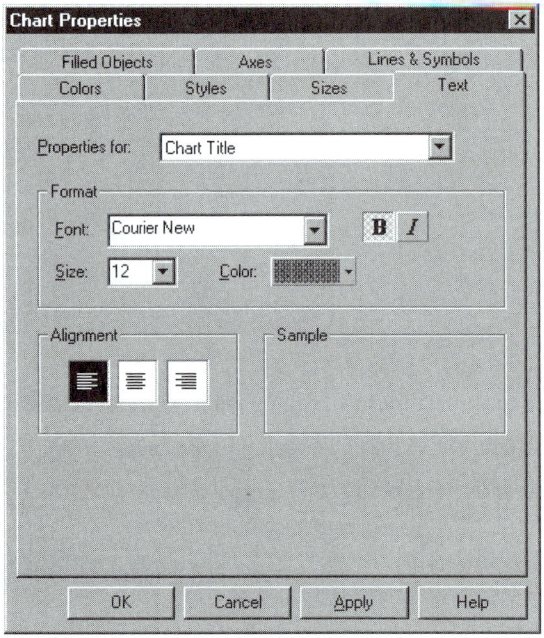


Text properties can be specified for each text object in a chart, including the chart title, chart subtitle, axis title, axis value label, category value label, legend title, legend item, key title, key text, element label text, and caption. When you select a text object from the drop-down list, its characteristics are displayed in the Format and Alignment boxes. The settings apply to the entire text object, even if only part of it is selected.

### To Change Chart Properties: Text

- Click the Text tab.
- Select a text object from the drop-down list.
- Select the desired properties for the text object.

Optionally, you can:

- Change the font, point size, and text color.
- Specify bold, italic, and underline.
- Change the text alignment.

## Chart Properties: Filled Objects

Figure 12-46
*Chart Properties: Filled Objects tab*

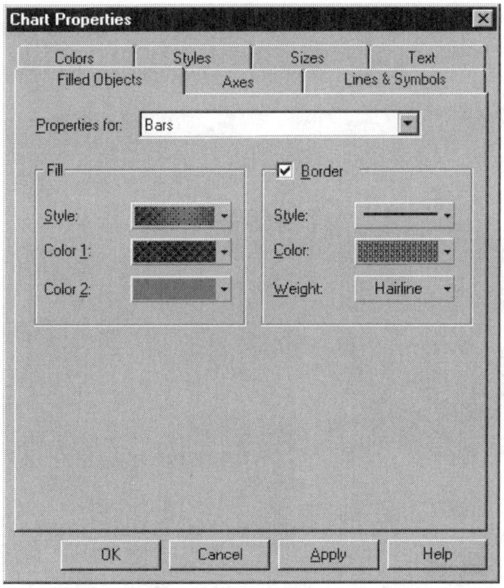


Properties can be specified for objects that have a fill and a border. These include bars, histograms, pie slices, boxes, surfaces, data region, legend frame, ribbons, and key frame. The applicable properties are displayed as you select each object from the drop-down list.

Fill specifications selected in this dialog box are applied to objects that are not affected by variable assignments. For example, if there is a variable assigned to the color legend, objects such as bars take their color according to the legend rather than the color assigned here.

### To Change Chart Properties: Filled Objects

- ▶ Click the Filled Objects tab.
- ▶ Select a type of filled object from the drop-down list.
- ▶ Select the desired properties for the type.

Optionally, you can:

- ■ Change the fill color or style.
- ■ Turn the border on or off and change its style, color, and weight.

## Chart Properties: Lines and Symbols

Figure 12-47
*Chart Properties: Lines & Symbols tab*

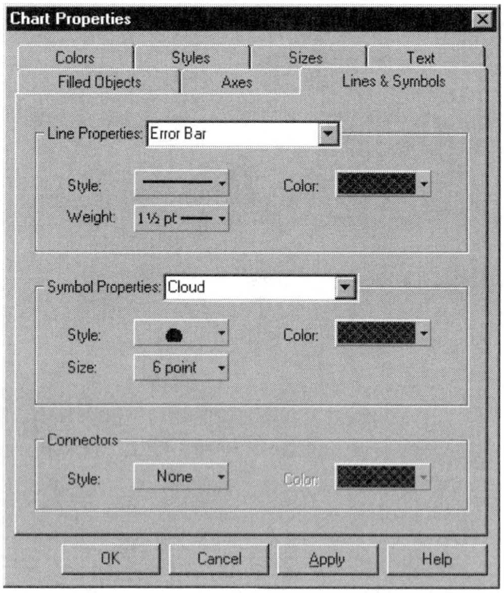


Properties for lines, symbols, and connectors can be specified for each ChartLook. Specifications that are selected in this dialog box are applied to objects that are not affected by variable assignments. For example, if there is a variable assigned to the style legend, symbols or lines take the style according to the legend rather than the style assigned here.

**Line Properties.** Lines include error bar, box median line, box whisker, smoother, regression, normal curve, drop line, and summary line element. For each type of line, you can choose the style, weight, and color.

**Symbol Properties.** Symbols include cloud, box outlier, box extreme, error bar (symbol in the middle), and dot summary element. For each type of symbol, you can choose style, size, and color.

**Connectors.** Connectors are used to associate a case number or a label with a symbol, bar, or other chart object. You can choose the style and color of connectors.

### *To Change Chart Properties: Lines and Symbols*

- Click the Lines & Symbols tab.
- Select a type of line from the drop-down list.
- Select the desired line properties.
- Select a type of symbol from the drop-down list.
- Select the desired symbol properties.
- Specify the style and color of connectors, used with labels.

Optionally, you can specify properties for each type of line, symbol, and connector that appears in a chart.

## Chart Properties: Axes

Figure 12-48
*Chart Properties: Axes tab*

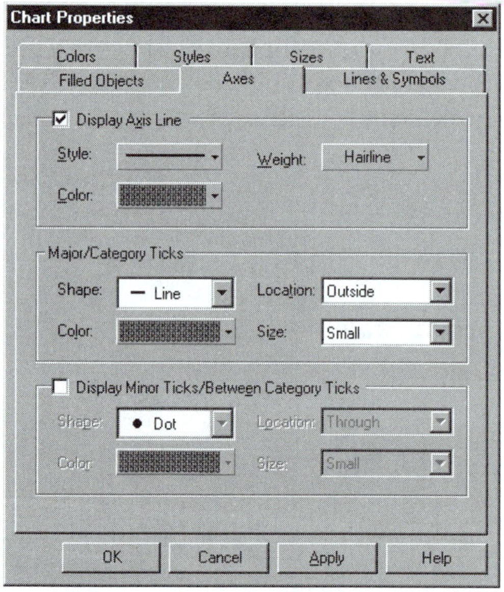


Properties on this tab apply to both scale and category axes.

**Display Axis Line.** The axis lines can be turned on or off. You can choose style, weight, and color.

**Major/Category Ticks.** For major ticks on a scale axis or category ticks, you can specify shape, color, location, and size.

**Display Minor Ticks/Between Category Ticks.** For minor ticks on a scale axes and between category ticks on category axes, you can specify shape, color, location, and size.

#### *To Change Chart Properties: Axes*

- Click the Axes tab.
- Specify properties for the axis line, major or category ticks, and minor or between category ticks.

  Optionally, you can change style, color, weight, shape, location, and size, as applicable.

## Colors and Styles

Objects in charts can have colors and styles assigned by using the properties dialog boxes for each type of object or by selecting the object and using one of the tools.

### Colors in Charts

Each chart has an attached color palette that is saved with the chart. The color palette can be used to color objects in the chart, including the fill of elements, lines, and text. Borders are colored using the Border Color tool. A filled object can have both color and style assigned. Color can be applied to chart elements, axes, text, the data region, or other chart objects.

| Tool | Icon | Description |
|---|---|---|
| Fill Color | 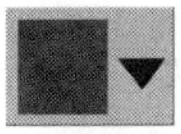 | Changes color of filled object, line, or text |
| Border Color |  | Changes color of border |

The Fill Color and Border Color tools each show a color that will be applied to any objects that are selected when you click the tool (tools show the color that will be applied; they do not show the color of the currently selected item in the chart).

Clicking the arrow attached to the Fill Color tool or the Border Color tool displays a palette of colors. The 48 colors at the top of the color palette are the standard program colors. Tool tips show either the names of colors or RGB values as the cursor passes over them. The 16 spaces at the bottom can be filled with custom colors for the current chart. Custom colors are defined by using the standard Windows color palette. If you define more than 16 custom colors, the seventeenth color replaces the first custom color, the eighteenth replaces the second, and so on.

Clicking a color in the palette changes the color of any selected items and changes the color swatch displayed in the tool. Clicking No Color makes the selected object transparent.

### To Change the Fill Color in Selected Objects

- Activate the chart (double-click it).
- Select one or more objects in the chart.
- Click the arrow next to the Fill Color swatch. This opens the color palette.
- Click the color you want applied to the selected objects and to the Fill Color tool.

*or*

- If the Fill Color tool already has the color you want, click the color swatch of the Fill Color tool.

This changes the color in all of the selected objects to the current color of the Fill Color tool unless their color is controlled by the data.

### To Change Border Color in Selected Objects

- Activate the chart (double-click it).
- Select one or more objects in the chart.
- Click the arrow next to the border color swatch. This opens the border color palette.
- Click the color you want applied to the border of selected objects and to the Border Color tool.

*or*

- If the Border Color tool already has the color you want, click the border color swatch of the Border Color tool.

This changes the border color in all of the selected objects that have borders unless their style is controlled by the data.

## *Styles in Charts*

The Fill Style tool shows the style that will be applied to selected objects when you click the tool (tools do not show the state of the currently selected item in the chart). The Symbol Style tool has a fixed design.

| Tool | Icon | Description |
|---|---|---|
| Fill Style | 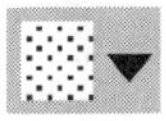 | Changes style of filled object |
| Symbol Style |  | Changes style of symbols |

For Fill Styles, you can choose a style from the palette, or you can click More Styles and select patterns, gradients, or textures. These are selected by clicking one of the following effects:

Figure 12-49
*Patterns effect*

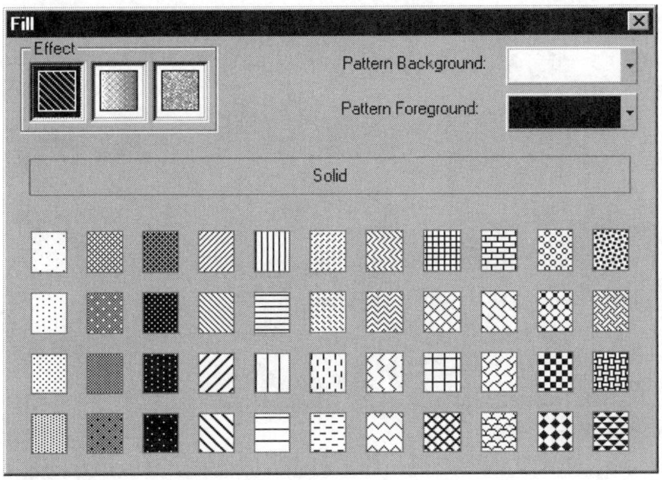


**Patterns** have foreground and background colors.

Figure 12-50
*Gradients effect*

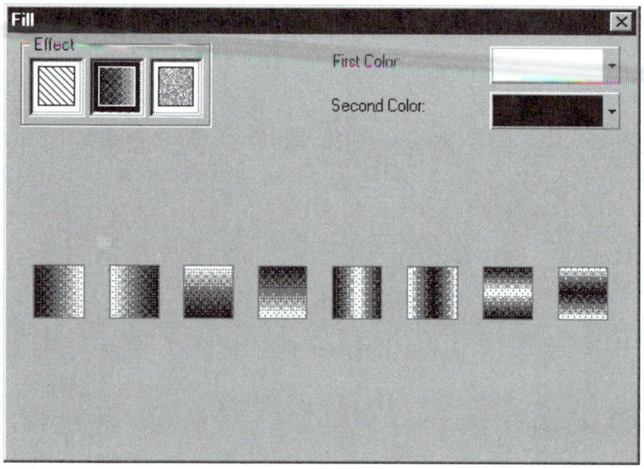


**Gradients** shade from one color to another. You can specify the colors.

Figure 12-51
*Textures effect*

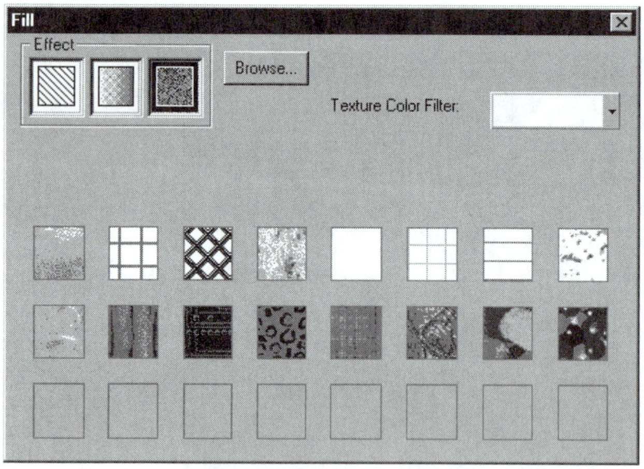


**Textures** can have a color filter. With a color filter, the texture is drawn in shades of the selected color. To display the texture with its original colors, the selected object should have no color.

**Custom textures.** By using the Browse button on Textures, you can insert any bitmap file as a texture. The bitmap should be square and sized to a number of pixels equal to a power of 2 (for example, 64 by 64 or 128 by 128). Otherwise, the program will clip the bitmap to the nearest lower power of 2.

### To Change Fill Styles

▶ Activate the chart (double-click it).

▶ Click the arrow on the Fill Style tool.

▶ On the Style palette, select a style or click More Styles.

When the Fill palette is displayed:

▶ Select the effect (pattern, gradient, or texture).

▶ Select the desired style.

Optionally, you can:

- Change the colors for patterns and gradients.
- Change the colors for some of the textures.
- Assign custom textures (click the Textures icon and then click Browse).

### To Change Symbol Styles

▶ Activate the chart (double-click it).

▶ Select the symbols you want to change.

▶ Click the Symbol Style tool and select a style.

This changes the style of all selected symbols unless the symbol style is controlled by variable assignment.

## Line and Connector Styles

**Line styles.** The Line Style tool can be used to change the style of selected lines. Line styles can be changed for axes, borders, chart element lines, error bars, and grid lines. (A 3-D object does not have borders.) Styles include a solid line and various dotted or dashed patterns.

**Connector styles.** Connectors are drawn between a graph object and a label. The style of connectors can be changed.

| Tool | Icon | Description |
|---|---|---|
| Line Style |  | Changes line style |
| Connector Style | 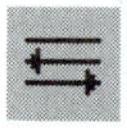 | Changes connector style |

### To Change Line Style

- ▶ Activate the chart (double-click it).
- ▶ Select one or more lines or objects with borders in the chart.
- ▶ Click the Line Style tool and select a line style.

  This changes the style in all of the selected objects unless their style is controlled by the data.

### To Change Connector Styles

- ▶ Activate the chart (double-click it).
- ▶ Select one or more connectors in the chart.
- ▶ Click the Connector Style tool and select a style.

  This changes the style in all of the selected connectors.

## Sizes of Objects in Charts

Sizes of symbols in scatterplots and boxplots can be changed. The weights of lines in the chart, borders, and other linear objects can be changed. (A 3-D object does not have borders.)

| Tool | Icon | Description |
| --- | --- | --- |
| Symbol Size |  | Changes symbol size |
| Line Weight |  | Changes line weight |

### To Change the Size of Symbols

- Activate the chart (double-click it).
- Select one or more symbols in the chart.
- Click the Symbol Size tool.

  This changes the size in all of the selected symbols unless their size is controlled by variable assignment.

### To Change Line Weight

- Activate the chart (double-click it).
- Select one or more lines or objects with borders in the chart.
- Click the Line Weight tool in the toolbar.
- Select a line weight.

  This changes the style in all of the selected objects unless their size is controlled by variable assignment.

# Modifying Text

You can change fonts and sizes in text by using a dialog box or the Text toolbar.

## Text: Font

Figure 12-52
*Text: Font tab*

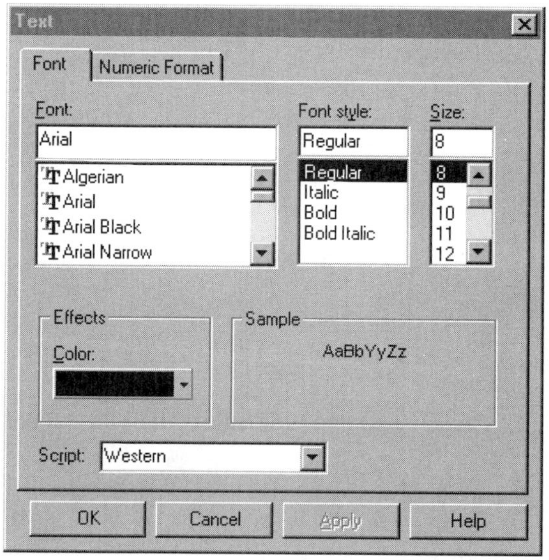


In the Text dialog box, you can change the appearance of a selected text object. You can choose a font, font style, point size, and color.

The Script drop-down list displays the available language scripts for the specified font. Select the one that is appropriate for your computer setup.

## Text: Numeric Format

Figure 12-53
*Text: Numeric Format tab*

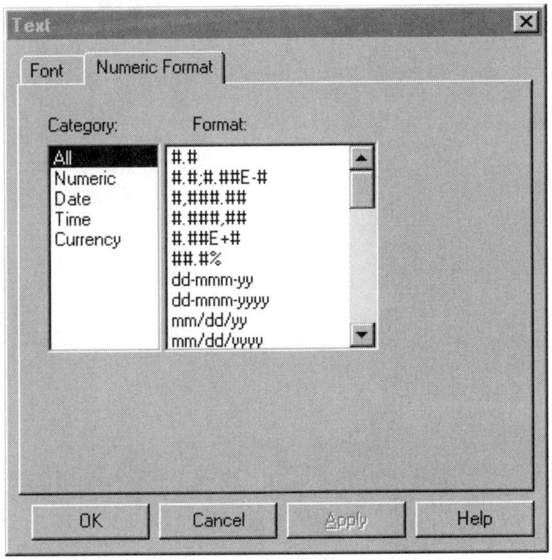


If the text is a number, the numeric format can be specified. The Category list allows you to group numeric formats.

### To Format Text in a Chart with a Dialog Box

▶ Activate the chart (double-click it).

▶ Select a text object.

▶ From the menus choose:

Format
 Text...

▶ Click a tab: Font or Numeric Format.

Optionally, you can:

- Select a different font, font style, size, color, or script.
- Change the numeric format.

### *To Format Text in a Chart with the Toolbar*

▶ Activate the chart (double-click it).

▶ From the menus choose:

View
  Toolbar
    Text

▶ Select the text you want to format.

Optionally, you can:

- Change the font.
- Change the size.
- Change the font style (bold or italic).

# Index